DATE DUE

NO 15 03			
JU 29 02			
DE 11 06			

DEMCO 38-296

EISENHOWER

EISENHOWER
The Prewar Diaries and Selected Papers, 1905–1941

DANIEL D. HOLT, *Editor*

JAMES W. LEYERZAPF, *Associate Editor*

Introduction by JOHN S. D. EISENHOWER

THE JOHNS HOPKINS UNIVERSITY PRESS

BALTIMORE AND LONDON

brary, Abilene, Kansas, by the Johns
Library is one of ten presidential
and Records Administration.

© 1998 National Archives Trust Fund Board
All rights reserved. Published 1998
Printed in the United States of America on acid-free paper
07 06 05 04 03 02 01 00 99 98   5 4 3 2 1

Frontispiece: Eisenhower with Tank Corps, Camp Meade, Maryland, 1919.

The Johns Hopkins University Press
2715 North Charles Street
Baltimore, Maryland 21218-4319
The Johns Hopkins Press Ltd., London

All illustrations in this volume are from the Dwight D. Eisenhower Library,
unless indicated otherwise.

Library of Congress Cataloging-in-Publication Data will be found at the end of
this book.
A catalog record for this book is available from the British Library.

ISBN 0-8018-5674-4

CONTENTS

Preface and Acknowledgments   vii

Editorial Method   xv

Abbreviations   xix

Chronology   xxiii

Introduction: The Eisenhower Diaries, 1929–1941   xxv
        by John S. D. Eisenhower

CHAPTER ONE / From Abilene to Leavenworth   1
        February 27, 1905–August 1926

CHAPTER TWO / The American Battle Monuments
                Commission   59
        March 15, 1928–September 5, 1929

CHAPTER THREE / Duty in Washington   99
        September 26, 1929–December 25, 1931

CHAPTER FOUR / Service with the Chief of Staff   211
        January 30, 1932–August 8, 1935

CHAPTER FIVE / Philippine Service   283
        November 1935–June 18, 1938

CHAPTER SIX / From the Philippines to the War Department   385
        June 26, 1938–December 12, 1941

Index   567

Illustrations follow page 282.

PREFACE AND ACKNOWLEDGMENTS

Dwight D. Eisenhower was born in 1890, at a time when American popular culture paid close attention to, and placed much credence in, the fictional successes of Horatio Alger. After the end of World War II, when Eisenhower revisited his hometown of Abilene, Kansas, to the cheers of his boyhood friends and neighbors, he recalled that he and all young boys of his generation had dreamed of going off to face stiff challenges and returning home a hero. The diaries and documents that make up this book depict a remarkable person and his military career taking shape—almost in Horatio Alger fashion. The 1905–41 Eisenhower papers certainly contain all the ingredients of rich historical fiction: the hard-working small-town boy; a plot replete with chance, hope, growth, intrigue, romance, disappointment, and triumph; interesting personalities, foreign travel, and events of considerable moment in the twentieth-century American experience.

It was as though his career path had been ordained, or at the least systematically planned. Eisenhower took all the steps that seemed necessary, in retrospect, to prepare him for the duties he took up during World War II. Though he had hardly any sense of training or of acquiring experience with future needs in view, as a young officer he did appreciate fully the opportunities the army placed before him. Some of them were certainly fortuitous. Early in his career, Eisenhower served as a training officer and troop commander. But along with field experience also came projects that required him to consider and reconsider military doctrine. He conducted analytical studies of army training, command, mobilization, procurement, and organization. By the late 1930s, Eisenhower already had studied and been exposed to what he would later term the "military-industrial complex." During his tenure in the chief of staff's office, he worked with or under important leaders in government and the armed forces. His ability to produce concise studies and compose documents and speeches in short order attracted increasing attention, and he was often called upon to use those talents.

Accompanying Douglas MacArthur to the Philippine Commonwealth between 1935 and 1939, Eisenhower helped to build and organize a defense force literally from the ground up. He accomplished this daunting task in a role that forced him to deal with various intractable elements—President Manuel Quezon, who might as well have been a foreign head of state; a highly difficult Philippine–United States political-military coalition; and General MacArthur himself.

Five days after the Japanese bombing of Pearl Harbor, on December 12, 1941, Chief of Staff George C. Marshall ordered Eisenhower to the War Department Plans Division. On that same day, Eisenhower's schedule included an address to army pilots graduating from Kelly Field in Texas. In composing his speech, Eisenhower used all the rhetorical skills he had developed and drew upon his military expertise and already deep devotion to duty. "This opportunity, that of becoming a real leader of fighting men," said Eisenhower, is "the part of soldiering that challenges the best that's in the officer—and it's the one part in which he must not fail! To gain the respect, the esteem, the affection, the readiness to follow into danger, the unswerving and undying loyalty of the American enlisted man. . . . It is his high and almost divine duty. It is the challenge to his talents, his patriotism, his very soul!" (Pre-pres. Papers, Eisenhower Library).

During the period from his 1915 West Point graduation through early December 1941, Eisenhower gained experience and developed associations that later enabled him to succeed in one of the most demanding posts any military man ever has held—directing the Allied invasion of Europe in 1944 and coordinating the defeat of Nazi Germany on the Western Front.

Arranged chronologically (from the earliest extant Eisenhower document in 1905 through December 12, 1941), the materials that make up this select edition provide a running account of the general's formative years and offer a far more detailed and highly developed picture of Eisenhower's prewar career than earlier has been available. Busy as he was with military duties and personal correspondence, as a young officer Eisenhower managed to maintain diaries that documented his work and private thoughts alike.

Five separate prewar Eisenhower diaries survive, covering much of the period from August 1929 to December 12, 1941. Eisenhower wrote his portion of the Gruber-Eisenhower Diary (August 28 to September 5, 1929) during a summer vacation he and Mamie took with William and Helen Gruber just before the end of his service with the American Battle Monuments Commission in Paris. Eisenhower kept the Guayule Diary in April 1930, during a trip to California and Mexico to inspect guayule rubber plant cultivation and processing operations on behalf of war mobilization planners at the War Department. The Chief of Staff Diary, covering the period from September 24, 1929, to June 8, 1934, was written while Eisenhower was working with the assistant secretary of war at the War Department and as a special assistant to

Chief of Staff Gen. Douglas MacArthur. Eisenhower kept the Philippine Diary while serving with the American Military Mission to the Philippines from December 27, 1935, to January 25, 1940. Afterward, the Fort Lewis Diary, covering the period from September 26, 1940, to April 18, 1941, recorded Eisenhower's thoughts during his brief service at Fort Lewis, Washington. Except for the Chief of Staff Diary—a second-generation typescript later prepared by a member of Eisenhower's staff, probably Kevin McCann—all the diaries are original texts.

After Eisenhower's death in 1969, the Eisenhower Library received fragments of a diary and two small books kept in 1938, that overlapped with the Philippine Diary. Until his death the general had retained them at his Gettysburg home. They include twenty entries dated December 1935 to July 1937; a diary of an official trip to the United States while Eisenhower was stationed in the Philippines from June 26 to November 5, 1938; and a diary of a family trip while visiting the United States on official travel from the Philippines, August 11–16, 1938. The editors of this volume have reintegrated these as part of Eisenhower's comprehensive Philippine Diary.

These valuable historical documents could easily have not been saved. Indeed, at one point the general ordered them destroyed. The Eisenhower Library received the Gruber-Eisenhower Diary, which Gruber had held in safekeeping, from the Gruber estate in 1980. The other diaries Eisenhower's staff, notably Kevin McCann, quietly saved from destruction. McCann's widow donated all four of them (plus a segment from a short diary Eisenhower began in January 1942) to the Eisenhower Library in 1981. That year, W. W. Norton published Robert Ferrell's *The Eisenhower Diaries,* which included Eisenhower entries dating from December 27, 1935, through November 5, 1938, most of them relating to the trip to the United States in 1938. They were, however, far less detailed and revealing than those in the Philippine Diary that McCann's widow turned over to the Eisenhower Library. The entries from the Ferrell edition are included but are drawn from the originals.

By 1982 the Eisenhower Library had processed all the Eisenhower diaries and opened most of them to researchers. Substantial sections of the Philippine Diary remained subject to copyright and invasion of privacy restrictions. With publication of this volume, all pre–World War II diaries at the Eisenhower Library through 1941 are open without limitation. However, five very brief segments of the Philippine Diary, which are open at the Eisenhower Library, have not been included in this publication because of copyright restrictions. They are located in the diary entries at August 25, 1937; October 15, 1937; December 13, 1937; February 15, 1938; and November 10, 1938.

Documents in this volume supplementary to the diaries fill in gaps and provide context for the diary record, permit detailed study of Eisenhower's early career, and help to demonstrate the process by which Eisenhower's expertise and character developed. Service in busy posts carried with it heavy correspondence duties and the writing of many policy statements. Eisenhower at the same time kept in close touch with family and friends, from whom he was often separated for long periods of time. The general later believed that many of these papers were lost to water damage during the trip home from the Philippines. "It is one of my deep regrets," Eisenhower wrote a friend in early 1966, "that all of my personal papers, accumulated during my entire army career up to 1941 [,] were lost in one of our frequent transfers of those days" (Eisenhower to Frank McCarthy, January 6, 1966, Post-pres. Papers, Eisenhower Library).

No doubt some of Eisenhower's early documents have been lost, but fortunately the Eisenhower Library preserves a substantial body of pre–World War II Eisenhower manuscripts. To assure that as many key documents as possible appeared in this volume, the library received assistance from twenty other repositories and in several divisions of the National Archives in locating documents. Dr. Daun van Ee, coeditor of *The Papers of Dwight D. Eisenhower*, generously made available an extensive file of pre–World War II Eisenhower documents, most of them from the records of the National Archives. The National Archives staff rechecked citations of these documents and conducted a search for others. Members of the Eisenhower family provided additional letters, as did many other supporters of the project.

The editors wish to acknowledge the critical assistance of John S. D. Eisenhower, who recognized the historical importance of the diaries and decided that they should enter the Dwight D. Eisenhower bibliography. He granted the Eisenhower Library permission to publish the Philippine Diary, and this volume would not have been possible without his cooperation. He also provided annotations when reading drafts of the book, and they have been incorporated into the footnotes. We wish to acknowledge the Johns Hopkins University Press for its willingness to publish documentary editions and specifically Robert J. Brugger, history editor. Dr. Daun van Ee of the Eisenhower Papers project and Dr. Larry I. Bland, editor of *The Papers of George Catlett Marshall*, read early drafts for this volume and made invaluable suggestions. The Eisenhower Foundation, Abilene, Kansas, provided financial assistance for preparation of the index and related costs. Projects such as this publication, as well as public programs and exhibits, could not be undertaken by the Eisenhower Library without the foundation's support. The National Archives Trust Fund Board, on behalf of the Eisenhower Library, negotiated a publishing contract with the Johns Hopkins University Press. No individuals or groups of individuals receive any proceeds from the sale of this publication. It is appropriate also to thank copy editor Katherine Kimball for her attention to detail, her nonintrusive editing, and above all her cooperative attitude.

Nearly the entire library staff assisted in some way, from those who absorbed the duties of Jim Leyerzapf and the editor so library work could continue to those who made photocopies, covered telephones, and accepted additional responsibilities so that others could assist with this project. Martin M. Teasley, assistant director, and Janet Whitehair, administrative officer, kept the library functioning and scheduled those who assisted the editors.

Other staff demand specific recognition. Michelle Kopfer, automation clerk and word processing genius, entered much of the manuscript into electronic form and proved to be an outstanding proofreader. Stacy Meuli, director's secretary, not only controlled the word-processing requirements and many other duties but also managed the time of those working on the project, including the library director. Tom Branigar, archivist, helped search the Eisenhower Library's collections and assisted in identifying archives elsewhere that might hold Eisenhower materials. His vast knowledge of the National Archives' holdings proved invaluable. Dwight Strandberg, librarian, whose knowledge of the OCLC system aided in our search for manuscripts located elsewhere and for obscure publications, provided major support. Kathleen Struss, audiovisual supervisor, and Hazel Stroda searched the library's massive photograph collection for appropriate illustrations, and Robert Paull, photographic laboratory technician, provided excellent prints from usually poor originals. Very early in the project, Susan Dyehouse assisted in the initial transcription of the handwritten and original documents into electronic format.

It is not often that volunteers work on such projects, but in this case Elinor Haas, a retired Abilene High School English teacher and library volunteer, contributed countless hours assisting in the search for documents and photocopying. She also assisted with proofreading document text. Her help was vital in completing this manuscript in a timely manner.

A very special thank-you to Timothy Connelly, assistant director of publications, National Historical Publications and Records Commission, for his dogged efforts in searching the National Archives' record groups in order to confirm, or where necessary revise, citations for documents obtained many years ago. He also searched for, and found, additional Eisenhower documents in a number of record groups the library had identified.

Dr. Richard Meixsel, assistant professor of history, James Madison University, whose field of study is the Philippine army, provided invaluable assistance with bibliography and assisted in locating biographical data on Philippine military and civilian officials. Elaine McConnell and her predecessor, Elizabeth Snoke, curator of archives, special collections, at the U.S. Army Command and General Staff College, Fort Leavenworth, Kansas, provided us with priceless assistance in finding biographical information on early-twentieth-century army officers and provided printed materials from old professional journals and army regulations. They were a constant source of information and always were efficient and prompt.

Alan Aimone, assistant librarian for special collections at the U.S. Military Academy, West Point, New York, not only searched manuscript sources but also cheerfully responded to our frequent requests for printed materials from both the academy's libraries and various administrative offices. James Zobel, archivist, MacArthur Memorial Archives, Norfolk, Virginia, with considerable patience and grace, endured countless telephone, faxed, and E-mail requests for document copies and other information. Diane Jacobs, archivist, Virginia Military Institute Archives, Lexington, Virginia, went the extra mile in locating important Eisenhower letters being held in temporary storage. Barbara Foltz gave the library many letters that had been given her by Mamie Eisenhower and that were critical to this publication.

Richard Sommers, archivist-historian, U.S. Army Military History Institute, Carlisle Barracks, Pennsylvania, and his staff often performed miracles for the library in locating documents and publications and providing general information. Jane Yates, director, archives and museum, The Citadel, Charleston, South Carolina, verified the great number of Mark Clark letters that were on microfilm at the Eisenhower Library and made copies of related materials available. Thanks also to Michael Kelly, curator of special collections, Wichita State University Libraries, Wichita, Kansas, for searching their files and furnishing documents. We are grateful to the James S. Copley Library, La Jolla, California, in particular Helen C. Copley and David C. Copley, for providing important letters, and to Carol Beales, library manager, for her cooperation. The Hoover Presidential Library, West Branch, Iowa, also provided documents.

There were also those important searches for materials that either did not produce documents or produced documents that could not be used. These searches were as important as those that produced substantive documents. Individuals involved were Christina Deane, public services assistant, special collections, Alderman Library, University of Virginia; James H. Hutson, chief, Manuscripts Division, Library of Congress; Daniel Luke, assistant archivist, Seeley G. Mudd Manuscript Library, Princeton University; Geoffrey Smith, curator, rare books and manuscripts, Ohio State University; Ray Teichman, archivist, Franklin D. Roosevelt Library; Thomas Camden, library director and archives curator of collections, George C. Marshall Foundation; Michael Dabrishius, head of special collections, University Libraries, University of Arkansas; Mary Hawkins, librarian, Kansas Collection, University of Kansas; Daniel Itzkovitz, reference intern, Special Collections Library, Duke University; Bradford Koplowitz, assistant curator, division of manuscripts, University of Oklahoma Libraries; and Dierdre Sullivan, reference assistant, Massachusetts Historical Society.

Lastly, we wish to thank Robert W. Richmond, Topeka, Kansas, for the unheralded job of indexing and Marilyn Holt, Abilene, who lent her editorial expertise to the entire project. There were many others who graciously accepted numerous inquiries for information or clarifications and are not named here. We thank them all.

EDITORIAL METHOD

In the case of the diaries, the selection process proved simple, for the editors of course included all of them. From among the many hundreds of additional documents one might select as supplemental to the diaries, the editors chose those papers that seemed to contribute substantially to the military biography of Eisenhower and to demonstrate his personal development. They include his earliest extant letter and a speech Eisenhower made as a high school student to a local Young Democratic Men's club. Other materials offer examples of the broad scope of military subjects Eisenhower became acquainted with, his breadth of duties, and the range of writing he did as a junior and field-grade officer—from personal to professional. A few documents demonstrate that the Eisenhowers, like other military families, faced some of the same personal problems that civilians did and tried to achieve a family and social life of their own, albeit restricted. Some personal and family letters from Eisenhower's West Point years and immediately thereafter that do not directly relate to his military career are not included but are referred to in notes.

As a fundamental rule, only documents that Eisenhower himself wrote appear in this volume. The editors have omitted almost all military orders or memorandums that were "by order" of Eisenhower (normally drafted by an adjutant or other staff person). In a few noted cases, the editors judged a "by order" document important enough in content surely to have merited Eisenhower's close attention and possibly his revision before being issued; those papers appear in this volume. The editors include here speeches and significant memorandums that Eisenhower demonstrably wrote for others, including the assistant secretary of war, General MacArthur, and members of the War Policies Commission. Eisenhower typically initialed the drafts as having been his work; in some cases he referred to his authorship in one of his diaries. The editors also have selected for this volume important Eisenhower publications and miscellaneous military presentations, which, though known to many specialists, are often difficult to locate. Some have never been published.

Ellipses in square brackets mark textual deletions that the editors believe justifiable for the sake of brevity or—in instances in the Philippine diaries—to honor the wishes of the copyright owner. The editors further abbreviated some of these additional documents by omitting, as indicated, appendixes, attachments, or enclosures.

In cases of undated diary entries or documents and where necessary in the text, the editors have supplied dates or probable dates in square brackets. Where necessary for clarity or definition, the editors have inserted a word or words in the text also by means of square brackets. In those few instances where Eisenhower's handwriting was illegible, the editors note the fact within square brackets.

Eisenhower was an excellent composer of the written word and an admirable speller; the editors have silently corrected his few misspellings of common words. If he misspelled a person's name, it stands uncorrected in the text but is spelled correctly in the notes. In his diaries Eisenhower made extensive use of dashes and some ellipses to separate thoughts. For the sake of sentence structure and clarity, the editors have rendered most single dashes as commas. Where Eisenhower clearly intended to end a sentence, the editors have transcribed dashes to periods. If Eisenhower clearly used ellipses or double dashes to change subjects, the editors have inserted a paragraph break. Double dashes that Eisenhower used for emphasis or expression remain. As a military man following the usage of his profession and time, Eisenhower capitalized all military terms; though cumbersome by our standards, these forms stand in the text as Eisenhower wrote them. In the case of the McCann diary typescript, the editors have rendered in lower case the nonmilitary words that Eisenhower in his handwritten diaries did not capitalize. Eisenhower often used underlining for emphasis, and the editors have let it stand.

The diaries overlap in places, and where they do the editors have arranged entries so as to maintain the chronological order of the materials in the volume. Obvious errors in the McCann typescript of the Chief of Staff Diary required moving several paragraphs to correct their chronological placement.

One undated, handwritten manuscript in the collection with the Philippine Diary the editors have treated not as a document but as a source. Philippine President Manuel Quezon requested of Eisenhower, probably in 1939 as he was about to depart for the United States, that he write confidential appraisals of individual Filipino military officers. These comments do not appear as a separate document but are excerpted in the notes to documents in which the names of these officers appear.

Of all the prewar Eisenhower documents (diaries aside) known to have survived, about one-half appear in this volume. Photostatic copies of all Eisenhower's prewar documents accumulated for this project now reside in a separate reference file at the Eisenhower Library. The original diaries are located in the following collections:

Eisenhower Diaries, 1935–1969; William R. Gruber Papers, 1929–1954; and Kevin McCann Papers, 1918–1981.

Eisenhower speaks for himself in these documents, but annotation helps to identify people and some obscure subject matter. The notes also provide clues to the nature and scope of work that Eisenhower accomplished. All notes pertain to the entry directly above. Notes for multiple diary entries with the same document number follow each dated entry, with the exception of the single-document Gruber-Eisenhower Diary. If no note is provided for identifications, information could not be located. The editors have omitted source citations for information in the notes that is readily available in standard reference works such as biographical dictionaries. Nearly all the biographical information for the Philippine officers and officials derives from Miguel R. Cornejo's *Directory of the Philippines: Encyclopedic Edition* (Manila, 1939).

Headnotes to each document provide its repository and collection or record group (fuller citations, including series and folder titles, are available at the Eisenhower Library). All documents are numbered for ease of reference; where more than one consecutive diary entry occurs, the document number of the first entry stands for those following until a nondiary document intervenes. The editors have standardized the textual treatment of letterheads, inside addresses, salutations, and complimentary closings. The editors have omitted signature blocks; unless otherwise noted, however, Eisenhower signed all the documents here printed.

In the notes the editors have identified terms or abbreviations that appear infrequently in the text. For common abbreviations and identifications of frequently used terms, see the list of abbreviations. This list also identifies those persons for whose names Eisenhower substituted initials or shorthand references.

Introductions to each of the six chapters provide context and background to the period the documents cover and Eisenhower's career during those years.

ABBREVIATIONS

Military, Government, General

A.A.	American Armament Company, also antiaircraft
AAA	Agricultural Adjustment Act
ABMC	American Battle Monuments Commission
A.E.F., AEF	American Expeditionary Force
AG	Adjutant general
AGO	Adjutant general's office
A.R.	Automatic rifle
A.S.W.	Assistant secretary of war
A.W.C.	Army War College
B of B	Bureau of Budget
Bn, Bns	Battalion, battalions
Brig., BG	Brigadier general
CCC	Civilian Conservation Corps
C.G.	Commanding general
C.O.	Commanding officer
C. of I.	Chief of Infantry
Constab.	Constabulary
Cos, C. of S., C.S., C	Chief of Staff
C.P.	Command post
CPX	Command post exercise
D.C.S., Dep. C. of S.	Deputy Chief of Staff
F.A.	Field artillery
F.D.	Finance Division
G-1	Personnel and administrative section of divisional or higher staff

G-2	Intelligence section of divisional or higher staff
G-3	Operations and training section of divisional or higher staff
G-4	Logistics section of divisional or higher staff
G.H.Q.	General Headquarters
G.S.	General Staff
H.C.	High commissioner, Philippines
Inf.	Infantry
I.R.C.	Intercontinental Rubber Company
M.G.	Machine gun
M.I.D.	Military Intelligence Division
Mil. Adv.	Military adviser
Misc.	Miscellaneous
Mss.	Manuscripts
M.T.C.	Motor Transfer Corps
NARA	National Archives and Records Administration
N.G.	National Guard
NRA	National Recovery Administration
NRC	National Recovery Commission
O.D.	Operations Division, also Ordnance Department
O.R.C.	Organized Reserve Corps
Ord.	Ordnance
OTAG	Office of the Adjutant General
P.A.	Philippine Army
PB	Planning Branch
P.I.	Philippine Islands
Pre-pres.	Prepresidential
President	In the Philippine diaries, the reference is usually to President Quezon of the Philippines.
PWA	Public Works Administration
Q.M.	Quartermaster
Q.M.C.	Quartermaster Corps
ROTC	Reserve Officers' Training Corps

Sec. of War, S.W., Sec.	Secretary of war
TAGO	The adjutant general's office
T.C.	Tank Corps
T.O., T of O	Table of organization
USMA	U.S. Military Academy
W.C.	War College
W.D.	War Department
W.D.G.S.	War Department General Staff
WPA	Works Progress Administration
W.P.C.	War Policies Commission
W.P.D.	War Plans Division

Personal

Bo	George "Bo" Horkan Jr., son of George Horkan
Dad	Usually John Doud, Eisenhower's father-in-law
Gee	Leonard Gerow
Gen.	Douglas MacArthur, also George V. H. Moseley
H	Gen. Lucius Holbrook
J, Jimmy	Jimmy Ord
M, Gen. M.	MacArthur, occasionally Moseley
Mac, Mc	MacArthur
Mother	Usually Elivera Doud, Eisenhower's mother-in-law
P.J.H.	Patrick J. Hurley, secretary of war
Q	Quezon
T.	Gen. Hugh Thompson
T.J., or TJ	Thomas Jefferson Davis

CHRONOLOGY

1890	Dwight David Eisenhower born, Denison, Texas (October 14)
1892	Family returns to Abilene, Kansas
1909	Graduates from Abilene High School; takes work as refrigeration engineer, Belle Springs Creamery, Abilene
1911	Enters U.S. Military Academy (USMA), West Point, New York (June 14)
1915	Graduates from USMA, commissioned second lieutenant of infantry (June 12); on leave, Abilene (June–September); to Fort Sam Houston, Texas (September 13, 1915–September 22, 1917)
1917	Promoted to captain (May 15); instructor, Reserve Officers' Training Corps (ROTC) camp, Fort Oglethorpe, Georgia (September 22–November 26); instructor, Army Service Schools, Fort Leavenworth, Kansas (December 1, 1917–February 28, 1918)
1918	65th Engineers, Fort Meade, Maryland (March 1–March 18); commander, Camp Colt, Tank Corps, Gettysburg, Pennsylvania (March 23–November 18); promoted to major (temporary) (July 18); promoted to lieutenant colonel (temporary) (October 14); troop commander, Tank Corps, Fort Dix, New Jersey (November 18–December 22); troop commander, Tank Corps, Fort Benning, Georgia (December 24, 1918–March 3, 1919)
1919	Tank Corps, Fort Meade (March 17, 1919–January 7, 1922)
1922	Executive officer, 20th Infantry Brigade, Camp Gaillard, Panama Canal Zone (January 26, 1922–September 19, 1924)
1924	Promoted to major (permanent) (August 26); III Corps Area, Fort Meade (September 28–December 15)
1925	Recruiting officer, 38th Infantry, Fort Logan, Denver, Colorado (January 25–August 2); student, Command and General Staff School, Fort Leavenworth (August 25)
1926	Graduates from Command and General Staff School (June 18); on extended leave, Doud residence, Denver, Colorado

(June 21–August 17); Assistant Post Executive Officer, Fort Benning, and commander, 2d Battalion, 24th Infantry (August 18, 1926–January 15, 1927)

1927   American Battle Monuments Commission, Washington, D.C. (January 21–August 15); Army War College, Fort McNair, Washington, D.C. (August 16, 1927–June 30, 1928)

1928   American Battle Monuments Commission, Washington, D.C. (July 1–30); American Battle Monuments Commission headquarters, Paris, France (August 9, 1928–September 17, 1929)

1929   Headquarters, American Battle Monuments Commission, Washington, D.C. (September 24–November 8); assistant executive to assistant secretary of war (November 8, 1929–February 20, 1933)

1933   Special assistant to the Chief of Staff, War Department General Staff (February 20, 1933–September 24, 1935)

1935   En route to Manila, Philippines (September 25–October 25); senior assistant to the military adviser to the Philippine Commonwealth (October 25, 1935–December 13, 1939)

1936   Promoted to lieutenant colonel (July 1)

1938   Procurement trip to the United States (June 26–November 5)

1939   En route from Manila to San Francisco (December 13–31)

1940   Temporary duty, IX Corps Area Headquarters, the Presidio, San Francisco (January 6–February 2); Executive Officer, 15th Infantry, and commander, 1st Battalion, Fort Lewis, Washington (February 3–November 30); appointed Chief of Staff, Headquarters, 3d Division, Fort Lewis (November 30)

1941   Chief of Staff, Headquarters, IX Army Corps, Fort Lewis (March 4–June 24); promoted to colonel (temporary) (March 11); Deputy Chief of Staff, Third Army, San Antonio, Texas (July 2–August 6); Chief of Staff, Third Army (August 7–December 12); promoted to brigadier general (temporary) (October 3); Deputy Assistant Chief of Staff, War Plans Division, War Department, Washington, D.C. (December 14)

INTRODUCTION

The Eisenhower Diaries, 1929–1941

JOHN S. D. EISENHOWER

The set of diaries published here begins as my father, Dwight D. Eisenhower, was preparing to leave his assignment with the Battle Monuments Commission in Paris (August 1929). After a brief and entertaining account of a trip through Germany and Switzerland, the diaries take him to the War Department in Washington. They then take him to the Philippines and end a year after the termination of that tour of duty, in early 1941.

The decade between the years 1929 and 1939 was extremely important in Eisenhower's career, for during that period he attained experience and sophistication in the ways of government at the highest levels. Chapters 3 and 4 are particularly interesting for their detailed and frank account of Eisenhower's duties and observations in the War Department between 1929 and 1935.

The pages of these diaries provide many insights into Eisenhower's attitudes, attitudes that he carried with him through life. His comments on the American political scene are remarkable because they were penned by a relatively young, forty-year-old major who harbored no expectations of reaching high office himself because of current Army promotion policy. His opinions of the various members of Pres. Herbert Hoover's administration, and later those of Pres. Franklin D. Roosevelt's, may surprise the student unfamiliar with Eisenhower's complex nature. The future Republican president's all-out support for Pres. Franklin Roosevelt's early policies, for example, may also startle some. A few of Eisenhower's assessments of his contemporaries are harsh, and many changed later, as Eisenhower was always open-minded. But these assessments were obviously honest, never intended for publication. Therein lies their value.

One myth will certainly be exploded in the eyes of anyone reading these diaries seriously: the myth that Eisenhower was politically naïve when he came to Washington as president of the United States in January 1953. He had witnessed, even studied, the prominent figures of government at first hand, and while he admired many of them, he viewed them with no reverence at all.

Eisenhower's self-confidence is sometimes astonishing in the way he praises or criticizes men of great influence—for his own private use, of course. In one instance, for example, he remarks icily that a certain official had reached his political peak, as that official, in Eisenhower's view, lacked the capacity to go further. The individual being referred to is no less than Patrick J. Hurley, secretary of war, whose position was second only to that of the president himself.

Such self-assurance was of course necessary in the positions Eisenhower held: Supreme Commander, Allied Expeditionary Force (1944–45), and thirty-fourth president of the United States (1953–61). Eisenhower's ability to move confidently from lieutenant colonel to commander of a theater of war in the fifteen months between March 1941 and June 1942 stemmed largely from his experiences as a major thirteen years earlier.

The second major portion of these diaries, beginning with Chapter 5, covers Eisenhower's tour of duty with Gen. Douglas MacArthur in the Philippines. MacArthur, retiring as Army Chief of Staff in 1935, was named military advisor to the president of the fledgling Philippine Commonwealth, Manuel Quezon. Eisenhower accompanied MacArthur as his senior U.S. Army assistant.

Eisenhower's account of this period is of interest primarily because of the light it throws on the difficult task facing the United States and the Philippines, that of developing a military force capable of defending those seven thousand islands after their projected independence from the United States in 1946. The budgetary constraints necessitated by the Great Depression made that task, so appealing in theory, almost impossible. The diaries also reveal the degenerating relationship between Eisenhower and MacArthur. The passages that deal with that phase of Eisenhower's job may titillate those who enjoy reading about personal conflict, but an examination of that dreary period, in which neither man shows up at his best, will reveal nothing new. It tells us little about the vain and theatrical MacArthur that has not become common knowledge. And by now Eisenhower's temper, along with his own formidable ego, are well known.

The relationship between the two future World War II leaders actually began in early 1933, at which time a considerable mutual esteem prevailed between them. Admittedly, that esteem degenerated. The two shared a mutual contempt for a while, but the most violent period had passed, at least on the surface, by the time that Eisenhower left the Philippines in December 1939. The off-and-on animosity that Dan Holt has aptly termed a "love-hate relationship" is well known; the degree of admiration and loyalty that Eisenhower felt for his chief in the early days of the War Department is not.

It is not generally recognized—probably neither MacArthur nor

Eisenhower realized it at the time—that this was a low period in both their careers, especially MacArthur's. Having left the exalted seat of power, where he had been the Army Chief of Staff in Washington, MacArthur was faced with the choice of accepting either a subordinate position in the Army or a position with President Quezon in the Philippines. He had chosen the position with Quezon, and though his position appeared to be luxurious to a subordinate such as Eisenhower, MacArthur was actually experiencing the frustration that Eric Hoffer, in *The True Believer*, associates with the "new poor." Eisenhower, on the other hand, was frustrated by MacArthur's sometimes exaggerated responses to the humiliations he was feeling at the hands of the officials in Washington—and to MacArthur's impatience with anyone who failed to see things his way. Faced with plenty of other frustrations in the job they were trying to perform, neither man seems to have made much effort to realize what the other was going through.

It is interesting to me, as Eisenhower's son, to see how different my father appears in these diaries from the man I saw as a boy. Eisenhower's diaries of the days in Washington all appear upbeat. They exude enthusiasm, and while Eisenhower sometimes mentions his long working hours, he never complains. In fact, the work schedule Eisenhower was subjected to in the offices of the assistant secretary of war and later the chief of staff nearly broke his health. In later years my father said, "I always resented the years I spent as a slave in the War Department."

On the other hand, the Dwight Eisenhower I remember in the Philippines was always cheerful. I had no inkling, when the two of us toured Northern Luzon in May 1938, that he was undergoing some of his worst moments in the Cuartel d'España, MacArthur's headquarters, at that time.

These diaries are valuable additions to our store of knowledge regarding Dwight Eisenhower principally and Douglas MacArthur secondarily. We can be glad that they were not (as Eisenhower once ordered) shredded, burned, and denied to history.

EISENHOWER

CHAPTER ONE

From Abilene to Leavenworth
February 27, 1905–August 1926

In the 1890s, as Dwight D. Eisenhower was growing up, the town of Abilene, Kansas, stood less than twenty years removed from its wild days as a railhead for Texas cattle and playground for gunfighters. The Abilene Eisenhower knew had evolved into a service center for the farms that lay in all directions. Members of the community epitomized the values we now associate with family farming, a barter as well as a market economy, and rural churches—trust (until betrayed) in one's fellow man, a commitment to Christian morality, a belief in democratic equality and the rule of law, an eagerness to learn, and, above all, a hearty work ethic. Growing up, Eisenhower became familiar with these virtues by dint of the house he lived in, the friends he made, and the air he breathed. Shaping him, they guided him throughout his life. Along with rock-solid rural values, the Kansas of Eisenhower's boyhood also offered an example of late-nineteenth- and early-twentieth-century American ferment. The state produced reform movements—some of them led by nationally known eccentrics such as Carry Nation—that promoted, among other causes, temperance, railroad-rate reform, and the right of women to vote.[1] Nationally, it was a time of progressivism, political and social reform, and economic experimentation. Young Dwight learned about and could express himself on such developments; he took an interest in politics.

After graduating from Abilene High School in 1909, Eisenhower spent two years working for his father's own employer at a local creamery. The young man planned eventually to apply to the University of Michigan, there joining his brother Edgar, whom the whole family assisted with financial support. A close friend changed Eisenhower's mind, planting the idea of seeking instead an appointment to the U.S. Naval or Military Academy. By happenstance, Eisenhower landed at West Point rather than Annapolis, and his graduating class of 1915 turned out to be the famous one "the stars fell on." So began a soldier's odyssey.

Lieutenant Eisenhower entered an army that long had been the subject of reorganization efforts and policy studies and that remained so after the crisis of world war. At the turn of the century, conflict with Spain and fighting in the Philippines had placed severe strain on a weak military structure. Elihu Root, secretary of war under William McKinley and Theodore Roosevelt, had created the Army General Staff and urged further change, which was partially accomplished by legislation in 1903. But nothing in the way of peacetime reforms had the impact of World War I, forcing as it did rapid enlargement of the army and also its reshaping—during the war and afterward. The Great War made a strong case for a better-trained professional army, supported by a reserve component and a national guard system. Dramatic improvements were frustrated, however, by lack of funding. Most Americans, predictably, had called for rapid demobilization and cutbacks in defense spending soon after the Armistice of 1918, and the public got its wish. Questions of army structure, peacetime policy, war preparations, and military-civilian cooperation remained unsettled in the 1920s and later.[2]

Eisenhower did not serve overseas in World War I—a fact he always lamented—but missed no opportunity to explore the many open issues the military faced in these years. He was fascinated with, and became an early proponent of, the use of tanks in warfare. Interested in transportation, he volunteered to be an observer on the Transcontinental Motor Convoy in 1919. It became clear early in his career that he had a special talent for managing, analyzing problems, and speaking and writing on how to solve them. Dwight and Mamie Eisenhower suffered the greatest tragedy of their lives when their son, Doud Dwight, died from scarlet fever at Fort Meade, Maryland, on January 2, 1921.

From January 1922 to September 1924, Eisenhower served under Gen. Fox Conner[3] in the Panama Canal Zone. Highly regarded in the service at that time, Conner became the young Eisenhower's mentor. After brief tours at Fort Meade, Maryland, and the army recruiting station at Fort Logan, Colorado, Eisenhower in 1925 entered the Command and General Staff School[4] at Fort Leavenworth, Kansas, graduating in June 1926, finishing first in his class.[5]

1. On the Kansas of Eisenhower's boyhood, see Michael Goldberg, *An Army of Women: Gender and Politics in Gilded Age Kansas* (Baltimore: Johns Hopkins University Press, 1997), and Robert W. Richmond, *Kansas: A Land of Contrasts* (Arlington Heights, Ill.: Forum Press, 1989).

2. For background on the U.S. military and military policy from the turn of the century to World War II, see (listed chronologically by date of publication) Elias Huzar, *The Purse and the Sword: Control of the Army by Congress through Military Appropriations* (Ithaca: Cornell University Press, 1950); Walter Millis, *Arms and Men: A Study in American Military History* (New York: Mentor Books, 1958); Samuel P. Huntington, *The Soldier and the State* (New York: Random House, 1964); Russell F. Weigley,

History of the United States Army (New York: Macmillan, 1967); Russell F. Weigley, *The American Way of War* (New York: Macmillan, 1973); James E. Hughes Jr., *From Root to McNamara: Army Organization and Administration, 1900–1963* (Washington, D.C.: Center for Military History, U.S. Army, 1975); Allan R. Millett and Peter Maslowski, *For the Common Defense: A Military History of the United States of America* (New York: Free Press, 1984)

3. Conner, an 1898 graduate of the U.S. Military Academy (USMA), probably influenced Eisenhower more than any other senior officer he encountered during his career. (See Dwight D. Eisenhower, *At Ease: Stories I Tell to Friends* [Garden City, N.Y.: Doubleday, 1967], 182–95.) Conner served in the Spanish-American War and as the G-3 (operations officer) of the American Expeditionary Force in World War I. As operations officer, Conner held one of the vital positions on the General Staff. Because of this previous prestigious position, it was an honor for Eisenhower to have been noticed by Conner. In 1925 Conner was promoted to major general.

4. During this time period, the officers' school at Fort Leavenworth was designated the Command and General Staff School. By 1946 it was generally known as the Command and General Staff College.

5. The editors relied on the following sources for general background information on Eisenhower: Kenneth S. Davis, *Soldier of Democracy* (Garden City, N.Y.: Doubleday, 1945); Kevin McCann, *Man from Abilene* (Garden City, N.Y.: Doubleday, 1952); Steve Neal, *The Eisenhowers: Reluctant Dynasty* (Garden City, N. Y.: Doubleday, 1978); Stephen E. Ambrose, *Eisenhower: Soldier, General of the Army, President-Elect, 1890–1952* (New York: Simon and Schuster, 1983); Piers Brendon, *Ike: His Life and Times* (New York: Harper and Row, 1986); and Merle Miller, *Ike the Soldier: As They Knew Him* (New York: Perigree Books, 1987). Combined, these works provide adequate information for the time period of this publication.

To Nettie Stover Jackson[1]

FEBRUARY 27, 1905

Dear Cousin: You will see from the date on my letter that I am slow. I received your letter two or three days ago, and one thing you said in it was unlucky. You know you said I must not get sick. Well I've got the worst sore throat that I ever had or ever hope to see again. Milton[2] asked for the picture you sent me and I let him have it and he said, "This looks like Nettie, is it her." Milton is much better but very weak and cannot walk. This old paper hasn't any lines and I feel miserable. Three boys came down there to the Reform School, from here for chicken stealing. I have not started to school yet. Arthur[3] intends to go to Kansas City in a few days. He is going to work at short hand. If Uncle Clarence and Aunt Alice[4] don't go before March 9th tell them to stop and visit here awhile because we will not be quarantined after March 9.[5] I'll bet this writing would take a prize anywhere and spelling too for all of that. Roy[6] and I have baked pies three times and a lady baked some once for us and my cousin baked for us today as well. Write soon even if I don't do it myself. It is 3 weeks today since Milton took sick from your cousin. <u>D. Dwight Eisenhower</u>[7]

1. This letter, which has not been published previously, is the earliest extant writing of Dwight D. Eisenhower. Nettie Stover was the daughter of Charles Wesley Stover, one of Ida Stover Eisenhower's brothers, who in 1905 lived with his family in Topeka.

2. Milton Stover Eisenhower, youngest of Dwight's five brothers, was born on September 15, 1899, in Abilene, Kansas. Milton was a close confidant of Dwight's and would be one of his chief advisers. Among Milton Eisenhower's achievements are director of the federal Agriculture Department's Information Division (1928–41); director of the War Relocation Authority (1942); associate director of the Office of War Information (1942–43); and president of Kansas State University and Pennsylvania State University as well as two terms as president of Johns Hopkins University. President Eisenhower utilized his brother in a number of capacities, including informal adviser, member of the President's Advisory Committee on Government Organization, personal representative to Latin America, and part-time speechwriter. He served on presidential commissions appointed by Lyndon Johnson and Richard Nixon, bringing to eight the number of presidents with whom he was associated in some capacity. He died in 1985.

3. Arthur B. Eisenhower, the oldest of the brothers, was born on November 11, 1886, in Hope, Kansas, where David Eisenhower and his partner, Milton Good, man-

aged a general store. Arthur's career began as a messenger boy at Commerce Bank, Kansas City. Eventually he became vice president. He also served on the boards of several Kansas City corporations. Arthur died in 1958.

4. Alice M. Stover Lucas was a half sister of Ida Stover Eisenhower.

5. Apparently the brothers were quarantined because they had scarlet fever. Milton's illness left him somewhat frail compared with his robust older brothers. See Eisenhower, *At Ease*, 34.

6. Roy J. Eisenhower was the fourth of the brothers. After graduation from pharmacy school in Wichita, he worked in an Ellsworth, Kansas, drugstore and eventually purchased his own pharmacy in Junction City, Kansas, only twenty-five miles from Abilene. A popular and prominent Junction City civic leader, he died unexpectedly in 1942 at the relatively young age of forty-nine.

7. Eisenhower's given name was David Dwight. Because he and his father shared the same first name, his mother decided to call her son by his middle name, Dwight. Eisenhower explained the reversal in a 1965 letter: "The revision took place when I entered West Point because having been called Dwight by mother all my entire boyhood I just assumed my name was Dwight David. Since I thus entered it into the official records I have continued to use this order." Eisenhower to David Silvette, January 8, 1965, Secretary's File, Post-pres. Papers, Eisenhower Library.

2   *Dickinson County News*, Abilene, Kansas
"The Student in Politics"[1]

November 18, 1909

Mr. Toastmaster and Gentlemen: An old proverb says: "As the twig is bent so will the tree be inclined." Nowhere does this quotation apply more forcibly than to "The Student in Politics." The young man just starting in politics is taking a very important step in life, and one which to all probability will determine his political standing forever. He will naturally line up with one of the two great political parties and the chances are will remain a life member of that party.

For, a man, after voting the straight party ticket for several elections, seldom changes from one side to the other. This fact is proven conclusively by a controversy now going on in the Republican party. You know there is one brand of Republicans, called Square Dealers, Insurgents, etc. and although these men are loud in their denunciation of Canon, Aldrich and a few others, who are hide bound party men, yet they refuse to join any other party, and at the elections vote for the Republican candidates. Thus, in reality, a man's party becomes a part of him as truly as he becomes a part of it, and he simply will not leave it.[2]

The average man ceases to reason fairly on the questions involved and always casts his vote as before. True he continues to discuss the political questions of importance but only in an obstinate and top sided manner of reasoning, in which he simply refuses to see any wrong in his party. Before each election he works himself into a frenzy of loyalty to his party, watches with feverish interest the returns from the different precincts, and then goes back to work in the same old way until another election. Remember however we are speaking only of the average voter, whose common place duties in life leaves him scarcely any time for politics.

So since a man rarely changes from one party to another, his first vote is probably his most important one, and the causes which influence his first vote are necessarily important to him. In choosing between the two great parties, a young man is often influenced by personal admiration for certain candidates or leaders of his party. A leader of a political party, who is a clean and fearless fighter and possesses a winning manner is undoubtedly the means of attracting a large number of votes to that party, for he is naturally the kind of man that young fellows idealize.

Then there is an inborn desire in all normal and healthy boys to help the smaller of the contestants in an uneven fight. A young man in speaking of the political situation the other day said, "My father is a Republican and so was his father, but I am going to vote for the Democrats at the next election because I think they need me and the Republicans do not."

But notwithstanding such reasons, as admiration, love of fair play, the parental vote and the like, a man's first vote is generally cast correctly. He has arrived at an age of great self confidence and has acquired a feeling of self importance for he figures that he will be about ⅟₁₅ of 1 millionth part of the voters of these United States and therefore must be very careful in choosing sides before he is willing to cast his vote either way.

He learns that one party (the Republican) protects our manufacturers by placing a high import duty on all manufactured goods. This practically blots out foreign competition in that line and enables the manufacturers to make enormous profits off of the U.S. citizens. He sees that the rich man would still make a good profit, if the duties were removed or at the least considerably lowered, and being young, impulsive, vehement and outspoken he calls this system, legalized robbery. He also finds that the other party (the Democrat) wants to remove these excessive duties and arrange a tariff that will bring revenue into the U.S. coffers and at the same time be easier on the great mass of citizens of this country.

In a further comparison, he learns that the Democrat party wants to make congress more truly representative of the people, by having the U.S. Senators elected by direct vote of the people. The other party opposes such a plan or at least has never endorsed it in any of their national conventions. The boy being rather shrewd, figures out that under such conditions it would be harder for the interests (the rich corporations) to control congress, and naturally concludes that this is the reason the Republicans oppose such a plan. The young recruit notices, that because one party has been in power for 50 years, with only two brief interruptions, many evils have sprung up in the machinery of the government, which a change in policy for a time would at least remedy if not blot out.

The young man also sees that the more honest and fearless of the Republican leaders have become disgusted with the policies and the actions of the party proper and branched off into, Square Dealers, Insurgents, Progressives and Reformers, though they still cling to the name Republican. He admires these men greatly but he cannot help but remark that they are fighting for many of the principles which the Democrat party advocates, among them being lower tariff.

So he naturally concludes, that with the Republican party splitting up and a number of honest and fearless ones tending towards Democracy, that the Democrat party deserves his first vote. And since the first vote generally determines his political standing, we find one more intelligent young man enlisted under the standard of Democracy.

1. Eisenhower was invited by the Dickinson County Young Men's Democratic Club to address its annual banquet, along with two other young men from the county and George H. Hodges of Johnson County, Kansas, a candidate for his party's gubernatorial nomination who in 1912 would win the governorship. Eisenhower chose the topic, "The Student in Politics." The *Dickinson County News* (Abilene) published the full text of the speech, along with Eisenhower's high school graduation photograph, on the front page of its November 18, 1909, issue. The editor wrote in the introduction to Eisenhower's speech: "The *News*. . . prints in full the speech of Dwight Eisenhower . . . not like it was much better than the others but the subject is one that every person should study." See also Robert H. Ferrell, "Eisenhower Was a Democrat," *Kansas History* 13 (autumn 1990): 134–38.

2. Eisenhower discussed several of the most volatile political issues of the day. The Republican sponsored Payne-Aldrich Tariff of 1909 dictated an average 40 percent protective tariff on imported goods. Duties on specific commodities and goods varied widely. Eisenhower's text reflects the Midwest's distrust of large eastern corporations, a distrust that prompted the reform movement of the Progressive Era. Joseph Cannon, to whom Eisenhower refers, was Speaker of the House from 1901 to 1910 and ruled the House of Representatives as a virtual dictator. In 1910 he was removed by allied insurgent Republicans and Democrats. Eisenhower incorrectly spelled Cannon's name.

To United States Senator Joseph L. Bristow[1]

AUGUST 20, 1910

Dear Sir: I would very much like to enter either the school at Annapolis, or the one at West Point. In order to do this, I must have an appointment to one of these places and so I am writing to you in order to secure the same.

I have graduated from high school and will be nineteen years of age this fall.[2]

If you find it possible to appoint me to one of these schools, your kindness will certainly be appreciated by me.

Trusting to hear from you, concerning this matter, at your earliest convenience, I am, respectfully yours

1. Joseph L. Bristow, U.S. senator from Kansas, was from Salina, a town only twenty-five miles west of Abilene. A prominent Kansas newspaper publisher and editor, he served as senator from 1909 to 1915.

2. Although Eisenhower's first preference was Annapolis, the Naval Academy would not accept for admission any man over the age of nineteen. Eisenhower would turn twenty on October 14, 1910, almost a full year before the class for which he was applying would enter Annapolis.

To Joseph Bristow

SEPTEMBER 3, 1910

Dear Sir: Some time ago I wrote to you applying for an appointment to West Point or Annapolis. As yet I have heard nothing definite from you about the matter, but I noticed in the daily papers that you would soon give a competitive examination for these appointments.

Now, if you find it impossible to give me an appointment outright, to one of these places, would I have the right to enter this competitive examination?

If so, will you please explain the conditions to be met in entering this examination, and the studies to be covered. Trusting to hear from you at your earliest convenience, I am, Respectfully yours[1]

1. On October 24, 1910, Bristow wrote to Eisenhower that he would send his name to the secretary of war as his nominee for a spring vacancy at the U.S. Military Academy and that the entrance examination would be held at Jefferson Barracks, Missouri, in January. The War Department would send instructions. Bristow requested that Eisenhower complete the War Department nomination form, including "a statement of your exact age, years and months, and a statement as to how long you have been an actual resident of Kansas." Bristow to Eisenhower, October 24, 1910, Joseph L. Bristow Papers, Kansas State Historical Society Archives. Eisenhower complied with the request the next day.

5   Kansas State Historical Society Archives
                         Joseph L. Bristow Papers

To Joseph Bristow

October 25, 1910

Dear Sir: Your letter of the 24th instant has just been received. I wish to thank you sincerely for the favor you have shown me in appointing me to West Point.

In regard to the information desired; I am just nineteen years and eleven days of age, and have been a resident of Abilene, Kans. for eighteen years. Thanking you again, I am Very truly yours

6   Kansas State Historical Society Archives
                         Joseph L. Bristow Papers

To Joseph Bristow

March 25, 1911

Dear Sir: Having learned from my parents, that you are again in Salina, I take this opportunity of thanking you for my appointment to West Point.

Although I wrote to you immediately after receiving the appointment last November, it's value to me has been greatly increased, since I was notified that I had passed the entrance examinations. I took the examinations at Jefferson Barracks, Mo., in January.

One of my alternates, Mr. Platner, did not pass, but I understand the other did. I have been ordered to report at West Point, June 14, this year.

So trusting that you will accept my heartiest thanks for the great favor you have conferred upon me, I am, Respectfully yours,

TO THE ADJUTANT GENERAL OF THE ARMY

AUGUST 9, 1915

Subject: Acceptance of appointment as Second Lieutenant of Infantry.
1. I accept the commission as Second Lieutenant of Infantry.
2. My legal residence at the time of appointment is, "201 E.S. 4th St, Abilene, Kansas."[1] My full name is Dwight David Eisenhower.
3. I am transmitting with this, an oath of office, and designation blank, as directed in your letter of August 4th.

> 1. Eisenhower wrote the above from his home in Abilene where he was spending the summer after his June graduation from West Point. The address of the home, 201 Southeast Fourth Street, today is the address of the Eisenhower Library. The "E.S." used in Eisenhower's letter was correct at that time.

8   Eisenhower Library
Ruby Norman Lucier Papers

TO RUBY NORMAN[1]

JANUARY 17, 1916

Dearest Ruby: 'Tis a long, long time since I've written you, n'est-ce pas? I've really started several times—but always something happens—and I get side tracked. It's 10 o'clock now—I'm on guard—and sitting down here in the guard house.

I scarcely even write a letter any more. Yes—I reckon you'll say—"Well what's the trouble"—but there isn't so much. One reason is this "You can't always hold what you have"—My life here, is, in the main uninteresting. Nothing much doing—and I get tired of the same old grind some times.[2]

The girl I run around with is named Miss Doud,[3] from Denver. Winters here. Pretty nice—but awful strong for society—which often bores me. But we get along well together—and I'm at her house whenever I'm off duty—whether it's morning-noon-night. Her mother and sisters are fine—and we have lots of fun together [. . . .]

My room mate is going into the aviation. I tried—but can't make it until next September. I'll get a lot more then—if I get in—and maybe I can make ends meet. Ha ha—You know me—I'll never have a sou [. . . .][4]

I coached a football team for a little school here this fall. They gave a dance not long ago at a big hotel, and I attended. When I entered the ball room everybody stopped and started clapping and cheering. I blushed like a baby—Gee! surely was embarrassed.[5]

I made a run for a corner, believe me [. . . .] I'll try to do better on writing hereafter—and sometime—if you're interested I'll tell you all about the girl I run around with. Good night.

1. Like Eisenhower, Ruby Norman (Lucier) was from the south side of town (in Abilene, the "wrong side of the tracks"). They became lifelong friends in public school, and they maintained an intermittent correspondence until Ruby's death in 1967. Evidently, she was the sister he never had at home. Eisenhower, *At Ease*, 3, 95. During Eisenhower's term at West Point, he wrote several letters to Ruby. This letter has been published but is included here in part because of the references to Mamie, aviation, and football (see below). The other letters have been excerpted in Ambrose, *Eisenhower*, 1:49–50.

Eisenhower's letters to Ruby Norman discussed West Point football games, smoking cigarettes (which was against West Point rules), and a variety of other matters. In a letter of November 5, 1913, he confessed that "West Point, N.Y. looks awfully nice as an address on an envelope." After Eisenhower had reinjured his bad knee dismounting from a running horse, he wrote on November 22, 1913, that it "seems like I am never cheerful anymore. The fellows that used to call me 'sunny jim' call me 'gloomy face' now. . . . I hate to be so helpless and worthless. . . . Anyway I'm getting to be such a confirmed grouch you'd hardly know me. Guess I'll come out of it soon though." His football days were over after this accident. When the cast was removed from his leg, he was informed he would never play again.

He also referred to the difficulties along the Mexican border when he wrote on November 24 that "the only bright spot is, just now, that trouble with Mexico seems imminent. We may stir up a little excitement yet, let's hope so, at least." Eisenhower's mood improved greatly when he wrote Miss Norman on November 30, 1913, that Army had "surely turned the trick" and had beaten Navy in football. He continued that it was "some game, some game! Just a small crowd saw us do it, you know, just 45,000 people. . . . You should have seen us after the game, oh, oh, oh! . . . I enjoyed myself. 'Course I couldn't raise a riot for I was in uniform—but I went down to Murray's in a crowd of four—and we danced and ate . . . the joy of the thing is too much—I feel my reason toppling." Eisenhower to Ruby Norman, November 5, 13, 20, 22, 24, and 30, 1913, Ruby Norman Lucier Papers, Eisenhower Library; and Ambrose, *Eisenhower*, 1:50.

Eisenhower also maintained a very private correspondence with Gladys Harding (Brooks) in 1915 after his graduation from West Point, which is not included here. The letters are quoted extensively in Miller, *Ike the Soldier*, 126–29.

2. During his two years at Fort Sam Houston, Eisenhower served as Inspector General for the Illinois National Guard, which had been mobilized in south Texas as part of President Wilson's show of force toward Mexico, then undergoing a revolution. He also served as provost marshal of the fort. His last assignment was supply officer for the 57th Infantry Regiment.

3. Mamie Geneva Doud was born in Boone, Iowa, on November 14, 1896, the

daughter of John Sheldon and Elivera Mathilda Carlson Doud. The family moved to Cedar Rapids, Iowa, in August 1897, and then to Pueblo, Colorado Springs, and Denver, Colorado, in 1905–7. Mamie Doud attended Denver Public Schools and Miss Wolcott's, a private finishing school. She met the then Second Lieutenant Eisenhower in October 1915 while she and her family were wintering in San Antonio and Mamie visited friends at Fort Sam Houston, Texas. Mamie and Dwight were married on July 1, 1916, in the Doud family home in Denver. Two sons were born to the Eisenhowers. The first, Doud Dwight Eisenhower, died of scarlet fever on January 2, 1921. The second son, John Sheldon Doud Eisenhower, was born in Denver on August 3, 1922.

Mrs. Eisenhower followed her husband to practically every post until Dwight was transferred to the Philippines in 1935. She remained in the United States a year before traveling to Manila with son John. When the attack on Pearl Harbor occurred, they were stationed at Fort Sam Houston. When Eisenhower was called to Washington, Mrs. Eisenhower moved to the Wardman Park Hotel, where she lived almost continuously throughout World War II during the general's absence. Mrs. Eisenhower performed volunteer work at canteens and for the Red Cross during the war. During the presidential years, Mamie appeared every year on the Gallup Poll's list of the Ten Most Admired Women in America. After the death of her husband, she continued to live on the Gettysburg, Pennsylvania, farm. Winter vacations were spent in California and Georgia. In the late 1970s she took an apartment in Washington, D.C. Mamie Doud Eisenhower died on November 1, 1979, in Washington, D.C., and is buried beside her husband and first son in the Place of Meditation at the Eisenhower Center in Abilene, Kansas. For a complete biography of Mamie Doud Eisenhower that covers this time period in detail, see Susan Eisenhower, *Mrs. Ike: Memories and Reflections on the Life of Mamie Eisenhower* (New York: Farrar, Straus and Giroux, 1996).

4. In February, just a few days after Eisenhower asked Mamie to marry him, he received notification that his application for the aviation section had been approved. His prospective father-in-law took a dim view of his daughter's marrying a man so reckless that he would want to pilot an airplane. Eisenhower complied with his father-in-law's request and did not enter pilot training. He would acquire his pilot's license while serving in the Philippines. See Eisenhower, *At Ease,* 117–18.

5. Eisenhower was well known for his ability to coach football. More than once during his early military career he received assignment requests because of his ability to coach the local army post team. While at Fort Sam Houston he coached football teams at San Antonio's Peacock Military Academy and St. Louis College. His success coaching the Fort Meade team from 1919 to 1921 led in part to his reassignment to Meade in 1924 and to his assignment to Fort Benning, Georgia, in 1926. See Eisenhower, *At Ease,* 180, 196–98, 203–4.

TO MAMIE EISENHOWER

SEPTEMBER 25, 1917
TUES. NIGHT, THE 25TH

Dearest Sweetheart: First of all I'll explain why I have not written. I arrived Sunday, and was sent immediately to the trenches, and didn't get out until tonight.[2] I could leave them under <u>no</u> circumstances. It was wet, cold, and rained the whole time. To complicate matters, my baggage has not yet arrived so I had nothing except what I had on when I left home. Just before I left the trenches, mothers[3] telegram was brought to me. You could have knocked me over with a feather. Why you sweet little old girl, somehow it doesn't seem possible. How I wish I could come and see you and "IT".[4]

I grabbed a chance to send you a telegram mon. eve, and I sent a night letter tonight. I surely hope you regain your strength soon. Gee! I'm crazy to see you.

So far I haven't had a minute to get in a pay voucher, but when I can, I'll have the money sent to Lockwood as usual.

Bless mother's heart, she sent me the sweetest telegram. Tell her I sure do "lub" her. And oh yes! Tell her please to mail the overcoat to me thusly—
Capt. DD, etc—
c/o Senior Instructor's Office
Civilian Training Camp,
Fort Oglethorpe, Georgia
Tell her "Thank you" for that.

Merillat[5] and I are living together in a nine by nine tent. He is a God send, for I'm using his stuff. I hope the Q.M. soon gets mine. I'm wondering exactly what you will call the BOY. I know it will be "Doud" for the sake of the Folks, and I think it will be fine. I hope you give him a middle name either beginning with D. or J. If it is D, then he can sign his name D Eisenhower, Jr., but if it is J. then it will be all same as my Dads, "<u>D</u>.J". Anyway, I'll love the name and Him, (no matter what you call him) but most of all, I'll love <u>YOU</u>.

I've sent you 100,483,491,342 kisses since I've been gone. I know that isn't very many sweet thing, but I've been so frightfully busy, and I had to send 'em when I could get a chance.

Please teach <u>our</u> son, to like "Sheltering Palms". Millions of kisses and lots of love to you and "mover". Your Lover—<u>YOU BET</u> [Marginal notes] Tell mother I signed the telegram "Dwight" cause the last word in the telegram was Ike and I wanted it to all get there.

13

I received you letter tonight. Gee! How I jumped for it. Ike.

1. Permission to reproduce or quote this letter must be in writing from the James S. Copley Library, La Jolla, California.
2. Eisenhower had departed Fort Sam Houston on September 22 for Fort Oglethorpe, Georgia, where he served through November as an ROTC instructor.
3. Elivera Mathilda Carlson Doud was born in Boone, Iowa, on May 13, 1878. She married John Sheldon Doud in 1894, just three months past her sixteenth birthday. Of the Douds' four daughters, Mamie was second-born. Tragically, the eldest daughter, Eleanor, and the third dauther, Eda Mae, died during adolescence. Mrs. Elivera Doud died in Denver, on September 28, 1960.
4. Mamie's mother had telegraphed Eisenhower to let him know that his and Mamie's first child, Doud Dwight, had been born September 24.
5. Louis Alfred Merillat graduated with Eisenhower in the class of 1915. Merillat served with the 38th Infantry Regiment, 3d Division, American Expeditionary Force. Badly wounded in France, he retired from the Army in 1922. In *At Ease,* Eisenhower recounts how in 1912 the Army football coach, who had learned a lesson from Army's loss to Knute Rockne's Notre Dame team earlier that year, developed a forward pass combination of quarterback Vernon Prichard to end Louis Merillat. The strategy, first used against favored Navy in the season's climactic game, resulted in a twenty-two-to-nine Army upset of the midshipmen. See *At Ease,* 15.

10 James S. Copley Library[1]

To Mamie Eisenhower

September 26, 1917

Dearest Sweetheart Darling: I am going to write this letter on the typewritter in order that you may have less trouble trying to read it. I received a letter from mother last evening and she said you had received no word from me. Since leaving home I sent a letter from a little town in Texas, then two telegrams from New Orleans, and two telegrams and two letters from here.[2] When I received mothers first telegram it was a day late on account of my being in the trenches. I didn't get a chance to answer until Tues. night and then I sent a night letter because I had too much to say to put in a straight telegram.

Mother told me what a brave girl you have been and said how proud she was of you. Why bless your heart, she isn't half as proud as I am.

I certainly hope that you are getting better fast and that you soon may be able to run out side the house again. Mother's letter was full of glowing descriptions of the youngster, and believe me I am surely anxious to see the young rascal. She said the doctor was awfully proud of the boy. Merry[3] wants to know the name of him and of course I couldn't tell him exactly. He thinks that is a crime and that I am a poor sort of a father not to know the name of our only boy.

I understand that Mr. Ike Jr. has my feet, hands, and shoulders. That must certainly take up the biggest part of him, for it certainly does of me. Just wait until I come home, if we don't have more fun with that boy than with a barrel full of monkeys, then I don't know a thing. Tell me, what does Dad[4] think of the new arrival, and are Bus and Mike[5] anxious to see the young giant.

You are probably wondering what I do all day long. I get up at 5.15 A.M. and go all day long. It is pretty hard to handle this thing, and it keeps a fellow busy right up to 9.00 P.M.

Give my regards to all your friends who come in and are nice to you. Any one who is nice to you is nice to me, and I am strong for them. Mother has been a peach. I am crazier about our muvver than ever.

It is now time for Sat. morning Inspection, and I must go and give the boys h———.

I'm sending you loads and loads of love and kisses. Then I'm sending some more for "Ikey" and barrels more for Mother. Tell her I love her so much I'm going to break all her ribs when I come home. Your devoted Lover "You BET"

1. Permission to reproduce or quote this letter must be in writing from the James S. Copley Library, La Jolla, California.

2. Letter was written from the Civilian Training Camp, Fort Oglethorpe, Georgia.

3. "Merry" was the nickname of friend and classmate, Louis Merillat.

4. John S. Doud, Mamie Eisenhower's father, was born on November 18, 1870, in Rome, New York. Married in 1894, he founded his own meat-packing company in Boone, Iowa, in 1898. In 1906 he moved the family to Pueblo, Colorado, then to Denver in 1907. Doud died in 1951. "Dad" in the diary text always refers to John S. Doud, unless noted otherwise.

5. "Bus" presumably was the nickname of Mamie's younger sister, Eda Mae, and "Mike" was the nickname of Mabel Frances, the youngest of the four Doud children.

11   James S. Copley Library[1]

To Mamie Eisenhower

SEPTEMBER 27, 1917

Darling Girl: Received Mothers letter (special) this morning and it was as enthusiastically received as it was sent. I'm surely glad the young scoundrel can <u>howl</u>—and as long as it is a boy—the big hands and feet can't hurt him much. Though how in the world mother can tell that it "looks like us both" is more than I can see. Just wait until I get home, I'll start teaching him boxing pronto.

I have been in such a terrible rush I can't get on my feet. I'll write to Dad as soon as possible—but I am even stealing the time to write you.

My baggage just arrived, and as it has rained steadily since I arrived, you can imagine what I look like.

I haven't been out of camp since arriving. Don't want to go—and wouldn't have time if I did.

Honey please don't try to walk around too soon, will you? You must be awfully careful, for you must be well and strong when I come home. We'll surely have a good time when I do come.

Mother has surely been sweet and lovely during it all, and tell her we "lub" her more than ever. We think she is great, don't we? Tell her I refuse to call her grandma.

I put in my pay voucher rather late, but had it sent to Lockwood as usual. So I reckon you'll have some money soon. When I get my travel pay, it will run me for a while.

I guess mother has sent my overcoat. It gets mighty cold here in the mornings and evenings.

The day Mr. Young One arrived in this world, his fond father was sloshing up and down the coldest, wettest, "slipperiest" trenches in the U.S. Gee! It was awful, and I slept a couple hours that night, with a little piece of canvas for a cover.

You tell mother you bet I'm a fond father.

Good bye for now—I love you—love you love you, awful much. Goodbye—love to mother and son. Your lover, Sheltering Palms, you bet. Sept. 24

1. Permission to reproduce or quote this letter must be in writing from the James S. Copley Library, La Jolla, California.

12   Eisenhower Library
                                                Pre-presidential Papers
"A MESSAGE TO THE MEN"[1]

JULY 1918

Under the present organization of the Tank Corps, it has been decided that the colors shall be red, yellow and blue. This combination is significant of the work the tank corps must do, for the colors represent artillery, cavalry, and infantry. In other words, the tank corps must be familiar with most of the details and the general plan of operation of these three branches, besides those peculiar to the tanks themselves. This, then, explains why this branch of the service needs men of unusual ability and why its <u>esprit de corps</u> must be of the highest standard.

By their very nature, tanks must work in conjunction with the three branches of service mentioned above, for while a tank can very often take a strong point or clear out a line of trenches, it cannot hold the position indefinitely, but must be supported by the other arms of the service—particularly the infantry and artillery.

We read on our poster—"Why walk to Berlin when you can ride in a tank?" This certainly is a strong appeal to the popular imagination, and has no doubt been the means of securing many men for the service. However, when these men enlist, their duties during their early training seem to be almost entirely along the lines laid down for the infantry, and many are prone to wonder if they have been misinformed as to the work involved.

Patience and perseverance ought soon to dispel this illusion, though, for both officers and enlisted men must have that fundamental military training, which only infantry drill can give. In other words, you cannot be a successful tank fighter without first being a good soldier, with the discipline and knowledge of military formations and minor tactics learned during infantry drill.

Bear this in mind then, and keep up the present high standard of spirit and efficiency. It seems perfectly safe to say that we have right here in Camp Colt one of the finest collections of men and officers anywhere in our army.

To a man making his first visit here is immediately borne the significance of the attitude of every man and officer in the camp. It means that the Tank Corps, although the baby branch of the service, is a baby only in name—perhaps a baby wild cat—and the slogan "Treat 'Em Rough" will prove to be a very appropriate phrase when the kitten has grown a bit more and sharpened his claws for the Boche.

1. On March 24, 1918, Captain Eisenhower received an assignment as commander of the new Tank Corps located at Camp Colt, Gettysburg, Pennsylvania. He would remain at Camp Colt until after the World War I Armistice was signed in November. His address to the men at Camp Colt was published in the camp newsletter *Treat 'Em Rough,* probably in July. John B. Shinn enclosed a copy of the newsletter in a letter sent to Eisenhower on November 14, 1946. Shinn File, Pre-pres. Papers, Eisenhower Library. The newsletter is not dated, but examination of prior and later issues indicate it was probably the July 1918 issue. Shinn served under Captain Eisenhower at Camp Colt in 1918 and after World War II sent memorabilia to the five-star general.

"OUR FLAG"

SEPTEMBER 10, 1918[1]

(On August 22d, the ceremony attendant upon the presentation of an American flag to the 330th Bn. was held. The flag was the gift of the parents of the Battalion Commander, Capt. Roderick Stephens. Major Eisenhower, Camp Colt Commander, made the speech of presentation which is printed herewith.)[2]

To the men and officers of the 330th Battalion Tank Corps, has been presented by the parents of the Battalion Commander an American Flag. To me has been accorded the great honor of making the formal presentation.

On such an occasion, it is entirely unnecessary and unfitting that I attempt to tell you of the ideals and principles for which this flag has unfalteringly stood. For over one hundred and forty years those ideals and those principles have been so gloriously symbolized by this flag that today, in the uttermost parts of the earth, it stands for justice, freedom and the right.

But it is fitting that we should here remind ourselves of the responsibilities devolving upon us, as we assume our American privilege of taking our stand under it as its defenders.

As members of the American Army we are soon to set foot on foreign soil. It behooves us to watch ourselves that no act of ours, however small, shall ever disgrace the unsullied reputation of this flag. Let us, therefore, resolve that at all times and places in whatsoever conditions we may be, we bear ourselves proudly and courageously, conscious of our duties and responsibilities, and of the great honor that fell to us when we were chosen to fight for our country.

Today the greatest war machine that lust, selfishness and sinful conceit could develop is striving to trample the flag in the dust.

Together with millions of others of America's Best, you have arisen to defiantly shout IT SHALL NOT BE DONE, and now you are offering your lives to prove your words.

And so men, as you go forth to take your part in this greatest war, may the ideals embodied in this flag sustain you. May you, when the work is done, return with it to your native land, but if God wills that you should stay, then let your comrades say that every man of the 330th showed in his every act all that America could ask of a Loyal son.

1. Eisenhower's message appeared in *Treat 'Em Rough* (see above entry) on September 10, 1918. A copy of the newsletter was sent as an attachment to a letter from

W. Louis Schlesinger to Eisenhower, on May 12, 1949. Schlesinger File, Pre-pres. Papers, Eisenhower Library. Like Shinn, Schlesinger had served under Eisenhower at Camp Colt.

2. The first paragraph was set off in parentheses by the newsletter editor as an introduction.

14   Eisenhower Library
                                                     White House Central Files

To Chief Motor Transport Corps

November 3, 1919[1]

1. I was detailed for duty as observer on Trans-Continental Motor Truck Trip[2] on the day that the train left its initial point, (Washington, D.C.). Being impossible to join the train before evening of that date (July 7), nothing is known by me of the preliminary arrangements and plans for the trip, nor of the start from Washington. I joined the train at Frederick, Md., the first night's stop out of Washington.

2. I have not at any time been furnished by any authority with information concerning the nature of the report desired; therefore, for purposes of this report, the subject is divided into the following general heads:

A - Matériel.
B - Personnel and Administration.
C - Roads.

REPORT
A - Matériel
1. The Trans-Continental Truck Train was composed of various types of light and heavy motor trucks, touring cars, special makes of observation cars, motorcycles, ambulances, trailers, tractor and machine shop unit. No attempt is made here to enumerate each one, nor to give specifications in detail, as this information is already in hands of Chief, Motor Transport Corps.

The vehicles were equipped with pneumatics, giant solids, dual solids and single solid tires. The Mack trucks represented the chain drive type, the F. W. D.'s[3] and Militor[4] represented the four wheel drive type, and various standard makes represented the two wheel, rear drive type.

Practically each of the above named types has its own most efficient speed rate, causing great difficulty in keeping the trucks properly closed in convoy formations.

2. Mechanical difficulties during the first part of the trip were slight, and easily overcome.

19

Reports of officers with the convoy indicated that the vehicles had not been properly tested and adjusted before starting the trip. This occasioned many short halts on the part of individual trucks, to adjust carburetors, clean spark plugs, adjust brake bands, to time motors and make minor repairs of this nature. It was evident though that many of these difficulties were caused by inefficient handling of the vehicle by the driver.

As the trip went on, it soon developed that difficulties arose much more frequently in some types than in others. The Garford trucks were particular offenders. While other makes and types had difficulties at times, so many repairs were necessary on the three Garford trucks as to justify the opinion that it is not so well constructed as other standard makes on this trip. One Garford[5] was compelled to abandon trip entirely.

In heavy going, such as sand and stiff grades, the heavy types were always in difficulty. Chain drive trucks would simply not operate in sand, and practically all of the heavy trucks had to be pulled through sand stretches. In such places, the lighter types, (1½ ton) usually went through without help. This was especially true of those mounted on pneumatic tires (ambulances). The heavy types also labored excessively of stiff grades. On a grade in California a Mack blew out a cylinder head. Travel on these grades necessitated constant work on the clutch assemblies of the heavy types. The heavies in these places slowed up the lighter and swifter light trucks; which type made all the grades easily. In this connection, I believe that the Riker[6] (3 ton), and F.W.D., had less difficulty in negotiating stiff grades, and sand stretches, than any other type of heavy truck.

On the very best roads, such as in Maryland, Pennsylvania and California, the heavies were not capable of the speed that the lighter types could efficiently maintain; showing that in general the two types should not be mixed for transport work.

The Militor, equipped with power winch and spade in rear, did wonderful work in pulling vehicles out of holes, sand pits, etc. The 5-ton tractor was also very efficiently used for this purpose. On one occasion at least, the Militor came into camp at night towing four trucks, showing that its power plant was almost perfect.

In the lighter types, very little difficulty was encountered. The only Packard trucks on the trip were three of the 1½ ton type. Mechanical difficulties in these were so few as to be negligible. A burned out wheel bearing, repaired at Carson City, was caused by an error in placing same when tires had been changed at Salt Lake City. These trucks surmounted the stiffest grades with motors running quietly and easily, and trucks in good condition. One Packard truck was badly overloaded during the entire trip. Its load was partially distributed in latter part, but when weighed near end of trip, its gross weight was still 1,500 pounds in excess of that of any other type of 1½ ton truck. The performance of these three trucks is considered remarkable.

The White 1½ ton trucks were also very good, and difficulties encountered with them were trifling. This also applies to G.M.C. type.[7]

Among the touring and observation cars very little difficulty was encountered. One Cadillac touring car required a timing chain, and in the mountains carburetors needed adjusting.

One White observation car (truck chassis) had frequent difficulty of a minor nature, due to stoppages in oil line. The same car burned out a wheel bearing and lost a rear wheel in Wyoming, necessitating the replacing of the whole rear end.

Kitchen trailers were of the two and four wheel type. The only one to finish the trip was one of the two wheel type (Liberty). The trailmobiles, four wheel type, were constantly in trouble. Officers of M. T. C.[8] maintained that these troubles were the result of improper trailer connections; proper ones not being provided. In my opinion neither type is suitable for transport work, and a better one must be devised.

Motorcycles had much trouble after getting in the sandy districts. Except for scouting purposes, it is believed a small Ford roadster would be better suited to convoy work than motorcycle side car.

In tires, the Giant solids gave better service than duals, and pneumatics were very successful. The Giant pneumatic is practically puncture-proof, admits of more speed than the solid, and prevents excessive vibration due to rough roads, etc.

The lessons drawn from observation of matériel are that the heavy area type is entirely unsuited for front transit work. A smaller type, not exceeding 2 tons, mounted on either solids or pneumatic tires, is essential. If deemed essential, these could be provided with folding seats for transporting personnel, accommodating twenty men. For such work, the light truck is so far superior to the heavy as to admit of no comparison. The heavy should be confined to rear areas, in supply depots and the like, on hard surfaced roads, and in general on short hauls.

Further, for any type of work, the two types should not be mixed in one train, as this impairs the efficiency of the lighter faster type.

B - Personnel and Administration.

1. The truck train was composed of two truck companies, a repair unit, engineer unit and medical unit. Officers stated that many men in the two truck companies were raw recruits, of no experience.

At the beginning of the trip, discipline among the enlisted personnel of the M. T. C. was almost unknown. The condition was probably the worst in the S. P. O. 595.[9] This lack of discipline was largely due to inexperience, and poor type of officers. It resulted in excessive speeding of trucks; unauthorized halts; unseemly conduct, and poor handling of truck in the convoy.

These conditions were vastly better in engineer and medical units.

The Commanding Officer stated that he had no opportunity of drilling and disciplining the men before starting, nor of choosing officers. He bettered conditions gradually, but was confronted with the problem of accomplishing this while maintaining a pre-arranged schedule of travel daily. In this connection, special mention should be made of a Lieut. Martin, who commanded one M. T. C. Company. He was an exception to the general rule, worked hard and was of vast assistance to the Commanding Officer.

It is not believed that the enlisted men were inferior in type to any other body of soldiers, but they lacked training and good officers.

2. In conducting this trip, two scouts were mounted on motorcycles who reconnoitered roads and placarded same for guidance of train. The engineer unit was charged with making bridges, culverts, etc., passable.

During the latter part of the trip an engineer truck was kept twenty-four hours ahead of train to perform this work, and this arrangement avoided many unnecessary delays.

3. The schedule of travel was easily maintained up as far as Omaha, Nebraska. A total delay of four days was accumulated after this point was passed, but all were unavoidable. It is believed the Commanding Officer would have been unwise in pushing on at any of the points where he delayed to make minor repairs and rest his men.

4. Lessons from observation of personnel are that officers and men should be thoroughly trained as soldiers before entrusting to them the valuable equipment of a motor train. This will prevent much unnecessary expense, due to breakage, speeding, etc., as well as preserve the standard of conduct essential to a good soldier.

Roads must always be reconnoitered and repaired far enough in advance of main body so that delays will be obviated.

C - Roads.

The Lincoln Highway was almost constantly followed after meeting same at Gettysburg, Pennsylvania. The road through Maryland was of concrete, and excellent in all ways, except that it is a little narrow for convoy work. Ten miles of dirt road from Emmitsburg, Maryland, to Gettysburg, Pennsylvania, had several old, low covered wooden bridges. They were too low to admit passage of high topped vehicles.

Road through Pennsylvania was almost entirely tarvia, and very good, though at some points, poorly graded.

Through Ohio and Indiana a great portion was paved and macadamized. In Illinois train started on dirt roads, and practically no more pavement was encountered until reaching California.

The dirt roads of Iowa are well graded and are good in dry weather; but would be impossible in wet weather. In Nebraska, the first real sand was encountered, and two days were lost in western part of this state due to bad, sandy roads. Wyoming roads west of Cheyenne are poor dirt ones, with weak culverts and bridges. In one day—14 of these were counted, broken through by the train. The desert roads in the southwest portion of this state are very poor.

In western Utah, on the Salt Lake Desert, the road becomes almost impassable to heavy vehicles. From Orr's Ranch, Utah, to Carson City, Nevada, the road is one succession of dust, ruts, pits, and holes. This stretch was not improved in any way, and consisted only of a track across the desert. At many points on the road, water is twenty miles distant, and parts of the road are ninety miles from the nearest railroad.

There exists at the present time a controversy between the Lincoln Highway Association and some of the people in the section west of Salt Lake City as to the best location for the Trans-Continental Road across this part of the United States. Many citizens informed members of the convoy that there existed across the northern part of the states of Utah and Nevada a good location for such a road. They state this route is free from grades and summits, is close to water and railroads, and is through a more thickly populated section.

At least, the Lincoln Highway over this portion of the country is so poor as to warrant a thorough investigation, of possible routes for building a road, before any government money should be expended on such a project.

The roads in California were excellent paved ones. No trouble in roads was experienced after surmounting the first grade of the Coast Range of mountains in California.

In observing the effect of the different types of road in progress of the train, it was noted that the trucks operated very efficiently and easily on the smooth, level types, but that on rough roads, sandy ones, or on steep grades the truck train would have practically no value as a cargo carrier. The train operated so slowly in such places, that in certain instances it was noted that portions of the train did not move for two hours.

It was further observed that some of the good roads are too narrow. This compels many vehicles to run one side off the pavement in meeting other vehicles, snipping the tire, [off] the edge of the pavement and causing difficulty in again mounting the pavement. This is especially true in a narrow concrete road. It causes fast deterioration of the road.

It was further observed that in many places excellent roads were installed some years ago that have since received no attention whatever. Absence of any effort at maintenance has resulted in roads of such rough nature as to be very difficult of negotiating. In such cases it seems evident that a very small amount of money spent at the proper time would have kept the road in good condition.

GENERAL SUMMARY

The truck train was well received at all points along the route. It seemed that there was a great deal of sentiment for the improving of highways, and, from the standpoint of promoting this sentiment, the trip was an undoubted success.

As stated before in this paper, it is believed the M. T. C. should pay more attention to disciplinary drills for officers and men, and that all should be intelligent, snappy soldiers before giving them the responsibility of operating trucks.

Extended trips by trucks through the middle western part of the United States are impracticable until roads are improved, and then only a light truck should be used on long hauls.

Through the eastern part of the United States the truck can be efficiently used in the Military Service, especially in problems involving a haul of approximately a hundred miles, which could be negotiated by light trucks in one day.

1. Eisenhower sent this report from the Rock Island Arsenal, Rock Island, Illinois. In addition to the written report, the Eisenhower Library also has the official army records of the convoy and a five-minute 16mm movie film, *1919 Transcontinental Motor Convoy,* produced by the Firestone Rubber Company, Akron, Ohio.

2. The Transcontinental Convoy was organized because the trucks used in World War I required roads far superior to those available at that time. In order to identify improvements needed, the federal government asked the army to undertake a motorized expedition over the planned Lincoln Highway. Not only did the convoy test the roads, but it also offered a test of the available motorized vehicles. Lieutenant Colonel Eisenhower, along with his friend, Maj. Sereno Brett, volunteered to be the Tank Corps's official observers on the convoy. His experience with the motor convoy and his observations of the German autobahns in World War II influenced his presidential support of the National System of Interstate and Defense Highways. See John E. Wickman, "Ike and 'The Great Truck Train'—1919," *Kansas History* 13 (autumn 1990): 139–148.

3. "F.W.D." refers to a four-wheel-drive truck manufactured in Clintonville, Wisconsin. "FWD" later became the company name. In 1920, the large truck division was absorbed by the Oshkosh Truck Company in Oshkosh, Wisconsin. Both companies still exist.

4. The "Militor" was the popular name for the army's wheeled artillery tractor, a wrecker-winch used by the convoy to rescue disabled vehicles.

5. The Garford was a two-ton cargo truck built by the Garford Motor Truck Company of Elyria, Ohio. Garford was eventually absorbed by Studebaker.

6. Rikers were three-ton cargo trucks built by the Riker Works, Elizabeth, New Jersey.

7. "G.M.C." refers to the General Motors Corporation.

8. "M.T.C." refers to the Motor Transport Corps, U.S. Army.

9. "S.P.O." is the abbreviation for the service and parts unit, Quartermaster Corps, that provided the mechanics for vehicle maintenance and repair.

15

Eisenhower Library
Pre-presidential Papers

To Chief of Tank Corps[1]

August 5, 1920

1. In compliance with instructions contained in first indorsement, the following report concerning Camp Colt, Pennsylvania, is submitted.

The site of Camp Colt, Pa. was used during the year 1917 by several Regular Army Infantry Regiments as a mobilization and Training Camp. These troops abandoned the site late in the year 1917 and transferred to Camp Greene, South Carolina. These troops left on the campsite a considerable number of open sided and floorless kitchens, and a few stables and warehouses. There were no other buildings on the grounds when taken over by the Tank Corps, in March, 1918.

The 301st Battalion, Tank Corps, was organized at Camp Meade, Md. and sent overseas from that camp. The personnel left over after this movement was transferred to Gettysburg, Pa. There it was joined by a small detachment from Camp Upton, N.Y., the combined troops immediately establishing Camp Colt, about Mar. 23, 1918.

The purpose of this camp was to receive and train recruits, and organize them into battalions to meet the demands for personnel, made by the Chief of Tank Corps, who was in the A.E.F. Authority was secured from the War Department to send out recruiting officers for the Tank Corps. These officers had authority to induct men into the service who came under the selective service law. Recruiting officers were specially instructed to accept only the best type of men for the Corps, and as a result, the type of enlisted men in the Tank Corps was of the finest.

Original instructions from the Chief of Tank Corps directed the shipment of a quota of men monthly to the A.E.F. On account of the fact that all space on vessels was needed for the shipping of Infantry units, there were no shipments of Tank Corps units during the months of April, May, June and July. During this time the Corps at Camp Colt was growing rapidly in size, and conforming to the provisional tables of organization the following battalions were organized.

Heavy Battalions (Approx. Strength per Battalion, 70 officers, 800 men.)

302nd Battalion	Captain Andrew Rollins, C.O.
303rd Battalion	Captain LeRoy Wilson, C.O.
304th Battalion	Captain Arthur Sheets, C.O.
305th Battalion	Captain Arthur Halton, C.O.

Light Battalions (Approx. strength per Battalion, 20 officers, 350 men)

326th Battalion	Captain John Farmer, C.O.
327th Battalion	Captain Edwin Robnett, C.O.
328th Battalion	Captain Edward Gruber, C.O.
329th Battalion	Captain Wallace Meyers, C.O.
330th Battalion	Captain Roderick Stephens, C.O.
331st Battalion	Captain William Willcox, C.O.
332nd Battalion	Captain Warren Day, C.O.
333rd Battalion	Captain Peter Tyler, C.O.
334th Battalion	Captain Laurence Brain, C.O.
335th Battalion	Captain Harry Dodge, C.O.
336th Battalion	Captain Leonard Murphy, C.O.
337th Battalion	Captain Claude Feagin, C.O.
338th Battalion	Captain Clarke Purcell, C.O.
339th Battalion	Captain Robert Ermis, C.O.
346th Battalion	1st Lieut. Milton Breschell, C.O.

There was also organized a number of special companies, which were not included in Battalions. Designations of the companies were as follows:

Repair and Salvage Companies.
307th, 316th 317th, 318th, 319th, 320th, 351st, 380th, 381st, 382nd, and 383rd.

Training and Replacement Companies.
376th, 377th, 378th, and 379th.

Centers. (Headquarters Companies.)
303rd, 304th, 309th and 310th.

Casual companies for overseas shipment.
Companies A, B, and C.

October Automatic Replacement Draft.
Companies A, B, and C.

November Automatic Replacement Draft.
Companies A, B, and C.

In addition to the above there was organized a number of units for purposes of administration in the United States. Those were:
201st Depot Company

Casual Company No. 1. (Depot Brigade.)
Development Battalion.

Tank Corps Training embraces both the basic or elementary military training common to all fighting units, and the training in special arms and equipment peculiar to the Tank Corps. Camp Colt was the station at which the recruit was to receive the first part; that is, the elementary training.

Infantry training, especially in close order formations were therefore the principal part of the work of the troops at this camp. The Tank Corps, as explained above, was very fortunate in the type of recruits received, rapid progress was made in infantry training, and organizations soon became very well drilled and disciplined units.

It was soon considered possible and expedient to give as many men as possible instruction in the special arms and equipment of the Tank Corps, preparatory to their work in the Tank Schools overseas. With this in view, schools in the following subjects were organized. Equipment and competent instructors were available, and rapid progress was made.

List of Special Schools.
Signal School:
(a) Telephone and Telegraph.
(b) Radio.
(c) Visual.
Mechanical.
Gasoline motors and accessories.
Machine Gun.
    All types except Browning. Included theoretical work and range firing, including firing from moving trucks.
    Light Artillery.
    Theoretical and practical work. Naval 3 pounder was equipment used.
37 mm. Gun.
    Theoretical and practical work.
Tank Operation and Driving. Care and upkeep.
    Only one Tank being available, instruction in this was limited to a very few men per company.
Pistol.
    Theoretical and practical work in use of pistol.

Officer Training.
The War Department early notified the Tank Corps in the United States that no Regular Officers would be detailed to the Branch. It was therefore necessary to secure officers from any place available, and to

fill large numbers of existing vacancies, it was necessary to establish Schools at Camp Colt for the purpose of selecting 2nd lieutenants from the enlisted personnel. This school was intended primarily as a place of elimination of unfit candidates for commission, and while as much instruction as possible was imparted in the short course, (6 weeks) it was purposely made as intensive as possible, in order to quickly eliminate the unfit. In this way a very good personnel was obtained for the grade of second lieutenant, but on account of inexperience, they were not suitable for promotion.

As many company officers as possible were sent through the schools enumerated above. Officer, as well as organization training, was very much handicapped due to the lack of competent instructors in military subjects. Although the camp grew to approximately 10,000 officers and men, there was never at one time more than four Regular Officers assigned to it. For the greater portion of the time, there were only two.

Camp Staff was composed as follows:
       Commanding Officer . . . Lt.Col.D.D.Eisenhower, Tank
                                Corps.(Capt.Inf.)
       Adjutant . . . . Captain Winfield S. Roberson,
                                Tank Corps
       Personnel Adjutant . . . . . Captain Sydney Weston
       Supply Officer . . . . Captain R.R. Whittingham
       Camp Inspector . . . . Major Norman Randolph,
                                Infantry
       Camp Quartermaster . . . Captain Frank Moore, Q.M.C.

The camp was discontinued on Nov. 17, 1918, and the troops in camp at that time were taken to Camp Dix, N.J. for demobilization.

   1. Eisenhower wrote this report while stationed at Camp Meade, Maryland, and sent it to Maj. Clark Chandler, Chief of Staff at Camp Meade. The history had been requested by the Pennsylvania War History Commission. The charts and exhibits accompanying the report are not included. They are available at the Eisenhower Library.

16

Infantry Journal
"A Tank Discussion"

NOVEMBER, 1920[1]

The Army Reorganization Act of June 4 provides that hereafter tanks will be a part of the Infantry Arm of the Service. It therefore becomes increasingly important for infantry officers to study the question of tanks; their capabilities, limitations, and consequent possibilities of future employment.

The tank, as a self-propelling, caterpillar type of weapon, was a development of the late war. Many officers who served with fighting divisions never had an opportunity to take part in an action supported by these machines, and their knowledge of the power and deficiencies of the tank is based on hearsay. Others took part in such combats, when the tanks were improperly used, poorly manned, or under such adverse conditions that they were practically helpless in trying to lend efficient aid to the Infantry. As the number of American-manned tanks that actually got to take part in the fighting with American divisions was very small, the number of officers of the Army who are openly advocates of this machine as a supporting weapon is correspondingly few.

As a result of these circumstances a great many officers are prone to denounce the tanks as a freak development of trench warfare which has already outlived its usefulness. Others, and this class seems to be in the majority, have come into contact with the tank so infrequently, and have heard so little either decidedly for or against it, that they simply ignore it in their calculations and mental pictures of future battles.

Believing that the man that follows this course of thinking is falling into a grievous error, this paper is yet no brief to try to convince a skeptical reader that tanks won the war. Tanks did not, and no one knows this better than the officers who commanded them. And just as emphatically no other particular auxiliary arm won the war. The Infantry, aided and abetted by these various arms, did, however, and it is safe to say that, lacking any one of them, the task of the Infantry would have been much more difficult. The sole purpose then of any discussion along these lines is to place such facts before the officer as will enable him to determine by sane and sound reasoning whether in future wars the tanks will be a profitable adjunct to the Infantry.

Briefly, the general capabilities and limitations of the tank are as follows:

(a) It can cross ordinary trenches and shell-pitted ground.

(b) It can demolish entanglements, and make lanes through wire for our Infantry.

(c) It can destroy by gunfire or by its weight pill boxes, machine-gun nests, etc.

(d) It can, by gunfire, force opposing infantry to seek shelter in dugouts, etc., until our Infantry can come up and occupy the position.

(e) It provides protection to its crew from small-arms fire, shrapnel, and anything except direct hit from any sized cannon.

Limitations:

(a) It cannot cross deep, unbridged bodies of water, rocky cliffs, nor deep bogs.

(b) It cannot penetrate forests of large trees, although it can break down isolated trees of great size.

(c) It has no power of holding a position it has taken.

(d) Its radius of action is limited by the amount of fuel it can carry.

The arguments usually advanced by those who believe there is no future for tanks are three, namely:

(a) Tanks are of value only in trench warfare.

(b) We will probably never again be engaged in truly "trench warfare."

(c) The tank is mechanically untrustworthy, and therefore unfit to be depended upon in a crisis.

Making every attempt to avoid a partisan attitude in the discussion of these arguments, let us take them up in the order they are set down above.

The idea of the tank was conceived and the first steps taken in its development during the progress of trench warfare. For this reason alone they are likely to be condemned as one of the necessary evils of that class of combat and sentenced without a hearing to eternal oblivion, as far as any other type of battle is concerned. Of course, it is true that tanks can cross trenches. Our small type can cross a 6-foot ditch and the large one a 15-foot. But this does not mean that they operate best in crossing trenches, nor that their usefulness is limited to the stabilized condition that "trench warfare" implies. Their ability to cross trenches is gained only by their much greater ability to negotiate less difficult ground. An automobile with chains is usually able to get through any mud road that it may encounter, but a good pavement enhances its mobility many hundred per cent.

As a matter of fact, bad trenches demand the utmost care in the manipulation of a tank, and, barring artillery, are their worst artificial enemy. In their efforts to aid the Infantry in its forward movement, their greatest use is the discovery and destruction of machine-gun nests. To do this, the faster they can move, the better, and, consequently, the better the condition of the ground, the greater the efficiency of the tank. Their ability to cut lanes through wire is of course not confined to trench warfare. As a military obstacle, wire has been used for many years, and undoubtedly will be so used in the future. The fact, then, that they were the only machine or weapon devised with the ability to cross the elaborate systems of German entrenchments should not be used as an argument in favor of the statement that they are of no value except in crossing such trenches.

The second argument is based on the grounds that probably never again will there be a battlefield occupied under the conditions that made a continuous and flankless line throughout its whole length possible. With Switzerland and the North Sea on the flanks, and a dense population on each side of the line capable of manning it to such depth that a break through was not possible until one side had secured a preponderance of numerical strength, it is easily possible that the battle conditions of 1915–1917 will remain a peculiar type, and never be duplicated in future wars. We must admit, however, that in all wars, trenches and entanglements will be as invariably a part of an army's defense as the rifle of the infantryman. Their efficiency and elaborateness of detail will be limited only by the time available for their construction.

In the large armies that will always be the rule in wars between two first-class powers, the Infantry must invariably expect to have to penetrate belts of wire and difficult system of trenches in the last stages of its assault. Under such conditions, what infantry commander is not going to thank his stars that he has at hand a number of tanks to lead and to support his unit through this stage of the attack? And on the way up to this main line of resistance, as he passes through the enemy outpost position and intermediate lines, composed in the main undoubtedly of hundreds of machine guns and automatic rifles; as he sees the tanks dashing back and forth in front of his assault battalions, crushing and obliterating those stinging pests, won't he be convinced that the tank was not a weapon that had both its conception and end of its usefulness in trench warfare?

And now we come to the soundest, and therefore the most difficult to answer, of all the arguments used against the tank, namely, the mechanical inefficiency of the tank. In the European War more tanks were put out of action, due to mechanical difficulties, than by all the measures of defense taken by the enemy. The general answer is this: The tank, in point of development, is in its infancy, and the great strides already made in its mechanical improvement only point to the greater ones still to come. Let us briefly review the progress of the large British tanks along these lines. The first ones were practically helpless. They carried a cumbersome and useless wheel on the tail for the purpose of steering the tank. In the next model this was abandoned and the principle of steering by alternate use of the driving tracks adopted. This series of tanks required four men for driving alone. In the next model this was corrected, and the controls and mechanism so altered that one man could drive the tank. It was then discovered that the tank was too short for the successful crossing of the Hindenburg system, and in the next model the length was made 6 feet greater. The principal defects noted in this type were:

    (a) Lack of power;
    (b) Engine interfering with the crew in fighting compartment;
    (c) Breaking of track plates;
    (d) Faulty shape of track housing.

The next series (American and British design, Mark VIII) corrected these faults. This is the type of heavy tank with which the American Tank Corps (Infantry) is equipped today.

Now, consider the conditions under which tanks to date have been built. After the conception of the idea, it became necessary to secure engines, transmissions, armor plate, guns, tracks, and all the special and particular material peculiar to the new machine. A suitable place for building and assembling had to be found, and the problem of placing the whole thing in to production had to be met. Necessarily it was important to utilize as many parts as possible that were already in production, in order that the tank in any numbers at all could soon take the place for which it was designed, on the western Front. This inevitably resulted in the frequent sacrifice of the ideal article in favor of one already in production that would probably answer the purpose. In other words, the tank of the present is not a product of years of development of the ideal article for each part of itself, but rather the emergency result of emergency methods.

It is believed by those most intimately acquainted with the tanks that the one model, Mark VIII, is too weighty, unwieldy and cumbersome. It is regarded as by far the best type of the heavy tank yet built, but not the ideal one for the varied conditions to be met in the next war we will have to fight. On the other hand, our small type, the Renault, is believed to be too short, underpowered, and deficient in fire power. The ideal type as expressed by these officers will be one of sufficient length to cross a 9-foot trench, a maximum weight of 15 tons, a fire power of one 6-pounder and two browning machine guns, sufficient power to run cross country at a speed of 12 miles per hour, and on good roads, with treads dismounted, at a rate of 20 miles per hour. Study, observation and correction of faults will easily place this tank on a level of mechanical efficiency with the best of our motor trucks of today. There is not the slightest doubt that such a tank can and will be built.

If the mobility and mechanical efficiency of such a machine will be admitted, let us try to see whether a weapon of this sort would properly fit into the organization of the division without any reduction in the mobility and flexibility of the whole.

As a basis from which to start, suppose we try to replace the Divisional Machine Gun Battalion by one company of these tanks. In making such a suggestion it should be understood that the idea is limited to the Motorized Battalion of the division. It is in no way meant to disparage the value of machine guns, and is not in conflict with the idea supported by some officers of enlarging and unifying the machine-gun units in the division. Neither is it to be understood that it is proposed to limit the use and organization of tanks to one company per division. There must always be a large unit of tanks as army troops which can be used at the point or points most desired. Further, it is not contended that the replacing of the Divisional Machine Gun Battalion is absolutely necessary in order to include the company of tanks in the divisional organization. But by making such a proposition, it gives a ground for comparison with an organization and weapon with which officers in general are more or less familiar.

The Motorized Battalion has 393 men and 57 motor vehicles of all kinds. It is available to the division commander for emergency use in strengthening a suddenly menaced part of his line; for fire of position, barrage fire, etc., in supporting his attack; for protection of his flanks or any other use to which he wishes to put its ability for concentrated small-arms fire. For transportation it has motor vehicles, mounted on wheels, which means that its transportation is of use to it only so long as it has the opportunity to use unobstructed roads. Thereafter it must abandon transportation and proceed to any selected position dismounted, a slow and tedious process at the best. It is of value in action only as it can bring its fire to bear upon the target selected. Any considerable changes of position in a short time are practically impossible.

The Tank Company would have a total of 220 officers and men and 26 motor vehicles of all types, which number includes 15 fighting tanks and 1 reserve. First of all they are available to the division commander as a powerful supporting arm to his infantry attack, as discussed above. With the type of tank we are now considering, each one can cover a frontage of at least 100 yards in assault, and furnish efficient protection from machine-gun nests to the Infantry attacking behind it. Allowing one platoon of five tanks in the second line to demolish nests missed by the front tanks, and for replacement of casualties, 1,000 yards of front would receive this aid in the assault.

But in using the tanks in this way, the division commander would not necessarily be sacrificing all the particular type of fire power that the Machine Gun Battalion afforded him. Each tank can carry one spare Browning gun complete, and on the outside of the tank a standard mount for the same. The personnel of the tank company, 200 enlisted men, is so devised as to provide the necessary personnel for these guns fighting separately. Thus the division commander would have a total of 16 machine guns, in addition to the strength of the Tank Company as a fighting unit to replace his old strength of one machine-gun battalion. Furthermore, in the question of mobility the 16 guns would be superior to his old battalion. In each tank company there will be unarmored tanks surmounted by large cargo platforms. In action two of these, after unloading their cargoes at the specified dumps, can be made available for the use of the 16 machine guns. Always remembering that on good roads the speed of this tank is equal to the best motor trucks, the instant it becomes necessary to leave such roads there is no comparison in the mobility of the two units. The unarmored tanks are enabled to proceed at a rate of approximately 12 miles per hour to any threatened or other point at which their fire power is desired. The ammunition supply of these guns is automatically solved, due to the enormous carrying power of the cargo tanks.

It has been practically an axiom that tanks are of use only on the offensive. With the improved tank now under discussion, it seems reasonable that this limitation will be removed in part, at least. The charge of a German cavalry brigade at Vionville, in 1870, against the flank of the advancing French infantry, saved an army corps from certain annihilation. In the same battle, on another flank, the charge of a squadron saved a brigade. There is no doubt that in similar circumstances in the future tanks will be called upon to use their ability of swift movement and great fire power in this way against the flanks of attacking forces. In making local counterattacks, the tank has already proven its worth, and the new tank will greatly increase the opportunities and effect of such actions. The clumsy, awkward and snaillike progress of the old tanks must be forgotten, and in their place we must picture this speedy, reliable and efficient engine of destruction.

One main point remains to be covered. It has been argued that this tank will be of such weight that many of our bridges and culverts in this country will not stand their crossing. The danger of breaking through the flooring of any bridge will be less with such a tank than with a loaded 5-ton truck. The weight is very evenly distributed by means of the tread, and the pressure bearing at any one point is less than with the truck. Bridges of such unstable character that a weight of 15 tons is liable to break the supports and stringers are generally the kind that span small ravines and dry creek beds. Under such conditions the tank needs no bridge. It is perfectly able to run off the bridge, cross the stream bed and rejoin the column, leaving the use of the bridge to the more helpless vehicles. Even granting that occasionally the tank company will be forced to construct its own temporary crossing over an isolated stream, such incidents are not insurmountable difficulties and are constantly being met in some form in warfare. Certainly if we are convinced of the truth of the arguments above, we cannot afford to allow the possible difficulty of crossing occasional poorly bridged streams to deter us from the use of these machines.

1. Eisenhower's "Tank Discussion" was published in the *Infantry Journal* 17 (1920): 453–58. He became interested in tank warfare when he trained tank units at Camp Meade, Maryland, Camp Colt, Pennsylvania, Camp Dix, New Jersey, and Fort Benning, Georgia. On a second tour of duty at Camp Meade in 1919, Eisenhower met George Patton, and the men had long discussions on tank tactics. Patton (USMA, 1909) gained his fame as a tank commander from World War I through his

World War II service, including the invasions of North Africa and Sicily, and in leading the Third Army in the drive into the heart of Germany. During the pre–World
War II period, Patton attempted to assist Eisenhower in receiving a troop or tank
command. Patton died on December 21, 1945, from injuries suffered in a car accident near Heidelberg, Germany. For additional biographical information, see
Carlo D'Este, *Patton: A Genius for War* (New York: Harper Collins, 1995); Martin Blumenson, *The Patton Papers, 1885–1940, 1940–1945*, 2 vols. (Boston: Houghton Mifflin, 1972, 1974); and Ladislas Farago, *Patton: Ordeal and Triumph* (New York: Ivan
Obolensky, 1963).

17

NARA
Records of the American Expeditionary Force

TO THE COMMANDING OFFICER, 306TH R. & S. COMPANY

JANUARY 25, 1921[1]

I have just learned that a letter sent by Mrs. Eisenhower and I to your
company about 2 weeks ago, thanking your company for the flowers
they sent to the funeral of our little boy,[2] has never been received by you.

We want you to know how much we appreciated the beautiful
roses, and the feelings expressed by them. They were very beautiful,
and it was very comforting to know that the men he liked so well remembered him at such a time.

Mrs. Eisenhower and I request that you express our thanks and appreciation to each member of your company. Sincerely

1. Eisenhower was stationed at Fort Meade when he wrote the letter.
2. On January 2, 1921, the Eisenhower's young son, Doud Dwight, whom they
had nicknamed "Icky," died at Fort Meade from scarlet fever contracted from a maid
the Eisenhowers had hired. The death of their three-year-old firstborn shattered
Dwight and Mamie. Doud Dwight was buried in Denver, then transferred in 1966 to
Abilene, Kansas, to be buried beside his father (1969). In his memoir, Eisenhower
referred to their loss as "the greatest disappointment and disaster in my life, the one
I have never been able to forget completely." Eisenhower, *At Ease*, 180–82.

18

United States Army Military History Institute
"Tanks With Infantry"

[MAY 1921][1]

1. <u>Tanks in co-operation with other Infantry weapons during the
World War.</u>

The tank in the World War was a new weapon, both to those actually using it, and to those with whom it co-operated. The plans under

35

which it was used were largely experimental. These plans varied in character from the highly spectacular, and practically independent attack of the entire British Tank Corps at Cambrai, to the assigning of very small numbers of them to an infantry unit, acting under the most detailed orders as to objectives, mission, route, and rate of advance.

Experience demonstrated that in order to overcome the anti-tank defenses of the enemy, special assistance and co-operation from the artillery and air service was absolutely essential. Further, Infantry and Tank Commanders soon learned that to obtain success from the use of their Tanks, they must operate in the closest coordination with the infantry they were supporting. Tanks were developed, and exist to provide a means whereby the infantry is enabled to assume the offensive against defensive zones organized in depth and using the power of the machine gun to repel assaults. Their development took place after massed artillery and poison gas had failed to make such offensive action of the infantry possible. In working out the best methods for the tanks to render this assistance to the infantry it was found essential that the maximum of mutual understanding and spirit of co-operation should exist between the infantry and its tanks.

During the World War the Division had no separate tank organization corresponding to the present Divisional Tank Company. All tanks belonged to a separate Corps and were Army Troops. For any action tanks were allotted to the different Corps, and to Divisions as considered necessary by Army Headquarters. One of the governing principles of this allotment was that tanks should be used in numbers, or not at all. Following this principle the allotment was usually made at the rate of one Battalion of Tanks per Division. This proportion of tanks allowed the Division Commander to demand from them a practically continuous support for his general infantry assault from the jump-off to the objective.

Tanks were not vulnerable to small arms fire nor to shrapnel, and their greatest enemy was the isolated guns and anti-tank rifles scattered through the enemy's defenses, which could fire on them over open sights. Tanks could cross ordinary trenches, and make lanes through enemy wire for our Infantry, and deliver fire against the garrison at deadly ranges. They could take a position but could not hold it, nor could they damage enemy personnel that had taken refuge underground. These facts were taken into consideration in working out the best methods of Tank and Infantry co-operation, the general principles of which were as follows:

GENERAL:
1. Front line tanks should support the infantry assault lines during an advance, and regulate their movements on the needs of the In-

fantry they are supporting. This principle properly makes tanks responsible for maintaining connection with the infantry and not vice versa.

2. Infantry must be constantly on the alert to take advantage of all opportunities of advance created by the tanks.

3. In situations where the infantry line is preceded by scouts, these scouts should be trained to locate accurately, and report or signal quickly to the nearest tank, the exact position of enemy resistance.

4. Riflemen should unhesitatingly open fire on an enemy regardless of the position of the tanks, as their fire will not damage the tank.

5. Tanks and infantry should advance by bounds. When resistance is located the tank should proceed at all possible speed to its destruction, and then patrol the vicinity until the infantry takes possession of the point by a similar bound.

6. Upon reaching the objective, tanks should patrol and exploit to the front until the position is consolidated by the infantry. The infantry Commander should then release tanks at once.

7. Infantry must avoid grouping behind the tank during an advance, as the tanks are sure to draw concentrated machine gun fire.

8. The infantry should aid the tanks against the nearer defenses of the enemy with all the weapons at its disposal.

9. Liaison measures between Infantry and Tanks must be thorough and workable.

1. SPECIAL WEAPONS:

1. Machine guns were frequently able to aid tanks by opening fire on enemy anti-tank guns, and maintaining same until the gun could be destroyed by a tank. Machine guns and tanks worked together because the machine gun fire could be kept up on any position regardless of the position of the tank.

2. It was found effective to use bombers to clean up an enemy garrison that had been forced into its dugouts by the action of the tanks.

3. When tanks were advancing through infantry lines to assist the infantry, the latter could frequently protect the advance of the tanks into action by use of smoke bombs.

4. The infantry 37 mm. and accompanying gun were frequently able to protect tanks by locating and destroying anti-tank guns.

2. TRAINING OF DIVISIONAL TANK ORGANIZATION.

(a) Characteristics of Divisional Tanks. (Present Type.)

The present Divisional Tank is known as the Renault Type.

Its overall length is 15½ feet and it weighs 6 tons.

It mounts one gun, either machine or 37 mm.

The gun is mounted in a revolving turret.

It can ascend a grade of ½, and a vertical wall of three feet.

It can traverse practically any ground the infantryman can except heavily timbered or bouldered ground, bad swamps, and unbridged streams of more than two feet in depth.

Its armor is proof against all small arms fire, (now 50 cal. machine gun excepted) against shrapnel, small shell fragments and splinters.

It is not proof against a hit from any sized cannon.

The crew is two men, one driver and one gunner.

Its speed varies from one to six miles per hour depending on the nature of the ground. It can operate in both mud and sand, but its speed and maneuvering ability is cut down by both.

On roads it is transported by truck. The divisional company is equipped with one truck for each tank. On long hauls it is carried by rail.

It can cross a six foot trench.

It can make lanes through wire except in very exceptional cases where the wire is particularly heavy, and the belt very wide.

Total number of tanks is twenty-five, divided as follows:

3 fighting platoons of five tanks each.

1 reserve and training section of 8 tanks.

1 company commander's tank.

1 signal tank. This tank can communicate with the Division and Brigade sets, but not with the Battalion and Regimental (Infantry) radio sets.

(b) <u>Missions assignable to Divisional Tank Company.</u>

Normally, when tanks are needed by the Division Commander to support his general Infantry assault, these tanks will be allotted to the Division by the Army Headquarters, for that particular action. Such a mission is not a normal one for the Divisional Company. This company will usually be in reserve at the beginning of any action. Its position will be such that it can readily answer to any call made upon it by the Division Commander.

It is apparent that even if tanks are not allotted from G.H.Q. for a particular action, the Division Commander will not usually commit his Divisional Company to the action in its early stages, due to their scarcity in numbers and difficulty of replacement, and the fact that they use themselves up rapidly in action due to mechanical deterioration. Rather he will hold it out for use when its particular kind of power will be imperative in some portion of the field. The missions to which he will usually assign them will be as follows:

1. To support the infantry in the assault of any position when the Infantry has been unable to take same without their assistance.

2. To assist in breaking up hostile counter attack.

3. For use in making counter attack against an advancing enemy.

4. In exceptional circumstances to aid in covering a withdrawal from action.

5. To accompany the Advance Guard when advancing, especially when contact with enemy is imminent.

(c) <u>Suggested methods for the accomplishment of above missions.</u> (note: See par. 1, above for co-operation between tanks and Infantry.)

1. When the Divisional Company is called on to aid the Infantry in reduction of some particular resistance they will do this by:

(a) Destroying enemy machine gun nests.

(b) Destroying enemy accessory defenses, especially wire.

(c) Forcing an enemy garrison to take cover in dugouts etc. until our infantry can occupy position.

(d) Patrolling and exploiting in front of objective until position is well consolidated by infantry.

(e) Increasing volume of fire of Infantry.

The following general rules for conduct of Tanks apply:

(a) All movements of tanks in front of railhead to be under cover if possible.

(b) Intervals between front line tanks determined by the total frontage to cover, and number of tanks assigned.

(c) The 37 mm. tanks and machine gun tanks to be arranged in the front line to mutually support each other.

(d) Tanks habitually maneuver to outflank an enemy's strong points, villages, woods and etc.

(e) Proper arrangements to be made with artillery and air service for special aid during combat.

(f) Proper use of terrain during all stages to prevent unnecessary exposure to observation of enemy, which will result in attracting concentrated artillery fire.

(g) Supply and repair measures must be well thought out to the end that all tanks will be constantly ready for action, and can be immediately repaired and re-supplied after an action.

2. To assist in breaking up hostile counter attacks.

Tanks will be especially valuable in assisting in breaking up hostile counter attacks immediately after a position has been taken, and before the infantry has had opportunity to properly consolidate it. During this period the tanks should be patrolling and exploiting to front and flanks. They must avoid concentrating, in order to reduce losses from the artillery preparations for the counter attack. At the instant the hostile infantry starts forward the tanks should advance upon it and with their gun fire, and crushing effect of the tank demoralize and destroy the formation. Their presence in this position will not interfere with the machine gun and rifle fire of our Infantry.

Care must be taken that the tanks, during this period, do not get out of control and can be readily rallied by their commander as soon as necessity for their presence at that point ceases to exist.

3. For use in making counter attacks against an advancing enemy.

(Tanks should be located under cover from hostile artillery fire as near as possible to the point selected for the counter attack, as early as practicable.)

General methods for normal attack apply, except that tanks should be allowed more latitude in maneuver and exploitation.

Tanks should make every effort to surprise any supports or massed troops of the enemy.

4. In exceptional circumstances to aid in covering withdrawal. The tank is essentially an offensive weapon, and its use in covering the withdrawal of a defeated force will be justified only when absolutely necessary in order to save a portion of such force. When however the Divisional Company is used for this purpose, the following principles apply:

1. To be launched at top speed directly upon, or on the flank, of that part of the enemy most dangerous to our troops.

2. All tanks used to be in assault echelon. No support platoon necessary.

3. Their mission will be to cause losses and demoralization in the enemy's advancing forces and not to take a particular position as in normal attack.

4. The company must be prepared to sacrifice itself entirely if necessary. They must depend upon their own efforts to accomplish withdrawal after their mission is complete.

5. To accompany the Advance Guard when advancing.

They will be invaluable in this position when contact with the enemy is imminent. The following is a normal method:

1. One platoon preceding under their own power with the support. Two of these should be with advance party, the other three with support.

2. Remainder of company, on trucks, with main body.

3. The front tanks are immediately available for demolishing resistance of small bodies of machine guns, auto-rifles, etc. One platoon is available to the advance guard Commander for use in attacking an enemy in considerable force who is attempting to delay main body.

4. The Division Commander retains control of the major portion of the Company, as described in par. 2 (b) above.

(d)[2] <u>Relation of Divisional Tanks to Infantry Rifle Company.</u>

The Infantry Company Commander will probably never have any tanks attached under his command. He must however be familiar with the capabilities and limitation of tanks. His company must be thoroughly trained in the methods of co-operation between infantry tanks as outlined in par. 1, above. Preceding any action, conference between him and the commander of the tanks in his front will insure better cooperation and better results from the efforts of the tanks to aid the advance of the company. Above all, the infantry must understand that the tank is not usurping the mission of the infantry, but is only trying to aid in its accomplishment. Therefore the infantry company fights its way forward in all respects as if the tanks were not present, and in so doing takes advantage of all opportunities created by the tanks.

(e) <u>Relation of Divisional Tanks to Infantry Battalion.</u>

When the Divisional Company is used in supporting an attack against a particular position at least one platoon will normally be attached temporarily to an Infantry assaulting battalion. During the action these tanks will be an integral part of the battalion, and must be released by the Battalion Commander upon the successful completion of the mission assigned before they may return to their rallying point. The Battalion Commander will therefore have at his disposal every type of infantry weapon. It is in this command that the final and detailed co-ordination of all these arms must be arranged. With his entire personnel thoroughly grounded in the principles of co-operation between tanks and infantry, the commander will be in position to arrange a sound play whereby the maximum results will be obtained. Liaison between the tanks and battalion commander throughout the action must be maintained, in order that he can use their power against an unforeseen obstacle, in coordination with the efforts of his infantry.

(f) <u>Relation of Divisional Tanks to Machine Gun Companies.</u>

Machine guns and tanks operate well together against targets within reach of both due to the fact that the fire of the guns may be kept up even when the tanks are in the position. The guns actually aid the tanks by keeping up their overhead and indirect fire while the tanks are in the enemy position before the infantry arrives at that point. Machine gun crews can further render invaluable aid to the tanks by watching for anti-tank guns and rifles and concentrating fire on them, until destroyed by our forces.

(g) <u>Relation of Divisional Tanks to Accompanying Gun.</u>

Accompanying guns attack enemy machine gun nests, hostile strong points and enemy tanks. The first two missions are identical with two of the missions of tanks. Therefore a thorough coordination of their efforts is essential. The gun should concentrate its efforts in the attack of a strong point upon the enemy guns and anti-tank rifles in the position. If the gun is successful in doing this, the tanks will be able to crush the machine gun nests, make lanes through the wire and force the enemy garrison into its dugouts or cause it to retire. Both the accompanying gun and the infantry 37 mm can lend invaluable aid to the tank throughout the action by locating and destroying the enemy anti-tank rifles and guns. Whenever possible assistance to accomplish the destruction of these defenses should be given by the "Infantry Batteries" detailed from the artillery.

3. General

As the mechanical efficiency of the tank, including speed, mobility and reliability is improved, its sphere of usefulness to the infantry will correspondingly grow. The missions assignable will increase in variety, and the probability of their accomplishment will be more certain. However, it is apparent that tanks can never take over the mission of the infantry, no matter to what degree developed. Advancing infantry will continue to be the deciding factor, and the tank should be carefully studied and developed as an important means of aiding this advance.

To sum up; efficacious co-operation of the tanks and infantry necessitates on the part of the latter a fixed determination to fight without waiting for the tanks to dispose of all the difficulties encountered, and on the part of the tanks, a determination to become acquainted with the needs of the infantry they are supporting, and to satisfy these needs.

1. "Tanks with Infantry" was found at the U.S. Army Military History Institute in a compendium of nine studies on various aspects of armored warfare. The compilation bears the notation, "The Command and General Staff School Library, 1932." Although the Fort Leavenworth Library had apparently assembled, bound, and cataloged the studies in 1932, the papers, only some of which are dated, were apparently written between 1920 and 1924. Eisenhower's article, while undated, almost surely was written during his Tank Corps service at Fort Meade (1919–21). Furthermore, as he signed his paper "Major Eisenhower" and had reverted to that rank from the temporary rank of lieutenant colonel on July 20, 1920, his study had to have been written after that date. As the following Eisenhower manuscript is dated August 13, 1924, the editors judged that placing the document here was most appropriate.

2. The original document is numbered in this manner. Obviously, the sequence was incorrect.

19 NARA
Records of the Adjutant General's Office

To THE ADJUTANT GENERAL, WASHINGTON, D.C.

AUGUST 13, 1924[1]

1. Request that I be designated to take the course at the Staff and Command School at Fort Leavenworth, Kansas, during the school year 1925–1926.

2. My tour of foreign service will expire Jan. 25, 1925, and in ac-

cordance with announced War Department policy, orders directing my transfer to the United States will be published in the near future.

3. Request for school detail is submitted at this time, since it is felt that if the request is approved it may affect the orders to be published for my next assignment to duty.

4. I am a graduate of no service school except the Infantry Tank School.

1. Eisenhower wrote this letter one month before departing Camp Gaillard, Canal Zone, Panama, for another tour of duty at Fort Meade. He was called to Meade principally to help West Point classmate Vernon E. Prichard coach the post football team. He later requested of the Chief of Infantry, Maj. Gen. Charles S. Farnsworth, an appointment to one of the army service schools, preferably the Infantry School at Fort Benning. Farnsworth turned him down and instead assigned him to Benning as a light tank battalion commander. Before leaving, Eisenhower received notice that the War Department had assigned him instead to Fort Logan, Colorado, as a recruiting officer. Disappointed at first, Eisenhower then learned that Gen. Fox Conner, his commanding officer in Panama and his mentor, had pulled strings at the War Department to remove Eisenhower from Farnsworth's control by placing him under the authority of the Adjutant General. Eisenhower left for Fort Logan in January. In April he received notice of his selection for the 1925–26 Command and General Staff School at Fort Leavenworth, Kansas. See Eisenhower, *At Ease,* 196–210.

20   NARA
Records of the Adjutant General's Office
Command and General Staff College Files
"On the Command and General Staff School"[1]

August 1926

This paper consists of an informal, and rather disconnected collection of observations and facts concerning the Command and General Staff School. Its purpose is to place before you as a prospective student at Leavenworth a reasonably accurate conception of the place, in order that you will not be compelled to undergo a more or less complete mental readjustment after taking up your studies there.

The belief is rather prevalent among officers who have never attended the school that the course can be mastered only through unnatural and strained exertions, that the instructors are tricky and mysterious, and that in fact the whole year is one of worry, fretting and nervous tension. Such erroneous ideas, especially when firmly fixed in mind, are bound to operate adversely against the student, particularly at the beginning of the school year. If they are not eradicated early in the course their effects may well be so serious as to actually spoil a year which should, and can be, one of the most enjoyable and in many ways the finest of an officer's peace time service.

It is hoped through this article to establish firmly in your mind that Leavenworth is in every way a reasonable and normal place, and that you should enter upon a year of duty there with the same viewpoint that you would entertain with respect to any other year of interesting duty. The importance of this idea lies in the fact that it has been proven time and again that the student who does so regard the school inevitably gains more in instruction, enjoyment, and in good marks than the one who persists in believing it a year of mental torture and ceaseless grind.

In order to present this picture of Leavenworth certain phases and particulars of the course are discussed in some detail. This is done only to point out some of the things which may be done to assist you in gaining and maintaining the desired mental attitude toward the school, and to indicate some of the details and incidents which, without this desired mental attitude, will prove irritating.

To insure that no essentially personal view of the school shall affect the general soundness of the ideas expressed or advice given herein, this article has been submitted to the graduates of Leavenworth whose names appear at the bottom of the paper, for criticism.[2] Anything to which they have not practically unanimously agreed has been stricken out. In addition you should understand that all contained herein will be presented to you either in the form of instruction or advice many times during the early part of any Leavenworth year.

By presenting these things to you some months in advance of your arrival at the school, thus giving you time to contemplate them at your leisure, it is believed that your efforts to drop quickly into a reasonable and profitable routine will be facilitated.

To begin with, then, it is desired to give the following as a bird's-eye view of Leavenworth:

The school consists essentially of a corps of instructors whose primary duty is to assist you in absorbing the subject matter of the course. As to the nature and scope of the work, many of our finest officers have been engaged for years in all capacities, ranging from the War Department General Staff to instructor in the school, in establishing and revising the course to the end that the student shall be benefited the greatest amount possible in the time available. Most of the officers now on duty there have had important battle commands. It is obvious that one cannot be greatly benefited if the volume of work is so great as to damage the health or the course presented in such a way as to be mystifying. As a matter of fact the course is comprehensive, but not burdensome. It has been devised to meet the needs of the average officer, and the daily demand it makes on the student is based on average capacity. You will have to work steadily and seriously, but never frantically. The aim of the school personnel is to instruct and assist, and not to harass and obstruct. <u>Any student of average intelligence, possessed of an enthusiastic and optimistic turn of mind, and with enough self confidence to trust his own common sense, will not only do well in the course, but have a most pleasant year while he is doing it.</u>

Based on the above I want to inject here my first, and by far most important piece of advice. TRUST INSTRUCTORS.

Failure to follow this dictum, especially when the failure becomes chronic is bound to result disastrously. The instructor from the standpoint of Leavenworth requirements must be considered as an expert in the subject he is teaching. He has himself been a student in the school, has unquestionably spent weeks in exhausting his subject, and is presenting to you its very essence.

Furthermore the ideas and principles he enunciates have been carefully scrutinized by the higher authorities of the school to insure that he does not deviate from the accepted teachings.

Very occasionally you may note, that in a subject with which prior study or experience in war or peace has rendered you thoroughly familiar, the instructor's statements on some detail will differ from your own understanding of the particular point. If you catch yourself taking mental issue with him on these differences, consider at once the relative unimportance of such details as compared to the principal theme of the conference. You cannot afford to get only a confused understanding of the whole subject just because the instructor may have misstated the effective range of a machine gun by 100 yards.

Again some students apparently fear they are failing to show their complete independence of thought, and their superior professional qualifications unless they constantly point out the fallacies expounded in a conference just attended. Don't let such people warp your judgment. Remember that your mission is to absorb what Leavenworth has to teach. The conference is the cornerstone on which the whole instructional structure is built. Devote your energies to assimilating the principles under discussion; don't magnify the importance of insignificant details, and don't worry about stultifying your mind or losing your power of independent thought. Get into the habit of listening to the instructor with an easy and open mind; believe what he says, and you have taken the first and greatest step in making your year a complete success.

Preparation for Leavenworth

Generally speaking, it is believed that the average officer who has completed the course at Benning has received the very finest preparation possible. This opinion is held in spite of the fact that some officers of one or two of the other arms point to their percentage of honor and distinguished graduates as evidence of the superior preparation they receive for the General Service Schools. I believe this view to be false. In the first place our educational system is not devised with the mission of turning out honor and distinguished graduates from Leavenworth. Rather it aims at the progressive improvement of officers professionally. The Chief of Infantry, as well as many other officers who have a hand in controlling our general policies, have announced time and again that Leavenworth class standing in itself is not a decisive element in determining an officer's rating. They want to know, instead, whether he has progressed steadily in general worth to the service as a result of the opportunities he has enjoyed. If any school slights the work for which it was established, in order to spend available time in preparing its students for a different kind of school, it follows that these students will eventually be less well rounded out professionally than graduates of both Benning and Leavenworth.

Secondly, from the narrow view of Leavenworth class standing the work at The Infantry School gives just as efficient preparation as any other. Correct habits of study; logical reasoning in the solution of problems; reasonable familiarity with the technique of writing orders and the tactics of small units, (particularly your own arm); and good health; are the prime essentials. Graduates of Benning should in the average case excel in all these.

For the officer who goes to Leavenworth without graduating from Benning I would advocate a reasonable course of study in solution of problems. A few solved in detail and compared later with school solutions will be of real benefit to you. But don't overdo it. Simply strive to get the broad principles exemplified, and by all means avoid memorizing the problem in the hope that you will get one like it at the school. In this connection it is worth while carefully comparing the "situation" with the "school solution", with the "discussion", and with the "comment sheet". In this way you will see that each statement in the situation means something, and has had its effect in the formation of a decision, and the disposition of the troops. Failure to consider any particular statement by the solver will be shown in the "comment sheet". When you select a problem (probably from one of the correspondence courses) for solution, stick with it until you thoroughly understand every detail connected with it. One problem correctly and thoroughly understood will prove much more valuable than a superficial acquaintance with a dozen. I would also advise the occasional copying in longhand of a school field order. This gives facility in order writing. Whatever you do, remember that it will be far better to do nothing at all than to work yourself into a hazy and doubtful frame of mind, whose clearing will have to be accomplished during the school term.

Reporting for Duty

Reporting for duty is made easy at Leavenworth. Quarters are assigned prior to arrival of students; your furniture will be in your house when you get there; your name plate will be on your door; and expert details will uncrate your effects very rapidly. Good exchanges and similar facilities are at hand, and servants who are of the usual run, are relatively easy to get. Within 48 hours after your arrival your housekeeping arrangements should be operating full blast. The bachelor will find good messes, conveniently located. Some families prefer to use these messes throughout the year instead of keeping house. In any event they are available for use until your cook gets on the job. In general, living conditions are splendid.

Orders are usually so written as to direct one to report at the school between August 20 and September 3. From every standpoint it is desirable to get there as soon after August 20 as possible. Recreational and athletic facilities are ample, and to report late is but to miss a bully good vacation time. In addition this period gives you time to become thoroughly acquainted with all the people and activities with whom you will have contact during the year, and also completely equip your study den for use during the year. Since a well arranged den is considered an absolute necessity it will be discussed under a separate heading.

The Study Den

Each set of quarters has one room which has been used as a study for years. This room will contain most of the necessary equipment, such as a desk, map table, beaver boarding and shelves. Plenty of light is essential. The necessary extension cords to insure that every part of the room will be well illuminated, may be obtained inexpensively from the Quartermaster. The most important single item in your study will be a simple and efficient filing system. Any plan will do so long as it is simple. A great many mimeographed documents of all sorts are issued. To be forced to decide in each case whether or not the paper should be saved, and if so, where to put it, consumes too much time and thought. The plan which works efficiently, and is easy to follow is this: draw from the quartermaster as soon as you arrive a marvel punch and about 15–16 shannon files. Put a dozen of these on nails conveniently placed about the room. As papers are received, and after each has served the immediate purpose for which issued, put it on one of these files. Each file should contain all the matter issued bearing on any particular general subject. If each file is so labelled that you can see its title from your chair, you can get all the data on any subject at a moment's notice, with the assurance that you have it all. Use two or three of the boards for miscellaneous purposes, such as filing of weekly schedules, "live" file, etc.

Each student uses slightly different equipment for study of texts and problems. Some people have very decided ideas as to what kind of maps, markers, tables, etc., one should use. Any system that suits you is all right. I would be sure that it is a system though, for the more systematic you become, even in so small a matter as the way you stake out your problems, the less chance there will be for careless errors, or irritation due to inability to find the things you want. So, in your den, have a place for everything, and strive to make it as efficient a work shop as possible. And do this before the course starts. Once the school is under way you don't want to be using your spare time for such matters.

Mental Attitude

Your year at Leavenworth should be regarded in every way as one of normal duty that should be approached with more than the usual amount of enthusiasm because it definitely results in personal benefit to the student. Many things will come up which will tend to load you into the habit of viewing the place from a warped or abnormal viewpoint. These must be recognized and guarded against. This question of mental attitude is of such importance that Leavenworth has been termed "not a place, but a state of mind". Luckily the proper state of mind is simply your normal one, and the school is so organized and administered as to minimize needless worry. Don't forget this one fact—IN THE LAST FOUR YEARS NO STUDENT HAS FAILED TO GRADUATE. This should convince you, not only of the eminent fairness and squareness of the school, but also of the certainty that you can meet the school's requirements for graduation. As stated above the daily work required of a student is not excessive. In addition there is academic work on only five days per week. Saturday and Sunday belong to you absolutely. There are no conferences or lectures on any afternoons. You will get two vacation periods of ten days each during the year. During these vacations your time is absolutely your own. No work of any kind is ever required of the student officer other than strictly school duty. All the agencies with which your family will come in contact in the ordinary activities of house keeping are most efficiently run, and you will almost never be bothered with such details. As a matter of fact the things which will disturb you at times are all of no real moment and at this distance you cannot well believe that they can ever possibly affect you.

Nevertheless, some and maybe all of them will at times disturb you, and for this reason a partial list of them is given as follows: worry over class standing; fretting over possible marks on problems turned in but not yet received back from the marking committee; useless striving to guess (G-2ing) what the next problem will be; worry over bad marks with a resultant loss of confidence in yourself; disturbance caused by unavoidable listening to some students whose views on the course are unsound and very much warped; worry caused by the belief (nearly always erroneous) that you have entirely failed to absorb the school instruction on a particular subject; and finally a feeling that you are being abused because you must study a little while each night with a consequent increasing mental reluctance to go to your study after dinner and settle down to work.

Some of these will bear a little discussion. It is obvious to anyone that there is no earthly use in worrying about something which is already an accomplished fact. So any thought and time expended in pondering or fretting over grades received, or to be received, on problems already solved is manifestly wasted. Worse than this it tends to depress you to a certain extent, and always takes away time that should be spent in regular study. In spite of the fact that this is the most useless of all mentally upsetting factors in the school, it is also the most common one. Only your own common sense and determination can prevent you from falling victim to the disease, and it is believed that a little thought given to the subject before you go there will do something to immunize you against it. If you will make it a practice to avoid conversation and argument with other students about past problems you will be less likely to acquire the disease in its virulent form.

G-2ing (guessing the next problem) causes much grief. In the first place you cannot do it except by accident. Some of your friends will explain their G-2 systems in great detail, and they will often sound more or less plausible. Pay absolutely no attention to them. Guessing has no place in a system, and though you might occasionally hit a problem exactly, you are bound, when you fail to guess it, to go to the problem room more or less prejudiced, and therefore not in the mental condition to do your best work.

Under the present system of marking used at Leavenworth it is impossible for any student to figure out his class standing. Being impossible of even approximate determination, conjecture and thought concerning it tends only to irritate. If a high class standing interests you personally in the slightest degree, the best way to attain it is to forget that such a thing exists, and bend your energies toward learning what the school has to teach. As you go through the course, if you can feel that you are really grasping your daily lessons, and slowly but surely learning what it is all about, class standing will take care of itself in a manner that will be very satisfactory to you at the end of the year.

As to the grade you may have received on a particular paper you will not be informed except that it is between 75–100% when you receive an "S". Speculation along this line is always interesting, but too much time should not be spent at it.

Some men spend considerable time in spouting bitter, caustic, and blatant criticism of the school. Occasionally they handle the English language clever enough to build up a very plausible case against the place. When you are feeling a bit low in the mind, their tirades may cause you to wonder whether it is all worth while, and may induce you to desert your normal routine for awhile in favor of a policy of "let her rip, and to h——, etc." When this happens to you try to recall the calibre of the men who have been, and are, responsible for the school, and the thousands who have successfully completed it ahead of you. Keep your feet on the ground.

By all means avoid feeling sorry for yourself because each evening you find it necessary to study for a couple of hours. One rarely gets stale, at least in nine months, doing anything in which a real interest is taken. It should be a religion with you to be interested in the next day's work.

As a matter of fact the central idea of this paper is to help you to get the right slant on your Leavenworth year. The purpose of routine, system, regular habits, and all the advice contained herein as to "do" and "don't", is simply to make it easier for you to preserve a normal, healthy mental attitude while a student at the school. It is almost certain that you will do some worrying, but you must adopt, as in the performance of any other serious duty, a philosophic frame of mind.

Habits

As in everything else, your daily habits at Leavenworth should be normal and reasonable. If you carry any one of your daily activities to an extreme, something else must suffer. If you study too much you will lose some of your ability to carry a fresh active mind to the problem room. If you sleep and exercise too little you will gradually lose health, or at least become irritable and stale.

Make for yourself a schedule and stick to it. For instance a reasonable schedule for school days is as follows: up at seven; at school at 8:30. The time from 8:30 AM to 5:00 PM generally speaking belongs to the school. Dinner at 6:00, and start study at 7:00 PM. Make the limit of study 10:15 PM. Get to bed at once and be sure you average a good solid eight hours sleep. Use your Saturdays and Sundays for exercise and recreation. Such a schedule is not strenuous, and can be indefinitely maintained with no loss of health. It gives all the study time you need, and toward the end of the year this study period will probably be cut down. At the beginning of the year there is often a temptation to overdo things. A man counts on getting a wonderful start by doing with less sleep and lengthening his study hours each night. He also cuts down his exercise and recreation to study some over the weekends. You should note the fact that knowledge alone will do you no good. You never get an examination at Leavenworth which consists of a list of questions to answer. Problems are so drawn that you are required to bring to bear your common sense and clear judgment in the application of the knowledge you have gained. If you are mentally fatigued or feel too stuffed up with facts and figures when you go to a problem, it is almost certain a poor mark will result. Cramming is even less profitable than in most other schools. This idea applies also to the hour preceding problems. These are solved in the afternoons, beginning at 1:00 o'clock. On such days morning conferences are finished at 10:45. The remaining time until the problem starts belongs to you. Take a nap or a walk, but do not study. One hour's study could be useful to you only in case you know the exact subject for the day's problem, and even this case the resulting damage would probably be greater than the supposed benefit. Go to the problem room in good health, fresh in mind and body, and with a reasonable understanding of the principles the school has been teaching, and the results you obtain will be more than satisfactory.

In this question of habits you should never forget that a routine based on common sense will yield for you far better results than any extraordinary and strenuous efforts toward "specking the course".

Methods of Study

There are three generally recognized systems of study in use at Leavenworth. These are called the single, the committee, and the pair or partner methods. Each has its adherents and its good points. The committee system is rather unwieldy, as there are too many men whose convenience and ideas must be suited. Too often when several men are working together some unfortunate characteristic of any one of them may vitiate the efforts of all. On the other hand if you work entirely alone you are more apt to go stale, to go to one extreme or the other in the hours you devote to study, and to consume too much time in working on details whose importance does not justify the effort made. The biggest advantage of this method is the independence in study enjoyed. The partner system has most of the advantages of the other systems and none of the disadvantages, provided the partners suit each other. Each serves as a check on the other, study is less monotonous, and much time is saved in the staking out and solving of conference problems, and in the assimilation of the broad principles of any subject. Studying with a partner does not imply a surrender of self reliance. It is simply a method of saving time and effort in assimilating the subject matter of assigned lessons. It has no effect whatsoever on your decisions and actions in the problem room, where all work is strictly individual. You need not feel that simply because you study with a partner, that you are depending on him to assist you through the school. The only caution to be observed is that the partners must not join up in haste and repent the rest of the year. The work at the beginning of the year is mostly review, and is sort of a shaking down process. If you have selected your partner by November 1, it will be in plenty of time. This gives you an opportunity to talk to many of your friends, and find the one who looks on the school about as you do, who likes to study the way you do, and who wants to devote to study about the same number of hours you do. Of course, if you already have a study partner whom you have been working with in Benning, and would like to continue the relationship, there is no reason that you should not work together from the first day. At least, you should consider this system of study, because every man I have known who used it was convinced it was the best of the three enumerated.

In addition to the instruction you receive in the conference room, during your study periods, and in the working of problems, you will gain a great deal by a method I call absorption. During recesses between conferences you have splendid opportunities of dropping into the office of any instructor you'd like to see. The little talks you will have with these officers who have been through the mill, and are now intimately connected with the school will prove invaluable to you. Instructors are anxious to help. You can ask specific questions or just sit around and listen to the general conversation. The insight into the school, and the understanding of the whole course you will pick up in this manner is remarkable. Do not carry this habit to dances, dinners, and the social gatherings. Their purpose is relaxation and recreation, not instruction. When you see instructors at such places avoid the school as a subject of conversation. In other words, during your working hours keep your mind in a flexible, receptive condition; and during play hours, forget the whole works.

There is some difference of opinion as to the proper subject matter for study during evening period, some people work on review subjects almost exclusively, others spend the major portion of the time on the next day's lessons. Those who advocate the review system maintain that time is saved by waiting to hear a conference on a particular subject before studying it individually. The time so saved is thus available for special work, especially on things in which the student believes himself behind.

The objection to this method is that the conference, which is of paramount importance in the school system of instruction, will not be thoroughly understood in the general case unless the student is well acquainted with the subject matter thereof, before it takes place. This method also places the necessity for choosing the subject for the evening's study on the student himself—and leads to haphazard work, and a dependence on G-2ing.

If the major portion of the evening is spent on the next day's lesson, the conference will so impress the essentials of the subject on the student's mind that necessity for review will rarely arise. Moreover, such a method fits in with a systematic scheme of study; the attention is centered more on absorbing the course, and less on doping out the next problem.

If two hours, on the average, is spent on the next day's lesson, there will be about an hour available for any special work you desire to do, and this will be found ample. Whatever you do, don't fall behind. Do efficient daily work to keep up with the school's schedule.

It is perfectly true that a man can go through Leavenworth with studying about 15 minutes per night, because he can to a great extent depend upon the conference alone. What is advocated here is neither one extreme or the other, but rather a reasonable system which will gain the most for you in instruction, and still make such moderate demands on you that you will finish the year in better health than you started it.

Solution of Problems

The instruction you will receive at Leavenworth in the proper methods of working problems is comprehensive and thorough, and identical with the instruction you have received on the same subject at The Infantry School. Therefore, there is no point in attempting in such a paper as this to go over the process in detail. A few general observations, however, may serve to emphasize several important phases of the work, and may help you to avoid some very common errors.

You will hear a great deal about the "common sense solution of problems" which means making a sound "estimate of the situation". In spite of all they tell you along this line, it is sometimes difficult to eradicate the belief that a spark of genius rather than prosaic common sense is the essential element in arriving at a good solution. Such a belief leads to guessing, which is fatal.

Among other things "common sense" will tell you that you cannot correctly solve any problem unless you thoroughly understand the situation issued to you by the school. Any one of the conditions imposed may decisively affect a problem. If the important detail should be overlooked, your solution may be a hundred per cent wrong. For instance, suppose a problem states, "The 1st Division, which marched from Chambersburg early on the 16th, went into bivouac near Gettysburg about 2:00 p.m. the same date." If you take only the present location of the division into consideration, it may very well be considered in the problem as available for any kind of duty. On the other hand if you at once check up the distance between its two bivouacs, you may find that to make the march described it had to start long before daylight and should be now almost exhausted, and unfit for any service except in an emergency. The illustration given is a most obvious one, and it does not appear possible to the average officer that he could make such errors. As a matter of fact, large or minor errors in the staking out and assimilation of the situation constitute the most frequent causes for incorrect solutions in the school. In all problems consider the map only as a chart to show you the terrain and the location of troops. When you order a certain action by your troops, regard it as an actual movement under actual conditions as portrayed in the situation. This is summed up by the school dictum, often repeated, "work yourself into the situation". Therefore, in the matter of understanding every part of the problem as issued, including the situation, the requirement and the time and place for turning it in, be absolutely certain you are right before you start the work of solving.

The situation understood, never forget that your assigned mission is always the sign post which must point your way as you proceed with your solution. Assimilate it, and thoroughly digest its meaning. In contemplating any action, do so in conjunction with your understanding of your mission. Keep it in front of you, literally and figuratively. Write it in large letters and prop it up on your map table directly in front of your eyes. And when you've arrived at your decision the first question you must ask yourself is "Does it carry out my mission?", or, if the accomplishment of the mission is now an impossibility, "Does it carry out the spirit of my mission to the limit of my ability?"

Two very important characteristics of every good solution are "simplicity" and "positiveness". Not only should the dispositions and actions ordered by you be simple, but your order or plan should be of the same character. It is difficult to overemphasize this point. You will sometimes hear students say "I would have done that too, but it looked so easy I could not believe it to be the correct answer." Common sense solutions are always simple, and stated in clear straightforward terms. It is the man who believes he is exhibiting a Napoleonic trend, who introduces some complicated maneuver or idea into his plan. No doubt it is a good idea to emulate Napoleon, but remember that his battle plans are among the simplest that history records.

Failure to couch your decision and plan in positive terms is fatal. The school will unfailingly brand such a solution unsatisfactory. Whatever you decide to do, state your decision in no unmistakable terms. Furthermore your plan itself should always take into account the axiom that "Positive results are obtained only through positive action".

If system and method are important in all Leavenworth activities, they are many times more important in this matter of solving problems than in any other thing you do. Routine will aid you in avoiding the commission of careless errors, will keep you from making an incorrect allotment of your time, and will assist you to solve the problem in a logical, orderly, and easy manner.

You will hear considerable conversation concerning "school set up", "school scenery" and the inevitable "—— in the wood pile". Those expressions are used to describe a very and most unreliable method (or lack of method) used by some students in working their problems. The idea is this: each problem is supposed to contain some little condition, usually expressed in a more or less stereotyped form, which to the discerning student in itself indicates the correct solution. By using the "common sense" method you will generally use the full afternoon to complete your solution. Quite often you will hear some student describe how <u>he</u> instantly hit the problem "right on the nose" because he had the acumen to detect the little point which showed him what the school wanted done. Remember, you are submitting <u>your</u> solution, not the one written by the school, and pin your faith to a sound, logical method of arriving at such solution, and not on a hide and seek system which will keep you "it" the great majority of the time. Make a real "estimate of the situation" and a reasonable answer will always result.

This subject of solving the problem is of course the one which interests the student more than any other. If you stick to the methods the school teaches, refuse to become disturbed by an occasional bad mark, and put your best efforts on each problem as it is issued, you will have no cause to fear for the result.

Some General Remarks

Under this heading it is desired to give you only some miscellaneous ideas which may serve to fill in a few of the gaps left in the picture which I have attempted to portray above.

This paper is not a "guide to Leavenworth". Furthermore, no article could be written which would be that. Rules will not serve the purpose. You will so often hear the expression "it depends upon the situation" that this remark actually becomes a by-word among students. Yet it is perfectly true. If tactical questions did not in general depend upon the situation, then one method of attack, defense or whatnot would apply to each, and warfare would be an exact science. In this event, the man who could remember all the rules would be the best soldier, and there would be no real need for the different qualities we believe a leader should have. You should therefore view with a great deal of caution any paper, or advice which lays down specific rules for use in Leavenworth. For instance, here is one; "when marching in two or more columns always make your main effort in an attack on the flank on which your tanks, 155-mm howitzers or other strong auxiliaries are marching". Now it is obvious that if other things are equal you would prefer to attack that flank, because less movement into position will be involved, and your whole plan will be simpler. But to take this as a rule to follow may well land you a nice fat "U" which would have been avoided had you studied the situation comprehensively. Another rule often quoted is; "always use as a reserve one regiment less one battalion." The theory is, that no matter what size of reserve the school uses, your solution will fall within the limits they will allow. Keep out the reserve you think proper under the existing conditions, and don't worry about the school answer to the same question. There are many others; such as "never penetrate"; "never attack unless you have 4 hours of daylight to push home the attack"; "when in doubt, attack"; etc. All of them belong to the same category, and taken in toto, most emphatically do not constitute the instruments needed to crack the Leavenworth nut.

Some people like to check their decision against the nine principles of war as given in Training Regulations 10-5. If you have time, I advocate this custom. Whether or not it ever results in calling your attention to some error you have made, the habit is a least instructional, and interesting. The principles can be memorized in a few minutes, and the idea involves no great effort on your part.

Some little difficulty is often experienced in writing decisions so that they will contain all that is necessary, and yet not be verbose. Whenever this subject is discussed from the platform, pay particular attention to the instruction. In addition it is a good subject for informal conversations with instructors. As a basis for thought, if you have any doubts about the matter at all, I suggest that you consider this idea (not original); my decision will be complete if I state, "what shall I do, how shall I do it, when shall I do it, where shall I do it, why shall I do it?"

Seemingly one of the hardest things for many students to do is to take the school as they find it and go quietly about their logical business of absorbing the course. They spend a lot of time and mental effort in cursing, criticizing, and working out reformations for the place. Nothing is better calculated to upset you all through the year than persistent habit of fault finding. If you won't take yourself too seriously, you won't be tempted to waste your time in this way.

The subject of "reclamas"[3] deserves mention. Whenever a comment on your papers is not understood, or you feel an injustice has been done, do not hesitate to make a plain, straight-forward presentation of the case in the form of a reclama, and you may rest assured your paper will receive the most careful consideration of the school authorities. To make a reclama the vehicle of an attack on the school, or an argument in favor of one's own opinion as opposed to doctrine of the school, or to submit a reclama for any purpose whatsoever other than to clear up a point on which you feel a mistake must have been made, is condemned. Think the matter over carefully and satisfy your-self that you are not "quibbling". Following this policy you will have no trouble in deciding whether or not to submit a reclama in any specific instance.

I have purposely avoided in this discussion any definite description of the curriculum. As a matter of fact, I have not intended to take up any of the details of the school itself, except such things as affect the routine of study, and have an influence on the student's attitude toward the place. You may rest assured that instruction in any subject will be given to you in such manner, and at such time, that you will be thoroughly familiar with it before you are called on to use it in the problem room. In addition, you are permitted to take with you to problems certain data, order forms, organization tables, etc., which make unnecessary the memorizing of most mere facts you will use. This is done because Leavenworth places more emphasis on principles than on technique; the memory is of less importance than common sense.

This paper can to a large extent be epitomized in a series of brief observations which on account of their conciseness may more succinctly convey the thought intended than when included in the longer discussion of the body of the article.

Therefore the following:

(1) Take Leavenworth naturally; the easier you take it, the harder you'll hit it.

(2) Trust not the G-2 artist; he fools himself, let him not also fool you.

(3) Believe in the humanity of the instructor; he gains nothing by tricking you into picking up one of the Leavenworth horseshoes. (U).[4]

(4) Don't spend your time in the problem room cursing the asterisk who made up this ditto problem; he is probably not psychic and therefore fails to suffer the discomfort of the place you've mentally consigned him.

(5) Give no thought to the wonderful marks of the assembly room orator; a fluent tongue is not always a veracious one.

(6) Be not too swift in turning in your solution; the habit may give you a reputation for brilliancy with your fellow students, but they don't award the marks.

(7) Don't worry about things which belong to the past; the water over the dam no longer turns the wheel.

(8) Avoid indulging yourself in the sport of chasing the Ethiopian through the timber; the man who has caught an elephant by the tail is always an object of ridicule.

(9) Don't be too critical concerning details with which you do not agree; it is possible to fail to see the forest because of the trees.

(10) Don't forget Jeff's famous supplication to Mutt; "Be reasonable".

(11) Also the philosophy of Molly-make-believe, "Now abideth faith, hope, and charity, these three—and greater than these is a sense of humor".

(12) Everybody graduates.

Finale

If you will accept the above as a fairly accurate depiction of Leavenworth, it must be apparent that you are undertaking nothing so unusual nor strange when you begin your study year. You are not going to a far country where the language is different, or the customs bizarre. You are going to a place where you'll be grouped with others of your own kind, and where those in authority know and appreciate your peculiar difficulties and are anxious to help you through them.

So have no hesitancy about going, nor doubts concerning your ability to absorb the instruction. Do your work, but do not slave; understand the teachings, but do not try to "speck" the course.

If you'll maintain this attitude throughout the year, Leavenworth, both while you are there and in retrospect, will in many ways be one of the brightest spots of your military career.

1. Eisenhower composed this essay either just after graduation from the Command and General Staff School in June 1926 or shortly after reporting for duty with the 24th Infantry at Fort Benning on August 18. The original draft is signed "Major D. D. Eisenhower, 24th Infantry." The draft of the essay was originally located in the Records of the Adjutant General's Office, Miscellaneous, Record Group 407, NARA, several years ago but can no longer be found; however, a copy of the draft is at the Eisenhower Library. A revised version was published with no authorship given (A Young Graduate, "The Leavenworth Course," *Infantry Journal* 30 [June 1927]: 589–600), but there is no doubt the "young graduate" was Dwight D. Eisenhower. Eisenhower sent the draft to Col. H. J. Brees, Assistant Commandant of the General Service Schools at Fort Leavenworth. Brees approved distribution of Eisenhower's commentary to incoming students in a letter of December 22, 1926. Brees served as Assistant Commandant of General Service Schools at Fort Leavenworth and as commandant of the Command and General Staff School from 1935 to 1936.

2. The names of the seven officers who reviewed the papers were listed on the last page and have been deleted here. Most could not be identified. Those reviewers included Brig. Gen. Edgar Collins, Commandant of the Infantry School, and Colonel Brees at Fort Leavenworth.

3. A *reclama* was a formal objection students could file in order to contest an instructor's criticisms of their papers.

4. The "U" stands for "unsatisfactory."

CHAPTER TWO

The American Battle Monuments Commission
March 15, 1928–September 5, 1929

After completing the Command and General Staff course in the summer of 1926, Major Eisenhower received orders to the 24th Infantry, Fort Benning, Georgia, where as commander of the regiment's second battalion (as well as assistant post executive officer), he temporarily realized his fondest dream—commanding troops. It proved to be a short assignment. In January 1927, at the request of Gen. John J. "Black Jack" Pershing, Eisenhower left for Washington, D.C., and the office of the American Battle Monuments Commission, which Pershing directed.[1]

Congress created the commission to establish and maintain cemeteries and erect monuments to the nearly 120,000 Americans who were killed in action or died from other causes during World War I and were interred in Europe. The commission also was to prepare a guide for those visiting the burial and battle sites. Pershing needed someone to complete this large and sensitive guidebook project, and Gen. Fox Conner, Pershing's operations officer during the war, had recommended Eisenhower. Conner believed him to be an officer gifted in writing and the other intellectual skills—as well as the energy and organizational talent—necessary to distill the mass of accumulated data into a helpful guidebook.[2] Eisenhower faced the daunting task of writing the guide within six months. Working long hours—often assisted by his brother Milton, then a journalist working in President Calvin Coolidge's Department of Agriculture—he completed the work on schedule in mid summer, and before the end of the year the volume appeared in print.[3] In August, Eisenhower left the commission for the Army War College, located in southwest Washington at the present-day Fort McNair. As he departed, Pershing praised him for his "superior ability not only in visualizing his work as a whole but in executing its many details in an efficient and timely manner." Major Eisenhower had demonstrated "unusual intelligence and constant devotion to duty."[4]

Graduating from the War College in June 1928, Eisenhower faced a choice of two new posts. The army offered him either assignment to the General Staff or a return to the Battle Monuments Commission, this time to its headquarters in Paris. Career ambitions drew Eisenhower toward the General Staff, but the Eisenhowers had spent time at dusty Fort Sam Houston and in steamy Panama; the family decided on a year in Europe. In late July, Major Eisenhower, Mamie, and six-year-old son John[5] sailed for France. There the major collected additional data for a revision of the battle monuments guide, which ultimately did not appear until 1938.[6] The fourteen months abroad made for a delightful interlude in the lives of the young officer, his wife, and their son. Four decades later, Eisenhower acknowledged that this may have been the family's happiest period together. John was enrolled at the McJanet School for American Children, and the family's apartment overlooking the Seine became famous as a hospitable haven for young officers and army friends who happened to be in Paris.[7]

Always eager to learn, Eisenhower took full advantage of his posting. He immersed himself in the culture, politics, and geography of France, and he studied the military history of World War I, both by reading and by inspecting battle sites. These lessons later served him well. While touring, the gregarious American major would stop along the road for lunch, often sharing his food and drink with the peasants and roadworkers of rural France. Frequently, he took along John and his son's friend, "Bo" Horkan, son of Eisenhower's army friend George Horkan.[8] Shortly before the Eisenhowers were to depart for home, Maj. William Gruber and his wife, Helen, friends whom Eisenhower and his wife had met at the Command and General Staff School, joined the Eisenhowers for a carefully planned motor tour of France, Belgium, Germany, and Switzerland. They embarked on this eighteen-hundred-mile, seventeen-day trip in late August 1929 and departed Paris for New York in September.

1. Gen. John J. Pershing (USMA, 1886) served as Commander in Chief of American troops in Europe during World War I. Earlier, he had served in several Indian Wars, in Cuba during the Spanish-American War, in the Philippines, and in the Mexican Punitive Expedition, which he led in 1916. He was appointed Chief of Staff in 1921, a position he held until 1924. Pershing died in 1948.

2. Stephen E. Ambrose, *Eisenhower: Soldier, General of the Army, President-Elect, 1890–1952* (New York: Simon and Schuster, 1983), 1:82.

3. American Battle Monuments Commission, *A Guide to the American Battle Fields in Europe* (Washington, D.C.: Government Printing Office, 1927).

4. Pershing to Maj. Gen. Robert H. Allen, Chief of Infantry, August 15, 1927, Pre-pres. Papers, Eisenhower Library.

5. John Sheldon Doud Eisenhower (USMA, 1944) was born in Denver, Colorado, on August 3, 1922. Except for the year in Paris, he spent his grade school years in Washington, D.C., attending high school at Brent School, Baguio, Philippine Islands. He served with the U.S. First Army during World War II, the Army of Occupation in Germany and Austria, the 15th Infantry Regiment, and then on the gen-

eral staff of the 3d Infantry Division during the Korean War. He joined the Joint War Plans Division, Army General Staff, in 1957–58 and retired from the U.S. Army Reserve as a brigadier general. He served as White House assistant staff secretary from 1958 to 1961 and as U.S. Ambassador to Belgium between 1969 and 1971.

6. American Battle Monuments Commission, *A Guide to the American Armies and Battlefields in Europe: A History, Guide, and Reference Book* (Washington, D.C.: Government Printing Office, 1938).

7. Dwight D. Eisenhower, *At Ease: Stories I Tell to Friends* (Garden City, N.Y.: Doubleday, 1967), 205–10; John S. D. Eisenhower, *Strictly Personal* (Garden City, N.Y.: Doubleday, 1974), 2–4; Rosalind Massow, "Mamie and Ike Talk about 50 Years of Marriage," *Parade,* June 26, 1966, 5.

8. George A. Horkan received his commission in 1917 and served most of his career in the Quartermaster Corps. He held the position of Chief Quartermaster, European Command (1948) and served as Quartermaster General of the Army (1951–52). Horkan retired from the army in 1952 with the rank of major general. Horkan and his wife, Mary, became acquainted with the Eisenhowers in the late 1920s, when Eisenhower was first detailed to the War Department. Horkan joined Eisenhower in the Paris office of the American Battle Monuments Commission. While in France, "Bo" (George Jr.) and John S. D. Eisenhower cemented what became a lifelong friendship. Eisenhower, *Strictly Personal,* 2–4.

21

United States Army Military History Institute
                        Army War College Curricular Files
     Memorandum for the Assistant Commandant, Army War College

MARCH 15, 1928

Subject: An Enlisted Reserve for the Regular Army[1]

I. [. . .]

II. The Problem Presented.

1. To determine the advisability of establishing an enlisted reserve for the Regular Army, and a practicable method of procuring and organizing such a reserve

Note: The major provisions of existing laws are accepted as those which will continue to form the basis for our military program. In the effort to make the conclusions practicable and reasonable, and applicable to present conditions, the subject is limited to a consideration of the effects on our military position that would be produced through the accumulation of an enlisted reserve for the Regular Army, and of economical and acceptable methods of securing it.

III. Facts bearing on the Problem

1. Missions of the Regular Army in an Emergency

a. Army Regulation 135–10 gives the following as the missions of the Regular Army:[2]

(1) To provide adequate garrisons in peace and in war for our overseas possessions.

(2) To provide adequate peace garrisons for the coast defenses within the continental limits of the United States.

(3) To provide personnel for the development and training of the National Guard and the Organized Reserves.

(4) To provide the necessary personnel for the overhead of the Army of the United States, wherein the duties are of a continuing nature.

(5) To provide an adequate, organized, balanced, and effective expeditionary force, which will be available in emergencies, within the continental limits of the United States or elsewhere, and which will serve as a model for the National Guard and the Organized Reserves.

b. The report of the Secretary of War, 1925, states, "The primary mission of the Regular Army is to provide a defensive force capable of defending the country on the outbreak of war against any force which could likely be brought against it before the civilian components could be prepared for battle".

c. The missions enumerated are each of such importance that no single one of them may be neglected safely.

Peace time garrisons for coast defenses in the United States must become the cadres for the formation of adequate war time forces at those critical points.

The task of developing and training the National Guard and Organized Reserves, important in peace, will demand intensified effort after the declaration of an emergency.

Organizational overhead is essential to the functioning of an administrative machine.

The importance of defending our territory and vital interests until the civilian components are prepared for battle is evident. Studies emphasize the fact that in certain situations immediate and energetic action by forces of moderate size is of the utmost importance. Initial successes under these conditions may relieve us of the necessity of waging a long and bitter war with large armies with its consequent losses in men, material, and money.

2. <u>Strength required to carry out the missions of the Regular Army upon the outbreak of an emergency.</u>

a. The strength required for the performance of the Regular Army missions will vary widely under different situations. Since, however, the reason for the existence of the army is national security, estimates should be based on a situation in which opponents are sufficiently strong to threaten our safety.

b. Studies made on this general subject are based on various assumptions.

One, which bases our requirements upon the carrying capacity of vessels available to possible opponents, concludes that to assure safety we should have concentrated within thirty days after declaration of war at least 300,000 men in a field army, with approximately 150,000 to 200,000 assigned on other missions. Under these conditions the minimum strength consistent with national safety which should be available to the Regular Army at the beginning of an emergency is 500,000 men.

c. Another study, based on the <u>minimum</u> situation in which our national safety could be menaced, estimates that we should make provisions upon the declaration of an emergency as follows:

Foreign garrisons (total)	35,000
Bridge heads at sensitive points	30,000
Vital operations	114,000
Secondary operations	35,000
Frontier defense in secondary areas	20,000
Strategic Reserve and frontier defense	50,000
	284,000

To these figures must be added the strength necessary for furnishing cadres for fixed coast defenses; manning anti-aircraft equipment in vital areas; personnel for organizing and training civilian components; necessary overhead and miscellaneous duties in Zone of Interior. It is estimated that these activities will demand the services of 40,000 to 50,000 men, some of whom can later be forwarded to the combat zone as replacements, and thus we have a total of about 330,000 men to accomplish the mission of the Regular Army upon declaration of such a war. Assuming that secondary and defensive missions could be performed by National Guard units and about one-half of the reserve could be furnished by them, we would still require an initial strength for the Regular Army of about 250,000.

The study quoted proposes the immediate preparation of two expeditions, the larger of which demands a force of 76,000 and the other 48,000. By providing for the larger only, and undertaking upon the outbreak of war only the one which promises the best results, we can diminish the 250,000 to about 200,000 men, although the larger number would be most desirable.

d. A third study places the minimum requirements of the Regular Army upon mobilization as 277,000 men.

e. A total strength of 200,000 trained men available to the Regular Army immediately upon the declaration of war is taken as the irreducible minimum consistent with national safety.

f. All studies examined emphasize the vital necessity for immediate operations by a moderately strong mobile force, upon the declaration of war. The Regular Army is the only component of our army available for immediate service in an emergency. (See par.5 b.)

3. Strength and organization of the Regular Army available to carry out missions.

a. The National Defense Act of June 4, 1920, provided that the enlisted strength of the Regular Army should not exceed 280,000 men and apparently contemplated that this figure would be approximated. By June, 1921, 214,000 men were in the Army.

b. This act repealed the laws of 1912 and 1916 which had provided for an enlisted reserve. It is evident that Congress considered, under the conditions existing at the time and in view of the other provisions it made for national defense, that there was no need for continuing the existence of the enlisted reserve.

c. [. . . .] At a time when we had approximately 4,000,000 trained veterans in the country, and when it was expected to raise the National Guard to a strength of 435,000, it was considered essential to provide for a Regular Army of 280,000. At present, with the contingent of veterans rapidly disappearing as a military asset, and with the National Guard less than one-half the strength it was expected to reach, the Regular Army has been reduced to about 40% of that considered necessary under the most favorable conditions.

This reduction has been occasioned by the necessity for economy in National expenditures, and there are no indications that the active army will be increased either now, or in the near future.

Any increase in the strength available to the Regular Army upon declaration of war must therefore be provided in some manner which will be much less expensive than that of maintaining greater numbers on the active list of the army.

d. Organization of present strength of Regular Army.

(1) The missions of the Regular Army, aside from that of providing an expeditionary force, are principally those connected with the organization and development of great civilian levies. For this reason, and to provide units in which officers and non-commissioned officers may secure essential practical training, the 88,000 soldiers in continental United States are organized into a large number of cadres, rather than in a small number of large units. Under the policy of the War Department, published August 15, 1927, the mobile force of the Regular Army is organized into six Infantry Divisions which are far below peace strength, and two reduced peace strength cavalry divisions.

(2) This system has the great advantage of providing a frame work into which large numbers of reinforcements who have received the training necessary in lower grades may be absorbed quickly, and also develops instructors and other key men for use with civilian components.

(3) If, however, trained reinforcements are not immediately available, then any expeditionary force, being composed of cadres only will remove from the Zone of the Interior too large a proportion of the very men who must be depended upon to assist in the development of civilian components.

Furthermore, the expeditionary force itself will be so weak that if opposed to any considerable army we can expect nothing but disaster in the beginning, and a protracted war with heavy costs in men and wealth.

4. Discrepancy between strength required and strength available.

a. The lowest possible estimate for a Regular Army which can assure comparative national safety is 200,000. With an actual strength of 125,000, including Philippine Scouts, it is seen that we require at least 75,000 trained reinforcements, immediately upon the declaration of war. A study made in G-3 Division, W.D.G.S.,[3] 1927, makes a similar estimate of our minimum needs. Considerations of economy must remain as a most important factor in fixing the maximum figure to be attained. While it is true that a nation's military problem is not based on its capacity to finance her efforts, yet needless military expenditures, if carried to the extreme, operate to defeat one of the purposes for which they are made; namely, the insurance of national prosperity.

b. Essential qualifications of reinforcements needed to fill discrepancy.

(1) The essential qualifications are:

(a) Immediate availability when called.

(b) Sufficient training to function in active field service.

(c) Good physical condition.

(2) The first of these is dictated by the fact that the vital missions of the Regular Army are to protect our interests and carry out necessary operations before the civilian forces can be prepared for battle, and to assist in the development of those components.

Essential training depends to some extent on the system under which the reinforcements are organized. If they are to take the field as units, then each of these should be advanced in training to approximately the same extent as our peace time Regular Army. On the other hand, if received as individuals and employed to fill up the existing Regular Army cadres, the training needed is only that which will enable the man to perform satisfactorily the duties of the lower enlisted grades of the unit to which assigned. For this reason they should be men of normal enlisted caliber who are well disciplined, and experienced in drill, maneuver, camping, firing, etc.

5. Means for providing the forces to fill the gap between the numbers required by the missions, and the strength available in Regular Army.

a. The Army of the United States consists of the Regular Army, the National Guard, and the Organized Reserves.

b. The National Guard receives annually the equivalent of one month's training, the units being maintained at reduced peace strength. The annual turnover in enlisted men averages about 60%. This means that at any time the average man in the Guard is about one month advanced in training. This amount has been shown by experience to be insufficient in which to inculcate in men the necessary standards of discipline, and give to them the practical instruction which will enable them to function satisfactorily even as replacements for active units. National Guard Officers state that if their units are permitted to remain near their home stations for about two to four weeks after beginning of mobilization, in the average case they will be practically filled up by the return of former enlisted men, and all will be afforded time to adjust their civilian affairs so as to work a minimum of hardship on the individual upon his departure.

In addition to the above consideration, National Guardsmen are engaged in all kinds of civilian pursuits, and in general will not be physically qualified for immediate field service until after they have undergone about one month's intensive training.

From every standpoint it is evident that the greater part of the National Guard should not be required to enter active campaign immediately upon declaration of war except in case of dire necessity. It has been officially stated that mobilization of the National Guard cannot be <u>completed</u> until eight months after the beginning of a war.

c. The Enlisted Reserve Corps consists at present of approximately 6,000 men. They receive no training, and in any event, may not be called to active duty until after an emergency has been expressly declared by Congress.

The Citizens Military Training Camps and Reserve Officers Training Corps are essentially training schools in which personnel is trained with a view of becoming officers or non-commissioned officers of the Organized Reserves.[4] The mission of this personnel is to fill key positions in our civilian levies after an emergency has been declared, and are not available for immediate field service.

Furthermore, students in these schools have not received the thorough training in the practical parts of the military profession which is essential in those intended for immediate active service.

d. As stated in paragraph 3c, it cannot be expected that the size of the active Regular Army will be increased under present conditions. Men discharged from the Regular Army, however, are qualified as to training for immediate service, and except for the active force itself are the only ones under our system who have received the requisite training. As long as no use is made of this class of men immediately upon declaration of war, we do not provide for making use of this important military asset in an effective way.

The reinforcements necessary may be provided by organizing these men into a reserve and requiring them under certain conditions to report immediately for active service. The availability of such men will be practically the same as that of soldiers in active service. Their physical fitness for immediate field service will remain, for several years after discharge from active training, much superior to that of the average civilian who has not had this training.

Experience has shown that the cost of maintaining a soldier in the reserve is only a small fraction of that necessary to maintain him in the active force. In 1912 the report of the Chief of Staff stated, "The economic effect of a reserve system therefore is to reduce the per capita cost of any given army, at the same time assuring maximum effectiveness in war. If we do not have reserves we are committed to a policy of maximum cost."

Under the Act of 1916 (discussed below) the pay of a soldier in the reserve was fixed at $24.00 per year. The cost to the Government of maintaining a soldier on the active list is about $1200.00 per year, not including overhead.

Some statistics concerning reserves raised under this general system are as follows:

(1) British—Most enlistments are for twelve years. Length of service with active army varies. The average is 7 years with colors, 5 years with reserves. Strength of reserves on April 1, 1927 was 92,000. Pay of reservist is from 25¢ to 37¢ per day. Reenlistments are permitted in the Reserves under certain conditions.

(2) Army Reserves under former laws in the United States.

The Act of August 12, 1912, effective November 1, 1912, provided for enlistment periods of seven years, either three or four with the colors, the remainder in reserve. No pay was provided, but each man, if called to duty, was to receive a bonus of $5.00 per month for each month spent in the reserves.

This law could not begin to produce a reserve until November, 1915. Its operation was suspended in May, 1916, when about 5,000 men had been furloughed to the reserve. In 1916, at which time the strength of the Regular Army was about 97,000, the Adjutant General estimated that under this law a reserve of about 60,000 would be maintained.

The law of 1916 revised this act in certain details. It provided for pay of $24.00 per year (equal in relative purchasing power to about $36.00 at present) but reduced the bonus from $5.00 to $3.00 per month.

(3) United States Navy

Under the Act of February 28, 1925, several classes of reserves have been provided for the Navy and the Marine Corps.

Certain facts relating to these reserves are worthy of note.

(a) One class is composed of men who have had sixteen to twenty years service when they enter the reserve, and a comparatively short period of usefulness remains to them. In general they will not be men who should fill the lowest enlisted grades if called to active service. With an active force of approximately 100,000 their numbers will always be small. The underlying idea of this reserve is more of reward to faithful sailors than that of maintaining a large reserve.

(b) Another class is formed from those men who have completed an enlistment in the Navy or Marine Corps. Their enlistment in the reserve is distinct and separate from that in the active force.

Pay is $25.00 per year and reserve enlistments are for four years each. The Marine Corps Reserve has 3,000 in this class. It is this class of reserves that the Marine Corps depends upon for immediate reinforcements in time of war.

The active strength of the Marine Corps is 18,000 at present.

6. Methods of Raising an Enlisted Reserve through utilization of the Regular Army itself.

a. By enlisting in a reserve such persons discharged from the active army as volunteer for this service. (This is the Marine Corps method.)

The size of such a reserve depends upon:

(1) Number of men discharged annually from the army, qualified for reserve service.

(2) Percentage of these who will volunteer.

(3) Length of reserve service.

The main advantage of this system is that the reserve service is a purely voluntary undertaking on the part of the soldier, entirely separate from his active enlistment. There can therefore be no objection raised to it on the ground that to enlist in the army a man is compelled to make himself liable to service for an unusually long period.

Another advantage is that this system begins to build a reserve immediately upon passage of law authorizing it.

Its main disadvantage is that the fullest possible use is not made of the capacity of the active force to feed the reserve. For many reasons, temporary or unimportant in nature, a discharged man may refuse to enlist in the reserve, and the total force is thus reduced in size by the number who annually do so refuse, multiplied by years of term of reserve service.

Another disadvantage is that it gives no opportunity to vary the size of the reserve as compared to the active force through varying by administrative action the length of service in each.

The experience of the Marine Corps is too limited to furnish sufficient data on which to base accurate estimates of the size of a reserve that the Regular Army could build up in this way. It would probably not exceed 20,000 men, under present conditions.

b. By making all enlistments for a stated number of years, part of which will be spent in active service, and the remainder in the reserve.

The size of such a reserve depends upon -

(1) The number of men qualified to enter the reserve, who are discharged annually from the active force, which in turn depends upon:

(a) Size of army

(b) Length of active service

(c) Various modifying factors

(2) Length of reserve service.

The main advantages of such a system are:

It assures that every man, trained in the active force at maximum cost, will be equally available for service in the reserves where he is maintained at minimum cost.

By authorizing the Secretary of War to vary the ratio of reserve service to active service in an enlistment period of a fixed total length, the total size of the force available may be varied to anticipate needs, or meet changing conditions.

The main disadvantage of this system is that it increases the length of the enlistment (if it is to be effective) beyond that of our present three year term. This point has aroused much opposition to this system and is therefore discussed as follows:

One argument advanced against the increasing of the term of enlistment is that it will increase enormously the difficulty of procuring recruits for the army, although during the years 1913–14–15, when enlistments were for a total of seven years, recruiting did not fall off. Under the law of 1912, no peace time pay was provided for reservists and therefore recruits during the years mentioned undertook an increased length of service with no additional inducement whatsoever. Even if some difficulty is experienced in this matter at first, if a modest amount is paid the reservist each year it appears probable that eventually the reserve feature may become an asset rather than a detriment in recruiting.

This possibility is substantiated by the fact that one of the classes in the British Reserve is constituted of men who voluntarily re-enlist therein. (Par. 5d) This system has been in operation in England for many years, and the public thoroughly understands the advantages as well as the obligations of reserve service.

Another objection advanced by opponents of the system is that the public will consider un-American any attempt to lengthen our present term of enlistment. Such objections apparently had no weight in 1912, and the final answer is that if the man who is undertaking such service does not object, the public will not concern itself in the matter.

Probably our people would object strenuously to instituting the twelve year period of the British, but a strong reserve can be built up with a period of half that length.

The following facts should also be noted:

Army regulations provide for discharge from the army on account of dependents, physical incapacity, etc., and these can be made to apply to reserves, and extended to include those persons who would be exempted under a draft law similar to that of 1917.

The reserve is intended for service only when we are facing a real emergency, and in general all men in the reserve would be called to military service with others through the operation of a draft law.

From the above it is seen that service in the reserve does not necessarily increase a man's liability for service, it simply advances the date on which he reports for duty.

Whatever pay is given the reservist during peace time is pay for this availability.

The results to be expected in the application of this general system to our present army are discussed in the next paragraph.

7. Factors bearing on the size of the reserve to be accumulated through the Army.

a. Assumptions -

(1) That the size of the active Regular Army will remain fixed at approximately its present strength.

(2) That all enlistments will be made for a certain number of years, part active and part reserve service.

b. If unaffected by other factors the number of men qualified annually for service in the reserve would be the total size of the active force divided by the number of years spent in active service. In practice this number is diminished by several factors.

(1) Reenlistments -

In our army at present the number of reenlisted men averages about 50,000, thus leaving about 65,000 as the actual source for a potential reserve.

A certain number of annual reenlistments are extremely desirable in order to fill key positions and promote stability in Regular Army organizations. Therefore, the active portion of any reenlistment period should be relatively long. From the standpoint of raising a reserve, there exists no reason for diminishing the three year term of active service in these cases, and any such reduction would needlessly increase expenses. However, if the requirements of the active army permit, the number of men passed into the reserve annually would be increased by limiting the number permitted to reenlist.

(2) Annual losses from other causes—

We also find in practice that the number of men honorably discharged (less reenlistments) from the army annually is less than 22,000 or one-third of the 65,000 left as the source of a reserve. One of the reasons for this is the large number of desertions. Any measure which will reduce this evil will therefore increase the number passed into the reserves. Available data shows that only 52% of men who enlist for three years are discharged per expiration of term of service, while of those enlisting for one year about 70% to 80% are discharged per expiration of term of service.

This indicates that a short term of active service will increase the number of men qualified for the reserve, both by increasing the capacity of the Regular Army, and by decreasing losses due to desertion.

Annual losses through discharge by purchase and for minority concealed at enlistment also diminish the number qualified annually for the reserve. These losses could be prevented in the first case by requiring all men who are discharged by purchase to complete the whole enlistment in the reserve. The same requirements could be made in discharge for minority, when desired by the government.

Losses due to death and disability cannot be prevented, but will remain about a constant.

c. Effect of the total term of enlistment, and the ratio of length of reserve service to length of active service.

(1) Other factors disregarded, the size of an accumulated reserve will vary directly as the ratio—length of reserve service to length of active service. Assume an army of 100,000, with total enlistment of three years, of which two years are spent in active service and one in reserve. The number qualified for reserve service annually equals 50,000, and since each man remains in reserve only one year, the accumulated reserve equals 50,000. If we reverse the length of the two periods of service, then one hundred thousand are qualified annually, and the accumulated reserve will equal 200,000. This demonstrates the great importance of the ratio, reserve service to active service, and, if we are to raise a large reserve, indicates that the first should be as large as possible and the second as small.

(2) As indicated in paragraph 6b, there is an objection to making total length of enlistment too great. The seven year period authorized by Acts of 1912 and 1916 is taken as the maximum limit in this study. Less opposition will be encountered if this figure can be diminished.

(3) Certain lower limits apply to the length of active service. Training requirements in the continental United States under present conditions indicate that it should not be less than one year. The requirements of garrisons in foreign possessions, because of time and money spent in transportation, demand a longer period than this, and for those stations two years is taken as the minimum.

It is also apparent that as the length of active service is diminished the annual number of replacements required for the army increases. Since the initial procurement, equipping, and transportation of the recruit is an item of expense, the reduction of the term of active service also increases the expenditures made in recruiting activities.

At present we obtain about sixty thousand replacements per year. It is estimated that if all enlistments (less reenlistments) were for one year active service, we would require about 108,000. Some difficulty might be experienced in obtaining this number, but on the other hand the opportunity to enlist for only one year of active service might well increase the number of applicants for enlistment.

(4) The length of reserve service is limited only by the limitations imposed on total term of enlistment, and the fact that men must not be so long in reserve service that they are no longer able because of lack of training to function in capacities required. In this connection, the average length of reserve service in the British Army is five years, and in some cases it is nine. . . .

d. The application of all the factors mentioned in paragraph 7b to present conditions in our army is shown in the following table, prepared in G-3 Division, War Department General Staff. (Based on average strength of 115,000)

Term of Enlistment	Years Reserve Service	Years Active Service	Estimated annual furloughs to Reserve	Estimated Annual Replacements	Estimated accumulated strength of Reserve. (No deductions due to death, disability, etc.)
3	2	1	54,852	108,086	109,704
3	1	2	24,401	70,296	24,401
4	2	2	24,401	70,296	48,802
4	2½	1½	34,772	82,273	86,930
4	3	1	54,852	108,086	164,556
5	2½	2½	17,892	63,750	44,730
5	3	2	24,401	70,296	73,203
5	3½	1½	34,772	82,273	121,702
5	4	1	54,852	108,086	219,408
6	5	1	54,852	108,086	274,260
6	4	2	24,401	70,296	97,604

All reenlistments in active force assumed to be for three years. While last column does not attempt to show natural attrition, neither does it show increases due to reenlistments in reserve when authorized.

e. In examining the above table to find those combinations which will provide a suitable reserve to meet our demands, and yet one which will meet requirements in the active army, and which will entail a moderate length of total service, it is noticeable that in the five year group all these considerations seem fairly well met. The two years active service and three years reserve give only 73,203 in the accumulated reserve, but the four and one division gives 219,408, and it is entirely feasible to use both these combinations in our army. Disregarding reenlisted men, and those on foreign service, about 50,000 men are in the active army, of whom any desired portion could be one year enlistments. One year enlistments are now provided by law, and apparently Congress intends retaining them. They will be made very advantageous to our defense program provided the four years service is required after discharge.

Exact results can be determined only by trial. The six year enlistment with the combinations four and two, and five and one, would insure more certain results but the six year total enlistment period should not be recommended to Congress until after the five year plan has been tested thoroughly.

f. Effect on annual expenditures.

Assuming that the strength and pay of the active army remain as at present, the authorization of a reserve would entail increased peace time expenditures as follows:

(1) Annual pay of the reservists

(2) Cost of procuring, equipping and transporting additional number of annual replacements caused by shortening of active service period. Under the general plan suggested in sub-paragraph "e" above, and assuming that about 25% to 30% of annual replacements would be for one year's active service, we would increase the present average number of replacements about 20,000.

The cost of procuring, transporting and initially clothing each will average $133.00, making an annual increase of $2,660,000. (This figure will be considerably reduced provided the average cost of procurement per man is lessened under the proposed system. The overhead for our recruiting system is already provided, and it is possible that the procurement of 20,000 additional men per year will occasion no increased expenditure.)

(3) Under the same plan it is estimated that 16,000 more would be transported home annually than at present. At $22.00 each, this would add $352,000 annually.

(4) Estimated cost of administration and supervision—$5.00 per year per man.

The plan under discussion it is believed would maintain an accumulated reserve of about 100,000 men, and $500,000 is the estimated cost of administration.

(5) Pay -

The matter of pay is most important. It must be sufficient to offer a real inducement for men of the average enlisted type, but must be small compared to active duty pay if Congress is to consider the matter favorably. The Marine Corps reservist is paid $25.00 per year, and fair results are achieved. The army has a much more difficult problem than the Marine Corps in securing adequate annual replacements because of its relative size. To secure a reserve of reasonable size the army is compelled to require each man enlisting in the active force to serve an additional time in the reserve. Reserve pay will have a direct effect on recruiting possibilities for the army, while in the Marine Corps, whose requirements as to numbers are much less, the purely voluntary system is used.

England pays reservists from $90 to $132 per year. (See paragraph 5d.)

Privates in the National Guard receive $48.00 per year, exclusive of allowances, and reserve pay should not be greater than this so that no antagonism or competition between these two components will be occasioned.

For purposes of completing estimate of total cost of reserve, it is assumed that pay of the reservist will be approximately $36.00 per year, or a total of $3,600,000.

(6) Adding the various items enumerated, we have a total of

$7,112,000 increased annual expenditures in peace time to provide an estimated accumulated reserve of 100,000 men.

This amount, compared to that necessary to maintain a like number on active duty, is insignificant.

It is, however, believed to be the maximum necessary, and through careful administration should be cut down.

8. <u>Factors bearing on administration and organization of enlisted reserve.</u>

a. Responsibility for administration.

(1) Administration of reserves by The Adjutant General at Washington has the following disadvantages.

(a) Concentrates administrative load and does not take advantage of existing facilities which are capable of performing a portion of this work with little or no increase in overhead.

(b) Controlling agency too far removed from individuals in outlying portions of United States, increasing difficulties of maintaining touch with them.

(c) Prompt collection of individuals in an emergency will be difficult.

(2) Administration of reserves by the unit from which the man is furloughed to the reserve is cumbersome and slow, and mobilization would be extremely difficult in an emergency. Units have not the facilities to exercise the needed supervision.

(3) Corps Areas are distributed roughly according to population and the headquarters of each is well placed to take care of the administration of the reservists in the particular area. Corps areas are now the agencies through which the mobilization plan is put into effect, and the added task of administering the reserve would occasion little disturbance in their programs. Plans for mobilization of the reserve could be prepared, and the men collected in a minimum of time for forwarding to the point desired. [. . .]

b. Principal administrative features.

(1) Peace time pay and war time bonus.

The amount of pay was discussed in paragraph 7f. By paying the reservists each quarter, authorities will remain in constant touch with them.

The 1912 and 1916 laws provided a bonus to be paid in case the reservist were called to active duty. Reservists are paid in time of peace for immediate availability, but the amount is kept as low as possible to meet budget requirements. A war time bonus of reasonable size, payable the instant a man enters upon active duty, will materially lessen any hardship occasioned by his inability to adjust private affairs because of lack of available time. The total sum involved will not be great and will be paid at a time when cost is not counted. This feature will also deter the Government from calling out reservists needlessly.

(2) Physical inspection -

Reservists are valueless unless in good physical condition. Yearly examinations may be made inexpensively by utilizing all stations and facilities in each Corps Area.

(3) Transfers, discharges, etc. -

These can be handled by the Corps Area concerned under regulations from the War Department.

Men, who for any reason become unavailable for immediate service, should be discharged. Change of residence from one Corps Area to another will occasion only a like transfer in records.

IV. Conclusions

1. The active strength of the army is at least 75,000 less than that essential to permit it to carry out its vital missions in an emergency, and there exists no feasible way of providing the reinforcements needed except by organizing all men discharged from the Regular Army into an Enlisted Reserve.

2. Recommendations should be made to Congress for the creation of a Regular Army Reserve by making all original enlistments in the Army for a period of five years, whether two or one with the active Army, and three or four with the reserves, the exact number of each to be determined by the Secretary of War.

3. All reenlistments in the active force should be for three years active and two years reserve service.

4. Upon completion of service in reserve, a man should be allowed to reenlist therein prior to becoming thirty-six years of age.

5. All men procuring discharge by purchase from the active army should be required to complete the full enlistment in the reserve.

6. Pay of the reservist should be $36.00 per year, payable quarterly, and each should receive a bonus of $100.00 which is payable immediately upon being accepted for active duty in an emergency.

7. The reservists should be required to report immediately to the proper station upon call of the President. They should be assured that they will not be called except when in the opinion of the President a national emergency exists in which the safety of the United States is likely to be imperilled.

8. All administration of the Enlisted Reserve should be intrusted to Corps Areas.

9. If it is found to be impossible to secure authorization for a reserve raised under the above general system, efforts should be made to secure authorization for one raised in a manner similar to that employed by the Marine Corps. Pay and administrative features should be as discussed above.

V. Recommendations

That efforts be made to secure authorization from Congress for a reserve created under the general system outlined in paragraph IV, sub-paragraphs 2–7- inclusive [. . . .]

PROPOSED AMENDMENTS TO THE NATIONAL DEFENSE ACT FOR THE PURPOSE OF CREATING A REGULAR ARMY RESERVE

Section 1. ENLISTMENTS IN THE REGULAR ARMY AND REGULAR ARMY RESERVE. On and after the ——— day of ———, 19—, all enlistments in the Regular Army shall be for a term of five years, of which, except as otherwise herein provided, two years shall be in active service, and the last three years in the Regular Army Reserve, herein created: Provided that, subject to the discretion of the President enlistments may be made for one year in active service and four years reserve service: Provided further that, subject to such regulations as the President may prescribe, upon the expiration of the active service portion of a first or any subsequent enlistment, a soldier may be re-enlisted for another period of five years service, of which three years shall be in active service, and the last two years in the Regular Army Reserve, and in which event he shall receive his final discharge from his prior enlistment: And provided further that, upon completion of any full term of enlistment any soldier not over thirty-six years of age may, subject to such regulations as the President may prescribe, be re-enlisted in the Regular Army Reserve for a period of four years.

Section 2. FINAL DISCHARGE OF ENLISTED MEN. No enlisted man in the Regular Army shall receive his final discharge until the termination of his five year term of enlistment, except as provided for in this Act, or as provided for by law for discharge prior to expiration of term of enlistment, but when an enlisted man is furloughed to the Regular Army Reserve his account shall be closed and he shall be paid in full to the date such furlough becomes effective, including allowances provided by law for discharged soldiers: Provided further that, in time of peace, the President may, under such rules and upon such conditions as he shall prescribe, permit any enlisted man to purchase his furlough to the Regular Army Reserve.

Section 3. COMPOSITION OF THE REGULAR ARMY RESERVE. The Regular Army Reserve shall consist of all enlisted men who shall hereafter become members of the Regular Army Reserve under the provisions of this Act.

Section 4. DUTIES AND COMPENSATION OF THE REGULAR ARMY RESERVE. In the event of an emergency declared by the President, the President may call into service the Regular Army Reserve in such manner as he may determine and thereafter retain it or any part thereof in active service for such period as he may decide the conditions demand, and the members of the Regular Army Reserve shall, so long as they remain in active service, receive the pay and allowances of enlisted men of the Regular Army of like grades: Provided that, upon reporting for duty in response to a summons by the President, a member of the Regular Army Reserve shall receive pay from the day he answers such summons to the date of his discharge or furlough to the Regular Army Reserve, and reimbursement for the actual and necessary cost of transportation and subsistence from the place at which he received such summons to the place at which he reported for duty and, if, upon examination, he is found disqualified for service, the actual and necessary cost of transportation and subsistence, to the place where he received his summons; and, in addition, shall, on reporting to duty, if found qualified for service, receive $100.00: Provided further that service in the Regular Army Reserve shall confer no right to retirement, retired pay, or longevity increase of pay, and members of the Regular Army Reserve shall become entitled to pension only through disability incurred while on active duty in the service of the United States: And provided further that, subject to such regulations as the Secretary of War may prescribe for their proper identification and location and physical condition, the members of the Regular Army Reserve shall be paid quarterly at the rate of $36.00 per annum while in the Reserve.

1. Eisenhower prepared this study while a student at the Army War College during the 1927–28 term. The commandant of the school at this time was William D. Connor. Although the memorandum to the assistant commandant is dated March 15, the study is dated March 20, 1928. By 1927, Congress had reduced the regular army to fewer than 120,000 men comprising nine skeletal divisions. Although the National Guard had an authorized ceiling of 435,000, the actual number was less than half that. The Officer Reserve Corps totaled 100,000, but there were virtually no troops to command. Eisenhower contended that a full mobilization of the National Guard required more time than an emergency would allow; he proposed that regular army enlistees serve, upon discharge, a term of either three or four years in an enlisted ready reserve. The total service obligation would be five years, including active duty and reserve time. See Benjamin Franklin Conkling, "Dwight D. Eisenhower at the Army War College, 1927–1928," *Parameters* 1 (1975): 26–36.

Endnotes, charts, graphs, and tables that accompanied the original report are not included here but are available at the Eisenhower Library. Some outline numbers and letters are no longer in sequence because of the omitted materials. Ellipses show where those were located in the original report.

2. Army Regulation 135-10 was issued on December 31, 1924. Eisenhower's summarization covers the primary points. The regulation was revised on June 21, 1929.

3. War Department General Staff.

4. The Citizens Military Training Camps originated with Army Chief of Staff Leonard Wood, who in 1913 proposed summer camps for high school and college

men where they would receive basic training from regular army officers. During the first three years of the camps, the trainees were expected to provide for all of their expenses. By 1915, five camps were in place, including one at Plattsburg, New York, for young businessmen. Initially funded by the trainees and by philanthropists such as Bernard Baruch, the camps were formally brought into the defense establishment by the National Defense Act of 1916. Funding from that point forward was provided by a congressional appropriation. By the eve of America's entry into World War I, twelve thousand young men had attended what came to be known as the "Plattsburg" camps scattered throughout the country. These citizens' military training camps remained active throughout the interwar period.

The Reserve Officers' Training Corps (ROTC) originated in a proposal made in 1915 by the War College Division of the General Staff to establish officer training programs in those colleges (for the most part land-grant institutions) that had army officers on faculty. Graduates of such programs would be commissioned as reserve officers. The National Defense Act of 1916 created the ROTC and provided for the detail of officers to colleges and military preparatory schools, along with appropriations for training equipment. The ROTC was divided into senior (college) and junior (preparatory) units. See Marvin A. Kriedberg and Merton G. Henry, *History of Military Mobilization in the United States Army, 1775–1945* (Washington, D.C.: Department of the Army, 1955), 208–9, 213.

22

Eisenhower Library
North Collection, American Battle Monuments Commission

To Major Xenophon H. Price[1]

July 3, 1928

Dear Xen: Was glad to note in your last letter that you were asking the General to request Captain Horkan's detail. I have made it a point to keep in touch with him and must say that I am very favorably impressed with his ability and personality. In his case I feel sure that you are making no mistake whatsoever.

With respect to the date on which he will become available for duty with the Commission, you will remember that, as I wrote you in my first letter, his year with troops will not be completed until September, the exact date being the 27th. However, to insure that a substitute will be brought into the office of the Assistant Secretary of War at once so that he can be relieved as soon after that date as possible, I believe it well to write the letter asking for him without delay. Major Schimmelfenig[2] estimates that the new man should be in the office approximately two months before Captain Horkan leaves. In short, I believe that the letter asking for his services should be written at once asking that the detail be made effective on or about October 1. I suggest that if this meets with your approval you send a cable stating "Horkan detail approved" and we will prepare the letter for the General and arrange all the details.

With reference to the second officer you require, who, I understand, must speak French fluently, and must have had some construction experience, I am not yet ready to make a final recommendation. I am trying to get a little more dope on Captain Beyette.[3] He suggests Colonel Van Duyne and General Harts[4] as references if you care to speak to those officers.

We will start looking at once for the two civilian engineers and the secretary you need. Hope to have something to report soon. Sincerely

P.S. By allowing Horkan to complete his year with troops, you will have him available a full four years.

1. Eisenhower returned to the commission from the War College two days before he wrote this letter. On July 31, he and his family left for Paris, France. The commission secretary was Maj. Xenophon Price (USMA, 1914). Although Price served with the Army Corps of Engineers, he was detailed for over ten years as secretary of the Battle Monuments Commission. Stationed in Paris in 1928 and 1929, Price served as Eisenhower's immediate superior. He was the only superior officer who gave Eisenhower less than the highest possible efficiency rating. Eisenhower, *At Ease*, 204.

2. Charles Adam Schimmelfenig (USMA, 1911) served in the office of the assistant secretary of war (1926–30). He was a major at the time of his death, on September 10, 1933.

3. Hubert Ward Beyette served with the Quartermaster Corps from World War I until he retired on October 31, 1946, with the permanent rank of brigadier general. Beyette was ultimately chosen for Eisenhower's Paris staff.

4. Following World War I, Frederick William Van Duyne (USMA, 1899) served with American Forces in Germany until 1920. He retired with the rank of colonel in 1939.

William Wright Harts (USMA, 1889) served as military aide to President Woodrow Wilson (1913–17), commanding officer of the District of Paris (1918–19), and as President Wilson's military aide during the Versailles peace negotiations.

23   Eisenhower Library
North Collection, American Battle Monuments Commission

To GENERAL JOHN J. PERSHING

JULY 21, 1928[1]

The second paragraph of the attached letter from Admiral Long[2] seems to imply that in the conference I held with him on the morning of July 19th, a tentative understanding was reached that eventually the

Navy chapter in the Guide Book would be more comprehensive than at present.

<u>The facts in the case are:</u>

At the beginning of the conference I carefully explained to Admiral Long my complete lack of authority to make any agreement of any description which could obligate the Commission to any form of action. He was told that I was representing the Chairman for one purpose only; namely, to request from the Navy corrections for the errors which that Department has stated exist in the Navy chapter at present. Admiral Long stated emphatically that the Navy view had always been, and still is, that the chapter should either be a fuller account of naval operations, or omitted entirely. He said that Naval authorities could under no conditions give their consent to regarding a mere correction of existing errors as an adequate revision of the narrative as a whole.

It was then explained to him that the present revision was little more than a reprint of the existing volume; that the Navy chapter could not, in such a reprint, be omitted without destroying the set-up of the book; that the Commission was anxious to eliminate all misstatements of facts; and that advantage was to be taken of the present reprinting to correct all known errors.

It was also suggested to him that in the event of a future revision the Commission would undoubtedly ask for the opinion of the Naval authorities, (as it has in the past), concerning any material dealing with that Department which might be included. Nothing at all was mentioned of the possible scope of such a chapter, other than Admiral Long's own statement, given above.

Upon receipt of this letter, immediate attempt was made to arrange another conference with Admiral Long. Due to his departing from the city at once, conversation could be had by telephone only.

In that conversation he stated in substance that the summary I have given above of the conference between Admiral Long and myself is substantially correct.

He stated that he had had the impression for some time, based on correspondence and conversation, that at a future date a general revision was intended, and that the second paragraph of his letter is nothing more than a reiteration of the Navy attitude that the chapter should be either enlarged or omitted.

In view of the above, it is suggested that simple acknowledgment be made of the receipt of Admiral Long's letter somewhat along the lines of the copy attached.

1. Eisenhower wrote this letter from the commission's office at the War Department.

2. This was probably Rear Admiral Andrew Theodore Long (U.S. Naval Acade-

my, 1887). He served as Commander, U.S. Naval Forces in Europe (1922–23) and, from 1924 until his retirement in 1930, with the Navy's General Board. Evidently, the U.S. Navy had complained about information contained in the guidebook.

24   Eisenhower Library
Pre-presidential Papers, Personal 201 File

TO FINANCE OFFICER

SEPTEMBER 1, 1928

1. The enclosed bill for excess costs in moving my effects from Washington is not understood for the following reason:

a. Under competent orders I reported for duty with the American Battle Monuments Commission at Washington, D.C., on July 1, 1928. That Commission, in turn, ordered me to Paris, France, for duty.

b. It is my understanding that the total authorized cost of my transfer is borne by the American Battle Monuments Commission, and not by the War Department. If this understanding is correct, then the bill for excess cost, if any, should be presented to me by the Commission.

2. It is therefore requested that the bill for entire cost of moving my effects be rendered to the American Battle Monuments Commission.

25   Eisenhower Library
Pre-presidential Papers, Personal 201 File

TO FINANCE OFFICER

NOVEMBER 15, 1928

1. Your letter of September 1, 1928, referring to excess charges amounting to $65.11 on bills of lading 1659471, 1662253, 1677724, and 1662226 was answered immediately upon receipt of same.

2. Because of the fact that I am assigned to the American Battle Monuments Commission, and not attached to the Military Attaché, Paris, France, I forwarded my reply through the Washington Office to that Commission.

3. It is my understanding that all costs of transportation of my effects from Washington, D.C., to Paris, France, are borne by the American Battle Monuments Commission, and not by the War Department. Therefore, in my former letter I requested that the total bill be transmitted to that Commission for payment, to whom it appears I should be responsible for any excess charges incurred in the transportation of my effects.

4. Because of the fact that your office has again written me a letter on this subject, and I therefore assume that settlement should properly be made through your office, I submit herewith my understanding of this case:

Upon being ordered to Paris, France, I consulted the Quartermaster at Washington, D.C., concerning the shipment of part of my property to storage, the remainder to Paris. He informed me that as long as the total cost of transportation of my effects was not in excess of the amount authorized for shipping 8000 lbs. from Washington to Paris, I would not be liable for excess charges. This information I understand has been rendered inaccurate by a subsequent ruling of the Comptroller General, which could not be foreseen. This apparently renders me liable for the shipment of effects which was in excess of an aggregate of 8000 lbs. (professional books excluded), no matter what the destination of the shipment.

5. If my understanding is correct then it appears that if I pay the cost of shipping the amount of excess over 8000 lbs. from Washington, D.C., to the New Cumberland depot, all requirements of the Comptroller General's ruling would be met. This amount, it appears, should be considerably less than $65.11, the amount of the bill your office has sent me.

6. I request your office consider the above suggestion and inform me whether the amount necessary for me to refund cannot be reduced. Upon receipt of your answer I will promptly forward the necessary amount to settle this matter.

26

Eisenhower Library
Foltz Papers

To John and Elivera Doud

April 26, 1929

Dearest Folks: Mamie is horribly rushed today—as she was yesterday, with the result that she cannot get off a letter to catch tomorrow's boat. I'm sending off this note to tell you everybody is well—and nothing so very startling has happened. She states she'll have a full letter on the Wed. boat.

Last eve, just as she settled down and started writing the Beyettes came in & stayed until 11.00. Today she had some marketing to do & has a luncheon at Mary's. Tonight we have Horkans to sauerkraut dinner & then are going to the theater for the first time since being in France, except twice as other people's guests. We are to see the show that has "Old Man River" in it—whatever that is.[1]

I am getting a new blue suit—my first since coming here. It will cost $33.00—and I hope will be satisfactory.

The weather is slowly improving and the trees and plants are very pretty.

I received dad's letter telling about the stockyards deal, and was very glad to learn the particulars. Certainly seems he did the only thing possible under the circumstances, and I am sorry that things had to turn out as they did. I feel confident however that something of interest to him will turn up.

So far have no further indication of the length of time we'll probably stay in France. Guide Book work is going slowly, and will take until middle of summer to finish. The only thing is whether they then want me to do something else.

I suppose Mamie told you about our trip into Belgium. She has now become interested in my battlefield trips, and looks forward to them. So does John.

Johnny's package came last eve & he had a great time. He says that tonight he's going to write Nana all about it. For my part I'm surely grateful for the socks which were most welcome.

It rained all the time we were in Belgium and I secured only 1 or 2 pictures. If Mame[2] ever gets an album we'll have quite a collection eventually. Love to all of you—& take good care of yourselves—your devoted Son.

1. Eisenhower referred to Oscar Hammerstein's musical *Showboat,* which opened on Broadway in 1927.

2. Eisenhower occasionally used "Mame" for Mamie, a possible intimate nickname within the Eisenhower family.

27   Eisenhower Library
                                          Gruber-Eisenhower Diary[1]

AUGUST 28, 1929–SEPTEMBER 5, 1929

Beginning of the Gruber-Eisenhower Expedition
Starting point. Paris—10:30 AM
Mileage at Gate—19389

The principal idea the four of us have upon starting this trip is to see something of France, Belgium, Germany and Switzerland, and possibly Italy or Austria. Due to the fact that Mame and I must sail on "Leviathan," Sept. 17, we are somewhat limited in our choice of itineraries, and we cannot tarry long in any one place if we are to complete the trip contemplated. On the other hand we have determined not to overdo—we have no intention of making the tour a disagreeable task.

We are "travelling light"—with very few clothes and intend to stay in reasonably priced hotels, and live very simply.

We put a baggage rack (price $4.00) on one running board where we put part of the luggage to relieve the congestion in the back seat of the car, which is a standard Buick coach.

Out of Paris we began having trouble with the fan belt which bothered us continuously until Bill had the happy idea of turning over the belt. No further trouble with that!

Route led us via Chantilly, Senlis, Compiegne–St. Quentin–Cambrai–Mons to Brussels, where we stopped at the Wiltcher Hotel. Rooms $2.70 each plus 10% taxes.

The most amusing incident of the day was the discovery by a Belgian customs official of a bottle of scotch we were carrying with us. We finally were permitted to carry it along upon paying 54¢ tax. Bill had a remarkably hard time opening the bag in which the whiskey was (we hoped) well concealed.

The prettiest sight of the day was the castle at Chantilly. We stopped at Mons for dinner, and arrived at hotel in Brussels about 9:00 P.M.
Distance—approx—180 miles
Spent during day—Lunch—gasoline—dinner—customs
taxes—about—15.00

On every corner we are reminded of Bill's song "Hello Fellers".

Expenses in France		approx
Gas - 30 liters	75 frs.	3.00
" 50 liters*	110 frs.	4.40
Lunch (including candy)	40 frs.	1.60
Fee at French customs	10 frs.	.40
One fan belt (leather)	16 frs.	.65
		$10.05

(*—really not more than 35)
(bad pump)

THURS—AUG. 29 BRUSSELS

Spent the day sight seeing in Brussels and the environs.

The most interesting thing we saw during the day was the "Grand Place" in the heart of Brussels. The guide books describe it as the finest example of a medieval square (outside Italy) in Europe. We agree!

The "Hotel de Ville" and the "Maison du Roi" were particularly interesting—while the various old "Guild Houses" also demand their share of attention.

The Botanical Gardens, the Palace of the King, the Arch and Buildings erected in 1905 (?) in commemoration of the fiftieth anniversary of Belgian independence, the Palais de Justice, and the Cathedral all interested us very much.

Had a nice luncheon, and the dinner, at the Cafe de St. Jean, afforded a lot of fun. The waiter was determined to sell us a huge lobster. He exclaimed over and over again "Bon"—"Good", "Nice", "You will like"—"tres bon," etc. etc. until we finally capitulated. It was excellent.

In the late afternoon we visited the battlefield of Waterloo. Bill and I enjoyed it. The "Lion of Waterloo", an English monument, weighs 70,000 pounds, and stands on a huge pyramid of earth, placed there for the purpose. It is situated at about the center of the Allied defensive position.

Returned to Wiltcher Hotel.

Expenses for day, lunch and dinner, about $7.50. Bought no gas today.

The girls saw lace makers in operation and bought some handkerchiefs.

Expenses in Belgium—Aug 28–30

		approx
Entrance fee (including tax on scotch)	64 frs	1.90
Hotel Bill - rooms - 2 nights - breakfasts		
taxes - bath - etc.	500 frs	15.00
Garage - 2 nights (can of oil) (air)	65 frs	2.00
Lunch (Namur) (29th)	30 frs	.90
Gasoline (leaving Brussels) 40 liters	120 frs	3.60
Lunch (29th)	100 frs	3.00
Dinner (28th)	115 frs	3.45
Dinner (29th) (lobster night)	160 frs	4.80
	1154 frs	34.62
Incidentals (Not counting personal expenditures)	75	2.25
	1229	$36.87[2]

Paid hotel bill—about 15.00—including breakfasts—taxes—etc. Put a can of oil in car—and paid garage rent—total about 2.00.

Left Brussels at 10.30 A.M. heading provisionally toward Cologne. For the first hour or so (through Namur) the road was very beautiful and picturesque. The wooded valleys and hillsides were particularly beautiful in the sunlight and the shaded roadway gave an impression that we were to discover something interesting around each turn of the road.

At the junction of the Sambre and the Meuse at Namur we saw the old fort high up on the prominent hill which rises between the two rivers. At the time of its construction its builders must have thought that it would be forever impregnable. The Germans reduced it easily in 1914.

From that point on we ran through a more uninteresting country. The towns were centers of industry and mining—the roads were poor and everything was dusty and dirty.

We "changed direction" at Liege and instead of continuing toward Aix-la-Chapelle and Cologne—we headed through Verviers toward Bonn.

Before reaching the custom house we stopped long enough to finish our scotch, determined to suffer no further embarrassment because of it.

We sailed through the customs with no examination, the German official being particularly courteous and obliging—not to say efficient in making out the great number of papers incident to bringing an auto into a European country. (Anyway the scotch tasted fine.)

We seemed to experience a very definite exhilaration upon leaving Belgium and entering the Fatherland. Maybe it's because both Bill and I have our family roots in this country, as our names testify.[3]

Immediately we came through the village of Montjoie (Monschau) and all of us were impressed with the picturesque quality of its beauty. We felt we had a fine introduction to this country.

We came on to Bonn, on the Rhine, and after searching a while found comfortable accommodations in the Hotel Goldenen Stern (Golden Stars). Mamie and I are in a room which is easily the largest hotel room we ever occupied, while the Bills are in a smaller connecting room.

The rooms themselves are not so cheap, but there is no tax and meals are very reasonable.

We spent today—(aside from those items listed above), 8.00 for gasoline and 1.50 at the customs.

Distance travelled, about 180 miles.

SAT—AUG 31—COBLENZ, GERMANY

We spent most of the day in Bonn. Helen was rather tired so we decided to take it easy. She and Mamie spent the morning in bed while Bill and I walked the streets to see the University, the Poppelsdorfer, the Hofgarten, and the shopping district. Just at noon we discovered that we had a broken spring, which the repair shop promised to have repaired by 3.30 P.M. We got the car about 5.00. In the meantime we had phoned to Paris and found that Johnny was well and happy.[4]

Finally at 5.00 P.M. we started southward along the Rhine. Along this part of the river there are many ruined castles on the heights bordering the stream. Just south of Bonn is a particularly beautiful one in the crags high up on the east bank.

In Andernach we stopped to examine the old wall which surrounded the city. The wall was built about 1200 and the city founded in 900 A.D. The gates were of peculiar construction, and are called double gates. A native told us this was the oldest of the Rhine cities.

Opposite this place is Neuweid and we tried hard to pick out the house beyond it where Bill lived for a period in late 1918. We couldn't see it—and so missed this famous spot.

We passed through Coblenz before dusk and were much impressed by the old fort on the heights opposite it.

Pushed on to Boppard where we thought we'd spend the night. It was filled with week-end vacationists and no decent accommodations were to be had, in spite of a diligent search. For the first time we got somewhat fed up with Germany and decided to go back to Coblenz, some 12 miles. Went to the Hohman Hotel. It was near the station and very noisy.

We were tired, dusty, and sleepy and the hotel did not help us in getting into a better humor.

Our hotel bill totalled about $18.50 including 3 meals and a telephone call and telegram. The broken spring cost us about 5.00. We bought no gas.

Distance—Bonn to Coblenz about 35 miles.

Hotel Kohlhof, near Heidelberg

Upon leaving the hotel at Coblenz we drove through the town to see the huge monument to Kaiser Wilhelm I (The Great). It is a magnificent thing at the junction of the Moselle with the Rhine River. Then drove up to see Ehrenbreitstein,[5] the fort on the east side which had attracted our attention the night before. It dates from the time of the Franks (486) and was restored about 1820. It is a great pile of masonry situated over 350 feet above the river, and over it, just now floats a French flag. From it we had a remarkably fine view of Coblenz and the Rhine River in both directions, as well as the lower stretches of the Moselle. We recrossed the river, to start south once more.

The bridge we used is a pontoon structure, the boats being of steel and quite large. A section in it is floated out to permit the passage of vessels up and down the river.

Saw lots of river-borne traffic. The current was very strong, and the tugs used are side wheelers of peculiar construction. The wheels extend out from the sides of the boats, giving them an odd appearance. They seem to be quite powerful and tow several loaded barges against the current.

As far as we are concerned, the least said about Boppard the better.

At St. Goar is the Rheinfels, once the strongest fortress on the river. It is by far the largest ruin we saw along the river, some of its massive walls still rising to unusual heights along the crests.

Both banks of the river along here, and as far south as Bingen, are covered with old castles. A few have been restored and are now being used. The bluffs in this stretch rise abruptly from the river along the edges of which is a very narrow shelf for the road, railroad and an occasional small village. Above Bingen the aspect changes noticeably, the slopes on each side being quite gentle in comparison with those on the lower side of that city.

From Mainz we went through a relatively uninteresting country until reaching Heidelberg which is a famous town on the Neckar River. We took a turn about the city and then climbed a steep road past the "Schloss" (castle) to a tea house where we sat on the edge of a bluff and looked down on the city and river, many hundreds of feet below us, and on the ruins of the Schloss. The whole pine covered valley is a most romantic spot.

The hotel is in the hills, on the opposite side of the range from the Neckar River. It is very quiet, we have good beds and should have a fine rest.

The trip today was tiresome, made so by the heat, dusty, and in some cases, poor roads, and the large numbers of automobiles carrying vacationists everywhere.

Spent 2.00 for gasoline
 .75 for oil
 8.00 for hotel bill
 2.00 for tea
 2.00 for lunch
Distance Coblenz—Heidelberg

Neustadt (In the Black Forest)

This morning we started early, much refreshed after a fine night's sleep.

We struck directly to Norzheim—where the girls did a little shopping. After an hour there we started southward through the heart of the famous Black Forest. The trip was beautiful. All of us agree it was the best day yet. The vistas through gaps in the dense forests which cover the heights, down beautiful narrow valleys beggar description. Little villages nestle along the rushing streams, and everywhere the countryside seems cool, fresh and clean.

We ate lunch by the roadside and voted it the best one we've had, all because the surroundings were perfect. Only a few of the roads are at all dusty, and the smell of pine, cedars and the freshly cut hay in the valleys adds to the feeling of peace and contentment a visitor is almost compelled to experience in this region.

We have been enthusiastic about Germany, the people as well as the beautiful landscapes. It is hard to describe the little differences which one detects between the people of one country and those of another. However, one of the big points we have noted is the friendly way we have been treated everywhere. Bill, in German which impresses the rest of us tremendously, has made inquiries of dozens and dozens of people as we have come through the country. Without exception we have received courteous and correct replies, and the informer has invariably paused sufficiently long to make sure that Bill has comprehended exactly. In fact, in many cases, when we've made inquiries of one person, another with a knowledge of the country has stepped forward voluntarily with information, always tendered in the most courteous way possible. We like Germany!

Expenses in Germany-from Aug 30–Sept 4. Mark = 24¢ (In pot 428 marks)

(Entrance fee & tip)		6.00
Aug 30	40 liters gas	13.20
	Miscellaneous	1.20
	Hotel Goldenen Stern (Bonn)*	74.55
	Guide book	1.50
31st	Garage and wash	5.25
	Car repair & tip	22.00
	Dinner (Boppard) (Aug 31)	12.10
	Hotel Hohman (Coblenz)	29.40
	25 liters gas (1 oil)	10.35
Sept 1	Lunch on Rhine (Sept 1)	10.80
	Tea (Mokenkur House at Heidelberg)	9.60
	Dinner Hotel Kohlhof	13.20
	Hotel Kohlhof	37.05
Sept 2	45 liters gas	15.50
	Lunch on road	6.80
	Hotel Adler (Neustadt)	
Sept 3	in Black Forest	36.65
	35 liters gas, 1 oil	14.35
	Miscellaneous	1.75
		321.25 = $77.10

We left Neustadt rather early heading toward Constance (Konstanz). The first town we reached was <u>Titisee</u> situated at one end of a beautiful lake, 2500 feet above sea level. On the slopes of the wooded hills which surround it are many stretches of grass land in which are built magnificent summer homes. We ran along the lake until we found a spot which commanded a view of the whole valley.

Brilliant morning sun. Tiny craft skimming the sparkling surface. Boatmen's bodies tanned to a nut-brown. Glistening green slopes. Exhilarating air.

What a wonderful start for a day's tour through this part of Europe!

At some points the highway is built into the sides of very steep slopes so that the view below is rather terrifying. After gazing into one of these chasms, Mamie suddenly announced that in case she fainted she would like us to know there were smelling salts in her hand bag! So far we haven't had to use them.

In Lenzkirch the signposts pointing out the roads to various towns are constructed in a unique manner. Each pointer bears on its top a series of figures in different costumes and poses. We took a photograph of one and bought some postcards depicting them.

At Oberwiese we left Germany and entered Switzerland. About noon, September 3. Shortly after lunching in a little wood by the roadside, we reached the southern edge of Lake Constance and followed it toward the city of the same name.

Just before entering that city we received a shock upon discovering that the city of Constance is in Germany, and to enter it would necessitate another ordeal with the customs officials. Rather than do this we skirted the city and started for Zurich which we reached about 5.00 P.M. It is a large city (250,000), very dusty and dirty, and seemed to us to be an average type of commercial center, whereas we were expecting to find a clean, picturesque town conforming more closely to our pre-conceived ideas of a Swiss city.

Our efforts to find good accommodations at reasonable prices were fruitless so we headed southeast along the southern side of Lake Zurich, and after many inquiries, much turning about and retracing of steps finally stopped at this little backwoods place. The hotel is poor, but the view over the lake is gorgeous. Thousands of lights around the shoreline twinkle through the darkness, and Bill is getting quite romantic under the influence of the place.

Spent about 5.22 for gas-

Came about 130 miles today.

September 4—Hotel Bellvue

Andermatt—(South of Lucerne)

The altitude here is about 5000 feet.

This morning I got down early and spent half an hour dusting off the car which had collected quantities of dirt from the Swiss roads. This is the first region in which we have travelled dusty macadam roads constantly, and motoring is less clean than in other parts of Europe we have visited.

Ran down to Lucerne where we arrived at 10.30 A.M. It is a very beautiful city on the western end of Lake Vierwaldstatter See.

Originally intending to stay but half an hour we became intrigued with the view, the quaint streets and the opportunities for shopping, so that we left the place about 3.15 P.M.

The road then follows along the lake for some miles and we were unanimous in the opinion that to date the scenery along this stretch of the route is the finest we've seen. The lake itself with steamers which in the distance appeared like toys puffing over its placid surface, the intensely green slopes of the bordering hills, and the great barren snow crested peaks in the background all combined to create a picture of appealing beauty. At several points we could not resist trying to record the scene on a kodak film, although all of us know that the results can give scarcely a hint of the beauty, the romance, and the splendor which Mother Nature has poured so lavishly into this spot. Helen, in particular, simply bubbled over with delight.

After leaving the lake the road led up the valley of the Reuss River through a canyon-like valley toward the backbone of the Alps. Mamie suffered her customary reactions when travelling a dangerous looking road and when ascending in altitude and as a result tonight has an attack of indigestion. We put up here at a splendid and expensive hotel, determined to have one evening when all modern comforts and conveniences were ours. Among other things we had our first high ball of the trip, and a little scotch certainly tasted great, even at 40¢ a drink.

So far we've averaged (from the point we entered Germany) over 14 miles to the gallon of gas, which considering the hills, towns and frequent stops is very good.

INTERLAKEN — THURS — SEPT. 5

Hotel du Nord

We arrived here at 3.00 P.M. after a trip of only 65 miles from the last stop, but one nevertheless which was chock full of thrills, and which both girls insisted lasted for some 10 years.

From Andermatt we continued southwest over the Furka Pass of the Alps. It is 2431 meters high and the road leading through it is constructed as is usual in such regions. Many hair pin turns, switch backs, steep banks on one side and sheer drops on the other, compel careful driving and strict attention to the road. Fortunately the car functioned perfectly.

We soon learned that neither of the ladies has any decided preference for driving in the mountains, and the farther we went the more caustic became the back seat remarks about husbands with such poor taste and lack of sense as to suppose for one second that their wives came to Switzerland to ride through the Alps. Cannot one see mountains from the bottom as well as from the top? Do you not know I'll be so nervous I won't be able to eat for a week? Think of the nightmares I'll have of this experience! My gosh, go into first speed! I'm going to shut my eyes! How much longer does this last?

These remarks, repeated in various keys and with many variations, were eventually succeeded by a profound silence, flavored with a distinct odor of smelling salts coming from the back seat area of the car.

And so we reached the summit!

By this time neither Bill nor I had the temerity to explain to the girls that we had to descend the Furka Pass (the second highest in the Alps) and climb immediately over the Grimsel Pass. We conversed (in tones we were sure they would overhear) concerning the slight climb we had next, and talked volubly of the fact that it was a full 1500 feet lower than the one we had just topped. (It actually is about 900 feet lower.)

We started the descent and Bill and I agreed that we'd be ultra-conservative, keeping the engine in first speed and proceeding so slowly that the girls could not possibly be frightened. All to no avail! Helen's difficulty comes from the fact that she hates any height, and in some places the drop on the exposed side of the road must be a full thousand feet. Naturally that seemed quite high. Mamie had no particular thing to complain of except that she hated it all, she was frightened, she was faint, and above all she was sure that we were headed for a nice plunge over the cliffs. The yawning chasms seemed to have a fascination for them both, and much as they dreaded the prospect they could not help gazing down into the terrifying depths. We noted however that both leaned well toward the inside, no matter how much they gazed out the other.

We met many cars and the huge busses filled with passengers required so much room to make the turns that it was possible to pass them only on the straight stretches, and then only in the wide parts, as the road as a whole is quite narrow.

We had a few moments of real thrills when, in attempting to pass one of these busses, its front wheel became engaged with the baggage rack on our running board. As we were on the outside, and the drop at the particular point was several hundreds of feet, it is not difficult to imagine that even skillful drivers like Bill and me were a little bit concerned.

Immediately they touched, both cars were brought to a dead stop and I hopped out to examine the situation. It was not serious and with slow careful backing while I beat the rack away from the bus wheel, we were soon able to get back into a little pocket where we remained while the bus went on past.

During the occurrence Bill and I were so busy that we had no time to consider all the various possibilities of the situation. The girls, however, penned in the back seat and perfectly helpless to do anything, could not be blamed for letting their imaginations run riot. Then and later we collected up their thoughts and reactions, and so were able to get a picture of the incident as it appeared to each of us.

Since Bill was behind the steering wheel, with the left side of the car against the bus, and his right front wheel very close to the edge of the precipice, he could do nothing but hold tight and wait for instructions from some one who could tell him how things stood.

I was the only one who could get out at once, and as quickly as I saw that the car was not in a particularly dangerous position, was concerned only in straightening out the mess. It was however useless to attempt an explanation to the girls, since from their restricted view they were in imminent danger of taking a nice drop down the mountain side.

Mamie's first thought was that she and Helen could not get out, and this idea naturally intensified the qualms and fears of the moment.

Since Helen realized that Bill had to stick with the car, her idea was to get Mamie out and then, come weal or woe, she and Bill would meet it together. One point not yet clear to any of us, including Helen, is how she expected to get Mamie out as long as she (Helen) stayed in, for Mamie's only possible means of exit lay directly through the point Helen was sitting.

Later, Helen surprised the rest of us by giving a minute description of the people in the bus, the actions of its driver, and the amusing antics of one passenger who stood up to address his fellow tourists and give them, in an excited voice, advice as to what to do at the moment.

It seems odd to us that these inconsequential things should have made such a clear cut and definite impression on her at a time when she felt there was an even chance that the next second would find her tumbling down the mountain side.

When finally we reached Gletsch, in a deep canyon on the headwaters of the Rhone, and the ladies realized that we had another tremendous climb in front of us, all criticisms previously made concerning the choice of the day's route faded into insignificance compared with the remarks addressed to us. Strangely enough, when they paused for want of breath, a lack of a sufficiently expressive vocabulary to give vent to their innermost feelings, the silence was more expressive, and more disturbing to us than were their most sarcastic remarks.

Although at the beginning of the day's trip, Bill and I had been more amused than otherwise by the girls' remarks which we felt were made mostly for our benefit, by this time we were not only convinced of their sincerity, but deeply concerned about the possible later reactions.

Fortunately for us all Grimsel Pass was baby's play after the Furka experience, and everything went off smoothly and pleasantly.

From the standpoint of scenery the trip was magnificent. Long deep pine-covered valleys extending away for miles, mountain streams tumbling down the mountain sides in precipitous falls of hundreds of feet, huge barren peaks frowning at us from the opposite sides of narrow gorges, their crests covered with snow and at their feet beautiful little mountain lakes all combined to make the trip one, which from the standpoint of scenic beauty, will never be forgotten by any of us. Probably the most interesting single thing was the Glacier du Rhone, a great glacier between Furka and Grimsel Passes in which the Rhone River has its source. Part way down the glacier the water melted from the great ice pack leaps out into space into a beautiful waterfall, only to disappear again beneath the ice and finally emerge again at the foot of the glacier and flow down the narrow canyon in which the village of Gletsch is situated. The river follows this canyon to Lake Geneva, which it feeds, and then continuing from the opposite end of the lake, empties it, through southern France into the Mediterranean Sea.

We viewed the glacier from many angles. While descending the Furka Pass we came to a point where we were level with the lofty crags of its highest part. From Gletsch we saw it from its foot, and while going up the Grimsel Pass the sun was exactly right to present to us its glistening pinnacles and deep dark crevices in gorgeous contrasts.

As far as Bill and I were concerned we experienced a very real and welcome reaction, when, the worst of the last descent being over, the girls began to yelp for lunch. We then felt sure that they were to suffer no damaging after results. About 1.00 p.m. we found a little roadside restaurant and each of us did justice to soup, steak, potatoes, salad and fruit.

Our hotel here is comfortable, reasonable in price for Switzerland, and we expect to lay over a day to give everyone a rest.

Interlaken is a summer resort town, consisting of 4–5000 permanent inhabitants and almost that number of hotels. The season is about over, and the hotel keeper says that soon everything will be closed for the winter. The girls say they will shop tomorrow.

Bill and I intended taking the train up the Jungfrau, but after learning the price decided to take the trip from our hotel windows, which afford a fine view of its snow covered crests.

Expenses to date in Switzerland

Swiss Franc = 20¢

	Hotel Shoenfels	41.40	
	35 liters gas	19.25	(very high in this country)
4 Sept	Lunch - Lucerne	10.70	
	Postcards	3.00	
	Oil	2.50	
	Mis	1.00	
	Hotel Bellvue (Andermatt)	107.00	
	30 gas	19.50	
5 Sept	Misc	2.50	
	Lunch (Meiringen)	18.00	
	Bottle Scotch	13.00	
		237.85	

Mileage to date – 106 miles – gas 83 gallons.

1. Eisenhower initially began to keep daily notes in order to record the trip's costs, so that expenses might be accurately divided at the end of the journey. But Eisenhower, struck by the scenery and amused by the Grubers' good-natured bantering, could not resist recording each day's more colorful events. The editors titled the document the Gruber-Eisenhower Diary because Gruber maintained the diary after September 5. Gruber served as an excellent tour guide, as he had served during World War I as an artillery battalion commander at St. Mihiel and in the Meuse-Argonne. During World War II, Gruber, by then a brigadier general, served as a divisional artillery commander in the China-Burma-India Theater and in the southwest Pacific.

In 1940, Gruber, who still held both his and Eisenhower's notes, added a retrospective narrative to his portion of the dairy. On November 11, 1955, Gruber sent Eisenhower a typescript of the notes, along with a letter asking Eisenhower's permission to publish them in full. In his reply of November 16, Eisenhower refused to allow publication of his diary entries, although he encouraged Gruber to publish his own notes and narrative. The typescript and accompanying correspondence were identified in 1975 by an Eisenhower Library archivist while she was conducting a search within the White House Central Files. The Eisenhower Library subsequently contacted Gruber's widow, Helen, who donated to the library the original manuscripts along with photographs taken during the trip.

2. Eisenhower did not add the costs correctly. The expenses totaled $34.65, making the grand total $36.90.

3. The precise location in Germany where the Eisenhowers (originally spelled Eisenhauer) lived before immigrating to America in 1741 has not been determined. Available evidence suggests, however, that the Eisenhauers probably lived in the Saar

area of southwestern Germany. When the Eisenhowers and the Grubers were in or near Heidelberg and Neustadt on September 1 and 2, they were in the general area where Eisenhower's ancestors had lived two centuries before.

4. John Eisenhower was left in the McJanet summer school, outside of Paris, while his parents were on the trip.

5. The fort was part of the Rhineland occupied by the French after World War I.

CHAPTER THREE

Duty in Washington
September 26, 1929–December 25, 1931

The military force in which Eisenhower served in the 1920s and early 1930s had been shorn of its world-war-time strength but at the same time loaded with new responsibilities. The National Defense Act of 1920 did prescribe a standing army larger than the prewar force, but the act also ushered in what some observers expected to be a new era of civilian control and participation. As part of its basic mission, the army was to train civilian components. Reserve units and reserve officers' training corps soon formed as part of this ambitious plan. The act placed procurement and mobilization under the assistant secretary of war. As the 1920s wore on, the army strengthened officer training and attempted to write mobilization plans. Nonetheless, suffering reductions in manpower, it did little to devise strategic war plans. Despite the consensus that amphibious warfare, tanks, and aircraft would be critical in any large-scale future conflict, most discussion remained at the level of theory and research, not development.

The hard times that began with the stock market crash of October 1929 severely crippled the nation's economy and therefore had a direct impact on the military establishment. Herbert Hoover's austerity programs made impossible any increase in the size of the army and prevented the operational exercises that would have helped prepare it for emergencies. After 1933, Franklin Roosevelt's New Deal enjoyed some success in improving the lot of the American workforce, but in the army Roosevelt maintained the status quo.[1] To offset curtailed funding (and attempt to avoid further cuts), military leaders in the early 1930s had to revise organizational tables, reexamine procurement policies, rely more on support from the Organized Reserve and National Guard, and downgrade preparedness as a priority. At the same time, suspicion arose that problems in Europe and the Far East might lead to a second world conflict.

On his return to the United States, Eisenhower remained in Washington with headquarters, American Battle Monuments Commission, devoting attention to the commission's work but also making preliminary inquiries into the current organization and management of the army. Frustrated by what he considered slow advancement, Eisenhower spoke frankly with his superiors. He craved a challenging position, either a troop command, for which Eisenhower was always eager, or high-level staff experience, which would also prove valuable to his future career. He was sent to the War Department. In early November 1929, he reported as assistant to Gen. George Van Horn Moseley,[2] principal military adviser to Frederick H. Payne,[3] assistant secretary of war. In addition to writing many reports and a short tour of duty with the Organized Reserves of the III Corps, Eisenhower also worked on the principal function of Payne's office—developing a plan for the mobilization of American industry and manpower in the event of world war. Eisenhower was now on the inside, observing the maneuvers necessary to match the army's growing needs with the politicians' demands for austerity.

Eisenhower and fellow officer Gilbert Van B. Wilkes,[4] a major in the Corps of Engineers, were charged with drafting the mobilization plan. The two traveled extensively, visiting industrial plants and talking with prominent American businessmen. During one of those inspection trips Eisenhower first met the head of the World War I War Industries Board and afterward longtime friend, Bernard Baruch.[5] Writing a mobilization plan required more than assessing industrial plant capacity and devising, on paper, administrative arrangements for wartime production. Planning for supplies of vital raw materials in time of war drew special attention.

1. On the U.S. Army's interwar culture, see the biographies and published papers of prominent soldiers, including Martin Blumenson, *The Patton Papers, vol. 1, 1885–1940* (Boston: Houghton Mifflin, 1972); Blumenson, *Patton: The Man behind the Legend, 1885–1945* (New York: William Morrow, 1985); D. Clayton James, *The Years of MacArthur, 1880–1941* (Boston: Houghton Mifflin, 1975); Larry I. Bland, ed., *The Papers of George Catlett Marshall: The Soldierly Spirit, December 1880–June 1939* (Baltimore: Johns Hopkins University Press, 1981); and Forrest C. Pogue, *George C. Marshall: Education of a General, 1880–1939* (New York: Viking Press, 1963).

2. Moseley (USMA, 1899) served in the Philippines, 1900–1907, wrote the Chamberlin Bill for Universal Military Service in 1916, served on the Mexican border in 1916–17, and worked with the American Expeditionary Force General Staff in World War I. In 1929 he became Executive Officer for the assistant secretary of war. From 1930 to 1933 he served as Deputy Chief of Staff of the Army and from 1936 to 1938 commanded the Third Army. In his memoir, *At Ease: Stories I Tell to Friends* (Garden City, N.Y.: Doubleday, 1967), 210–13, Eisenhower noted his high regard for Moseley, who died in 1960.

3. Assistant secretary of war from 1930 to 1933, Frederick H. Payne was a self-made millionaire who began his career as a bank examiner and went on to become a tool company executive and prominent Boston and New York banker. A major in army ordnance during World War I, he served as a district procurement officer.

4. Gilbert Van Buren Wilkes (USMA, 1909) spent his entire army career in the Corps of Engineers (thus Eisenhower in his diary entries placed "C.E." after his name). Wilkes retired as a colonel in 1946.

5. Bernard M. Baruch, wealthy Wall Street investor, served several presidents as counsel and special assistant. In 1916 Woodrow Wilson appointed him to an advisory commission to the Council of Defense, and he chaired the War Industries Board. He became known as an expert on wartime economics.

28

SEPTEMBER 26, 1929[1]

Yesterday Mamie, Johnny and I landed at New York after spending over a year in France with the American Battle Monuments Commission.

My work during the year consisted mainly in studying American Battlefields, and preparing accounts of American operations there.

This material is intended as a partial revision of a book "A Guide to the American Battlefields in France," which I assisted in compiling during 1927.

The year was very interesting to me, in spite of the old maidish attitude of my immediate superior, the Secretary of the Commission.[2]

I was not so successful as I should have been in concealing my impatience with some of his impossible ideas and methods of operating. However, we are good friends—in spite of the fact that from the standpoint of piling up a <u>perfect</u> record in the W. D. I was not sufficiently suave and flattering.

Other officers serving in France on construction work for the Commission were of very high caliber, particularly Maj. W.D. Styer,[3] Corps of Engineers.

I hope to keep in touch with him—as he has the qualities to carry him a long way—in or out of the Army.

Last night I drove from N.Y. City to Washington between the hours of 6:00 P.M. and 4:00 A.M. Was all alone and had never been on that road before on the other side of Pennsville.

Mamie and Johnny came down by train with Kathryn Gerow,[4] who met us at the dock.

Capt. Skerry[5] and his wife, friends of Styers, also met us—so we had plenty of help getting out of the city.

Staying at Gerows temporarily, but expect to take an apartment in the Wyoming.

I have a few little things to clean up for the Commission, and will soon be available for duty with the Army—much to my delight.

1. This is the first entry of the Chief of Staff Diary. The "chief of staff" diary designation is used for Eisenhower's service throughout his term in the War Department.

2. The "secretary" reference is to Maj. X. H. Price.

3. Wilhelm Delp Styer (USMA, 1916) served most of his career with the Corps of Engineers. From 1928 until 1931 he was an engineer with the American Battle Monuments Commission. Appointed Chief of the Quartermaster Corps in 1941, he became Chief of Staff, Army Service Forces, in 1942. He retired in 1948.

4. Kathryn was the wife of Lt. Gen. Leonard Townsend "Gee" Gerow, perhaps Eisenhower's closest friend during the interwar period. Gerow, whom Eisenhower first met at Fort Sam Houston when both were assigned to the 19th Infantry, graduated from the Virginia Military Institute. Unlike Eisenhower, he saw service overseas during World War I. After the war, their paths crossed several times, including during the 1925–26 school year at the Command and General Staff School. At Leavenworth the two were study partners, thus cementing a friendship that had begun a decade before. In December 1940 Gerow was named Chief of the War Plans Division. When Eisenhower assumed this position twelve months later, Gerow became assistant to the Army Chief of Staff, George C. Marshall. In 1942, Gerow assumed command of the 29th Infantry Division and in July 1943 commanded the V Corps, which on D-Day, June 6, 1944, was part of Omar Bradley's First Army. Gerow participated in the European campaign from Normandy to the Rhineland and was the first American general to enter Paris. After the war he was commandant of the Command and General Staff School at Fort Leavenworth and commander of the Second Army. He retired in 1950 and died in 1972.

5. Col. Harry Allen Skerry served with the Corps of Engineers from 1917 until his retirement in 1947.

29

Eisenhower Library
North Collection, American Battle Monuments Commission

To Maj. Xenophon H. Price, Secretary

September 26, 1929

Dear Xen: After my first hasty inspection of the activities being carried on here, I cabled you today and am writing this letter to inform you generally of the factors affecting the major problems of the office.[1]

(a) <u>Lists of Missing</u>. I find that the lists now in the possession of the Commission, which were prepared by the War and Navy departments, are reported officially by those departments as correct in every detail. The whole file of correspondence with the Secretary of the Navy, however, leads to the conclusion that many errors probably still exist in their lists.

The proposal to check these records by communicating in each case with the nearest relative of the deceased is, so far, a proposal only, and nothing whatsoever has been done to accomplish it. In fact, the lists of the nearest relatives have not yet been prepared and it appears that this can not be done except by the Veterans Bureau, which organization can begin work on this task October 1. Mr. Mangum[2] conferred yesterday with the Veterans Bureau and, based on the information he secured, I estimate that the Brookwood list could be submitted to this check, typed and forwarded to the architect by November 8. Other lists could follow the first one at irregular intervals, depending upon the length of the particular list. With proper arrangement of work, the Suresnes and Waereghem could follow almost immediately.

It appears to me that the checking of these lists by communication with the nearest relatives is extremely desirable, but nevertheless a step which can be dispensed with if deemed necessary. As far as the War and Navy Departments are concerned, the name of the missing man is that carried in the records of those two departments. These men were enlisted and paid under such names and, generally speaking, final settlement with their nearest relatives made under the same names. To accomplish the proposed check will necessitate a certain delay, and, undoubtedly, annoyance to the architects who are attempting to finish this part of their design.

If we receive cabled instructions from you directing the check, we will turn the whole office force on this work with a view of performing it in the quickest possible time. Whether or not we make the check, the three critical lists will be prepared first.

(b) <u>Historical Section</u>. With the present help, the work of this section can not possibly be accomplished during the ensuing year, according to the standards we expect. In my opinion, it would be rank injustice to Cahill[3] to hold him in this office after June 30 of next year in view of the fact that he expects to go to school on the first of September.

While it is true that Cahill expects second revisions to go rather rapidly, he has in my opinion failed to present to you the serious nature of the problem as it now exists, considering the amount of work yet to be done and the personnel on hand to accomplish it. First revisions under the present schedule will not be completed by Yeuell and Cahill before the first of the year, if then. If we should start today to make second revisions, and edit each summary carefully at the same time, we would have to finish them at the rate of ten per month in order to complete the job before Cahill will leave the Section. There is, in my opinion, no solution possible except as follows: First, Yeuell and Cahill to start immediately on second revisions; second, secure at least two good lieutenants who, under the supervision of Cahill, can complete the first revisions and be trained sufficiently well to carry out the many unfinished tasks which will be left in the section after Cahill departs.

These tasks will include final checking of maps; placing retained records in proper shape for use; proof reading in connection with printing of summaries and maps; miscellaneous work in connection with Guide Book, particularly double checking for historical accuracy, etc., etc.

Since the A.G. told me that he would detail two lieutenants without waiting for a formal letter from the Chairman, I am now trying to get hold of them. One man, whom Cahill recommends is now in Montana and there seems to be no objection by the War Department to making the detail. I'm having some difficulty in getting hold of a second one immediately, but am keeping after them all the time. If the General's letter comes in soon, it will help immeasurably in speeding up the A.G.

As far as I'm concerned, I've been offered three jobs in Washington, two of which look very attractive. My own branch, as well as others here, discourage any attempt to go with troops in the expectation of getting an interesting job. I suppose I'll settle down here for a while, but feel I should stick long enough to insure that both the lists of missing and the historical work are placed on a basis which will insure their early completion.

The trip home was uneventful. I found that quite some few people on the boat had secured accommodations only several days before sailing. I think the company rather ignored Mr. Dennis in that they made no attempt to better my accommodations, and in view of the fact that the Commission paid $775.00 for my passage as well as some $175.00 for the auto, they could well have afforded to make more of an effort than they did.

The customs officials were very kind and courteous, and I had no trouble whatsoever, except the long delay occasioned by the enormous crowd.

By the way, the room I had was really for two people, according to the steward. The third bunk was so poor that we could not keep John in it even by using the chairs to pen him up. Consequently I had to use it, much to my own discomfort. I believe Mr. Dennis should be a bit more hard-boiled with them.

Hope to have an answer to my cable today, and that answer may occasion some additions to this letter, but I'll have it typed up ready to send immediately upon receipt of your cable.

My best to everyone in the office. Sincerely

1. On September 16, the day before Eisenhower left France, Price handed him a memorandum outlining the tasks he was to accomplish when he returned to the commission's Washington headquarters. Eisenhower was to check on the status of the missing-in-action lists, as the architects needed the names to complete the memorial chapels in Europe; obtain two lieutenants to assist Cahill and Yeuell with their research; oversee the preparation of a model map and battle summary "suitable for publication"; assume temporary charge of the Historical Section of the commission; and let Price know what new job prospects Eisenhower had found so that "a decision [can] be made concerning your assuming permanent charge of the Historical Section." The documents dated September 26 through October 28, 1929, contain Eisenhower's reports on these matters. See Price to Eisenhower, September 16, 1929, North Collection, Eisenhower Library.

2. James E. Mangum, a civilian, served as an executive assistant to the commission's Historical Section.

3. Capt. Howard F. K. Cahill served as a research assistant with the commission for several years. Tired of the work, Cahill had asked for a transfer.

30   Eisenhower Library
North Collection, American Battle Monuments Commission

To Maj. Xenophon H. Price

October 8, 1929

Dear Xen: I have run into a few snags in the accomplishment of the specific jobs you gave me to do, but none that have acquired any great importance to date.

In selecting the officers for Cahill, we ran afoul of a few War Department "policies," but this morning I feel that we will soon secure the necessary approval. I've tried to push the War Department in this because time is such an important factor. To date I've had conferences on this subject with the Office of the Chief of Infantry, the Adjutant General, G-1 Division, G. S. and finally with the Secretary of the General Staff. With some of these I've talked many times. There is in existence an authorized allotment of six officers for the A.B.M.C. Who authorized it I've been unable to find out. This point came up after I last wrote you saying that the A.G.O. had told me the matter was settled. At any rate this put the question of detailing additional officers to us on a very special basis, involving long studies in each section concerned. No one section or department seems to have any authority whatsoever, but today I have the promise that the orders will be telegraphed this afternoon.

The officers are: Lt. John R. Vance, Ft. Missoula, Montana; and Lt. Percy E. Hunt, Jefferson Barracks, Mo.[1]

I insisted on obtaining infantry officers if possible for the very good reason that our studies are essentially infantry ones. I also insisted on getting graduates of Benning and officers of good record. Vance was specially requested by Cahill, and Hunt recommended by the Chief of Infantry.

Unless something unexpected comes up in this case, I will write you no more about it.

The lists of missing are being processed, and by the time I can get an answer to the letter I wrote recommending my relief from duty with the Commission, I shall have been able to supervise the whole operation in the first list except the forwarding of the same to the architect. This list is by far the most difficult one (Navy) because of the many times we've had to send it back to the Navy Department, and our consequent belief that even now it contains many errors.

Once the first list has been processed, all others are mere routine.

This week I hope to have completed one map and summary for mailing to you, and thus finish up the special tasks you've assigned to me. Therefore, unless you want me to do something else of a special nature, I'll be ready for relief soon.

In this connection, my assignment upon relief from the Commission is to be in the Office of the Assistant Secretary of War, on special work as an assistant to General Moseley. Being in the same building I will be more than glad to help out on anything you may want done for I'll always have a very great interest in the task of the Commission; so don't hesitate to call on me for anything in which I can help. This is sincere, and I expect you to take advantage of it if anything arises on which you'd like me to do a little work.

John has started going to the Kalorama School, and we are taking a rather large apartment in the Wyoming. All of us are in good health, but miss the gang at Rue Molitor, Vingt.

Good luck and best regards, As ever

P.S. When your letter arrives releasing me, I'll send you a copy of the order from the A.G.O. so that you can make out my report to include the correct date.

1. John Raikes Vance (USMA, 1919) served in Army Finance throughout his army career. He retired in 1954 as a colonel.

Percy Emery Hunt (USMA, 1919) retired because of disabilities in 1939. Hunt died December 21, 1940.

31
Eisenhower Library
North Collection, American Battle Monuments Commission

To Major Xenophon H. Price

October 15, 1929

Dear Xen: So far I have told you twice that the detail of the two lieutenants to the Commission was assured. Both times I had been told by persons who I supposed knew whereof they spoke that everything was approved.

After waiting twenty-four hours after the last of these reports I again went to the Secretary of the General Staff, only to be told that the Chief of Staff was out of town and the Deputy Chief of Staff could not act on this. That entailed an additional delay of three days. After the Chief of Staff returned I again started after the Secretary and finally got the report that while the Chief of Staff personally favored this detail, he could not act on it and had to put it up to the Secretary of War. Today I am informed that no information will be forthcoming until after the meeting of the War Council at 1:30 p.m.

I tell you all this to explain the delay in a matter which looks so exceedingly simple and easy.

We have already proved that the decision to send the lists of missing to the nearest relatives was a wise one. Yesterday we received a communication informing us that the body of a Navy man reported as missing by that Department had been returned to the parents and was now buried in Baltimore, Md. We've always been suspicious of the Navy list.

Incidentally the Veterans Bureau is cooperating splendidly.

I understand Mr. Mangum is keeping you informed of the progress of this whole project. Seems incomprehensible to me that such little tasks could take so much time. I still believe, however, that by the time your letter releasing me arrives here, every thing will be in tip top shape, and completion merely a matter of routine.

Adamson[1] is much better and I suppose will be out in another ten days. As ever

1. This was probably Godfrey Douglas Adamson (USMA, 1920). He was retired as a major for disabilities in 1940.

32   Eisenhower Library
North Collection, American Battle Monuments Commission

To Major Xenophon H. Price

October 18, 1929

Dear Xen: Today, after many conferences, arguments, useless talks, and irritating delays, the Adjutant General of the Army is ordering in 1st Lieuts. Hunt and Vance to go to work in the Historical Section. At the last minute, they waited to send Vance, now at Fort Missoula, Montana, by water, which would mean that he could not get here until December 15th at the earliest.

We therefore wrote another letter, in your name, requesting that he be sent by the fastest available transportation. Copy of letter enclosed. On this letter he will be ordered in by rail.

I could never have believed that this job could have been such a difficult one to perform.

In order that these two officers understand clearly their position before reporting, I have drawn up simple orders in your name, copies of which are enclosed. These will be handed to them upon their arrival in Washington. I was careful to make the orders brief and definite so that you could amplify or modify as you choose if you consider necessary.

Day by day we are getting additional proof of the wisdom of sending the lists of missing to relatives. The Veterans Bureau also has uncovered many mistakes. In two cases in the Navy, parents have reported that men carried as missing have actually been brought home and buried in family plots!

As far as the system is concerned, it is working perfectly, and no further delays will occur in getting out the lists.
Sincerely,

33
Eisenhower Library
North Collection, American Battle Monuments Commission

To Major Xenophon H. Price

October 28, 1929

Dear Xen: In my past week's work on the model map and summary I have become convinced that editing of the summaries will be a task requiring good solid work, and should preferably be done by someone outside of the Historical Section.

We have been working on one of the less complicated operations, namely that of the 28th Division in the Aisne-Marne. Yet, aside from a few very small corrections, I have found two places in which the meaning itself is obscure. In my opinion we cannot afford to permit years of work in obtaining accuracy as to fact to be vitiated by looseness in expression. Exactitude is the primary consideration and should take precedence over all others.

I have talked at length with Cahill about this and he, of course, agrees in principle. However, the people in that section have studied the facts in the case so carefully that they <u>know exactly</u> what happened in each instance. This knowledge colors their criticism of their own work, with the result that things stated in a loose or even incorrect manner escape their notice. I quote two instances below:

"On July 26th the 28th Division, assigned to the XXXVIII French Corps, was ordered to make a night attack on July 27th, and relieve the 39th French Division by a passage of lines. . . . ."

With your knowledge of tactics you appreciate of course that the passage of lines necessarily preceded the attack. But the construction of the sentence indicates to the layman that it was a subsequent operation, or one of the results to be accomplished by the attack.

In military orders we often say "The 1st Division will attack at daylight and promptly capture Hill 208".

Another instance: "On the afternoon of July 29 the 2d and 3d Battalions, 110th Infantry had been in line, side by side over 24 hours."

An order for an attack at 3:00 P.M. is described in this manner:

"The 55th Brigade was again ordered to attack at 3:00 P.M. in conjunction with the 3d Division on the right. The 3d Battalion, 110th Infantry, on the left, was ordered to advance and dig in. The 2d Battalion was ordered to execute a passage of lines of the 3d Battalion and make the main attack".

I doubt whether anyone can decide from the description given just what was intended in the attack. Since our maps do not show regimental and battalion boundaries, they do not help to clear up the meaning of the paragraph.

These instances are given only to illustrate my idea that some one should go over each operation carefully. In my opinion no one could be better qualified for this than Jones, provided that eventually he has the time to do it. The statements quoted were in a summary which Yeuell and Cahill had already turned over as complete in all details.

I do not believe the matter should be mentioned to Cahill. He, as you know, is working hard and incessantly, and these points, which escape his notice, can be corrected in editing. When more information is necessary in order to make such correction the historical section can simply be asked to simplify the particular paragraph or sentence.

You will note I say nothing about style, etc. That is a matter for your personal decision, and I therefore confine myself to considerations affecting the meaning of each sentence in the summary.

I have nothing but praise for the way Cahill and Yeuell are working, and am confident, that with the help of the two lieutenants they will perform their part of the work to your complete satisfaction. Sincerely,

34

NOVEMBER 9, 1929

I reported for duty in the office of Assistant Secretary of War yesterday. Apparently I am to be a direct assistant to General Van Horn Moseley, and will spend my time principally on studies connected with "Industrial Mobilization." Except for the fact that I do not like to live in a city I am particularly pleased with this detail. The General is alert and energetic and certainly enjoys a fine reputation for accomplishment in the Army. I am also looking forward to the opportunity of learning something about the economic and industrial conditions that will probably prevail in this country in the event of a major war.[1]

Gee and Ham[2] are also on duty in this office. Gee has been my best friend for years—and he, Ham and I are very close. We all once served in the 19th at Fort Sam Houston in Texas.

I think Mamie is glad to stay in Washington—and of course it's all the same to Johnny.

1. Eisenhower's title in his new posting was "Assistant Executive, Office of the Assistant Secretary of War." Officially, his primary duty was the "preparation of special staff studies," according to his officer efficiency report dated December 20, 1930. He held this position until February 20, 1933, when he was assigned to duty as special assistant to Army Chief of Staff Douglas MacArthur. His primary duties prior to joining MacArthur were to prepare plans for mobilizing the nation's resources, including raw materials and manpower in the event of another major war, and to provide staff support to the War Policies Commission.

2. Lt. Gen. Wade Hampton "Ham" Haislip (USMA, 1912) served at Vera Cruz in 1914 and with the General Staff in World War I. From 1928 to 1931 he held several administrative posts, including one in the Budget and Legislative Planning Branch of the War Department. During World War II he served under Eisenhower, commanding the 85th Infantry Division and then XV Corps, which he led from Normandy until the German surrender.

35   National Archives and Records Administration (NARA)
Records of the Secretary of War

MEMORANDUM FOR THE CHIEF OF ORDNANCE

FEBRUARY 3, 1930

1. The Assistant Secretary of War recently received information from Smith & Wesson, Inc., that at 10:30 A.M., February 6th, there will be held in Room 450 at the State House in Boston a hearing on a bill to prohibit the manufacture of pistols and revolvers, before the Massachusetts Legislature.

2. The Secretary of War has written to Smith & Wesson, Inc., setting forth his views concerning this type of legislation. A copy of his letter is inclosed. It has occurred to this office that the Ordnance Department's representative in the Boston Procurement District might be able to assist the Committee holding the hearing to appreciate the importance of munitions production to national defense. If, in your

opinion, such action is advisable, it is suggested that you forward this correspondence to him immediately together with any suggestions you may care to make consistent with the Secretary's views on the subject. Geo. Van Horn Moseley[1]

1. Eisenhower initialed this memorandum, indicating he wrote it for Moseley. The wave of criminal violence resulting from Prohibition led to public outrage about easy access to firearms, particularly handguns. The Massachusetts legislation proposed a shutdown of handgun manufacture in that state, which was particularly troubling to the army because the state was home to four of the nation's handgun manufacturers, including Smith and Wesson. The legislation was defeated.

36

To Smith and Wesson, Incorporated

FEBRUARY 4TH, 1930

Gentlemen: Your action in forwarding to the War Department information concerning the bill to prohibit the manufacture of revolvers and pistols, now pending before the Massachusetts Legislature, is greatly appreciated.

The War Department is naturally hesitant to express its views on any matter which is apparently the sole concern of one of the several states and believes it is not justified in doing so unless the matter in question has some direct bearing on the common problem of national defense.

In this case the War Department's concern arises from the fact that under the law it is charged with the "assurance of adequate provision for the mobilization of matériel and industrial organizations essential to war time needs." Since, in any future emergency, the Nation would be absolutely dependent upon private industry for 90% of the pistols and revolvers necessary to munition our forces, it is essential, in the interest of national defense, that existing establishments for the manufacture of these weapons remain in being. On the other hand, the War Department is in entire accord with the efforts being made to prevent the acquisition of firearms by our criminal classes, but trusts that the various legislative bodies will find a way to accomplish this without lessening the ability of the country properly to arm its citizens in case we are forced into a war.

In short, the Department would like to conform its policy to the best thought on the subject consistent, of course, with the recognized necessity for the use of such arms in the event of a national emergency. Sincerely yours, Patrick J. Hurley, Secretary of War.[1]

1. Eisenhower wrote the letter for Hurley. It was sent to Smith and Wesson's headquarters in Springfield, Massachusetts. From 1929 to 1933 Patrick Joseph Hurley served as Herbert Hoover's secretary of war and as chairman of the War Policies Commission (1931–33). During World War II he served as personal representative of Gen. George C. Marshall to the Far East and as President Franklin Roosevelt's personal representative to the Soviet Union and to several Middle Eastern countries. He was a delegate to the Republican National Conventions in 1952 and 1956.

37

NARA
Records of the Secretary of War

MEMORANDUM FOR GENERAL MOSELEY

MARCH 22, 1930[1]

1. Mr. Carnahan[2] decided to make his visit to the Departments of Agriculture and Commerce very informal, and, at his suggestion, I did not accompany him. He stated that, at the direction of the President, he had extended the invitation to visit his plants to the War Department, and that if he attempted to arrange anything with another department, it might be considered unwarranted interference.

2. From his standpoint, as long as the War Department is sufficiently interested to examine the project, the organizing of the inspection party should be left entirely to us.

3. He believes that if the Secretary of War requests such help from the Department of Agriculture as is desirable there will be no trouble about obtaining it—and believes, also, that instead of detailing a Washington man, the Agriculture Department will detail local men in the southwest. Mr. Carnahan emphasized over and over the confidential nature of the inspection—and urged that no publicity of any kind be given it. This is because of the fact that publicity would probably occasion a rise in land prices which either his company or the Government might wish to acquire later.

4. He is most anxious that if possible you accompany the inspection party. He said that in his opinion it would be better to delay the trip as long as April 15th if by so doing you could get away to accompany the party.

5. Attached hereto is a suggested letter to the Department of Agriculture.[3]

1. This memorandum refers to Eisenhower's forthcoming trip to inspect the guayule rubber industry. He began his diary of the trip two weeks later. The mechanized, twentieth-century army had made access to supplies of raw rubber critical. This fact placed the United States in a precarious strategic position: rubber supplies

were vulnerable to interdiction by an enemy because the primary supply source was the distant East Indies. Even the secondary source, Latin America, could be cut off by an enemy with naval superiority. The military's concern proved to be justified when, during World War II, Japanese control of large portions of Southeast Asia created a shortage of natural rubber. Fortunately, the petroleum-based synthetic rubber technology that had emerged during the 1930s proved sufficient for the nation's needs.

Early in the twentieth century the American rubber industry had discovered that the sap of the wild guayule plant of the Mexican deserts contained an acceptable rubber substance. By 1910 rubber processed from guayule had been produced on a limited scale by American firms operating in Mexico. When the Mexican Revolution of 1911 led to an era of government policies hostile to foreign capital, American producers abandoned most of their Mexican operations. To offset these losses the Intercontinental Rubber Company of New York attempted to cultivate guayule near Salinas, California, and in the Laredo, Texas, area. When, in 1930, the company became aware of the military's interest in rubber reserves, it invited the War Department to evaluate its operations in the United States and Mexico. Eisenhower and another officer were detailed to conduct the inspection. After returning to Washington, Eisenhower prepared a report of their findings that is located at the June 6, 1930, entry.

2. George Holmes Carnahan worked in the mining industry in Colorado, Ecuador, and Mexico. In 1915 he became president and chairman of the board of the Intercontinental Rubber Company. Carnahan and Dr. David Spence, vice president, invented the extraction process for removing rubber resin from the wild guayule plant.

3. Eisenhower noted in his draft that the War Department was convinced that an investigation of the guayule industry was warranted to develop a supply of raw rubber "in the event of a grave national emergency" and that the "assistance of the Department of Agriculture would be highly appreciated." See Secretary of War to the Secretary of Agriculture, March 25, 1930, Records of the Assistant Secretary of War, NARA.

38   Eisenhower Library
                                                         Guayule Diary[1]

APRIL 8, 1930–MAY 7, 1930

April 8. Left Washington at 3:20 P.M. on Liberty Limited for Chicago. Dad and Mamie brought me to train, where I met Wilkes. Turned in early—quite chilly.

1. That Eisenhower maintained a diary of the guayule inspection trip became known when his speech writer, Kevin McCann, quoted from the Guayule Diary in his 1952 campaign biography, *Man from Abilene.* (Kevin McCann, *Man from Abilene* (Garden City, N.Y.: Doubleday, 1952). Its whereabouts were unknown for three decades after the biography's publication. Eisenhower had given McCann access to

his personal papers during his research for the book, and McCann sprinkled the biography's text with excerpts from numerous manuscripts, including the diary. McCann felt that the diary of the rubber inspection trip "revealed a typical American sensibility—a man of simple tastes, eager to do his job and return home as quickly as possible" (McCann, *Man from Abilene*, 92). In 1981, McCann's widow, Ruth McCann, donated his papers to the Eisenhower Library, and archivists discovered that McCann had kept not only the Guayule Diary but also several other Eisenhower diaries among his own personal papers.

WEDNESDAY, APRIL 9

Arrived Chicago, 9:10 A.M. Had breakfast on train. Took Parmolee bus to Dearborn Station. Walked up street to a movie which was <u>terrible.</u> Party Girl!! Bah-!!
Called Louise—Euclid 37985. No luck.
Had lunch and got aboard Santa Fe train "Navajo."

It is a poor train—and not their best one. Such a crowd!! Getting warmer all the time and I feel sure I'm going to wish for summer clothes.

THURS, APRIL 10

Up at 7:00 to get breakfast at Hutchinson. Played baseball in that town 21 years ago.[1] Lunch at Syracuse after going through Dodge City. I loath this hopping off to eat business. Boy how hot it is—the country is dry & parched—and everybody on the train is sweltering. Next time I go west in summer, I'll take a northern route.

Went to bed early. Right side of my head has become irritated from coal dust—or possibly I'm developing a cold. Feel miserable—with my insides not too good.[2] Boy—'tis hot!

1. Eisenhower was an outstanding high school athlete, starring in both football and baseball. One of his boyhood aspirations was to be a major league baseball player like his idol, Honus Wagner. Stories have circulated that between his high school graduation in 1909 and 1916 he played several semiprofessional baseball games in Kansas under an assumed name. Documentation concerning this allegation is more suggestive than definitive.

2. The diaries contain repeated references to gastrointestinal problems that plagued Eisenhower most of his adult life. A 1923 episode was so severe his appendix was removed even though physicians believed that evidence of appendicitis was less than substantial. Attacks continued every year between 1927 and 1933 and again in 1937 and 1938. Several more incidents occurred between 1946 and 1956. In 1956 the disorder was finally diagnosed as Crohn's disease (chronic regional enteritis). Within a month of the diagnosis, he underwent major surgery to alleviate an acute intestinal obstruction caused by scarring that typically results from the disease. For additional information see Robert E. Gilbert, *The Mortal Presidency: Illness and An-*

guish in the White House (New York: Basic Books, 1992); Robert H. Ferrell, Ill-Advised: Presidential Health and Public Trust (University of Missouri Press, 1992); and Thomas L. Mattingly, Medical History of Dwight David Eisenhower, deposited in the Eisenhower Library.

FRIDAY — [APRIL 11]

Long hot day. Our car was put on a siding at Seligman—and picked up 30″ later by another train.

The train following us hit a bus this afternoon, killing 19–20 people. Happened west of Albuquerque, N.M.

A man named Gene Harris—owner of "Club Alabam" in Chicago is on the train. He is a very interesting character, but gets terribly tiresome at times—Have worn my old suit ever since we left Chicago—and it looks like h—.[1]

Cold no better—and my insides have been acting like nobody's bug!

1. John S. D. Eisenhower states that in most of his father's writings and diaries he never spelled out expletives. Dwight Eisenhower retained the practice all his life.

SATURDAY, [APRIL 12]

30 miles from S. F.[1] Almost at end of journey and had our first little shower. Ran out of it in 2 minutes, but it was a welcome relief. Things in California are quite green—a real contrast to the long dusty miles in Kansas—Colo—N.M. & Arizona.[2]

Will put on my tweed to get off. We stay in S.F. 2 hrs and then hit the trail again for Salinas, where we are due at 1:00 A.M.

Arrived Salinas as per schedule. We have connecting rooms & 1 bath. Bath & to bed.

1. San Francisco.
2. Eisenhower's comments regarding the "dusty" miles refer to the Dust Bowl era in Kansas, beginning in 1930.

SUNDAY — APRIL 13

About 9:00 AM. Dr. Spence[1] called us up from Pebble Beach where he lives. Invited us to stay at a club there as his guests—we declined. At noon Mr. Williams resident Manager of American Rubber Producers, Inc. called. He returned at 3:00 P.M. with Dr. McMullins, the company botanist. We examined several fields of guayule from 1 month to 7 years in age. They told us about climate—soil conditions, etc. etc.

Rode to Monterey & Presidio with these two—(19 miles away) Beautiful scenery. Returned & went to "Inn Santa Lucia" for dinner with these two men, and Mr. & Mrs. Yeandle, the people who are in charge of Mexican Branch.

Nice dinner, and all of them nice people. Home by 10:00 & to bed.

1. Dr. David Spence became director of research and development for the Diamond Rubber Company, Akron, Ohio, in 1909 and was later chief of research and development for B. F. Goodrich. In 1925, as vice president, he directed research and development at Intercontinental Rubber Company, New York, N.Y. During World War II he served as a consultant on rubber to the War Production Board.

Had a very interesting day. Mr. Williams called for us at 8:00 AM, and we went at once to the guayule nurseries, a short distance from Salinas. The principal officials on the grounds are Mr. Spence: Vice Pres., I.R. Co. & head of chemical research. Mr. Yeandle, Vice Pres. I.R. Co. & head of Mexican Division. Dr. McCallum, Chief Botanist of I.R. Co. Mr. Williams, in charge of local operations of Co.

These men are undoubtedly high grade—intelligent & honest. They are very frank—and discuss failures as well as successes. They took us to many fields of guayule. Apparently there are now about 6500 acres (net) planted in this valley. The character of soil, amount of rainfall, and even the climate seems to vary between wide limits within a very small area. While some spots seem ideal for valuable lettuce crops, others are suitable only for beans—barley—etc. It is in these latter places that the Co. is trying to introduce guayule. Of the land now in guayule about 1500 acres are owned by the Co.—about 200 acres are on a share & share or contract basis—the remainder is leased. Rentals run from $7.00 to $15.00 per acre per year.

Much of that planted in former years is still on a commercial experimental basis. Consequently some fields (because of unsuitable types of plants) do not have as good stands as do others. However, the men now seem certain that three varieties (out of hundreds experimented with) are commercially practicable. One of these is particularly suited to irrigation methods. We have been promised a detailed map of region—cost sheets—pictures—etc.

It is needless to describe the milling method used in the experimental plant here. Wilkes & I traced the process from shrub to completed sheets, ready for shipment. We are convinced (now) that this is a real and growing industry. Land values may prevent any great expansion here, but we feel certain that with the return of normal prices in crude rubber, the production of guayule rubber will be started in many parts of the U.S.

Went to a movie tonight, Punk, as usual. Lord but they are banal.

117

Finished up our work in this area—but found out that Mr. Yeandle cannot reach El Paso until the 21st. We are both thrown out of schedule by this fact—and more than a little peeved, since it means hotel bills that are useless. Don't know what we'll do. Could run up & visit S. F.—but that could be quite expensive. Guess I'll figure on going to El Paso tomorrow night.

Went to a movie this eve which was quite good—don't know the name.

WEDNESDAY—[APRIL 16]

Went to plant & gathered up some loose ends of information. About 11:00 AM Mr. Williams took us out in the company Essex to see something of the countryside. We went first a few miles beyond Santa Cruz—where we visited a forest of red-wood trees. The tallest was 306 feet—about 66 feet in circumference. The oldest one is estimated at 5000 years.

This is not the most famous forest in California, but being handy we visited it instead of going to see the large trees in Yosemite Valley.

Then went to Santa Cruz for lunch—All this was on north side of Monterey Bay. After this we went around to south side of bay and along the famous 17 mile drive. Saw Monterey—Del Monte—artists colony at Carmel—the Monterey Cypress grove—wonderful beaches—country clubs—homes etc. This section—(had one a lot of money)—would be ideal for a home—hope to bring Mamie there some time.

THURSDAY (LATE WED. NIGHT) [APRIL 16–17]

Left Salinas for El Paso. One hour & 45 minutes in Los Angeles. Stayed in station. Hot dusty trip across desert.

FRIDAY—[APRIL 18]

Arrived El Paso after a hot dirty trip. Cleaned up and went to Juarez for a bottle of beer. Ate dinner there. Most expensive bust I've been on this trip—spent over 5.00. Won't do that again.[1]

Went to bed early—and read until 2:00 AM.

1. Dwight Eisenhower's concern with his finances was not only a result of his frugal upbringing but also because army officers were not well paid. This issue concerned him often before World War II and caused him to consider other employment at times during his early career. During his service with the War Department in the early thirties, Eisenhower's military expertise and writing skills brought him to the attention of a newspaper chain whose management offered him a job as mil-

itary editor at a salary five times his major's pay. Later, in Manila, friends he had made in Manila's Jewish community approached him in 1938 with an offer to head an effort to settle Jewish refugees from Germany in the Far East. Eisenhower turned down their offer of sixty thousand dollars per year plus expenses, which must have seemed like an astronomical sum at the time.

SATURDAY, APRIL 19

Went to post to look around. Fort Bliss[1] is now commanded by Brig. Gen. Symmonds[2] who is due to retire shortly. He seems a very affable man—not too energetic, but still a very fine man.

Gen. Short[3] is next ranking officer and everybody hopes he will get the command when Gen. Symmonds retires.

Gen. Short had us to luncheon—and he and Mrs. Short were more than nice to us. The General took us all over the post after lunch and explained the construction program to us. All of them are devoted to Gen. Moseley—which made a hit with me.

The rain in this section (such as there is) falls between July and October. Right now things look pretty dry although they do what they can with irrigation. Some thousands of dollars spent in additional wells & water systems would do wonders to this place.

Morale seems to be high—but everyone is terribly anxious about the pay bill. Wish I could be more optimistic about it—but I believe the chances are so slim that it would be only raising a false hope to tell people that "in Washington it is believed a pay bill will pass soon"— Certainly if we don't get one soon we are going to get only those men in the Army who are sons of wealthy families.[4]

1. Fort Bliss, five miles from El Paso, Texas, in 1930 was in the Eighth Corps Area and home to the 1st, 7th, and 8th Cavalries.

2. Brig. Gen. Charles Jacobs Symmonds (USMA, 1890) served in Cuba during the Spanish-American War, in World War I, and as commandant of the Army's Cavalry School (1927–29). He retired in 1930.

3. This probably was Walter Cowan Short, a brigadier general who served in World War I. He retired in 1934.

4. Legislation providing for new rates of pay and allowances was under consideration by Congress. Eisenhower was correct in his belief that no new legislation would pass in 1930; it would be June 16, 1942, before any change in pay and allowances occurred.

SUNDAY—APRIL 20

It seems useless to say that by this time we are getting terribly bored. My hotel room is so very unattractive & "smelly" that I hate to stay in it—but after all I'm more comfortable here than anywhere else.

119

Bob Strong[1] is to come for me before noon & take me to Post for dinner. Had my dark gray suit pressed for the occasion.

It is puzzling to know what to take to Mexico with me. Guess it will be the two dark gray suits—one good—one awful!!

A night letter from Mamie this A.M. Guess I'd counted on "selling" the articles more than I'd thought—for I feel very downcast that nothing has happened to them.[2] However!!!!! Doesn't seem quite so hot this morning, probably because I've not yet been out in the sun. I'll be glad to see Bobby—but wish I did not have to go out to Post. <u>I seem to want to grouch</u>!

1. Brig. Gen. Robert William Strong (USMA, 1915) served during World War I with the Army General Staff. In July 1942 he was assigned to the North Africa Theater as Eisenhower's Chief of Staff, U.S. Army Forces. In February 1943 he returned to the states as commanding general, Cavalry Replacement Center, Fort Riley, Kansas. He retired in 1950.

2. The letter from Mamie has not been located; however, apparently Eisenhower was referring to writings that he had submitted for publication. In 1931 he had an article published in the *Cavalry Journal* titled "War Policies." The article is included at the November 1931 entry.

MONDAY—APRIL 21

Left El Paso at 12:40 P.M.—Hot dusty day. In Washington, and at the hotel in El Paso we were told again and again that we needed no passport or other official papers to make a trip into Mexico. Two hours before train time we found that we needed a "tourist's passport"—and out we flew to get it. This we finally did.

After the train crossed the river we waited interminably in Juarez for inspection of baggage, passports, etc., etc. Eventually we got started. Have seen nothing but desert—The people in this section seem impoverished—and dejected. Under the best of conditions it would appear no easy task to wrest a living from this desert region—But with no capital, and handicapped by ignorance and traditions of serfdom (or near serfdom) these people will certainly be years in attaining any degree of comfort & conveniences in living conditions.

Train stopped for 20 minutes at a little station where the 2nd class passengers bought supper. Tortillas—enchiladas—hot tamales—milk—coffee—etc. were served by swarms of women and little boys & girls running up and down the train.

There is one Pullman Car on the train, & one combination club & dining car. Prices in the latter are exorbitant . . . much higher than in the states. A skimpy dinner cost me 1.80 gold—Wearing old suit, with no vest—but still swelter.

Arrived Torreón,[1] 12:20 and came out to Mr. Yeandle's establishment for lunch. The town is entirely different from anything we saw all the way down. Paved streets—trees—grass—nice buildings etc. are common although the town is situated in the middle of the desert.

Mr. Yeandle took us to the Army Post where a Colonel ——[2] conducted us all over the place. He spoke English very well and seemed quite well educated.

We saw the carbines & rifles now being manufactured by the Mexican govt. itself. According to this officer they have made them for about a year.

The carbine is very short. Both weapons are 7MM calibre & look like serviceable guns. Horses were in fair shape—guns & weapons were rather sloppily kept—the post itself is of good buildings—all in all—under a good leader the command could probably give a fair account of itself.

A regiment is not left long in any one locality. This is to prevent fraternization & fomentation of rebellion. Neither, according to Colonel ——, are officers left very long with a regiment—for somewhat the same reasons.

We saw polo fields—basketball courts—baseball fields—radios—schools—etc. Also visited the Torreón Air Port.

From here one co. runs five air lines—1 to El Paso, 1 to Mex. City, 1 to Mazatlan, 1 to Brownsville, 1 to ——.

The other runs to San Antone & San Luis Potosi.

The big Co. has 19 planes—the best being Lockheed—they still have some Ryans (Lindberg type) but these are now emergency ones only.

One accident since they started operating. 4 months ago they lost 1 pilot and 4 passengers. Went up to Yeandle's residence for dinner.

1. Torreón, in the state of Coahuila, is located on the central plains of Mexico, due west of Monterrey.
2. The blank underlines are Eisenhower's. Evidently he did not know the colonel's name.

WEDNESDAY APRIL 23

Spent morning examining factory at Torreón. It is not running at present and is undergoing some repairs. Gave us good chance to examine machinery.

Left Torreón at noon for Cedros Ranch. We went by train to Camacha (5 hours south of Torreón) and then cross country 65–70 kilometers in a Chevrolet. Oh boy what roads!!!! Arrived ranch 9:00 PM—supper & to bed.

The general manager of the Ranch is Mr. Selden Kirby-Smith, a son of Gen. Kirby-Smith[1] of Civil War. Quiet, unassuming & gentlemanly. He is about 55 (?) and has spent the major portion of his life in the wilds of Mexico.

His wife is in El Paso when his children are in school. They come down in summer time.

This A.M. we went out with Messrs. Yeandle & Kirby-Smith in an effort to get an idea of the general nature of ranch.

Total—1,800,000 acres.

Largely desert. Supports a growth of palms—cacti—desert shrubs, etc. The ranch buildings (some of which were built in 1732) were located here because of a fine spring.

Los Cedros means "The Cedars"—which at one time surrounded the spring and pond. The Spaniards had a silver mine here—their buildings, viaducts, etc. are now in ruins, but recognizable. There are great piles of slag, which contain 9% lead.

When the Madero Revolution started the Co. had some 250,000 goats—thousands of horses & cattle. Today there are practically none of these. In addition the Mexican "Land Laws" make it unsafe to risk any considerable money in this country.[2]

The guayule experiments near the ranch houses have been fairly successful. When the shrub is harvested, lots of seed remain on the ground. In the plots near the house these seeds have germinated well, and produced quite heavy stands of shrub. The original plants in these patches were set out as seedlings from other beds.

The seeding or reforestation experiments in the field have not been very successful to date. We saw a large field (100 acres) on which seed was spread a year ago and very few plants are standing on it. However, Mr. Yeandle believes that he will ultimately be successful in reforestation of large areas.

1. Selden Kirby-Smith's father was Confederate States of America general Edmund Kirby-Smith. Kirby-Smith, like some other Confederate soldiers, had moved to Mexico at the end of the Civil War.

2. Beginning with the Madero Revolution of 1911, Mexico underwent a series of political and constitutional upheavals. The 1917 constitution proclaimed that private ownership of land was subordinate to the public interest and provided for expropriation of large private landholdings by local villages. Millions of acres were turned over to Mexican peasants by 1940. The constitution also provided that all mineral rights were inalienable national property, leading to conflict between the government and the large multinational petroleum companies with holdings in Mexico.

We continued looking over the place—examining fields, etc. There are now four guayule extraction plants in Mexico. These are at Torreón (the largest), Los Cedros—Catorce and Cedral. Two others have been abandoned.

The combined capacity of these four plants is about 40,000 tons of shrub per year (12,000,000 lbs of rubber). These four Mr. Yeandle believes can be run continuously & profitably on the basis of 20-cent rubber, with only natural reproduction of the shrub.(?)

One of the great difficulties in the way of expansion (aside from crude rubber prices) is the uncertainty of the future of property rights in Mexico. There is no great incentive to put more money into a project which might be wiped out at any time by action of the Mexican authorities.

Went shooting with Mr. Kirby-Smith early this A.M. Got a glimpse of a deer in the brush and fired twice, but missed.

Still at Cedros.

Left Cedros at 8:30 A.M. to come to Catorce in Chevrolet. 6 hours over a twisty dusty trail. Luckily the day was overcast & therefore we were not uncomfortably warm.

Here we struck the railway again. This is the branch which runs via Laredo–Monterey–Saltillo to Mexico City. At Torreón we were on the El Paso–Mex. City line.

The plant is running full blast. We will inspect tomorrow.

Today for the first time we went through a plant actually making rubber commercially. This plant (Catorce) is running night & day, its capacity being about 10,000 tons of shrub per year. Its best month to date was March of this year 290,000 lbs of dry rubber. This month it will make about 210,000, having been shut down a week for boiler repairs.

None of the shrub milled here is raised on land owned by the I.R. Co. or its subsidiaries. It is obtained on sliding scale contracts from ranch owners—dependent on the price of rubber. The gathering and hauling are big items. Inasmuch as Mr. Williams, in Salinas, gave us confidential memos setting forth the costs of various steps of production, I believe Mr. Yeandle will do the same for Mexican production (from here).

The factory process (primary) is as follows:

The brush is parboiled to coagulate the rubber in each individual cell. It is dried and baled. The shrub goes into the factory about 20–30 days after gathering.

The bales are broken open and the shrub fed at a uniform rate onto a belt conveyer which carries it to a roller crusher. The shrub, accompanied by a flow of water passes through two sets of rollers and is then fed into a long tube mill filled with pebbles and water. In this mill the shrub is thoroughly pulverized and the tiny rubber cells gathered into little rubber worms. At the exit of the tube mill the mixture is passed into a settling tank. The rubber worms retain air and float, the fibre, bark, etc. which have been water logged in the tube mills sink to the bottom. (Some of the cork, etc., still floats.) The rubber is skimmed off mechanically and the refuse taken out at the bottom by a screw.

The rubber is then taken to a screen and the excess water drained off. It is then carried to a boiler where it is heated to 212 degrees(?) and a water pressure of 300 lbs applied. This process water logs the remaining cork, bark, etc. It next passes into a settling tank to permit the water logged material to separate from the rubber. The latter is skimmed off and goes into a washer, where it is agitated by mechanical beaters to assist the cleansing process. It is skimmed off from this tank and passes through two more settling tanks before it is drained and passed through a roller washer under a spray of water. It then goes through a roller wringer to shape it roughly into sheets and take out some of the water. It is then dipped into a preservative solution.

It next goes into ovens (heated by steam) and in which a partial vacuum is maintained to dry it out.

After this it is weighed and packed.

Along the line of the continuous process described, various operations are repeated on the material remaining in a tank after the top is skimmed off. These secondary operations are simply to recover whatever rubber is not obtained by primary methods. The waste solids are dried out in basins and used for fuel. Thus additional secondary processes cost nothing except the wages of men necessary to manipulate the machines. The waste water is used in irrigating a farm near the factory.

TUESDAY [APRIL 29]

Left Catorce late last night, catching a train for Laredo. Early this morning we came down off the plateau (crossing the costal range) onto the Monterey plain, a drop of 7–8000 feet in 3 hours. From then on it was very hot—and the slow passage through the international boundary red tape was very tedious. In Laredo Texas, had to change trains and wait ½ hours. Wired both Mamie and Mike.[1] Arrived at Dilley at 6:00 P.M. Tomorrow we inspect the sample plots around this town—next day those at Lind—etc. This will complete the work except writing of report & possibly accumulating some statistics from various agencies in Washington.

Left San Antonio Monday morning [May 5]—9:45 AM—Due to arrive Wash. 12:05 noon—Wednesday [May 7][2]

1. Mabel Frances Doud Gill, "Mike," was Mrs. Richard Gill, Mamie Doud Eisenhower's sister.

2. Eisenhower kept a separate diary book for his rubber inspection trip. On May 8, 1930, he returned to his original diary, now identified as the Chief of Staff Diary, and included a summation of the inspection trip. Eisenhower and Wilkes submitted their official report on June 6, 1930.

39

MAY 8, 1930

Returned today from a month's trip which I made, in company with Major Wilkes, (C. E.) through California, Mexico and Texas.

The object of the trip was to gather first hand information concerning the guayule rubber industry that has been under development in Mexico and southwest United States for some years.

The points at which we spent the most time were, Salinas, California, Torreón, Los Cedros and Etacion Catorce, in old Mexico; and Dilley, Texas.

The guayule shrub is native to Mexico—where it grows wild over a vast area in the northern desert.

The Intercontinental Rubber Co. (N. Y. City) and its subsidiaries have been engaged for some years in efforts to cultivate the plant in the U.S.

The plant contains a large percentage of rubber—which is extracted mechanically through a crushing, rolling and washing process. With the labor saving machinery they have developed—the company officials believe they can produce rubber in the U.S. (figuring in land values) at 12 cents per pound.

So far the extraction process does not produce as good a brand of rubber as is obtained from the plantations in southwest Asia and adjoining islands.

I visited Mike and Dick for three or four days in San Antonio, Texas.

Officials of the Intercontinental Rubber Co. were:

Mr. George C. Carnahan, 175 Broadway, New York City

Dr. D. Spence, c/o American Rubber Producers, Salinas, Calif.
Mr. William H. Yeandle, Torreón, Coahuila, Mexico.

40

To Assistant Secretary of War

June 6, 1930

REPORT OF INSPECTION OF GUAYULE RUBBER INDUSTRY[1]

I. INTRODUCTION

Interest of War Department in Domestic Rubber Production.

1. The United States is at present dependent for its supply of raw rubber on outside sources, principally located in southeastern Asia and in the islands adjoining. From that region is obtained the "plantation" or "hevea" rubber, the best grades of which establish the commercial rubber standards of the world. Should our sea communications with that region be cut in an emergency, shortage of rubber in the United States would rapidly become acute.

2. We import annually about one billion pounds of raw rubber. Perhaps, under war time regulations, our necessities could be met by an annual supply of less than 300,000,000 pounds (150,000 tons) but under the assumed conditions the procurement of even this amount would be almost an impossibility.

3. Because of the great importance of an adequate rubber supply the Secretary of War is vitally interested in any project which offers a reasonable opportunity for the production of raw rubber in continental United States.

History of Guayule Rubber Industry.

1. The bone dry guayule shrub contains from eleven to fifteen per cent of rubber. The plant exists in a wild state in large areas in northern Mexico and in a small portion of southwest Texas.

2. When a practicable commercial method was developed, some twenty years ago, for extracting the rubber from the guayule plant, several companies were formed to furnish the product to consumers. During the first years following the establishment of these factories there appears to have been little or no effort made to domesticate the shrub, or to reforest the areas constantly denuded as the result of the operations of the producers. Unlike the method used in extracting latex from the rubber tree, the extraction process used in the guayule industry entails the destruction of the plant itself. Thus it is apparent

that eventually the industry was doomed to extinction, unless methods were developed for cultivating the plant, or operations were limited to the harvesting of the shrub at a rate not exceeding that of natural reproduction.

3. Beginning in 1911 harvesting operations had to be materially curtailed due to the outbreak of revolution in Mexico, and by 1915 all extraction plants were practically closed down. A company which is now controlled and owned by the Intercontinental Rubber Company brought seeds to the United States and began a long series of experiments designed to determine whether or not the plant could be domesticated in the United States and rubber produced economically through cultivation.

4. Experiments have been most exhaustive, and have covered every phase of the industry from the germination of the seed to the best methods of vulcanizing this particular brand of rubber. The company has employed experts of the highest type, and has established experimental stations in various parts of Texas, Arizona and California.

5. At the beginning of 1930 the Intercontinental Rubber Company informed the War Department that experimentation and development had demonstrated the commercial practicability of producing rubber from guayule cultivated in the United States, and invited an inspection of the company's properties by Government officials.

6. Accordingly, an inspection party composed of
Major Gilbert Van B. Wilkes, C.E.,
Major D. D. Eisenhower, Infantry,
was directed to visit the projects of the Intercontinental Rubber Company connected with the production of guayule rubber.

The localities visited were:

The Salinas Valley (about one hundred miles south of San Francisco.)

The semi-desert region between Torreón and Estacion Catorce in northern Mexico.

The general area, Pearsall, Laredo, San Diego in southern Texas.

The officers detailed on this inspection are not technically trained in rubber production. The inspection was for the purpose of gaining first hand information of conditions as they now exist and impressions as to personalities, etc. On this account, it is considered best to make the report an informal narrative and to cover in the appendices most of the details which are usually found in a technical description.

II. REPORT OF THE INSPECTION.

In this area we visited in succession the city of Torreón, Los Cedros Ranch (located some sixty miles east of Camacho), and the village of

Estacion Catorce. This region lies between the two great coastal mountain ranges of Mexico and is semi-arid in nature. It supports a heavy growth of mesquite, greasewood, cactus, palms, century plants, etc.

The Intercontinental Rubber Company operates in this region through its subsidiaries the Continental Mexican Rubber Company and the Cia. Ganadera y Textil de Cedros, which it owns and controls.

The company has obtained guayule shrub through harvesting operations on its own land, and by contract with private owners throughout the region. Los Cedros, the largest ranch owned by the company is almost 2,000,000 acres in extent.

We saw guayule shrub in the wild state. In none of the localities visited, however, did we see any heavy stands of the shrub, nothing like the stands described by Lloyd as existing in 1907–08 for instance. It seems to occur mainly in scattered patches along the hillsides throughout the area. It was impossible for us to make even the roughest kind of approximation of the amount of guayule now growing in Mexico. The officials of the Intercontinental Rubber Company stated, however, that to date there has been no difficulty in obtaining all the shrub, through contracts with owners, that they were willing to mill. The aggregate annual capacity of their mills in Mexico is about 10,000,000 pounds of rubber. In 1927 the company operated all its existing plants at capacity.

In recent years considerable attention has been given to reforestation of the shrub on Los Cedros Ranch. We inspected several areas where attempts along this line have been made. In the larger fields where seed has been sown the most meager results have been secured. However, the company officials have been greatly encouraged by success in one or two small plots and by new developments in planting methods. They believe that reforestation on a considerable portion of the range will eventually be successful. Under present conditions in Mexico the major portion of the cost of guayule rubber is incurred in the purchase and harvesting of the shrub and transporting it to the extraction plants. (None is now being harvested on the Los Cedros Ranch, owned by the company.) Reforestation, if successful, will not only increase the amount of shrub available but will cut down materially the harvesting and transportation costs.

The Company owns four extraction plants in Mexico, situated at Torreón Los Cedros, Estacion Catorce and Cedral. We visited the first three of these. Those at Torreón and Los Cedros are not operating at present, the one at Torreón is partially dismantled. At Catorce we examined in detail the extraction process, and witnessed actual packing of rubber for shipment. This plant has a capacity of 10,000 pounds of dry rubber per day. It produced about 280,000 pounds in March and about 210,000 pounds in April. Because of the present low prices in rubber, this plant will soon be closed down, and the Intercontinental Rubber Company will be producing no rubber in Mexico.

The extraction process is relatively simple and is almost completely mechanized (Appendix B.) [. . . .]

2. In the Salinas Valley of California the Intercontinental Rubber Company has planted approximately 6,500 acres of guayule shrub, all of which we inspected. This land, except for 200 acres, is either owned or leased by the Intercontinental Rubber Company. Near the town of Salinas we went through their principal experimental station. Exhaustive research has determined that out of the thousand or more varieties and sub-varieties of guayule shrub analyzed or developed, three of them offer the greatest commercial possibilities as a cultivated crop. These three, each adapted to slightly different conditions of soil and climate, are characterized by hardihood of plant, high percentage of rubber content, and large size of shrub. The shrub now being planted in the Salinas Valley is the variety best adapted to the climatic conditions and soil of the region. The area near the town of Salinas has a sandy, loamy soil, and about ten to fourteen inches of rainfall annually, which occurs mainly in the winter and early spring months.

The price of land in this rather restricted valley varies within wide limits, depending upon the suitability or unsuitability of each area for the production of such high priced crops as lettuce, artichokes, etc. In those sections which will produce these crops, land is valued as high as $800 per acre, while those adapted only to the production of barley, beans, etc., average $100 to $150 per acre. The latter class of land appears to be well suited to the production of guayule shrub.

The guayule plant requires three to five years to reach maturity. The areas now under cultivation in the Salinas Valley have been planted at various times so that at present there is in this region guayule shrub varying in age from a few weeks to more than five years. Thus, we were able to see the plant from the seed bed to maturity. In the Salinas area the seeds are planted during the spring months in specially prepared beds, which are irrigated. During the following winter the fields to be planted are plowed, harrowed, and levelled. In the succeeding February and March the plants in the seed beds are cut off and then transplanted. From planting until maturity the fields are cultivated frequently to eliminate weeds and other competitive growths.

After transplanting in the Salinas properties, it is said that the weight of actual increases annually on each average acre about as follows; (Gain results from growths of plants and increase of rubber percentage in each to end of fourth year—thereafter, only by growth of plants).

Gain per acre per year			Accumulated Total (Rough approximation based on experiments).	
1st year	300–400	pounds	300–400	pounds
2nd year	300–400	"	600–800	"
3rd "	400–400	"	1000–1200	"
4th year	400–400	"	1400–1600	"
5th "	200–300	"	1600–1900	"
6th "	200–300	"	1800–2200	"
7th "	200–300	"	2000–2500	"
8th "	100–200	"	2100–2700	"
9th "	100–200	"	2200–2900	"
10th "	0–100	"	2200–3000	"

The officials of the company are convinced that the maximum figures given here are only an average under the present stage of development, and soon will be substantially exceeded on the average acre of Salinas ground.

The information gained during the long period of development work has enabled the company officials to make rather accurate estimates of the cost of producing guayule rubber in that region. (There is no factory yet established in this region, but extraction costs are based on the company's experience in other places.)

3. The Salinas experiments have convinced the officials of the Intercontinental Rubber Company of the following: (From such observation as we were able to make in the limited time available, we believe, these conclusions to be correct.)

a. That the guayule shrub can be domesticated.

b. That it can be produced in commercial quantities in the Salinas Valley and in certain other parts of the United States.

c. That under proper conditions domestication of the plant does not injure its rubber producing qualities.

d. That shrub can be produced without irrigation at the approximate rate of four to five tons (dry weight) per acre in a four year cycle, and that (assuming normal prices for raw rubber) the economic time for harvesting is at the end of the fourth or fifth year.

e. That almost complete mechanization of the production process is feasible.

f. That the cost of producing guayule rubber (delivered in New York) is no greater than for an equal amount of hevea rubber.

g. That guayule shrub has no particularly bad effects on soil.

h. That by the application of the methods developed during the years of experimentation, an average stand of 92 to 96 per cent of all plants set out is practically assured in the Salinas Valley.

i. That with raw guayule rubber selling at an average level of twenty-five cents per pound, (corresponds to about thirty cents per pound, standard smoked sheets of hevea) Salinas Valley land producing guayule shrub should yield per acre a minimum of $20.00 net returns per year or a net profit of about $10.00 on the basis of $10.00 per acre. (This is much higher/average yield than is now secured from some tracts planted in barley, beans, etc.) For an individual farmer this revenue would of course depend upon the terms of his contract with the producing company.

j. That certain varieties of the plant do well under irrigation—that a sandy, loamy soil is best for its growth—that only a light rainfall is necessary (ten to fourteen inches per year)—that light frosts or at least spells of cold weather are necessary to its development and that the plant is singularly free from pests, parasites, diseases, etc.

4. The Intercontinental Rubber Company has planted several experimental plots in the southern part of the state of Texas. The area in which they are particularly interested is roughly the triangle—Pearsall–Laredo–Rio Grande. On one of these plots the guayule shrub is two years of age, on the other only a few months. We considered the guayule stands on these plots to be as fine as any of similar age we saw in the Salinas Valley. Results secured to date have convinced the Intercontinental Rubber Company that the region is particularly suitable for the raising of one of the varieties of guayule shrub developed by the company.

In this region are great areas of undeveloped or partially developed land. We saw much under a growth of mesquite while other tracts have been planted in cotton, corn, and onions. In favorable years onions are a very profitable crop. Citrus fruit has not done well in the region, due to the occasionally severe winters. Land varies considerably in price, but in general it may be said that the sandy, loamy tracts in this area run from $10.00 per acre (uncleared and off of main highways) to $40.00 or $50.00 per acre for the cleared areas lying close to the highways. Some of the uncleared land in this region rents (for grazing) as low as twenty five to thirty cents per acre per year.

The existence of vast areas of cheap land undoubtedly suitable for guayule production is the feature which makes this region particularly interesting to the Intercontinental Rubber Company.

<u>Quality of Rubber Produced from Guayule.</u>
5. (Except as otherwise stated, all information in this paragraph is furnished by the Intercontinental Rubber Company.)
The best hevea (plantation) rubber contains about
    4% resin
    4% other water insolubles

1% water

9% total foreign matter.

Guayule rubber from Mexico as marketed today has about

20% resin

8% other water insoluble

1% water

29% total foreign matter.

The basic price of guayule is about eighty per cent of the market price of the best hevea rubber (See Appendix G.) [. . .] It is marketed with this percentage of impurities because of the fact that consumers have need of a certain amount of raw rubber of this type, thus making it commercially profitable for the company to sell the rubber in this state. We were told that there has been proved out a simple and inexpensive process for reducing the percentage of impurities to the approximate level of that contained in the best hevea rubber. The greater portion of Guayule has been marketed under the trade name of Duro and is used in mixture with plantation rubber. The Intercontinental Rubber Company introduced in 1927 a superior grade known as Ampar for which they demand a premium of one and one half cents per pound. Apparently the only real difference in these is the somewhat smaller percentage of impurities in Ampar, attained by more careful methods of milling. The Ampar grade is also treated with a preservation solution prior to shipment. It has a higher tensile strength than the original Duro grade.

In this connection Dr. D. Spence the chief chemist of the Intercontinental Rubber Company stated to us that even better results would be obtained when the best vulcanization methods had been worked out. In other words, he intimated that even with exactly the same percentage of impurities in Guayule rubber as are contained in hevea, the two products must be treated somewhat differently in the vulcanization process in order to secure the best results from each. In spite of the fact that the best methods of vulcanization have not been determined exactly, one set of experimental tires and tubes made wholly from Guayule rubber gave satisfactory results. We saw a letter from Mr. Thomas A. Edison to the Intercontinental Rubber Company in which he stated that he had tested another set of tires made from Guayule for 14,000 miles and that they still appeared perfectly sound in every respect.

III. GENERAL CONCLUSIONS CONCERNING GUAYULE AS A PRESENT AND FUTURE SOURCE OF A RUBBER SUPPLY FOR THE UNITED STATES.

　　1. Supply Source Under Present Conditions.

At present the only capacity of the Guayule industry to furnish quickly an <u>emergency</u> supply of rubber is represented by the shrub actually growing in California and Mexico.

It may be assumed that from the Spring of 1931 and after, there will exist continuously in the Salinas Valley a minimum of about 4,500 acres of Guayule at an average age of three and one-half years. At 1,600 pounds per acre, this would total less than 6,000,000 pounds of rubber.

We could obtain no estimates on the amount of Guayule shrub now existing in northern Mexico. In 1911 Dr. Lloyd estimated that there were 500,000 tons in the country originally and possibly one-half had been already used. Under the stimulus of emergency prices whatever shrub does exist could be collected and milled. If 100,000 tons exist at present the rubber yield would be about 25,000,000 pounds.

2. <u>Consideration Affecting Probabilities of Expansion of Industry.</u>

a. In Mexico the probability of expansion depends upon three factors. These are:

Stability of government and fair treatment for investors.

Success of Guayule reforestation efforts.

Price of raw rubber.

b. In the United States expansion depends solely upon the price of rubber. (Assumption is made that the claim of the Intercontinental Rubber Company, supported by findings of Bureau of Standards as to complete suitability of Guayule rubber for all uses is correct.)

c. Under the laws and general political conditions now existing in Mexico every business concern is bound to be reluctant to invest any large additional sums in that country. Until assurance is given that property rights are to be respected no steps toward the development of guayule industry requiring considerable outlays of capital will be undertaken. Because of the nature of the climate, there is at present no belief that guayule can be domesticated and cultivated in Mexico, at least under methods similar to those used in the Salinas Valley. Reforestation schemes are limited to plans for clearing land and broadcasting seed which will then be allowed to develop without further attention. Some of the company officials are quite hopeful that these measures will produce results which will exceed materially the initial average yield of the wild guayule. At least thirty per cent of the nearly 2,000,000 acres in Cedros Ranch are considered suitable for guayule. If 600,000 acres could be reforested and produce an average of thirty pounds of rubber per year, this alone would make an annual rubber production of 18,000,000 pounds. Success in reforestation over the vast tracts in northern Mexico on which the plant grows wild would insure a supply of rubber of considerable proportions.

d. In the United States the whole project sifts down to obtaining a price for raw rubber which will assure the farmer in the regions effected a larger net return from a guayule crop than he can obtain in any other way. Previous contracts with farms (200 acres only involved) made by the Intercontinental Rubber Company have assured growers a price of $25.00 per ton of standing shrub with a bonus of $1.00 per ton for each cent the price of rubber is in excess of twenty-eight cents per pound at the time of harvest. Costs of soil preparation, of plants, of planting, and even of cultivation have been advanced by the company. Just what offers will be made to farmers in the future is not known. In view of the cost analyses furnished to us, it would appear that a minimum of $30.00 per ton could be offered for shrub. This would necessitate a price for the raw rubber corresponding to about thirty cents for plantation rubber. The fact that to date farmers in the Salinas Valley, where land prices are high, have shown little interest in the project. When rubber is actually being milled and shipped from California it is probable that more interest will be shown. Cooperation by farmers is essential if the industry is to grow and be maintained in the United States. The only other alternative is the outright purchase of ground by the developing company, on which to raise the shrub. At an average price of $40.00 per acre for suitable cleared ground, 250,000 acres (sufficient to produce annually one tenth of our present consumption) would cost $10,000,000 while initial planting and first year cultivation would cost another $10,000,000. With the present lack of stability in the raw rubber market, this is too great a risk for one company to take.

3. Conclusions as to Probabilities of Expansion.

Our conclusions on this subject, based on the information gathered through observation, conversation, and reading, are as follows:

a. The Intercontinental Rubber Company has too great an interest in the Guayule industry to abandon it definitely, and will continue to operate on a relatively small scale in the hope of a rise in raw rubber prices.

b. The research departments of the company (Botanical and Chemical) will continue to seek improved varieties of plant, methods of production, and means of improving the quality of the finished product.

c. Under prevailing rubber prices the Intercontinental Rubber Company will not undertake any definite expansion. If rubber prices around twenty-five to thirty cents per pound prevail for some years we personally believe the industry will experience a considerable growth. Such expansion, if it takes place at all, will probably be in southern Texas.

d. No organization other than the Intercontinental Rubber Company is at present in a position to undertake a Guayule development project in the United States. One of its principal assets is the tremendous amount of pertinent information accumulated through its years of experimental and development work together with control of seed supply of special varieties. Methods of germinating the seed—caring for the seedlings transplanting into fields—cultivating—harvesting—treating shrub before milling—crushing—agglomerating—cleaning—etc., have all been changed materially since the industry was first begun. Much of the machinery used is patented, and efforts have been made to patent the varieties of plant developed for commercial use. Certainly, no competitor will appear in this field as long as rubber prices are low—and under high rubber prices any competitor, under existing conditions would be greatly handicapped.

e. Unless some method is found of aiding the industry as a whole (both the producing company and cooperating farmers) no material progress in its development will be made in the near future.

IV. DISCUSSION OF POSSIBLE CONNECTION OF UNITED STATES GOVERNMENT WITH GUAYULE INDUSTRY.

1. It would appear that the Government might be interested in encouraging the Guayule industry in the United States in view of:

a. The opportunity to build up a domestic source of supply for rubber so that in a grave emergency we would not be wholly dependent on southeast Asia and the adjoining islands for this important raw material.

b. The Opportunity to build up a domestic source of supply of rubber so that American consumers would have some protection against possible commercial combines between the great rubber producing companies of the Far East. (The United States at present uses about sixty per cent of the annual rubber output of the world.

c. The possibility of building up an industry in the United States that would give profitable employment to some thousands of American farmers, mechanics, and laborers. We send some two to three hundred million dollars annually to foreign countries to pay for the rubber we import.

d. The opportunity of occasioning a measurable reduction in the acreage now devoted to such crops as cotton, corn, and small grain of which we usually produce a surplus; and increasing the acreage devoted to a product for which we are almost completely dependent on overseas sources.

e. All our vegetables and field crops have been developed in the course of thousands of years of cultivation in the humid areas of Europe and Asia and are not adapted to the conditions found in the dry areas of southwest United States. Farmers in these regions are constantly faced with the failure of a large percentage of their crops and when conditions are just right for production their produce must be sold in an already well supplied market. Guayule is a plant indigenous to just such regions and is by nature adapted to the vicissitudes of the climate. No desert plant so far as we know has been made the subject of so much research and study and offers such possibilities for the farmers of our semi-arid southwest.

f. The precarious position of the United States in depending entirely on the continued health of hevea trees in the Middle East now producing ninety-six per cent of the World's supply of rubber.

g. Adding even ten per cent to the total annual supply of rubber by means of cultivated Guayule would mean much lower prices for the remaining ninety per cent, with the United States, as a consuming country, greatly benefited.

2. Building up a Rubber Reserve for Use in an Emergency.

a. The specific concern of the War Department is centered almost wholly in the first of the considerations enumerated above. While naturally interested in the general prosperity of the country, and the betterment of economic conditions for various groups, these matters are the direct concern of certain other departments of the Government.

b. It is difficult to make an estimate of the extent to which the Guayule rubber industry must expand before it would prove to be a material factor in our problem of providing an emergency supply of rubber. Studies have indicated that, considering: stocks on hand and afloat at any one time; the proved practicability of using reclaimed rubber extensively; the estimated extent to which rubber could be saved by effective conservation methods; the possibility of synthetic rubber serving as an inferior substitute for some purposes; and the fact that even under the worst conditions unusually high prices would attract some rubber to the United States through neighboring neutrals; there would be no critical situation with respect to rubber shortage created in the United States during the first twelve to eighteen months of an emergency. Thereafter the situation might become very acute. The Guayule plant is of relatively slow growth and consequently if we are to count on Guayule rubber as an emergency supply a considerable acreage of the growing shrub should exist before an emergency arises.

The question of an emergency supply of Guayule rubber is therefore almost solely a question of the acreage devoted to the industry in the United States.

At present no one believes that the United States will, in this or the next generation, produce annually the major part of the rubber we consume. But if the Guayule industry could develop to the point where approximately 400,000 acres were devoted to the growth of Guayule we would produce annually almost 160,000,000 pounds of rubber, and have in reserve at all times not less than 250,000,000 pounds. The existence of these conditions would in the event of a war where our overseas communications were interrupted be of inestimable value to the Nation. A 400,000 acre tract in one block would equal an area 25 miles square.

V. MEANS FOR STIMULATING THE GROWTH OF GUAYULE INDUSTRY IN THE UNITED STATES.

1. a. The necessary acreage could be planted by the Government itself. Under such a scheme the Government would have to enter into contracts for the clearing of land, planting, caring for and harvesting the shrub, and for its sale to the factory.

b. A tariff on raw rubber imports could be imposed.

c. The production of rubber in the United States could be encouraged by offering the use of public lands for this purpose at a nominal rental.

d. The United States could guarantee a reasonable price for all rubber raised and milled in this country.

2. The first method of stimulation listed above would have obvious disadvantages and is subject to criticisms directed at other schemes for putting the Government in business. Moreover, it would tend directly to encourage the milling side of the industry alone and would encourage the planting of the shrub by independent agencies indirectly only.

The second method would have the effect of laying a tax on a large volume of an essential commodity in order to increase the price on home rubber which is bound to be negligible in quantity for many years.

The third method would encourage the growth of Guayule to the extent to which the public lands are suitable and available. The suitability of the lands available in the southwest is still a matter of considerable doubt and it is scarcely probable that outside interests would be willing to take the chances involved in the industry. The amount of assistance that would be afforded by furnishing rent free land in this section of cheap lands would probably not outweigh other disadvantages inherent in the localities available.

The fourth method listed seems to us by far the most practical and in line with recent farm relief legislation.

3. We are personally convinced that under real encouragement the production of Guayule rubber would develop rapidly into an important industry in the United States. We further believe that an offer of the United States Government to purchase during the next fifteen years all rubber raised and milled within the continental limits of the

United States at a price based on standard smoked sheets hevea rubber of thirty cents per pound would certainly furnish this stimulus. The present price of crude rubber is unreasonably low. Similar prices obtained in 1921–1922 followed by an increase to $1.20 per pound in 1925. Judging from past history it appears probable that the average price for the next fifteen years would be greater than thirty cents.

Such a scheme would amount to the Government paying to producers for each pound of rubber actually produced within the United States the amount that the market price was below the guaranteed amount at the time of delivery. It would be necessary to draw standard specifications for the grades of rubber entitled to the guaranteed price or prices and to provide for inspection and certification. A guaranteed price of thirty cents per pound for instance, would be allowed for a rubber as suitable for all uses as standard hevea, while a corresponding price for instance, twenty-four cents would be allowed for a rubber such as the present Duro grade, suitable as a useful material in admixture with hevea. Such prices would enable the producing company or companies to make such favorable contracts with agriculturists that the area devoted to rubber production in the United States would steadily expand.

It would not be necessary to specify Guayule or any other plant as the source of the rubber is guaranteed. Euphorbia Intisy, Golden Rod or American Hevea rubber answering the standards could be furnished as well as Guayule.

1. Several statistical appendixes were included with the official report in the Forest Service records. Ellipses indicate where Eisenhower referred to them.

41   NARA
Records of the Secretary of War
"Fundamentals of Industrial Mobilization"[1]

To Frederick H. Payne

June 16, 1930

In the brief period that has elapsed since I was appointed the Assistant Secretary of War and became legally responsible for making provisions for industrial mobilization in war, it has obviously been impossible for me to become familiar with all the problems involved in the performance of this task. Necessarily, I have devoted most of my attention to a study of the basic provisions of the plan begun in 1920 and whose development has continued steadily, if slowly, ever since. Broadly speaking, the plan concerns itself with the fundamental relationships that should exist in war between Government and industry, and with the methods whereby military forces will secure necessary munitions from industrial establishments.

In attempting an analysis of these matters, I find that now I am approaching many of the same questions from the standpoint of a governmental official which formerly I studied almost solely from that of an industrial executive. Possibly for this reason I find that the problem of industrial mobilization holds for me a peculiar and natural interest.

By studiously avoiding the manifold and intricate details, I have succeeded sufficiently in absorbing the fundamental principles of the plan adopted by my predecessors to state that they have my entire approval, and will receive my hearty support as long as I retain the responsibilities devolving by law upon the Assistant Secretary of War.

In discussing the plan, first it is necessary to obtain a clear conception of the results we are trying to secure. In other words, what do we mean by industrial mobilization? Do we imply that in an emergency national industry should be marshalled into a military or semi-military organization, subject to the necessarily strict and direct discipline of armed forces in the field? Do we contemplate that presidents of corporations will be made colonels in the Army, or shop foremen, chief petty officers in the Navy? Do we insist that all industry should be compelled in war to operate under uniform production, sales and accounting systems laid down by the Federal Government in Washington? Most emphatically we do not.

Our purpose is simple—to see to it that every individual and every material thing shall contribute, in the manner demanded by inherent characteristics, their full share to the winning of any war in which we may become involved. Simplicity and practicability are the foundation stones of the plan through which it is proposed that this result shall be attained.

Before 1914 military men had but dimly perceived the tremendous influence that industrial and economic factors would exert in a modern war. Probably more striking than any other single lesson of the late war was that, when great nations resort to armed conflict today, the readiness of each to meet promptly the needs of its armed forces in munitions, and of its civilian population in the necessities of life, may well prove to be a decisive factor in the contest. Today a nation faced with a grave military emergency must look as anxiously to her capacity to forge the weapons of war as she does to the ability of her Army and Navy to use them. Consequently, when the emergency comes, we cannot with impunity cripple any essential industry. If its ability to produce the articles upon which our armed forces depend is weakened by a lack of skilled labor, by a shortage of money, or because it is forced to operate under unaccustomed or inappropriate methods, then we are lessening our own chances of victory just as surely as though we deliberately should sink a fleet of our own troop laden transports in the middle of the Atlantic.

The industrial establishments of this country have been built up through decades of experiment and development. They have become efficient, each in its own line, because inefficiency means financial loss and eventual extinction.[2]

The paths of industrial currents are rather definitely fixed. The flow of trade involves: the movement of raw materials and of finished articles along accustomed routes; financial arrangements almost permanent in their periodical renewals; concentration of labor at strategic points; development of power systems to meet the needs of particular areas; and the gearing of industrial establishments to meet the requirements of a continuing demand. All these are interdependent—violent disturbance in any one of them entails a dislocation in the whole.

As a first principle then we must adjust the war load to our productive facilities in such a way as to occasion the minimum of disturbance in the ordinary industrial processes of the country. To accomplish this the Office of the Assistant Secretary of War as a first step has taken the great shopping list containing the estimated war time requirements of the Army and through representatives stationed in all parts of the country, has parcelled it out in accordance with the capacity of each part to absorb the additional load assigned to it. Furthermore, in order to occasion, in an emergency, the minimum of disturbance in production methods, the Army has substituted as far as possible, items in commercial use for those articles of equipment whose manufacture demands alterations in shop layouts, methods, and so on. This, of course, cannot be done in the case of ammunition, guns, bayonets, fighting planes, and similar essential items whose employment is limited strictly to combat.

Through "Gentlemen's Agreements" made in peace with individual establishments we are able to insure the speediest possible initiation of a production program in war. It is true that these agreements have no binding force but they serve to show us what can be done, and forewarn the manufacturer of the job that will probably fall to his lot. No agreement is made by the Army with an industrial establishment particularly adapted to meet the needs of the Navy, and in no case is more than half of the normal capacity of a plant obligated. These measures will enable the manufacturer to supply, on a reduced basis, his civilian customers during a war, and will facilitate the return to normal peace time business after the war is completed. Moreover, under the policy outlined, there will exist a great reserve production capacity which could be drawn upon should the emergency become so grave as to demand its use.[3]

Gratifying progress has been made in working out the details of this munitions procurement program. We certainly will not be faced again with the necessity of rushing frantically to the commercial world with our war time shopping list in an attempt, through the offer of exorbitant prices, to make good deficiencies in peace time planning.

However, no matter how efficiently we distribute the munitions production task to industry, as quickly as plants begin work on the millions of articles needed, there will be created some shortages in secondary requirements, and disturbances in the whole industrial fabric of the Nation. If sea trade is not maintained shortages in certain critical raw materials will rapidly become acute. Rubber, tin, nickel, iodine, manganese, and some few others are either not produced in our country or are produced in insufficient quantities to meet the needs of the country in war.

Where possible, plans must provide for substituting plentiful raw materials for scarce ones—for conserving critical materials for essential uses—and for increasing sources of supply. Prices must not get out of hand. Experience has shown that when prices begin to rise in war they rush in dizzy spirals to heights that cannot fail to have the most demoralizing influence on the whole population. Mounting prices entail an unequal distribution of the war burden, and a sapping of morale among those whose efforts and hardships are apparently capitalized by others whose situation enables them to take advantage of the emergency conditions. Obviously a systematic and effective control of our industrial and economic resources will be necessary in a major war. Such control can come from the central Government alone. In no other place can there be found a knowledge of the Nation's requirements as a whole, or can there be placed the requisite authority to insure compliance with the directives and orders that will necessarily be issued.

Consequently, in the event of war, a great industrial organization will certainly be a part of the Federal Government during the period of the emergency. This organization must be made up of leaders in all the branches of industry. Representatives of labor, of manufacturers, of financiers, of the professions, of agriculturists, of producers of raw materials and so on must combine in an organization under the President to guide our industrial effort along those lines that will insure speedy victory—and justice to every citizen.

Thus the existing plan for industrial mobilization is seen to be simple in conception. It provides for making peace time arrangements to insure prompt initiation of munitions production in the event of war; for the determination of methods whereby men, money, and materials may be set to work in the interest of the whole Nation; and for setting up an industrial organization to administer and carry out the execution of the war time industrial task. But the complete preparation of such a plan is a most intricate and difficult work. Studies to determine how the various desirable results may be attained—plans to make promptly effective the schemes adopted—constant experimentation with new materials—accumulation of gages, tools, jigs, and fixtures, and other equipment to install quickly in new or converted establishments—insuring the existence of the skilled labor required in non-commercial processes—all these and more must be carried on continuously.

Needless to say, without the hearty cooperation of patriotic civilians the task would be a hopeless one. But with this help, unselfishly given, progress is being made. Today we cannot say that we are ready to the last cartridge box—we never will be—but we have a clear understanding of the capacity of the Nation to make cartridge boxes. What is more we have the assurance that the Army, the Navy, and industry can promptly undertake their respective tasks in an orderly and efficient way, if unhappily we must again take up arms in the defense of our Country and its institutions. Prepared by Maj. Eisenhower

1. Eisenhower wrote this article for Assistant Secretary of War Payne to submit to the *Army Ordnance* magazine (Frederick H. Payne, "Fundamentals of Industrial Mobilization," *Army Ordnance* 11 [July–August 1930]: 7–8). This draft was sent to Payne on June 16, and received in Payne's office on June 17. The draft is signed "Prepared by Major Eisenhower." The article was published as drafted except for the changes noted below. In his introduction to the essay, the journal's editor, L. A. Codd, stated that "*Army Ordnance* is privileged to present to its readers as the leading article of this, its tenth anniversary number, a statement on industrial preparedness from the pen of Frederick H. Payne, recently appointed Assistant Secretary of War." The Eisenhower Library has a copy of the full 180-page report that was obtained from the Hoover Presidential Library. Cabinet Offices, War, Plan for Mobilization, 1930, Hoover Presidential Library.

2. This paragraph was deleted in the published version.

3. The last sentence was deleted in the published version.

42

Eisenhower Library
Chief of Staff Diary

SEPTEMBER 18, 1930

On Thurs. Sept. 11, General Moseley and I left town on the B & O to make an inspection of Camp Perry, Ohio, where the National Matches were in progress.[1]

The trip was enjoyable and instructive. We went to dinner at a shooting club on the Sandusky River as guests of Mr. Benedict Crowell.[2]

With him was a Mr. Otis, a very interesting personality, who had experience in 1918 on War Industries Board.[3]

We visited the various activities in Camp Perry on the 12th and 13th—and also went through the Erie Ordnance Depot, which adjoins Camp Perry. A Capt. Brown,[4] in charge, seems very efficient.

Col. Osmund Latrobe[5] served this year as Executive Officer of the National Matches. I lived in a tent with a Lt. Col. Bump.[6] Capt. Paul Hudson[7] acted as General Moseley's aide during the visit.

We returned to Washington Sat. morning, Sept. 14.

1. Camp Perry, adjacent to the army's Erie Ordnance Depot near La Carne, Ohio (thirty miles east of Toledo), has been the home of the annual national pistol and rifle matches for more than eighty years. Civilians as well as military personnel may compete.

2. Benedict Crowell served as assistant secretary of war (director of munitions) during World War I and as a regional director of the National Recovery Administration during the Roosevelt administration. He was coauthor, with Robert Frost Wilson, of *How America Went to War* (New Haven: Yale University Press, 1921).

3. The War Industries Board was established by Congress in 1917 to coordinate the production of war materials during World War I. The board, headed by Bernard Baruch, allocated raw materials, organized production, and fixed prices for both raw materials and finished products.

4. Col. John Edward Brown received his commission during World War I and served with the Ordnance Department until he retired in 1944.

5. Col. Osmund Latrobe, a veteran of the Spanish-American War and World War I, retired in 1938.

6. Col. Arthur Leroy Bump entered the cavalry in 1901 and retired in 1932.

7. Lt. Col. Paul R. Hudson enlisted in the Coast Artillery in 1911, was commissioned a second lieutenant in the infantry in 1917, and retired in 1941.

43

NARA
Records of the Assistant Secretary of War

To Colonel Hasson[1]

SEPTEMBER 26, 1930

1. Attached hereto is the draft of letter prepared by Captain Hagen,[2] addressed to Editor, <u>The Times</u>, Manitowoc, Wisconsin.

2. General Moseley considers that the facts in the case are well presented in Captain Hagen's letter, and is returning it for rewriting as suggested by you yesterday. When the letter is written in final form, please have it prepared for General Moseley's signature.[3]

3. He also believes that it might be desirable to send a copy of this letter to the Editor of the <u>Nation,</u> with the notation that an editorial

in the Manitowoc <u>Times</u> indicates that the <u>Nation</u> has been misinformed concerning the activities of the War Department in preparation for industrial mobilization. If this is done, the letter to the <u>Nation</u> should be conservative in tone and carry the assumption that the Editor of that paper would welcome receipt of correct information on the subject. Your recommendation on this is desired.

4. The General was favorably impressed with your suggestion of enlisting the services of Fred W. Wile,[4] to counteract the effect of publicity such as that contained in recent editorials in the <u>Nation</u> and in the Manitowoc <u>Times</u>. It would be quite desirable to have some person, not connected with this office, take sufficient interest in these matters to place before the public correct information concerning our efforts to prepare adequate plans for industrial mobilization.

1. John Patrick Hasson served most of his military career with the Quartermaster Corps. He retired in 1942 with the rank of colonel.

2. This was probably Harry Edgar Hagan, who served in the Quartermaster Corps during World War I. He retired as a lieutenant colonel in 1942.

3. On September 3, the Manitowoc, Wisconsin, *Times* published an editorial titled, "A Startling Change," alleging that the War Department already had dealt out munitions contracts for the next war, without the knowledge of Congress or the public. The editor wrote: "Modern wars are brought on by greedy self-seekers who intend to enrich themselves by destruction and misery . . . . the only safe way for the public is to 'take the profit out of war' by outlining a definite policy of conscripting wealth. . . . From the facts at hand, it would appear as if the war department has been guilty of an outrageous assumption of power." The *Times* based its editorial on an article by Forest Revere Black, "The Profits of War," published in the *Nation* magazine, on August 27, 1930. Black alleged that an anonymous source within the War Department had provided him with documents relating to "Adjustable Price Contracts," which already had been awarded in the event of a future war emergency. Black considered that the contracts provided the "merchants of death" with incentives to provoke another world conflict.

On October 2, Moseley sent a rejoinder, based on Hagan's draft, to the *Times* editor. Moseley asserted that in fact the War Department's mobilization planning efforts were undertaken pursuant to Congress's National Defense Act of 1920 and were not secret activities undertaken without legislative authorization. Furthermore, Moseley explained that one purpose of such planning was that, "in another war, there may be avoided inequities and difficulties resulting from the types of contracts used in the World War." Moseley also sent a copy to the editor of the *Nation* "in view of the fact that the editorial . . . was largely based upon an article published by you." Moseley to Editor, Manitowoc, Wisconsin, *Times,* October 2, 1930, and *Nation,* October 2, 1930, Records of the Assistant Secretary of War.

4. Frederick William Wile, a noted journalist, served as Berlin correspondent for the London *Daily News,* the *New York Times,* and the Chicago *Tribune* during World War I and served with general headquarters as an intelligence analyst. He then directed the Washington bureau of the Philadelphia *Public Ledger* until 1923, when he

joined the National Broadcasting Company as a radio political analyst. He joined Columbia Broadcasting System in 1929, serving as a radio political commentator.

44

NOVEMBER 12, 1930–DECEMBER 11, 1930

November 12. Have been working for some weeks on a study in which we hope to include the gist of a <u>complete</u> industrial plan for war.

Many difficulties encountered—particularly in selection and arrangement of material. First effort of Planning Branch of little value, whereupon Gen. M. directed me to do it. With some assistance from Maj. Wilkes got out a draft in a week.[1]

Conference yesterday with Bureau of Efficiency on the general subject of coordinating govt. effort in preparing for war. Gen. Moseley presented his idea frankly and completely. Gist of idea is—setup an executive asst. for President, with Cabinet rank, to act for President on all nat. def. matters.

Maj. & Mrs. Price returned from Paris several weeks ago. They will be in this country a month or so. The Paris colony seems to be going strong.

1. By the end of the year the assistant secretary of war had forwarded to President Hoover the finished document, titled "Plan for Industrial Mobilization, 1930." The Planning Branch was not preparing a suitable draft, so Eisenhower, according to this diary entry, wrote the draft, with help from Wilkes. The plan covered all facets of mobilizing the American economy in the event of war. It examined price and trade controls, procurement of raw materials, labor, utilities, transportation, organization of the Executive Branch to coordinate efforts and even included draft legislation authorizing the creation of special agencies. During his studies at the Army Industrial College, Eisenhower wrote a paper that probably was based upon this work for the Planning Branch. The paper is located at the October 2, 1931, entry. The reference to "General M." is Moseley. Eisenhower used the "M" designation for both Moseley and MacArthur.

NOVEMBER 14 [1930]

Letter from Dad last eve says he is holding
500 shares Grt Wes Sugar at 18⅛
500 shares No. Am. Aviation at 8¾
200 shares Com. & South at 12⅞
100 shares Republic Steel (preferred) at 87
100 shares Stand. O. N. J. at 65½
225 Cities Service at 28

Gen. M. sent for me last eve and we had a long conversation at his house. He informed me of impending change in his assignment—and was apparently anxious that I do not feel as if I'd been stuck here and forgotten.

He also said that Asst. Sec. of War would not permit me to leave his office coincidentally with the General's departure. Further, Mr. Payne said he wanted me to take over Gen. M's work as Executive, and wanted to know <u>how</u> they could go about making me a Brig. so the assignment would be an appropriate one.

When the General explained this to be an impossible thing he insisted that whatever could be done for me should be done at once.

The Gen. says he will put the above remark on my efficiency report.

However, it seems I'm to be stuck here, in spite of fact that I'd always understood I was to leave whenever the Gen. did.

I like Mr. Payne—and if new exec. is a fine man the work should be pleasant enough—but much of the kick will be gone because I'm particularly keen about working with Gen. <u>M.</u>

Gen. Moseley will take over duties as Dep. C. of S. on Dec. 22. Col. Irving J. Carr[1] will take the General's place as Exec. for A.S.W.

Yesterday the General took a small group to lunch at Carlton.

Present:　　Mr. Payne
　　　　　　Maj. Lombard (French Army)
　　　　　　Col. Hodges[2]
　　　　　　Maj. Kroner (G-2 Div)[3]
　　　　　　Mr. P. Lloyd-Smith, Editorial Staff Time & Fortune
　　　　　　(Lloyd-Smith committed suicide about Jan. 1932)[4]
　　　　　　General M. and myself

Mr. Lodge[5] is writing an article on "Industrial Preparation" for "Fortune". I conferred with Mr. Smith on project and assigned Hartrick[6] to job of looking up suitable pictures.

The Planning Branch has forwarded completed plans to this office. General M. wants to have one bound in leather to present to President Hoover. He will meet expenses involved. Have assigned Hartrick to job of looking up suitable binding in Washington book stores.

Working on "different" speech for Mr. Payne at War College.[7]

1. Maj. Gen. Irving J. Carr entered service in 1898. He served in the Philippines, the Punitive Expedition to Mexico, and World War I. He directed the Army Industrial College from 1926 to 1930 and was Chief Signal Officer of the Army from 1931 until his retirement in 1934.

2. Brig. Gen. John Neal Hodges (USMA, 1905) served his entire career with the Corps of Engineers. He retired in 1944.

3. Brig. Gen. Hayes A. Kroner served as military attaché, London, from 1934 to 1939. In 1941 he was appointed Chief of the British Section, Military Intelligence Branch, War Department General Staff, later becoming Chief of the Intelligence Branch, a position he held until the end of World War II.

4. Eisenhower noted Lloyd-Smith's death on the margin.

5. Lodge is probably Henry Cabot Lodge, who, two decades later, would serve Eisenhower as a member of the inner circle of advisers during the 1952 presidential campaign and as his representative to the United Nations (1953–61). By this time Lodge already had worked for the New York *Herald-Tribune,* covered the London Naval Conference of 1930, written for *Harper's* on the Kellogg-Briand Pact of 1928, and published an article in the January 1930 issue of *Harper's* entitled, "Our Failure in the Philippines."

6. Guy R. Hartrick served during World War I in the Ordnance Department. He died while in the service in 1935.

7. The speech Eisenhower refers to follows.

45

United States Army Military History Institute
Army War College Records

ADDRESS BY HONORABLE F. H. PAYNE[1]

JANUARY 6, 1931

I was originally scheduled to address this class last fall on the functions of my office and the plans being developed for industrial mobilization. I understand that your investigation and research on these subjects have, in the meantime, been largely completed. A detailed exposition concerning them, given at this late date, would probably be little more than a repetition of facts and opinions that you have already considered.

Consequently, I have decided not to confine myself strictly to any particular subject today, but rather to present my personal views and impressions on some of the questions that have come to my attention in the War Department. Although my remarks will be grouped roughly around the functioning of the Office of The Assistant Secretary of War, I shall not hesitate to bring up any other matters that may occur to me as possessing general interest. I am speaking to you frankly as an individual, and am not delivering a formal address as an official in the War Department. I shall ask you to view my statements in this light.

The background of experience and knowledge that each of us brings to the consideration of his problems is different from that of every other person faced with the same responsibility. In general, my background is that of the industrial and commercial world. In the

World War I assisted, as did many other business men, in the task of procuring from industry the material things demanded by the Army, and in recent months I have been a transplanted business man in an administrative post in the War Department. I speak of these things in order to explain my viewpoint on some of the problems you gentlemen will be called upon to help solve during the remainder of your active careers.

One question that bobs up time and again within the War Department concerns the desirability of having an Assistant Secretary of War responsible for procurement, and for developing the plans for procurement of munitions in war.

I have heard it said that the only reason Section 5-a was written into the National Defense Act[2] was because the General Staff, in the fourteen years of its existence before our entry into the World War, had failed to make provisions for the munitioning of an emergency army. If this were the only reason, it was certainly not an adequate one. It is true that prior to 1917 there had been prepared no comprehensive procurement plan for the Army. Neither did we have a suitable mobilization plan for personnel, nor a well-considered program to govern the purely military activities we were forced to undertake. Everything had to be extemporized; we had failed to prepare plans to meet the situation that actually confronted us, and we paid the price of that failure in time, in money, and in lives. There is no need to try to fix the blame for this failure. Certainly, it would seem that military officials were no more responsible for it than were our political leaders.

In 1920 Congress endeavored to apply the lessons of the World War in directing a reorganization of the War Department. In doing so it did not consider for a moment the abolition of the General Staff as a planning agency for <u>military</u> matters simply because strategic and mobilization plans were lacking in 1917. Why then was there set up a special agency for developing plans not strictly military in nature?

When a military man considers questions of supply he is principally concerned with its storage, transportation, and distribution stages. In bygone times, when munitions were largely obtained by individual effort, or by capture from the enemy, the military man could also largely accept responsibility for the procurement stage of supply. <u>But today satisfaction of military requirements in munitions demands the properly coordinated employment of a nation's productive resources.</u>

Modern war is thus essentially dual in nature—combatant and industrial. Planning for war should take into consideration this dual character of war itself. That is, the Federal Government in time of peace must devise methods for organizing industry promptly upon the outbreak of war, as well as for placing properly trained armies in the field. I think it is obvious that the men who will assist a war-time

President in directing our industrial effort into proper channels must be leaders in the business world. Long ago bitter experience impressed upon us the necessity of entrusting our armies and navies only to the leadership of trained commanders. We visualize the business of armies and navies in war as fighting—and we demand as leaders those men who have studied combat operations throughout their careers. In the same way the men who must direct our industrial effort must be those who are experienced in the methods and customs of business.

The Army's supply services, under the direction of The Assistant Secretary of War, will form the weld—the cementing material—between industry and the fighting land forces. The group developing the plans for procurement, and which will carry on the task of Army procurement in war, must be familiar with the needs and methods of each of the great bodies with which it deals. Actual procurement, being the initial phase of supply, is the point where supply fits directly into the industrial body, and it partakes far more of the industrial than of the military in its character.

Here, then, are demanded the services of specialists—both in the planning and operating stages of procurement. For this purpose a specially trained staff is necessary to the Army, a group that might be termed the War Department Economic Staff. This staff is being gradually built up of selected officers in our procurement services. Its efforts do not duplicate those of the General Staff. On the contrary, it is carrying on vitally important duties in preparing for the procurement of Army supplies in war that are supplementary to the planning work of the General Staff. The things that chiefly concern the War Department General Staff are mobilization of personnel; military organization; operations; questions of strategy; tactics; training, and supply in its storage, transportation, and distribution stages. It cannot be expected to develop solutions to the industrial problems that war will bring to us.

In addition to planning for procurement of Army munitions, the law places within the War Department the responsibility for developing plans to mobilize national industry in war. That is, Congress recognized that the civilian leaders that would be made responsible for our great industrial establishment would need plans, studies, data, and a well-developed organizational program in order to insure the prompt coordination of our economic resources in war. In the work of preparing these plans the Navy has the same interest as the Army, though possibly not in the same degree. The nature of naval equipment requires that the peace-time strength of the fleet approximate its contemplated combat strength much more closely than is the case in our land forces. Consequently, the Army has a far more serious problem in providing for its own prompt expansion in time of war than has the Navy, and is more deeply concerned in assuring that our industrial establishments be put to work speedily and efficiently.

The magnitude and scope of the task almost stagger the imagination. It will never be satisfactorily performed except through the development of an energetic, able, and specialized staff whose members can devote to it the major portion of their active years.

What was more natural, in visualizing the building up of such a staff, than to head it by a civilian? In this age in industrialization and specialization a combat soldier must not be diverted from his mission of organizing and leading armies in order to attempt the solution of all the other National problems we will face in war. The military man has small interest in the mine, the farm, and the factory. On the other hand, the manufacturer loses interest in an article when it has been produced and placed in the hands of the user. Consequently, the civilian viewpoint at the top of a staff, which is charged with a mission more industrial than military in character, would seem to be desirable in the larger aspects of war planning.

Many interesting and important problems must be studied jointly by the two War Department planning staffs. Mobilization of personnel is of course the direct concern of the General Staff. Another General Staff responsibility is that of determining upon types of equipment and the amounts of each type needed in war. But these two problems, especially when considered together, affect our economic situation to the extent that there comes a point when adjustments and coordination become mandatory. The economic staff is primarily the servant of the General Staff. Its job is to procure what the General Staff wants, at the time desired. But let's consider this a little more specifically.

Within recent years we've heard much of motorization and mechanization and have witnessed an increasing tendency to visualize the next war as one of machines. With the growth of this idea the mobilization plans of the General Staff must provide for greater and greater numbers of skilled mechanics, drivers, electricians, machinists, and all other types of skilled workers in the mechanical sciences. Obviously, we cannot strip industry of these classes of skilled workmen if we are going to produce the machines that will be necessary. It seems to me that tactical doctrine cannot be developed independently of, and with no regard for, the production possibilities of the equipment required thereunder. Every feature must be considered—and the plan adopted must contemplate America moving forward against the enemy as a vast integrated machine—all our capabilities and our limitations must be considered.

Such plans as these are not made in a day. In fact they can never be wholly completed. Conditions change. New inventions open up new possibilities and require a complete review of former programs and possibly dictate the adoption of some other line of action. All such questions must be viewed from every angle, and unified War Department opinion concerning them must be developed.

To adjust diverse viewpoints and develop a unified opinion within the War Department is at present not such an easy matter. The War Council, established by law, is an agency for effecting an adjustment between military and non-military questions within the Department. The Council is predominantly civilian in composition, and it cannot be expected to conduct a searching analysis into the details of the important questions brought before it. As a result, many matters affecting mobilization, industrial preparation, our development in aviation, and many other things, are presented to the War Council without any more prior coordination than is obtained in the normal contacts and conferences among junior officials of the Department. I am particularly pleased to learn that General MacArthur is taking steps looking toward the establishment of a military body to serve, under his direction, as an important adjunct to the War Council. This body, I am informed, will be sort of an interlocking directorate composed permanently of the heads of General Staff sections and representatives of the two Assistant Secretaries of War. For the study of any particular question the chief of arm or service, or other official who has a direct responsibility in the matter, will also sit as a temporary member. This proposal envisions a true meeting of minds. It promises the assurance that all important questions in the Department will be studied and analyzed from a comprehensive military viewpoint before being presented to the War Council. Naturally, it will not formulate decisions. The power of decision must, as always, remain in a single head. But its considered recommendations will carry such weight and prestige that higher authority will act contrary to them only after long and earnest study. You may allege that such a body is actually a super-general staff. I am perfectly willing to have you call it what you will. But I am also perfectly certain that properly used under the guidance of enlightened leadership it will be of inestimable value to the War Department.

Another question affecting both the economic and the general staffs is that of Governmental organization for war. Admitting that the central Government must exercise a more definite control over the vast resources of this country in war than it does in peace—how is this going to be done? My attention has recently been directed to a study prepared by an individual officer, which was included in an official report. Briefly, his scheme consists simply in assigning necessary war functions to existing Governmental departments, which will be required to perform the necessary planning duties involved, as well as exercise the corresponding controls in war. The idea appeals because of its apparent simplicity. Its author even intimates that to question the entire suitability of our peace-time Governmental set-up to carry on war is to attack the sacredness of our Anglo-Saxon institutions. By implication we become long-whiskered bolshevists when we contend that, though war is a political act and a continuation of Governmental policy, its successful conduct demands an organization apropos to its nature. His views are not novel. His idea was tested by England in the late war—and rejected when disaster almost caught up as a result. Long and exhaustive studies made in my office have caused us to abandon this scheme as an entirely impractical proposal. The General Staff has reached the same conclusion, as a reference to the General Staff Handbook will demonstrate. We should not quibble about details of organization, but we should have a due regard for experience in adopting a basic scheme for setting up the necessary administrative machinery. Let me quote from a paper prepared in the General Staff.

A Government at war is now confronted not only with a military problem, but with an industrial problem of a nature wholly different from that confronting it in peace. Indeed its attitude toward industry is largely reversed—from one of reliance upon private initiative it becomes one of extreme paternalism. For in peace the commercial and industrial activities of the nation flow from the working of the economic law of supply and demand, with a minimum of interference by governmental regulation. In war this law must be displaced in a large measure by that of military exigency. Some activities take on a much greater importance than others; so some must be expanded, others curtailed, and still others set in entirely new directions, and many must be re-grouped in new relationships. The impulse for this and the subsequent guidance and control of the national activities in their new channels and new relationships, must come from the central Government, which alone can determine how the exigency can best be met. This necessarily entails material changes in the administrative machinery of the Government.

In any event, the brief report to which I have referred is a suggestion only. The work necessary to develop the suggestion into adequate plans is tremendous in volume, and it is to be done in many departments of the Government. All such partial plans are inter-related and inter-dependent. The success of the whole depends upon the success of each of its principal component parts. Any of you that have had experience dealing with the high officials of our Government know that these men are harassed and driven from day to day with current business, be it administrative, political, or personal in nature. Of all these our President is the busiest. If we scatter the responsibilities of the Federal Government in war, and that of preparing adequate plans for war, throughout all these independent departments—how are we going to get our plans prepared? Who is going to have the responsibility for their sufficiency? Certainly we're not going to permit a Chief Coordinator, set up to coordinate current and routine administrative business in the several departments, assume responsibility for the safety of this Nation!

Perhaps the setting up of a peace-time assistant to the President for this one purpose might solve the planning difficulty—but it would not improve the suitability of a cumbersome Governmental organization to carry on the vital executive functions of war.

If the General Staff has an interest in these things, and to my mind there can be no question on this point—there should be exhaustive and complete General Staff studies on the subject. No single man, in one year, or in five years, can study and analyze the applicable factors and considerations that must be weighed before even an outlined plan can be accepted.

My office also has an interest in these matters, particularly from the angle of determining what kind of an organization will be necessary for industrial control. The function of my office is to be ready to turn over to the President and to his industrial organization such plans, studies, and data as we believe will assist them to initiate our industrial effort on a sound basis. I suppose you are familiar with the essentials of the plan we have tentatively adopted. It is proposed that a great industrial body, somewhat similar to the War Industries Board of late 1918, will be the President's medium for exercising general control of industry. Certain related special agencies will undoubtedly be set up, depending upon the desires of the war-time President. Studies setting forth the relationships that should exist between the Federal Government and industry in war, the controls that must be exercised by the President, and means and methods for making Governmental instructions effective, are gradually being developed into concrete plans.

The proposals of my office in these matters have been furnished to the General Staff and informally to the Navy Department. We hope before long to have substantial agreements between these two departments and to be able to submit our conclusions to those other departments that must assist us in the larger phases of preparing for war. In line with this idea we will keep appropriate committees of Congress constantly advised of the contents of bills we expect to submit to that body immediately upon the declaration of a major emergency. Our aim is to have ready at all times such a reasonable, practicable, and sound system for controlling the Nation's industrial effort in war, that it can go into effect without friction and with the complete prior approval of all interested parties.

Thus we see that the development of adequate war plans in the larger sense demands real cooperation. We must attain unity of effort—in no other way can we progress. This idea of cooperation is one on which we can devote some thought with profit to ourselves. In the past year one thing has particularly impressed me. There is distinctly noticeable in this city a "spirit of bureaucracy." This spirit, under my definition, consists in the jealous guarding by every bureau or department of its real or fancied rights, privileges, and prerogatives. Infringement of these by another agency, no matter how excellent the result obtained thereby, is considered a major crime.

From this spirit we in the War Department are not entirely free. I believe of course in orderly distribution of duty and responsibility. But I think also that all of us would make more real progress if we could keep our eyes glued on our mission and pay less attention to the methods used by our contemporaries in contributing their efforts toward the same end.

When we are settling one of our own problems, or when we are dealing with the Navy and other departments, let us remember that we are all in the service of the United States. We must assume that the other fellow is giving his best to his job, and is as deeply interested as we are in arriving at a correct answer to the particular question involved.

In this school and in the Army Industrial College much is being done toward giving to embryo General Staff officers and to procurement personnel an appreciation of the other fellow's problem. In the Industrial College we are particularly pleased that an increasing number of line officers are submitting applications to enter as students, and that the Navy Department is sending a larger number than ever before. The Navy Department has also detailed a splendid officer as instructor in the college. Thus our contacts with naval procurement activities are continuous, and appreciable progress is being made toward synchronization of the procurement plans of the two sister services.

By all means this idea of cooperation must include the Army's civilian components. These organizations come constantly to my attention because of the fact that the Secretary of War has delegated to me responsibility for matters connected with them. Whenever we have a problem before us connected with these components, I believe we should always approach it in the spirit of making the greatest progress possible under the system prescribed by law. We should guard against being hyper-critical in individual cases. We are counting upon Reserve officers to fill most of the positions in the Army's procurement organization in war. On the combat side you will be equally dependent upon them and the National Guard. Let us use every practicable means, within the limits of available funds, to prepare them in every possible way to carry the war load that will be thrust upon them. Particularly we must make every effort to assign every man to the right place to do the job for which he is best fitted.

This question of assignment to duty suggests a peace-time person-nel matter that to me is most interesting. The Army's rigid seniority system has come forcibly to my attention at various times when I have attempted to assign my assistants to posts in accordance with my opin-ion as to their suitability. In some cases I have been informed that the relative rank involved would not permit the contemplated action.

The seniority system of course has certain advantages, and to some extent is used in business. Favoritism is at least partially abolished—but so also is the ability to use a specially qualified individual in the po-sition you desire. Certainly seniority should prevail through those stages that will give the normal man ample opportunity to demon-strate his ability. But in the Army each man is carried forward by ros-ter until he is some fifty or sixty years old, and he is assured of reach-ing the grade of colonel. If it is best for all concerned that the seniority system apply to this extent, should there not be more flexibility in mak-ing assignments? While these things are largely fixed by law, we know that Congress reopens such questions at irregular intervals, and when it does the War Department must be ready to submit well-considered recommendations. Of course this particular matter does not involve me or my office except as we are governed by the law in building up our own organization. But you men will be senior commanders and high ranking General Staff officers, and it will be your duty to assist in the development of War Department conclusions affecting them. My personal opinion, while not definitely crystallized, leans toward the idea that the present system affords too little leeway to encourage abil-ity and effort.

In concluding I'd like to say that my pride in being associated with the Regular Service in equalled only by my high expectation for its fu-ture accomplishments. You are not to imply from my rambling re-marks that I believe anything to be seriously wrong in our Department. On the contrary, I have been continuously impressed by the general worth of our personnel and by the loyalty and efficiency displayed by all ranks, often under adverse and discouraging conditions.

A complete evaluation of the War Department's peace-time work is of course impossible except in the acid test of war. In this we are total-ly unlike industry, which has at all times a definite measure of its own success. The business man's primary interest is to show a profitable re-turn on invested capital—and to do this he strives to produce materi-als or service in the most efficient way possible. The Army's profits must be shown in a constantly increasing excellence in our person-nel—and in the efficiency with which we—without burdening the Country with useless expenditures—make adequate provision for this Nation's defense under any and all circumstances.

I regret that I cannot stay this morning to discuss any questions that might be brought up concerning the matters I have touched upon. But whenever you have the time I wish you'd pay a visit to the Industrial College, the Planning Branch, and the other divisions of my office. I have there a corps of hard-working officers of whom I'm rather proud, but you will find that not one of them will ever be so busy that he won't be glad to lay aside his work to discuss industry and war. In these things all of us must have an interest—and the more we get together to consider them the more surely will we develop satisfactory solutions to the War Department's many problems connected with National Defense.

1. On January 6, 1931, Assistant Secretary of War Frederick Payne delivered a speech based on Eisenhower's draft to the Army War College. Upon return to his office, Payne sent a copy of the speech and a cover letter to the commandant, Maj. Gen. William D. Connor. Payne wrote: "After talking the matter over with Colonel Carr and Major Eisenhower on the way to the office, I am sending you a copy of my talk, as I thought there might be certain parts of it that you would wish to read over. I do not wish to have it printed for distribution, however, as it was meant to be a collection of rambling remarks on my personal impressions, and not a speech. This explains my original reluctance to part with a copy of the manuscript." Payne's letter was attached to the speech copy he sent to the War College. "Functions of the Office of the Assistant Secretary of War," by F. H. Payne, January 6, 1931, 325-D-26, Records of the Army War College, U.S. Army Military History Institute.

2. In the National Defense Act of 1920, Congress reduced the power granted the Army General Staff by the 1916 Defense Act and decentralized army organization. The 1920 legislation fixed responsibility for industrial mobilization and military procurement in a civilian, the assistant secretary of war. In a real sense, Eisenhower's position at this time derived from the 1920 legislation.

46

Eisenhower Library
Chief of Staff Diary

FEBRUARY 3, 1931

Mr. Payne delivered his speech at A.W.C.[1] on Jan. 6. He did not do as well as he usually does, because he read too rapidly and pitched his voice too low. However, he was better than many I've heard there.

Had an attack of "flu", fortunately not a heavy one. Was sick in quarters for a week, returning to duty on Jan. 31. Seems to have weakened my eyes temporarily.

1. Army War College

To Elivera Doud

February 5, 1931

Dear Nana: Out of deference to your eyes and patience this will be a typewritten one. Should I attempt to use a pen it would be worse than useless to expect you to figure out what, if anything, I had to say when you are lying in a hospital bed and probably have lots more interesting things to read. I rather imagine that Mamie has kept you informed of such local news as we have. However, I guess that some of it can bear repeating.

Jim Stanley[1] has been in Washington on and off for about two weeks. He is representing a company that has large holdings along the Mississippi River that are affected by the flood prevention projects in that region. The law provides that the land owners will be reimbursed for damage done their property, and as general counsel of a group of these people he is here trying to make settlement with the government. We have not seen a great deal of him because we do not play very much bridge any more. In fact, I think we have played about twice since we came back from France, and then just for the fun of the thing. We saw Mrs. Robbie one evening when we went to dinner at the Shoreham. Her time, as usual, is taken up playing bridge, and naturally we see very little of her.

The principal topic of conversation in Washington these days is politics. You enjoyed going to the Senate and House so much that it is a shame you had to miss this particular session of Congress. The personal and political differences seem to be more bitter than usual, with the result that various members take great delight in calling names and hurling vituperations at one another. I suppose most of it is done for effect, but nevertheless it makes splendid headlines for Washingtonians to read the following day. Katherine[2] and Mamie are fully determined to go down to the Senate soon and spend a whole day.

I suppose you heard that I was laid low for a little while with flu. The doctor kept me in bed about a week and finally told me that I was a well man and could go back to work. Luckily neither Johnnie nor Mamie showed any signs of catching the disease.

As you know, Johnnie is now in the high third in school. Naturally, no one is quite as insignificant in his eyes as a child in the lower third. He speaks of them as "those little children" and really seems to pity them that they have not done a little better and gotten along further in school. Of course he just left the lower third about a week ago. His last report card was the best one he had received. He knows that I take a great deal of interest in it, and when I came home on the evening it had been handed to him he rushed up with all the excitement in the world in his voice and announced that he had seven A's and three B's. As a matter of fact, he is doing perfectly well in all his studies except writing. He seems to have inherited my helplessness with the pen or pencil. As you know from the letters he sends you his writing is still much more of a scrawl than it is legible penmanship. He has been remarkably free from colds this winter. He plays outside every afternoon and comes in almost exhausted with his cheeks red, and dirty as only a boy can be after digging around in the dirt for an hour or two.

Social demands have been quite heavy this winter, but we have succeeded in ducking some of them, either because of friends in town or some excuse of illness. Next week I think we have four engagements, all late parties. I will be glad when that's over.

We have been expecting Earl[3] to come down from Pennsylvania to spend a day or two with us but have not heard from him in a month. As a matter of fact, we have been expecting him ever since January 1st. He will probably drop in some day and very casually remark that he is here, and whatever prior notice we have will be nothing more than a telegram that will antedate his arrival by an hour or two.

We are very glad that the most recent letters from you and from Dad indicate that you are showing lots of improvement. I certainly hope you take it easy and do not undertake anything for a long, long time that is going to tax your strength unduly. I know you must be looking forward to the trip south in March. We are counting on your spending the month of May with us, and as you know very well, the whole gang will be struggling to keep you here as long as they possibly can.

I went to a luncheon yesterday at the Carlton given by General Moseley in honor of General MacArthur. The Secretary of War and two Assistant Secretaries were also guests. Altogether there were eighty guests at the luncheon. Since I was sick I have not been working very hard, but it is about time I was starting in again, as I have a speech or two to write besides other things to do that require some time and effort. I have not had a leave since the summer of 1926 and am getting a little bit tired of losing a month each year. If things turn out like I hope they will, I am going to take a month and a half or two months sometime this summer. If I do we will have to figure out some interesting expedition to go on and organize a convoy with you, Dad, and the G's and ourselves.

The above may not be so interesting, but what there is of it, you can read. Hurry up and get well, and come flying to Wash. as soon as you possibly can. You know the cherry blossoms come out sometime in

Apr. I think. If we don't have a little more winter weather it will be earlier than that this year.

Lots of love and kisses from your devoted son

P.S. Please give my best to Dr. & Mrs. Black[4]—and say that nothing would please me more than to take him up on his fishing invitation. Don't see how I can do it though!

1. James G. Stanley served as general counsel for the Continental Oil Company of Denver, Colorado, from 1920 until 1928. From 1928 to 1938 he practiced law, specializing in petroleum law. Eisenhower's reference to Stanley probably indicated that the Douds knew him socially from his years in Denver.

2. This was Kathryn Gerow, wife of Leonard Townsend Gerow.

3. Earl Dewey Eisenhower, the second youngest Eisenhower brother, was born in Abilene in 1898. He left Abilene in 1917 for Washington state, where he lived with his brother Edgar while attending the University of Washington. After graduating from Washington with a degree in electrical engineering, he moved to Pittsburgh, Pennsylvania, where he worked for thirty years with the West Penn Power Company. In 1955 Earl moved to LaGrange, Illinois, where he served as business manager of the *Suburban Life* newspaper organization. From 1964 to 1966 he served one term as a Republican member of the Illinois House of Representatives. He died on December 18, 1968.

4. Dr. Herbert A. Black was the long-time family physician for John and Elivera Doud.

48

MEMORANDUM FOR THE ADJUTANT GENERAL

FEBRUARY 14, 1931

1. The Assistant Secretary of War desires that orders be issued directing Lieut. Col. Townsend Whelen,[1] Ordnance Department, to proceed from Springfield Arsenal to Boston to carry out instructions of the Secretary of War, and upon the completion of such duty to return to proper station.

2. By confidential letter, instructions similar to the following should be given to Colonel Whelen:

The inclosed correspondence sets forth the attitude of the War Department concerning proposed legislation having for its purpose the abolition of the arms industry in the United States. It is understood that a committee of the Massachusetts legislature will hold a public hearing in Room 450, State House, Boston, at 10:30 a.m., February 18, 1931, on a bill to make illegal the manufacture of hand arms in that state.[2]

You are directed to attend this hearing, and if called upon by the committee to do so, will explain the importance to national defense, particularly from the standpoint of procurement, of keeping civilian arms factories in being. The War Department's attitude on this subject is briefly set forth in attached copy of letter from the Secretary of War to Smith and Wesson, dated February 4, 1930. In general, your testimony, if given, should follow the lines of your explanation of this subject given to a committee of the Massachusetts legislature under similar circumstances in February, 1931 [. . . .]

Upon completion of the duty described it is desired that you render directly to The Adjutant General a brief report of the action taken, and submit a recommendation as to the advisability and necessity of having an officer of the Regular Army attend hearings in similar cases in the future.

3. Attached hereto are duplicate files of correspondence, one of which should be forwarded to Colonel Whelen. If the other is not desired for The Adjutant General's files, it should be returned to this office.

4. When Colonel Whelen's report has been received it is desired that it be transmitted promptly to this office.

5. Attention is invited to the necessity for expediting issue of above orders and instructions.

By direction of The Assistant Secretary of War

1. Col. Townsend Whelen served in the Philippines and in World War I. In 1920 he was assigned to the Ordnance Department and remained with the department until his retirement as a colonel in 1935.

2. See documents of February 3, 4, 1930, relating to the Massachusetts legislature's earlier attempt to ban the manufacture and sale of handguns. In 1931 similar legislation was introduced that excepted the manufacture and sale of handguns to the federal government and to state and local law enforcement agencies. Whelen to Adjutant General, February 19, 1931, and Payne to Dudley Harmon, February 14, 1931, Records of the Adjutant General's Office, NARA.

49
NARA
Records of the Secretary of War

MEMORANDUM FOR GENERAL MOSELEY

FEBRUARY 17, 1931

Subject: Special measures to assemble and arrange material for presentation to Commission.[1]

1. Conference with heads of General Staff Sections.

a. Explain that task given to General Moseley by Secretary of War is <u>not</u> to develop any plans, but to search out, assemble, and arrange pertinent parts of existing plans for presentation to Commission.

<u>b</u>. Point out the detailed and difficult nature of work, and necessity for promptness. In order to relieve Chiefs of Divisions of as many details as possible, suggest forming of a small committee composed of one officer from each General Staff Division to assist the Deputy Chief of Staff in the work.

<u>c</u>. Request the cooperation of all chiefs in facilitating the work of these representatives.

<u>d</u>. Explain that through the formation of such a committee a body is provided that can appropriately confer with a similar committee in Office, Assistant Secretary of War—also one that can perform detailed work for Deputy Chief of Staff, and for Secretary of Commission.

<u>e</u>. Explain that in any case where there is discovered apparent discrepancies or contradictions in existing plans, the matter will be brought to the attention of appropriate chiefs.

<u>f</u>. If above is agreed to in principle would like to have the following designated by their respective chiefs for this work:
As head of Committee—Major Hughes, G-1[2]
Committee Representatives:
Major Cox, G-1[3]
Major Crane, G-2[4]
Major Fuller, G-3[5]
Major Crawford, G-4
Major Hickam, WPD[6]

2. If Chiefs of General Staff Divisions agree to proposals made in 1, above, call conference as early as practicable of members of subcommittee. If desired, Major Wilkes and his committee also to be present. Discuss problem with these officers. They must understand that no <u>definite</u> directive can be laid down in advance. Their job is as much to discover and decide <u>what</u> to present, as it is to develop the most practicable way of doing so. Undoubtedly the Commission will, from time to time, make demands that will upset a settled routine, and probably disarrange programs. These demands will have to be met. Imagination and intelligence demanded.

3. There should be discussed briefly the procedure to be observed and <u>necessity for cooperation between committees.</u> Each officer should study the resolution itself. Point out particularly that the two committees are to develop a <u>unified</u> War Department presentation.

4. If desired it might be stated that Major Eisenhower has a file on what has gone before, including a synopsis of minutes of previous meetings. Also, that he is familiar with general views of Deputy Chief of Staff on this subject.

1. Moseley's staff served as liaison between the War Department and the War Policies Commission. Eisenhower and his associates coordinated the commission's requests for information from the department, represented the department to the commission, and performed general staff work for the commission.

Congress created the commission in 1930 to define basic national mobilization policies should there be another major war. The impetus for its creation came from the conviction of many Americans that World War I had resulted in large part from lobbying by industrial interests who stood to profit from American involvement. By 1930 a powerful political groundswell pressured Congress to take steps assuring that never again would America be led to war by the "merchants of death" and that if war did come, sacrifices, as well as profits, would be distributed equitably. The War Policies Commission, chaired by Secretary of War Patrick Hurley and consisting of five other cabinet members, four senators, and four congressmen, was tasked with studying such issues and developing policy guidelines for any future mobilization.

2. Everett S. Hughes (USMA, 1908), a close friend of Eisenhower, served with the Army Ordnance Department during World War I and with the War Department's General Staff from 1928 to 1932. During World War II he served as Deputy Chief of Staff, European Theater of Operations (ETO), and Special Assistant to the Theater Commander, ETO. At the end of the war, Hughes was appointed Inspector General of the Army. From 1946 until his retirement in 1949, Hughes served as the Army's Chief of Ordnance.

3. This possibly was Richard Ferguson Cox. He enlisted in the army in 1910 and retired as a brigadier general in 1940.

4. This possibly was John Alden Crane. He served in the Philippines twice, from 1908 to 1910 and from 1919 to 1921, and in World War I. He retired as a brigadier general in 1946.

5. Several Fullers and Crawfords held officers' ranks at this time and any of them could have been detailed to the War Department.

6. This likely was Horace Meek Hickham, who served during World War I with the Army Air Service. Eisenhower evidently misspelled the name. From 1919 to 1923 he was detailed to the office of the chief of the Army Air Corps. From 1932 to 1934 Lieutenant Colonel Hickham was commanding officer of the Corp's 3d Attack Group. He died in an airplane crash on November 5, 1934. Hickham Field, Hawaii, was named in his honor.

50

NARA
Records of the Secretary of War

Memorandum to General Moseley

February 18, 1931

Subject: Conference with committees organized to assemble material for presentation to Commission.

1. All members of both committees should be present at a conference to be held as soon as practicable after conference with Assistant Chiefs of Staff. While it is expected that this work will take most of the

time of officers, it is not desirable to issue formal order placing them on special duty. In many cases things with which no one else is familiar can be handled by these officers in a few minutes. Good judgment and tact and cooperation of chiefs will solve difficulties.

2. Discuss problem with these officers. They must understand that no <u>definite</u> directive can be laid down in advance. Their job is as much to discover and decide what to prepare, as it is to develop the most practicable way of presenting it to Commission. Undoubtedly the Commission will, from time to time, make demands that will upset or disarrange programs. These demands will have to be met. Imagination and intelligence are demanded.

3. There should be discussed briefly the procedure to be observed and <u>necessity for cooperation between committees.</u> Each officer should study the resolution itself. Point out particularly that the two committees are to develop a <u>unified</u> War Department presentation. Also, whenever it appears desirable the committees should confer with representatives of other departments.

4. If desired it might be stated that Major Eisenhower has a file on what has gone before. Also, that he is familiar with general views of Deputy Chief of Staff on this subject.

51

NARA
Records of the Secretary of War

MEMORANDUM FOR GENERAL MOSELEY

FEBRUARY 25, 1931

1. I was informed by Mr. Martyn that he believes Mr. Baruch made a definite recommendation to the Secretary of War concerning a suitable person to fill the job as executive assistant to Mr. Hadley[1] on the Commission. Effort should be made to find out whether this is true, and if so the person concerned should be communicated with immediately. From an informal note furnished me from the Secretary of War's office, I am of the opinion that Mr. Baruch recommended a man named <u>Robert Montgomery.</u>[2] I looked up this man in Who's Who and believe that from the training and experience he would be <u>eminently satisfactory</u> if he would consent to serve. Certainly the particular matter of selecting the executive assistant should receive prompt attention, as Mr. Hadley's secretary informs me that he intends to do nothing pending the naming of such an assistant.

2. I am just in receipt of a telegram from the Commander of the American Legion.[3] Due to other engagements he cannot arrive in Washington until 11:00 o'clock on the morning of the 5th of March,

but states that he will be available to the Commission at any hour during the rest of the day. He requests immediate telegraphic information as to the hour his appearance is desired. In view of the fact that we have received answers from neither General Pershing nor the Commander of the Veterans of Foreign Wars,[4] there might be some difficulty about giving the American Legion Commander a morning date, and it seems to me that to be safe the hour of 2:00 P.M. should be designated.

3. The question concerning the appropriation of $50,000, of which I spoke to you this morning, can be handled by the designation of the Finance Officer of the Army as the disbursing officer for the Commission. Colonel Truesdell[5] states that this is perfectly feasible and will occasion no difficulty in spite of the fact that the appropriation will actually be authorized under the Independent Offices Bill. May I draw up a telegram to this man?[6]

1. Lindley Hoag Hadley of Washington state served nine terms in Congress (1915–33). He was appointed one of the four House members on the commission and also served as the commission's secretary.

2. Robert H. Montgomery, an attorney and accountant, directed procurement for the Army General Staff in 1918 before moving later that year to the War Industries Board as a member of the Price-Fixing Committee. The secretary of war followed Eisenhower's recommendation and appointed Montgomery to replace Hadley.

3. Ralph Thomas O'Neil, a veteran of World War I, was national commander of the American Legion (1930–31).

4. Paul Wolman, a World War I veteran and a Baltimore attorney and civic leader, was national commander of the Veterans of Foreign Wars.

5. This probably is Karl Truesdell. From 1927 to 1931 he was detailed to the War Department General Staff, where he served as chief of budget and legislation. Truesdell retired in 1946 as a major general.

6. Eisenhower scribbled this last sentence as a marginal note next to Montgomery's name.

52   NARA
                                                  Records of the Secretary of War

FEBRUARY 27, 1931

Subject: Notes on conference held by the Secretary of War at noon February 27, 1931, and attended by Major General Moseley and Major Eisenhower.[1]

1. The Secretary of War was informed that the Commander of the American Legion, Mr. O'Neill, had expressed his intention to appear before the Commission at 2 P.M., March 5th. The Secretary was also

informed that none of the other persons invited to appear before the Commission on that date had so far accepted. These persons are: Mr. William Green, President, American Federation of Labor; General John J. Pershing; Mr. Paul Wolman, Commander, Veterans of Foreign Wars; Mr. Bernard M. Baruch.

2. The Secretary directed that a telegram be sent immediately to Mr. Benedict Crowell,[2] inviting him to appear before the Commission at 10 A.M., March 5th. He also directed that the Commander of the Military Order of the World War (General Delafield)[3] and the Commander of the Disabled Veterans of the World War be invited to appear before the Commission later, on the same morning.

3. The Secretary directed that Mr. Baruch be invited to appear before the Commission at 10 A.M., March 6th. He directed further that invitations be extended to Mr. Newton C. Baker, Mr. Frank Scott, and Mr. Brookins,[4] and any other persons that might be able to assist the Commission in its investigations.

4. The Secretary stated that an opening statement for the March 5th meeting should be prepared, to be delivered by himself. He wished to emphasize in this statement that preliminary meetings of the Commission for purposes of organization and for discussing the general nature of the problem in hand had been held and that the present meeting was the first open hearing conducted by the Commission, and lastly that the statement include a public invitation to all interested persons to appear and offer their opinions and ideas to the Commission concerning the work to be performed.

1. Evidently this was a memorandum of the conference for Eisenhower's files or for the official office file of the assistant secretary of war.

2. Benedict Crowell served as assistant secretary of war during World War I. He later served as a regional director of the National Recovery Administration and in 1940 as a consultant to the secretary of war.

3. John Ross Delafield, a prosperous New York attorney and oil company executive, served during World War I as a colonel in the army's Ordnance Department and as chair of the War Department's Board of Contract Adjustment. From 1923 to 1926 he was president of the Reserve Officers' Association and from 1930 to 1933 served as commander of the Military Order of the World War.

4. Newton Baker served as President Woodrow Wilson's secretary of war from 1916 until 1921. Appointed to the Permanent Court of International Arbitration at the Hague in 1928, Baker was a strong contender for the Democratic presidential nomination in 1932. Baker died in 1937.

This probably was Frank Augustus Scott, who in World War I was chair of the General Munitions Board.

This may have been Homer DeWilton Brookins, who was the business manager of the *Christian Inquirer* (later the *Watchman-Examiner*). Brookins died on April 3, 1938.

To Herbert E. Swope[1]

MARCH 11, 1931

Dear Mr. Swope: Mr. Montgomery informs me that you desire a short explanation of the proposal for an office of "Public Information" as shown in the tentative industrial plan prepared in the office of The Assistant Secretary of War.

While I cannot give you any authoritative "War Department opinion" on this matter, I can give you my personal understanding of it as gathered in many conferences during the time the personnel of this office was engaged in assembling the tentative plan. In fact I doubt that there can be said to be any approved War Department policy affecting the whole subject. Plans have been made in detail to meet our own publicity needs in an emergency, but in the broader sense current proposals should be considered only in the nature of suggestions.

Fundamentally the purpose of the tentative plan in this respect is to indicate the desirability of an organization through which a war-time President may be enabled to maintain a unified public opinion in support of the war effort. It is assumed that war would be declared by this country only in response to a definite expression of the popular will, and it is obvious that without the support of public opinion no program for the conduct of war can succeed. While true that in a long and exhausting war public opinion will support war measures only if the population is confident that the whole program is sound and ably administered, it is also true that discriminatory publicity, propaganda, and censorship are powerful agents in molding and sustaining the desired national attitude toward war. Policies affecting these must be formulated and unified by someone directly responsible to the President.

The organization set up to assist in the formulation and execution of these policies will have primary contact with all existing publicity organizations, such as newspapers and periodicals, radio, motion pictures, and speakers' bureaus. The susceptibility of these to Federal control should be as great as will that of ordinary industrial establishments.

The principal functions of the President in this respect have to do both with positive and with negative information, that is, with publicity and with censorship. Whether or not he will center responsibility for both in one man, or provide for two separate organizations to be coordinated by the President in person, seems relatively unimportant.

While I personally believe one man, under the President, should have this responsibility, I admit it could be worked otherwise.

The idea is to <u>unify</u> our efforts in this field under the direction of an expert. Some means must be provided to keep our population informed of important happenings, but we must guard against a trend toward hysteria on one hand and pessimism and defeatism on the other. We want one hundred and twenty million people to think alike, and along those lines that will make possible a unified and continuous military, economic, industrial, and moral effort.

I realize that the above is in the main more a repetition of glittering generalities than it is an exposition of concrete proposals. In a letter of this sort it could not well be otherwise. We have our detailed plans for setting up the War Department publicity agencies, and, as indicated in the tentative plan prepared by The Assistant Secretary of War, these agencies are expected to be subsidiary and subordinate to the central publicity agency set up by the war-time President. We are principally concerned in demonstrating that the moral force of the Nation is in the end a <u>basic</u> force, and that this force will be developed to its full possibilities only if the program that it must support is <u>sound,</u> and if adequate measures are adopted to unify and control the agencies principally responsible for the development of public opinion.

While I could send you some of the detailed studies that have been prepared in the War Department on this subject, I believe they would be of little assistance. We cannot expect any Commission to recommend to the Congress the adoption of anything more specific than basic principles. Those are important and lasting—organization, methods, and detailed plans must be adopted to the exigencies of the moment.

Mr. Montgomery would very much like to have you appear before the Commission either Monday, the 16th of March, or Wednesday, the 18th, preferably the former. The meetings will start at 10:00 A.M., and while we have so far scheduled two or three other witnesses, none of them will probably use more than a few minutes.

Will you please wire Mr. Montgomery, Room 157, State, War, and Navy Building, informing him whether or not we can count on your appearance before the Commission on either of the dates mentioned?

1. Herbert Bayard Swope was noted for aggressive journalism. After working on several major newspapers, Swope worked for Joseph Pulitzer's New York *World* in 1909. From 1914 to 1916 he covered the European War and in 1917 won the first Pulitzer Prize for journalism. He led the American press delegation to the Paris Peace Conference, arguing successfully against the conference's prohibition against press representatives covering conference proceedings. During World War II he served as a personal consultant to the secretary of war. In 1946, President Tru-

man appointed him to the U.S. delegation to the United Nations, which proposed the so-called Baruch Plan for the international control of atomic energy.

54

MARCH 13, 1931–MAY 18, 1931

MARCH 13

The Commission created by Public Resolution, 98,—71st Congress, started holding public hearings on March 5, in Senate Office Building. I am sort of a "working" Secretary for the Commission but with no official title or authority.

Sec. of War Hurley is Chairman
Senator David A. Reed[1] is Vice-Chairman
Congressman Lindly H. Hadley is Secretary (also a member)
Robert H. Montgomery of New York is Executive Secretary.

He has secured offices in State War & Navy Bldg. and Capt. Hartrick and I have done all the secretarial work to date. We are not detailed to him as assistants—but through an understanding with Mr. Hurley and Gen. Moseley we keep on the job with him.

Major Wilkes and Maj. Hughes head two committees in the War Dept. to prepare a War Dept. presentation of plans that have been developed in the last 10 years.

The purpose of the Commission is:
to promote peace
to consider amending the constitution to provide
that private property may be taken by Congress for public use during war;
to study and consider methods for equalizing the burdens and removing the profits from war;
to study policies that should be pursued in the event of war.

Many interesting witnesses have been heard. Among these are:
Bernard M. Baruch*
Honorable Newton D. Baker*
Daniel Willard*[2] (B&O)
Leonard Ayres*[3]
George N. Peek*[4]
Mr. O'Neil (Commander American Legion)
Mr. Kirby (Rep. Disabled Veterans)
John Ross Delafield
Admiral McGowan[5]
John M. Hancock*
Mr. Ashton (President Am. R.R. Assn.)

Other prominent men will be heard next week.

On the Commission are 6 Cabinet Officers, 4 Senators and 4 Congressmen. *Those starred have impressed me as particularly able men. I have been impressed by

Mr. Hurley

Senator Robinson (Arkansas) [6]

Mr. McSwain [7]

Senator Vandenberg [8]

Ross Collins [9] of Mississippi is either stupid or a shrewd charlatan.

Several members have never attended a public hearing. Among these are Sec. of Ag. Hyde—Sec. of Commerce Robert P. Lamont, Sec. Adams & Attny. Gen. Mitchell. Also Senator Reed. [10]

1. David Aiken Reed, a major in World War I, served two terms as a U.S. senator from Pennsylvania (1923–35). A delegate to the 1930 London Naval Conference, he also served as a member of the American Battle Monuments Commission (1923–47).

2. A prominent railroad executive, Willard was president of the Baltimore and Ohio Railroad from 1910 to 1941 and on the board of directors of several other railroads. During World War I he served as chairman of the President's Advisory Commission to the Council of National Defense before his appointment to the War Industries Board. Willard died in 1942.

3. Leonard Porter Ayres became director of education and statistics with the Russell Sage Foundation in 1908. He served as director of the Division of Statistics, War Industries Board, and as chief of statistics, U.S. Army, in World War I. After the war he was economic adviser to the Dawes Commission. He died in 1946.

4. George Nelson Peek, an executive with both the Moline Plow Company and the John Deere Company, served with the War Industries Board in 1918 as commissioner of finished products and from 1925 to 1928 was president of the American Council on Agriculture. He was one of the leaders in Alfred Smith's 1928 presidential campaign. In 1933, President Roosevelt appointed him administrator of the Agricultural Adjustment Administration. He died in 1943.

5. Rear Admiral Samuel McGowan served as Paymaster General and Chief Supply Officer of the Navy during World War I. McGowan retired in 1920. He died in 1934.

6. Robinson served in the U.S. House of Representatives from 1903 to 1913 and in the U.S. Senate from 1918 to 1937. He chaired the Democratic National Conventions in 1920, 1928, and 1936. In 1928 he was Democratic presidential candidate Al Smith's vice presidential running mate. He was Senate majority leader at the time of his death in 1937.

7. John J. McSwain, an attorney, served in World War I. He was elected to Congress from South Carolina in 1921, serving continuously until his death in 1936.

8. Arthur Vandenberg, editor and publisher of the Grand Rapids, Michigan, *Herald,* was appointed to the U.S. Senate in 1928, serving until his death in 1951. A leading isolationist early in his political career, by 1945 he had changed his thinking. In 1946, when serving as chairman of the Senate Committee on Foreign Affairs, he was instrumental in securing the passage of the Marshall Plan. His support of bi-

partisanship in foreign policy during the early years of the Cold War won him the gratitude of internationalists such as Eisenhower.

9. Ross Alexander Collins, attorney general of Mississippi (1912–20), was elected to Congress for seven consecutive terms (1921–35). After suffering defeat in a bid for a Senate seat, he ran again for Congress, serving from 1937 to 1943.

10. Arthur M. Hyde, governor of Missouri in 1921, served from 1929 to 1933 as President Hoover's secretary of agriculture. He died in 1947.

Robert P. Lamont achieved the rank of colonel as Chief of Procurement, Army Ordnance, in World War I. President Herbert Hoover selected him as his secretary of commerce (1929–32). Lamont died in 1948.

Charles Francis Adams, great-great-grandson of President John Adams, served from 1929 to 1933 as secretary of the Navy and played a prominent role in the 1930 London Naval Conference.

William DeWitt Mitchell served as President Coolidge's solicitor general, a position he held until Hoover's election. Hoover appointed him attorney general.

MARCH 28

Lots of troubles with my insides lately.[1] Have been bothered for 5–6 years with something that seems to border upon dysentery. Doctors have come to the conclusion that it is a result of nervousness, lack of exercise, etc. Am taking some medicine at the moment that for a day or so seemed to be exactly right—but now am apparently no different from usual.

Gen. Moseley presented me with a nice brief case lately.

Talked on telephone with Joel Carlson[2] last night, who is much alarmed about Mother Doud's condition. We wired Dad at once (who is in Pueblo at Hospital with Mother) to see whether Mamie should go out there.

1. Eisenhower refers to his chronic stomach and intestinal problems. See also entry of January 31, 1938.

2. Joel Carlson, or "Uncle Joel" as Mamie always called him, was the brother of Mamie's mother, Elivera M. Carlson Doud.

APRIL 27

Doctors report, after long X-ray exam. that they can find nothing wrong with my insides.

Mr. Payne, Mrs. Payne and Lt. Kimble[1] left for Panama in Ford plane Apr. 8. Arrived there about 14th. After a week's stay the Paynes & Bill Gruber (who had gone down by boat) returned by boat acct. of troubles in Central America. Supposed to arrive at port today, I believe.

The W.D. program (plans, etc.) is to be presented to War Policies Commission by Gen. MacArthur on May 13. Gen. M.[2] expects me to prepare the paper, after all facts have been submitted by Wilkes & Hughes.

1. Brig. Gen. Frederick von Harten Kimble (USMA, 1918), like Eisenhower, was an aide to General Moseley. From 1929 to 1934 he served as an aide to the assistant secretary of war and to the White House. From 1940 to 1941 he was an aide to the Chief of Staff of the Army Air Corps. During World War II he commanded the Tuskegee Flying School at Tuskegee, Alabama. He retired in 1953.

2. The "Gen. M." reference is to MacArthur, who had assumed the position of Army Chief of Staff the previous November, after the expiration of his tour of duty as commander of the Philippine Department, Manila. He served as Chief of Staff until the late summer of 1935, when Roosevelt appointed MacArthur as Military Advisor to the Philippine Commonwealth.

The W. D. presented its story to the War Policies Commission on May 13. General MacArthur read the statement. The material for the presentation was proposed in General staff and office of Asst. Sec. War. I worked for 10 days (and nights) getting it ready.

Everything went off splendidly. Gen. MacA. said the paper was "masterly"—and it seemed to make a general hit. We summarized it in a press release—and Gen. MacA. is to make a short movie-tone of a synopsis.[1]

1. It is difficult to determine the authorship of MacArthur's long statement read to the War Policies Commission on May 13. Eisenhower's diary entry indicates that at a minimum he coordinated a staff effort that produced the document. He may have been editor only; he may have authored portions of it; or he may have written the entire twenty-four-page statement from staff papers on various subjects addressed by the final document. The style of the report seems much like Eisenhower's. The War Policies Commission had been created in response to powerful pacifistic currents in America, particularly the widespread opinion that American industry's enormous wartime profits were at best unconscionable luxuries and at worst incentives for the powerful to push America into the European slaughter. MacArthur's statement attempted to address such concerns. But the statement also expressed the War Department's interest in a more realistic view of national security preparedness. The following quotation is taken from the statement's introduction, "Promotion of Peace."

> As the passage of time thrusts our war experience further into the background of the national memory, more and more is forgotten of the tragedy of suffering, waste, and deprivation that war entails. . . . But through the very nature of their profession, Army and Navy officers are not allowed to forget the true meaning of war, nor to fall into a state of mind that will permit them to contemplate with indifference or complacency the horrors of war, or the possibility of its recurrence. . . . The Department holds to the belief, so often reiterated by our first President, that a reasonable preparation for defense is one of the best guarantees of peace. . . . In our attempts to equalize the burdens of, and remove the profits from, war, we must guard against the tendency to over-emphasize administrative efficiency and under-emphasize national effectiveness. The objective of any war-

ring nation is victory, immediate and complete. . . . It is conceivable that a war might be conducted with such great regard for individual justice and administrative efficiency as to make impossible those evils whose existence in past wars inspired the drafting of Public Resolution 98. . . . It is also conceivable that the outcome of such a war would be defeat. With defeat would come burdens beside which those we are considering would be relatively insignificant.

Public Resolution 98, referred to above, authorized the War Policies Commission. Statement of Douglas MacArthur, Chief of Staff, U.S. Army, before the War Policies Commission, May 13, 1931, Records of the Secretary of War, NARA.

55   United States Military Academy Library
                 Sixty-Second Annual Report of the Association of Graduates

"To the Graduating Class"

Address by the Honorable Frederick H. Payne[1]

I am sure that for many months you members of the graduating class have been looking forward eagerly to June 11, 1931, and I am happy to be a participant in this momentous event in your lives. Judging from my contacts with older graduates, I feel safe in saying that in your retrospections during the years to come this date will lose none of its present importance. Today you change the color of your uniform and leave this spot to follow your respective destinies to the far corners of the earth. Yet in a very real sense you will forever be an inseparable part of this institution. Wherever you go you will be known as West Pointers—whatever you do will effect, for good or for ill, the reputation of West Point. The privilege that has been yours of attending the Military Academy as a cadet has imposed upon you a corresponding obligation to her that must remain with you to the end.

You could not expect me, as a layman, to attempt an interpretation of West Point's ideals, of her traditions, and of her standards, to you who have just undergone a four years' enriching experience within her walls. But I welcome this opportunity to pay my sincere tribute to your Alma Mater and to what she stands for in the minds of loyal Americans. From West Point graduates the Country has learned to expect a high standard of accomplishment—accomplishment in its broadest sense. Fundamentally, it is for this reason that this great school holds such an enviable and almost unique position in our national pride and traditions.

The majority of you will continue in the military service, but others, due to a variety of circumstances, will, as is always the case, find yourselves sooner or later engaged in civilian activities. Whether your paths lead to the varied duties and far-flung stations of the Army—to the marts of trade—to the factories of industry—to the laboratories of science—or to the farms and fields of our great agricultural regions, there will be expected of you the kind of accomplishment that is based on self-application, on integrity of purpose, and on firmness of character—a character too bold supinely to suffer wrong, too upright purposely to inflict wrong.

Those of you who remain in the service will become at once important members of the Regular Army, in control of men whose loyalty and devotion will be won and held by their recognition of like qualities in you. Later years will bring wider responsibilities and corresponding promotion—but only as a lieutenant will you be privileged to exercise immediate command over those composing the rank and file of the Army. No matter if you should be the youngest soldier in your platoon—you must aspire to, and reach the position of "the old man." The troubles of your men must be yours—you must take their burdens upon your shoulders, and their welfare must become your very reason for existence. You must continue to develop yourself to meet every requirement made upon the platoon commander in garrison and in the field. The sergeant with his rows of service stripes and the rawest recruit must alike look to you as leader. When you have bound them to you with ties of mutual confidence and esteem—you will have done your part in making your unit worthy of its place in an Army justly proud of its traditions and of the real leaders it has produced.

The Regular Establishment is, of course, but one of the components of the Army of the United States. The members of the others—the National Guard and the Organized Reserves—are not professional soldiers as you will be. But their zeal, their patriotism, and their abilities are, equally with yours, devoted to the best interests of our Country. America's wars have always been fought and won by a citizen soldiery. If we are ever forced to fight again, the same conditions will hold true, and the nucleus of the land forces we would need exists today in the three components.

Because of the special training you receive you will serve as technical instructors for the citizen elements of the Army. By your efficiency, by your spirit of helpfulness, and by your respect for the opinions and feelings of others, you will assist in developing a national defense system that, if need be, will stand all tests, even to the ultimate test of war. In this task the prestige of West Point and the Regular Army training will be yours. The citizen soldiers with whom you work will be contributing voluntarily from their time and talents to an unselfish and patriotic purpose. They will be more than ready to meet you halfway in your efforts to provide for the continued safety of the Nation. In these positions it will be particularly important that you do not become dogmatic. Progress toward the basic objective of instruction is more to be sought than perfection in mechanical detail. Not only will duty with the citizen components furnish some of your greatest opportunities for service, but it will bring to you a particular broadening and valuable personal experience.

It has been charged that Army training tends to limit the mental horizon and to restrict the viewpoint, and perhaps this may have once been partially true. It is not so now. To be worthy of his commission the officer must delve into questions unlimited in their diversity and scope. For modern war is a struggle of peoples—it is no longer a semisporting contest between professional armies. To meet the demands of armed conflict every material resource, and every individual in the state must be called upon to bear a proportionate share of the burden. As a consequence, the study of warfare today includes the consideration of methods for unifying and utilizing the efforts of a whole nation to protect itself against aggression. An officer passing through a complete military educational system is concerned with financial, industrial, social, and governmental questions, for all of which he must have due regard as he solves his own problems in actual tactics and strategy. He must appreciate the aspirations of our people, and understand the governmental institutions created to promote the realization of those aspirations.

Ours is a peace-loving nation. The professional officer above all others should visualize clearly the sufferings and hardships of war, and should be active in studying methods by which such catastrophes may be avoided. And I would ask you to remember that the Army points with pardonable pride to the services it has performed in the interests of peace and of pacification. Having once fought to victory in the cause of Country, the American soldier has ever been ready to lay aside his arms and devote his efforts to the alleviation of suffering and to the betterment and uplifting of humanity.

In this Country there is no room for the jingoist, least of all among the paid public servants of the Government. Our Army is maintained to preserve the peace—not to provoke war. It keeps itself ready, and as far as possible the Nation ready, to defend our liberties and our rights, but under our national policies it can never be an instrument forged to violate the rights and liberties of others. Your words and deeds must reflect a clear appreciation of this truth.

I would impress upon you then that you are at the threshold of a continuing task that will demand the best from each of you. Today your names are entered on the rolls of the officers of the Regular Army in the order in which you have stood in your class. Time will bring changes in that order. There will be those who display such outstanding ability as leaders that there will come to them positions of the greatest responsibility, and the world will confer on them the honors they have earned. West Point lessons in good sportsmanship will cause you to rejoice in the success of your fellows as much as you will in your own.

And now on behalf of the Secretary of War and every one of his subordinates, I bid you welcome to the commissioned ranks of the Army. Because of those qualities that have enabled you to attain the standards West Point establishes for graduation, we expect much from you. My heartiest congratulations and best wishes go with you.

1. Eisenhower had drafted Payne's speech (see diary entry of June 17), but since the draft did not survive it is impossible to determine how closely Payne's address to the class of 1931 conformed to what Eisenhower had given him. The speech text included here is from the *Sixty-Second Annual Report of the Association of Graduates of the United States Military Academy at West Point, New York, June 10, 1931* (Chicago: Lakeside Press, R. R. Donnelley, 1931), 45–48.

56 Eisenhower Library
Chief of Staff Diary

JUNE 17, 1931–JUNE 25, 1931

JUNE 17

Lately have prepared a good many addresses for Mr. Payne, including the graduating talk at West Point given June 11. According to his story he received many compliments on it.

Have made arrangements to take a 2 mos. leave this summer, leaving here on or before July 1. Everything seems to be pretty well up to date in the office.

Capt. Bomar[1] will report for duty here shortly after July 1.

1. Col. Ernest C. Bomar entered service in 1917. In 1931 he served in the Ordnance Department. He retired in 1952.

JUNE 25, 1931

Went to Aberdeen Tuesday, June 23, with Gen. Moseley to see a demonstration of some new tanks. One, the T-2 was of medium weight—and of Ordnance manufacture. The other was a British Cardan-Lloyd—6 ton. The latter has flexible track-engine on side to lower profile and very capable tank. The medium was a powerful tank and operated well.[1]

1. Eisenhower's interest in tank warfare began in 1918 and 1919 when he trained tank units at Camp Meade, Maryland, Camp Colt, Pennsylvania, Camp Dix, New Jersey, and Fort Benning, Georgia.

"BRIEF HISTORY OF PLANNING FOR PROCUREMENT
AND INDUSTRIAL MOBILIZATION"[1]

[OCTOBER 2, 1931]

In preparing a synopsis of ten years' progress in procurement planning and preparation for industrial mobilization it is rather difficult to follow a rigid chronological sequence, or to demonstrate each event to be the logical result of a preceding cause.

While the record of what took place is usually available, a statement of reasons therefore is not often found in existing documents. At times it is even impossible to discover any exact account of significant incidents.

For the purposes of this discussion Section 5a of the National Defense Act of 1920 is taken as the genesis of our present system of procurement planning. That law contains an ambiguity. It charges the Assistant Secretary of War with responsibility for "the assurance of adequate provision for the mobilization of matériel and organizations essential to war-time needs", but it also directs the General Staff "to prepare plans for . . . the mobilization of the manhood of the Nation and its material resources in an emergency."

With nothing but this law to guide him, a student of today would certainly be at a loss in determining a proper boundary between the functions of the General Staff and those of the Assistant Secretary of War. But, as you know, the Harbord Board was convened very soon after the passage of that act, and one of its tasks was the establishment of such a boundary line. General Orders No. 41, 1921, gave force to the conclusions of the board. That portion of the order dealing with the mobilization responsibilities of the General Staff omits the words "and of its material resources." This was done deliberately, as is evidenced by the fact that these words appear in the original drafts of the board's conclusions, but were omitted in the final document. Thus a question that might have become most vexing was settled administratively in such a way that the two principal sub-divisions in the War Department could be perfectly sure of the missions with which they were respectively charged.

In spite of this, the misunderstandings that have at times arisen with respect to the proper spheres of the General Staff and the Assistant Secretary of War form an interesting chapter in the history of procurement planning. Nevertheless, the provisions of G.O. No. 41 (which have been incorporated in Army Regulations) remain in force. Furthermore, there is an encouraging tendency among all officers, both in and out of the procurement services, to look upon Section 5a as furnishing a logical solution to procurement problems, and not as an arbitrary directive to be grudgingly accepted simply because "it is the law".

One illustration of this changed attitude was afforded some months ago by the smooth collaboration between the Assistant Secretary of War and the General Staff in the preparation of a unified War Department planning policy to be enunciated before the War Policies Commission. Another is found in the substance of a recent talk by the Deputy Chief of Staff before the Army War College. I understand that he is to address this class at a later date, and I feel sure he will reiterate his opinion on this matter.

The creation of the General Council early in 1931 accelerated this tendency. Composed of the Deputy Chief of Staff, the heads of the General Staff sections, the chiefs of arms and services, a representative of the Assistant Secretary of War, and one or two others, it formulates advisory opinion as to War Department policies. This course of action has gone far to eliminate friction between the Assistant Secretary's office and the General Staff.

With this dividing line once clearly defined, the first job of the Assistant Secretary in 1921 was to analyze his job, determine its principal parts, and set up an organization to aid him perform it. An appropriate name for this chapter in our history is the "period of conferences." The Assistant Secretary had been given a task without parallel or precedent in any peace-time army organization. His first move was to obtain opinions from all authoritative sources regarding organization and methods best adapted to the accomplishment of his mission.

Numerous conferences were held with prominent civilians who had served on the War Industries Board. Liaison was maintained with engineering societies and trade associations. Opinions and recommendations from many sources are set forth in the early records of the office.

A staff of civilian advisors was appointed, composed largely of former War Industries Board personnel. The Chiefs of supply branches were directed to establish procurement planning sections in their respective offices. An early task of these sections was the study of strategic raw materials. Frequent meetings were held between the personnel of these sections and that of the Assistant Secretary's office. Indeed in October, 1922, apparently taking a page from the book of the Lion Tamer's Club, an officer order was issued inaugurating a monthly luncheon schedule at the Army and Navy Club to be attended by all personnel on this duty.

From these early beginnings the office developed rapidly. The first heading under which we will examine our ten-year progress is that of organization. Just because I take this first, do not accuse me of worshipping too devoutly at the altar of the great god "Organization." So-called "correct organization" is, of course, no sure cure for every evil in operation. But in discussing other subjects it is necessary to refer by name to some of the agencies brought into being in response to the provisions of Section 5a. Accordingly, we will examine at once their origin and reasons for existence.

Mr. Wainwright,[2] the first Assistant Secretary of War appointed following the passage of that act, took up his new duties in March, 1921. Colonel H.B. Ferguson[3] was the first officer designated to act in an executive capacity for the Assistant Secretary in carrying out duties imposed by law. He was given the title "Director of Procurement", and gradually accumulated a group of assistants.

The "procurement planning sections" in the offices of the supply chiefs, which I have already referred to, were set up in May, 1921. Five months later was published the first order governing the organization of the office of the Assistant Secretary. The Planning Branch and the Current Supply Branch were established, the former being divided into ten sub-sections. The first reorganization took place the same year. Changes were frequent and some of them were drastic.

The Commodity Committees were added in 1922. The policy of allocating facilities was inaugurated that same year. The War Department Procurement Districts were set up in 1923. These frequent changes continued until 1925. This is perhaps only natural, since the period may be designated as one of "shaking down" during which personnel was becoming more intimately acquainted with the task in hand and adjusting the machinery better to carry out that task.

In the latter part of 1924 we find the first move was made to organize the Planning Branch into the four principal divisions that exist today. Since that time the organization has been relatively stable.

When compared to the experience of the General Staff, it would seem that the Assistant Secretary did remarkably well to approach stability in the organization of his planning staff in four years. The General Staff was established by law in 1903, but was not finally organized along its present lines until after the submission of the Harbord Board Report in 1921. During the seventeen intervening years reorganization was the rule rather than the exception. You understand I am not predicting there will be no further changes.

Before leaving the subject of organization and growth I want to trace briefly the principal events in the format of the Army Industrial College. It was organized initially in 1924 for the purpose of training personnel to carry on the various procurement activities in the office of the Assistant Secretary and in the procurement services. At first it operated under a rather informal arrangement between the Assistant

Secretary and the various chiefs of services, and the course of instruction was limited to a few months. Students were assigned to the offices of their respective chiefs of branches and were simply placed on temporary duty in the school. From this beginning the school has gradually developed until today it is recognized as one of the important general service schools of the army.

In May, 1924, an Advisory Board, consisting of the chiefs of supply branches, was formed to assist in the determination of policies relating to curriculum and the qualifications of student personnel.

In 1930 the War Department established a policy of giving preference to supply branch graduates of the Army Industrial College for student detail to the Army War College. The Assistant Secretary of War usually also fills his two vacancies at <u>that</u> school from graduates of <u>this.</u>

In 1931 the Navy created a vacancy in the Naval War College to be filled each year by a selected graduate of the Army Industrial College.

Certainly in recent years at least, we can see the Assistant Secretary of War and his associates have taken an intense interest in the prestige and influence of this school. To bring the discussion absolutely up-to-date on this point, I shall read a short memorandum signed by the Deputy Chief of Staff this morning. (Read)

An unofficial, though most important, function of the school is that of providing a focal point for the discussion of principles, doctrine, and methods applying to the great subject of procurement in war. These come from the various branches of the Army, the Navy, other governmental departments, and from civilians. I know that the present Assistant Secretary and his three predecessors and their executives have often stated most emphatically that the free opportunity offered here for the adjustment, coordination, and assimilation of divergent views is of the utmost importance to the student body, to the Army as a whole, <u>and to the development of logical thought on the problems involved in industrial mobilization.</u> Before leaving this subject I might remark that the Assistant Secretary of War is now considering the advisability of establishing a "Munitions Staff Eligible List", to be comparable in its own field to that of the General Staff Eligible List in the tactical field.

One major aspect of our present organization is sufficiently interesting to absorb our attention for a moment. The division of the office into a Planning Branch and a Current Procurement Branch has been observed since the beginning, but the <u>relationship</u> between these two branches has undergone very distinct changes.

Both branches were originally organized as component parts of the Procurement Division of which Colonel Ferguson was the head. Current Procurement matters were handled initially by a single officer who served in an advisory capacity to Colonel Ferguson.

It seems apparent that Colonel Ferguson's attention was concentrated principally on the great task of developing plans for use in the event of another emergency. The written record throws very little light upon the supervision of current activities during this period. However, decisions affecting them were rendered by Colonel Ferguson. He, above all others, was in position to see that such decisions were definitely coordinated with procurement plans.

It appears, however, that during these years the Assistant Secretary of War in person became increasingly interested in the problems constantly arising in connection with "current activities". These are the problems that demand immediate answers and the ones from which repercussions are most frequently felt. Human beings react more rapidly to the facts of today than to the probable consequences of next year. It was unquestionably this feeling that impelled Mr. Davis to select an officer to act as his immediate advisor in matters affecting current procurement.

An office memorandum written in 1925, apparently by Colonel Ferguson, indicates that as a result of this action a distinct cleavage between the Procurement Division and the Current Procurement Branch had occurred. This memorandum recites that, while the original order of 1921 had never been revoked, verbal instructions of the Assistant Secretary had operated to change relationships existing between Procurement Planning and Current Procurement. Each of these branches had been given a head office in the State, War, and Navy Building. While Colonel Ferguson apparently did not approve of the practice, his memorandum indicates that the chief of each branch was authorized to report directly to the Assistant Secretary of War. We know that this was the actual method of operation.

A memorandum of 1926, written by Assistant Secretary MacNider, confirms this arrangement and designates the Chief of the Current Procurement Branch, Lieut. Col. E.D. Peek,[4] as "Director of Purchase" for the Army. Such an organization implies almost a total lack of relationship between current procurement and procurement planning, since there is no coordinating head provided short of the highest authority—the Assistant Secretary of War.

This sharp cleavage in the office existed until General Moseley became Executive to the Assistant Secretary in 1929. In this position he represented the Assistant Secretary of War in all matters coming within the jurisdiction of that official. He was thus in a position to effect a closer coordination between current and future operations. I may add here that succeeding executives, General Carr and Colonel McFarland,[5] have had the same conception of their responsibilities. Even this organization, of course, does not bring the several sections of the

Current Procurement and Planning Branches into direct and continuing contact.

This particular point in the organization of the Assistant Secretary's office has been frequently criticized. The most pertinent arguments against the present arrangement are: First, that it disregards the distinct relationship that should exist between current procurement activities and war-time procurement; second, that advantage should be taken of current procurement operations to train personnel for war activities; and third, that a reorganization and readjustment of the office of the Assistant Secretary at the beginning of an emergency will be required as its result. It has been held by many, however, that any reasonable amalgamation of the two offices is impossible because of their diverse viewpoints affecting procurement. Another reason in favor of observing such a sharp distinction is that of expediency. When any officer is compelled to work upon the details of both current and planning problems, the planning usually suffers. The critic's retort to this argument admitting the truth of the premise, is that groupings can be made along functional lines without having the same individual responsible for detailed work in both current and planning matters. I believe this particular point in the existing organization will come to your attention in studies this year. I want only to say without regard to the correctness or incorrectness of the present set-up that in my opinion it results, in part, from the personalities of two men who appeared on the stage at a critical period. Methods of operation adopted because of these personalities have left a lasting imprint upon the organization of the office of the Assistant Secretary of War.

We will now attempt to trace briefly the subject of the changing conception in the office of the Assistant Secretary of War, of the mission given that official by law.

It has always been appreciated that the duty of planning for the procurement of army munitions in war was distinct from, although related to, that of providing for assurance of an adequate mobilization of industry to meet war-time needs. The first activity relates to the army alone; the second involves coordination of all material resources and agencies of the Nation. From the very first there has been a very definite accord respecting the responsibilities devolving upon the office in formulating complete procurement plans for the Army itself.

There is also evidence that as early as 1921 the Assistant Secretary believed that his duty with respect to preparing for industrial mobilization forced him to make plans for the establishment of governmental super-agencies over which the War Department could have no control in war. There is on file a memorandum of that year enumerating by name the men the Assistant Secretary of War expected to recommend to the President in emergency as suitable for occupying positions in the various super-agencies. There is no indication, however, that Colonel Ferguson or the Planning Branch believed it necessary to proceed further in this matter.

It is clear from many of the documents left by Colonel Ferguson that he personally believed super-agencies would be necessary in a great war. Aside from the record of his expressed opinions on the matter, we find in the War Department Handbook of 1923 the following quotation:

"The Assistant Secretary of War is the custodian of the records of the Council of National Defense and of the War Industries Board. The only peace-time existence of these war-time super-agencies is in his office, and it devolves upon him to draw plans for their operation in war.

"There are certain other super-agencies of the business of war that existed in the last war and which must exist again in the next. The Assistant Secretary of War cannot give 'the assurance of adequate provision' for industrial mobilization unless he plans for the recreation of these agencies."

This was, of course, inserted with the entire approval of the office of the Assistant Secretary of War. In spite of this recognition of responsibility in the matter, there is no evidence that any definite steps were taken at that time for meeting that responsibility. It is easy to see why this should have been so. At that time the many civilians who had occupied positions in the super-agencies during the World War were still in the prime of life. It was a foregone conclusion that if any emergency should occur in the near future many of the same men would be called back and placed in jobs similar to those they had left a few years previously. These men needed no organizational or operational plans. They did not need to be told how to work with other governmental agencies, nor where to secure the technical and administrative help that would be necessary.

Consequently, the great task facing the Army at that time was to find out exactly what the Army would require; to prepare specifications for the articles needed; to find out where these articles could be purchased; and to evolve an organization that could execute that portion of a war program for which the Army itself would necessarily be responsible. Too much emphasis placed upon super-agencies at that time might easily have induced Army personnel to pin its faith in them, and caused a neglect of those procurement plans whose existence will be vital to us in any major war. Because of all these reasons, there appears very little in the records of the whole period 1921–1929 concerning super-agencies or the control of national industry in war. It is true advisory committees of civilians were formed, and to a certain extent used, but their attention, like that of Army personnel, was directed more toward the Army's munitions plans than toward the broad aspects of industrial mobilization.

As a consequence it became the fashion, both in and out of the Army, to say that the War Department <u>disapproved</u> of the idea of having super-agencies in war. Former members of the Planning Branch and civilians who then came in contact with Colonel Ferguson, have informed me that this was his attitude, but the record gives indisputable proof that these impressions were erroneous. <u>It seems to be a fact, however, that this impression became so general as to be an accepted belief in the Army.</u> Colonel Ferguson has rightly been honored with the name of "Father of Procurement Planning". The widespread belief that he was opposed to this particular idea influenced to a marked degree the thoughts and actions of his contemporaries in the Planning Branch, and probably of his successor as Director of Procurement. That successor was Colonel Wooten, now retired.

Colonel Wooten <u>definitely</u> stated that the initial formation of industrial super-agencies in war should not be contemplated, and gave as his opinion that they would not be organized until such time, if ever, that the course of events in the war became so unfavorable as to alarm the people and compel the organization of such bodies. In other words, we see that by this time—late 1928—such faith was placed in the efficacy of detail procurement plans made up in the Army and Navy respectively that a general supervisory control over industrial activity was considered to be unnecessary, and even objectionable.

As we noted before, General Moseley became Executive to the Assistant Secretary in 1929. His views concerning the necessity for providing for a strong administrative control of all the national resources in war were diametrically opposed to those of Colonel Wooten. He not only believed with Colonel Ferguson that super-agencies would be necessary, but insisted that the time was ripe for developing plans to govern their organization and operation. He insisted that no matter how carefully and exactly were the various procurement plans of the Army and Navy prepared, the absence of a national control body would be quickly felt in war and would tend to lead the Nation toward chaotic conditions.

<u>At that time General Moseley went even further than this.</u> He was of the belief that the <u>actual procurement</u> of munitions in war should be removed from the Army and Navy and put into a separate "Department of Munitions". He thought this could be easily accomplished by detaching from the Army and Navy those officers engaged in these activities, giving them the plans already prepared within the two departments, and permitting them to function under a separate department head set up for the purpose.

Further, he believed it was the duty of the Assistant Secretary to prepare, in as great detail as practicable, the necessary operational and organizational plans for the industrial super-agency and for the department of munitions, and to accumulate data and statistics in time of peace to assist the early functioning of those organizations.

General Moseley immediately initiated a new series of conferences with the Planning Branch, with the chiefs of all procurement services, with the General Staff, and with many civilians whose war experiences were such as to make their opinions of value. As a result he abandoned the idea of establishing a department of munitions. The controlling argument that caused his change of view in this regard was that to regroup all operating organizations in new relationships upon the outbreak of war would only enhance the confusion, doubt, and uncertainty which to some extent must occur in any transitory period of this nature.

It is of course axiomatic that any plan developed for the control of industry in war, and which will have a direct bearing on the activities of the Army and Navy in war, must reflect the views of all three of these groups. A plan of this nature, to be of any value, must be a joint Army-Navy-Business Man's plan.

The conception, then, of the Assistant Secretary of War's mission that was finally adopted during the winter of 1929–1930 was that in addition to his duty of supervising the preparation of all plans for the procurement of army munitions, he is responsible for cooperating with the Navy, with Industry, and with all other interested agencies in developing plans for the control of industry in war. It has also been adopted as basic doctrine that war-time industrial control will be exercised through emergency organizations specially set up to assist the President. The acceptance of this doctrine by the Assistant Secretary of War and the General Staff was not accomplished without a struggle. If anyone is particularly interested I will be glad to take up this matter further during the question period. The Assistant Secretary of War has the further responsibility of seeing that these broad plans are in suitable form for placing before the President in case of war. Since that date the fundamental conception of the job of the Assistant Secretary of War with respect to his war-planning duties has remained about as I have given it.

An early agency set up to promote cooperative action was the Army-Navy Munitions Board, consisting of an Assistant Secretary from each department. It was organized in 1922. There was set up under it many committees, each of which was given the task of coordinating the procurement programs of the two services in a particular direction. That progress in such coordination has not been entirely satisfactory has long been recognized in the two services. Neither the Army-Navy Munitions Board nor its subsidiary committees have been particularly active during the last nine years, nor have they always been able to settle controversial questions placed before them.

In view of this lack of progress both services began to devote much thought to the matter some two or three years ago and through a series of conferences and conversations have gradually smoothed out many of their difficulties.

During the current year, by mutual action of the two services, the Board was completely reorganized and is undoubtedly better suited now to carry on its functions than it previously was. More important than this, however, is the growth of a mutual understanding between the two services that will make possible some solution to the many problems that heretofore have defied our efforts. Correspondence between the two services, referring to the presentation of an industrial mobilization plan to the War Policies Commission, of which I shall speak presently, gives indisputable proof of this growing accord. Captain Gage and Captain Pence,[6] to mention only two of the Naval officers engaged in this work have never hesitated to meet us more than half-way.

Having discussed origin and growth—inter-office relationships—and changing conceptions of responsibility—I wish finally to draw your attention to relatively recent events—principally to the formation and activities of the War Policies Commission. Ever since the war there has been a continuous effort made by various veterans organizations to secure legislation generally known as the "Universal Draft". The battle-cry of these advocates has been "The Nation must not require one man to give his life in defense of his Country while another is permitted to make a huge profit at the expense of his Country." No one, of course, has ever disagreed with this generalization in principle, but it has been difficult to secure any unanimity of opinion concerning methods for putting it into practical effect. Various bills have been introduced into Congress, some of which were referred to the War Department for comment and criticism.

Finally, since there seemed to be no concerted opinion as to what was needful, Congress determined in its past session to appoint a commission to investigate the whole subject of profiteering and the use of property in war. This implies an investigation of all industrial activity in war. The first hearings of the commission were held in March, 1931. It seems almost unnecessary to point out that the subjects it was forced to consider are identical with many that present themselves to the Assistant Secretary of War.

As a consequence, the War Department prepared a statement of its opinions and beliefs concerning these matters and presented them to the commission when called upon to do so in June of this year. As a further instance of the complete accord between the office of the Assistant Secretary of War and that of the Chief of Staff, I digress here long enough to say that at Colonel Payne's request General MacArthur presented the industrial plans of the Department, as well as the munitions plans. Our great interest in the commission's activities is occasioned by two things; first, it became a sort of forum before which all the conflicting views of the country bearing upon industrial activity in war could be heard and digested; and second, no matter what recommendations are finally made to Congress, the mission and operation of the office of the Assistant Secretary are likely to be directly affected.

I understand that a complete set of the hearings of the commission form part of the desk library of each student. Consequently, I do not intend to discuss at any length the evidence presented. From our standpoint, however, a very pertinent fact is the almost universal approval given by conservative thinkers to the activities now being carried on under the supervision of the Assistant Secretary of War. Such people as Howard Coffin, R.H. Aishton, Daniel Williard and Walter Gifford[7] insisted that this work was necessary, and at least some of them have expressed the opinion that it was being satisfactorily performed.

In this connection I would like to call your attention to the testimony of Mr. Baruch. Most people have seemed to think that Mr. Baruch is antagonistic to the work of the office of the Assistant Secretary. Reference to some of his past lectures would appear to substantiate this belief. It must be remembered, however, that he made those statements at a time when he was laboring under the impression that the Army intended to resist the formation in war of a body similar to the War Industries Board. This, above all other things, was anathema to Mr. Baruch. There are on file, however, letters from Mr. Baruch written during the past two years in which he heartily endorses the work being done in this office.

It has also been erroneously believed that Mr. Baruch's complete plan for industrial mobilization in war consists in freezing prices by law, and then setting up a War Industries Board to run the Country. A careful reading of his testimony shows that this is not his belief at all. Before the War Policies Commission he stressed the necessity for exact preparation in the field of munitions procurement. In many conversations with General Moseley and with other high officials of the War Department he has elaborated on these views much more than he did before the commission.

It must be remembered that Mr. Baruch's so-called "price freezing" scheme is simply a measure that he advocates as an additional means for preventing inflation in war. His initial suggestions in this field were opposed by the War Department, but these suggestions were somewhat modified later. In this connection I invite your attention to a letter to Mr. Baruch signed by General Moseley, found on page 830 of the commission's hearings.

One of the most encouraging impressions to be gained by a reading of the hearings is that there seems to be developing a general agreement among the Army, the Navy, and Industry as to the broad outline of the system that will finally be invoked in war to assist the President in controlling national resources. Without such agreement it would be practically impossible to make any real progress in these broader planning questions. Under the law the Assistant Secretary of War believed that it is his responsibility to be able at any moment to present such a plan to the President. <u>But he is aware also of the fact</u> that if the broad plan so presented were objected to in principle <u>by the Navy</u> or by <u>the principle figures in Industry</u> the whole plan would be absolutely useless. Army and Navy officials have agreed that, since no other agencies of government are charged with direct planning responsibility with respect to war, it is their common duty to have on hand at all times a broad plan that meets their own specific needs and is in entire consonance with the views of the men who will have to execute the industrial program in war.

There are several very obvious comments to make concerning the plan known as the "Industrial Mobilization Plan, 1930". First of all, in form it is rather a study containing a tentative plan than it is a concise plan itself. This is because the document was expected to have a certain educational value among people not intimately acquainted with the problem at hand, and it was thought best that the first edition should be more a narrative than a strict directive. Second, the plan indicates that many subsidiary plans must be prepared before the general scheme proposed can come into full effect. On some of these subsidiary plans very little has so far been accomplished, but on others a great deal has been done. These include the Army and Navy procurement programs; the plans prepared by the American Railway Association in cooperation with the War Department for the operation and control of railways; and a labor plan, in whose preparation the representative of this office had the advice and assistance of the Department of Labor, the Federation of Labor, and others. There are other plans under development. There have also been accumulated and analyzed many vital statistics and data that would be essential to the intelligent operation of any national industrial program in war.

To summarize all of the above in brief fashion I may say that the period 1921–1925 was one of shaking down, both with respect to organization and to an analysis of the job to be performed. In 1925 practical stabilization in organization took place, and the Army's procurement plan has developed in this office and in the procurement services steadily and without interruption since that date. The period 1929–1931 has been one in which the Assistant Secretary of War has attacked with renewed vigor the job of preparing for industrial mobilization. This period has also witnessed great progress in developing unanimity of opinion among the Army, Navy, Industry, and possibly also legislative and executive departments of the government respecting the scope and nature of the task.

Finally, there has been prepared an Industrial Mobilization Plan which expresses, at least approximately the composite views of these several agencies. Such a plan, no matter how incomplete it may be at present, is absolutely essential to the further development of a unified program for industrial mobilization. I shall be glad to attempt the answer to questions with which I may have some acquaintance.

1. Eisenhower prepared this paper while he was a student at the Industrial War College. Undoubtedly, in writing this paper he drew on his experiences in preparing the official report on procurement and mobilization for the War Policies Commission (see diary entry of May 18, 1931). Eisenhower included margin title heads for paragraphs. Those have been deleted.

2. Jonathan Mayhew Wainwright served from 1921 to 1923 as assistant secretary of war. In 1923 he was elected to Congress from New York, serving until 1931. Wainwright died on June 3, 1945.

3. From 1921 to 1926 Harley Bascom Ferguson (USMA, 1897) directed planning for industrial mobilization in the office of the assistant secretary of war. He was largely responsible for organizing the Industrial War College.

4. Ernest Dichmann Peek (USMA, 1901) served from 1924 to 1928 in the office of the assistant secretary of war. He retired as a major general.

5. Earl McFarland (USMA, 1906) served in the War Department as executive officer for the assistant secretary of war (1931–36).

6. This was possibly Harry Langley Pence, who graduated from the Naval Academy in 1906. Captain Pence served with the Navy until 1945.

7. Howard Coffin, who had held positions as chief engineer of the Olds Motor Company, vice president of Hudson Motor Company, chief executive officer of National Air Transport, and chairman of the Aircraft Board of the United States, was regarded as one of the nation's top experts on transportation engineering.

R. H. Aishton became president of the Chicago and Northwestern Railway in 1916. In 1920 he was appointed president of the American Railway Association, a position he held until his retirement in 1935. Aishton died on October 3, 1946.

Walter Sherman Gifford, a prominent statistician and executive with American Telephone and Telegraph, served as an adviser to a number of federal agencies. His last government appointment was as U.S. ambassador to Great Britain (1950–53).

58

To Elivera Doud and Eda Carlson

October 17, 1931

Dearest Mother and Auntie: I received your birthday presents and needless to say both were more than acceptable. In addition to Mother's check and the tie from Auntie, Mamie gave me a fine new traveling bag just like Dad's little one except that mine is calf skin instead of black leather. It is a beauty and I feel that I must make a trip soon in order to show it off. Johnny gave me a pair of suspenders, and I had a big birthday cake at the office. Everybody participated in its eating, but I saved two pieces to take home to Mamie and Johnny. That made a big hit, particularly with Johnny.

I do not know what I could have said with respect to Mamie's general condition that seemed to alarm you and Dad. Both of you in recent letters have remarked about it. All I meant to say was that she had occasional little spells when she did not feel quite up to par and suffered slight attacks of indigestion. These are nowhere near as serious as those she had before the operation, and all in all we think she is doing splendidly.[1]

Naturally she has been under some little strain from time to time due to effort she had to make in connection with the visit of my Dad and Mother and Solo, but all of these she has come through very nicely.

All the woodwork in our apartment has been painted. They also painted the bathroom and kitchen completely. We are to have some little reduction in rent, probably about $10. This is particularly acceptable, and we are only hoping that our allowances are not reduced this winter, a possibility which has been talked about a great deal. If they are reduced I am going to ask for immediate relief from Washington.

Mamie fired Lulu about four days ago because she got so worthless that she had Mamie worried all the time. The same day she picked up another one named Edith. She seems to be very fine and so far we are mighty pleased with the change.

Mamie has all her curtains up and yesterday got all the rugs from storage. Her house is looking very well indeed, and she is now resting on her laurels. So far we have had a lovely fall. It has been warmer than usual, but the days have been beautiful. The trees are still almost as green as during the summer.

Mother's room is empty and waiting for her any second she can get here. Lots of love to you all - As ever your devoted

1. Eisenhower may have been referring to Mamie's gall bladder condition. See diary entry dated July 31, 1938.

59

NOVEMBER, 1931[1]

For ten years several of the veterans' organizations have persistently advocated legislation intended to eliminate, from any future war, opportunity for profiteering and to insure an equitable distribution among all citizens of the burdens that must inevitably accompany war. The worthiness of this objective has been universally recognized, but it has been difficult to secure any substantial agreement on measures for its attainment. As Congressman Laguardia[2] once very aptly remarked:

" . . . the subject of equalizing the burdens of war and minimizing the profits of war is about the easiest of any to make a speech on, but probably the most difficult to work out in detail."

These difficulties arise from a variety of causes. Pertinent statistics of past war experiences are by no means complete, nor are they easy to interpret intelligently. Every proposal made must rest to some degree upon abstract reasoning, and even on pure conjecture. Class fears and prejudices are easily aroused—while a mass inertia engendered by the feeling that "any war is a long way off" has likewise contributed to the defeat of efforts to secure decisive action.

It gradually became apparent that no progress would be realized unless the many factors involved were thoroughly investigated and a comprehensive plan presented to Congress that would embody the considered opinions of those best qualified to speak.

War Policies Commission

Finally, in June, 1930, by a Joint Resolution entitled "To Promote Peace," Congress created the War Policies Commission. It was directed to consider amending the Constitution "to provide that private property may be taken by Congress for public use during war;" to study methods for equalizing the burdens of and removing the profits from war; and to develop "policies to be pursued in event of war." The Secretary of War is Chairman of the Commission, which is composed of six Cabinet officers, four Senators, and four Congressmen. During open hearings held in March and May, 1931, the Commission listened to some fifty witnesses, many of them nationally prominent citizens.

The press has devoted much space to the Commission's activities, both in news columns and editorially. War Department interest in the proceedings is quite natural, as the subjects under consideration by the Commission constitute some of the most vexing problems confronting the Department in the preparation of war plans.

An interesting feature of the testimony presented at the hearings was the great diversity of individual opinion expressed concerning the tasks confronting the Commission. In general, each witness gave his own interpretation to the resolution creating the Commission. For example, a considerable number insisted that the entire effort should be devoted to the promotion of peace,—some even going so far as to say that investigations carried out under the remainder of the Congressional directive would adversely affect our friendly relations with other powers.

Methods for Preventing War

Among those who confined their attention almost exclusively to methods for preventing war were a retired admiral of the Navy, two ministers of the Gospel, a leader of the Socialist party, an oculist, editors of magazines of so-called "pacifist" leanings, and officials of various peace associations.

Admiral Samuel McGowan advocated amending the Constitution of the United States,

" . . . so as to require that before war can be declared or participated in (except only in the event of attack or invasion) there must be a referendum . . ."

He was supported in his view by a later witness, Dr. Thomas Shastid, who heads an organization known as the "War-Check-Vote, Incorporated." Both of them argued that the people that have to fight the battles never desire war—that they are rushed into hostilities by "big interests" and governmental officials. In the Admiral's words:

" . . . the only good war is a war that doesn't take place; and it will never take place in this or any other country, if the people back home, the mothers . . . all through the country, are allowed to have their say."

In response to questions by Commission members, other witnesses vigorously opposed this proposal. Newton D. Baker, Ex-Secretary of War, voiced the substance of this opposition as follows:

"If the question were submitted to popular vote in the United States—shall the United States go to war with X—and we had a great debate about it over the United States, . . . country X would in the meantime be . . . making all the preparations, and we would not be making any until we found out what the vote would be. Our people would be separated into opposite camps about war, and if a small majority decided in favor of war, it would be a practical advantage to our adversary by our going to war with a divided people whose feelings were split wide open; it would put us in a very weak situation."

Neither Admiral McGowan or Doctor Shastid advocated disarmament as a definite means of preventing war. The latter, although intensely interested in methods for maintaining the peace, characterized many of the so-called peace movements as futile "gestures." Among these he included the League of Nations, and disarmament.

Dr. Arthur Call,[3] Secretary of the American Peace Society, concluded, as did the others of this group, that the only real solution to the problems given the Commission was through positive prevention of war. Unlike most of the others, however, he believed that conditions of the "living world" were such as to require the maintenance of military force of approximately the size now existing in this country. He said:

"I am quite of the opinion that the 'reasonable defensive posture'; as phrased by President Washington, remains still a necessary posture on the part of our people . . . we could not wage a war in a foreign country by our Navy alone; it has to be waged by the Navy in cooperation with the Army. Since our Army is as small as it is, I am of the opinion that our Military Establishment, as is, does not constitute, therefore, a menace to the peace of the world and that it is not necessary to think that it does."

On the other hand Rev. John Sayre, representing the Fellowship of Reconciliation; Tucker Smith, Secretary of Committee on Militarism in Education; and Miss Dorothy Detzer, Secretary of the Women's International League for Peace and Freedom, bitterly attacked our present military program. They said that it was a hindrance rather than a help in maintaining the peace; that it tended to make our population "war-minded;" and that it encouraged the adoption of economic and imperialistic policies likely to lead us into war. While it was generally agreed that there was small chance for other countries to take measurable steps in disarmament at present, it was nevertheless urged that America should by "example" show its complete reliance upon the Kellogg-Briand peace treaty—a document by the way that came in for considerable discussion before the Commission. Mr. Smith had the following to say about military preparation:

" . . . your report must recognize that military preparedness that envisions the ability to strike hard and fast makes peace almost impossible in a crisis, and that the task before humanity is a task of getting a degree of disarmament that will prevent that situation; . . . "

Surprisingly though, Mr. Smith did not concur in the popular assumption that the hope of profiteering by "business" has a great effect in influencing us toward war. In this he differed sharply with the following statement of policy contained in the Democratic National Platforms of 1924 and 1928:

"In the event of war in which the man power of the Nation is drafted, all other resources should likewise be drafted. This will tend to discourage war by depriving it of its profits."

Miss Detzer likewise did not entirely agree with Mr. Smith on this point. She contended that the searching for trade by the munitions industry in time of peace, and its hope of large profits in war, both tend to bring on conflict.

Most of the witnesses just named advocated adherence to the World Court and to the League of Nations; withdrawal of Marines from Nicaragua; independence of the Philippines; recognition of Soviet Russia; and revision of national policies with respect to Latin American countries. Some also recommended cancellation of war debts. They opposed the development of any "policies that should be pursued in the event of war." They insisted that to admit the possibility of war was to make war more likely, and helped to make our people "war-minded." Such expressions as "peace-minded," "war-minded," "atmosphere in the psychology of war," "peace policies," and "preparation for peace" were used repeatedly, but no attempt was made to define them.

A listener gained the distinct impression that the members of this group, with possibly one or two exceptions, were earnestly and unselfishly laboring for the promotion of an idea in which they implicitly believed. One—Dr. Mercer Johnston—wore in his lapel the ribbon of the Distinguished Service Cross, won while serving with the A.E.F. in 1918.

Equalization of War's Burdens

Other witnesses addressed themselves to the more specific tasks laid down in the resolution creating the Commission. They urged the intensive study in time of peace of the serious economic, industrial, and social disturbances that are certain to occur in war, and the development of a comprehensive program designed to minimize the effects of these disturbances. They believed the Commission's efforts to do this were perfectly proper and could not logically be interpreted by any foreign nation as indicating "double-dealing" by the United States. Congressman Laguardia said:

"As I understand the purpose of the resolution . . . it is entirely separate and distinct from the question of the prevention of war . . . The mere fact that one takes an interest in the purpose of this resolution is no indication he is . . . not doing all he can to avoid war. Anyone who contemplates the terrors of another armed conflict, I believe, will see the necessity of providing ahead of time, as far as we can, for equalizing the burden of war."

Bernard M. Baruch, Chairman of the War Industries Board in 1918, stated a similar view even more emphatically:

"I take it that we are of the common belief that war ought to be avoided if possible, but that we must plan in such a way that, if war comes, we shall meet the enemy with our maximum effectiveness. . . .

"War on this vast modern scale has hitherto so violently disturbed the pattern of the normal economic structure of belligerent nations that, . . . the aftermath of the struggle prostrates both the conqueror and the conquered. With these most serious considerations you must deal. . . . The neglect of them is, in my opinion at least, one of the most threatening aspects of our governmental policy. It is for these reasons that I regard the work of this commission very seriously . . . "

Proposals concerning these matters naturally varied as widely as did those submitted by the "peace" contingent. On one question, however, witnesses were divided of necessity into two camps. This question was: "Should the United States, in the event of war, actually seize, and take title to, all private property during the period of the conflict?"

Congressmen Frear and LaGuardia, as well as Dr. Shastid and others, took the affirmative. Congressman Royal C. Johnson and Past Commander P. V. McNutt[4] of the American Legion, approved the idea in principle, but expressed doubt that it would be accepted by the majority of the people.

Directly opposing the idea of actual seizure of all property were Newton Baker; Daniel Willard, President of the Baltimore and Ohio Railroad; Commander Ralph O'Neil of the American Legion; Walter S. Gifford, President of the American Telephone and Telegraph; Dr. Leonard P. Ayers, Statistician and Economist; A. H. Griswold, Executive Vice President of the International Telephone and Telegraph; C.B. Robbins, Ex-Assistant Secretary of War; William Green,[5] President of the American Federation of Labor, and many others.

Since the American Legion has long advocated "Universal Draft" in time of war, Commander O'Neil's testimony was particularly interesting from the standpoint of establishing just what was meant by the phrase. Remarking that this term had been used largely as a "symbol," it developed that he did not believe in the actual confiscation of private property, but rather in a strict governmental control over it. The true purpose of the program he advanced was clearly stated in answers he gave to questions by Commissioners:

Mr. Collins. And in event of war, you think they (Producers of munitions) ought to be paid up to 7 per cent per annum!

Mr. O'Neil. That is a fair return; yes. If they do not get any more than that, it will help considerably. That is a maximum, you understand.

Senator Vandenberg. You are talking about taking the exploitation profits out of war?

Mr. O'Neil. That is what I am trying to do.

Mr. McSwain. In other word, eliminating what is ordinarily called profiteering; that is, unreasonable and excessive profits?

Mr. O'Neil. Yes.

Some witnesses maintained that the recognized right of government to tax wealth to any extent it saw fit, and to commandeer property for public use, was in fact a recognition of the principle of "conscription of wealth." This view was rejected by those who want to extend materially the right of government to seize private property. Mr. LaGuardia was in favor of a constitutional amendment to "give the government the broad, all-sweeping powers that it needs to take over property, nationalize industry, stop speculation, and suspend all normal gains and profits; nothing short of that will equalize the burdens of war."

Mr. Frear was in substantial agreement with this suggestion. It is curious to note, in view of this statement of Mr. LaGuardia's that he later disclaimed any intention of "equalizing the burdens of war." He put it thus:

"If any plan is to go through to take the profits out of war, it must do just that thing. . . . everybody in the United States, whether in the infantry, in a bank, or in a factory, will enter the service of the country, taking all the chances of war and chancing the inequalities that war brings. In other words, to do this we have to nationalize all of the industries and militarize everybody from Texas Guinan[6] to J. Pierpont Morgan. . . .

"It is difficult, and it is going to involve a lot of details and perhaps chaos. . . .

"Now, it is quite possible that one man's factory will be used and abused and he may come out of the war almost ruined, while another man's factory may not have been used at all—yet no one will have made any profits. . . .

"You can not stop and worry . . . Whether one is going to suffer more than the other . . . "

The opponents of actual conscription of property based their arguments largely upon their convictions of its impracticability in operation. Mr. Baruch summarized his reasons as follows:

"Nobody with any familiarity with industry could seriously urge a wholesale assumption by any Federal Bureau of the responsibility for management of any or all of the vast congeries of manufacturing establishments upon which we must rely for extraordinary effort in event of war. Even if such bureau management could prove adequate to the task (which it could never do) the mere process of change would destroy efficiency at the outset."

He said that when similar suggestions with respect to specific industries were made during the World War the proposal split upon the rock of the following argument:

"Who will run it? Do you know another manufacturer fit to take over its administration? Would you replace a proved expert manager by a problematical mediocrity? After you had taken it over and installed your Government employee as manager, what greater control would you have then than now! Now, you can choke it to death, deprive it of transportation, fuel, and power, divert its business, strengthen its rivals. Could any disciplinary means be more effective? If you take it over, you can only give orders to an employee backed by threat of dismissal, and with far less effect than you can give them now."

No witness that advocated an actual seizure of all private property without giving owners the "just compensation" required by the 5th Amendment to the Constitution came forward with a detailed plan for administering the system. Statements were made that the population should be rationed—that the government should put our 125,000,000 people on its pay roll—that money would cease to circulate, or be used only by the government in foreign trade—that property would be returned to the original owner at the end of the war on an "as is" basis—but no one explained through what agency all this should, or could, be done.

Finance and Price Freezing

With respect to the use of money in war, Mr. Eugene Meyer, Chairman of the Federal Reserve Board, expressed an interesting view.

". . . The obvious lesson is that the course of war depends upon resources in man power, supplies, and morale, and that finance is only incidental to these, for, after all, money is only a medium of exchange, and to the extent that men, material, and morale are available some medium of exchange will be available or will be developed so as to permit their continued functioning to the maximum limit."

Mr. Meyer thus indicates that under certain conditions something might be substituted for money as a "medium of exchange." With a system of universal conscription this medium could scarcely be anything else than governmental orders.

Mr. Baruch advocated a so-called "price freezing" system. Because this proposal came in for much discussion during later meetings of the Commission, newspaper accounts presented it generally as constituting the whole of Mr. Baruch's plan. Actually, it was only one of the features of his complete proposal. He favored the development in peace of broad plans for setting up promptly in emergency an administrative machinery corresponding generally to that existing in the fall of 1918—and the preparation of specific plans for procuring the supplies that would be needed initially. He praised the work now being done along this line in the War and Navy Departments and emphasized the necessity for its continuance. His "price freezing" plan was advanced as an added means of securing justice and efficiency, and was proposed particularly to assist in preventing inflation. Simply stated, the proposal is to place on the statute books a law that would empower the President in emergency to declare that the maximum prices existing in each locality for all services and things, at the time of the promulgation of the order, should not be exceeded during the war. A "Price Fixing Board" would be created to adjust prices where found necessary. The serious effects of rapid inflation in war, which the "price fixing" scheme is intended to eliminate, are described by Mr. Baruch as follows:

"Inflation enormously increases the cost of war and multiplies burdens on the backs of generations yet to come. The war debt of the nation is necessarily incurred in terms of debased dollar values. In the inevitable post-war deflation the debt, of course, remains at the inflated figure. Thus the bonds that our Government sold in the World War for 50-cent dollars must be paid through the years by taxes levied in 100-cent dollars."

Much discussion centered about the constitutionality of this part of the plan. At first it was thought Mr. Baruch intended that the government should compel the sale of private property to individuals or to the government at prices fixed by fiat, thus constituting a "taking" of property without according what the owner might consider "just compensation." Later it was explained that no compulsion was intended—it was expected only to prohibit a buying or selling at a higher price than that specified. Doubt was expressed by some witnesses as to the possibility of administering such a law. Objections of other kinds were raised—objections that Mr. Baruch in a second hearing attempted to meet by presenting an additional brief in support of his idea.

Aside from Mr. Baker and Mr. Baruch, many other witnesses had unusual experience in the World War, from which they were able to offer valuable suggestions. Among these were Daniel Willard; Walter S. Gifford; William Green; and Howard Coffin, head of the Aircraft Production Board during the World War, and a devoted advocate of industrial preparedness long before we entered that conflict. Others were J. Leonard Replogle,[7] Director of Steel Supplies, War Industries Board; George N. Peek, Commissioner of Finished Products, War Industries Board; Herbert Bayard Swope, prominent newspaper man and editor, and Benedict Crowell, Assistant Secretary of War during the period 1917–1920.

Mr. Willard and Mr. R.H. Aishton, President of the American Railway Association, outlined the program the railways have developed in cooperation with the War Department to insure the effective use of transportation systems in emergency. Assistant Secretary of the Treasury, Arthur Ballantine,[8] discussed the operation of tax laws in war. Clyde B. Aitchison,[9] member of the Interstate Commerce Commission, described the proper functions of that body under emergency conditions. Honorable William Ramseyer,[10] Member of Congress, presented an interesting paper on "Paying for War as You Go." In the World War about 27 per cent of current expenses were met by current taxation—the remainder of loans. It is Mr. Ramseyer's view that all of the expenses should be paid for out of current revenues. He argued that by taxing incomes heavily enough to do this, people would not have money to spend freely, inflation would be automatically prevented, expenses would be kept to a minimum, and there would be no serious aftermath to the war.

On May 13, 1931, General Douglas MacArthur discussed before the Commission the principal features of War Department plans for the mobilization of men and material in emergency. In describing the premise on which these plans are built he said:

"We have a General Mobilization Plan. This plan does not envisage any particular enemy. It contemplates the mobilization, by successive periods, of six field armies and supporting troops, or approximately 4,000,000 men . . . This general plan establishes the basic policies for a . . . systematic mobilization of the manpower of the United States. Being arranged by successive periods, the mobilization plan is flexible and can be made to fit the manpower needs of any military situation . . . "

The press generally jumped at the conclusion that in any emergency the War Department would insist upon raising immediately an army of 4,000,000 men. The language quoted above, of course, conveys no such meaning. Other remarks of the Chief of Staff further emphasize his real intent.

"An emergency involving no more than the Regular Army, raised to its full strength and perhaps strengthened by some National Guard units, would cause scarcely a ripple in American life and industry. . . . there would be no occasion for the application of any governmental control not usually applied in peace. . . ."

After discussing the basic provisions of the selective service system that the War Department believes should be applied if it ever becomes necessary to mobilize large land forces, General MacArthur took up those portions of the plan, prepared under the supervision of the Assistant Secretary of War, that affect the economic problems of war. He described the effects that proposed measures would have in war in equalizing burdens and minimizing profits.

The War Department Plan provides in detail for the orderly procurement of all supplies it will need so as to occasion the minimum of disturbance in the normal economic life of the nation. Beyond this it provides for a civilian organization to exercise, under the President, an efficient control over all resources. It makes provision for setting up promptly, in an emergency, all the administrative machinery that will be necessary. The plan conforms to existing constitutional provisions and to the laws that could be reasonably expected to be passed promptly in an emergency. General MacArthur's address—which, with the War Department "Plan for Industrial Mobilization," is published in Part II, Hearings before the Commission authorized by Public Resolution 98—contained these general conclusions:

"Modern war demands the prompt utilization of all the national resources. Measures for transforming potential strength into actual strength must work in emergency with the utmost speed and effectiveness. . . .

"The human burdens of war must be equalized in so far as possible. To this end liability for combat service must be determined under a selective service system developed along the general lines of that used in the World War.

"The economic burdens must be equalized through:

a. Systematic registration of wealth and all accretions thereto during the period of the emergency; and tax legislation framed to place an equitable burden thereon.

b. Orderly and economic procurement by the government itself.

c. Strong and intelligent leadership . . . exercised through an organization adapted to the purpose.

d. Application of governmental controls . . . to prevent any profiteering at the national expense.

e. Prompt resumption of normal peace conditions upon the termination of the war. During the progress of any war the President should appoint a committee to study and prepare plans for demobilization. These plans must facilitate the reemployment of men returning to civil life from the Army and Navy, and the freeing of industry of the accumulations of stocks produced to meet war requirements. "All of the above demand an intensive and intelligent planning program carried out continuously in time of peace. Because of their peculiar responsibilities, the War and Navy Departments must be definitely required to carry on this work as the agents of the whole government. "Congress should satisfy itself at frequent intervals as to the progress of plans under development by requiring their presentation to appropriate committees of Congress."

In commenting on the War Department plan, many witnesses, including a representative of the Navy Department, gave their endorsement to its general provisions. Mr. Coffin, a thoughtful student who has had a wealth of experience, studied the whole plan carefully and expressed the opinion that it is splendidly conceived, and practicable in every respect. He believes that, in case of need, it would work with the maximum speed and effectiveness, with the least possible injustice to individual citizens.

After acknowledging the debt of the Department to the many public spirited civilians who have been of so much assistance in bringing plans to their present state of development, General MacArthur said:

"It must be apparent to the Commission that the principles on which War Department plans are based do not differ essentially from those expressed by the majority of the witnesses who have previously appeared before you. The goal we seek is that sought by the men responsible for the drafting of Public Resolution No. 98. Our plans simply set forth the methods whereby it is believed these principles and theories could be applied in the event of another great emergency."

1. Dwight D. Eisenhower, "War Policies," *Cavalry Journal* 40 (November–December 1931): 25–29. This article is based on notes that Eisenhower maintained of several meetings of the War Policies Commission and from official records of the commission. The ellipses and quotation marks used in the quotes are Eisenhower's.

2. Eisenhower refers to Fiorello LaGuardia, who served in Congress from New York from 1917 to 1919 and again from 1923 to 1933. From 1934 to 1945 he was the highly popular, and sometimes flamboyant, mayor of New York.

3. Arthur Deering Call became executive director of the American Peace Society in 1912 and represented the society at the Paris Peace Conference (1918–19). From 1919 to 1930 he served as director of the International Peace Bureau, Berne, Switzerland. He died on October 23, 1941.

4. Royal Cleaves Johnson represented South Dakota in Congress from 1915 until 1933. Johnson died on August 2, 1939.

Paul V. McNutt served two terms as governor of Indiana before joining the Roosevelt administration as high commissioner to the Philippines (1937–39) during Eisenhower's service with the American Military Mission. After World War II he returned to the Philippines, first as high commissioner (1945–46), then as the United States' first ambassador to the new republic (1946–47). McNutt retired from public life in 1948.

5. Augustus H. Griswold was vice president of International Telephone and Telegraph from 1928 to 1935, and again from 1938 until his death in 1940.

Charles B. Robbins, a civilian aide to the secretary of war from 1924 to 1927, was appointed assistant secretary of war in 1928.

In 1924, William Green succeeded Samuel Gompers as president of the American Federation of Labor, a position he held until his death on November 21, 1952.

6. Mary Louise Cecilia "Texas" Guinan, known in the 1920s and the early 1930s as "Queen of the Nightclubs," owned nightclubs in various locations throughout the United States.

7. Jacob L. Replogle, a prominent executive with several steel companies, served during World War I as director of steel supplies for the War Industries Board.

8. Arthur Atwood Ballantine, an expert on taxation, advised Congress on tax problems and in 1931 was appointed assistant secretary of the treasury, becoming undersecretary in 1932.

9. Clyde B. Aitchison, appointed to the Interstate Commerce Commission in 1917, served until 1952, including four tenures as commission chairman.

10. Christian William Ramseyer served in Congress from Iowa from 1915 until 1933. In 1933 he was appointed to the U.S. Court of Claims.

60   Eisenhower Library
                                                                Foltz Papers

To Elivera Doud, John Doud, Eda Carlson

                                                        November 12, 1931

Dearest Mother, Dad, & Auntie: Mamie told me that she had written you lately saying that I had forwarded to you a copy of a letter I'd recd from Gen. MacArthur.[1] I had promised to do so—it is time—but it had entirely slipped my mind. Anyway here it is!! I think Mamie had a cheap frame put on the original simply to preserve it. By the way Mother, have you the original of a letter I recd from Gen. Pershing several years ago?[2] I don't know where it is but thought possibly you had it along with a few other keepsakes of mine!

Johnnie and I are giving Mamie 3 knives & 3 forks of her new silverware. I got hold of a little money of which she knew nothing. Therefore she'll be all the more surprised & delighted with the present, I think. Johnny is all excited & very mysterious about it. We'll do a lot of marching & singing anyway. I think Mary, George, and Bo[3] are to be in to dinner, so Johnny's party will be complete.

Have worked like a dog ever since I came back to work—but things are easing up a little now, I think, and I intend to do some soldiering about the office.

Dad's birthday is next then. Wish we could be there to give him the necessary <u>walloping</u> where it would do the most good. We are certainly thrilled Mother will be here for Xmas & are only sorry dad cannot come too. We've had 2 bottles of alleged champagne lying around for years. We could open them to see whether they were better than the one we opened some years ago in Denver. Remember? Lots of love to all of you—as ever, Your devoted son

> 1. MacArthur wrote to Eisenhower on November 4, 1931:
>
> My Dear Major: I desire to place on official record this special commendation for excellent work of a highly important nature which you have just completed under my personal direction. You not only accepted this assignment willingly—an assignment which involved much hard work—performing it in addition to your regular duties in the office of the Assistant Secretary of War, but you gave me a most acceptable solution within a minimum of time.
>
> This is not the first occasion when you have been called upon to perform a special task of this nature. In each case you have registered successful accomplishment in the highest degree.
>
> I write you this special commendation so that you may fully realize that your outstanding talents and your ability to perform these highly important missions are fully appreciated. (MacArthur to Eisenhower, November 4, 1931, Pre-pres. Papers, Eisenhower Library)

Eisenhower refers to this letter again on December 1, 1931.

2. The Pershing letter referred to was sent to Chief of Infantry Maj. Gen. Robert H. Allen on August 15, 1927, praising Eisenhower's work with the American Battle Monuments Commission. The letter is quoted, in part, in the introduction to chapter 1. Pershing wrote of Eisenhower's "superior ability not only in visualizing his work as a whole but in executing its many details in an efficient and timely manner" and his ability to produce excellent work under short time deadlines. Pershing concluded that the "work he has done was accomplished only by the exercise of unusual intelligence and constant devotion to duty." Pershing to Allen, August 15, 1927, Pre-pres. Papers.

3. Eisenhower is referring to his close friend George Horkan, his wife, Mary, and their son "Bo."

61   NARA
                                          Records of the Adjutant General's Office

MEMORANDUM FOR THE ADJUTANT GENERAL

NOVEMBER 25, 1931

I. The policy of the Assistant Secretary of War governing the selection of students for the 1932–1933 course of the Army Industrial College is outlined below.

1. The following approved policy with reference to the apportionment and selection of student officers for the Army Industrial College, school year 1932–1933, is communicated to you for your information and guidance.

  a. The apportionment of students to the Supply Arms and Services will be as follows:

                Quartermaster Corps 9
                Medical Department 2
                Corps of Engineers 4
                Ordnance Department 9
                Signal Corps 2
                Chemical Warfare Service 2
                Air Corps 4

<u>b</u>. No quotas are fixed for the
Infantry
Cavalry
Field Artillery
Coast Artillery
Adjutant General's Department
Inspector General's Department
Judge Advocate General's Department
Finance Department
    Chiefs of these Arms and Services desiring to send officers to the
Army Industrial College will submit appropriate recommendations to
The Adjutant General.
    2. Students will be selected from officers:
    <u>a</u>. Having a general efficiency rating of at least "excellent".
    <u>b</u>. Within the following maximum age limits:

                Lieutenants 42
                Captains 45
                Majors 50
                Lieut. Cols. and Colonels 54

    In recommending officers for detail as students, Chiefs of Arms and
Services should give consideration to the mission of the college and to
the nature and scope of its curriculum. Only a relatively small student
body can be accommodated, and it is essential that officers be selected
from those deemed especially qualified for this particular type of duty.
    3. Attention is invited to the policy outlined in War Department
memorandum of March 4, 1930, which provides that certain proportions of the officers from the Supply Arms and Services recommended for detail as students at the Army War College will be Industrial College graduates.
    4. Recommendations for officers to attend the Army Industrial
College will be submitted to The Adjutant General as soon as practicable, but not later than January 15, 1932.
    II. The Assistant Secretary of War desires that these instructions be
given appropriate circulation.

To COLONEL ROBERT H. MONTGOMERY

NOVEMBER 27, 1931

Dear Colonel: After talking with you this morning on the phone, I had a long discussion with Congressman Hadley. After I had explained the situation fully to him, he was reluctant to authorize a reprint of the tentative draft solely for the purpose of setting forth Mr. McSwain's personal suggestions. He pointed out that this would be establishing a precedent that might prove embarrassing in case a number of the Commissioners desired to follow Mr. McSwain's example. In view of the possible cost involved, he felt we should be rather conservative along this line.

As an alternative method for handling the question I proposed to Mr. Hadley that I secure from the Public Printer 20 additional copies of the tentative draft as it now stands. On these I will have the girls in the office note each of the suggestions offered by Mr. McSwain, and forward a copy immediately to each member of the Commission. This should require an expenditure of very little money. Mr. Hadley agreed to this proposal. To make sure that Mr. McSwain would approve I called him on the phone and told him what I was doing. He gave his full approval to the scheme and requested that I send with each of the corrected copies a short memorandum setting forth his idea in asking for this circulation of his proposals.

I am enclosing the note I received from Mr. McSwain this morning, as well as a copy of the memorandum I sent to each member upon his request. I am not sending you a copy of the draft as corrected by Mr. McSwain for the reason that the girls will be very busy getting the necessary ones to the Commissioners and you will be able to digest their import very easily upon your arrival here at the beginning of the week.[1]

Mr. McSwain told me on the phone that he was anxious to eliminate from the report anything controversial in nature, unless its inclusion was vital to the report. Most of his suggested changes consist in deletions. Sincerely

1. The enclosures are not included. Eisenhower was directing and coordinating much of the work of the War Policies Commission, which was not his responsibility.

DECEMBER 1, 1931

Had 2 months leave this summer, returning to office on Sept. 1. Lt. Col. Earl McFarland,[1] O.D.[2] is now exec. for A.S.W. <u>Fine man!</u>

I have a new assistant named Bomar—also of O.D. He is a splendid type—I am lucky to get him.

This fall have been particularly engaged in writing annual reports for Mr. Payne, General MacArthur and Mr. Hurley. The last one was a revision of a report written in Press Relations.

All went through as written—and I received from Gen. MacA. a very splendid letter of Commendation. Mamie had it framed!!!

Have also done lots of work for War Policies Commission. That body is now trying to hold its final executive meetings in order to arrive at general conclusions. So much trouble is being experienced in securing the attendance of a quorum that it looks at times a report will never be completed. I have assisted Col. Montgomery in getting out a suggested report.

1. Brig. Gen. Earl McFarland (USMA, 1906) served during World War I in the ordnance service. From 1931 to 1936 he served as the executive officer to the assistant secretary of war.

2. "O.D." refers to the Ordnance Department.

To COLONEL ROBERT H. MONTGOMERY

DECEMBER 8, 1931

Dear Colonel Montgomery: We have just received a letter from Senator Robinson in which he makes certain suggestions concerning the alterations proposed by Mr. McSwain in the original tentative draft of the report.

I am sending you a copy of his letter, together with the report in which he made his suggestions.

In addition to the above, he wrote a personal letter to the Secretary of War. In his letter to the Secretary he discusses only the matter taken up in the second paragraph of his letter to you.

I have studied this matter rather completely and am inclosing herewith a draft of reply which I believe suitable for you to make to Senator Robinson. Very sincerely

(Draft)[1]
Hon. Senator Joe T. Robinson,
United States Senate.
My dear Senator Robinson: I have received the copy of the Tentative Report containing certain suggestions by you. While a revised edition of the draft has already been printed, the changes you suggest can be included in a later one. You are undoubtedly aware of the fact that the Commission has requested an extension of ninety days in order to give further study to its conclusions and recommendations, particularly as they deal with the constitutionality of price fixing in war.

It had not occurred to me that the paragraph to which you particularly referred might reopen an old controversy. I shall eliminate it at once.

I do not anticipate any objection to your proposal to couch the approval of War Department planning in more general language, and am proceeding to re-write the affected paragraphs. In this connection the War Department plans were made the subject of a separate conclusion solely in order that the Commission might present a definite program affecting the organizational, administrative, and functional matters that must form part of any complete set of "policies to be pursued in event of war." Since the War Department plans concerning these subjects seem to conform generally to the testimony of the several witnesses that discussed them, my purpose in drafting these paragraphs was simply to suggest to the Commission a method for covering this phase of the problem presented.

Many of the suggestions made in the original draft by Congressman McSwain are included in the present revision. The particular one affecting War Department planning had not been so included simply because no discussion concerning it arose at the meeting of December 1st.

I note that you apparently approve Congressman McSwain's suggestion to eliminate the recommendation dealing with a war-profits tax. I feel that this subject must be covered definitely in the Commission's report. In view of the fact that Congressman McSwain had made no suggestion in the paragraphs entitled "Function of War Taxes", beginning on page 32, I had retained the particular recommendation, pending final decision of the Commission. So many of the witnesses regarded the taxing power as the only applicable method for eliminating profiteering that I believe it must form some part of the whole program proposed by the Commission.

I understand that the next meeting of the Commission will not be held until after the Attorney General submits an opinion on the general subject of the constitutionality of "price-fixing in war". Before that time I hope to forward to you a revised draft of the report. Sincerely,
R. H. MONTGOMERY

1. The draft letter for Montgomery's signature was contained within the text of Eisenhower's letter.

65

DECEMBER 20, 1931

Went to office of C. of I.[1] the other day and placed informal request for assignment to San Antonio. Made up my mind to do so only after a long struggle as I hate the heat, etc. Family was so insistent thought it best thing to do. Mamie is concerned chiefly with getting a post where servants are good—cheap—plentiful. I'd like a place that offers some interesting outdoor work. Dad, Mother, & Mamie have talked about S. A. until it is apparent that they're going to be all down in the mouth with any other selection. So I asked for it. Now I hear Charley Howland[2] is going there. What a break!! It would be a good excuse to ask for something else—but as far as the family is concerned the conditions have not changed materially. So I guess he will be just another thing for me to worry about.[3]

1. The Chief of Infantry at this time was Maj. Gen. Stephen O. Fuqua, who entered West Point in 1892 but did not graduate. He participated in the Spanish-American War, received his commission in 1901, and moved through the ranks to become a major general in 1929, when he was appointed Chief of Infantry. Fuqua retired in 1938 to become military affairs editor of *Newsweek*.

2. Charles Roscoe Howland (USMA, 1895) served in the Philippines (1898–1902) as aide-de-camp to Gen. Arthur MacArthur (Douglas MacArthur's father, 1903), and as Assistant Judge Advocate General (1907–12). He retired in 1935 as a brigadier general.

3. Evidently Eisenhower did not relish serving under Howland and saw this as a bad "break." He was also considering not taking the San Antonio assignment because of this situation; however, Mamie's wish to go to San Antonio, and Eisenhower's expression that it would "be just another thing [. . .] to worry about," seems to have persuaded Eisenhower to go ahead with the assignment.

66

TO ELIVERA DOUD

[DECEMBER 25, 1931]

Dearest Min: I am writing you my first letter on my new typewriter, which it seems you, Mamie and John enticed old Santa to send me. Of course

I've wanted one for a long time, but I think I never was more surprised in my life with a present. They certainly guarded the secret well around this house.

As I look over my list I find that your name appears with a regularity that is quite startling. Socks, underwear, ties and pajamas have all come to my house with your name attached to them. I appreciate them all and thank you a lot for all of them. Auntie sent me some socks, Unk and Carolyn[1] gave Mamie and me a fine set of bookends, and Mike and Dick[2] sent us some large pieces of that silver Mamie is collecting. We also had silver from pupah who sent on a check for the Eisenhower family and we decided we wanted to spend it that way. From that same source John got a new pair of corduroy pants. Mamie tells me also that you were responsible for a fine fruitcake we found under the tree this morn.

Mamie of course is fairly hysterical over her tablecloth. She spread it out on the table at once and walked around and around getting the view from every angle. She has been terribly busy since she recovered from her attack of flu because that put her far behind on her Christmas schedule. I think she looks very well at that.

We had the Hodgsons[3] over to dinner last night. Johnny has made P.A. his particular hero these days, and he is forever urging us to get them over here. They are fine and are quite keen on John— so everything is lovely.

We had a big snow last week, but it has since turned warm and most of the snow has disappeared. For a couple of days traffic was in a terrible snarl, and there were many minor accidents.

Mamie just informs me that it is time to go to see Milton and Helen, as well as the McCammons.[4] She also says to tell you she will surely write today or tomorrow.

I am very glad that Mike has decided to throw her party the first thing New Year's morning. One is always searching for new ways of entertaining their friends while they are sitting around to hear the chimes and firecrackers—and her suggestion strikes me as having a real air of originality. I'll be writing to her very soon. I know she'd appreciate some advice on this matter—and I see no reason why I should get snooty and refuse to give it.

Well as you can imagine everybody is quite excited around here this a.m. (My golly, I see I skipped a whole line. I wonder how that happened?) Johnny says his first X-mas letter will be to you and that he intends writing it on this machine. If he is as awkward as I am you will be getting another weird and wonderful affair. Anyway he'll get a wonderful thrill out of picking it out, and you can devote your daily crossword period to <u>puzzling</u> it out. (I don't know just what hour you will use for <u>this</u> effort.)

Lots of love from all of us to you, Mike and Dick. Thanks again for all the lovely presents.

As ever, Your devoted son

P.S. Your special delivery just arrived. Mamie just finished reading it to Johnny and me.

1. "Unk" is another nickname for Mamie's Uncle Joel Carlson; Carolyn was Joel's wife.

2. "Mike" was the family nickname for Mamie's youngest sister, Mabel Frances Doud Gill; "Dick" was Richard Gill, her husband.

3. Col. Paul Alfred Hodgson, native of Latham, Kansas, shared a room with Eisenhower at West Point until their graduation in 1915. In later years Eisenhower would characterize Hodgson as the kind of roommate—scholarly, conservative, well-disciplined—that he needed as a steadying influence on his own tendencies to be impulsive and a little too fun-loving. Hodgson spent World War I working with training units in the United States. Between the wars he served with the office of the assistant secretary of war. In 1942 he returned to the Army, serving as the executive officer at Fort Sam Houston until his retirement in 1946.

4. Helen Eakin Eisenhower was the wife of Milton Eisenhower. John Easton McCammon may be the person referred to. He served in the Army from 1917 until he retired in 1951 with the rank of colonel.

CHAPTER FOUR

Service with the Chief of Staff
January 30, 1932–August 8, 1935

Eisenhower remained at the office of the assistant secretary of war until February 1933, when he was transferred within the War Department to be a special assistant to Chief of Staff Douglas MacArthur.[1] This assignment formalized an arrangement that had been informal for more than a year; beginning in January 1932, Eisenhower had worked on a number of projects that related to MacArthur's office and the War Department General Staff. In the assistant secretary's office and then with MacArthur, he developed a reputation for being an officer who could accomplish many different tasks and successfully work with people at all levels—from the lowest-ranking soldier to high-level officials.

Eisenhower's diaries in these years expressed his concern about the continuing effects of the Great Depression on the military and his views of the Roosevelt administration, which employed the army to manage the Civilian Conservation Corps and the Public Works Administration at the time of their creation. The military later provided major support to the Works Progress Administration and conducted a variety of government studies. All such unusual service may have saved the military from deeper budget cuts than it suffered.

Meanwhile, as the army endeavored to develop wartime mobilization plans, Eisenhower produced some of his most important analytical writing. He noted that American industrial leaders avoided military procurement commitments unless guaranteed large profits; they were fearful of military controls and otherwise reluctant to engage in definitive strategic planning. Problems of procurement and mobilization planning brought Eisenhower face to face with what he later called the "military-industrial complex." War Department policies and politics grew increasingly interwoven, and Eisenhower found himself at the center of action.

As MacArthur's assistant in Washington, Eisenhower enjoyed a cordial relationship with the Chief of Staff. Eisenhower seemed genuinely flattered to work with the general; the position also enhanced the reputation the younger man had built in the assistant secretary of war's office and which no doubt had commended him to MacArthur.[2]

1. According to Eisenhower's personnel records (Records of the Adjutant General, Eisenhower Library), he bore no formal title during this term of service. His efficiency reports for 1933–35 simply describe him as "on duty in the Office of the Chief of Staff." In *At Ease: Stories I Tell to Friends* (Garden City, N.Y.: Doubleday, 1967), 213–19, Eisenhower shed no light on the subject. In his diary entry for March 15, 1933, however, he refers to his being appointed "senior aide." His last day in the chief of staff's office was September 24, 1935.

2. For general background on Douglas MacArthur, and the Philippines, the editors have relied on the following sources (listed chronologically by date of publication): George E. Taylor, *The Philippines and the United States: Problems of Partnership* (New York: Praeger, 1964); D. Clayton James, *The Years of MacArthur, 1880–1941* (Boston: Houghton Mifflin, 1975); William R. Manchester, *American Caesar: Douglas MacArthur, 1880–1964* (Boston: Little, Brown, 1978); and Carol M. Petillo, *Douglas MacArthur: The Philippine Years* (Bloomington: Indiana University Press, 1981). Citations to these sources occur only for either direct quotations or specific information.

67   Eisenhower Library
Mamie Doud Eisenhower Papers,
Family Correspondence File

To John S. Doud

[January 1932]

Dear Dad: Since writing you recently our tentative plans for the coming year have been completely changed. As you know we were counting on going to San Antonio—being particularly anxious to lead an outdoor life for a couple of years and above all to be so located that the whole family could have some real reunions.

As you know I was basing my excuse for leaving here this summer on the fact that I will be due for duty with troops July 1. I have not, however, completed a four year detail since I returned from France. General MacArthur discovered all these facts the other day through questioning the Adjutant General (the official who is custodian of all records). He also found out that the troop duty matter could be cleared up by assigning me to additional duty with the troop units in this city.

He then sent for me, and expressed his desire that I remain on my present job. He was very nice about it all, and discussed my future assignments very frankly. He repeated many of the same things he put into that letter of commendation you saw some months back. Finally he told me to talk it over with Mamie and let him know the answer.

To say that we were surprised is putting it mildly. We had had no prior hint that such a thing was even considered. Of course we were flattered that he liked my work well enough to want to keep us, and had interested himself personally in seeing how it could be done. It was, on the other hand, hard to give up our anticipated pleasure in going to S. A. All in all there was nothing else to do. It is an opportunity that comes rarely, and when Gen. Moseley, the A.G. and Gen. MacA's aide all told me that they knew he really <u>wanted</u> us to stay—why I just marched back in to his office and said "O.K. General." So that's that!!

There are many angles to it that you will like to hear when we get to talk it over. They help to make the whole matter interesting for the family—but are too long and involved to write about. Please send this letter on to mother so she'll know what has happened. I rather think that just like us she will be disappointed that the S. A. detail fell through—but I know she'll get a great kick out of knowing the circumstances under which we were kept here.[1] As ever your devoted Son

1. In his diary entry of February 15, 1932, Eisenhower refers to a meeting with MacArthur on "Saturday (13th)" about his immediate career plans. The date was January 13. In December 1931, Eisenhower tried to obtain a troop command at Fort Sam Houston, San Antonio. Although he was not enthusiastic about the prospect, he chose that station because Mamie and her parents, who wintered in San Antonio, preferred that posting to any other. MacArthur, already aware of Eisenhower's unusual talents, used all of his charm and force to persuade Eisenhower to remain at the War Department and offered hope that he would soon find even more rewarding work in Washington. A year later, MacArthur chose Eisenhower as his principal assistant in the chief of staff's office. Eisenhower, knowing the Douds were anxiously awaiting word on his next assignment, would likely have written to his in-laws shortly after this meeting with the Chief of Staff, therefore, the presumed date of this letter.

68

Eisenhower Library
Chief of Staff Diary

JANUARY 30, 1932–FEBRUARY 15, 1932

JANUARY 30

There has been informally put up to me the proposition of going to West Point for the purpose of relieving Maj. Fleming[1] as graduate manager of athletics in 1933. Had two talks with Gen. Connor (W.D.)[2] who is to be the next Superintendent.

The Chief of Staff & Gen. Moseley both disapproved.

Also considered (after a talk with Gen. Heintzelman)[3] the possibility of going to Leavenworth as an instructor and as Commander of the Inf. Bn. located there. This also was disapproved very luckily. The dual job would undoubtedly prove very confining.

1. Maj. Gen. Philip Bracken Fleming (USMA, 1911) became deputy administrator of the Public Works Administration (1933), coordinator of the Resettlement Administration (1939), and in 1941, administrator of the Federal Works Agency. He retired from the army in 1947.

2. Gen. William Durward Connor (USMA, 1897) served in the Philippines and as Commandant of the Army War College (1927–32). From 1932 until his retirement in 1938 he served as Superintendent of West Point.

3. Maj. Gen. Stuart Heintzelman (USMA, 1899) served in the Philippine Insurrection and in World War I. From 1921 to 1924 he held the position of Assistant Chief of Staff, U.S. Army, and from 1929 until his death in 1935 was Commandant of the Command and General Staff School at Fort Leavenworth.

Just completed a report on the Philippine Islands. I worked under the direction of the Chief of Staff—the report being intended for the signature of Sec. War.

The C. of S. was very much pleased with it—and I heard that the Sec. War also liked it. However, I also understand that the Sec. has not yet signed it.

The report advocates continuance of status quo for the present, and denies the ability of Filipino masses to express intelligent opinion on the many questions involved until they shall have reached a substantially higher cultural plane.

On Saturday (13th) Gen. MacArthur called me to his office for a short conference relative to my prospective transfer to the duty in July. He called attention to the fact that though I would be due for duty with troops this summer I will not have completed a 4 year detail in this city until Sept. 1933.

He suggested that I go on additional duty with organized reserves on July 1 and stay here for 4 years. Gave me until today to think it over— and also informed me that at the end of 4 year detail he would give me Ft. Washington to command.[1] I talked it all over with Mamie, with Gen. Moseley, Gen. Bridges and Capt. Davis[2] (Aide to Gen. MacA).

This A.M. told the General I would be glad to stay. While I do not think I'll want to go to Ft. W.—that's a long way off—anything can happen.

Gen. MacA. was very nice to me—and after all I know of no greater compliment the bosses can give you than I want you hanging around.

1. Fort Washington, Maryland, located ten miles south of the District of Columbia on the east bank of the Potomac, was home at that time to the 3d Battalion, 12th Infantry.

2. Maj. Gen. Charles Higbee Bridges (USMA, 1897) became Assistant Adjutant General of the Army in 1927 and Adjutant General of the Army in 1929. He died in 1948.

Thomas Jefferson Davis, one of Eisenhower's good friends and professional colleagues, participated in World War I. After the war he remained in Europe with the Army of Occupation until 1923. During the 1930s he served as one of MacArthur's aides, both in Washington and, at Eisenhower's request, in the Philippines. In 1940, Davis returned to Washington from Manila and worked in the office of the adjutant general. Brigadier General Davis served Eisenhower as Adjutant General, Allied Forces, North Africa (1942–43) and as Adjutant General, Supreme Headquarters, Allied Expeditionary Forces (1944–45). In August 1945 he accompanied Eisenhower to Russia. Davis served as Assistant Adjutant General of the Army from 1946 until his retirement in 1953.

69   National Archives and Records Administration (NARA)
Records of the Secretary of War

To Congressman Lindley H. Hadley

February 25, 1932

Dear Congressman: I telephoned the offices of all the members of the Commission this afternoon informing them of the meeting tomorrow [. . . .] [1]

In most instances I was unable to secure definite information that members would attend, but I am promised that the indicated information will be conveyed to the various members by their respective secretaries. I suggest that if you have the opportunity it would be well to remind the House members of the Commission in person concerning this meeting. In view of the unavoidable absences there is likely to be some difficulty in obtaining a quorum.

May I remind you again that since I have no official connection with the Commission it will not be appropriate for me to attend an executive session. If you could have a stenographer take such rough notes of the proceedings as may be necessary, I will be available to assist you in the necessary redraft of the report.

In confirmation of telephonic conversation I sent a note similar to the one inclosed to each member of the Commission.
Very truly

1. Even though Eisenhower remarked that he had no "official" position with the commission, it is apparent that he had assumed a key role in the organization and execution of the commission's work.

70

To COLONEL R. H. MONTGOMERY

FEBRUARY 26, 1932

Dear Colonel: Everything concerning the Commission was put off until the last minute. Now there has developed a mad rush to get everything finished as quickly as possible. It is apparently expected to complete the report by March 6, which date marks the expiration of the three months extension requested last December.

I have not seen the opinion prepared by The Attorney General, but have had several conversations with Colonel Hurley. I gather that the chief criticisms of The Attorney General will be directed more against the method of presentation of the report than against any specific recommendation made.

There is to be a meeting this afternoon and indications are that a quorum will be present. Mr. Hurley went over with me the general tenor of the recommendations he wants to submit, and I have gotten them ready for him. He is against any Constitutional amendment, but otherwise has no ideas particularly different from those set forth in the first revision. He directed me to place the recommendations in a slightly more detailed form so as to explain exactly the program that he believes should be followed.

If any definite action results from the meeting this afternoon I will forward to you promptly complete information concerning it.

The oranges and limes arrived yesterday afternoon. They are delicious, and we are eating them very rapidly because our ice box is too small to take care of them all. Mamie and I thank you a lot. With best wishes, Sincerely

MARCH 5, 1932

Turned in final recommendation of W.P. Commission. Have a few other documents that I must fix up and get ready for submission within a few days. Except for that the long siege with the W.P.C. is completed.

72   NARA
                            Records of the Secretary of War
                        Report of the War Policies Commission[1]

TO THE PRESIDENT

MARCH 5, 1932

The Commission appointed under Public Resolution No. 98, 71st Congress, entitled "Joint Resolution to promote peace and to equalize the burdens and to minimize the profits of war", respectfully submits the following report and recommendations:

First, we recommend in order to eliminate all doubt concerning the extent of the power of the Congress to prevent profiteering and to stabilize prices in time of war, that a proposed Constitutional amendment clearly defining such power be submitted by the Congress to the States.

Second, we further recommend that until a Constitutional amendment be adopted clearly defining the power of Congress to prevent profiteering and to stabilize prices in time of war, the following program be adopted as governmental policy in order effectively to minimize the profits of war and to distribute its burdens and sacrifices equitably:

(a) That the Congress should empower the President, in the event of war, to institute a program under which prices may be stabilized and thereafter adjusted at such levels as will minimize inflation and will secure to the Government the use of any private property needed in the prosecution of the war without affording the owner thereof profit due to the war. It should be clearly stated that such a program will not be placed in operation until Congress specifically directs it as a necessary measure in the conduct of war.

(b) The Congress should empower the President to make, in war, such readjustments in, and additions to, the Executive Departments of the Government as are necessary to assure adequate control of all National resources. The President should be empowered also to fix the status, for the period of the war, of personnel transferred under this authority, from one Bureau or Department of the Government to any other.

(c) Existing law empowering the President to compel acceptance of war orders and to commandeer property should be continued.

(d) In addition to all other plans to remove the profits of war, the Revenue Law should provide that, upon any declaration of war and during the period of such emergency, individuals and corporations shall be taxed 95 per cent of all income above the previous three-year average, with proper adjustments for capital expenditures for war purposes by existing or new industries.

(e) In time of peace continuous planning by the Federal Government, particularly by the War and Navy Departments, should be directed toward insuring:

(1) That upon declaration of war there shall be immediately available to the Congress accurate and detailed estimates concerning the man-power and material needs of the military and naval services, together with detailed studies and recommendations concerning the most applicable methods for mobilizing the necessary men and procuring the required munitions.

(2) That there shall be no competitive bidding between Government agencies for the products of industry.

(3) There shall be no placing of contracts in excess of needs.

(4) That cost plus percentage methods of purchase shall be eliminated.

(5) That the munitions production load shall be distributed properly over the United States.

(6) That the governmental organizations required in the administration of war functions shall be set up promptly.

(7) That the necessary controls respecting prices, raw materials, transportation, priorities, war trade, finance, and related matters shall be continuously studied, so that in the event of war the will of Congress may be promptly and efficiently administrated.

(f) Plans prepared in the War and Navy Departments for the accomplishment of the above should be continuously revised to meet changing national and international conditions, and should be thoroughly examined and revised at least every two years by appropriate Congressional committees.

Third, we recommend that no Constitutional amendment to permit the taking of private property in time of war without compensation be considered by the Congress.

Respectfully submitted

(Signed)

Patrick J. Hurley, Chairman; David A. Reed, Vice Chairman; Joe T.

Robinson; John J. McSwain; Arthur H. Vandenberg; William Mitchell; C. F. Adams; R. P. Lamont; Wm. B. Holaday; Arthur W. Hyde; W. N. Doak; Lindley H. Hadley, Secretary.

To the President: [Minority Report]

The purpose in creating the so-called War Policies Commission was to "study and consider amending the Constitution of the United States to provide that private property may be taken by Congress for public use during war and methods of equalizing the burdens and to remove the profits of war, together with a study of policies to be pursued in the event of war".

I take it that the object of the Resolution creating the Commission deals solely with the purpose of eliminating profits that accrue to certain classes of individuals and corporations during war and that "a study of policies to be pursued in the event of war" relates to policies to be prescribed by Congress either through a Constitutional Amendment or by legislation for the purpose of eliminating war profits.

As the Constitution of the United States is now drawn, I am convinced that the only way to eliminate war profits is through the adoption of a Constitutional Amendment so as to enable Congress to pass legislation creating an agency to fix prices of commodities either for the purpose of keeping profits at a minimum or the entire elimination of them. I heartily favor the adoption of a constitutional amendment to carry out this object.

I do not believe it was the intention of Congress that the power to fix prices of commodities should be delegated to military men. I believe that such administrative matters should be entirely in the hands of civilians and I object to any recommendation that would tend to confer upon military men the power to regulate prices or the activities of the civilian population during war or at any other time. I am firmly convinced, whether intended or not, that any war planning as now carried on by the War Department will in the end result in the administration of price fixing laws and the regulation of civilian activities by military and naval officers if the recommendations of the majority members of the Commission are finally adopted by Congress.

I regret that I am unable to follow the majority of the Members of the Commission upon all of their proposals and respectfully submit to you this dissent.

Very respectfully, Ross A. Collins.

1. Eisenhower wrote and initialed the commission's report, indicating he wrote the document. He probably prepared the minority report as well, because it is part of the same document.

Records of the Secretary of War

MEMORANDUM FOR SENATOR ARTHUR VANDENBERG

MARCH 7, 1932

1. Referring to the subject of appropriate legislative action in support of the recommendations made by the War Policies Commission, I bring the following to your attention:

In its second recommendation, sub-paragraph (b), the Commission stated:

"The Congress should empower the President to make, in war, such readjustments in, and additions to the Executive Departments of the Government as are necessary to assure adequate control of all national resources. The President should be empowered also to fix the status, for the period of war, of personnel transferred under this authority from one Bureau or Department of the Government to any other."

This apparently means that a law similar to the war-time "Overman Act" should be placed on the statute books now.

Mr. Baruch in his testimony said:

"In addition to some such statutes as these, the essential principles of the Overman Act (approved May 28, 1918) should be reenacted authorizing the President in time of war to make such redistribution of functions of Executive Departments as he may determine."

2. Of the several proposals advanced by the Commission (excepting those dealing with a Constitutional amendment and with taxes) this is the only one in which Congressional action is apparently contemplated in advance of an emergency. A bill providing for this transfer of executive functions and personnel might be introduced. This, taken in conjunction with the amendment and the resolution concerning the drafting of the tax laws, might be considered as giving complete force to the Commissions recommendations. The general resolution I suggested to you this morning would be discarded. Respectfully

JOINT RESOLUTION[1]

Proposing an amendment to the Constitution of the United States providing for the fixing of prices in time of war and the prevention of profiteering.

Resolved by the Senate and House of Representatives of the United States of America in Congress assembled (two-thirds of each House concurring therein): That the following article is proposed as an amendment to the Constitution of the United States which shall be valid to all intents and purposes as part of the Constitution when ratified by the legislation of three-fourths of the several states:

ARTICLE

At the end of the Fifth Amendment change the period to a semicolon and add the following:

"Provided, however, that in time of war Congress may regulate or provide for the regulation of prices, rent, or compensation to be exacted or paid by any person in respect of the sale, rent or use of any real or personal property, tangible or intangible, without regard to any limitation contained in this Article or any other Article of the Constitution."

1. Eisenhower signed the document, then sent it to Vandenberg. He also prepared the proposed resolution for a constitutional amendment.

74

NARA
Records of the Adjutant General's Office

To United States Senator David I. Walsh[1]

May 27, 1932

Dear Senator Walsh: Elaborating further on the subject matter of our conversation this morning, I am giving below a summary of facts that bear directly upon the proposition of retiring two thousand officers from active service.

The National Defence Act of 1920, adopted by Congress after an exhaustive analysis of the lessons of the World War, provided for a Regular Army of 18,000 officers and 280,000 enlisted men. Through successive reductions since that time the numbers are now approximately 12,000 officers and 125,000 enlisted men. These depletions have served to throw a more highly concentrated load upon the remaining officers, for it is to be remembered that administration and training of Regular Army units constitute only one of the duties of the professional officer corps. Other duties comprise many kinds of preparation for mobilization, such as civilian training, experimentation, planning, and research. The importance of national security of these activities of course has been intensified by the reductions made in the forces immediately available to us in event of war.

There are now 12,133 officers on the active list. Of these, 5,031 are serving in tactical units of the Regular Army, while another 1,200 are serving in capacities directly connected with the local sanitation, administration, and training of these troops. The number assigned to tactical units is 1,300 short of their actual requirements, which shortage is occasioned by the need for officers in other essential activities.

1,653 Regular officers are serving with the citizen components—National Guard, Organized Reserves, and Reserve Officers' Training Corps. This work is of primary importance. Through it there is being developed a nucleus of partially trained personnel to assist in the intricate organizational and training tasks inherent in a general mobilization of an untrained citizenry.

On school duty, including the faculties and student bodies of all military educational institutions, there are about 2,400 officers. Our military educational system proved its value on the battlefields of the World War, and since that conflict it has been vastly improved in quality. Through it the whole Army is kept abreast of the times in tactical methods, and our officers are developed into skillful and capable leaders. Such institutions as the Infantry School at Fort Benning, the Field Artillery School at Fort Sill, and the Cavalry School at Fort Riley, furnish, with the aid of the model units maintained thereat, as practical a training for our combat officers as anything short of actual war can provide.

The technical branches, such as the Medical, Engineer, and Ordnance Departments, require a considerable number of officers. The duties they perform are of a specialized nature, both in current administration and in preparing to meet the great problem of munitions production in war. Successful functioning of all our technical branches would be vital to the operation of large armies in emergency. The officers assigned exclusively to this work, added to all those engaged in a variety of miscellaneous though most important tasks, including duty in the War Department and on civil works, total about 15 per cent of existing strength.

To carry on efficiently all the essential duties that devolve upon it, the War Department has estimated, after repeated studies, that approximately 14,000 officers are necessary—3,000 more than are now available. Consequently there is a shortage of officers in every category of activity I have mentioned. Nevertheless, it has been alleged that our officers outnumber those of the British Army, the only other military force among the great powers maintained by voluntary recruitment. Such statements are absolutely without foundation in fact, yet apparently they have had considerable weight among the uninformed. I am attaching hereto pertinent statistics on this matter.

This country, because of its particular situation, does not need a large standing army nor tremendous reserves in munitions. The American system properly places ultimate responsibility for the defense of the country in a citizen soldiery, raised, trained, and equipped after the beginning of any emergency. But the success of such a system depends upon the continuous existence of a trained nucleus of reasonable size. Of this nucleus the professional officers corps is unquestionably the most essential part. In this body reside the expert knowledge, the specialized training, and the peculiar ability necessary to the successful operation of the whole.

The trained officer is the one element of an army that cannot be improvised. Like all other professional men, he is the product of his own study, research, and experience. It would indeed be a short sighted policy of economy that made further inroads into this already weakened vital element of our defense structure. Very sincerely yours, F. H. PAYNE, The Assistant Secretary of War.[2]

On Administrative Duties		
War Department	525	
Corps Areas & Overseas Departments	337	
		862
At Service Installations		
Development, Supply, Transportation and Finance	810	
Medical and Welfare	926	
Recruiting	99	
Military Attaches	32	
		1867
With the Civilian Components		
National Guard	466	
Organized Reserves	472	
Reserve Officers' Training Corps	715	
		1653
At Schools (West Point, War College, Service Schools, etc)		2395
On Civil Duties (Public Works, etc)		268
With Troops		
United States	3155	
Overseas Garrisons	1876	
		5031
Miscellaneous		57
TOTAL		12133

1. David I. Walsh served one term as governor of Massachusetts (1914–15) and in the U.S. Senate from 1918 to 1924. He returned to the Senate in 1926 to fill the unexpired term of Henry Cabot Lodge. Reelected in 1929, he continued in the Senate until his defeat in 1946. Walsh died June 11, 1947.

2. Additional attachments accompanying the letter are not included.

75

JUNE 14, 1932–AUGUST 10, 1932
JUNE 14

Twenty-one years ago today I entered West Point.

The past few months have been hectic ones for those charged with Army Administration. The general economic situation has been such that "pacifistic" propaganda and efforts have been more effective than ordinarily is the case. All our appropriations are to be cut substantially under pending legislation—and right now the Senate and the House are fighting it out to see whether or not 2000 officers are to be retired.

All salaries are to be reduced—apparently about 10%. The outlook for an Army officer on "city" duty is none too cheering.

Rode to work with Helen and Bill[1] this A.M. They were having an argument concerning moths in clothes. Which reminds me that Mamie had cleaned before putting away for the summer only my two old tweeds and my tails. All overcoats and uniforms she put into cedar bags without cleaning. We'll see how this works out.

I expressed fear we'd regret it—but she's perfectly confident that all will be well. (Jan. '33—It was!)[2]

1. William and Helen Gruber.
2. The January 1933 entry is a margin note that was added later.

JUNE 15

Occurred to me I might jot down from time to time impressions of people with whom I came in contact. Sometime in the future it will be fun to review these to determine whether my impression was a permanent one.[1]

Notes on Men.

There are no "great men" as we understood that expression when we were shavers. The man whose brain is so all-embracing in its grasp of events, so infallible in its logic, and so swift in formulation of perfect decisions, is only a figment of the imagination. Yet as kids we were taught to believe in the shibboleth of the "super-man"—possibly because it is easier to exaggerate than not.

In spite of this some men achieve goals for which numbers have been striving—and it is interesting to look over those qualifying for "Who's Who" or who have attracted special attention in some field, to try to make an estimate of their character, their abilities and their weaknesses. In succeeding pages I shall jot down some notes—many made on poor info—but nevertheless representing <u>my impressions</u> as they are formed.

It will at least be amusing to see how the months or years change my own opinions.

Maj. Gen. R.E. Callan G-4[2]

Energetic—keen—and very serious minded, verging toward pomposity. I do not know him very well.

Maj Gen. Edgar Collins—G-2[3]

Keen, positive, impulsive and mentally honest. Progressive in his thinking—firm in his likes and dislikes and an officer I admire tremendously. He believes in "selection" and preaches it day and night—even to the C. of S.—who is diametrically opposed to him in this matter. Died Feb. '33

F. Trubee Davison, Asst. Sec. of War for Air[4]

A nice little boy! Courteous, well bred, and tactful. Ambitious politically, and being a man of real wealth and of Republican convictions (or affiliations) he will probably some day hold a responsible position in American political life. A bit petulant—but not so much so as Mr. Hurley.

He is now about 35–36 and since the Republicans have dominated national politics about 75% of the time in the past 60 years, it can be expected that he will have many opportunities during the next 30 years to attain his ambitions. In the Democratic landslide of this fall he was defeated overwhelmingly as candidate for Lt. Gov.

Brig. Gen. C.E. Kilbourne, W.P.D.[5]

A hard working, modest, and essentially sound individual who appears to have little imagination or mental keenness. I hear him spoken of principally as the fine "wheel horse" type.

Moseley, Maj. Gen. Geo. Van Horn

Thin, wiry and very alert type. Generous to a fault—and extremely appreciative of efforts of subordinates. Consequently is likeable and has the affection of everyone with whom he comes in contact.

Works "personally" as opposed to "organizationally"—a trait that grinds the soul of some of our "so-called" Gen. Staff people, particularly those whose god is "ritual".

Has an enormous circle of friends—many made while he was G-4 of A.E.F., 1917–18. Essentially honest and straightforward—very sensitive but not unduly avid for self-advancement.

Worries somewhat about things and circumstances over which he exercises and can exercise no control. For example—in our present situation (1932) he sees many common sense measures that could be applied nationally to the great benefit of the whole people. These engage his attention and time and make him fret somewhat that he can do nothing about it. This trait, taken in connection with the fact that he performs daily an enormous amount of work, constitutes a drain on his strength. However, he does not seem to weaken under it.

He is now 57. His only chance of any further advancement (he is now Dep. Chief of Staff) is to be made Chief of Staff in November 1934. If he keeps his health and gets the job he'll be a peach. He is a rabid "selectionist".[6]

Among the senior officers of the Army he has been my most intimate friend and one for whom I have great admiration and esteem.

A wonderful officer—a splendid gentleman and a true friend. Mentally honest and with great moral courage he is well equipped for any task this govt. can possibly give him.

Brig. Gen. Andrew Moses G-1[7]

Affable, likable, and possessed of a fund of common sense. Barring accident will probably be made a Maj. Gen. in due course but in event of war I would not expect to see him one of the men who would go to the top quickly.

F.H. Payne—A.S.W.

A typical New Englander about 56–8 years of age. Little academic training but lots of common sense and very shrewd. Tall thin in appearance, he is straightforward and direct in action. Very much intrigued with the social side of Washington official life and attends every dance—tea—reception, etc. to which invited. Likes also to appear at conventions, dinners and etc. where he is invited to speak but cares very little what material appears in the speech. His thrill comes from the invitation itself—which he considers a recognition of his prominent position in the official world—and from meeting people. Devoted to his family. Friendly in all his contacts. An old-line Republican. Anti-prohibitionist. My principal contacts with him are through writing all his speeches.

Col. A. T. Smith—G-2[8]

Courteous and gentlemanly and particularly assiduous in trying to anticipate the desires of his superiors. Has been named for advancement to Brig. Gen., but has not yet been confirmed. He is one of the officers recommended by Gen. MacA. for promotion that do not, in the opinion of most people, stand out as worthy of this recognition. At times he appears slow, if not stupid.

Maj. Gen. Fox Conner

Cmdg. 1st Corps Area.

A wonderful officer and leader with a splendid analytical mind. He is as loyal to subordinates as to superiors, and like Simonds,[9] Moseley and others of our finest is quick to give credit to juniors.

This summer (1932) he has been in bad health but I sincerely trust is fully recovered. I served as his brigade exec. for 3 years in Panama and never enjoyed any other 3 year period so much. Devoted to his family and to the service, he is a credit to both as well as to his country. He has held a place in my affections for many years that no other, not a relative, could obtain. Only a few others have ever meant so much to me personally. These include Gerow—Moseley.

Maj. Gen. W.D. Connor, Commandant, West Point[10]

Mentally alert—ambitious—physically trim—straightforward in his thinking and acting, he is one of our best. He'd make a fine Chief of Staff—and if he ever gets the job (he is now 58) he'll be a real success at it. I like him and would be glad to join his command any time in peace or war. He believes in promotion by "selection". By many considered arbitrary—unfair and egotistical. I do not agree.

George H. Dern—Sec. War., Ex-Governor of Utah[11]

About 56–57 years of age. Slow, ponderous, and with a love of stilted phraseology that so often characterizes the "heavy" speaker. Honest, thoughtful and straightforward—he is, all in all, a cautious but sound person.

From my few contacts I have learned to like him—and believe that in a real pinch he would be sturdy as a rock—but he could never be a warm advocate of a lost cause. There is nothing of the romantic in his makeup—so far as can be seen from surface and casual observation.

He shows up best in producing an analytical paper on a subject requiring elucidation. He is painstaking in research and logical in his mental processes. He is poorest when making a public address. His love of quotations, of generalization and of platitudes is nothing less than remarkable.

Hugh Drum[12]

Gen. Drum became Dep. Chief of Staff last February. My room is located between his and that of the C. of S.—so I get to see a great deal of him. In addition, in my capacity as Senior Aide (Military Secretary) to C. of S. I am in on many of the important conferences.

Until this year I had known Gen. Drum only by reputation and, to some slight extent, socially.

He is able, industrious, efficient and likable. Beyond doubt he is one of our best, and his ability is universally recognized. Except for Gen. MacA is the youngest of our Maj. Generals (54 now) and will probably be C. of S. someday. He is a "selectionist"—at least to the extent of wanting to find some way of getting rid of dead wood.

<u>Major L.T. Gerow</u> Inf.

My best friend. A graduate of V.M.I. about 2 years older than I. He is intensely loyal—painstaking, energetic and possessed of a sound analytical mind. Once in a while I think he is a little too respectful of rank, but this fault, if it is a fault, is very nearly the only one with which he has been cursed. I know of no job in the Army, either in peace or war that he could not perform brilliantly—and given a few months to size up new situations there are mighty few in civil life that he could not master completely.

Of medium size—handsome, courteous and with a splendid personality he is liked as well as respected by both seniors and subordinates.

If "Gee" does not eventually hold one of the highest positions in the Army—it will be because circumstances, such as linear promotion or health, intervene and prevent. I have no language sufficiently forceful to describe his efficiency and general worth.

Kathryn (Gee's wife) died June 17, 1935.[13]

<u>Patrick J. Hurley, Secretary of War</u>

About 49 years old. Affable but rather petulant, courteous but unappreciative of good work on the part of subordinates. His interests seem almost wholly political—and he has sufficient wealth to take full advantage of every opportunity offered along this line. Keen on favorable publicity and always solicitous of members of the press—no matter what the occasion. Meticulous as to details of dress and personal appearance—sometimes characterized by the unfriendly sections of the press as a "dandy", "Fop", etc.

I do not believe he will go any higher in the political world although he is very ambitious.

My prediction is that whenever the Republicans are in power he will have a cabinet post—ambassadorship—or other appointive position—or may possibly show up later in the Senate.

He is not big enough to go higher.

Unquestionably he has decided that his one chance of political advancement is as a henchman of Pres. Hoover. Consequently in public utterances he is slavish in his support of the Pres. He is jealous and unstable.

In June, 1932 Mr. Coffin and Dr. Mortin, both former members of the Advisory Commission of the Council of Nat. Def. submitted their resignations to the Sec. of War—also, by law the Chairman of Council. Although the Council has been inactive since 1921 both gave as the ostensible reason for the resignation the fact that the slate of the Council should be clear. Actually they were probably caused by the refusal of the Pres. to utilize the Council as a means of combatting the present economic emergency.

I prepared drafts of proposed replies—conservative, but acknowledging the services performed by the 2 men in the past. P.J.H.[14] wants to put in a par.[agraph] that is insulting and needlessly belittling. Probably because it is generally understood that the Pres. heartily dislikes Mr. Coffin.

Harold Ickes, Secretary of Interior, Chairman Public Works Board Director, Oil Conservation.[15]

Essentially a small man if newspapers portray him as he is. More concerned in looking well in the public eye than in doing his job without regard to personal fortunes. I have never seen anything published about him that indicates ability—bigness—or even common horse sense. I think he is the poorest, but still one of the most powerful figures in the government.

Hugh Johnson[16]

When I was serving with the "War Policies Commission" (1930–31) I quite often ran into Gen. Johnson, who then was the right hand man of Bernard Baruch. During the World War he met Mr. Baruch and immediately thereafter resigned from the Army (he was West Point Class 1903) and ever since has been associated with Mr. Baruch's interests.

He is now the Director of the National Recovery Administration. The purpose of the body is to establish codes of business practice among our various trades associations, with the idea of shortening hours for labor and so spreading employment—and of raising prices of raw materials and wages for labor. As in all other ideas of the President's that have been translated into actual national effort—the announced objective is a most desirable one. But much resistance to the methods employed has been encountered—and apparently in some instances Johnson has had to use bulldozing methods to secure even outward agreement. In fact, Henry Ford has definitely refused to sign a code on automobile manufacturing.

The picture being built up in the public mind of Gen. Johnson through the enormous amount of publicity now naturally attaching to him is a rather peculiar one. He seems to be considered a brilliant diamond in the rough—indomitable in will—ruthless in action, and possessed of a remarkable insight into American economic processes, their difficulties and their needs.

I think he is quick of mind, a gambler by instinct, intolerant of others and their opinions, but all in all about as good a man for the job he has, as could be found. One thing is sure, he will never admit failure until ingenuity has been exhausted and every artifice of a fertile brain and lively imagination has been employed.

Douglas MacArthur, General, Chief of Staff

Fifty-two years old. Essentially a romantic figure. I have done considerable personal work for him, but have seen far less of him than of other seniors now in the dept. Very appreciative of good work, positive in his convictions—a genius at giving concise and clear instructions. Consideration of the principal incidents in his career leads to the conclusion that his interests are almost exclusively military. He apparently avoids social duties as far as possible—and does not seek the limelight except in things connected with the Army and the W. D. Magnetic and extremely likable. Placed a letter of commendation on my record—and has assured me that as long as he stays in the Army I am one of the people earmarked for his "gang".

In my opinion he has the capacity to undertake successfully any position in govt. He has a reserved dignity—but is most animated in conversation on subjects interesting him. I doubt that he has any real political ambition—and in these days of high powered publicity and propaganda—I do not expect to see him ever prominently mentioned for office outside the W.D.

Most people that have known Gen. MacA. like and admire him to a degree. These same people, however, almost without exception profess themselves to be incapable of understanding his policies with respect to the Army's commissioned personnel. The mention of any kind of promotion system involving selection seems to be anathema to him—and he will tolerate no suggestion of "forced elimination." Generally speaking in naming officers for promotion to Brig. Gen. he seems to select the older and senior ones—regardless of qualifications.[17] In this one thing even those who have known him longest seem to consider him reactionary and almost bigoted. In my own part, while some of his "makes" have astounded me, I know that there is nothing personal in his attitude toward this matter, and that the policy he is following has been adopted only after careful study and consideration on his part. The chief of these reasons I believe to be a hatred of favoritism and special privilege.

He is impulsive—able, even brilliant—quick—tenacious of his views and extremely self-confident. It might be remarked too that he has not appointed some of his new Brigadiers under any delusions as to their abilities. He is too shrewd for that!! The answer is that, in his opinion at least, he is pursuing a course representing the lesser of two evils.

Brig. Gen. George Simonds, Head of War College

Loyal—intelligent—appreciative and considerate of subordinates—energetic and possessed of a fund of useful information and sound common sense. There is no military position, either in peace or war that he could not fill with honor to his country and to himself. A fine type! Outstanding qualification—mental balance; judgment.

Harry Woodring, Asst. Sec. War[18]

For the past six weeks his office has been under investigation by the grand jury for alleged irregularities in the handling of Govt. contracts, of which the A.S.W. has complete jurisdiction, so far as the W.D. is concerned.

Mr. Woodring himself is a small, rather effeminate appearing person—but quick—almost intolerant—and with an obvious love of publicity. He has been governor of Kansas. Right now he is undoubtedly worried, for while his own actions may have been above reproach in the alleged speculation—some of his known friends are prominently mentioned in the newspapers as liable to be indicted by the grand jury.

The whole story (or rather what I know of it) is too long to set down. But one thing is certain. If Mr. Woodring comes through perfectly clean—he is not going to act hereafter without paying some regard to the advice of his assistants.

1. John S. D. Eisenhower believes the introductory three paragraphs to the "Notes on Men" "show Dwight D. Eisenhower at his best," for both his judgment of men and his analytical ability. Dwight Eisenhower made these observations sporadically, and many are undated. Most probably they were written in 1932, although some had to be in 1933 or later.

2. Robert Emmet Callan (USMA, 1896) served in the Spanish-American War; with the Philippine Department's General Staff (1915–17); and in World War I. In 1931 he was appointed Assistant Chief of Staff, War Department, a position he held until his retirement in 1936. He died later that same year.

3. Edgar Thomas Collins (USMA, 1897), who had prior service during the Philippine Insurrection and World War I, commanded the Infantry School from 1926 to 1929. In 1932 he became Assistant Chief of Staff (G-3, Organization and Training), War Department, a position he held until his death in 1933. Eisenhower noted in his diary that Collins was G-2, Intelligence, while in fact he was with G-3. Eisenhower added the date of Collins' death later in a marginal note.

4. Frederick Trubee Davison, a New York assemblyman in 1922, was appointed assistant secretary of war for air in 1926. He left the War Department in 1933. During World War I he served with the U.S. Navy Air Service and during World War II held a variety of staff positions with the Army Air Corps.

5. Charles Evans Kilbourne served in the Philippines, World War I, and as Assistant Chief of Staff, War Plans Division (1932–35). Major General Kilbourne retired in 1936.

6. "Selectionism" was the term applied to those (like Moseley and Eisenhower) who opposed the current officer promotion system, which was based entirely upon seniority calculated from the date of initial appointment in the regular army. Pro-

motions within the army up through colonel are generally automatic if an officer maintains a good record and receives good evaluations. That was true in this period, if one lived that long. The real "selection" process began at the step from colonel to brigadier general.

7. Andrew Moses (USMA, 1897) served twice as director of the Army War College (1921–23 and 1928–29) and as Assistant Chief of Staff, G-1, Personnel and Administration (1931–35). Moses died in 1946.

8. Alfred Theodore Smith achieved the rank of brigadier general in 1933. A veteran of the Spanish-American War, he was Assistant Chief of Staff, G-2, Intelligence, and Chief of the Military Intelligence Division of the War Department General Staff (1931–35).

9. George Sherwin Simonds (USMA, 1899) participated in the suppression of Aguinaldo's rebellion in the Philippines and in World War I. From 1927 to 1931 he served as Assistant Chief of Staff, War Plans Division, War Department, Commandant of the Army War College (1932–35); and Deputy Chief of Staff, War Department.

10. Connor was Superintendent of West Point from May 1, 1932, until January 17, 1938. Previously he had served as Commandant of the Army War College, leaving there for West Point on April 30, 1932. Eisenhower evidently confused the position terminology. The commandant at West Point is similar to a dean of students.

11. George H. Dern worked in the mining industry, inventing several silver extraction processes. Elected governor of Utah in 1924, he served in that office until his appointment by President Roosevelt as secretary of war in 1933. He held this position until his death in August 1936.

12. Hugh Aloysius Drum, a veteran of the Spanish-American War, served as Assistant Commandant of the Command and General Staff School (1912–14). He was Pershing's Assistant Chief of Staff in 1917 until his appointment as Chief of Staff of the First Army in 1918. He held a number of important commands, including the First Army during the Normandy invasion. Drum retired in 1944 as a lieutenant general.

13. Eisenhower's note regarding Mrs. Gerow's death was added later as a marginal note.

14. "P.J.H." is Eisenhower's abbreviation for Patrick J. Hurley.

15. Harold Ickes was chair of the Public Works Administration, not the Public Works Board. When Roosevelt appointed Ickes, a former Republican, secretary of the interior in 1933, he charged him with directing the Public Works Administration's massive building program.

16. Hugh Samuel Johnson (USMA, 1903) served as acting quartermaster officer in charge of refugee relief work after the 1906 San Francisco earthquake and fire. During World War I he served as deputy provost marshal of the Army, charged with implementing military conscription. He also performed staff work in logistics for the Army General Staff and assisted Bernard Baruch on the War Industries Board. In 1919 he resigned from the Army and joined Baruch as an industrial and economic adviser. Roosevelt appointed Johnson director of the National Recovery Administration in 1933. He resigned in 1934 and by the late 1930s had become an outspoken critic of Roosevelt's New Deal. Johnson died in 1942.

17. See note 6, above.

18. Harry Hines Woodring failed to complete public school but became a

prominent Neodosha, Kansas, banker. Elected governor of Kansas in 1930, he was appointed assistant secretary of war by Roosevelt in 1933. In 1936 Roosevelt appointed him secretary of war, but Woodring's isolationist, anticonscription views were increasingly at odds with those of the president. Woodring resigned from the administration in July 1940 and by 1944 openly opposed Roosevelt's nomination for a fourth term.

AUGUST 10

As Gen. MacA's aide took part in Bonus Incident of July 28, a lot of furor has been stirred up but mostly to make political capital. I wrote the General's report, which is as accurate as I could make it. I kept a copy, including most of the enclosures.[1]

1. The report follows.

76

Eisenhower Library
Pre-presidential Papers, Bonus March File

TO SECRETARY OF WAR

AUGUST 15, 1932[1]

Dear Mr. Secretary: On the afternoon of July 28, 1932, in response to your instructions, Federal troops entered the District of Columbia for the purpose of assisting civil officials in restoring order in certain sections of this city where considerable bodies of persons had successfully defied police authority and were then engaged in riotous activity.[2]

Within a few hours this mission was substantially accomplished and with no loss of life or serious casualty, after the arrival of the troops, among either the civilian or military elements involved. By July 30th all Federal troops were withdrawn to their proper stations, and the local situation was under the complete control of the civil authorities.

I am giving below a comprehensive account of this incident, to include the sequence of events leading up to the employment of Federal forces, the authority under which the troops acted, the principal troop movements involved, and the results accomplished. Attached as appendices are copies of official communications having an immediate bearing upon the incident; a detailed report of Brigadier General Perry Miles,[3] who was in direct command of the Federal Troops; a photographic record of particular phases of the operation, and typical newspaper articles and editorials dealing with the affair.

The purpose of this report is to make of permanent record in the War Department an accurate and complete description of a particu-

233

lar employment of Federal troops on a type of activity in which elements of the Army have often been engaged since the founding of the Republic.

REPORT FROM THE CHIEF OF STAFF, UNITED STATES ARMY, TO THE SECRETARY OF WAR ON THE EMPLOYMENT OF FEDERAL TROOPS IN CIVIL DISTURBANCE IN THE DISTRICT OF COLUMBIA, JULY 28–30, 1932

GROWTH AND ACTIVITIES OF SO-CALLED BONUS ARMY

During late May, 1932, large groups of practically destitute World War veterans, self-styled the "Bonus Army", or "Bonus Marchers", began arriving in the City of Washington with the announced intention of conducting an aggressive lobby in favor of the immediate payment of Veterans' Adjusted Compensation Certificates, commonly called the bonus.

With no normal means of support, they established themselves, with the consent of local authorities, in vacant areas and abandoned buildings, principally governmentally-owned. Subsistence and supplies were obtained through donations from local and outside sources, and for the large majority the only protection from the elements were rude huts constructed from scrap material. The largest of these encampments was named CAMP MARKS,[4] situated on an alluvial flat on the left bank of the Anacostia River, northeast of the Bolling Field area. In the same vicinity was Camp Bartlett,[5] on privately owned ground. A portion of the Bonus Army took possession of an area southwest of the Capitol, where demolition activities incident to the Federal Government's building program had already begun. Smaller detachments were located in other parts of the city. The aggregate strength of the Bonus Army gradually increased until it reached an estimated maximum of some ten to twelve thousand persons, including in some cases families and dependents of the veterans.

Speaking generally, all their early activities in the city were peaceable and lawfully conducted. They organized themselves under leaders of their own choosing, and these cooperated reasonably well with the civil authorities in the preservation of order. Manifestly, however, in a large body recruited as was this one, the inclusion of a lawless element was inevitable. As the Bonus Army's increasing size gave to the members thereof a growing consciousness of their collective power and importance in the community, efforts to solve acute problems of existence often went beyond the limits of legality. Individual solicitation for material assistance was frequently couched in terms of demand rather than of request. In some cases merchants and others, when called upon for contributions, were confronted with covert threats which amounted to nothing less than a system of extortion or forced levy. But the principal and most weighty objection to the concentration of such a force in the District of Columbia was occasioned by the deplorable conditions under which these people were compelled to live, entailing an ever-present danger of disease and epidemic.

Until the end of the Congressional session the marchers used every possible influence to secure support for their project among members of Congress. Even after the proposal was decisively defeated in the Senate on June 17th, these efforts were continued, and recruits for their cause were sought throughout the United States. Meanwhile the sanitary conditions under which they lived, with the arrival of the summer heat and rains and the further crowding of the occupied areas, rapidly grew from bad to worse.

After it became apparent that Congress would not favorably consider the bonus project there was of course no longer any legitimate excuse for the marchers to continue endangering the health of the whole District population by the continued occupation of these areas. From another viewpoint also the concentration in one city of so many destitute persons normally residing in other sections of the Country was exceedingly unwise and undesirable. The natural outlets through which they could benefit from the resources heretofore made available for the care of the needy by the charitable instincts of the American people were the local institutions of their respective communities. In their own communities they and their relative needs were known or could be investigated, and each could receive assistance accordingly. By coming to Washington they deprived themselves individually of this assistance, while collectively they presented to the charitable resources of the District a problem of insurmountable proportions. But though the necessity for the dispersion of the Bonus Marchers daily became more evident, its accomplishment was plainly to be accompanied by many difficulties because of the destitute circumstances of the great majority. In appreciation of this fact Congress, just preceding its adjournment on July 16th, provided funds for transporting them to their homes, and some fifty-five hundred took advantage of this provision of law.

As this partial evacuation took place an influx of newcomers occurred, in many instances later arrivals being of radical tendencies and intent upon capitalizing the situation to embarrass the Government. Former leaders of the Bonus Army lost, to a considerable degree, the authority they had so far exercised over the mass, and the subversive element gradually gained in influence.

During the whole period of its stay in the city the Bonus Marchers were assisted in various ways by the local police force. Help rendered included the collection of clothing, food, and utensils; permitting the use of vacant areas and abandoned buildings; providing some medical service, and securing the loan of tentage and rolling kitchens from the District National Guard. In this matter the efforts of the police were humanitarian and more than praiseworthy. In the light of later events, however, it is likely that a portion of the marchers interpreted this attitude as an indication of timidity rather than of sympathy, and were ready to take advantage of this supposed weakness whenever it might become expedient to do so.

(Immediate cause of riots.)

In late July the evacuation of certain of the occupied areas in the vicinity of the Capitol became necessary in order that the Government's parking and building program might proceed. On July 21st the Bonus leaders were formally notified by the police of this situation and requested to make prompt arrangements for the removal of occupants from the affected areas. Although there still remained ample time for veterans to apply for Government transportation to their homes, these requests were largely ignored. Prolonged negotiations were productive of no real results.

Since the projected operations were part of the program for unemployment relief they could not be indefinitely delayed, and finally the District Commissioners directed the police to clear these areas, using force if necessary. Accordingly, on the morning of July 28th a considerable body of police went to the encampment near Pennsylvania Avenue and 4½ Street and compelled the trespassers to evacuate. Within a short time large groups of men arrived from other camps, apparently under some pre-arranged plan, and a struggle for the possession of the disputed territory ensued. The police were overwhelmingly outnumbered and were quickly involved in a serious riot. The mob, composed of veterans and others who had intermingled with them, was incited by radicals and hot-heads to a free use of bricks, clubs, and similar weapons. Several policemen were hurt, one most seriously, while another, in defending himself, was forced to shoot and kill one of the Bonus Marchers. In the pictorial supplement attached hereto are several photographs showing the desperate nature of these encounters.

OPERATIONS OF FEDERAL TROOPS
(Message to President from District Commissioners)

The situation rapidly assumed such a threatening aspect that the District Commissioners reported to the President their inability longer to preserve law and order in the areas affected and requested immediate assistance of Federal forces. They gave it as their opinion and that of the Superintendent of Police that if such help failed to materialize, considerable bloodshed would ensue. A copy of the letter they sent to the President is attached hereto.

The President promptly directed the Secretary of War to cooperate with the civil authorities in restoring law and order in the District of Columbia. The issue had now become a broader one than that of the simple expulsion of recalcitrant persons from an illegally occupied area in which they were physically interfering with essential Government activity. By their open and determined defiance of the Metropolitan police the members of this mob, recruited from all or most of the bonus camps in the city, had threatened the integrity of Federal authority within the confines of the Federally-governed District of Columbia. The dispersion and expulsion from the District of the force became thus the only logical answer the Government could make to the mob's action.

At 2:55 P.M., July 28, 1932, the following order was handed me by the Secretary of War:

To: General Douglas MacArthur, Chief of Staff, United States Army.
The President has just informed me that the civil government of the District of Columbia has reported to him that it is unable to maintain law and order in the District.

You will have United States troops proceed immediately to the scene of disorder. Cooperate fully with the District of Columbia police force which is now in charge. Surround the affected area and clear it without delay.

Turn over all prisoners to the civil authorities.

In your orders insist that any women and children who may be in the affected area be accorded every consideration and kindness. Use all humanity consistent with the due execution of this order.
PATRICK J. HURLEY, Secretary of War.

The legal sufficiency of these successive steps as authority for the employment of Federal troops in civil disturbances in the District of Columbia is clearly set forth in a memorandum from the Judge Advocate General of the Army, attached hereto

Upon receipt of the Secretary's order I designated Brigadier General Perry Miles, Commanding the 16th Brigade, as the officer in direct charge of all elements of the Regular Army to be employed. The troops selected for immediate use were:

1 Battalion 12th Infantry, stationed at Ft. Washington, Md.

1 Squadron 3rd Cavalry, stationed at Ft. Myer, Va.

1 Platoon Tanks, temporarily stationed at Ft. Myer, Va.

Headquarters Company, 16th Brigade, stationed at Washington, D. C.

Simultaneously orders were issued for the concentration of a reserve at Ft. Myer to comprise troops from Ft. Geo. G. Meade, Md., Ft. Howard, Md., and Ft. Humphreys, Va.

(General plan for troop employment.)

The Brigade Commander was directed to give his attention first to the requirements of the situation near Pennsylvania Avenue and 4½ Street, where, according to reports, rioting was still in progress. My general plan was to clear that area, turn then to the encampment, alleged to be occupied by Communists, at 13th and C Streets, after which I intended to move against the Anacostia contingent. A point on the Ellipse, a short distance south of the State, War, and Navy Building, was designated for concentration of these units so as to insure, prior to any contact with the rioting groups, complete organization of the force and proper issue of necessary instructions.

I accompanied the troops in person, anticipating the possibility of such a serious situation arising that necessary decisions might lie beyond the purview of responsibility of any subordinate commander, and with the purpose of obtaining a personal familiarity with every phase of the troops' activities.

The Cavalry Squadron and Tank Platoon arrived at the Ellipse about 3:00 P.M., and the Infantry Battalion about 4:20 P.M. The Brigade Commander issued necessary instructions, particularly cautioning subordinate commanders to avoid rushing tactics and undue haste as likely to provoke useless conflict with the rioters. General Miles proceeded correctly on the theory that a demonstration of overpowering force, accompanied by sufficient time to permit dispersion of the rioters, promised the surest, simplest, and safest results in this situation. Necessary special equipment was issued to the troops, particularly tear gas bombs.

(Understanding with civil police.)

While essential preparations were in progress I was in receipt of several messages from members of the police force concerning the existing situation. About 3:45 P.M., General P. D. Glassford,[6] Superintendent of the Metropolitan Police, contacted me, and the projected troop movement was discussed. At my request he undertook the special and immediate mission of notifying leaders of all bonus groups that Federal property in the District would have to be evacuated before nightfall. This I considered important, since in the chaotic conditions then prevailing there was grave danger of many innocent or neutral persons becoming involved in difficulties because of a lack of understanding of the orders under which the troops were operating.

Unfortunately, the leader of the bonus movement had apparently lost all control of the situation. According to reports made to me he had stated he was no longer able to handle his men and had withdrawn from the scene of operations. I vainly sought him during the entire operation so that I might utilize his influence towards pacification of the situation.

At this conference General Glassford also reported that his men were exhausted by long hours of continuous duty and by their strenuous efforts of that day in the riot on lower Pennsylvania Avenue. It was apparent to me that unless assistance was quickly forthcoming there would probably be permitted a situation to develop involving the gravest consequences.

Promptly at 4:30 P.M. the troops began moving east on Pennsylvania Avenue, the Cavalry and Tanks leading; the Infantry following in extended formation.

The march to the Capitol area was made without incident. Upon arrival there, and while troops were taking up designated positions, repeated warnings to disperse were given to a large crowd of spectators on the north side of the Avenue. These people were in no sense lawbreakers and their dispersion was desired only to safeguard innocent bystanders from accident incident to subsequent activity. These warnings were temporarily ignored, but later when it became necessary to release tear bombs against the rioters, the prevailing wind carried a light gas concentration into the crowd of spectators and the area was quickly cleared.

(Troop employment.)

The rioting elements were immediately ordered to evacuate the area south of the Avenue, which order they ignored. In line with my determination to give a reasonable time to any and all groups to disperse, no troop movement was initiated against them until 5:30 P.M. At that moment they were still apparently determined to hold their ground.

It is to be remembered that for many weeks members of the Bonus Army had seen all their wishes and desires, as far as the local situation was concerned, acceded to by civil officials, and more recently they had successfully defied constituted authority and withstood police efforts to evict them. It is doubtful, therefore, that when the Regular troops were deployed in their front, the rioters really believed that the eviction order was to be definitely enforced. At least it is a fact that as the troops started to move forward the mob showed a surly and obstinate temper, and gave no immediate signs of retreating. As the soldiers approached more closely a few brickbats, stones, and clubs were thrown, and it became apparent that some hint must be given of the determination underlying the employment of Federal troops in this contingency. This hint was given through the medium of harmless tear gas bombs. A number of these were thrown by the soldiers among the foremost ranks of the rioters, and from that moment little organized defiance was encountered.

Troop operations were strictly confined to evacuation of Governmentally-owned tracts. A short distance south of Pennsylvania Avenue was a bonus detachment reported by the police to be occupying leased property. These men were not molested. For the same reason no action was taken against a small group of bonus seekers on the 7th Street Wharves—a detachment brought to my attention by General Glassford in person.

The program previously outlined for the day's activities was carried out expeditiously, albeit with a leisureliness that permitted every member of the Bonus Army ample time to make his unhindered way, if he was so minded, out of the path of the troops. I was particularly desirous that the drift of the dispersed groups be toward the Anacostia encampment and away from the principal business and residence sections of the city. This was accomplished through appropriate dispositions and movements of the troops.

That ample time was accorded everyone to remove himself and his belongings from affected areas before the arrival of the troops is evidenced by the general time schedule of the movement. At 3:45 P.M. word had been sent to all detachments of the Bonus Army to evacuate Governmentally-owned ground. It was 5:30 P.M. before the first movement started against the occupants of the area in which rioting had taken place during the day. It was another hour before the so-called Communist area, at 13th and C Streets, was reached. This, incidentally, had already been evacuated.

Here the troops were rested and fed, affording the Camp Marks occupants additional time for evacuation. I held personal conferences with subordinates and with representatives of the police. At this point General Glassford called my attention to one group of Government buildings occupied by women and children and asked my instructions concerning them. I informed him that not only would they be unmolested, but that I was prepared to furnish a guard for their protection if he so desired. He replied that the police could take care of this activity, and stated that the Red Cross had volunteered assistance in caring for these groups.

The march toward Anacostia was resumed about 9:10 P.M. Upon arriving at that camp half an hour later the eastern end was found vacant. Almost immediately there reported to me a man who gave his name as Atwell and his position as commander of CAMP MARKS. He asked for an additional delay of an hour to complete the evacuation of that encampment, to which request I promptly acceded and directed the troops to halt and bivouac for the night.

Bonus detachments at Camp Meigs, Camp Sims,[7] and near the Congressional Library were not evacuated that night, although I was in receipt of several specific requests from the District Commissioners to clear out these places. I did, however, send the occupants of those camps a message to the effect that the troops would move against them the following day if not previously evacuated.

Because of the relative slowness of their general advance, and their calm and unhurried demeanor at all times, the troops largely avoided actual physical contact and conflict with rioting elements. In isolated instances it was necessary to threaten individual members of the mob, and upon several occasions troops were subjected to showers of brick and stones. The report of the Brigade Commander gives the details of these incidents.

(Burning of encampments.)

Invariably, as each area was evacuated during the afternoon and evening, fires broke out among the shacks previously occupied by the marchers. Constructed of highly inflammable materials, these structures stood so close together that the spread of the flames was extremely rapid. In each instance, however, the troops and the Fire Department prevented any damage to permanent buildings in the vicinity. Considerable argument has obtained concerning the origin of these fires, and I therefore give below the facts, as far as I have been able to determine them.

At no time did I give orders to subordinate commanders that could have been construed as authorization for initiating the destruction of the encampments, and investigation has failed to reveal a single instance where a subordinate gave any such instruction. The first of these fires came to my notice within a few moments after the troops began their initial advance against the rioters on lower Pennsylvania Avenue. Personally stationed at that time within a few yards of the spot where this occurred, I was under the distinct impression that, in view of the proportions the fire quickly attained, it must have been ignited at least several minutes before the foremost troops reached it. The District Fire Department came immediately to the scene, and a considerable number of shacks in that general vicinity were not harmed by fire on the evening of July 28th.

My arrival at the encampment at 13th and C Streets was almost simultaneous with that of the leading troops. The area was practically deserted and already dotted with fires, started, in my opinion, by the former occupants. Under the circumstances the only feasible action was to hasten the spread of the flames so that danger to neighboring areas would be minimized and personnel relieved from the necessity of standing guard. This the troops did.

At Camp Marks, by far the largest of the encampments, responsibility for firing the main camp lay definitely with the Bonus Marchers. The troops entered the area at the eastern tip, descending onto the flats through a steep, poorly conditioned road. This portion of the area was completely deserted, and one or two abandoned and partially demolished shacks in the vicinity of the Anacostia Bridge were fired to illuminate the immediate surroundings and permit orderly disposition of the troops. It was in this area, completely outside of the main part of the camp, that the troops were halted by my order to afford more time for evacuation. During this period of inaction the firing of CAMP MARKS began, apparently by concerted action of its occupants, for within a few minutes the blaze was general throughout the area.

In this area was a considerable amount of Government property, previously loaned to the veterans by the National Guard, which we had contracted to recover. Consequently, when the fires started the Brigade Commander directed his troops to proceed into the camp, now obviously abandoned, to save as much of this property as possible, and to clear the area of possible stragglers. Reported subsequent burning of individual shacks by soldiers, if authentic, was for the purpose only of hastening the destruction of a camp already doomed by the action of the Bonus Marchers themselves.

In the process of mopping up the various areas the following day the troops discovered here and there various partially burned or destroyed hovels. The destruction of all these was completed with a view of facilitating the clearing up process which must inevitably follow.

During the night of July 28–29 groups of rioters on the heights east and south of Camp Marks attempted to initiate attacks against isolated detachments of soldiers. They were dispersed with a few tear gas bombs, and no further trouble was experienced. Searchlights provided by the District Fire Department and by the National Guard were helpful in maintaining proper outposts. Troops were placed at critical points to prevent the return of Bonus Marchers, either individually or collectively, toward the business centers of the District.

In employing Federal troops for reestablishing law and order, there had been no occasion for a declaration of martial law, so that responsibility for general control of traffic and spectators remained with the police. Congestion of the most serious kind occurred in the streets and areas around the Anacostia Bridge—a condition that kept the police extremely busy until a late hour at night. In some instances they were forced to use tear gas bombs, but by morning approximately normal conditions in this respect were restored.

During the day of July 29th the troops completed the task laid out for them. Stragglers near the Capitol and in other areas were evacuated and order restored throughout the city. The details of these movements, all of which were accomplished without unusual incident, are given in General Miles' report. Isolated shacks were demolished, and the troops, as a precautionary measure, remained on guard that night.

The following day, July 30th, all troops were withdrawn. The mission given them had been performed loyally and efficiently and in accordance with your personal injunction to use all humanity consistent with the execution of this order. They had neither suffered nor inflicted a serious casualty. They had not fired a shot, and had actually employed no more dangerous weapons than harmless tear gas bombs. Even these were not used in heavy concentrations, or over periods more than a few minutes each, and any contention that injury to individuals was caused by them is entirely without foundation. This is evidenced by the fact that in several instances individual officers and solders remained, without masks, in the midst of gas concentrations throughout their duration.

(Cooperation with civil agencies.)

At every stage of this operation the cooperation received from the Police and Fire Departments of the District of Columbia was all that could be desired. Their help in transmitting messages, controlling fires, providing transportation, furnishing searchlights, and in similar activity was freely given and deeply appreciated. The Commanding General of the 16th Brigade has written letters of appreciation to them, as he did also to the Commanding Officer of the National Guard of the District of Columbia, who assisted by furnishing searchlight service on the night of July 28–29.

GENERAL OBSERVATIONS
(Value of discipline.)

From the standpoint of the Army one of the outstanding features of this entire incident was the exemplary conduct of the rank and file of the units employed. Compelled often to act entirely on their own responsibility, and frequently under extreme provocation, the enlisted men exhibited a patience, a forbearance, and a sympathetic though determined attitude that won the praise of every impartial observer. The value of obedience, cohesion and discipline, all products of intelligent and thorough training, was again exemplified and emphasized. This leads to a reiteration of the axiom, so well understood by military men, that whenever necessity arises for employment of Federal troops in civil disturbance, only such units should be used as are known to have attained a high degree of excellence in training and discipline.

Noticeable also were the efficiency, good judgement, and tireless devotion to duty displayed by commissioned personnel. From officers we expect, as a matter of course, the utmost in loyal and intelligent service. Yet situations of this kind invariably present to all unit commanders problems of extreme delicacy, characterized more by rapid and kaleidoscopic change than by predictable detail. The possibility of errors in judgement, with far-reaching and serious consequences, is always present. I report with real gratification that during this whole affair there came to my attention no instance warranting the slightest criticism of the action of any officer, from the Brigadier General commanding to the Second Lieutenant latest commissioned.

(Adequate force minimizes casualties.)

It is almost superfluous to say that in employing troops to quell civil disorder the prevention of casualties among civilians and soldiers alike is a consideration of the utmost importance. This end is best attained through the concentration of a force strong in apparent as well as in actual power. Suspected weakness on the side of law and order encourages riotous elements to resist, usually resulting in open conflict, while obvious strength gains a moral ascendancy that is normally all-sufficient.

These truths were strikingly illustrated in the events of July 28th on lower Pennsylvania Avenue. By 3:00 P.M. of that day the police were almost exhausted, after hours of failure to make headway against a mob of overwhelming numbers. This was not due to any fault of the police force, for the members of which I have nothing but praise. The real cause for failure lay in the great disparity in apparent power—a disparity that could be made good only by the use of deadly weapons. This, obviously, was a method of last resort—a circumstance of which the rioters advantaged themselves in refusing to evacuate disputed territory. Even so, casualties were serious on both sides, resulting in the immediate death of one man and the subsequent death of another.

But within a few minutes of the first definite advance by Regular troops this area was hastily vacated and with no casualty worth the name. The rioters lost heart in the face of a power they could recognize as overwhelming, even though numerically their advantage was still some five or six to one. But the combination of sufficient numbers, proper equipment, concerted action, and solid discipline are not to be withstood by any mob.

For the reasons I have been discussing, tanks are particularly valuable in quelling civil disorder. They create an impression of irresistible and inexorable power, and being visible from some distance they create apprehension in the rear as well as in the front elements of a mob. This is important, for thus is avoided any tendency of a mob to force its forward elements into a fight because of physical pressure from those who imagine themselves to be in an area of comparative safety in the rear. Cavalry also, aside from its mobility, is useful for similar reasons.

Most efficacious of all weapons in such circumstances is the tear gas bomb. In the hands of well trained infantry, advancing with an evident determination, this harmless instrument quickly saps the will to resist of unorganized and unprepared bodies. Its small smoke cloud is visible from some distance, and its moral suasion thus extends over a far greater area than does its actual effects. It creates an irresistible desire to run from rather than toward the scene of its use.

We are led then to a second observation applicable in situations of this kind. Having selected well disciplined troops, it is desirable and necessary that they be concentrated in sufficient strength to awe the opposition, and that they be equipped with such weapons as tend to increase the impression of irresistible power. The greater the real and apparent strength of the force on the side of law and order, the smaller will be the casualties among the disaffected elements.

(Newspaper representatives.)
Finally, I desire to invite attention to the handling of representatives of the public press during this affair. Employment of Federal troops on an occasion of this kind is essentially disagreeable and repugnant to the units involved, and the natural impulse is to attempt to hold newspaper men at a distance. Any such attempt is a fundamental error. Incidents of this character are of intense interest to the public, and accurate information concerning them should appear in the columns of the daily newspapers.

The conduct of military units must be such that when accurately reported no fair-minded person can justly criticize them. The logical answer therefore is to accord to representatives of the press the utmost freedom consistent with the requirements of the military task to be accomplished. In this instance this procedure was used. All reporters were invited to go to any spot at any time they desired, and to see everything they possibly could. Arrangements were made to assist in their transportation during moves of considerable length, and no attempt was made to confuse or deceive them as to the details of any phase of the operation. As a result there appeared in the daily press, except for a few obviously prejudiced accounts, a very fair presentation of the facts as they were seen and interpreted by the reporters.

Occasion for the necessitous employment of the army in service of this character must be universally deplored. It is indicative of a temporarily unhealthy condition in the body politic, no matter how localized may be the inciting cause. For the Army itself there is involved a task of the most unwelcome sort. It nevertheless constitutes a duty that must be performed with loyal determination, but without harshness or brutality. The objective to be attained is prompt restoration of law and order, with a minimum of physical violence and with the least possible interference in the normal activities of the civil community. By adhering firmly to these methods military units will not only serve best the public interest, but will win for themselves the renewed respect and appreciation of public-spirited citizens.

In the case at hand these standards of conduct were rigidly observed by the Army. Its allotted tasks were performed rapidly and efficiently, but with the maximum consideration for the members of the riotous groups consistent with their compulsory eviction. The results speak for themselves. Within a few hours a riot rapidly assuming alarming proportions was completely quelled, and from the moment the troops arrived at the scene of the disorder no soldier or civilian received a permanent or dangerous injury. Thus a most disagreeable task was performed in such a way as to leave behind it a minimum of unpleasant aftermath and legitimate resentment.

DOUGLAS MacARTHUR, General, Chief of Staff.[8]

1. Eisenhower wrote the report for MacArthur.

2. In May 1932, seventeen thousand unemployed veterans of World War I descended on Washington, demanding that the government pay immediately the $3.5 million in veterans bonuses legislated in 1924 and 1931 but which were not to be paid until 1945. Although the House of Representatives passed legislation on June 15 granting the veterans' demand, on June 17 the Senate voted the bill down. At that point, most of the protestors who had camped on the Anacostia River flats near the Capitol left town. But a small band of intransigent veterans, joined by their families, refused to leave, vowing to "stay 'till '45." When the District of Columbia police attempted to evict the ragtag "Bonus Army" from the city on July 28, several policemen panicked, shots were fired, and several occupants of "Bonus City" were killed or wounded. At that point, District of Columbia commissioners asked for the army's aid. President Hoover issued orders for army intervention, and MacArthur's troops, bayonets drawn and using tear gas, drove the protestors from several downtown buildings, pushed them across the Anacostia River bridge to their encampment, and set fire to their tents and shanties. Hoover and MacArthur were pilloried by the press for overreacting and using excessive force. Major Eisenhower had accompanied MacArthur to the forced eviction.

The many items listed as appendixes in the report are not included in this book but are available at the Eisenhower Library. See Roger Daniels, *The Bonus March: An Episode of the Great Depression* (Westport, Conn.: Greenwood, 1971), and Donald J. Lisio, *The President and Protest: Hoover, Conspiracy, and the Bonus Riot* (Columbia: University of Missouri Press, 1974).

3. Maj. Gen. Perry Miles (USMA, 1895) served in the Spanish-American War and in World War I. He retired in 1937.

4. Camp Marks, with an estimated population of fifteen thousand, by far the largest Bonus encampment, was named by the veterans in honor of District police capt. S. J. Marks, whose Eleventh Precinct adjoined the camp. Like Glassford, Marks was patient and generous with the veterans.

5. Gen. John H. Bartlett, a former postmaster general, allowed the Bonus Marchers to camp on a wooded lot he owned overlooking the Anacostia Flats. The marchers named their camp for him.

6. Pelham D. Glassford (USMA, 1904) during World War I became the youngest brigadier general in the AEF. In 1931, Glassford took an early retirement in order to receive an appointment as chief of the District of Columbia's police force. Glassford won the everlasting gratitude of the encamped veterans—and the everlasting enmity of the Hoover administration and Congress—by trying to take a low-keyed, empathetic approach to the Bonus Marchers. On October 20, three months after the event, the District commissioners asked for his resignation. Glassford returned to the army during World War II, serving as director of internal security, Office of the Provost Marshal General.

7. Camp Sims, a National Guard installation near Anacostia, was used by the veterans with the permission of the District's National Guard commander. Camp Meigs was a small camp more than a mile from the Anacostia encampment.

8. The many enclosures that accompanied the report are not included but are available at the Eisenhower Library.

77

Eisenhower Library
Chief of Staff Diary

NOVEMBER 30, 1932–DECEMBER 9, 1933

NOVEMBER 30

This year I wrote the Annual Report of the C. of S. and edited the reports of the Sec. War and the A.S.W.

The report of the C. of S. consists in a review of W.D. opinion of all the controversial matters that have engaged the attention of the dept. during the past year.

Chief among them are: Reduction of 2000 officers; Consolidation & W. & N. Depts.; Abolition of Army Transport Service; Promotion; Pay; Suspension of Civilian Training; Mechanization.

The published report has evoked much favorable comment.

Have been very busy on political papers (before the Democratic landslide of Nov. 8) and in preparation of many explanatory letters to Congressmen, etc., concerning military subjects of various sorts.

While I have no definite leanings toward any political party I believe it is a good thing the Democrats won—and particularly that one party will have such overwhelming superiority in Congress.

It will be most interesting to watch the results obtained by the new administration, and I hope they are only ¼ as successful as they said they would be!

FEBRUARY 28, 1933

When the current depression has once been conquered and easy money and prosperous times are again with us there will be many persons saying "I told you so," and recalling that they had predicted the event with a nicety and exactness little short of the miraculous.

I have heard men say that in May, 1918, when the Allies were staggering back from the Aisne under the blows of the German Army, they themselves saw with a clear vision the Allied victory of that fall. During the course of the current depression I have also heard men say that they foresaw it some years ago—that anyone of sense must have known the inflation of 1927–28–29 could not possibly endure.

The fact is that in the spring of 1918 everyone on the Allied side was badly frightened, and showed it. People were too busy praying to do much predicting. The first signs of German deterioration, which appeared in the late summer, were greeted with sighs of relief and with renewed hope.

In the same way the talk of 1928 was that a new economic era was upon us. Roger Babson,[1] the only man who then publicly expressed the view that deflation and depression were in the offing, was laughed off the stage. Just a reactionary and an old fogy were the names applied to him.

Right now everything is pessimism. For the past few days banks have been suspending payments in Michigan, Ohio, Maryland, Indiana—and finally this morning a large bank in D.C. followed suit. Today I've heard people advise holding all money in gold—eschewing bonds, bank deposits, stocks and all other types of money credit. Their feeling is that virtual panic is upon us—and their battle cry is "Save himself who can."

I wonder how prevalent this feeling is. Of course if everyone gets to believing the same way there is bound to be a panic, because all banks will be called upon simultaneously to pay off depositors. The effect can scarcely be imagined.

My own belief is that if things should get as bad as some predict then cash in hand will be no more valuable than a worthless check. So why all the concern in drawing money out of the bank? A socialistic or communistic regime would be forced to confiscate or disregard money—one or the other!

I am going to sit tight in the boat.

Just when this depression and this pessimism will cease no one can foretell. But when it does there will be plenty who will claim that in Feb., 1933 they had already figured out exactly what was going to happen—and acted accordingly. The dirty liars!

But right now I'm going to make one prediction. Things are not going to take an upturn until more power is centered in one man's hands. Only in that way will confidence be inspired; will it be possible to do some of the obvious things for speeding recovery, and will we be freed from the pernicious influence of noisy and selfish minorities.

For two years I have been called "Dictator Ike" because I believe that virtual dictatorship must be exercised by our President. So now I keep still—but I still believe it!

1. Roger Ward Babson, a prolific writer on business, business statistics, investments, and religious subjects, founded Babson Institute, the Midwest Institute, and *Babson's Reports.*

MARCH 6

The inauguration is over. The President has issued a proclamation suspending until next Thurs. <u>all</u> bank payments. This is a hopeful sign, for while the moratorium itself is only a delaying action, yet its announcement shows that the Pres. is going to step out and <u>take</u> authority in his own hands. More power to him!! I wonder who the people are that are urging him on. He will have to cut down expenses, stamp out crime, consolidate transportation systems and keep credit liquid by an exercise of the same kind of authority.[1]

1. The day after Franklin Roosevelt's March 4, 1933, inauguration, he invoked obscure provisions of the Trading with the Enemy Act as authority to proclaim a bank holiday, closing the nation's banks until Congress reconvened on March 9. The measure was intended to restore confidence in the banking system and to buy time for his advisers to formulate banking reform legislation and have it ready for submission to Congress by the following Thursday. Roosevelt's treasury team submitted a bill on March 9, and Congress passed the legislation the same day.

MARCH 10

Yesterday Congress met and gave the Pres. extraordinary powers over banking. Now if they'll just do the same with respect to law enforcement, federal expenditures, trans. systems, there will be such a revival of confidence that things will begin to move.

My own salary will be cut some more if these things come to pass. I cannot afford it, and will have to ask for relief from this city. Nevertheless he <u>should</u> do it—and if he doesn't I'll be disappointed in him.

The papers have begun seriously to mention the desirability of extending the President's powers along many lines as has been done in the case of banking. It's funny—as soon as the pocketbook is definitely hit—then demagogy is not so popular and people begin to talk common sense.

MARCH 15

About three weeks ago I was appointed senior aide to the Chief of Staff—Gen. MacArthur. My duties are to be those of a military secretary, working on confidential or special missions for the General.

Today I actually start to move my office, since Gen. McCoy[1] had been occupying the one next to the C. of S. that is assigned to me.

1. Maj. Gen. Frank Ross McCoy (USMA, 1897) served as aide-de-camp to Gen. Leonard Wood in the Philippines and to President Theodore Roosevelt. His distinguished service with the General Staff, AEF, led after the war to a variety of diplomatic assignments in which his exceptional political and diplomatic skills were employed. These included membership on the League of Nation's Lytton Commission, which in 1932 investigated Japan's aggression in Manchuria.

MARCH 15

I was brought into Gen. MacA's office not long ago with the title of "Senior Aide." My work will apparently be little different from that I have been performing for him for two years but he alone will be my boss—and I'll be more available for every kind of duty.

APRIL 3

The past week was a very busy and exciting period. The W.D. received instructions from the Budget Bureau directing that a schedule of reductions in the 1934 appropriations be prepared for affecting a $90,000,000 saving in the $271,000,000 provided. This of course represents practical scrapping of the preparatory program we have been trying to carry out, since the $271,000,000 is in itself far below the amount necessary to develop a well rounded army of the size we now have (125,000 regulars—190,000 Nat. Guard—100,000 O.R.C.).

The schedule submitted by Gen. MacA. did not provide for cutting military personnel. Training supply—replacements—etc. are eliminated—so that our army will quickly be nothing but men.

Unfortunately, however, this is the yardstick the ordinary civilian uses in measuring military strength—therefore his impression will be that we have not been cut at all.

Psychologically (not considering the effect on army morale) it would have been wise to cut deeply into personnel, retaining a maximum degree of what might be called "invisible" or "unnoticed" preparation. But considering how this program would have affected the morale of the service it probably could not be adopted.

I hope that a new directive does not now come to us directing a _further_ cut to reduce personnel.

I still have some hope that we will not suffer the full cut so far directed. Anyone not familiar with the problem would have difficulty in appreciating the extent to which this project cuts into military effectiveness. For instance, practically the whole of the Army's corps of expert civilian technicians must go. The men that for many years have been trained in gun and ammunition manufacture—test, etc. We have engineers and scientists of all kinds—and they are not only efficient—they are vitally necessary. To disrupt this corps will be well-nigh fatal. It would take years to reestablish it. We will have left only a shell of a military establishment.[1]

1. Eisenhower's fears were well founded. The War Department's budget was cut from $455 million in fiscal year 1933 to $348 million in fiscal year 1934. As a percentage of total federal expenditures, the military's budget fell from 9.4 percent in 1933 to 4.4 percent in 1934. By 1936 the War Department's appropriation had shrunk even further, to 3.9 percent of the federal budget. Military expenditures would not exceed (as a percentage of the total budget) the 1933 figure until 1940, when it reached 11.9 percent. By contrast, the percentages for the years of World War II were: 31 percent (1941); 64 percent (1942); 49 percent (1943); 59 percent (1944); and 23 percent (1945).

APRIL 10

Gen. P.L. Miles has an aide—Lieut. John B. Sherman[1]—who appeals to me as a fine type. I'm going to try to keep an eye on him, for if a chance comes I'd like to put opportunity in his path. Seems honest—intelligent—energetic and loyal.

1. John B. Sherman (USMA, 1918) served in World War I. During World War II he served directly under Eisenhower as senior U.S. representative to Belgium. Beginning in 1947, he worked for the Central Intelligence Agency (CIA) until he retired in 1951.

APRIL 20

Yesterday the nation, by order of the President, officially went off the gold standard. That is, export of gold is prohibited and technically our currency is no longer backed by a 40% gold reserve.

This seems to me that the Pres. is definitely choosing the road toward internationalism rather than nationalism in working out economic troubles. I rather think a bitter economic war is in the offing, unless the forthcoming "Economic Conference" (to be held here soon by invitation of President) does more than such bodies usually do. I still believe that the best way to get out of trouble is to deal within ourselves—adjust our own production to our own consumption and cease worrying about foreign markets except only those necessary to pay for essential imports—manganese, nickel, rubber, sugar, wool, iodine, and a few others.

We have a greater per capita wealth in natural resources than any other nation. Very well—let's shut others out and proceed scientifically to adjust economic activity within our own country so as to enhance the general standard of living to the greatest extent possible. Otherwise there will be levelling off of living standards throughout the world, in which process we will necessarily suffer.

Economists say it cannot be done!! Revival of world trade is their battle cry. Practically speaking we've got a whole world of our own within the area over which we exercise political control. Our plan should be to attempt economic control only to political boundaries. That way we have definite rather than indeterminate factors in the problem.[1]

1. Ironically, Eisenhower's autarchic views at this time were not unlike those of the post–World War II Republican "Old Guard," which would attempt to frustrate his pursuit, as Military Commander of the North Atlantic Treaty Organization (NATO) and as president, of collective security and free trade policies.

JUNE 2

Major Fleming, representing the head of the Emergency Construction Administration,[1] came to my office and tendered me the job of Office Manager and Executive.

Not knowing what Gen. MacA's reaction would be I did not commit myself. When the General arrived I went in and explained the situation. He emphatically refused—so that's that! Probably it would have been a marvelous opportunity in some ways—but—I'm glad I'm staying with the General.

1. There was no New Deal agency named the Emergency Construction Administration. Given the fact that Fleming was deputy administrator of the Public Works Administration, Eisenhower must have been referring to the PWA.

JUNE 18

The CCC[1] has been the big activity engaging the Army's time this summer. I've written a preliminary report for inclusion in Annual Report of C. of S.

Gen. MacA. finally won the most important phases of his fight against drastic cutting of National Defense. We will lose no officers or men (at least at this time) and this concession was won because of the great numbers we are using on the Civilian Conservation Corps work and of Gen. MacA's skill and determination in the fight.

On Sat. the President announced that the Army could use $225,000,000 for 1934. This is almost $40,000,000 more than we would have received under the original orders for the cut.

On the same date (June 10) the Pres. announced his reorganization plan. It vitally and adversely affects the Army, particularly in procurement. Since the Congress had previously given the Pres. almost autocratic power in this matter there is little hope for its defeat or postponement. Nevertheless we are trying—mainly by getting Senators and Congressmen to refuse to adjourn.

The plan would put all Army procurement under the Treas. Dept.— a cumbersome and expensive system in peace, and an impossible one in war. My God, but we have a lot of theorists and academicians in the administration!

1. The Civilian Conservation Corps (CCC), another of Roosevelt's "first one-hundred days" programs, was designed to address the economic and social problems of the millions of youths between the ages of fifteen and twenty-four who were neither in school nor employed. Civilian Conservation Corps work centered upon restoring America's natural environment. The Department of Labor recruited CCC workers, the War Department transported recruits to camps, which military officials administered, and the Departments of Agriculture and Interior designed and managed the work projects.

OCTOBER 24

Sent Gen. MacA's 1933 annual report to the Public Printer. Had hoped to have the document completed about three weeks earlier, but a combination of extra work, slow action on the part of G-1 and G-4, to say nothing of stenographic difficulties, slowed up the whole task. Ordinarily the report would have been turned in on Nov. 15, in company with all other documents to be included as parts of report of Sec. of War. About middle of Sept., however, Gen. MacA. had to have his report published separately, and at the earliest possible moment.

I am curious to find out what comment it will inspire, as it is a frank presentation of our situation with respect to military preparedness.

For the past three weeks I have acted as Gen. MacA's personal aide (while T.J. Davis was on leave) as well as doing my own work. I have been busy—to say the least.

OCTOBER 29

As I look back over the past few months I have to laugh at the antics we go through in support of a shibboleth. Specifically the word "dictator" has always (and properly) been anathema to the Average American. So today, when in some respects we have the strongest possible form of dictatorship—we go to great lengths to congratulate ourselves that we have not fallen for the terrible systems in vogue in Italy, Germany, Turkey, Poland and etc. True, in outward form, and in certain fundamental individual rights, so far preserved to us, we are not under a dictator. But President Roosevelt's power is of tremendous extent—greater by far than is realized by the average citizen.

This is so much true that Henry Ford's current struggle with the N.R.A.[1] administration is looked upon as a bold and almost foolhardy action. Yet he is simply pursuing a course that three years ago would have been unquestioned, either by the govt. or by any private citizen.

I believe that unity of action is essential to success in the current struggle. I believe that individual right must be subordinate to public good, and that the public good can be served only by unanimous adherence to an authoritative plan. We <u>must</u> conform to the President's program regardless of consequences. Otherwise dissension, confusion and partisan politics will ruin us.

So I think Ford theoretically right—very much so—but I hope his differences with the N.R.A. may be composed under some plan that will not weaken Presidential prestige.

1. The National Recovery Administration (NRA) was created by the National Industrial Recovery Act of 1933. The NRA's objective was to stabilize the economy by overseeing the drafting of industry-wide "codes," or rules, that, it was hoped, would increase production, raise wages, and generally get the economy moving again. The net effect of the rules was to circumvent antitrust laws and encourage cartelization of American industry. Although codes were aimed at recognizing labor's right to organize and bargain collectively, labor actually benefited little. In May 1935 the U.S. Supreme Court held the NRA unconstitutional. The agency was abolished.

DECEMBER 9

Publication of Gen. MacA's annual report elicited a volume of press comment throughout the country. In general this publicity was sympathetic and favorable, although half a dozen editorials were distinctly hostile. I think that the C. of S. is, on the whole, much pleased with the reception his report experienced.

DEC. 9 [SECOND ENTRY]

Criticism of the "New Deal" has been growing in volume, much of it being directed against the monetary policies of the Administration, generally described (by the Adm.) as a definite move toward a "managed" currency.

Another inspiration for much unfavorable comment is the failure of many of the so-called Emergency Administrations to accomplish their purposes and attain their objectives as speedily and definitely as expected.

For example; Mr. Ickes and his Public Works Administration[1] were given $3,300,000,000 to initiate a program of public works, which, it was promised, would rapidly relieve unemployment—and initiate an era of industrial revival. Hundreds of unforeseen difficulties were encountered, and effects have been only gradually felt. Many alibis have been advanced by Mr. Ickes and his group—some of which have been indignantly denied by people upon whom he was apparently seeking to throw some of the blame.

Regardless of responsibility for failure, some acknowledgement of disappointment on the part of the Adm. was exhibited in the formation this fall of another agency charged with spending money for the specific purpose of reducing unemployment. This is the Civil Works administration,[2] given $400,000,000 to spend apparently on anything and everything that could be remotely classed as "public". Even this C.W.A. organization, although seemingly operating under even fewer restrictions than apply to the P.W.A., has not been able to put men to work as rapidly as was originally promised.

It seems strange that people responsible for such efforts do not see and make allowances for the necessity for preparation. In the C.C.C. project the original plan put principal functions in the hands of persons who necessarily had to begin the building up of operating organizations. As the prospect of failure became more and more imminent the wisdom of turning much of the job over to an existing organization, specifically trained and prepared for tasks of the kind involved, became more and more apparent. Then was when the Army really became responsible for all the organizational and administrative phases of the mobilization. (Of course the thought was probably also entertained that if failure should be experienced, there would be a fine scapegoat.) But the Army fully succeeded—and to date it stands as the only organization that has fully and completely attained the objectives set for it by the "New Deal". This fact of course has not been publicized. It will not be. But the need for a trained organization for administering huge operational tasks should be obvious.[3]

The N.R.A. (Gen. Johnston's outfit) has apparently been making progress more in line with what was expected, than has any other. While he had to develop an organization he has had so much experience that he quickly utilized existing agencies to a considerable extent. The program of establishing industrial codes has occasioned lots of argument, but a lot of this can undoubtedly be attributed to Johnston's proclivity for talking. He has a ready tongue and a facile imagination. His expressions of "small man", "dead cats", etc. etc. have excited comment and ridicule—and this last is one of the greatest enemies to any effort depending upon public opinion. But the basic soundness of his methods (and I assume also of the principles of the N.R.A. effort) are demonstrated by the fact that in spite of all this ridicule the mass of our newspapers agree that the N.R.A. is really making headway.

The Agricultural Adjustment Administration, on the other hand, has experienced the same difficulties as have the P.W.A., C.W.A. and so on. The papers are just now full of stories concerning an alleged fight going on between Mr. Peek, head of the A.A.A.,[4] on the one hand, and Mr. Wallace and Mr. Tugwell,[5] Sec. & Asst. Sec. of Agriculture respectively, on the other. The mere fact that such a fight can begin and rage between two principal agents of the President, both responsible for important phases of his program for agricultural rehabilitation, is evidence of faulty organization. Only history can render a verdict as to the wisdom of Pres. Roosevelt's policies. But—as definitely as has ever been done in this country—the people gave the Pres. a mandate to revise our economic processes and to take charge of our nation in leading it out of the wilderness of depression. <u>The only chance</u> for success is <u>to follow where the Pres. leads</u>. No matter what other scheme may be theoretically more applicable to our difficulties, the fact remains that this is the only one that can be tried during the next three years. Therefore unified support <u>must</u> be given.[6]

I do not decry the value of proper criticism in the newspapers and elsewhere. The advocates of money stabilization should be heard, as should all others who have definitely formed ideas to advance as substitutes for portions of the President's program. But bitter attacks carrying no thought but "it is all wrong" do not help, and can only serve to destroy the solidarity of public support which <u>alone</u> can bring us out of current troubles.

1. The Public Works Administration (PWA) was created in 1933 to stimulate the economy through large expenditures of public funds on such projects as public buildings, highways, power plants, sewage systems, levees, bridges, and docks. It constructed the aircraft carriers *Yorktown* and *Enterprise*, built more than fifty military airfields, and improved thirty-two army bases. Among its greatest achievements were much of the Tennessee Valley Authority (TVA) system, as well as Grand Coulee, Bonneville, and Boulder dams.

2. The Civil Works Administration (CWA), established in 1933, served primarily as a work relief program to provide immediate employment—at make-work projects, if necessary. Headed by Harry Hopkins, the CWA improved one-half million miles of secondary roads, built or improved thousands of small schools and airports, improved parks and playgrounds, and employed three thousand artists and writers. The agency was liquidated in July 1934 and its functions either terminated or transferred to the Federal Emergency Relief Administration.

3. Eisenhower's military background, with its training in the fundamentals of organization, fitted him well for working in the large bureaucracies that characterized twentieth-century America, whether it was the U.S. Army, Columbia University, or the presidency. Furthermore, his experiences posited such values as cooperation, moderation, consensus-building, and a conservative reluctance to initiate major changes in American institutions. Eisenhower's understanding of political economy and the impact of that understanding on his policies as president are described

in Robert Griffith's "Eisenhower and the Corporate Commonwealth," *American Historical Review* 87, no. 1 (1982): 87–122.

4. The Agricultural Adjustment Act (AAA) was intended to alleviate agricultural depression through production controls and marketing agreements. By the end of its first year the AAA had removed forty million acres from production, and farmers had received several million dollars in relief. The net effect was to double the annual income of America's farmers by 1935. After the Supreme Court ruled the act unconstitutional, Congress passed a second AAA, providing for federal crop insurance, parity payments, and even stricter marketing quotas and acreage allotments.

5. Henry Agard Wallace, the son of Henry C. Wallace, secretary of agriculture in the Harding and Coolidge administrations, edited the family's publication, *Wallace's Farmer,* from 1929 until Roosevelt appointed him secretary of agriculture in 1933. In 1940 he became Roosevelt's third-term running mate. In 1944 Roosevelt dropped him from the ticket, replacing him with Senator Harry S. Truman of Missouri. Wallace remained as secretary of commerce until President Truman asked for his resignation in September 1946. Wallace ran against Truman as a Progressive Party candidate.

Rexford Guy Tugwell, a professor of economics at Columbia University, joined the Roosevelt administration in 1933 as one of the key members of his "brain trust." One of the authors of the AAA, he helped administer it as assistant, then undersecretary, of agriculture. From 1936 to 1938 he served as administrator of the Resettlement Administration.

6. Many scholars who have studied the Roosevelt administration have concluded that Roosevelt deliberately cultivated conflict among subordinates so that he would have available many policy options and be in a position to make all vital decisions. For more information on this matter, see Richard E. Neustadt, *Presidential Power: The Politics of Leadership from FDR to Carter* (New York: W. W. Norton, 1980); Richard Tanner Johnson, *Managing the White House* (New York: Harper and Row, 1974); and Roosevelt's major biographers, Arthur Schlesinger Jr. and James MacGregor Burns.

78

To GENERAL GEORGE VAN HORN MOSELEY

JANUARY 6, 1934

Dear General: I have had some difficulty in obtaining material that would be of any help to a newspaper man in making an analysis of our Congressional friend.[1] I have picked up a few things here and there and which I inclose with this letter. Major Hedrick is running through his file to get together a few of Mr. Collins' speeches, but as usual seems to be taking ten days to do a ten-minute job.

I went to see General DeWitt[2] about the anonymous letter. He told me that the information he received was on a confidential basis and that he could not possibly be quoted. The letter of which he had knowledge referred to the Gold Star Pilgrimage[3] and was admittedly written by Mr. Collins to himself for delivery in the House. The letter to which I believe you are referring was one read during the effort to accomplish the retirement of 2,000 Regular officers. I had this letter copied from the Congressional Record along with a few of the remarks made by other members following its delivery. You will find this among the attached papers.

The other documents I have attached are simply given to show the existence at least of an entente cordiale between Mr. Collins and one of our principal pacifist organizations.

The only person I know in Washington who might be of any help in furnishing the writer the necessary leads is Major Molter of the Reserve Officers' Association. The Congressional Directory of course gives a very brief biography. It would seem to me necessary, though, that the writer of the article find some friend of Mr. Collins who could furnish some of the more intimate details of the man's life. As a matter of fact, I have no doubt that Mr. Collins himself would jump at the chance to furnish all the information requested. He is a publicity seeker and would be highly pleased to find his name in print. The best thing to do with such a person is to ignore him. Sincerely

1. The "congressional friend" refers to Congressman Ross A. Collins of Mississippi.

2. Probably Gen. John Lesesne DeWitt, Quartermaster General (1930–34). Eisenhower would have contact with him a few years later when, from 1936 to 1937, DeWitt commanded the Army's Philippine Division at Fort William McKinley, Manila. DeWitt did three tours of duty in the Philippines from 1899 to 1911.

3. This likely was a peace demonstration sponsored by the American Gold Star Mothers, an organization created in 1928 by mothers of World War I veterans who had died in service. The organization is still in existence.

79   Eisenhower Library
                                                    Pre-presidential Papers

To James Van Fleet

January 15, 1934

Dear Van: I have not forgotten your ambition to get to Fort Leavenworth very soon. As you know, I have no official authority in making the details but I have done my best to learn as much as I can about your chances. The impression I get is that the authorities are considering you more definitely for the 1935 class than for the 1934 one. Howev-

er, I do not know this to be a fact and it is possible that you may make the grade this year. At least I will stick in a good word whenever I get the opportunity.[1]
With best regards, As ever

1. Apparently, Van Fleet sought Eisenhower's support in attempting to secure admission to the Command and General Staff School. Van Fleet was a West Point classmate of Eisenhower's. During World War II, he commanded the 8th Infantry at Utah Beach on D-Day, then became commanding officer of the 90th Division, which played a key role in the Ardennes counteroffensive. In March 1945 he assumed command of the III Corps, which spearheaded the Allied drive from the Remagen Bridge across Germany. During the Korean War, Van Fleet commanded the Eighth Army and received his fourth star. He retired in February 1953, when Maxwell Taylor was appointed as his replacement. Van Fleet died on September 23, 1992.

80

To Everett S. Hughes[1]

January 18, 1934

Dear Everett: Time and again within the past two weeks I have been just on the point of starting a note to you but always something has intervened. Actually, of course, I suppose there is no news other than that you have seen in the papers, but nevertheless, I have the uneasy feeling that much has happened of which I should have given you a report.

First of all, I am anxious to know how you are coming on your building program. Did you find any way of getting around the matter of excessive bids on your officer's quarters? Would there have been anything unethical in coupling a given number of sets of quarters with some other large construction project on the post in asking for bids? On that basis the contractor could have distributed itemized costs as he saw fit and possibly on a bulk order would have been disposed to have brought the bids for quarters within the legal limit. Anyway, I am curious to know how you solved the problem.

There seems to be only a Chinaman's chance of getting the pay cut reduced more then 5% or of having the pay freeze repealed. The Senate will undoubtedly have something to say on these matters but I doubt that any substantial amendment to the House bill will be adopted by the Senate or even if adopted can get by conference.

You have probably seen dispatches to the effect that Mr. McSwain is going to conduct a searching investigation into the War Department organization, particularly with the view of setting up a separate department for air. This particular attack looks to be somewhat more strongly organized than similar ones in the past but I don't believe he can put it over. Fundamentally, the inspiration for such efforts comes from air corps officers who are determined to set up a separate pay and promotion list for themselves.

I understand that hearings on the Army Appropriation Bill are to begin next Monday. General MacArthur has prepared a rather comprehensive statement dealing with the Army's situation and principal needs and I hope it will have some effect upon Mr. Collins' sub-committee. Mr. Powers and Mr. Bolton,[2] two of the members of the sub-committee, seem to be very favorably disposed towards the Army.

I think it is high time that you and Kate were running down here to look us over. While I understand that you have a date for the 19th, after all, there are seven days in each week and you are just as welcome on Tuesdays and Thursdays as you are on Saturdays and Sundays. A day's leave once in a while would do you both good. Best to you both. As ever

1. Hughes was stationed at Aberdeen Proving Ground, Maryland, at this time.
2. David Lane Powers of New Jersey served four terms in Congress (1932–45).
Chester Castle Bolton, a steel executive, served with the War Industries Board and with the Army General Staff and in 1928 was elected to Congress from Ohio. After his death in 1937 his widow, Frances Bolton, filled his unexpired term and went on to a long and distinguished career, serving fourteen terms from Ohio's Twenty-second District.

81   Eisenhower Library
                                                    Pre-presidential Papers

TO MAJOR LELAND S. HOBBS[1]

JANUARY 23, 1934

Dear Leland: While the War College list is still being ground painfully and slowly through the Adjutant General's office and G-1 I thought I would drop you a note just so you would be sure that I have not forgotten your anxiety for news. I believe that within a week or ten days the slate should be completed and as soon as anything definite is known Madison Pearson[2] or one of us will drop you a note.

I think you are just a little bit mistaken in your estimate of the causes lying behind the changed methods in the office of the Chief of Infantry.[3] I think the present Chief takes a very definite personal and detailed interest in all assignments made through his office and as a result Colonel Crea, Benny Ferris[4] and the rest of them are often not in a position even to give an intelligent guess as to what will happen in a particular case.

So far as I know Colonel Wilson of G-3 has nothing whatsoever to do with the selections. On the other hand he undoubtedly has some splendid friends in G-1 and might do something from that angle. But my honest opinion is that the best thing to do is to simply sit tight in the boat and let it pitch. It is all going to be over soon and you will either know the best or the worst. Both Pearson and I are hoping that everything will be O.K., and certainly if a good word stuck in at an opportune time will help out you can be sure that we will put it in. With best regards

1. Leland Stanford Hobbs (USMA, 1915) evidently was seeking Eisenhower's assistance for an appointment to the Army War College. Hobbs was a student at the Command School at Fort Leavenworth at this time. After graduating from the Command School, he attended the War College, graduating in 1935. During World War II he commanded the 30th Division, ETO.

2. Madison Pearson entered service as an enlisted man and was commissioned in 1917. He retired in 1944 as a colonel.

3. The Chief of Infantry at this time was Maj. Gen. Edward Croft.

4. Harry Bowers Crea (USMA, 1908) served from 1919 to 1922 with American Forces, Germany. He retired in 1944 as a colonel.

Benjamin Greeley Ferris (USMA, 1915) served in the office of the Chief of Infantry during the 1930s. He was associated with Eisenhower as director, Civil Affairs Division, Headquarters, European Command, from 1949 until his retirement in 1951.

82   Eisenhower Library
                                                              Pre-presidential Papers

To General George V. H. Moseley

January 24, 1934

Confidential

Dear General: I have not yet learned of your first impressions of your new command.[1] I am sure, of course, that you are having a good time because you always take so much delight in plunging into the problems brought by a new task. I hope Mrs. Moseley and Jimmy soon join you there.

While I gathered up and sent to you a number of documents that might be of some value to a writer making an analysis of Mr. Collins, I was very sorry that I could not uncover more "leads". Here and there someone would tell me a story (for illustration, the anonymous letter stories) but each person did so on a confidential basis, and was unwilling to let it be repeated.

I miss the talks we used to have on such subjects as "the state of the nation"—and all included matters. So much is happening that is going to be of the utmost significance to our country for generations to come that I would like very much to discuss with you the motives, purposes and methods of some of the actors now occupying the national stage.

Hearings on our supply bill have not yet begun. I don't see how the committee can extract much more from our budget, so possibly the sessions won't be of as long duration as formerly. I hear that Mr. McSwain is going to propose a sweeping and exhaustive investigation of the cost of national defense—in accordance with one of the planks of the Democratic platform. Of course, the real purpose will be to obtain some personal publicity, plus the chance for furthering his pet scheme of abolishing other arms in favor of a unified air corps.

It appears more or less certain that the Navy is to secure another great building fund. I notice that even the Marine Corps will probably be increased by 1,000 men. The War Department, as usual, is struggling to prevent further deterioration.

I am sending to Bomar today a couple of documents distributed by the Committee for the Nation,[2] on the general subjects of finance and banking. It struck me that you, as Corps Area Commander, might have reason to mention such subjects occasionally in formal or informal addresses. He may be able to dig something out of these particular ones that will be of value to you. With best regards, Sincerely

1. At this time Moseley was commanding general of the IV Corps Area, Atlanta, Georgia.

2. Eisenhower probably was referring to the Committee of the Nation, consisting of prominent business leaders, investment bankers, and journalists who lobbied to have the United States abandon the gold standard, thereby devaluing the dollar, which would place more money into circulation.

83   Eisenhower Library
                                                    Pre-presidential Papers

To Dr. Herbert Black

JANUARY 24, 1934

Dear Dr. Black: Your letter served to clear up in our minds some of the things that have been most puzzling to Mamie and me. But we were startled and disappointed to learn, not only of your fears in Dad's case, but also of your deductions as to Mother's condition. Some specific questions occur to us, and we feel that we must trespass on your time for additional help and information.[1]

To start with, it was news to us that Dad intended going back to Boone in the near future, even for a temporary visit. The first questions we have apply to his condition. Will it take any appreciable time to determine whether the internal condition is really malignant in character? If so, is there any possibility of curing or allaying its progress? If it should prove to be trouble of this kind, would there arise immediate danger to him or would it mark rather the initiation of a protracted difficulty? Do you expect anything, of any kind, to develop from your current investigation that will lead you to urge Dad to give up his present intention of making a temporary visit to Boone?

Mamie has for a long time been holding herself in readiness to leave for home on a moment's notice. But not knowing the answers to the above questions it is difficult for her to arrive at any decision.

Now with respect to Mother. You recommend rest and frequent check-up. Where should she go for this? To the hospital? Or do you mean rather that she should go to bed at home—or possibly come on here or go to San Antonio? We realize that both of them need care and constant observation, but you know as well as we how difficult it is to get them both to relax and take the necessary care of themselves. I feel it should be done on a basis that will so far as possible, keep them both contented. I feel also they should not be separated by any great distance for any length of time.

Naturally we cannot write in any detail to Dad and Mother. In fact, we will not tell them for the present that we have heard from you—as they would probably become alarmed. But we are anxious to encourage them to do whatever is best for them, and I feel that if we have your frank opinions we will be in better positions to propose and urge a suitable plan upon them.

Unfortunately Mamie cannot afford to run back and forth at will, and although ready and anxious to do anything that will help, she feels the need for the very best information possible in order to lay plans that may possibly extend over some months.

We are grateful indeed to you for all the trouble you are taking. Please give our love to Mrs. Black, and with best regards for yourself,
Sincerely

1. It is not known for certain what John and Elivera Doud's illnesses were that family physician Dr. Black wrote about to Eisenhower.

To General George V. H. Moseley

February 21, 1934
Dear General: Literally things happen so rapidly these days that it seems hopeless to give any coherent account of events, and of their reactions in the War Department.

You have read, of course, about the current investigation into the activities of the Assistant Secretary of War. The Grand Jury has had a number of officers before it in an effort to find out whether there has been anything irregular in awarding War Department contracts involving motors and other items. Through the newspapers the names of Mr. Payne, Mr. Woodring, Mr. O'Neill, Joe Silverman and one or two others have been dragged into the matter, but so far as I know there is no intimation or insinuation that any Army officer is even remotely connected with any culpability that may exist.[1]

This morning I notice that Mr. McSwain has announced an intention to investigate the same and similar matters. I suppose this will have the effect of dragging the whole matter out indefinitely, whereas our hope has been that they arrive at a definite and complete answer without delay.

All our contacts with the Military Affairs Committee of the House this year have revolved around air problems. Unfortunately, we seem to be handicapped, as usual, by a senseless, but very active, resentment against the General Staff. The words themselves are sufficient to bring a sneer upon the faces of many of the people with whom we deal, including some few, of course, in the Army itself. It is strange how often prejudice completely overwhelms knowledge and judgement. I believe that many Congressmen think, if they give the matter any thought at all, that the General Staff is a body of academicians, selected from the Army and permanently stationed in Washington for no other purpose than blocking progress in the rest of the organization. It is an easy excuse for failure to say: "The General Staff would not let us do that."

For a while we thought the chances were bright for securing a substantial increase in the authorized strength of the Air Corps, and in such a way as to make good in other branches, the losses they have sustained in building up the Air Corps. But extremists were so anxious to butcher the rest of the Army in order to get up an entirely impossible organization for an aggrandized Air Force, completely independent of the Chief of Staff, that it looks like the whole project will be lost.

The Air Mail probe and the substitution of the Army Air Corps for civilian firms in flying the mail has caused lots of work and much discussion pro and con in the newspapers. I firmly believe we'll do a good job, though I hope we don't have to continue it too long.[2]

I liked your instructions concerning reserve assignments, and have no doubt as to their good effects. I also saw an order you published regarding rotation of Reserve officers on Civilian Conservation Corps duty. They struck me as being perfectly sound, and based upon a clear analysis of fundamental considerations.

I hope business will bring you this way again in the near future, since the subjects that engage our attention these days are much better topics for conversation than for correspondence.

Please pay my respects to Mrs. Moseley and with best regards for yourself. Sincerely

1. Assistant Secretary of War Harry Woodring's principal duty was to manage military procurement. In the spring of 1934 the House Military Affairs Committee charged that the law requiring competitive bidding in the procurement of airplanes and aviation equipment had been violated by Woodring's office and the arms and bureaus he supervised. Shortly after these charges were made, another House committee revealed that the Quartermaster General's office had formulated specifications that excluded all but one truck manufacturer from the bidding process. See James, *Years of MacArthur* 1:439–40.

2. In January 1933 the U.S. Senate created a special committee chaired by Alabama senator Hugo Black to investigate the awarding of airmail contracts. Black's committee accumulated substantial evidence that Hoover's postmaster general, Walter F. Brown, had ignored competitive bidding in the awarding of airmail contracts in order to favor large commercial airlines. Graft was not the primary concern; it was simply that Brown, like Hoover, gave a lower priority to competition than to order, stability, and rational growth in the nation's corporate economy. Brown believed that government promotion of the larger carriers through subsidization would accelerate the development of a national air transport system. Small independent carriers were enraged by the Black Committee's revelations, which confirmed their worst suspicions.

In January 1934, Black confronted Roosevelt with his committee's findings, suggesting that the president cancel all contracts immediately. Roosevelt agreed, and on February 9, 1934, he voided all contracts and charged the Army Air Corps with the responsibility for airmail service until new contracts could be let later in the year. The inadequately trained Air Corps suffered a rash of deadly accidents in the four months it carried the mail, and the Roosevelt administration suffered its first public relations defeat. By early summer commercial firms were again awarded all airmail service, but through competitive bidding and with much smaller subsidies. The War Department suffered severe criticism for the sorry performance of the Army's air arm (Gen. Billy Mitchell seized on the accidents as proof of his claim that a reorganization and expansion of the Air Corps was vital to the national interest). Responding to the criticism, the Roosevelt administration set up a special board chaired by Newton D. Baker to study the Army Air Corps and its needs. See Arthur

M. Schlesinger Jr., *The Age of Roosevelt: The Coming of the New Deal* (Boston: Houghton Mifflin, 1959), 446–55.

85

TO ISAAC MARCOSSON[1]

MARCH 5, 1934

Dear Mr. Marcosson: I am somewhat at a loss in attempting to make reply to your inquiries concerning the size of the organization now running the Air Mail.

When responsibility for the air mail was assigned to the Air Corps, it immediately proceeded to the accomplishment of this mission prepared to use whatever number of officers, men and airplanes might prove necessary. In all three categories, many temporary and part-time assignments have been made which will eventually be discontinued, and I believe also there is still some question as to the exact number of mail lines that will be operated. As a consequence, the organization has not yet been definitely crystallized, and probably an additional week or two will elapse before the figures you want can be supplied. I have not felt justified in requesting the Air Corps to make a survey of their field agencies in order to prepare an official estimate of the numbers that will be needed, since officers and men are naturally extremely busy in meeting the initial strain of the situation.

I am sorry that I cannot be of more assistance to you on this point. Sincerely

1. Isaac F. Marcosson began his career in journalism with the *Louisville Times* and became a staff writer for the *Saturday Evening Post* (1913–36). A prolific writer, he published books on business and commerce, including a history of Anaconda Copper, and biographies of Gen. Leonard Wood and David Graham Phillips.

86

TO FRANK J. WETZEL[1]

MARCH 27, 1934

Dear Frank: I have just received a letter from my brother Edgar, who, as you may know, is an attorney in Tacoma, Washington. He is also a part owner of a considerable lumber brokerage business.

He has just learned that the Pennsylvania Railroad makes some of its lumber purchases on the West Coast and is going to write to you to find out the name and address of the official responsible for your lumber purchases.

He has no intention of embarrassing you by asking for special favors, but since, under the code, all mills must charge identical prices, he feels that the quality of their product and the service they can give may well obtain for him a portion of the Pennsylvania Railroad business on the West Coast.[2]

The purpose of this note is just to warn you that he will probably send you a letter in the near future and to tell you that when you see his name you will know it is from my brother and not from some more distant relative.

A recent spell of cold weather probably set our cherry blossoms back a few days but of course Lane Powers will let you know when to expect them. There is no question but what we will have a fine time when you all come down. Sincerely

1. Wetzel was serving as special representative, Pennsylvania Railroad Offices, in Trenton, New Jersey, at this time. The Douds owned some stock in the railroad.

2. The "code" to which Eisenhower referred probably was one of the price-fixing codes promulgated by the National Recovery Administration.

87

To General Fox Conner[1]

April 23, 1934

Dear General: I've heard lots of nice things about your recent talk at the War College. You made a great impression on the class.

There has been some little stir caused by a bill (introduced by Congressman Clark Thompson of Texas) to increase the Army to 14,000 officers and 165,000 enlisted men. It quickly reached the stage of holding hearings—which is more progress than we originally anticipated. Provided no opposition from administration leaders is encountered it should at least come up on the floor for discussion.[2]

The Appropriation Bill still carries a provision requiring us to get rid (before September 30th) of some 300 officers commissioned prior to June 1, 1924 and replacing them with new lieutenants. Voluntary retirements, physical disabilities and Class "B" procedure will have to provide the vacancies.

Mamie has just returned from San Antonio, and is looking well. All of us send our best to you and Mrs. Conner. As ever

1. Conner commanded the I Corps Area headquartered at Boston, Massachusetts, at this time.

2. Thompson's bill failed to pass, and the army's officer corps fell from 13,761 in 1934 to 13,471 in 1935, although enlisted strength grew nominally, from 124,703 to 126,015. The army's appropriation, however, did grow substantially, from $408,587,000 in 1934 to $487,995,000 in 1935. See Russell F. Weigley, *History of the United States Army* (New York: Macmillan, 1967), 561, 568.

88   Eisenhower Library
                                                Chief of Staff Diary

APR. 26, 1934

I intended to go to Kansas on leave about May 3. Helen, Milton, Buddy[1] and I are to make the trip in Milton's car. We expect to be gone somewhat less than a month.

Two newspaper men of the lower order (scandalmongers) named Pearson and Allen[2] have been consistently attacking General MacArthur for many months. They publish a column in the Hearst papers and are known as the authors of a book that appeared some two years ago under the name of "Merry-Go-Round".

There seems to be no logical reason for their continued outpourings of innuendo, insinuation and even falsehood against a man who never has injured them. It appears probable that one of two theories may apply. First that their assault is inspired—perhaps by someone to whom these two busybodies look for favors. If this is so the one involved <u>may be</u> a man named Early[3] who is one of the President's Secretaries. Several times he has tried to get the W. D. to pull chestnuts out of the fire for him, and he probably suspects that Mr. Dern's canny refusals are inspired by the C. of S. This could of course make him furious, since he appears to be one of the small fry suffering from illusions of grandeur. Moreover, much of the material that comes out in the muckraking column drags the "White House" into the matter.

The second theory is simply that the two men are innately cowards (which they are) and are giving expression to an inferiority complex by ceaseless attempts to belittle a man recognized as courageous, if nothing else.

I personally think that both of these theories are involved.

1. Milton Eisenhower Jr.

2. Drew Pearson and Robert S. Allen wrote a syndicated "gossip" column, "Wash-

ington Merry-Go-Round." In 1941, Pearson publicized Eisenhower's prominent role in the Louisiana Maneuvers and his promotion to brigadier general, thus bringing Eisenhower's name to the American public's attention for the first time. Pearson continued to play an unsolicited role in publicizing the general when in 1951 he joked with Eisenhower while they were being filmed for a newsreel, saying that he hoped Eisenhower would seek the presidency. John Eisenhower notes that Pearson became a chronic nuisance to his father.

3. Stephen Early worked for the United Press International from 1908 to 1913 before joining the Associated Press. In 1927 he worked for Paramount News, and in 1933 Roosevelt brought him to Washington as assistant press secretary. In 1937 he became press secretary to the president, a position he held until Roosevelt's death in 1945. Early also served from 1949 to 1950 as deputy secretary of defense under President Truman.

89

To Captain J. C. Whitaker[1]

May 31, 1934

Dear Jack: It was indeed a shock to learn that you had been placed provisionally in Class "B".[2] I feel like you, that your unfortunate position on the promotion list as compared to your age must have been a very large factor in the decision of the Board.

As you know, the War Department as an administrative agency has nothing whatsoever to do with the classification of officers. It rests entirely with the Board convened under the provisions of the law and no interference with their action is permitted within the Department.

When we were both serving in the office of the Assistant Secretary of War I know that your reputation was a splendid one. I, of course, did not serve in the particular section under which the Board for the Promotion of Rifle Practice functioned, but I was in very close contact with Haislip and Gerow and of course also formed my own impressions from meeting you often in the normal course of our respective duties. Certainly it was always my fixed impression that you were officially considered one of the splendid officers under the jurisdiction of the Assistant Secretary, and I know that I have that distinct conviction personally. Incidentally, it occurs to me that Colonel Coward,[3] Major Haislip and Major Gerow should all be possessed of all detailed official knowledge on which to express a similar opinion to the one I have just voiced.

You are quite correct of course in your observation that your age was a matter as well known on the date that you were commissioned as it is now. On the other hand, there is ample evidence that a great deal of attrition was expected in the Army's commissioned strength than has actually taken place during the last fourteen years, and consequently it was thought that promotion would be somewhat more rapid. The Department has given a great deal of study to the matter of age-in-grade, and I suspect that the board of general officers very likely gave this factor considerable weight. My own impression is that your little difficulty of some years ago at Walter Reed would have little, if any, bearing on the matter.

A considerable number of those who have been placed provisionally in Class "B" I suppose will apply for physical retirement. I should think the Department would have to be very liberal in such cases and have no doubt that many officers will be, to protect their complete equity in their retired pay in following that route.

I scarcely need say that my very best wishes are with you in the affair. I stand ready to do anything that I possibly can but of course any official testimony that I would be called upon to give would have to be limited to that based upon general contact and impression as I have explained above, rather than upon any kind of direct observation and responsibility. With best regards and good luck, As ever

1. John C. Whitaker received a commission in 1903 with the District Of Columbia's National Guard Quartermaster Corps and transferred to the Quartermaster Corps of the regular army during World War I. He served with the Quartermaster Corps until his retirement on September 30, 1934. At this time he was serving with the Michigan Reserve District in Detroit.

2. Apparently Whitaker's age (fifty-eight) at the time of his correspondence with Eisenhower explained his relegation to a secondary promotion list ("B" list), although Whitaker believed that a single critical efficiency report in 1921 had unfairly prejudiced his prospects for promotion. See Whitaker to Eisenhower, May 29, 1934, and Whitaker to John M. Carson, May 26, 1934, Pre-pres. Papers, Eisenhower Library.

3. This probably was Jacob M. Coward, who enlisted in the New Jersey infantry in 1898 and achieved the rank of lieutenant colonel during World War I. Although he spent most of his army career with the Coast Artillery Corps, he apparently had drawn, in 1932, a desk assignment at the War Department.

90 Eisenhower Library
Chief of Staff Diary

June 8 [1934]

Gave Capt. Greenwell[1] some estimates (furnished by Capt. Wonal of F. D.)[2] on cost of increases provided by Thompson Bill.[3] The total annual cost involved was something under $40,000,000. But I believe that actual experience would raise this figure by 20%.

History of cut made by Bureau of the Budget in the sums appropriated by Congress for maintenance of the Army for fiscal year 1934.

About April 1, Director of the Bureau of the Budget (Lewis Douglas)[4] informed the War Department that the War Department would be permitted to withdraw from the Treasury, during the fiscal year 1934, only about $180,000,000 of the $271,000,000 previously appropriated by Congress. This meant virtual destruction of the Army, involving retirement of about 3500–4000 regular officers, discharge of 12,000 enlisted men, and almost complete withdrawal of support from all civilian components.

In addition procurement and maintenance of matériel would have had to be abandoned, and almost the whole of the Army's corps of civilian experts in ordnance and other departments would have been discharged.

The Chief of Staff fought this program bitterly, finally inducing the President, in a personal interview, to direct a reconsideration of the whole subject.

As a result there followed a long drawn out struggle between the Budget Bureau and the War Department. On May 30, General MacArthur obtained a promise that discharge and retirement of regular personnel would be avoided, and early in June was informed that the War Department would be permitted to withdraw during 1934, $225,000,000 (approximately). This sum is about $110,000,000 less than was provided for the Army in 1931—and the appropriations of that year were based upon a military program that has seen us go steadily backward in its degree of readiness for emergency.

While General MacArthur's fight, conducted incidentally with no effective help from anyone, including the Secretary of War, has saved some $45,000,000 and prevented complete emasculation, yet apparently this country is going back to 1898 in a military way.

There is some hope that this situation will be remedied by the devotion of considerable sums under the Public Work's Program (part of the Administration's scheme for economic rehabilitation) to the manufacture and maintenance of needed military equipment.

1. Col. Samuel Alexander Greenwell enlisted in the army in 1904 and in 1918 was promoted to major in the Army Signal Corps. He retired in 1944.

2. "Wonal" is probably Col. John James Honan. "F. D." refers to the Finance Department. A typist that Eisenhower used to transcribe this passage probably could not make out Eisenhower's sometimes difficult handwriting. Honan served in World War I. After the war he served in the army's Finance Department and the judge advocate general's division, where he worked until his retirement in 1951.

3. The Thompson Bill sought to increase the number of officers in the army.

4. Lewis William Douglas was elected to Congress in 1926. President Roosevelt appointed him director of the Bureau of the Budget in 1933. After serving as Gen. Lucius Clay's adviser on the German Control Council, Douglas was appointed ambassador to Great Britain, where he served until 1950.

91

Eisenhower Library
Pre-presidential Papers

To Everett Hughes

SEPT. 9, 1934

Dear Everett: I've just returned from the wars. The guns are silenced, the flags are furled, the weary soldiers turn their eyes longingly and expectantly to almost forgotten pleasures of home, of sweethearts and of bootleg liquor. In emulation of thousands of equally obscure and unimportant participants in cataclysmic (look up the spelling of that word in the little book you carry) struggles of the past, I am hastening to record for posterity (No, I know you don't qualify under that classification, but please quit interrupting) my profound impressions of the dramatic incidents, outstanding characters, (except that this is not really an autobiography) and lasting lessons of the late conflict. Casting a calculating eye toward experiences of the past I feel that I am justified in hoping the world will, momentarily at least, unsuspectingly measure the extent of my influence on the events of which I write by the speed with which I break into print.

Still mindful of the methods of my predecessors I must immediately, though of course modestly and reluctantly, confess that my intimate and continuous association with the principal figures of the war gave me "unusual and often unique opportunities to observe and perhaps even at times to influence" the actions and decisions of leaders who the world already has come to recognize as men of destiny. Am I to be deterred by the fear of criticism from those mean spirited cynics who will suggest that an aide is only a tail to a cow, or at the best nothing more than a visible warning to the meek and lowly that the brass hats are on the way? Ah, my friend, I need not say to you that the jibes and jeers of such can touch me not! Duty (hell I should have used capitals on that word) is to me a sacred thing—the world shall not lose the message that only I can bring it. And besides, many times before now gullible publishers have paid handsomely for documents having no other claim to fame than the extravagant admiration of their authors. Yes, the path is plain before me; let fortune frown, let friends desert me, let the world condemn me, but I follow it to the end. (To be read in a low voice, somewhat tinged with melancholy.)

And so to work! Perhaps I should take time to say that in this magnus opus there shall be no hint of plagiarism; from my own mind and from my own inspired thoughts shall flow every phrase, idea and word that I here set down in my keen realization of profound obligation to my fellow men. Genius at work cannot of course pause to consider the probability that kindred spirits of the past may have used identical or strangely similar phraseology in the expression of burning inspiration. Indeed should this be cause for wonder? Rather should we not realize that, cascading down from Olympian slopes, the molten lava of their genius must occasionally find eventual identity in form and shape even as it invariably does in beauty and in grandeur? Away then with all concern for the carping critic who finds in similarity of language evidence of feeble imitation! From these we find refuge in the nobility of our purpose and our self-dedication to its accomplishment.

There remains of course the possibility of challenge as to fact. Always we must realize that doubting Thomas did not depart this world with a consistent record for failure in procreation. His progeny plague us and insult us—they laughed at Fulton; they imprisoned Bunyan; they burned Joan d'Arc, and they invented the Bronx Cheer!!! I say to them in advance, that their attacks against the product of my pen, might with equal reason and presumption be directed against the works of some of my most illustrious predecessors, to all of whom I unhesitatingly acknowledge that close kinship which their demonstrated genius so clearly indicates. But who, for instance, can take his oath that one man and one only was so rude as to draw aside his curtain when the beautiful Godiva rode so hopefully around the streets of Coventry? What woman whose charm (and figure) had been so indifferently ignored by the whole manhood of a great city would have failed to leave for our edification an embittered and outraged commentary on the discernment and faded instincts of her male contemporaries? Preposterous? Of course. Yet the faithful historian could do no more than to record with precision and accuracy that which he himself saw, (And what a break it was to be an historian on that day and in that town.) Who can prove that the lovely Portia won her case solely by her knowledge of the law and her skill in debate? Would not an experienced judge have quickly penetrated her thin disguise and by an exchange of winks assured her client of acquittal and himself of a date—regardless of the logic of her argument? Sticklers for petty facts in Moses' day undoubtedly asserted that his flight from Egypt was inspired more by his fear of a shot-gun wedding than by his unalterable determination to give the Israelites a swim in the Red Sea. And from what we know of the habits of the Pharohettes, we are constrained to acknowledge the plausibility of this contention. The lesson is that fact and history are not necessarily synonymous terms—the artist is not to be confused with the statistician. Now the task I have set for myself is writing the history of the great Blue-Black and Tan War of 1934, and of my own participation therein. Why should I quake in terror of the anticipated attacks from those who will try to confound me with facts? The most they will be able to prove is that my participation was nil, that there were no Blues, nor Blacks, nor Tans, and that in truth there was no war.[1]

What on earth has happened to you and Kate? We've constantly been expecting to see you drop in here if for no other reason than to thumb your noses at us. I returned from Raritan last eve and we were so concerned as to your undetermined fate that we agreed to mount the Plymouth this morning and play Stanley to your Livingstone. We failed to do so only because we were afraid you'd be off on some jaunt and we'd get neither a drink nor a feed to help us on the return journey. Since we are expecting John by next Saturday we are toying with the idea of running up there one afternoon this week and staying over the next day. That would compel me to take only one day off, which I could manage I think. This subtle hint for an invitation is not nearly so plain as I could make it, but having implicit faith in your mental alertness and fine discernment, I am putting it this way in complete confidence that you will not miss the point. But of course, as long as things are hinted at, one can always conveniently duck disagreeable prospects by assumed denseness. And no umbrage can be taken by the hinter! Love to you both and for cripes sake come on in and see us, As ever

1. Eisenhower had witnessed the turmoil that plagued the War Department during the past year and in September probably had begun to prepare the Chief of Staff's annual report. As he compiled material for the document and reflected upon the year, he may have been unable to resist the urge to describe to a trusted friend the madness he had observed. In his humorous missive, Eisenhower alluded to budget battles with Congress and the White House, seemed to hint at the airmail scandals and congressional inquiries into War Department contracting, and may even have alluded to the Nye Committee's sensational inquiry into munitions profiteering. But there probably was more to the letter than his effort to capture the year's events in figurative language. The literary allusions, colorful metaphors, and extravagant use of adjectives almost surely mock his superior's flamboyant language. In *At Ease*, 223, Eisenhower wrote that MacArthur "spoke and wrote in purple splendor."

92

To John "Johnnie" Conklin[1]

September 21, 1934

Dear Johnnie: In the thought that anything postponed is very apt finally not to be done at all, I have started a hurried first draft of a letter to be sent to the Association of West Point Graduates as an obituary for Eddie Bethel. I am giving you this simply with the idea that it may suggest a few thoughts to you and would be very appreciative if you yourself would develop a letter you consider suitable and send it to the Association.[2]

The Class of 1915 bows in submission to the inscrutable decision that took from among our number Eddie Bethel whose unswerving path of success was leading him straight toward the highest places in his profession. Brilliant, upright, considerate, modest, and understanding, his brilliant record of attainment is fully accounted for in the rounded fullness of his character. No wonder that a sense of futility overpowers the pen in attempting to express in words the feeling of loss that his passing inspires.

Nothing I can say will assuage in even a small degree the grief of his devoted family, to whom his own devotion was complete. But for his classmates there is a certain satisfaction in the knowledge that he answered the last rollcall in full realization of a long-held ambition. This was a detail as a student at the Army War College. Having graduated brilliantly from Leavenworth and the Echole de Guerre he rightfully felt that in view of his unbroken record of service he was richly entitled to the assignment he sought. Though recommended consistently by his chief, unusual combinations of circumstances—Fate apparently—for several years denied him the opportunity, but the fall of 1934 found him in possession of the prized detail and his happiness was apparently the greater because of the frustration he had endured.

Hardly had he entered upon the course when the blow fell. If he himself had warning his demeanor never disclosed it. A few days before his death he took part in the field maneuvers in New Jersey and, forward looking as ever, he found in them an inspiration for future investigation and study.

But his work is done. Though reason refuses to accept the thesis that no need remain for his acknowledged talents, yet, the comforting thought comes that already there stood to his credit a whole lifetime of accomplishment.

And so we blow the trumpet and fire the vollies, a soldier's goodbye, to our friend and classmate. He would not have wanted more.

1. This was probably John French Conklin, a 1915 graduation classmate of Eisenhower's at West Point. In 1934, Conklin was the class of 1915's Association of Graduates representative.

2. It was common practice for West Point graduates to write obituaries for the Association of Graduates' annual reports. Eisenhower sent the obituary to Conklin. Eisenhower's was not published in the *Sixty-Sixth Annual Report of the Association of Graduates of the United States Military Academy at West Point, New York, June 11, 1935* (Newburgh, N.Y.: Moore Printing, 1935), as the Bethel obituary bears the initials "J.B.W" and "R.W.S." The "J.B.W." probably was John Beugnot Wogan, also a 1915 graduate. The only 1915 class member with the initials "R.W.S." was Robert William Strong.

93

To GENERAL GEORGE V. H. MOSELEY

SEPTEMBER 24, 1934

Dear General: As you know I am back to my desk, although I am not feeling like any colt just out of the pasture. The doctors found absolutely nothing wrong with me organically and seemed to think that the aches and pains I suffered probably result from injuries and congested tendons that were originally hurt many years ago. Certainly the doctors didn't take the thing anywhere nearly as seriously as I did.[1]

You can well imagine the War Department is rife with gossip these days, all centering principally around the prospective Chief of Staff. Since you know how the place runs here you know that we have even less information than people do out in the field. I hear your name mentioned possibly more frequently and more favorably then anyone else's, but I honestly think that no one but the President knows exactly what is to be done and he will make his announcement in his own good time.[2]

General MacArthur told me that Mr. McSwain had paid you a visit. I sincerely hope that you were able to convince him that the War Department is honest and straightforward in its dealings with his committee. He has always seemed to be extremely suspicious and prejudiced. At least if anyone could convert him to a sane view of things, you could, and I will be watching for beneficial results.

I miss the long talks we used to have and would very much like to be able to drop in on you and have a few days in which to bring up again many of the subjects we used to find worthy of talking about.

I had a note the other day from Bomar who said Mrs. Moseley was still in Long Island. I suppose with the approach of cooler weather she will be coming home and I know you will be looking forward to seeing her and the youngster.

I am working very hard to make sure that everything is cleaned up and in tip-top shape before the 20th of November. Actually I hope to be finished two or three weeks ahead of that time so that I can take a short leave and do some real loafing.

With cordial regards, as always

1. During the summer of 1934 a chronic problem with lower back pain and stiffness had become so severe that physicians confined Eisenhower to quarters. When he failed to improve, he was admitted to Walter Reed Army Hospital, where he spent four weeks (July 17–August 14) undergoing evaluation and treatment. During the hospitalization, army physicians also sought an explanation for his intermittent gastrointestinal distress and performed a general medical evaluation. Analysis of X-rays found a congenital anomaly in a lumbosacral vertebra, almost surely the cause of his discomfort. In 1934, however, medical science did not acknowledge that such a condition would produce severe symptoms. Instead, the army physicians diagnosed his condition as "chronic arthritis." Furthermore, the attending physicians, believing that simple arthritis did not adequately explain the severity of Eisenhower's subjective discomfort, diagnosed his complaints as in part neurotic, an explanation they also used in accounting for his puzzling intermittent gastrointestinal disorders. In any event, long bed rest on a stiff board, diathermy, massage, and aspirin alleviated the condition sufficiently to enable him to return to work. Eisenhower's disabling condition and long absence from his office may explain, in part, the long hiatus in his diaries following the June 8, 1934, entry. See Musculoskeletal System File, Thomas L. Mattingly Medical History of Dwight D. Eisenhower, Eisenhower Library, and Robert E. Gilbert, *The Mortal Presidency: Illness and Anguish in the White House* (New York: Basic Books, 1992), 80.

2. This reference concerned the rumors as to who would become the new Chief of Staff replacing General MacArthur. Ultimately, Gen. Malin Craig Sr. received the appointment.

94

Eisenhower Library
Pre-presidential Papers

To GENERAL GEORGE V. H. MOSELEY

NOVEMBER 23, 1934

Dear General: Events of the past few weeks have kept us all in a state of indecision and turmoil. We are still completely in the dark concerning what is to be done with respect to the Chief of Staff appointment, and so of course all questions that project themselves any distance into the future become especially complicated and difficult. Three months ago we were proceeding in normal and orderly fashion to make our expected exit on November 20th, but when there was raised the possibility of reappointment, we had to begin a policy of watchful waiting which has become quite wearing. The situation is particularly irritating for those of us that have leases, schooling for children and similar things to think about.[1]

There is no use in repeating any of the gossip that is constantly being circulated with respect to the President's eventual decision. Not only is it based upon the wildest kind of rumor, but I have no doubt that you hear the same tales that we do.

It is wholly impossible for me to express in words the great pride I take in knowing what a high estimate you place upon my professional qualifications, even though I know that during the whole of your recent tour in the Department your generosity always impelled you to give me credit where none was due except to yourself. But in asking me to give you the name of an officer who could serve in the same kind of confidential capacity under you that I occupied for three years I think I know what you have in mind. As I understand it, you want a man who is mentally alert, who thinks logically, and who will not only absorb your ideas and conceptions but will apply himself with sufficient energy and persistence to translate them into directives, memoranda or analyses which are direct, clear and coherent.

One officer I mention only briefly because you are already well acquainted with him. This is the older Gerow. (By the way, his detail to your Headquarters has already been approved.)

Major James B. Ord,[2] Infantry, now an instructor at the War College, is a superior type in every respect. There is nothing too good to say about him, and if you ever get a hold of him you will never willingly let go. His professional background is particularly broad—and all in all, I'd say that he is probably the most ideally equipped man to meet your needs that I know.

Another man you should not overlook is Major F. G. Bonham,[3] Infantry, now a student in the War College. He has a great record, both peace and war. You cannot go wrong on him—he's one of the finest in the Army. He has had considerable service as instructor in schools, and I have heard from others that he writes very well indeed.

Major W. E. R. Covell[4] of the Corps of Engineers is another officer of unusual qualifications. He is now on duty in Panama, but has been there almost two years, I think. He is brilliant, ambitious, energetic and of fine personality. He has not yet attended the War College.

Captain Oscar B. Abbott,[5] Infantry, now on the War Department General Staff, has a fine record and is extremely able. He has a keen mind, is a great student and very energetic. You would like him a lot.

If I should be called upon to establish a priority among these people on the basis of <u>my opinion of their qualifications to meet your requirements</u>, it would be as follows:

Ord, Bonham, Gerow, Abbott, Covell.

You know how tremendously I admire Gerow, and in explanation of the third place I give him, I should say that while he expresses himself clearly and logically, writing is nevertheless a rather laborious task for him. Consequently, the documents he prepares usually lack spontaneity. In almost every other respect I'd place him No. 1. All of these are men of the highest character, and are "superior" in every sense of the word.

There are several things I'd like to discuss with you. They are, however, so involved and they ramify in so many directions that it is completely impossible to take them up in a letter. I had counted on taking a leave this winter and going to that station you have in Florida where they tell me Army officers enjoy life at reasonable cost. Plans for such a trip of course included a projected stop in Atlanta, where I visualize our going over many matters at our leisure and in detail. But it looks now as if vacations for this winter are not to be.

Give our love to Mrs. Moseley and Jimmy when you write, and, as always, affectionate regards for yourself. As ever

1. Eisenhower's comments concerning "reappointment" refer to MacArthur's request to Roosevelt for a short extension of his tour of duty as Chief of Staff. When in September 1935 Eisenhower and MacArthur sailed for the Philippines with the American Mission, Roosevelt's announcement of MacArthur's replacement, made shortly after MacArthur departed, immediately caused a controversy (see Chapter 5).

2. Maj. James Basevi Ord, a West Point classmate of Eisenhower, was one of Eisenhower's closest friends. He participated in Pershing's Punitive Expedition to Mexico and from 1917 to 1918 served as an instructor at West Point. A bright, promising young officer, Ord studied from 1922 to 1924 at the Ecole de Guerre, Paris. In 1928 he returned to Paris as assistant military attaché, a position he held until 1932. Eisenhower prevailed upon MacArthur to have Ord assigned to the Philippine Mission, where he would work as Eisenhower's virtual equal in devising a defensive plan for the islands. Ord was a lieutenant colonel at the time of his 1938 death in a plane accident in the Philippines. In later years Eisenhower often said that in losing Ord, the army was deprived of an officer who would have achieved high distinction had he lived to participate in World War II.

3. Francis G. Bonham (USMA, 1917) served as commanding officer of an anti-tank battalion at Fort Benning in 1939, where he died suddenly at the age of forty-seven.

4. William E. R. Covell (USMA, 1915) retired as a major general in 1948.

5. Oscar B. Abbott served in World War I. He retired as a brigadier general in 1950.

To Colonel Daniel VanVoorhis[1]

June 5, 1935

Dear Colonel: Upon receipt of your wire I tried to prepare a telegram to
send you but finally decided that I could not possibly give you a correct impression of Kathryn's[2] condition in a short message.

First of all, please consider this letter as a confidential one because
Gee is making every effort to keep from Kathryn any definite knowledge of the seriousness of her condition.

As you probably know, Kathryn underwent a very radical operation
immediately upon arriving in Washington. Some weeks thereafter she
went with Gee to Atlanta where he was to have a job on the Corps Area
staff. Almost immediately she had some recurrence of her former
trouble and had to return to Washington. The doctors decided that
the only treatment possible under the circumstances was to use the X-
ray and that further operation was out of the question. They insisted
also that she stay close to Walter Reed.

When Gee learned of this diagnosis he asked for transfer to Wash-
ington and is now on duty in the War Plans Division of the General
Staff. They have taken an apartment in the St. Nicholas on California
Street, where Kathryn is now confined to her bed.

Of course I am not a doctor and you know how reluctant the
medicos are to make definite statements about such cases. I infer, however, from what I have heard that she is very seriously ill and is certainly
making no apparent improvement.

On the other hand Kathryn herself is brave and hopeful and when
not suffering excruciating pain is very lively and vivacious. Mamie, Gee
and I all try to do what we can in keeping up her spirits and in occupying her time pleasantly.

She is receiving no medical treatment at present since it is apparently impossible to use the X-ray method for long periods of time. The
doctors of course keep in close touch with her and furnish medicine
to alleviate the distress she so frequently feels. In talking to a doctor
the other day he told me he saw no reason to expect any sudden
change one way or the other in her condition, but in my opinion spoke
of the case most pessimistically. The above represents my understanding of her condition. As you know, I would not try to conceal from you
the critical nature of her illness but on the other hand I neither want
to alarm you unduly. We are all perfectly certain that everything that
medical science can possibly do for her has been or is being done and

we must take whatever comfort we can from that knowledge. I repeat that we are doing our best to keep her reasonably happy and her mind free from worry.

The rest of us are about as usual and send worlds of love to you, Edith and the children. As ever

P. S. Please give Jimmy Ulio[3] and George Patton my regards and pay my respects to the General.

1. Daniel VanVoorhis served as Chief of Staff, Hawaii Department, at Fort Shafter, Hawaii. He achieved colonel's rank during World War I and by 1940 was a major general.

2. Kathryn died later that year.

3. Col. James Ulio, an assistant adjutant general, was a close friend of Eisenhower.

96

TO ELIVERA DOUD

AUGUST 8, 1935

Dearest Mother: The check I am inclosing is to pay for John's tennis lessons. He said in a letter he could get 10 at 50¢ each. So long as he seems to take such an interest in the game I'd like to help him get the right start, so that he doesn't form bad muscular habits. If he stays here next year tennis will be one of his principal games with Bo, who I understand practices all the time. So I want John to be able to hold his own. Of course I do not want to force him to do anything, and even more I do not want to put you to any extra trouble. But if he can go on his bicycle to get the lessons it should be a simple matter. If you decide that he should not take them, for any reason at all, then just use the check to help pay his expenses home next month. My whole point is that if this could cause no inconvenience I'd like very much for him to have the opportunity to keep up with these boys who will delight in beating him when he returns.

I was surprised to learn that he was to go to a camp for two weeks in addition to his visit at Abilene. I thought the visit rather took the place of camp—or that at the most he'd be gone again for only a week. But undoubtedly it will do him much good to mix with a crowd of boys for that period and I deeply appreciate your generosity in arranging the experience for him.

I miss him more this year than ever before. Possibly its because I've got this Philippine thing staring me in the face and realize that we'll be separated for many months at the very least. I hate the whole thought—and know that I'm going to be miserable. On the other hand Mamie is so badly frightened (both for Johnnie & herself) at the prospect of going out there that I simply cannot urge her to go. My thought is that either I will be able to send her favorable reports as to conditions of health, education etc. that she will be willing to come next June, or that I will come home within a reasonably short time. I can only hope for the best, as the idea of being separated from my family has nothing for me but grief.

We had a very nice time at the Beyettes and would have liked to remain longer. However, we had to come on back here as I have lots of work. I rather think I'll leave here a few days before the rest of the party and come through Abilene and Denver before joining the group in Cheyenne for the trip out to the Orient. If this plan matures I'll see you along about Sept. 28, or 29.

As you know Mamie considered several plans for her winter's sojourn, including Denver, San Antonio & here. She chose the last because of John & his convenient schooling here with old friends—as well as for the fact that it may avoid an extra move. But I do hope that you & Dad or you alone or Auntie[1] can spend almost the full time with her. I think she will be writing you today or tomorrow. With lots of love to all of you. As ever your devoted son

1. "Auntie" referred to Eda Carlson, Elivera Doud's unmarried sister, who lived in Denver with the Douds.

Eisenhower's 1909 high school graduation photograph. The photo was also on the front page of the *Dickinson County News*, Abilene, November 18, 1909, accompanying the text of Eisenhower's speech to the Young Men's Democratic Club.

Above: While stationed at Fort Sam Houston (1915) Eisenhower (*first row, left*) coached San Antonio's Peacock Military Academy football team. *Below:* Fort Sam Houston, San Antonio, 1916. Eisenhower inspects trenches dug by troops of the Illinois National Guard stationed there. The guard unit was called to active duty during the Mexican border difficulties in 1916.

Transcontinental Motor Convoy, 1919. Sign on first truck reads "We're Off to Frisco." Location unknown.

From left, Maj. Sereno Brett, Harvey Firestone Jr., and Lt. Col. Dwight Eisenhower at the Firestone home, Columbiana, Ohio, taken during the 1919 Transcontinental Motor Convoy.

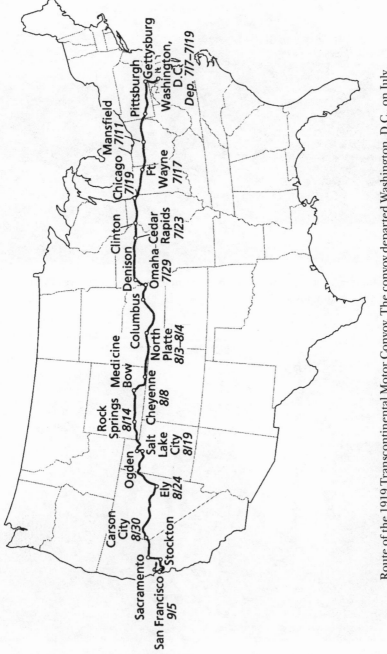

Route of the 1919 Transcontinental Motor Convoy. The convoy departed Washington, D.C., on July 7, and Eisenhower joined it at Frederick, Maryland, on July 8. The route followed the proposed "Lincoln Highway," paralleling or following modern Interstate 80. Map by William L. Nelson.

Above: George "Bo" Horkan Jr. *(left)*, and John S. D. Eisenhower, Paris, 1929. Photograph courtesy of John Eisenhower. *Below: from left,* Mamie and Dwight Eisenhower, Helen Gruber, on Rhine River above Coblenz, September 1929.

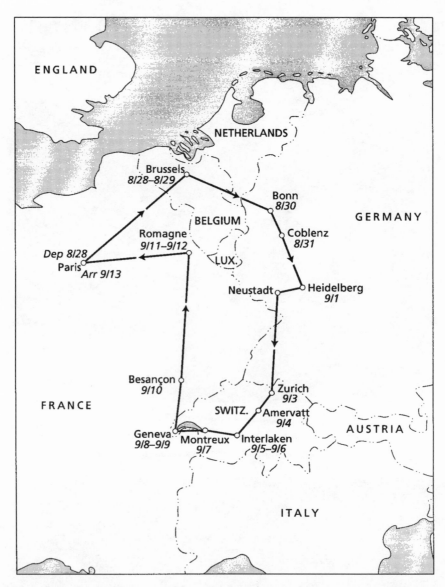

Route of the Gruber-Eisenhower motor tour, August 28 to September 13, 1929. Map by William L. Nelson.

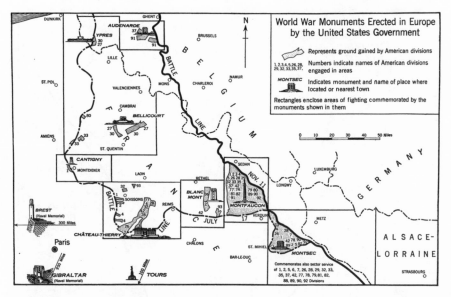

Eisenhower's work on the American Battle Monuments Commission included mapping of the American monuments and cemeteries in Europe. Even though his work was completed in 1929, the guidebook was not published until 1938. These maps show the location of American World War I monuments (*above*) and military cemeteries (*below*) in Europe. American Battle Monuments Commission, *A Guide to the American Armies and Battlefields in Europe: A History, Guide, and Reference Book* (Washington, D.C.: Government Printing Office, 1938), 477.

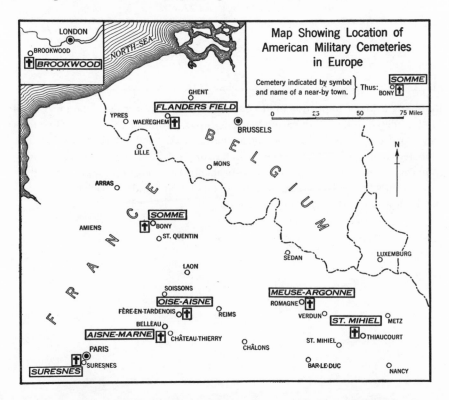

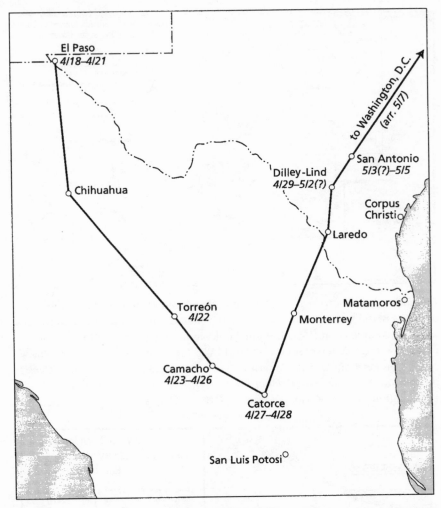

Route of the Mexican portion of Eisenhower's guayule rubber inspection trip, April 21–28, 1930. Eisenhower departed Washington, D.C., on April 8, traveling first to San Francisco, then south to Los Angeles, and on to El Paso, Texas, on April 18. He returned to the United States at Dilley, Texas, on April 29. The diary dates became somewhat confused at this point, but he probably visited Fort Bliss, May 3–4, and San Antonio, May 5. He arrived in Washington on May 7 and was back in his office the day following. Map by William L. Nelson.

Secretary of War George Dern *(front row, center)* visited a CCC camp at Fort Meade, Maryland (c.1933–34), accompanied by Gen. Douglas MacArthur *(front row, left),* Brig. Gen. Perry Miles *(second row, left),* Maj. Gen. Paul Malone *(first row, right),* and Maj. Dwight Eisenhower *(third row, center).*

Eisenhower, Lt. Col. James Ord *(center)*, and Capt. T. J. Davis, on redoubt outside Gen. Douglas MacArthur's office at No. 2, Calle Victoria, Manila, Philippines, 1936.

Above: Dwight, Mamie, and John Eisenhower, at the walled city of Manila, August 4, 1937. *Below:* Eisenhower golfing in the Philippines, 1937. Both photographs courtesy of John Eisenhower.

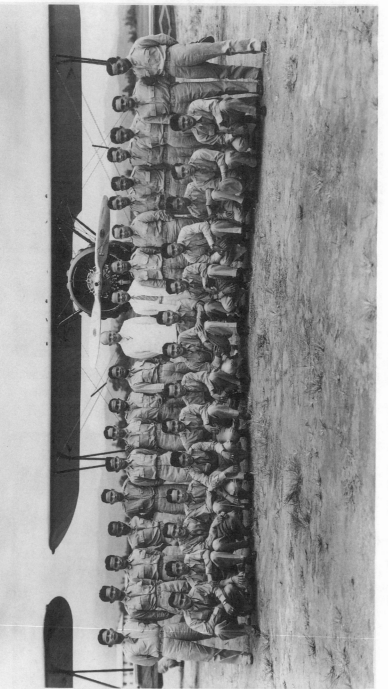

Farewell review of the Philippine Air Force held for Eisenhower (*center left, in white suit*) at Camp Murphy on December 11, 1939.

CHAPTER FIVE

Philippine Service
November 1935–June 18, 1938

By means of the Philippines, Eisenhower's relationship with Mac-Arthur lasted for nearly seven years, all of them tense and eventful. When, in the fall of 1935, Eisenhower departed for Manila, the world was in turmoil. Two years earlier, both Japan and Germany had withdrawn from the League of Nations. The World Disarmament Conference of 1934 had produced no happy results. Japan that year denounced the Washington and London naval treaties; in 1935, when Italy invaded Ethiopia, Germany declared itself unbound by the disarmament clauses of the Versailles treaty. Throughout Eisenhower's stay in the Pacific, discord worsened. The Spanish Civil War raged for three years, beginning in 1936. Japanese troops landed in Manchuria in 1931 and attacked China in 1937.

Such wars and rumors of war might have caused alarm in the isolationist United States, but by and large they did not. The military establishment continued to practice theoretical strategic planning rather than direct preparation for war. The 1935 Neutrality Act and the War Policy Act of 1937 maintained this restrictive posture. MacArthur's successor as Chief of Staff, Gen. Malin Craig,[1] attempted to revise training and prepare the army for possible combat operations. He had only modest support.

While serving on MacArthur's staff, Eisenhower became acquainted with the issue of Philippine independence and the problem of creating an army adequate for defense of the islands—a burden the United States assumed as a legacy of acquiring the islands after the Spanish-American War. Congress in 1934 had assured the Filipinos of independence in 1946 and pledged to assist the Philippine government in making preparations. Until then, the Philippines received commonwealth status.[2]

Even earlier, in an act of 1926, Congress authorized the sending of military advisers to certain friendly countries. The act originally did not include the Philippines, but with an amendment of 1935 it permitted a military mission to the commonwealth, primarily to create an army for defensive purposes. The Philippine legislature in 1935 adopted a National Defense Act specifying (at MacArthur's urging) that the U.S. adviser designated be a "field marshal" in the Philippine Army, and the stage was set for MacArthur's mission.

Eisenhower arrived in the Philippines on October 26, 1935, after an enjoyable voyage that a companion recorded in his own diary.[3] As usual, Eisenhower had hoped for a troop command, but MacArthur had insisted that he accept a staff assignment—assistant military adviser, U.S. Military Mission to the Philippines—and he had reluctantly agreed. Eisenhower recognized the valuable experience that building an army would entail. Besides his stipend of $980 a month, he received a welcome extra allowance for living expenses. MacArthur, as head of the mission, collected an additional $3,000 a month, making him apparently the highest paid military officer in the world. Two military headquarters operated in Manila: the MacArthur Mission and Headquarters, Philippines Department, U.S. Army. Unconnected, the two groups made an effort at cooperation but frequently failed.

MacArthur himself eventually became an issue in the War Department because of his enmity for his successor, General Craig, and for Washington more broadly. The outgoing Chief of Staff had tried to effect the appointment of Maj. Gen. George Simonds as the next Chief of Staff. Secretary of War George Dern had notified MacArthur in September that he would be relieved effective December 15. While traveling by train on his way to California and the voyage to the Philippines, MacArthur learned not only that Craig had been appointed new Chief of Staff but also that the move would be effective October 2—two months early. Failure rankled him. Worse, MacArthur learned that he would revert to his permanent rank of major general. Eisenhower noted later that when MacArthur learned of the army's decision, he launched a tirade directed at the government that was "an explosive denunciation of arrogance, unconstitutionality, insensitivity, and the way the world had gone to hell."[4] Then in August 1937, Craig ordered MacArthur to return home at the end of his two-year tour of foreign duty. Rather than suffer the humiliation of returning stateside to a subordinate command, MacArthur retired. As of New Year's Day, 1938, MacArthur—then a retired U.S. Army officer—remained military adviser to the Philippine government while serving as a field marshal in the nascent Philippine Army.

Against this backdrop of increasing vanity, and while the Pacific edged closer to full-scale war, Eisenhower received his most important preliminary training. He served as assistant military adviser from October 25, 1935, to October 12, 1937, when MacArthur named him his chief of staff. His duties included oversight and coordination of all planning. On July 1, 1936, he was promoted to lieutenant colonel, and when MacArthur retired from the service in 1937, Eisenhower became senior U.S. Army officer of the mission.

It was not unusual for U.S. Army officers to serve in the Philippines; between the Spanish-American War and World War II, more than half of the future "builders of the modern army" served there. Eisenhower's duties were more than routine, however. In the Philippines he learned to build and train an army from practically nothing while being as politically and diplomatically sensitive as possible, negotiating difficult logistical circumstances, and working with hair-trigger personalities.[5]

1. Craig (USMA, 1898) served with the 4th Cavalry in Santiago in 1898, with the 6th Cavalry in the 1900 Peking Relief Expedition, and with American forces suppressing the Philippine Insurrection of 1900–1904. During World War I he was chief of staff to Gen. Hunter Liggett. Afterward he directed the Army War College, commanded the cavalry school at Fort Riley, Kansas, spent more time in the Philippines, and commanded the Panama Canal Department and, from 1930 to 1935, the IX Corps Area, San Francisco. Craig returned to active duty during World War II, serving as chair of the War Department's personnel board. He died in 1945.

2. MacArthur remained a field marshal in the Philippine Army until July 26, 1941, when, with tensions mounting in the Pacific, he was recalled to active duty to command the U.S. and Philippine troops in preparation for war.

3. James B. Ord kept an intermittent diary of the mission's trip to the Philippines that included notes on the seven-day train trip from Washington to San Francisco (September 29–October 5). Eisenhower, who had enjoyed a short visit with the Douds in Denver, boarded the train in Cheyenne on October 2. That day, the mission received a telegram announcing that Roosevelt had appointed Malin Craig as the new Chief of Staff. Ord wrote: "Ike and I wired both Craig and Simonds. We sat up and jawed about it all until 2:30 A.M. Ike & I got our messages off at Big Springs, Wyoming." Ord also commented in his diary on the failing health of MacArthur's mother, who died five weeks after the party's arrival in Manila. Except for the party's concern for Mrs. MacArthur, the group seemed to have a relaxing three-week voyage. While enjoying a stopover in Honolulu, Eisenhower received from his old friend George Patton two quarts of his favorite scotch. On October 14, Eisenhower's birthday, he received gifts that Mamie and John had sent with Ord. When the group arrived in Manila on October 26, President Manuel Quezon and his staff boarded the ship to greet the mission before the party left for quarters in the Manila Hotel, which Ord described as "punk" (see McCann Papers, Eisenhower Library).

4. Dwight D. Eisenhower, *At Ease: Stories I Tell to Friends* (Garden City, N.Y.: Doubleday, 1967), 223.

5. On Eisenhower's Philippine service, see also Daniel D. Holt, "An Unlikely Partnership and Service: Dwight D. Eisenhower, Mark W. Clark, and the Philippines," *Kansas History* 13 (autumn 1990): 154–55.

NOVEMBER 1935 –MAY 29, 1936
NOVEMBER 1935

Draft[1]

In the early fall of 1934 the Army was agog with speculative gossip as to the identity of the new Chief-of-Staff, soon to be appointed. General MacArthur, counting upon an early departure from Washington, personally penned a good-bye to the Army to be attached to the Chief of Staff's annual report, and selected Governors Island as his next station. An elaborate, week-long, General Headquarters Command Post Exercise was staged in New Jersey, intended as a practical test of the revolutionary theory of the 4-Army Organization, expounded and supported by General MacArthur during his entire tour as Chief of Staff.[2] The Secretary of War—genial, honest, lovable George Dern— attended the maneuvers. There, in the evening isolation and homey atmosphere of a fire-lighted Army bungalow he referred frequently to the questions plaguing him for answer, to the problems nagging him for solution, and, coming back again and again to the same theme, to his reluctance to make any change, at a time he considered critical, in the identity of his principal military assistant. In conversation this reluctance seemed gradually to develop into a lively apprehension as to consequences, and there finally generated in his mind a hope that a way out could be found. With crystallization of desire he gave definite orders that, upon returning to Washington, every possibility would be explored to determine his right to continue as Chief of Staff in office beyond the four years then generally accepted as the legal limit. General MacArthur was charged with responsibility for conducting the necessary investigation.

No great difficulty was experienced in securing affirmative legal opinions, armed with which and with arguments presented to him in a number of memoranda, the Secretary directed a series of insistent recommendations to the President. Authority was finally granted at the White House to postpone, temporarily, the Chief of Staff's relief. This authorization was renewed from time to time, and so it came about that in the spring of 1935, at the moment Manuel Quezon, then President of the Philippine Senate, arrived in Washington to discuss matters of state, General MacArthur was still occupying the post to which he was first appointed in November, 1930.

This was not the first time, during General MacArthur's term as Chief of Staff, that the Philippine question came before the highest councils of the War Department for intensive discussion. During the administration of President Hoover, the Secretary of War, Mr. Hurley, journeyed to the Philippine Islands, to make a personal investigation of their readiness for independence—and to make a report on the matter for the benefit of Congress, before which, at the time, was one of the constantly recurring bills intended to cut the islands adrift. Upon Mr. Hurley's return the task of writing his official report was thrown up on the Chief of Staff, who supervised its preparation in every detail. This report was completely negative. It proved, or it purported to prove, that the Islands were not prepared economically, industrially, educationally, governmentally or militarily for independence. It even repudiated the thought that any definite date, no matter how remote, could then be fixed when the Philippines might, with some assurance that they could so maintain themselves, be constituted as a completely independent nation.

This report was, through inept handling, never presented to Congress and to the public as an entity, and whatever force it may have attained under more skillful procedure, was definitely and irrevocably lost. At the time the Philippine question was being intensively propagandized by interested blocs and personalities in the United States, and eventually there was passed and approved in the United States, and accepted in the Philippine Islands, the Tydings-McDuffie Act.[3] This law granted independence to the Islands, subject to a ten year span of Commonwealth Government, intended as a preparatory and transitory period.

At the time of his Washington visit Mr. Quezon was assured of election as President in the Philippine Commonwealth, scheduled by the Tydings-McDuffie Act to come into being on November 15th that year. He was attempting to foresee and prepare for the tasks with which he would inevitably be confronted, none of which, he said, gave him more concern than that of developing for the Philippines the security forces necessary to independent existence. Through correspondence he had already expressed to General MacArthur a hope that the General would come to the Philippine Islands as "Military Adviser", a post which he hinted would carry great prestige and emoluments. To discuss this subject further he called personally at the office of the Chief of Staff.

With characteristic directness and frankness, President Quezon bluntly phrased this question, "General, in your professional opinion, can the Philippine Islands defend themselves in an independent status?" The instantaneous answer was—"I know they can." Many times, since, General MacArthur has explained in detail the basis for his unequivocal reply, and since those reasons are pertinent to this narrative of later events in the Philippines, it is no digression from the main theme to enumerate them here.

General MacArthur had, he said, pursued a profound study of the Philippine Islands since the days of early American occupation. He had, through every possible contact, including tours of duty in the Islands, given earnest consideration to Filipino resources, psychology, geographical advantages and disadvantages, the fighting qualities of its soldiery, and the economic capabilities of its soil. His conclusions were that there existed, or could be developed among Filipinos a fervid spirit of nationalism, ready to express itself in a unified and continuous effort to preserve the independence they were shortly to obtain; that military preparation in the Philippine Islands need seek no more ambitious objective than a passive defense of territory; that by training the citizenry throughout every portion of the archipelago any hostile attempt at landing would be instantly met by intensive fires at the beach; that defensive concentrations at critical stretches of these beaches would be in overwhelming strength; that the economic resources of the Philippine Islands could be so developed as to sustain the population, and the defending army, through a long period of blockade; and, finally, that the anticipated yearly income of the new government would sustain indefinitely the costs of peace time preparation. At no time has General MacArthur intended that the P.I. could defend themselves against a major assault conducted with the full military, naval and aerial strength of one of the great powers. He has consistently decried, however, the possibility of invasion being undertaken on this scale, in the belief that world conditions would not justify such an attempt by any nation. His discussions and pronouncements have therefore ignored this possibility because of his conviction as to its remoteness, and his statements on the subject have visualized only a raiding or secondary effort.[4]

The next question, "If the matter can be arranged with the President of the United States, will you accept the post as Military Adviser, taking charge of all defensive preparation in the Islands?", was answered in the enthusiastic affirmative. Reasons, again, were later explained by the General. The offer came at an opportune time, as it was not considered possible, to secure indefinite extension of White House authority for postponing designation of a new Chief of Staff. In fact, because of the attractiveness of the new offer, effort was now directed toward retention of the Chief of Staff Post only to the moment that the new assignment could take effect, obviously not before November 15, that year. Acceptance of the post would avoid stepping down to a subordinate position in the hierarchy of the American Army. The position might well prove to be spring board for attaining an even more desirable position in official or industrial life. A large degree of independence was promised in administering the Philippine Army.

With the conclusion of this verbal agreement, it became necessary to initiate a stream of correspondence, all of it carefully calculated to inspire official confidence in the undertaking, so that no objection from an unforeseen source would arise, at the last moment, to wreck the project. As an opening gun in the campaign, a letter was drafted to the Secretary of War for Mr. Quezon's signature, setting forth in detail the intricacies of the defense problem facing the new nation, and requesting the help of the War Department in its solution, specifically soliciting the detail of General MacArthur as Military Adviser, effective upon completion of his tour as Chief of Staff. Study of all laws bearing upon such assignments indicated the advisability of requesting an amendment to an old law which authorized the President of the United States to lend to countries of South and Central America, personnel of the Army and Navy for advisory functions in military preparation. The amendment sought was to specify the Philippine Islands as an included country in the general authorization, and appropriate request was inserted in Mr. Quezon's letter. In order to assure Congress of the propriety of the suggestion, letters were to the Navy and State Departments, and their concurrence secured. Letters were likewise written to the respective Chairmen of the Senate and House Committees on Insular Affairs, and in every possible way the path was cleared for securing enactment and approval of the amendment. It passed without provoking comment in any quarter.

The next problem was to secure authority for specific assignment of General MacArthur. To this proposition the Secretary of War readily agreed, since, in addition to his personal inclination to comply with the desire of General MacArthur, he felt a certain obligation due to his belief that only because of his own insistence had the General agreed to the earlier extension of the tour of Chief of Staff. Proper opportunity was assiduously sought for presenting the matter to the President, which was found. The President gave his approval to the request, thus clearing the way for initiating a horde of studies, plans and conferences on many matters connected with the prospective assignment.

The first decision made was that, so far as possible, all necessary studies, plans, laws, proposed speeches and other essential documents would be prepared prior to General MacArthur's departure from Washington. Manifestly the W.D.G.S. could not be used as a body for this purpose, while the group of special assistants attached to the Chief of Staff was too small and too busy to perform it. A way out was found by requesting the Commandant of the War College to set up a special committee in that school to undertake the work. To this committee several of the ablest officers of the Army were assigned, with Major J.B. Ord, then an instructor at the [War College], designated as Chairman.

Initially the Committee was given a free hand in working out the problem, subject to Gen. MacArthur's instructions. That conscription would be made the basis of military training in the Philippines, and that preliminary military training would be made a definite function in the public school system.

In the absence of exact information the Committee was forced to base many of its conclusions upon estimates—as for example the number of young men arriving annually at a given age in the P.I.

1. Although Eisenhower's draft is undated, it is included here because it serves as a suitable preface to the introduction and diary that follow. Eisenhower may have written the draft before his departure, during the voyage, or even much later when he realized that the substantial diary he had compiled required background for the events described therein.

2. In 1932, MacArthur changed the Army's organization, making the nine corps areas subordinate to four armies he had created. Each army had a regional mission (northeast, northcentral, Gulf of Mexico and southwest, and the Pacific Coast). The Chief of Staff felt that such centralization would expedite mobilization in the event of war. See D. Clayton James, *The Years of MacArthur, 1880–1941* (Boston: Houghton Mifflin, 1975), 367–68.

3. The Tydings-McDuffie Act of 1934, also known as the Philippine Independence Act, granted commonwealth status to the Philippines and promised full independence ten years after the creation of a commonwealth government. The act provided that, with the exception of certain naval bases whose status would be negotiated later, all U.S. military bases in the Philippines would be closed after independence. The Philippine legislature was empowered to convene a constitutional convention to formulate a basic governing document; however, the constitution had to include provisions similar to those of the U.S. Constitution. In return, the commonwealth government was to relinquish its free trade privileges in the American market, and its governing authority was subject, in certain areas, to the veto of a U.S. high commissioner. The legislation virtually promised independence in 1946.

4. Although Eisenhower had typed most of the document, the last three paragraphs were handwritten. Where the editors found particular words difficult to decipher, the most plausible words were chosen, based upon context.

Introduction

As an introduction to a diary of the American Military Mission to the Philippines, there is summarized here General MacArthur's conclusions as to the national and international implications inherent in the granting of independence to the Philippines.

The approval of the Tydings-McDuffie Act definitely established a terminating date for American political domination in the Philippines, and marked the culmination of a unique experiment in colonization.

American Activity in the Philippine Islands

From the moment that the United States acquired from Spain the legal title to the Philippines in 1898, its general policy with respect to these Islands has been based upon an underlying purpose of preparing them for, and finally to confer upon them, complete independence. Evidence of the existence of this policy is found in the public utterances of Presidents from McKinley to the present, and was definitely expressed in the form of legislative intention in the Jones Act of 1916.[1]

Administration of foreign possessions with such an objective was in itself a departure from international custom. Historically, European nations have looked upon the possession of outlying territories as an opportunity for their own economic betterment and have always fought against relinquishment of title to such properties. Since maximum profit from colonization ventures required rigid political control from the seat of government, every concession to local autonomy was, in general, granted slowly and reluctantly. American expressions of an opposite purpose were habitually viewed, therefore, as political duplicity, designed only to deceive the inhabitants of the Philippines, and minimize the possibility of rebellion. Nevertheless, the policy was pursued steadily and honestly.

The American effort in the Philippines was naturally influenced by the political concepts underlying the progress of civilization in the United States. Three controlling principles in the American development have been personal liberty, religious freedom, and the maintenance of democratic institutions that insure to every citizen a voice in his own government. These conceptions are often epitomized in the expression "Government only by the consent of the governed". In pursuance of its policy of preparation for Filipino self-government, the United States established a system of public education in the Philippines, assisted and encouraged the development of agriculture and industry, and accorded to natives a constantly increasing degree of autonomous government. As a result of thirty-five years progress under these liberal policies, the Philippines gradually became an outpost of European civilization in the Far East. The standard of living was raised to a higher level than that enjoyed by any other Asiatic country. The degree of individual liberty and religious freedom enjoyed by Filipinos equaled that of any other country of the world. Illiteracy was gradually diminished. Finally there was developed within the Islands a government that, except for the control represented in the power of an American Chief Executive, was, for all practical purposes, purely Filipino.

During this development period the United States had retained full responsibility for the defense of the Islands. For various reasons it had never been considered expedient nor desirable to compel or to authorize the Filipinos themselves to organize and maintain strong military forces. Such native regiments as were established were officered principally by American personnel and were incorporated bodily as part of the American Army. The number of troops so maintained usually represented practical equality with the number of American troops stationed in the Islands.

As the general result of this development the Islands, in 1935, could be considered as generally well prepared politically to assume responsibility for their own government. Economically they had prospered to an extraordinary degree, and the only weakness in their situation in this regard was their extreme dependence upon free access to the American markets. This freedom of access would, of course, be lost with the gaining of complete independence. But in the fundamental obligation of sovereign government, namely that of providing for the common defense, the Filipinos were completely unprepared for independence.

The future ability of the Philippines to defend themselves has a very obvious interest for the United States. The Islands represent an outpost of American civilization in the Far East and the relative advantages they now enjoy have been gained through thirty-five years of liberal instruction, patient training, and material as well as sentimental investment. Not only would the growth of democracy and democratic institutions in the Western Pacific be completely destroyed should the Philippines ever fall under the domination of a neighboring Asiatic country, but American pride and American prestige would receive a severe, if not unendurable, blow. Local unrest and strained international relationships would almost certainly create an embarrassing situation for the United States and might conceivably draw us into a major war. On the other hand, if the Filipino people can be, within the next ten years, thoroughly prepared for their own defense and given an unquestioned ability to make a determined resistance against any type of attack, they should continue to flourish as a product of Western civilization and contribute to stability and peaceful relationships in the Asiatic area. It was in the belief that the development of adequate defense forces in the Philippines would constitute a distinct service to the United States, as well as to the Islands themselves, that General MacArthur consented to act as the Military Adviser to the new government.

The announcement of General MacArthur's acceptance of this post was not made until the termination of his tour as the American Chief of Staff, about the 1st of October, 1935. Sometime before that, however, he had conferred with the President of the United States, who gave his enthusiastic approval to the project. The months intervening between the receipt of this approval and the time when General

MacArthur actually left Washington to undertake his new duties were utilized by him in preparing a basic defense plan for the Philippine Islands.

1. The Jones Act of 1916, also known as the Organic Act of the Philippines, committed the United States to eventually grant Philippine independence and initiated immediate political reforms designed to prepare the native population for self-government. Filipinos were integrated into the civil service at all levels, with the objective of eventually giving the native population total control of the bureaucracy. It also granted increased government responsibility and authority. For a thorough description of the Philippine government, see Carol M. Petillo, *Douglas MacArthur: The Philippine Years* (Bloomington: Indiana University Press, 1981), and George E. Taylor, *The Philippines and the United States: Problems of Partnership* (New York: Praeger, 1964).

DIARY–OF THE AMERICAN MILITARY MISSION IN THE PHILIPPINE ISLANDS[1]

The first entry in this book is made as of December 27th, 1935. The Military Mission, headed by General MacArthur, landed in Manila two months ago, on October 26th. It has been the intention from the start to keep a brief narrative record of the principal recommendations and activities of the Mission. Due to unsettled conditions, there has been, up to this time, no opportunity to make a methodical record of events. The first installment, therefore, is intended to summarize briefly the outstanding incidents of the past two months, with the intention that hereafter this journal will represent a daily running account of the Mission's activities.[2]

The group is so organized that the detailed work connected with the development of the Philippine Defense Plan falls principally upon Major James B. Ord (in this narrative referred to as "Jimmie") and myself. Captain T.J. Davis serves as General MacArthur's aide, is the administrative officer for the whole group and is in charge of such matters as motor transportation, clerical assistance, normal administrative contacts with the Philippine Department and so on. Major Howard J. Hutter,[3] Medical Corps, is specifically charged with the development of a sanitary plan for the Philippine Army and in addition serves as personal physician for the group.

General MacArthur is the head of the Mission and is officially designated as the MILITARY ADVISER TO THE PHILIPPINE GOVERNMENT. He directs policy and, except in matters of detail, does all the contact work with the President of the Commonwealth.

The principal features of the Philippine Defense Plan were developed in Washington, beginning about the first of November, 1934.

293

General MacArthur announced that the defense system should be based primarily upon universal conscription and should be so devised as to require the minimum of expenditure. He gave as the basic mission of the plan the development of a defensive force that would assure maximum local protection in every Island, District and Province of this country.

Specifically, he recognized, from the beginning, the impossibility of developing a defensive force in the Philippines capable of concentrating its full potential power at any threatened point of attack. In other words, from a strategic viewpoint, a cordon system of defense was practically forced upon the Islands due to the impracticability of developing naval forces to preserve inter-island communications against any powerful attack by water. The objective, then, of the Defense Plan is to ensure such an excellent defense of each portion of Philippine Territory that the cost of its subjugation would exceed the potential rewards accruing to any aggressor.[4]

Manifestly, such a system cannot protect any Island Nation against the consequences of a blockade by sea. However, it represents the ultimate that a small and relatively poor nation can hope to accomplish and at the very minimum gives to such a nation the hope that through preservation of territorial integrity it may, in the event of prolonged blockade, acquire powerful allies before the moment of final starvation arrives.

In addition, the plan contemplates the development of an air corps, the threat of which will be sufficient to keep major portions of a hostile navy completely outside these Territorial waters.

Based upon these conceptions, the details of the original plan were worked out by Ord. He had intermittent assistance from personnel in the War College, where he was then on duty, and kept in close contact with General MacArthur and with myself.

It included tables of administrative and tactical organization; progress charts showing in detail the anticipated growth of the new army; and maps showing the location of each unit to be raised. It included also drafts of laws prescribing the Army's basic organization and methods for registering and inducting trainees into the Army; establishing a system of military instruction in public schools; and appropriating necessary funds for the development.

Cost estimates were prepared on the following basis: Ord first prepared a plan based upon maximum practicable results, taking into consideration only such elements as population strength, local geographical and climatic conditions and with only a secondary purpose of minimizing expense.

General MacArthur then directed Ord to revamp the plan with the idea of attaining the same results so far as ultimate strength in personnel was concerned, but making cost the predominating factor otherwise. On this basis, Ord and I worked for some time. We cut periods of training; cut down on pay and allowances; eliminated particularly costly elements of the Army, and substituted conscripts for professionals wherever we considered it safe to do so. We retained as the minimum strength of the Professional Force 1500 officers and 19000 enlisted men. On this basis we arrived at a minimum yearly estimate of 22,000,000 Pesos.[5] The General then decided that this figure must be cut to 16,000,000 Pesos, still without reducing the total number of trained men finally to be incorporated into the Army. We reduced the Regular Force to 930 officers and about 7000 enlisted men, substituting for the enlisted men so eliminated an equal number of conscripts that are to be retained in the service one year; we extended the munitions procurement program to attain fruition in twenty instead of ten years, and made important deferments in the development of an Artillery Corps and so on. While Ord and I expressed the conviction that with this kind of organization it would be difficult to sustain efficiency because of the lack of professional personnel, it was the basis adopted because of the savings represented. The cost estimates were thus reduced to 16,000,000 Pesos annually.

We landed in the Philippines with the various portions of the Defense Plan prepared as completely as was possible before gaining an intimate knowledge of local conditions. Among other things, we had written for the President[6] a long explanatory address, intended for delivery to the National Assembly upon submission to that body of the plan. This speech was delivered by Mr. Quezon about November 22nd. The language of the address committed the President to enthusiastic support of the basic features of the plan.

Before landing, General MacArthur was very hopeful that the proposed bills we had prepared would be accepted practically as written, and could be enacted into law no later than November 20th, that is, within a very few days of the inauguration of the Commonwealth Government. It soon became evident that the bill would have to be rewritten insofar as arrangement and much of its language was concerned. Its basic provisions were, however, retained intact; that is to say, universal service, a stabilized budget of 16 million Pesos, and the proposed scheme of organization were fully accepted by the President and the Assembly. A series of conferences, beginning even before November 15th, were held with officials of the Insular government and later with the National Defense Committee of the Assembly. The bulk of this contact work fell upon Ord. The plan, somewhat revised as to detail, was finally approved on December 21, 1935.

A question arising soon after our arrival was that of devising a practicable method whereby Philippine Scout[7] officers could be incorporated into the new army. Many factors were involved and these became the subject of frequent conferences between Ord, myself, and individual Scout officers. To date (January 1, 1936) the question has not been completely and satisfactorily settled.

Soon after our arrival also, General MacArthur announced his intention to secure the appointment of Colonel Paulino Santos as the Chief of Staff, and of Brigadier General Valdes[8] as Deputy Chief of Staff. We based all plans and conferences on this understanding until about December 28, 1935, when we received information that this arrangement might prove unacceptable to the President. For political, personal or other reasons the tentative slate on which we are now working is to appoint Jose de los Reyes[9] as Brigadier General and Acting Chief of Staff, and Colonel Santos, General Valdes and Colonel Francisco[10] as his immediate assistants. No formal appointments to this effect have as yet been made.[11]

Another question requiring much study was that of planning for the organization of the Regular Division, provided for in the Basic Defense Act.[12] Originally we had hoped to locate this unit as a well concentrated force in the Island of Luzon. For two reasons we were forced to abandon this idea temporarily. The first reason involved the lack of quarters and other accommodations in the Island of Luzon. The second was the necessity for supporting Constabulary elements in other sections of the Philippines, where existing units must be substantially reduced in order to form the nuclei of the new army. Tentatively, therefore, we propose to organize one regiment at Camp Murphy, just outside of Manila; one at Camp Keithly on Mindanao, and one in the Island of Cebu.

We have had many conferences concerning such subjects as the preparation of a suitable building for the Central General Staff and other elements of a War Department; the pushing of construction at Camp Murphy to establish a satisfactory flying field and providing quarters for a considerable body of troops; the selection of officers to fill key positions in the War Department and tactical units, and the procurement of armament, particularly rifles, with which to equip new units as they are formed. In this connection, we are very hopeful that the United States Government will agree to sell to us, at a nominal price, 300,000 of the Enfield rifles left over from the World War. A radio request to this effect has been submitted to the War Department.

To sum up: The first of the year, 1936, finds us with less definite accomplishment to our credit than we had hoped to attain by this time, when we landed more than two months ago. The Philippine War Department is not yet organized and responsible officials have not been set up to undertake the many planning, administrative and organizational tasks with which the Commonwealth Army is faced. Necessary proclamations have not been drawn up, regulations have not been prepared, and under present conditions, it is even impracticable to use any of the money that has been appropriated for the development and maintenance of the Army.

On the other hand, the Mission itself has become better acquainted with local conditions and personalities, and is much better prepared to go ahead with the work, once the various developments indicated above can be initiated. Since the first registration of man power is scheduled to take place in early April, these many problems must soon be solved or the schedule of development contemplated in the law and in the plan will require drastic revision.

We—at least Jimmy and myself—have learned to expect from the Filipinos with whom we deal, a minimum of performance from a maximum of promise. Among individuals there is no lack of intelligence, but to us they seem, with few exceptions, unaccustomed to the requirements of administrative and executive procedure. When any detail is under discussion, they seem to grasp the essentials of the problem, and readily agree to undertake accomplishment of whatever decision may be arrived at in conference. But thereafter it is quite likely that nothing whatsoever will be done. Moreover, it often develops that the decision itself has not really been accepted by them, even though at the time they appeared to be in full agreement. The whole matter must then be gone over again. These peculiar traits we are learning to take into account, but obviously they impede progress.

Jimmy and I have worked a great deal with General Valdes and Colonel Santos. With the possible exception of the President, they are the two most able executives we have met here. We earnestly hope they both will accept positions in the Army Headquarters.

We have prepared a succession of slates for the important subordinate positions in the War Department. Each one so prepared was supposed, at the time, to make the best possible use of available personnel, and to conform to the ideas and desires of the President. Each, in turn, has proven unsatisfactory. This must be settled soon.

1. The format of this entry, with its formal, typed (in caps) heading, suggests that Eisenhower intended to prepare from time to time periodic summaries of events for a rather straightforward, factual narrative. This long entry, for example, provides additional background information about the mission and summarizes its first two months. As the mission evolved, however, his periodic summaries became distinctly more personal and subjective as serious problems arose involving resources, organization, politics, and personalities. Before long, the diary began to serve not only as a record of the mission's operations but also as a cathartic device for a man undergoing great stress. Many of the records of the Philippine govern-

ment and the U.S. military were lost during World War II. For an analysis of the Philippine Mission records that have not been recovered after World War II, see Holt, "An Unlikely Partnership," 150–51.

2. While Eisenhower obviously began writing this first entry on December 27, he evidently did not complete the entry for several days, as he notes the date of January 1, 1936, within the text. He most likely began the entry and continued to write until January 20, 1936, when he again dated an entry.

3. Col. Howard Joseph Hutter served his entire career with the Medical Corps. Early in his career he became associated with General MacArthur, first as a friend, then as his personal physician. MacArthur requested that Hutter accompany him to Manila because of the general's concerns for his mother's fragile health. Hutter retired from the army in 1947.

4. John Eisenhower believes that "this report had to justify the use of a cordon defense. A 'cordon,' or 'linear,' defense, lacks depth and reserves, and the professional military employs it only when absolutely forced to do so. Nevertheless, this concept for the Philippine defense was unavoidable, as the forces on one island were in no position to reinforce those on another island. Given that situation it makes the whole idea of a 'defensible' Philippines against a major force questionable, at best."

5. The peso was officially set at fifty cents against one dollar, U.S. currency.

6. "President" refers to President Manuel Quezon. Born in 1878 on the island of Luzon, Quezon fought against the American forces during Aguinaldo's 1899 Philippine revolt. Jailed for six months for his participation in the revolt, he entered the University of Santo Tomás and in 1903 received a law degree. Elected provincial governor of Tayabas Province in 1906, he then ran successfully for the Philippine Assembly and was elected floor leader of the Nacionalista Party in 1907. From 1909 to 1916, as resident commissioner with the Philippine Commission in Washington, D.C., he effectively lobbied for Philippine independence, including passage of the above-cited Jones Act of August 29, 1916. After his return to Manila he was elected president of the Philippine Senate and became leader of the Nacionalista Party in 1922. During negotiations on the Tydings-McDuffie Act of 1934, he spent considerable time in Washington working closely with Senator Millard Tydings in drafting the legislation. When the Philippines achieved commonwealth status, Quezon was elected president.

Often described as a strong and sometimes ruthless leader, Quezon appointed himself chairman of the Council of National Defense and divested the Speaker of the Assembly of his role as head of the governing party, claiming that position for himself. With this power and a large patronage machine, Quezon wielded immense authority and influence. After the Japanese attack on Pearl Harbor, Quezon, Vice President Sergio Osmeña, and several other Philippine leaders left the Philippines ahead of the advancing Japanese forces. They awaited the outcome of the war in Washington, D.C. Quezon died in Washington in August 1944, on the eve of MacArthur's return to the Philippines. Vice President Osmeña accompanied MacArthur and through succession became the commonwealth's second president. In his diaries, Eisenhower frequently refers to Quezon as "Q."

7. Philippine Scouts were units of Filipinos serving in the U.S. Army.

8. Paulino Santos entered the Philippine Constabulary (see below, note 11) in 1914. Considered highly able, he rapidly received promotions to the rank of colonel and served from 1924 to 1930 as the Constabulary's adjutant. In 1930 he retired from

the military to assume the post of director, Philippine Bureau of Prisons. In 1935, Quezon, with MacArthur's support, persuaded Santos to return to military service, promoted him to the rank of brigadier general, and appointed him Acting Chief of Staff of the new Philippine Army. In May 1936 he became Chief of Staff. When Santos left the army in 1938, he became director of the National Land Settlement Administration. He remained in the Philippines during the Japanese occupation, in which he served the puppet Laurel administration as commanding general of the Constabulary. He died with Japanese forces on Luzon in August 1945.

Basilio Valdes, born in 1892 on Luzon, served with the French Red Cross as a medical doctor in Europe during World War I. In 1921 he became medical inspector for the Philippine Constabulary, later rising to the presidency of the Board of Medical Examiners. In 1934 he was made chief of the Constabulary. On January 11, 1936, Quezon appointed him brigadier general and Deputy Chief of Staff of the Army. On January 1, 1939, he became Chief of Staff. Valdes accompanied Quezon to the United States during the president's exile during World War II.

Shortly before leaving the Philippines in December 1939, Eisenhower drafted a confidential memorandum for Quezon in which he evaluated key Philippine Army personnel (Memorandum on Philippine Officers, undated, McCann Papers, Eisenhower Library). Although it is difficult to determine precisely when the memorandum was prepared, his letter of December 30, 1939, to Quezon's secretary, Jorge Vargas (see letter under that date), indicates he wrote the appraisals just before leaving Manila or, perhaps, aboard ship. The undated document was found in the McCann Papers. Because Eisenhower's analysis of these persons is important to the context of the diary, excerpts from Eisenhower's comments on each officer are added to the notes at first mention.

In the memorandum Eisenhower wrote of Valdes:

> A high-minded man who, if assured of presidential confidence, is capable of doing splendid work in his present position. His devotion to the President is so absolute that he is frequently reluctant to present [to] higher authority his own views with the force and logic of which he is capable. Place all proper details in his hands—particularly everything pertaining to the control, assignment and handling of military subordinates—and he'll be a good chief of staff. Through the Secretary of Defense, delegate complete responsibility for these matters, together with commensurate authority, to General Valdes, and I believe that many existing difficulties and irritations will disappear.

9. Jose de los Reyes entered the Constabulary in 1901 as an enlisted man and had risen to the rank of lieutenant colonel at the time of his retirement in 1930. In 1936, President Quezon appointed him Acting Chief of Staff of the Philippine Army with the rank of brigadier general, then Provost Marshal General. He retired in August 1938. De los Reyes collaborated with the Japanese during World War II and was assassinated after the war by Hukbalahap rebels.

10. Guillermo Francisco, commissioned in the Constabulary in 1908, became a brigadier general in 1935. In 1936 he served as commanding general of the 1st Regular Division at Camp Murphy, Rizal. Eisenhower wrote rather critically of Francisco in his undated memorandum, describing him as "honest but stubborn," but "satisfactory when closely supervised by a competent supervisor" (see Memorandum on Philippine Officers, McCann Papers).

11. The Constabulary was established at the end of the Spanish-American War

as a quasi-military internal security force. When the Philippine Provisional Government was established in 1935, Constabulary members became the nucleus for the new army, with a portion remaining as a civil police force although still very much organized as a military system. For a useful study of the Philippine Constabulary, see Harold H. Elarth, *The Story of the Philippine Constabulary* (Los Angeles: Globe Printing, 1949).

12. Eisenhower's reference to the "Basic Defense Act" is probably to the Philippine Assembly's December 1935 legislation that codified the defense plan MacArthur's staff (primarily James Ord) had formulated before the Military Mission left the United States. The "Regular Division" was probably the projected eleven-thousand-man regular Philippine Army that was to be developed, as opposed to the forty-thousand-man reserve force the mission also was tasked with creating.

JANUARY 17, 1936

Major problems that have engaged our attention from the beginning involve construction of necessary facilities for the new army; procurement of necessary munitions; establishment of a satisfactory officer corps; and the development of rules and regulations for the administration of the Army and to govern registration of conscripts as well as their induction into the service, and final incorporation into the Reserve.

The critical factor in the first two of these problems is money. When Jimmy began the process of budget trimming in Washington, two of the items that had to suffer severely were construction and armament. The first was cut to the bone while the allotments for the second were reduced so as to provide for the accumulation of the necessary reserves in twenty years rather than in ten, as first contemplated.

We were somewhat disappointed to find that the quarters, barracks and warehouses available to the Constabulary are not suitably situated to serve the needs of the new army efficiently. In most cases, reservations that had been set aside for the use of the military are far too small. We found Camp Murphy, just outside of Manila, to be in the process of construction. It is intended for a landing field and flying school as well as a garrison for a regiment of troops and a division headquarters. It has only fifty hectares, or somewhat over one hundred acres of ground. If we are not successful in securing Camp Keithly in Mindanao, and in addition some suitable quarters in the Island of Cebu, we are going to be badly handicapped during the years 1936 and 1937. The Military Academy at Baguio[1] must be expanded somewhat so as to take care of the additional cadets required until such time as the Commonwealth Government acquires title to Camp John Hay. All of these things have been given to the Staff for study, with directions to prepare a complete building program for the next two years.

In the matter of armaments, the chief incident to date has been a continuing effort to secure some 400,000 Enfield rifles from the United States Government at a nominal cost. This rifle would be a very good one for our purposes and since it is practically obsolete from the standpoint of the American Army, it has been our hope to buy them at a cost of not over two dollars each. The matter has been the subject of some radio correspondence between General MacArthur and the War Department, and finally the President himself became involved in the discussions. Our budget had been based on the assumption that every material assistance in the armament question would be forthcoming from the United States and if this support should be denied, we are going to be very badly handicapped.

The establishment of an officer's corps presents most serious problems. Some of the senior officers in the Constabulary have considerable individual ability, but are practically without experience in the administration of large organizations. We are struggling now to get the Staff properly organized and working so as to determine our exact needs in commissioned personnel, and to devise means and methods for procuring individuals capable of filling the vacancies. (NOTE: The appointments to the higher positions in the Army were finally made by the President about January 10th. He appointed Jose de los Reyes as a Brigadier General and Acting Chief of Staff and assigned Brigadier General Valdes and Colonel Francisco as Acting Assistant Chiefs of Staff. It is around this nucleus we are attempting to develop and organize a General Staff.)

The development of rules and regulations to govern the new army as well as to establish the processes of registration and induction into the service has been turned over to the Staff for study. This is a matter of primary importance and considerable progress has been made on it. Forms for registration cards, military register, and general instructions to registering officers have been approved by this office and proof copies have already been printed. The President has issued a proclamation directing the registration of young men of military age during April, but there has as yet been no effective steps taken to organize the administrative machinery to accomplish registration. This must be done within the next few weeks or the registration in April will be a failure.

1. Camp John Hay was a small U.S. Army post located in the resort town of Baguio. Baguio was also the location of the Brent School, which John Eisenhower attended. It was located not far from the temporary home of the Philippine Military Academy, a spot called "Teachers' Camp." John Eisenhower commented about this location: "I personally thought that the Teachers' Camp was an admirable location for the Philippine Military Academy, and this is the first time I ever heard of turn-

ing Camp John Hay, primarily a vacation spot, over to the Philippine Army, though of course that must have been a consideration." Camp John Hay became a U.S. Air Force base after World War II and remained in U.S. hands until recently.

At this moment the mission is engaged principally with questions that have arisen out of our request to the American Government to furnish the Philippine Army with Enfield rifles at nominal cost. Knowing that this item of equipment is considered an obsolescent one in the American Army, we supposed, at the time the request was submitted, that the only question that would arise would be one involving unit cost. Actually, when the request was received in Washington, it was apparently looked upon as one involving major policy and was referred to the President[1] for decision. We are at a loss to determine exactly what the question of policy may be, whether it involves domestic politics or whether it is supposed to have somewhat of an international tinge. For example, the President may be concerned as to the effect upon the pacifistic group in the United States of announcing a decision to furnish considerable quantities of arms to the Philippine Commonwealth. Again, it may be that he has some fear of disaffection among important groups in the Islands and would look upon a distribution of arms throughout the various provinces as an opportunity for these groups to revolt against the central government. It has even been suggested that the Filipinos as a nation would in a crisis turn against the United States and we would have the spectacle of a people who had been armed and equipped by American effort and largely at American expense becoming an active opponent of the United States. It has been suggested also that the Administration at home might fear the effect upon American relationships with Japan should our government show real determination to assist the Filipinos in becoming relatively strong defensively in this region. Finally, there is the possibility that with arms embargo and neutrality legislation attracting so much Congressional attention, that the announcement of the sale of obsolete arms to the Philippine Government might be construed as a flagrant violation of the spirit of Congressional intent.

All these questions, upon analysis, fail to furnish any satisfactory explanation of what seems to us to be a short-sighted policy on the part of the Administration. The matter is purely a domestic one, involving relationships between the United States and one of its own political sub-divisions. It conforms entirely to the announced policy of making the Filipino capable of independent government within ten years. It does not concern the munition industry in the United States since the items requested are now in storage and are, generally speaking, useless for future American use. Whether or not disaffection in the Islands will finally grow to a point where a major revolt might take place is a question that should have been settled before the passage of the Tydings-McDuffie Act. It is too late now to consider such a possibility as a decisive factor in preventing the Filipino people from arming themselves in accordance with a sound and economical plan for defending their future independence.

Regardless, however, of the motives actuating Washington, or of the soundness of our own views in the matter, the pertinent fact is that the question has been referred to the High Commissioner[2] by the President,[3] and the General has been instructed to confer with the Commissioner as to the necessity for the amounts of munitions requested in our telegrams to the War Department. The High Commissioner is, of course, a politician—not a soldier. His views as to the political and international aspects in the matter will be particularly valuable to the President, as also his conclusions as to the danger of general revolt of the Filipinos against constituted authority. However, when it comes to the question of the number of rifles and automatic rifles furnished to the Army, there seems to be no reason for making the High Commissioner the arbiter in the matter.

In this situation, we can only do our best to secure some favorable expression of opinion out of the High Commissioner and hope that the language of his report to Washington will be such as to secure substantial approval of the proposition we have already submitted. At the minimum, if we are successful in obtaining some 40,000 or 50,000 rifles during the current calendar year, there is no reason to despair as to ultimate success. There may be a change of Administration after next November and in any event, even if the present Administration is re-elected, there may be a definite change in attitude towards this matter. We must never forget that every question is settled in Washington today on the basis of getting votes next November. To decide this matter completely in our favor would gain no votes, while to disapprove the request and give the matter some publicity might be considered as a vote getting proposition among the pacifists and other misguided elements of the American electorate.

Our attitude now should be that we have given our best professional advice on the subject, and that no matter what decision is rendered, we stand ready to make the best of it for the time being. If need arises, the General can always find reasonable excuse for going to Washington and attempting through personal persuasion to straighten the matter out and secure the announcement of a definite and favorable policy in this regard.

It is rapidly becoming apparent that either here or somewhere else it will be advisable for me to keep some notes that I cannot, with propriety dictate. The General is more and more indulging in a habit of damning everybody, who disagrees with him over any detail, in extravagant, sometimes almost hysterical fashion. I've seen him do this, second hand, in the past, but now he seems to consider that the combined use of his rank, a stream of generalizations that are studded with malapropos, and a refusal to permit the presentation of opposing opinion will, by silencing his subordinates, establish also the validity of his contentions. The case at hand involves his authorized rank of Field Marshal—and his determination to make this a "30 Division" Army. I'm coming to believe that the 30 Div. plan is adopted, not because he believes there is any honest possibility of attaining it, but to justify the early appointment of a Field Marshal. After days of wrangling and arguing on the subject he gave J. and me a ridiculous lecture on "sufficiency in strength" of armies. We want to train 20–25,000 men yearly, with a minimum period of 10½ months. We want to make our announced objective 10 Res. Divs.—1 Regular (of real efficiency, particularly in artillery) strong auxiliary services, a large pool of trained reservists, an air corps of at least 50 bombers and 30 other planes (aside from primary trainers) and an off shore patrol of about 30 boats. We are convinced that the figure given us by a local source as the price for a patrol boat (60,000 pesos) is far too small. Consequently the General's talk about 30 Divisions, 250 planes, and 60 boats is just talk. But he is adamant on the 30 Div. stuff, so we can just go ahead. He makes nasty cracks about "technicians" and "small-minded people" when we try to show that we are simply arguing from the standpoint of the amount of money available.

1. The "President" references in this paragraph are to Franklin D. Roosevelt, not Quezon. Eisenhower designated both Roosevelt and Quezon often just as "president."

2. The high commissioner took the place of the governor general as the senior U.S. official in the Philippines. The high commissioner, however, had a much narrower role in government. Frank Murphy was the first U.S. high commissioner of the Philippines (1935–36) and was later a justice of the U.S. Supreme Court.

3. President Franklin D. Roosevelt.

FEBRUARY 6

Authority was finally received from Washington to purchase 100,000 Enfield Rifles during the current year, with a statement of policy to the effect that in the absence of drastic change in the general situation an additional 300,000 rifles could be made available to this government over a period of 8 years. This decision was undoubtedly influenced by the cable report submitted by the High Commissioner to the War Department. We held several conferences with the High Commissioner and with members of the staff, and his office became convinced that our request was entirely reasonable. The only real disappointment for us in the decision rendered by Washington was the price fixed for the Enfield Rifles. We had hoped to obtain them at a price of about 8 pesos, laid down in Manila. Actually they will cost us about 18 pesos. Even so, the saving represented is a very considerable one when compared to the price of the Springfield which is approximately 65 pesos each, delivered in Manila. The mechanical differences between the two rifles is far too small to justify any such differences in prices.

We have encountered many difficulties already, mainly occasioned by an almost total lack of administrative ability in the higher officials of the government and of the army. From the President down each official seems to act individually and on the spur of the moment with respect to any detail in which he is interested, and without regard for possible effects upon other activities or upon the army as a whole. Moreover, the orders given by the President at the time he installed General Reyes as Acting Chief of Staff, and General Valdes as his principal assistant, have caused additional trouble. Those instructions required General Reyes to act as Provost Marshal General and to supervise only in a most general way the processes of organizing the Philippine Army. In actual practice, however, General Reyes has issued specific orders involving assignment and re-assignment of personnel, which practice has at times rather badly handicapped current work. General Valdes has been resentful and even went so far as to report one incident to General MacArthur. The President, during a visit to the Military Academy at Baguio, issued such sharp reprimands to the faculty, in the presence of the student body, there was no other recourse than to replace the superintendent and all his assistants since, under the circumstances, their usefulness in that school was obviously ended. This morning, February 6th, we have word that the President has, in company with the Chief of Staff, gone to southern Luzon with the idea of establishing an entirely new site for the Military Academy. We have no idea as to the reason for this move nor what the result will be, but the fact remains that if any major construction project of this kind is undertaken with the funds now available, all other building will have to stop. This will be a calamity.

Jimmy and I still stick to the conclusion we formed as long ago as early November, last year, which is that Colonel Santos is the only logical person to serve as Chief of Staff of the Philippine Army. He understands organization and the necessity for systematic procedure in handling an army. He appears to us to be essentially an energetic worker who has a sound, logical head and who always keeps the main objective in view. General MacArthur agrees with this conclusion but appreciates also that the time is not yet ripe when a change of the kind indicated can be insistently urged upon the President.

I have recently completed a speech for the President to be delivered before the faculty and students of the Philippine University. The draft was accepted by the President and upon delivery of the speech the plan is to distribute copies to every unit in the public school system of the Islands. Its purpose is educational and was written in the hope that through its wide distribution a better understanding of the defense plan and of the duties and obligations of private citizens will obtain. I am now engaged in writing a talk along similar lines to be given before the teachers' convention in Baguio in March or April.

Jimmy is principally engaged in assisting Colonel Aguilar[1] and Colonel Francisco in the development of studies and plans applying to procurement, financing, preparation and revision of regulations, construction, and final distribution of available troops.

1. By 1938, Miguel Aguilar became acting chief, Quartermaster Service, Philippine Army. In his memorandum for Quezon on Philippine Army personnel, Eisenhower spoke favorably of Aguilar. Although he expressed concern about Aguilar's health, Eisenhower praised the officer for showing "remarkable progress in handling his extremely important and difficult duties. No suspicion of dishonesty has ever attached to his administration of the q.m. service. . . . Every effort should be made to keep him. . . . hard working, loyal, competent" (see Memorandum on Philippine Officers, McCann Papers).

FEBRUARY 15

Recently a subject that has been much discussed among members of the Mission is the advisability of accepting higher rank for each of us under the provisions of the National Defense Act. To any such thought I have been unalterably opposed from the start, and have in fact gone so far as to inform the General that I personally would decline at this time to accept any such appointment from the Philippine Army in the event it were tendered to me. Although in one of the early discussions of this matter Captain Davis informed the General, in my presence, that his action in the matter would be governed by the General's personal desire, he has since then swung around definitely to my view of the matter and now stands with me in direct opposition to the proposal. Jimmy also, though in somewhat less positive fashion, stands with Captain Davis and myself.

The principal reasons for our opposition are two. In the first place we believe that in a locality where we are serving with so many American officers, most of whom believe that the attempt to create a Philippine Army is somewhat ridiculous, the acceptance by us of high rank in an Army which is not yet formed would serve to belittle our effort. Moreover, it would seriously handicap every effort on our part to secure necessary cooperation from commanders and staffs in the American Army. Secondly, we believe that in dealing with Philippine Army Headquarters our position is unassailable as long as we purport to be nothing but assistants to the Military Adviser. If, however, we should accept military titles in the Philippine Army, the authority and soundness of our advice would be measured, in the minds of Philippine Army officers, by the rank held. We believe this would create an anonymous situation and would handicap our efforts to assist, advise and direct the efforts of Army Headquarters and subordinate officials.

Captain Davis and I have in addition strongly advised General MacArthur to decline, for the present, the acceptance of the title tendered him as Field Marshal.

Recently Jimmy and I have been urging upon General MacArthur the advisability of his making an early trip to Washington. It is becoming more and more evident that there is no basic appreciation in the War Department of the local defense problem, at least as we see it. The Tydings-McDuffie Act so clearly contemplates the employment of the Philippine Army by the President of the United States, in the event of a national emergency, that we believe the American War Department could make a definite effort to develop the strength and efficiency of this military adjunct. For the next ten years complete responsibility for Philippine Defense resides in the American Government, and since weakness in the local defenses would involve extreme embarrassment in the event of war, it seems to us to be the part of wisdom for the American Government to take positive and appropriate action in the matter. Specifically, we believe that the local reserves of the American Army in weapons and ammunition should be substantially increased and the stocks so accumulated should be made available for the training of the Philippine Army. We believe such a policy should apply particularly with respect to those weapons in the possession of the American Army that are becoming obsolescent from the view point of the American Army. In this category are such things as Enfield rifles, hand weapons of the revolver type, Lewis machine guns, Infantry mortars and British type 75mm. guns. Jimmy and I believe that if this whole matter were clearly explained to the American Chief of Staff and Secretary of War, that very substantial and effective assistance would be forthcoming. Such assistance would not involve any weakening of the United States defenses at home, would materially strengthen them in this outpost, and would not involve any straining of international relationships. In addition to the reasons given above for the making of a personal visit to Washington by General MacArthur is the fact that Department Headquarters has shown a disposition to question the legality and propriety of the letter of September 18th, written by the Acting Secretary of War to Department Headquarters. That letter directs the Department Commander to cooperate with the Military Adviser in every possible way to insure the rapid development of the Philippine Army. Under it the Department Commander is authorized to use personnel and property to accomplish this end, and if the legality of the order is to be called into question, it is highly necessary that the whole subject be completely clarified in Washington.[1]

All these views have been presented to General MacArthur, but he has stated that he has no intention of going to Washington before the late fall of this year.

1. Eisenhower is referring to Headquarters, Philippine Department of the U.S. Army, also located in Manila. The department oversaw not only the army's Philippine Division (commanded by General DeWitt) but also all American troops in China. Although MacArthur's military mission was organizationally independent of the department, the mission often relied upon the department for men and matériel. On February 13, 1936, Gen. Lucius R. Holbrook (USMA 1896) took command of the department.

MARCH 1

General MacArthur has been considering the various reasons advanced by Jimmy and myself in urging him to go to Washington at an early date. In lieu of such a visit, he has determined to have prepared a rather exhaustive treatise on the whole subject of the Philippine Army. While the document is to be labelled a report, it will actually constitute a comprehensive argument to support the efficiency and soundness of the Philippine Defense Plan, and the idea that the American War Department should cooperate efficiently toward its development. I have been assigned the duty of preparing this paper.

MAY 29

Registration was carried out during the month of April and the total number registering was considerably in excess of our original estimate. Jimmy and I are quite doubtful, however, that all of the 150,000 who registered are actually 20 years old this year. We are inclined to the belief that many men both younger and older than this entered their names on the rolls. Only future registrations can establish the accuracy of this estimate.

As a result of the large registration General MacArthur has quite suddenly decided to make a material change in the plan for the year 1937. He has decided to take in the full quota of 40,000 conscripts during the year instead of the total of 6,000 contemplated under the original plan. This decision, of course, tremendously increases the estimated outlays for immediate construction and procurement of supplies. Its general effect is to increase, during the next four years, our training program by approximately 94,000 individuals. Disregarding entirely the cost of arms and ammunition for these men after they have been trained, the additional training and maintenance cost involved will be about 10,000,000 pesos. In other words, a ten million peso additional cost has been placed upon the ten-year plan while no additional revenues have been provided. Another acute embarrassment arises from the fact that we have no money whatsoever immediately available for construction. Before January 1, 1937, we must have selected something over 125 sites for Training Cadres, erected the necessary buildings and procured the additional amounts of supplies that will be required. Since sums for all these things were not included in the 1936 budget there is nothing to do but to await the meeting of the National Assembly in June and secure from them the necessary authorization to go ahead. Other new problems created by this decision are those of providing and training instructional staffs for Training Cadres and of establishing an expanded overhead to take care of administration and maintenance.

The purpose of increasing the number of men to be trained in 1937 had been previously advanced by General MacArthur, who at first thought this could be accomplished through the American Army. As early as January we initiated detailed conferences with the Department Staff[1] in an effort to have officers and enlisted men in considerable numbers trained in 1937 at the various army posts. General MacArthur was of the opinion that as many as 15,000 could be trained during the year under a suitable arrangement. After exhaustive study of the proposition by the Department Staff it was found that a very complicated administrative arrangement would be involved, that the number possible to be trained would be limited to some five or six hundred enlisted men and that the per capita cost would be high. For these reasons General MacArthur advised the Department Commander that the proposal would be dropped. In lieu of that plan it was requested that a considerable number of Philippine Scout enlisted men be detailed for duty under the direction of the Military Adviser. It was recommended that they serve as instructors in training cadres. This request was approved in principle and plans are now developing to train in our own stations 40,000 men in 1937, beginning with the first contingent of 20,000 on January 1st.

The matter of higher organization in the Philippine Army was finally brought to a head upon the insistence of Jimmy and myself in early May. The President finally accepted the slate as recommended by General MacArthur and issued the necessary orders to appoint Santos, Valdes and De los Reyes as Major Generals, and Francisco as a Brigadier General. This was a slight change from our recommendations as we did not contemplate the promotion of De los Reyes. Santos is now serving as Chief of Staff.

In the long negotiations with Philippine Scout officers a definite plan was evolved in early April setting forth the various conditions under which a Scout officer might serve with the Philippine Army. Several acceptable sets of conditions were developed and stated as follows:
a. Any native-born officer of the Philippine Scouts electing to retire from the American Army would be tendered a commission by the President of the Philippines on the day of his retirement (radio grams received from the War Department state that a retired Philippine Scout officer who accepts a commission in the Philippine Army could continue to draw retired pay from the American Government as long as the Commonwealth status of government exists. After termination of the Commonwealth form of government, the individual, under existing law, will either surrender his retired status in the American Army or his commission in the Philippine Army).
b. Any Philippine Scout officer who desires to remain for some time in the American Army in order to acquire retirement privileges may either remain on duty with the American Army or may take a detail with the Philippine Army pending his retirement.
c. Any officer resigning from the American Army will be immediately commissioned in the Philippine Army.

In all these cases it is understood that no additional compensation is to be paid such officers from the military appropriation of the Commonwealth, no officer is to be detailed for duty with the Philippine Army except with his own consent, and each is to be informed prior to his retirement of the exact place on the Philippine promotion list that he will occupy. In addition, General MacArthur stated that officers of this group accepting commissions in the Philippine Army would be credited for pay purposes with the amount of service each has to his credit in the American Army, but that his retirement credit will begin from the moment he accepts his commission in the Philippine Army. In this last connection, the General has agreed to support legislation to the effect that whenever any officer of this group should lose his retired status in the American Army because of his commission in the Philippine Army he will then be credited for retirement purposes from the Philippine Army with all service performed in both organizations.

MAY 29 (SECOND ENTRY)[2]

Jim and I undertook to get the general to modify his order to call twenty thousand men next January. We insisted further than the general thought we should, and he gave us one of his regular shouting tirades. He seemed particularly bitter toward me. Jim knows the objections as well as I. We cannot possibly get the money for some time yet. We cannot select each site carefully and provide proper technical supervision for each construction project. There are 128 of them. Each needs water, roads, lights, drainage, etc., etc. Camp Murphy, plus about ten well-selected sites, should be all that we try to develop this year. We have no officer corps to supervise organization on such a scale, and officers cannot be produced out of thin air. We have no comprehensive supply system, and we've not yet had a chance to develop the overhead that can absorb, train, segregate, organize, and maintain reserve units! I argue these points with more heat and persistency than does Jim—consequently I come in for the more severe criticism.

We've tried also, time and again, to get the general to stay in closer contact with Q. Things happen, and we know nothing of them. We're constantly wondering whether the President will approve or disapprove. We ought to <u>know</u>! We could if the general would take the trouble to see Q weekly—but he apparently thinks it would not be in keeping with his rank and position for him to do so!!!!!

1. Philippine Department, U.S. Army.

2. Eisenhower's diary dating is somewhat confused at this point. Both May 29, 1936, entries were published in Robert H. Ferrell, *The Eisenhower Diaries* (New York: W. W. Norton, 1981), 18–20. The McCann Papers include a typescript copy of the first May 29 entry but no copy of the second. Eisenhower also made two entries on January 20, 1936 (see above). The original first entry was available to Ferrell, who published it. The original second entry of that date and a typescript of the first entry were found later in the McCann Papers. From May 29 onward there are no more dual entries.

MEMORANDUM FOR GENERAL MACARTHUR

JUNE 15, 1936

Subject: Cost of Defense Plan.[1]

1. The commitment made last November by the Military Adviser as to the development of security forces in the Philippines is paraphrased as follows:

Conditioned upon the prompt enactment into law of the defense plan submitted to the President by the Military Adviser, and upon subsequent financial support of the plan by the annual appropriation of 16 million pesos, there will be established in the Philippines by the end of 1945, a defensive force capable of assuring a high degree of security for each inhabited island in the Archipelago, against either foreign aggression or internal disturbance.

2. In subsequent statements the Military Adviser has described the general character of the military establishment, capable of assuring reasonable protection for the Philippines, as follows:

a. An Air-Force and a Marine Detachment that will constitute a distinct threat to any hostile surface craft attempting to operate in Philippine waters.

b. A Land Force to consist of:

(1) A professional establishment of minimum necessary size.

(2) A Reserve Force of such size and efficiency as will result from the annual training, equipping, and organizing of approximately 40,000 conscripts.

3. General description of plan:

a. This plan is based on a 30-year program conforming to the number of years the citizen is obligated to military service. It is divided into three 10-year phases, commencing January 1, 1937. The first phase is the development phase, during which the three essential elements of the national defense are brought into being, namely, the land forces, the air forces and the off-shore patrol. The second phase is the expansion phase, during which reserves in equipment, and in organized trained man power are built up. The third phase is the consolidation phase, during which the national defense is extended to include all men of military age, and may be further enlarged as demanded by the growth and wealth of the nation.

(1) First Phase:

The objectives of the first phase are as follows:

(a) Train annually 40,000 men and organize all effectives from this group into combat units.

(b) Organize an air-force of 1 air battalion.

(c) Organize an off-shore patrol of 4 flotillas.

(d) The budget for the first phase contemplates the expenditure of 160,000,000 pesos, plus savings in kind and money from 1936 of about 5,000,000 pesos. The assumption is made that from the annual class of 40,000 trainees about 31,000 effective soldiers will be produced. Of these, 30,000 will be assigned to divisions, while 3,000 will be available for the organization of special troops, such as air corps and off-shore patrol, and service units such as Quartermaster, Engineers, Medical and so on. In addition, these 3,000 will, after the first year, balance annual attrition in combat divisions.

(e) <u>Combat units</u>. The combat unit adopted is the Infantry Division of approximately 10,000 officers and men, organized as shown in Annex 1. This strength includes a 33% local replacement reserve.

(f) <u>Territorial organization and development of Combat Units</u>:

1. The Commonwealth is to be divided into 10 Military Districts, each of which will provide approximately 15,000 men of military age each year. Each district is to raise 3 Divisions at 3 year intervals, with one year available for adjustment, replacement, or for the organization of additional central reserves.

Each division is eventually to contain 10% of each class, starting with the class of 1916. The first division organized in each District is to take all of the classes of 1916, 1917 and 1918. Thereafter, classes will be reassigned at 3 year intervals so that by the end of the development period each Division will represent every class of the First Reserve.

This group of 30 Divisions will be known as the Divisions of the Line. The re-assignments necessitated under this plan will, of course, have some effect in retarding the growth of divisional esprit. However, it is deemed necessary to work toward the ideal of proportionate distribution of age groups in each division. To assure the early development of a few complete units, as well as to minimize initial demands in officers and overhead, the 10 division organizational pattern is deemed the most ambitious that should be undertaken.

2. In general, training is accomplished through establishments known as "Training Cadres", each with an average annual capacity of 155 men. On this basis approximately 13 training cadres are initially required in each divisional district, which number will be permanently sufficient. The actual total planned is 128.

3. The number of mobilization centers needed mounts with the number of divisions established in each area. For each division approximately 15 mobilization centers will be required—although where justified by density of population some construction costs will be saved by consolidation of two or more of these under one roof.

4. Analysis of First Phase costs:
(a) Construction of training cadres:
The estimated construction cost of a training cadre is 17,000 pesos each. On this basis the initial cost of providing training cadres will be 2,176,000 pesos, which cost is non-recurrent.
(b) Construction of mobilization centers:
On an estimated unit cost of 10,000 pesos, the total cost of the 150 mobilization centers to be provided in the first three years will be about 1,500,000 pesos. In the interests of eventual economy, each of these should be sufficiently commodious to accommodate at least 3 battalions, that is one battalion from each of the three divisions eventually to be organized in the particular district. This could possibly be done at a unit cost of 16–18,000 pesos, but the necessity of minimizing expense during the first three years precludes adoption of this plan. The most that can be done is to assure that the ground acquired will be extensive enough to permit erection of subsequent centers. Another pertinent fact is that construction money available in 1937 will permit the erection of only 27 mobilization centers. These will have to be exclusively used temporarily as storage for equipment. Consequently, the annual training of units previously organized will have to be almost completely omitted during 1938. In that year 60 more mobilization centers will be built, and the remaining 63 in 1939. On this modified basis construction costs for training cadres and mobilization centers in 1937, 1938 and 1939 will be:

1937	P2,446,000.00
1938	600,000.00
1939	630,000.00

P3,676,000.00 total development of 10 divisions, during first three years.
Estimated total initial cost of 30 division plan in training cadres and mobilization centers construction: 6,176,000 pesos.
  NOTE: The estimates shown do not include cost of land, and only a small amount for labor, the great bulk of which is to be performed by military or prison personnel. (For each 10 divisions the approximate additional cost in mobilization center construction will be 1,500,000 pesos, less what savings can be made through consolidation.)
(c) Training Cadre Equipment:
  To the construction costs of training cadres must be added costs of station equipment and of individual equipment maintained there for the training of annual increments. These expenditures are non-recurring, although some money will be required for maintenance.

Under station equipment is included a considerable list of items which has a total cost of about 1,200 pesos. For 128 cadres the cost is: 153,600 pesos.

Under non-recurring items of individual equipment we have the following:

1 bolo	P2.50
1 rifle	18.25 (cost here with spare parts)
1 belt and strap	4.30
1 gun sling	2.55
1 oiler	.73
1 haversack	2.98
1 meat can	1.07
1 canteen	1.24
1 cup	.87
1 knife, fork and spoon	.36
2 cotton blankets	5.34
1 mosquito bar	2.41
1 locker	4.24
1 bowl, enamel	.30
1 plate, "	.30
	P47.44

Average initial cost of individual equipment in 1 training cadre: P7,353.20 (or approximately 7,350.00).

For 128 training cadres the total cost will be P940,800.00

(d) Recurring costs of trainee instruction:

Once the plant and immediately necessary equipment has been provided, we proceed to an estimate of the annual cost of trainee instruction in cadres. This is analyzed as follows:

Subsistence, 165 days @P.30	P49.50
Transportation	3.00
Medical	1.00

Clothing as follows:

1 stocking puttee	P .50
2 khaki shirts	2.04
2 overalls	2.14
1 hat and cord	1.00
1 pair shoes	4.60
1 pair canvas shoes	.91
6 pair socks	.78
3 drawers	.96
3 undershirts	1.47
3 towels	.86
6 handkerchiefs	.54

collar ornaments	.34
2 pair shorts	3.00
Clothing Total	19.14
Pay, 165 days @ P .05	8.25
Welfare, recreation and miscellaneous	1.00
Training ammunition	2.00
Grand total, recurring costs	P83.89

P83.80 × 40,000 = P3,355,600.00

To this must be added as a minimum, if the full number of 40,000 is taken in annually, one-half the pay and subsistence costs of maintaining conscripts attached to the Regular Force, because they serve 11 months instead of 5½:

Total . . . . P 231,000.00

NOTE: No additional sums are provided for training of trainees as officers and non-commissioned officers. It is hoped that this cost will be balanced by savings made through personnel losses incurred during training periods. Under the conditions described, the annual recurring costs of trainees will be:

3,586,000 pesos. For the ten-year period this cost will be: 35,866,000 pesos.

(e) Miscellaneous construction throughout the Army:

Pending exhaustive study of construction needs for the Army, which study must take into consideration the organization of existing posts occupied by the American Army, it is impossible to make any accurate estimate of detailed construction needs. Obviously, however, satisfactory posts must be provided for the various elements of the Regular Divisions, and some additional storage, school and technical structures must be provided. To set aside 1,250,000 pesos for this purpose appears a most conservative procedure.

(f) Regular Army costs for pay, subsistence, clothing, etc.

(NOTE: In the following discussion those Reserve officers that are on extended tours of duty with the Regular Army are counted as part of the Regular establishment.)

Certain variable factors enter into computation of costs under this item, among which may be mentioned the size of the Off-Shore Patrol and of the Air Force. To establish one composite air battalion of the modest size hereinafter indicated will require 79 officers and 340 enlisted men, of which number a large proportion must be regular troops. Sixty (60) MAS[2] boats will require 420 men, also largely from the Regular Force. In addition, each mobilization center must have a minimum of 2 enlisted men from the Regular Army, which sets up requirements that will eventually reach 900 men.

All these requirements are in addition to those initially considered in determining upon Regular Army distribution. Allowing 250 men to the air battalion, and the same number to the Off-Shore Patrol, these additional requirements total 1400.

These requirements will come into existence only as the organization and facilities indicated are acquired. Since time will assure increased professional efficiency in every activity in the Army, some saving in Regular personnel may be effected with safety by reducing the number allotted to training cadres and to police work. Consequently, the requirements just indicated will compel an increase in the Regular Army of possibly not over 1,000 men.

Another eventual drain upon the Regular Army will be in assisting to man the defenses of Corregidor. During the years 1944 and 1945, at the latest, strong contingents must be stationed there so as to acquire some skill in the technical phases of operating that establishment. Assuming that at least 40% of the garrison must be professional, an additional 1,200 men will be needed in the Regular Army.

Thus the strength requirements of the Regular Army will vary between the 716 officers and 7,500 men who will be assigned to it by December 31, 1937, and the 930 officers and about 10,000 men that will represent minimum needs when the whole defense plan is in operation. For 1937 the cost of maintaining the Regular Army will be:

Pay of officers	P2,006,034.00
Pay, subsistence, hospitalization and clothing of enlisted men	3,300,989.00
Total	5,307,023.00

The average costs represented are respectively P2,807.00 and P439.00.

Assuming that these figures given on a basis for estimate, the maintenance cost of the Regular Army in 1945 would be:

For Officers	P2,606,732.00
For enlisted men	4,388,489.00
Total	P6,995,221.00

The mean between these 2 totals is about P6,151,000.00, but since the increases indicated will be deferred as long as possible, the average annual cost is estimated at somewhat less than the mean—or roughly, P6,000,000.00.

For 10 years the maintenance cost of the Regular Army will be approximately P60,000,000.00.

(g) <u>General Administrative & Maintenance Charges, other than Pay, Subsistence and Clothing:</u>

(1) <u>Regular Army:</u>

<u>Transportation:</u>

Mileage and per diem	P270,000.00
Transportation of supplies	85,000.00
Upkeep of motors	105,000.00
Maintenance of animals	45,000.00

| Maintenance of water craft | 25,000.00 |
| Total | P530,000.00 |

Training:
Maneuvers, etc.	P67,000.00
Cadets (other than costs already given)	30,875.00
Other Army schools	10,000.00
Total	P107,875.00
Civilian Personnel, pay:	268,690.00
Pension Retirement Fund:	300,000.00
Replacement of Q.M., Ordnance, Engineer and other technical equipment:	93,000.00
Total (annual)	P1,299,565.00

TOTAL, REGULAR ARMY, 10 YEARS: P12,299,650.00
(NOTE: The total cost of Regular Army for current year (less cost of airplanes) is P 6,606,565.00; including charges for pension retirement.)

(2) Preparatory & Teacher Training:
Non-recurrent (principally equipment for R.O.T.Cs., including 10,000 rifles)	P597,000.00
Recurrent (P64,000.00 × 10)	640,000.00
Total ten-year cost	P1,237,000.00

(3) Estimated annual maintenance of training cadres and equipment there at, & MOBILIZATION centers: P300,000.00
| Total ten-year charge | P3,000,000.00 |

(h) Non-recurrent initial cost per division:
Enlisted actually assigned to units	=	7,239
33⅓% local reserve	=	2,413
Officers	=	428
(approximately 10,000)		
Clothing @ P25.44 per man	=	P254,300.00
Equipment (bolo, haversack, mess, belt and straps) @ 13.32	=	133,200.00

Organizational equipment:
6,900 rifles (Infantry 3,639; Cavalry 400;
Engineers 321; Artillery 500; Transportation
Bn. 200; Division Hq. 50; Communication
Company 68; 5/7 of replacements 1722)
@ 20.42	=	140,898.00
492 pistols @ 50.00	=	24,600.00
(428 officers, 15% replacement)		
431 machine rifles @ 500.00	=	215,500.00
(374 assigned, 52 replacement)		
54 machine guns..@ 576.00	=	31,104.00
18 Stokes Brandt 81mm @ 200.00	=	36,000.00

24 Stokes Brandt 120mm @ 4,000.00 .... = 96,000.00
Signal equipment (50% of normal
allowance) .... = 45,000.00
Fire control equipment .... = 60,000.00
Medical equipment .... = 50,000.00
Quartermaster equipment per Regiment
P 2,400.00 (⅓ of estimated needs) .... = 12,000.00
                                                                                P1,098,602.00

Ammunition:
.30 caliber, 1,000 per machine
gun or auto-rifle   = P38,800.00
200 per rifle (6,900)   = 110,400.00
50 per pistol (492)   = 738.00
.81mm. 100 @ P 20.00   = 36,000.00
.120mm. 100 @ 56.00   = 134,400.00
                                    P320,338.00
Ammunition Reserve 10%   = 32,033.00
TOTAL AMMUNITION   =   352,371.00
P1,450,973.00 × 30 = P 43,529,190.00   P1,450,973.00

NOTE: It should be noted that the divisional armament provides no weapon capable of effective defense against armored vehicles. If only a few of such vehicles were landed the defensive forces would be badly embarrassed, and possibly demoralized. As a defensive weapon against tanks nothing has greater value than the .50 caliber machine gun. Moreover, mounted on the dual purpose cradle it is effective against both the airplane and the tank. It would be highly desirable to include in the Artillery Regiment another battalion made up of 3 batteries of 4 guns each in the .50 caliber type. For each gun about 5,000 rounds should be provided, since this ammunition is not interchangeable among various types of weapons as is the case in .30 caliber. This would add a total cost to each division (rough estimate) of:

Guns P24,720.00
Fire control equipment 10,000.00
Ammunition 14,440.00
                        Total P49,160.00

Personnel could be taken from the local 33-⅓% replacement pool. For 30 divisions the total additional cost would be roughly: P1,474,800.00

(i) Recurrent (training) charges of each organized division of Reserves:

The following estimate is based upon the minimum program which it is believed can possibly sustain divisional efficiency. It involves only 10 days training—or a fixed subsistence charge of P30,000.00. For transportation P2.00 per man is allowed; for ordinary Quartermaster supplies P0.50 per man; for ammunition 20 rounds per rifle; 100 per automatic weapon, and 5 rounds per mortar; P0.50 per man is added for wear and tear on equipment, and a total of P 1,500.00 for rental of transportation.

Manifestly, certain of these charges can be saved if divisional training is considered unnecessary—particularly the cost of transporting individuals to and from camp. <u>Efficiency will seriously suffer</u> under such a scheme:

Subsistence, 10 days annual training	P30,000.00
Transportation	20,000.00
Ammunition and supplies	28,590.00
Replacement of mobilization equipment	5,000.00
Rental of animals & transportation	1,500.00
Total	P85,090.00

Assuming that 10 divisions will exist for 7 years; 10 for 4 years, and 10 for 1 year, the total charge will be: P10,210,800.00.

(NOTE: It should be noted that on and after the 10th year the training charge for 30 divisions will involve an annual expenditure of P2,552,700.00).

(j) <u>Air Corps Battalion</u>:

The Battalion will be the basic Air Corps tactical and administrative unit and consist of:

(1) Headquarters and Headquarters Company.
(2) 4 Tactical Companies.
(3) 1 Service Company.

Bombardment airplanes:	26 @	P70,000.00	=	P1,820,000.00
Light bombers & fighters:	30 @	50,000.00	=	1,500,000.00
Cargo airplanes:	2 @	50,000.00	=	100,000.00
Long range observation airplanes:	4 @	70,000.00	=	280,000.00
FOR AIRPLANES				P3,700,000.00

As attrition in airplanes is conservatively estimated at 20% yearly, we necessarily provide for this attrition if we are to attain the indicated totals at the end of the period. Adopting only a gradual rather than immediate procurement program this attrition total is kept to a minimum. Under this plan, it is believed that attrition can be kept down to about 50% of the total: **P1,850,000.00**

TOTAL FOR COMBAT GROUP	P5,550,000.00

Primary training planes (including washouts)

20 @ P 25,000.00 each:	P500,000.00

We can use expeditionary type planes for basic and tactical training. Maintenance, repair and operation for all the above planes cannot be accurately predicted. This will be determined by the amount of operation.

Estimated at (10 years)	P4,000,000.00
The prices for airplanes include original installation of armament and radio, and wear and tear of this type of equipment (estimated)	30,000.00
Ammunition and bombs (estimated) for tactical training and reserves	300,000.00
Radios, for planes and ground stations	100,000.00
Photographic equipment	50,000.00
Hangers and other buildings	150,000.00
Landing fields (construction, wind cones, T's, and field lighting)	500,000.00
Flying equipment (parachutes, helmets, goggles, etc., including replacements of this equipment)	75,000.00
AGGREGATE TOTAL	P11,255,000.00

(NOTE: This does not provide the air strength deemed essential to Philippine security. However, it entails, after the 10th year, an annual maintenance cost of roughly P2,000,000.00 in view of other large maintenance costs that will be incurred after the expiration of a few years, no additional expenditures for air force are now recommended, although a minimum of P20,000,000.00 during the first phase would more nearly represent actual needs.)

(k) Off-Shore Patrol:

Organized in 4 flotillas, each of which will be organized into squadrons of 5 boats each.

60 sea-sleds (with torpedoes)	@	P75,000.00	P4,500,000.00
6 patrol bases	@	40,000.00	160,000.00
Cumulative maintenance on basis of acquiring boats as per following schedule: 1 in 1937; 5 in 1938; 8 in 1939; 16 in 1940; thereafter 5 per year: (estimated)			2,136,000.00
TOTAL 10 YEAR COST			P6,796,000.00

(NOTE: After the 10th year the annual maintenance cost will be at least P 360,000.00.)

(l) Summary of ten-year costs under complete 30 division plan:

Construction of 128 training cadres	P2,176,000.00
Construction of 450 mobilization centers	6,176,000.00
Station equipment at training cadres	153,000.00
Cadre equipment (individual)	930,800.00
Training conscripts (10 year total for subsistence, pay, clothing, transportation)	35,866,000.00
Miscellaneous construction during 10 years	1,250,000.00
Regular Army maintenance, (pay, subsistence, clothing)	60,000,000.00

Regular Army—administration, training, Military Academy, maintenance (including Quartermaster and other supplies)	12,995,000.00
Preparatory and teacher training	1,237,000.00
Maintenance of cadres and mobilization centers	3,000,000.00
Equipment of divisions	43,529,190.00
Subsequent training of Reserve divisions (on schedule as shown)	10,210,800.00
Air Corps	11,255,000.00
Off-Shore Patrol	6,796,000.00
TOTAL	P195,574,790.00

5. Estimated 10 year Deficit:

Estimated savings in kind and money for 1936: P5,000,000.00, including rifles already purchased. Total visible assets = P65,000,000.00 − P195,574,790.00 − P165,000,000.00 − P30,574,790, or an approximate deficit of P30,600,000.00

6. Recurring (or annual) Costs After 1945:

Regular Army, including all training, etc., Military Academy, transportation	P7,000,000.00
Maintenance of Plant and Equipment in all Stations	500,000.00
Conscripts	3,800,000.00
Air Corps	2,000,000.00
Off-Shore Patrol	380,000.00
Divisional Training	2,500,000.00
TOTAL	P16,160,000.00

It will be noted that this rough estimate shows that the full anticipated appropriation will be used up in maintenance of the permanent plant and personnel strength built up by the end of 1946. It provides nothing for replacement of weapons, ammunition and ordinary equipment; and does not touch the vital matter of accumulating adequate ammunition reserves.

7. In general the following armament is provided in the above estimate:

(a) With Reserve Divisions:

Rifles:	
With Reserve Divisions:	207,000
Pistols:	14,760
Mortars:	
120 mm	720
81 mm	540
Machine Rifles:	12,950

Machine Guns:	1,620
Bolos:	300,000

Ammunition:

Caliber .30	61,545,000
.120 mm.	79,200
.81 mm.	59,400
.45	811,800

(NOTE: The estimate provides also for an annual training allowance for each division of 186,500 caliber .30; and 120 and 90 rounds for the .120 mm. and .81 mm. mortar respectively. These amounts of training ammunition roughly provide for a twenty-year turnover in the total ammunition kept on hand in each division.)

(b) For Training Cadres:

Rifles	23,000
Bolos	23,000

(Annual training amounts only.)

(c) In the R.O.T.Cs. and Teacher Training Camps:

Rifles	10,000

(Annual training amounts.)

8. Additional equipment for R.O.T.Cs. and teachers, and for equipping the Regular Division is to come from that which was on hand on November 1, 1935—plus whatever may be secured at nominal cost from the United States Army.

Possible Savings:

9. In preparing this analysis quantity estimates have, in almost every case, been materially reduced below the amounts deemed necessary to produce units of normally desirable efficiency. In other words, little if any additional money can be saved by a general application of percentage reduction to all estimates, except at a serious cost to efficiency of the whole. A more drastic process, eliminating whole items or units is obviously necessary.

As an approach to this problem, the following reductions are suggested as those likely to occasion the least damage to the plan as a whole:

ELIMINATE THE FOLLOWING	SAVING

Divisional Equipment:

Artillery in 10 Divisions	P1,320,000.00
Automatic weapons in 10 Divisions	2,466,040.00
Medical equipment in 10 Divisions	500,000.00
Signal and fire control equipment in 10 Divisions	1,050,000.00
Ammunition (except for rifles) in 10 Divisions	2,309,000.00

Other savings:

Adopt policy (after 1937) of having total of
20,000 conscripts in training at any one time
  (saving) 3,000,000.00
    Fix maximum size of Regular Force enlisted at
9,500. Since increases were deferred in estimates, total
saving would be
  approximately: 2,000,000.00
Eliminate 3 mobilization centers for each division through
consolidation (total 90) 900,000.00
Eliminate 10 MAS boats (total savings
including maintenance) 900,000.00
Assume an average savings of P 500,000.00
in rations 5,000,000.00
    TOTAL SAVINGS P19,445,000.00

If all suggested savings are approved, the remaining deficit will be: P30,600,000.00 − P19,445,000.00 = P11,155,000.00.

(NOTE: To this deficit must be added any expenditure for additional equipment such as gas masks, .50 caliber machine guns, etc.)

10. Recommendations:

Since the total necessary reductions cannot be affected by the method indicated, nor can the total future annual income of the Commonwealth be meaned today, the following recommendations are submitted:

(a). That the 10 division pattern be adopted with objectives of the first phase as follows:

(1) 30 Divisions.

(2) 1 Composite Air Battalion.

(3) 4 Off-Shore Patrol Flotillas.

(b). That the first 10 divisions of the line be fully equipped and maintained in a high degree of training.

(c). That adjustments to meet income after 1939 be made the following ways:

(1) Delay organization of 2nd and 3rd Echelon Divisions.

(2) Reduce equipment assigned to these divisions.

(3) Scale down, if necessary, the program in all its parts—Regular, Trainee, Divisional, Air Corps and Off-Shore Patrol.

(4) As an alternative to the lines of action suggested in

(3) above, the Military Budget must be increased.

ON HAND IN PHILIPPINE DEPARTMENT		REMARKS
Rifles, caliber .30	58,553	53,118 U.S. Army
Bayonets	70,888	
Rifles, automatic, caliber .30	3,449	1,665 surplus

Pistols, caliber .45	25,698	3,700 caliber .45 revolvers surplus
Machine Guns, caliber .30	646	136 surplus
Machine Guns, caliber .50	16	None
Guns, .37 mm	63	None
Mortars, 3" MK I	53	
Guns, .75 mm	126	
Guns, 2.95 pack	52	
Guns, .155 GPF	32	
Carts, machine gun	202	
Radio, SCR 131	42	
Radio, SCR 161	229	
Radio, SCR 171	65	
Radio, SCR 177	2	
Radio, SCR 198	2	
Radio, SCR 203 (pack)	16	
Communication carts	0	
Masks, gas	24,441	
AMMUNITION		
Caliber .30	65,103,000	
Caliber .45	4,500,000	
Caliber .37 HE	53,500	
.81 mm. Mortar	0	
.120 mm. Mortar	0	
.75 mm. Gun	288,000	

Practically all equipment except reserve surplus, where noted, is in the hands of organizations or in Post Reserves.

1. Five annexes, not written by Eisenhower, accompanying this document are not included but are available at the Eisenhower Library. Eisenhower's outline numbers and lettering are not in sequence but are left as they appear in the document.
2. The exact identification of "MAS" boats has not been located. Given that they would transport only seven men per boat, they must have been a type of patrol boat or motorized assault craft.

99   Eisenhower Library
                                                          Philippine Diary

JULY 1, 1936–JANUARY 23, 1937
JULY 1

The report of the Military Adviser already referred to in this diary was published in June. It obtained considerable space in the local press and quite a good bit of favorable comment. Simultaneously with its submission to the National Assembly, the President also designated General MacArthur as a Field Marshal in the local army. The question of local rank for General MacArthur's assistants was happily not again brought up and we sincerely hope that the action in the case of the General will not create any unfavorable impression. By this time the General himself [has] become very reluctant to accept the title, although originally, of course, he was very determined to do so. He feels now, however, that he could not decline it without offense to the President. Anyway, he is tickled pink, and feels he's made a lot of "face" locally.

The most notable development in recent weeks has been a very marked change in the attitude of the Department Commander and his staff toward cooperating in our effort. General Holbrook sees the entire problem exactly as we do and is doing everything possible to assist us, even including the presentation of his views in forceful fashion to the American War Department. We are hopeful of more rapid progress under the new understanding.

AUGUST 15

For the past six weeks various phases of the problem of completing construction before January 1, 1937, have practically engaged our entire attention.

Through negotiations with the Department Commander it was arranged to place 8 of our training cadres on a portion of the Fort Stotsenburg Reservation.[1] Authority of the War Department was secured to this proposal and these particular cadres are to be trained by the American Army as artillerists and machine gunners. Seven of the units concerned were scheduled, under the original plan, to be stationed at Camp Murphy, the other one was one of the three scheduled for San Fernando.

Other changes will probably be necessary to accommodate a similar plan for placing several cadres at Fort McKinley,[2] where men will be trained by the American Army for the Signal Corps and as other types of specialists. This latter scheme has not yet been agreed upon between Department and ourselves.

All these things require alterations in construction plans, which have been further complicated by the extreme slowness of the Assembly in acting on the budget. Since the annual appropriation bill has not yet been passed, the only way money could be made available for this work was to have the Assembly authorize the use of unexpended balances in the 1936 appropriations. This authority has now been secured and construction will proceed as rapidly as possible.

Hasty inspections, made principally by Jimmy, have brought out the fact that some of the sites selected for locations of training cadres are entirely unsuitable. This puts another unexpected obstacle in the path of our program since we had thought this was one task District and Provincial Commanders could carry out without serious error.

We have found that the mortar equipment with which we had hoped to arm Philippine Divisions is much more expensive than we had originally thought. Prices quoted by a representative of the Stokes Brandt Company make it appear impossible for us to procure this equipment in the amounts we had intended. At the same time, the American War Department has informed us that they could not manufacture this type of equipment in less than a year, and that it would be very expensive.

In this situation we have sent urgent messages to the American War Department recommending that the reserve stocks of the Philippine Department be materially increased by the addition of Enfield rifles, Lewis machine guns, Stokes mortars, and British model 75 mm. field cannons. From the standpoint of the American Army all this equipment is obsolete or obsolescent. If the War Department agrees to this suggestion (which recommendation has been strongly supported by the Department Commander) we will undertake to revise the armament plans for the whole Philippine Army so as to take advantage of the availability of this material. In this way more money would be available for the purchase of ammunition both for training and reserve purposes.

Recently some adverse comments in the newspapers have disturbed General MacArthur very considerably. Jimmy, TJ, and myself have not taken these items very seriously and have constantly recommended against any attempt to answer them. The General, however, has taken an opposite view, believing that by circulating favorable publicity we can neutralize criticism directed against the soundness and efficiency of the defense plan. In line with this, we prepared one rather lengthy document which was released as an address by General MacArthur and sent it to the States. It was also released locally. The General has also made one or two shorter statements which he has furnished to the local press.

Recently a report appeared in the papers that the Appropriation Committee of the Assembly was investigating alleged corruption in the purchase of Army supplies. The Chief of Staff promptly appeared before the Committee with complete analysis of all Army purchases so far made, and fully satisfied the Committee that Army Headquarters had been guilty of nothing irregular or illegal in the procurement of supplies. On the contrary, [he] had been very solicitous in protecting the interests of the government. While we do not know what inspired the Chairman of the Committee to initiate the investigation or to make any statement concerning it, it would appear from surface indications that his actions were governed by nothing else than ignorance and stupidity and possibly some hope for publicity. Jimmy studied the reports rendered by Army Headquarters and is convinced that the supply division is operating efficiently and properly.

1. Stotsenburg, near Angeles, Pampanga Province, was the post that spawned Clark Air Force Base. Clark Field was constructed in 1919. Before World War II it was a primitive dirt landing strip.
2. Fort William J. McKinley was the major U. S. Army center in the Philippines, located near Manila. Stotsenburg was a respectable second. McKinley had two regiments of Philippine Scouts.

SEPTEMBER 26

TJ and I came in for a terrible bawling out over a most ridiculous affair. The Gen. has been following the Literary Digest poll, and has convinced himself that Landon[1] is to be elected, probably by a landslide. I showed him letters from Art Hurd,[2] which predict that Landon cannot even carry Kansas, but he got perfectly furious when TJ and I counselled caution in studying the Digest report. I don't believe it reached the great mass of people who will vote for the incumbent. We couldn't understand the reason for his almost hysterical condemnation of our STUPIDITY until he suddenly let drop that he had gone out and urged Q. to shape his plans for going to U.S. on the theory that Landon will be elected. Possibly he will—I don't know. But I hear the General is trying to bet several thousand pesos on it. He'll look fine, both here and at home if his calculations, based on his ravings about "least squares" and the accuracy of the Digest figures as a proper index, are proved unfounded. But WHY should he get sore just because we say "Don't be so d— certain, and go out on a limb unnecessarily"???? Both of us are "fearful and small minded people who are afraid to express judgments that are obvious from the evidence at hand." Oh hell.

1. Alfred Landon, the 1936 Republican presidential candidate, lost in a landslide election to Franklin Roosevelt. Landon, a prosperous Kansas oil producer, served as the state's governor from 1933 to 1937.
2. Arthur Hurd, born in Abilene in 1878, was a brother of Bruce Hurd, who graduated with Eisenhower from Abilene High School in 1909. Both Arthur and Bruce joined their father's law practice, Arthur remaining with the firm until his death in 1943. Bruce left the firm in 1933 to practice law in Topeka and would later become solicitor for the Santa Fe Railroad. At the time of Hurd's death, Eisenhower noted that he had been "one of my very best friends in Abilene and the one with whom I

most often exchanged letters." Eisenhower to Gertrude Verna Gough, August 5, 1943, Pre-pres. Papers, Eisenhower Library.

NOVEMBER 15[1]

Boy, did the General back pedal rapidly. I hear he went out to Q. on the first or second and "took back" what he had said at first. Accused the <u>Literary Digest</u> of "crookedness" when he heard Wall Street odds had gone up to 4–1 on Roosevelt against Landon. Now he's scared Roy Howard[2] will "tell on him" in Washington, for his former views were well advertised by H.[3] But he's never expressed to TJ or to me any regret for his awful bawling out of a couple of months ago.

1. Although Eisenhower made no reference in his diary, Mamie and son John arrived in the Philippines in late October 1936.
2. Roy Wilson Howard began his journalism career in 1902 with the Indianapolis *News*. By 1907 he had become New York manager of United Press International (UPI) and by 1912 president and general manager of UPI. In 1922 he became chairman of the board of Scripps, McRae, which later became Scripps-Howard. Long a friend and admirer of Douglas MacArthur, he was one of several publishers, including William Randolph Hearst and Col. Robert R. McCormick, who boosted MacArthur for the Republican nomination in 1944.
3. "H" refers to Howard.

CHRISTMAS 1936

Thought I'd write a summary of progress—but I'm too weary!! Most of our stations will not be ready for receipt of recruits in Jan., and we've found that many of them are unsatisfactory as to site and as to location on the site. Many places will be without water, roads or light. In addition, the hasty way we went at the job boosted costs, which, even without the aggravation are much higher than we originally estimated on info. given us here.

J. and I still believe that the plan emphasizes strength and numbers too much at the expense of efficiency—and that, even with an unsatisfactory standard of training, the program is going to run far in excess of the 160,000,000.[1] The Gen. admits this but says he has so informed Q. and that the money will be forthcoming. When the blow-up comes I wonder how he is to convince anyone that the present plan can be executed for a total ten year cost that he originally fixed as a maximum!!

1. The 160 million peso amount was for the entire ten years. The peso had been set by law by this time, tied to the American dollar at fifty cents; therefore, this amounted to $80 million.

329

Notes during Ord's absence in States.

Gen. MacA. with T.J. and Hutter accompanied Q. to States in spring of 1937.[2] They were absent about 4 mos., during which time we simply carried on plans and policies previously laid down by MacA.

1. Eisenwhower did not keep a diary during Ord's visit to the United States. See note below.

2. In early January 1937, Franklin Roosevelt appointed former Indiana governor Paul McNutt the new Philippine high commissioner. McNutt invited President Quezon to attend the swearing-in ceremony in Washington. Quezon used the opportunity to lobby for his plans for early Philippine independence. He also traveled to Japan, Mexico, and Europe, ostensibly to learn about other nations' military forces. A large entourage accompanied Quezon, including prominent Manila businessmen, leaders from the National Assembly, MacArthur, and several members of the military adviser's staff, including Ord. Upon arrival in the states, Quezon announced that he wanted the date for independence moved to 1938. MacArthur, concerned that Quezon had not received an invitation from the White House, went to Washington to implore Roosevelt to see the Philippine president. Roosevelt agreed to meet with Quezon but refused the request for early independence. When Quezon continued on his travels, MacArthur and his staff remained in the states to fight a fruitless campaign with the War Department to provide additional equipment for the Philippine army. On April 30, MacArthur stunned everyone, including his own staff, the press, and the public, with his marriage to Jean Faircloth. The MacArthur party returned to Manila shortly thereafter. See James, *Years of MacArthur,* 1:510–15.

100   Eisenhower Library
                                          Pre-presidential Papers

To General George V. H. Moseley[1]

April 26, 1937

Dear General: Lately I have become increasingly conscious of a lapse in our correspondence, which, so far as I am concerned, has already been far too prolonged, so this morning I determined to take the time to do something about it.

Recently I had a very splendid letter from Bomar. Won't you please tell him that I appreciated it keenly and very soon will get off a reply to him?

Ever since Mr. Quezon went to the States I notice that Philippine affairs have been obtaining considerable space in the American Press. So I doubt that I can give you much new information concerning local political affairs. However, you may be interested in my personal slant on some of the questions that are constantly under discussion here. The first of these involves the advancement of the independence date for the Philippine Islands from 1946 to 1938 or 1939. This suggestion was made by Mr. Quezon after his arrival in the United States, and it certainly gave birth to a wealth of furious discussion, pro and con, in Manila.

Naturally, the American investors in this country are solidly against any material shortening of the transitional period. Presumably they have laid their plans either for liquidating existing businesses at the end of the ten years or for using that length of time in adjusting their offices to anticipated conditions under independence. This applies not only to the sugar and other basic industries but also to individuals in the department store, brokerage, banking, and other types of business. Supporting this group is another that comprises investors from other countries, as well as some of the wealthier Filipinos themselves. All these people fear that termination of political connection with the United States will mean also the loss of all preferential trade, and in this result they foresee the complete economic ruin of the country. Certainly, to the innocent bystander there appears to be much weight in their arguments, especially when one notes the extent to which Filipinos are dependent, for cash crops, on sugar, copra, hemp and minerals.

The arguments advanced by those on the other side of the question are that so long as the Filipinos remain a dependency of the United States they are helpless to defend themselves against any unfair legislation on the part of the American Congress. They allege that the Tydings-McDuffie Act was in fact a covenant between the two countries and as such no amendment to it is morally possible without the consent of both governments. Since the excise tax on coconut oil was imposed by the American Government without the consent of the Philippines this particular group argue that the Tydings-McDuffie Act has already been scrapped, in principle, by the United States and that the Philippines can expect nothing but a progressively unfavorable economic position with respect to United States trade until such time as these matters can be crystallized in the form of treaties between independent nations. They argue, also, that in granting Philippine Independence at an early date the United States would, as a matter of justice, continue preferential trade agreements for a number of years. Whence comes the bases of this argument, I do not know.

The great mass of the population, that is the farmers and workers in the outlying areas, takes very little interest in such questions. You are well acquainted with the Philippines and I do not have to explain anything concerning the lack of communications in great portions of the islands. In many areas the people do not even know that such subjects as these are up for decision.

The outcome is something that I would not be bold enough to predict but I do feel sure that if the transitional period is shortened materially many grave problems will automatically arise for which no immediate solution is in sight. For example, our defense plan was conceived and initiated on the basic assumption that a minimum of ten years would be available for its development. If this period should be shortened to two or three years, the picture would be radically altered. Manifestly it is possible that the increased risk would have no bad effects on the Philippines, the hope being that there would be no occasion to employ this army before it had attained the maximum state of readiness of which it is capable. When one discusses such questions he, of course, enters the field of international possibilities, and I have never yet heard of an infallible prophet along that line.

The two great obstacles to success in the military effort in which we are engaged are insufficient finances and the difficulty of developing an efficient officer corps. Although I have been here for a year and a half I am not one of those who attempt to ascribe to the Filipino any racial defect which would make it impossible for him ever to become a good officer. Genghis Khan produced one of the finest military machines the World has ever seen, and the only material he had was nomadic tribesmen of Central Asia. I do not know of any local Genghis Khan to serve as the military leader of the army we are trying to organize, but at least his success proved that education and a highly level of civilization among a whole population are not essential to the development of a powerful military organization. In spite of these comforting reflections, however, I must say that I have been disappointed in the result of our efforts to galvanize the officer corps now available to us into intelligent and efficient action. The other day I read a comment by an eminent Chinese educator. He said that the Oriental is satisfied with things that are good, but that the American is always striving for the best, with resultant bad effects upon his blood pressure, happiness, and longevity. It may be that this difference in basic character is one that we are unwittingly combatting as we struggle to produce a body of officers capable of carrying on their work in the manner we think they should.

In some lines the job we have undertaken is no more difficult than we anticipated. To say the least, it is a most interesting experience to start from the beginning in the task of developing a defensive force for a new country. You notice I have not expanded upon the first difficulty I mentioned, namely, that of insufficient finances. Nothing I could say could add to your comprehensive understanding of the difficulty we have in attempting to build up an army on a total annual appropriation of eight million gold dollars.

So far the Philippines has not seemed to agree with Mamie. She has had a spell of bad health and is still under the observation of the doctors because of trouble with her digestion. On the other hand, John is developing rapidly and is enthusiastic about his school at Baguio. He is doing well in his studies and is very anxious to remain out here for at least another year. General MacArthur will be back from the States in another month and I have no doubt will bring to us a wealth of interesting news affecting you and our other old friends in the War Department. With warm regards to you and your family, Cordially

1. Moseley, headquartered in Atlanta, Georgia, commanded the IV Corps Area.

101   Eisenhower Library
                                                        Foltz Papers

To John Doud[1]

Dear Dad: As I read the sketchy news we receive from the United States I get the impression that this is rather a nice corner of the world from which to watch the things that are going on. Gold policies, supreme court legislation, agricultural laws, and mounting taxes, to say nothing of the thousand and other one important subjects that appear to be in an unsettled state, must cause the ordinary citizen to wrinkle his brow and shake his head. Here we are so isolated that we feel more like spectators than participants in American activity, and generally speaking, know so little of what is happening that we are spared the worry of wondering, doubting and questioning.

Of course, we have our own troubles. But in these we are ordinarily interested as they affect another people—at the most, the probable success of our job—and again are saved from the wearing worry of attempting to provide for our own future security and welfare.

There is going on here a very interesting experiment in self-government. Altogether there are some 15,000,000 people in the Islands. The ruling, or office holding group, is relatively small, and comprises in general the mestizo class, the product of Malay and Caucasian cross-breeding. Many of these mestizos are exceedingly smart, quick and shrewd. Their main interests seem to be political. Many of them are very wealthy (planters—mine owners—hemp producers—etc) and others are very competent professional men, particularly in the law. But acquisition of political power seems to be their fundamental ambition, and out of this ambition has undoubtedly come much of the clamor for independence. Their difficulty is the solution of econom-

333

ic problems that independence will bring. Before the date for complete independence arrives they must have found something to substitute for the revenues they now get out of a free market in the United States for sugar, copra, and hemp. They have been greatly encouraged by the developing mining industry, which many believe will finally supplant sugar as the principal revenue producer in the Islands. The country is flooded with American Mining Engineers and some mines are really producing gold on a very profitable basis. Two of these have gone far past the speculative stage and their stock sells normally on a basis of about 11% returns on the investment. I think the gross production from all mines last year was almost 30,000,000 pesos and this year it will be much greater. But there is no assurance, as yet, that mineral production, which includes gold, silver, chromite and manganese, will reach a level where governmental income can be based principally on taxes from that source.

Leaders are preaching diversification of crops so as to make the Islands more nearly self-sustaining in the matter of food, and thus decrease dependency on imports, which must be paid for in exports. To date they've been backward in this regard. For example, rice is the great staple article of food, yet much must be imported yearly. In other items it is the same story.

Under existing laws they have ten years to revamp their national economy, and to prepare themselves in all respects to carry on as an independent power. Our work, preparing their national defense, is only one direction in which they have a stupendous task.

A certain group of Americans and Europeans habitually sneer at the Filipino—challenging his sincerity, integrity and ability—and claiming that this whole situation is the result of the crooked scheming of politicians to get more personal power. But possibly a lot of other so-called reforms and developments have grown out of the same source. In any event they've started something, and it is most interesting to be here watching the early stages of a development that is certain to have far reaching effects in the coming years.

Mamie writes home regularly, so I doubt that I can give you any news of a family variety. She has had some of her old trouble with digestion, but after an exhaustive survey—X rays and so on, the doctors can find nothing wrong organically. Johnny is fine—and loves his school, where he is doing very splendidly. All of us send our love to you both, and hope that you are in fine health and spirits. Our best to Mike, Dick and the youngsters, with a particular message of "Bon Voyage" to Mike and Dick on their European trip. As ever your devoted son

1. Doud was at the Gunter Hotel, San Antonio.

TO THE ADJUTANT GENERAL

MAY 3, 1937

Subject: School records of Philippine Army officers attending United States Army Schools.

Under specific agreements with the War Department certain officers of the Philippine Army are to be trained annually in American military schools.[1] In addition, six officers of the Philippine Scouts are now taking the course of instruction at the Command and General Staff School, and one other officer of the Scouts will enter the same school with the next class. It is requested that, upon completion by each of these officers of any of the prescribed courses of instruction, a full report of his school record be furnished to the Military Adviser. This record will be of considerable value in determining an appropriate assignment in the Philippine Army of the individual affected.

1. Eisenhower also sent a list of fifteen Filipino officers selected to attend schools in the states to the Adjutant General on April 30, 1937. The officers' expenses were to be paid by the army. They were slated to attend the infantry, artillery, cavalry, quartermaster, air corps, and support-service schools. See Records of the Adjutant General's Office, Philippine Islands, April 30, 1937, NARA.

103   Eisenhower Library
Philippine Diary

JUNE 21, 1937–JULY 1, 1937

JUNE 21

Gen. MacA. decided the budget must be revised to provide sufficient money for mobilization equipment for complete class of 1936 and first half of 1937. This means a total (average of various estimates) of approx. 4,500,000 pesos, whereas budget, as at present constituted sets up only 1,150,000 for this purpose. Mob. equip.,[1] according to Gen. MacA. must take precedence over all other charges except those that are fixed, such as pay of personnel. He said that to fail to do this was to defeat his whole plan.

1. Mobilization equipment.

Showed General how we could re-arrange budget to obtain maximum amount in item "mob. equip."
This consists in:

a. Elimination of principal Ord. items, including
    8 howitzers 75mm. approx.   600,000
b. Cutting down Signal Corps, approx.   300,000
c. Revise savings estimates in purposes
    I and II to add approx.   900,000
d. Reduce purpose III by   100,000

It was explained to Gen. MacA. that nothing was to be gained in reduction of construction costs, since under present arrangement with B. of B. these costs are charged against surplus, and assembly will not be asked to appropriate for this item.

This scheme would place a total of about 3,000,000 in mob. equip.

Gen. rejected that part of ordnance savings involving 75 mm's by saying this equipment equally necessary with mob. equip. This cuts down projected shift of amounts to about 500,000 from that item. It was explained to him that by making maximum estimates on this year's savings in Purposes I and II[1] we ran the risk of going broke in those items before end of 1938, which would require discharge of trainees and relief of Reserve Officers. In this connection, however, I am not listing these estimates of savings at anything like the amounts given in a statement from Victoria. I am making a compromise between his figures and the ones we used originally, which were vastly smaller.

Altogether I think I'll add to the "mobilization" items by 1,500,000. The general frankly said this mobilization was for "psychological" reasons, giving this answer to silence my strenuous objections, on account of cost.

1. The reference to "Purposes I and II" was obviously to a report Eisenhower had given to MacArthur. A report to match these references could not be located.

a. In a conference with Gen. Grunert[1] agreed that 20 McKinley trainees will be instructed in Motor Transport work.

b. Gen. MacA. read Ord's preliminary study on Nov. 15 concentration. Agreed to it except that we, instead of improvised staffs, must do the work. Ordered an immediate beginning, so I gave the paper to Harrison and told him to go ahead.

c. Agreed with Colonel Hodges[2] and General Humphrey on composition of next camp at Dau. General H. (artilleryman) has authority, during first six weeks of camp, to transfer up to one hundred men, if he finds this necessary.

1. George Grunert was assigned to the Philippines (Mamie and son John Eisenhower arrived in the Philippines on the same ship as Grunert, in October 1936) as second in command to Maj. Gen. John L. DeWitt, commander of the Philippine Division at Fort William McKinley. From 1940 to 1941, Grunert served as commander of the Philippine Department, a position in which he repeatedly voiced to his civilian superiors his concerns about the islands' vulnerability. He would serve under Eisenhower as commanding general, First Army, from August to October 1943. He retired in 1945.

2. Courtney H. Hodges attended the U.S. Military Academy for two years before leaving in 1906 to enlist in the 17th Infantry. From 1936 to 1938 (he arrived in the Philippines on May 2, 1936) he served at Fort William McKinley in the Philippine Division as assistant chief of staff for intelligence and Assistant Chief of Staff for operations and training. In 1938 he was detailed to the Infantry School at Fort Benning, Georgia, as Assistant Commandant. In 1943, as a lieutenant general, he commanded the Third Army. In 1944 he assumed command of the First Army when Gen. Omar Bradley took over command of the Twelfth Army Group in Normandy. General Hodges retired in 1949.

JUNE 25

General MacA. disturbed by some criticism in local press and says that all misstatements must be answered. I am to prepare a statement at once showing that we've fed men well and that this army has very low proportion of professional officers, particularly in higher grades.

JUNE 26

Boy Scout argument up again, with the general seriously concerned about it.[1] Has appointed me, Santos, Segundo[2] as representatives of army to meet Boy Scout executives in conference. Mr. Vargas, upon hearing of this, said to lay off conferences until Stevenot returns.[3]

1. Evidently, the concern over the Boy Scouts was based on the fact that Quezon was honorary president, Osmeña honorary vice president, Jorge Vargas first vice president, Vicente Lim treasurer, and Carlos Romulo second vice president of the scouts. The executive board of the scouts also included Paulino Santos and Basilio Valdes from the army. This situation may have created concern that officials of the Philippine government were attempting to utilize the Boy Scouts in a military fashion or enlist them in the reserve forces.

2. Fidel Segundo was Assistant Chief of Staff for intelligence, the operations, and training divisions of the Philippine Army General Staff. Eisenhower wrote of Segundo:

In certain respects the most able officer in the army. Forceful, direct, and especially well trained, particularly in the tactics and techniques of the several combat arms. His greatest defect is that he does not devote himself exclusively to his own tremendous job, but is constantly getting into other tasks and activities, both in and out of the army. This habit has kept him from becoming the great progressive force in the army that he easily could be. . . . It irritates others and even creates a suspicion, in the minds of some people, as to the purity of his motives. My current conclusion is this: Teach Colonel Segundo to devote his vast fund of energy to the essentials of his own job and he will be brilliant in any position, including the highest. A superb commander (Memorandum on Philippine Officers, McCann Papers).

3. Jorge B. Vargas, a distinguished jurist and politician, was prominent in social circles. A member of the Philippine Assembly, he was also secretary to President Quezon.

J. E. Stevenot was president of the Philippine Boy Scouts and president and general manager of the Philippine Long Distance Telephone Company. A longtime resident of the Philippines, Stevenot had joined the Philippine National Guard in 1917 and served with the U.S. Army as a pilot in World War I. By 1937, he had become one of Manila's more prominent businessmen, serving on the boards of numerous utility, transportation, and financial firms.

JUNE 28

a. General has directed me to get up estimates on total needs in mobilization equipment for next two years, to end of 1939. This amount, he says, he's going to get Mr. Quezon to donate from "oil" money.[1] If this is so, then we ought to return to original composition of budget. Says he's been promised minimum of thirty million extra to finance plan.

b. General Santos has shown again that he will not stand fast on any project when appeals are made to him by subordinates.

He agreed to assignment of Garcia[2] as district commanding officer, then weakened under maudlin appeal from Garcia and promised him he could stay as G-3.

He also came up with a plea to send school officers to states via tourist accommodations on Coolidge[3] instead of dormitory accommodations on transport. He had a dozen reasons, but the real one is, as usual, "face". I'm weary trying to save money when everyone else wants to spend it, so I said, "Do as you please".

c. General MacA. wants to get at construction of addition to this office for use of engineers that are to come over in October. He said, "My real purpose in having them here under my thumb is that, though paid by funds of the Power Development Corporation, I can use them to help us out whenever they are not busy on other work." I am to go get Mr. Vargas's permission to build the addition in the old wall.

1. The commonwealth government had levied a heavy excise tax on coconut oil, drawing almost one-third of its revenue from this single source. The effect of the tax

was to slow the growth of one of the most promising sectors of the Philippine economy. See Theodore Friend, *Between Two Empires: The Ordeal of the Philippines, 1929–1946* (New Haven: Yale University Press, 1965), 159–60.

2. Col. Raphael L. Garcia was Assistant Chief of Staff, Supply and Personnel Division, Philippine Army. Eisenhower's appraisal of Garcia was somewhat critical. He wrote: "Pleasant personality and good appearance. Slow in grasping new ideas and works better in operating capacities than in general staff position. In my opinion he would make a fine district commander, which we sorely need, but it is only a waste of time and effort to try to make a real General Staff officer out of him." Memorandum on Philippine Officers, McCann Papers. Evidently, the Philippine Army combined personnel and supply divisions, something the U.S. Army did not do in its staff system.

3. The *USS President Coolidge* was a President Lines ship.

JULY 1

Prepared the statement on accomplishments of the Philippine Army during the past 6 months. My original intent was to write it as a summarized report from Chief of Staff to Malacañan and to furnish copies to papers for their use. When the General read it he liked the tone and immediately said <u>he'd</u> issue it in his own name. With this purpose in view he desired an expansion of the paper to include additional subjects, air corps, offshore patrol, tributes to American Army and Navy, etc. I protested that the paper lost all value and became just another <u>report</u>. He insisted, so today he is to give it as an "<u>interview</u>" to the <u>Herald</u>. I fear that one of these days some Editor will flatly refuse to take such statements for publication, because of little or no news value.

We have not yet gotten permission to increase revolving fund by 2,000,000 pesos with which to buy mobilization equip.

Have told Harrison that he could have Bailey for a while to help prepare plans for concentration in Manila on November 15.

Finally authorized Hutter to send his detachment to Corregidor for training. Against my better judgement—but haven't the time myself to conduct the research and investigations necessary to establish the facts as to whether or not the expenditure is justified.

Big conference at Army Headquarters on June 29 of all staff officers and District Commanders (10). I talked at meeting on duties, responsibilities and importance of new District Commanders. Answered questions for an hour. I did all I could to get these officers to take hold of job and carry it through. Informed conference of General's decision to eliminate Scout enlisted instructors next January.

To James Ord[1]

July 8, 1937

Dear Jimmy: The General received this morning the letter you wrote shortly after reaching Washington, and it has been circulated about the office. Last evening Emily handed me the one you enclosed for me in a letter to her.[2]

It was quite a shock to learn that we are to get none of the coconut oil money, but if the President can make good on his promise to provide money from some other source I guess that is all we can expect. What you had to say about the attitude of the Chief of Staff, Deputy Chief of Staff, and the head of the Insular Bureau was more than interesting to me. My previous understanding of that attitude was considerably different from the one apparently existing, and I hope that you are successful in your efforts to change it.

With respect to the things you can do there in addition to finding out about 75 mm howitzers, I simply want to recall to you the desirability of a continued supply of $8.00 ammunition and of getting some more 2.95 ammunition. The Department is getting low in this last. In connection with the item of ordnance the Department Commander has just received a letter from the War Department limiting to 1,000 the number of automatic rifles that may be loaned to us. You might look up the reason for this restriction since the Department, as I understand it, had already reported to the War Department that they had 1,200 available for loan. Incidentally, you might make some inquiries about the stocks of Lewis guns that we originally thought were available in the United States.

In the matter of personnel please ask The Adjutant General to make arrangements for the Commandant of the General Staff School to send us the detailed records on the Scout officers who attended there last year. Also try to make similar arrangements for all schools that our officers will attend in the future.

Now for local news. An irritating job that I acquired immediately after you left was a partial revision of the budget. You will recall that altogether we were able to put only something like one million pesos in the item "Mobilization Equipment". When I explained to the General that this would provide equipment only for the half class that has already graduated he became much disturbed and directed a drastic revision of the budget to supply sufficient money in this item to take care of all men to include all of the 1938 class. When I showed him just what this meant in the matter of cutting down ordnance purchases, pay for personnel, transportation and so on, he modified the instructions by omitting the 2nd half of the 1938 class. As you well know, even this more limited objective cannot be fully attained. I did, however, succeed in getting something more than three million pesos in this item. I did it by knocking off P300,000 from the Signal Corps; about P500,000 in special ordnance items, particularly fire control sets for machine guns; reducing the number of field glasses from 1690 to about 200; and then by making another survey of the surplus expected at the end of the year. In addition I ran up the total amount asked for to the point where subtraction of the "Permanent Items" under Purpose V will leave us almost exactly P16,000,000 over and above savings. This last increase I made only this morning after receipt of your letter indicating that the President would stand behind a larger budget. I do not need to recall to you how pitifully small the appropriations still are in all such items as ordnance, signal, medical and chemical property.

Reports received so far indicate that the new class of trainees assembled promptly on July 6th. I have no detailed statistics as yet but the general information I get from Army Headquarters is that practically 100% of those selected arrived on schedule. I have grave doubts as to the accuracy of this information.

Our little schools at Dau and Iloilo were unquestionably a success. Both Colonel Ramee and Captain Whatley rendered quite enthusiastic reports and I believe we will realize something on that particular investment.

The opening of the Reserve School at Camp Keithley had to be postponed two weeks. This order was issued without my knowledge and, while I raised some fuss about the manner in which the thing was done, it was unquestionably necessary. I am convinced that institution is badly placed because it is so far off center, and we will have to find a better location next year.

The other day General Santos came to the office to beg off from a couple decisions we had made. He wanted to permit Garcia to remain as G-3 and wanted to send officers to the U.S. tourist class passenger service instead of on the Transport. I listened to his stories and at first declined to entertain his suggestions. I then discovered that he had already committed himself on both propositions and told him we would stand back of him on his actions, but indicated clearly that I was not very impressed by the habit of folding up whenever people came to him with tears in their eyes.

Personally I have been swamped with work as you can well imagine. What with dealing with Malacañan, Army Headquarters and Department Headquarters, to say nothing of the thousand and one details that come up in the office, I am pretty much on the run most of the time. On top of all this, we have had an unusual splurge of social activities, including formal dinners that it was impossible to duck.

Emily has been in quite a nervous state. I have talked to her several times and so has Mamie. I called up the other morning to find out whether there was anything the office could do in the way of providing transportation or other assistance in the manhandling of baggage and she said she was getting along fine from that standpoint. She is unquestionably in bad health but I am hopeful will get on the transport on the 10th in a better frame of mind.

So far as the market is concerned there is nothing unusual to report. I am enclosing a clipping of the market pages of today.

There are, of course, dozens of things which would be of some interest to you if I could only think of them, but as usual my mind (no conceit intended) is a whirl of confusion and entirely incapable of orderly employment. So if you want to know anything you will have to ask specific questions. These I will process to the Great General Staff and send you an answer that will be a source of some astonishment even if not of information.

1. Ord had barely settled into his old duties after returning from the United States when MacArthur sent him back to Washington in another attempt to get additional military assistance from the War Department. Ord's wife, Emily, had become quite ill and would soon leave Manila for the states to undergo surgery for a diseased gall bladder and other gastrointestinal problems. The Ords would not return to Manila until September. See Eisenhower to Ord letters at entries dated August 13 and September 1, 1937.

2. In his June 27 letter to Eisenhower, Ord complained of the War Department's resistance to providing supplies for the Philippine Army. He wrote: "Boy, they are from Missouri—and make no mistake." Ord still held out hope that he would obtain 75mm artillery, automatic rifles, and machine guns. One reason Ord might have sent the letter through his wife was his revelation that High Commissioner Paul McNutt was "in bad [with] the soldiers. Why, everybody is just cussing the devil out of him." Also, Chief of Staff Malin Craig had told Ord that he recently had received a complaint from Philippine Department Commander Lucius Holbrook about "something MacA wanted to do." Ord's reference to "soldiers" means the War Department leadership. Ord to Eisenhower, June 27, 1937, Records of the Philippine Military Advisor, MacArthur Memorial Archives.

105

Eisenhower Library
Philippine Diary

July 9, 1937

Informed this morning by T.J. that the General called him in for a long talk. Subject was the General's readiness to dispense, at a moment's notice, with the services of any or all members of mission. The occasion for the conversation was speculation on Ord's possible permanent stay in United States, and the General's expressed irritation at what he termed the "conceit and self-centered" attitudes of various members of the mission. Said too many individuals were acting as if they were indispensable, and remarked that each was selfishly "looking out only for himself".

It begins to look as if we were resented simply because we labor under the conviction, and act on it, that someone ought to know what is going on in this army, and help them over the rough spots. However, from the beginning of this venture I've personally announced myself as ready and willing to go back to an assignment in the United States Army at any moment. The General knows this if he knows anything, so I guess I don't have to make an issue of the matter by busting in and announcing it again.

106

To James Ord

JULY 14, 1937

Dear Jimmy: This morning I received the copy of the short letter you sent to the General, concerning .30 caliber ammunition. The conditions laid down by the War Department with respect to this particular ammunition are entirely satisfactory and we can meet them with no difficulty.

From what you say about the organization of our artillery regiment I rather think it may have slipped your mind that we had to revise our items on the organization of this particular unit. You will recall that when we were counting on putting 81mm mortars in the artillery regiment we assumed that we were going to have the 3″ Stokes in almost unlimited quantities for use in the infantry regiment. When we learned that this assumption was an erroneous one we tentatively decided we would have to put 6 of the 81mm in each infantry regiment. Such a solution would automatically eliminate the need for the 81mm in the artillery. On this basis we were counting on having 8 75mm howitzers in the division artillery, with a provisional battalion of 4 to 8 .50 calibers and either 8 or 4 .30 caliber machine guns forming a special battalion.

Immediately after you left I reopened this whole question and discussed it with several officers of the department and with Segundo. Because of the effective range of the 81mm and the small size of our division, it looks like a reasonable solution might be to take the mortars away from the infantry and to keep them in the artillery. A compromise idea would be to cut down the allotment to the infantry and placing a few of them in the artillery regiment. This compromise has obvious disadvantages by complicating supply and in disbursing training activities. All in all, I must say that my inclination at present at least is to take them away entirely from the infantry and including them in the artillery at the rate of 8 or 12 per division. Each infantry regiment should have 2 of the .50 caliber and the artillery should have at least 4. This is the plan that I now favor, although I have not discussed the question in detail with the General. That I expect to do this morning and will add a postscript onto this letter before mailing.

I sent you a radio yesterday stating that the formal request for mobilization equipment that we expect to get through the American Army are being submitted. As I explained in the radio, the requisitions are being divided in two parts. The first part includes those items that are essential to the November concentration, involving principally shelter tents and individual and company mess equipment. In order to arrive in the Philippines on time these particular items will have to be shipped commercially since the Grant does not come back here until October 26th. Other items may await available government transportation.

New items keep bobbing up for inclusion in the budget while demands keep arising which tend to diminish our expected surplus at the end of the year. In this connection Captain Magtoto[1] and the Finance Section have been urging on me the advisability of carrying our expected surpluses in lump sum at the end of the budget instead of estimating them under each purpose. They maintain that this is the method followed by the Bureau of the Budget and the Auditor General, and would simplify our accounting system, as well as provide us more flexibility in the spending of money next year. I confess I don't understand some of their arguments and so far have refused to agree to their recommendations. I have a conference fixed up with them later in the morning and will try to get through my head exactly what they are talking about. The biggest reason that I do not want to propose any change is that every such change has to be explained in detail to the Assembly and gives them the idea we are trying to put something over on them.

P.S. I have just talked over the question of organization with the General. He has approved as a basis for planning an organization that removes the mortars from the infantry regiments entirely—leaving them only rifles, bayonets, automatic rifles, machine guns, caliber .30, and 2 .50 caliber machine guns. The artillery regiment will have 8

75mm Howitzers, 12 81mm mortars and either 4 or 8 .50 caliber machine guns (this particular point to be determined later). I am sending you a radio today giving you the gist of this decision.

Just as this letter was ready for mailing your radiogram arrived asking for list of U.S. Army equipment loaned to the Philippine Army. I will get it off by the next clipper.

1. Capt. Amado B. Magtoto served at this time as budget officer of the Philippine Army. In his memorandum on Philippine officers, Eisenhower wrote that Magtoto "is doing a fine job as head of an important Gen. Staff Division. Has studied the military profession, earnestly, all his life, and with noticeable success. I believe that he and Col. Martelino, P., should go to Leavenworth whenever that school reopens after February 1940. Thorough—loyal—gentlemanly." The "P." refers to "Pastor." See Memorandum on Philippine Officers, McCann Papers.

107

Eisenhower Library
Philippine Diary

JULY 20, 1937

Army Headquarters is moving into its new building. A week or so ago the General called for a detailed statement of expenditures from Military Adviser Fund. After going over it <u>he directed that all scout N.C.O.'s[1] be dropped as of next January 1</u>. They cost us 50,000 per year, and this drain on the fund cannot be longer sustained. I've given orders to this effect, <u>hoping</u> that cadres will be able to function without scout enlisted men next year.

Because of current expenses the General directed that Whatly[2] be given only 5.00 per day instead of the 8.50 that all other liaison officers get, and that we attempt to get the services of a signal officer at 3.00 per day.

1. Noncommissioned officers
2. This possibly was Vachel Davis Whatley Jr., (USMA, 1927).

108

MacArthur Memorial Archives
Records of the Philippine Military Advisor

TO JAMES ORD

JULY 29, 1937

Dear Jim: You have been fine about keeping us informed of everything going on in Washington. We have been intensely interested in everything you had to say not only concerning official matters but the gossip as well.[1] The only reason I have not written to you more regularly is the fact that until we received your radio a day or so ago I had no idea as to how long you would be in Washington.

I will first list for you a few of the incidents connected with the Army that have engaged our attention from time to time since you left. Most of these are totally disconnected and I will not attempt to make any running narrative out of it; merely by giving you the facts I am sure you will paint your own picture of such changes as have occurred in our general situation in the last month or so.

We failed to get student bodies at San Miguel and Lanao of the size we anticipated. 207 men reported at San Miguel and 152 at Lanao. The latter school was delayed in starting and even now is not functioning well because of lack of facilities at that station. Fellers[2] has just reported back from Mindanao and believes that the school will soon be established on a good basis due to the ability of the man detailed to command. This is Captain Dumlao,[3] of whom I have spoken to you before. We had to modify our plans for the General Service School at Baguio due to a lack of qualified students to enter on that course in September. We are running one more of the Reserve officer classes which will end on December 15th. On January 1st the General Service School will start and for the first year will end after seven months instruction. According to the report submitted to me yesterday, the Construction Fund is now about ₱70,000 in the red and many bills are piling in on us from the Bureau of Public Works, some of these bills being a year old. To provide the money for the cost of mobilization equipment we are now buying we had to have many conferences with the Auditor-General. Finally someone discovered an old law whereby money appropriated for personnel may be transferred under the authority of the President to the purchase of equipment and supplies. Consequently, we are using savings under Purposes I and II to buy these articles. Naturally this operation reduces by the amount we spend the expected savings for the year. However, since whatever system of financing we might use constitutes nothing more or less than borrowing from next year's anticipated appropriations, the plan evolved by the Auditor-General and Aguilar is as good as any other. As you well know I am personally opposed to this method of financing and believe that the longer we use it the more we confuse and fool ourselves. In addition we are failing to inculcate in Army Headquarters the strict regard for proper accounting methods and for appropriation law that they must have if we are ever to get upon a completely sound administrative basis.

With regard to the cadres the early inspections have been disappointing. In Southern Luzon conditions were found by Whatley to be very unsatisfactory. The constant rains are of course partially responsible for this but many other defects were traceable to neglect on the part of cadre officers and in some instances to distinct failures on the part of our Army Headquarters. As an example of these latter failures the Ordnance Department had failed to ship cleaning and preserving materials to the cadres during the month of June and the Quartermaster Department had not supplied uniforms. The excuse given was that "requisitions had not been received". I believe though that we have finally got into the heads of Aguilar and Cunanan[4] that articles such as these must be furnished automatically and requisitions are neither necessary nor desirable. One cadre, that at Canlubang, was found to be vastly improved and Whatley was really encouraged after going through it. Our needs in barracks and grounds improvement are just as urgent as ever and just as impossible to fulfill. I was compelled to approve a request for twelve additional gun bays at Stotsenburg although the money had to come out of the maintenance item. Many cadres are sunk in a sea of mud and there is very little we can do about it. We ought to undertake improvement projects at once that would cost us no less than three or four hundred thousand pesos.

I am negotiating now with Division to get the services of a Signal officer. The General will not permit me to get him on full time so I am trying to get him for additional duty in the afternoons only, and on the "Inspector" basis that has already been approved by Department. Apparently a lot of red tape is involved because the request has been in for ten days and I have heard nothing of it. For the concentration in Manila this Fall we will use all the active cadres between Tarlac and Batangas including Dau, McKinley and Murphy. Outside of this particular area we will use only Reserve units, omitting all those where particularly difficult transportation problems are involved. We are now working on a total strength basis of from eighteen to twenty thousand. The plans are rather well advanced and so far I figure that the additional cost, over and above normal mobilization and training requirements will be around P250,000.00. I haven't the foggiest idea, as yet, as to where this money is coming from.

I think I told you that Marabut[5] instructed us to figure our personnel costs of the basis of 100% pay instead of the 85% on which we had been operating so far. For the whole Army this involves an increase on the Budget of P670,000.00. I am carrying the increase as a separate entry under each item affected and carrying similar separate paragraph in the justifications. I think I told you that by slashing many items to the bone I finally succeeded in getting something over P3,000,000.00 in the item "Mobilization Equipment". Frankly, I feel that our greatly increased budget is going to take a lot of defending before the Assembly this year but I am encouraged by your report to believe that the

President will put his influence behind it and that we will get it through. If we don't we are going to have to pull in our horns very markedly all along the line.

It is obvious, without my saying, that your trip to the States has been extraordinarily successful. As I indicated to you in a long telegram I got off today, I am completely out of sympathy with the idea of providing a large number of pistols or revolvers for our Reserve divisions, unless these are obtained without cost. There is no sense in putting 4,000 of these in each division when we are already providing complements of rifles for the Artillery and Engineers, and are giving one to every Infantryman that is not operating some other weapon. On the basis I figure, the 1,950 pistols or revolvers per division will be ample. In addition I am somewhat doubtful as to the wisdom of getting a bunch of the 3″ mortars unless the ammunition for them can be obtained at considerably lower prices than have been quoted to us here. As I recall the figures, these prices are only about $1.00 gold lower than those obtaining for the ammunition to be used in the improved 81mm mortar. If this understanding is correct then I would far rather pay the extra money for the new mortar and avoid confusion and additional cost in our ammunition supply system. Likewise I am somewhat doubtful about the wisdom of asking for any 2.95 guns unless we are assured that ammunition for them will be forthcoming. If we can arrange to have reasonable supplies of ammunition manufactured in the United States then I am heartily in favor of taking over whatever number of these guns we can get and using them as the artillery component of a corresponding number of Reserve Divisions.

We have not heard a word about Emily since she left. I hope that by the time you meet her in San Francisco she will be feeling fit and optimistic.

We have had recently a rush of social activity and I am exceedingly weary of it. However Mamie says that there is a lull coming for which I am duly grateful. Mamie seems to be in reasonably good health and is taking much better care of herself than formerly. John is visiting at Stotsenburg with his friend, Cook. The day he arrived there he came down with dengue[6] but is now up and about once more.

Everybody in the office is on the job and going along about as usual. Sincerely

1. Ord had written Eisenhower on July 13 about his efforts to obtain additional supplies and equipment from the War Department during his second trip to Washington. The factors delaying any loans to the Philippines were Japan's aggression in China, the possibility of a war in the western Pacific initiated by Japan, and unsettled questions about the future political status of the Philippine Commonwealth. The U.S. Army was reluctant to commit a portion of its limited supply reserve to the

Philippines when the matériel might be needed elsewhere and when the possibility of early independence could lead to difficulties in securing its return. Ord reported, however, that he had obtained medical supplies and the loan of a thousand Browning automatic rifles. He doubted that he could obtain 75mm pack howitzers because they were no longer manufactured in the United States and the U.S. Army was short of them. Ord to Eisenhower, July 13, 1937, Records of the Philippine Military Advisor, MacArthur Memorial Archives.

In his letter of July 18, Ord reported that the army had promised twenty 75mm field guns. General Headquarters wired Philippine Department Commander Holbrook, ordering the department to lend as many 75s as possible from its reserves and its Corregidor armaments. If Holbrook was unable to commit the full number, the remainder would be sent from army reserves in the states. Again, Ord related his frustrations in dealing with the profound skepticism at the War Department about the Philippine Mission. Ord planned to go again the next day to the War Department to request a study of the Philippine Army "and have it included in the War Plan Orange." War Plan Orange was the War Department's elaborate plan for defending vital U.S. interests in the Far East, including the Philippines, in the event of an all-out Japanese attack. Ord to Eisenhower, July 18, 1937, Pre-pres. Papers.

2. Capt. Bonner Fellers (USMA, 1918) joined MacArthur's staff in 1935. One of his first assignments was to organize a reserve officers' school in Baguio. By 1937, however, he was performing liaison duties between the military adviser's headquarters and Malacañan Palace. Very early, Fellers became one of MacArthur's favorites. In 1940 the War Department assigned him to North Africa, where he served as U.S. military attaché in Cairo. Soon after MacArthur's evacuation from the Philippines to Australia in 1942, MacArthur had Fellers reassigned to his headquarters staff. Fellers would remain with MacArthur through 1946.

3. Capt. Amando Dumlao was Philippine Army provincial military commander.

4. Lt. Hugo V. Cunanan, a former Constabulary officer, had been promoted to acting chief of the Ordnance Service in April 1937. In Eisenhower's 1939 memorandum for Quezon, he recommended that Cunanan, by that time Chief of Ordnance and a captain, be promoted as soon as possible to the rank of major. Eisenhower wrote: "He is a well trained officer, but would probably much prefer to serve in the line than in his present position. But there is no one else in sight to fill this important post, and it should be made attractive to him." Memorandum on Philippine Officers, McCann Papers.

5. Serafin Marabut served in several positions within the Philippine bureaucracy. These included service with the Provincial Treasury of Rizal, the Bureau of Commerce and Industry, and the Philippine Budget Commission, where he was serving as departmental undersecretary when Eisenhower made this entry. A leader in the Nacionalista Party, he served several terms in the Philippine legislature and as a delegate to the 1934 constitutional convention.

6. Dengue fever is a tropical, epidemic flulike illness characterized by high fever and severe joint pain. While rarely fatal, it is severely disabling during its one-to-two-week course.

JULY 31, 1937

Have begun a campaign to instill in Philippine Army, particularly in officers, a higher regard for regulations, orders, and care of government property. Recently two or three instances have come to my attention of officers using government property for unauthorized projects. Have recommended in each case that the guilty officer refund the amount to government. Have further recommended that an officer who used a truck for ten days improperly be fined and reprimanded. Have urged Chief of Staff to stop approving requisitions for property unless accompanying documents show a real need for same. Directed a thorough investigation of typewriter situation, including a physical inventory of machines charged to offices in Manila, and personal payment for any that is missing.

Heard a bunch of gossip today (via TJ) that this mission is bitterly resented by H.C.[1] That office is supposed to be particularly peeved at salary of Chief and his penthouse. The H.C. is also supposed to have written letters home to the President and Secretary of War demanding relief of mission. O.K. by me!! I'm ready to go. No one seems to realize how much energy and slavery Jim and I put into this d— job.

The General got quite disturbed upon learning of Army Headquarters[2] plan to make a Mr. Melchor (head of Math. Dept. at P.M.A.)[3] a major in Aug. He talked on subject for 1/2 hours—I'm trying to get legislation creating a corps of professors.

Radios from Jim (in Washington) indicate he is getting along pretty well in arranging extensive loans of ordnance from U.S. Army. He's doing lots of good work, though why it was not done when General was in States is beyond me. Jim expects to sail Sept. 8, don't see how he can predict his date of departure when Emily's condition will not be known for some weeks. The sooner he comes the better for me, I'm tired. Over a year and a half at this slavery in this climate and no leave!

The mobilization for this fall, particularly the Manila concentration, is to be a much smaller affair than originally ordered. The General has finally become convinced that his idea of doing the job for next to nothing is out of the question. So after doing weeks of work on a 20,000 concentration (instead of the 25,000 the Gen. ordered) we are directed to come down to the 15,000 Luzon concentration, that I originally urged. We are told to keep additional expenses within the 100,000 pesos limit, as the maximum.

1. "H.C." was Eisenhower's shorthand for the high commissioner of the Philippines. Frank Murphy, the first U.S. high commissioner (1935–36), disliked

MacArthur and may have been behind the recall letter to MacArthur of August 1937 that ordered him back to the states. After that letter, MacArthur resigned from the U.S. Army and remained in the Philippines as a field marshal in the Philippine Army.

2. Eisenhower refers to the Philippine Army Department.

3. Philippine Military Academy.

110

MacArthur Memorial Archives
Records of the Philippine Military Advisor

TO JAMES ORD[1]

AUGUST 13, 1937

Dear Jim: At last I have the two essentials which should permit me to get off a letter to you. The first is some knowledge of your probable address a week or ten days hence; the second is a bit of time during which I'll probably be undisturbed. It's exactly 7:15 a.m. and there's no one else in the office except Eddie. In all Manila, except our office, today is a holiday—Occupation Day. So perhaps I'll be let alone for an hour or so.

A recent message gave your radio address as Saratoga, care of Seventh Corps Area, but that means nothing to me. Where is Saratoga, anyway? Unless I'm completely crazy—which is a more probable contingency than even you might suspect—the Mayo Clinic is in Rochester. So there is where this will be sent.

First: The General, following suggestions of mine, has written a couple officers in the G. S. to find out whether or not they would be interested in coming out here to serve on his staff next year. One he wrote to is Peabody,[2] in the office of the Secretary of General Staff. So, while this information is of course confidential, if he should begin to bombard you with questions, you'll know what it's all about.

The matter came up in a discussion of future plans and I put in the thought that sooner or later you and I would be due to go back to the States, if for no other reasons than those of health. He seemed a bit surprised but understood the point. So his letters to the two officers in the States were written with the idea of being sure of replacements in the event we should want to leave next summer. (Incidentally, he stated that both of us had a job with him as long as we desired.) Later he changed his ideas somewhat and proposed a plan for organizing this office parallel to the General Staff at Army Headquarters, one officer as G-1, 4, and director of the Budget; another as G-2, 3; you and I to be a sort of dual Deputy and War Plans; Harrison and Whatley to be used on whatever work we desired. He's told me to budget probable expenses incident to such a plan and find out whether we could fi-

351

nance it. Naturally I told him that, assuming we stayed on, such an organization would be a great relief to us. TJ is of real assistance. He does very little "aide" work now, except as to running appointments and so on in the office. But he handles everything that can be classed as Adjutant General work, and takes a lot of irritating details off my neck.

The budget is in the hands of Marabut. I sent it over with the information that I'd come over to see him whenever he wanted me—but so far have had no call. Everybody in the government is too busy preparing a royal reception for Quezon, who arrives Monday, the 18th. Apparently they are determined to fire twenty-one guns, but they are following our suggestion to wait until the President enters the portals of Malacañan before turning them loose. I hope there will be no resentment, which I fear there would have been if 21 had been fired at the water front. But to get back to the Budget for a moment: After deducting "expected savings" it totals about P20,600,000. After taking off "construction" it still runs about P16,750,000. It will be quite a lot for the boys to swallow, but I don't see where we can cut it. You will recall that the amounts shown in the left hand column is the 1938 estimate under each item. The total of this column runs about P25,000,000. That is, it is the aggregate of the amounts we'll have available in 1938, <u>including</u> savings. But since this column shows also the desired <u>distribution</u> of the aggregate available it was necessary to include language that would prevent dislocation due to the <u>actual</u> distribution of 1937 savings. We took care of this adequately, I hope.

The Department is insisting more and more on conducting independent inspections of property loaned to us—and that means more money. I added 5,000 pesos to Purpose I, with an authorization to pay inspection expenses of U.S. Army Officers looking after U.S. property loaned to us. I lumped the amounts for flying pay and pay of Air Corps instructors and added P5,000. This I did in order to increase Lee's[3] per diems, who, at the General's suggestion, is to stay on for a while.

I'm living in terror of what the President is going to do to our scheme for incorporating Reserve officers. Old General Alejandrino[4] has been attacking us through the press for "political" appointments and so on. These politico may get scared, although our procedure is not only efficient it demonstrates clearly the unbiased manner in which the whole thing has been handled. We've recommended five Captains for transfer to the Regulars—all the others are Lieutenants, to a total of some 135.

I sent you two radios about extractors. Since we had some doubt as to your address at the time they were sent, I'm enclosing copies. As you can see, the first purpose is to have the War Department authorize the free issue of the 50,000 already here as replacements for those broken in the first 75,000 we bought. The second is to anticipate certain future requirements for the 300,000 rifles still to come, and arrange to get them at the lowest possible cost. In my opinion, if they won't let us have them gratis, we should pay not over 25% of initial cost which is about the ratio of actual to initial cost represented in the $7.50 price for the rifle itself.

The information on the patrol boats staggered me a bit. The cost of the two ships will be 500,000 pesos, dangerously close to the total sum we have in the item for Off-Shore Patrol, including armament, repairs, etc., etc. Incidentally, upon receipt of your radio on the subject, I went down and transferred P50,000 from other items into the Off-Shore Patrol. I don't see the real advantage of getting two, particularly as they are pilot, which means experimental, models. Huff[5] is writing a long letter to Capt. Chantry, asking questions about points we do not understand. It strikes me that if the only real advantage in purchasing two is the saving of some P50,000 on the total cost of two, then, under the circumstances, it's not a good bet. Of course, if the model should turn out perfectly, then we'd be that much ahead, and we'd win on the gamble. But I'm afraid of "bugs" and consequent necessary revision in design. Please don't get the idea I'm worrying about this—whatever you do is o.k. by me—and we'll make it work out to our satisfaction.

In this connection we must be sure, after your return, to have the P70,000 available this year actually transferred to the Navy before January 1, so that it cannot be counted in our lump sum savings for this year. If carried over as a saving it disappears as a separate item and, together with new money appropriated, is distributed according to the estimates in column 1. We are assuming that all, if any, purchases of new dies, jigs, etc., actually charged by the Navy against the cost of these boats, will become our property to be transferred later to Cavite and used there in later manufacture.

I'm enclosing the latest available copy of market quotations. As you'll see, stocks are still in the doldrums.

Haven't heard a word concerning Emmy since she left. Hope she stood the trip in good shape and that her morale is on the up and up.[6] Incidentally, I don't see, personally, how you can count with certainty on catching the Sept. 8th Clipper. Keep me informed of your situation, radioing through JIMIKE if necessary. The $500 was transferred as you requested—which I suppose you know by this time.

Also, whenever you see anyone that you know to be a friend of mine, give them a personal greeting for me.

My best to you, Emmy and Tish. How is Jimmy doing, and has he a chance for West Point?? Good luck. As ever

1. Ord wrote three letters after Eisenhower's letter of July 14. In his correspondence of July 27, August 9, and August 10, Ord reported again on his attempts to

procure supplies and munitions. He was particularly enthused about the Navy's offer to build two patrol boats at $112,000 each. The most vexing problem continued to be resistance within the War Department to providing scarce equipment when there would be no assurance the equipment would ever be returned, or compensation paid, once the Philippines achieved independence. Maj. Gen. Walter Krueger, Assistant Chief of Staff, War Department, was especially hard to convince. Krueger felt that to arm the Philippines was to provide the means for an insurrection against the United States. Ord had some success, however, convincing many officers on the General Staff that the Philippine Army could be a useful reserve force for the American Army in the Far East. Ord wrote on August 10 that the War Department was about to order Philippine Department Commander Holbrook to transfer twenty additional 75mm artillery pieces, as well as all of his 2.95-inch guns, to the Philippine Army. Ord also demonstrated his impatience with the department commander when he wrote of Holbrook: "He and the Dept. staff must be made to realize that whatever defense plans they have—we constitute the 'means for its execution,' the better prepared we are for immediate field service, the more efficient their plan becomes." Ord to Eisenhower, July 27, August 9, 10, 1937, Records of the Philippine Military Advisor, MacArthur Memorial Archives.

2. This probably was either Hume Peabody or Paul E. Peabody. Hume Peabody (USMA, 1915) entered the Air Service in 1920 and remained with the air arm until his retirement in 1946. Paul E. Peabody served in World War I and during World War II obtained the rank of major general. Paul E. Peabody retired in 1950 with the permanent rank of brigadier general.

3. William Lee reported to the Philippines on November 23, 1935, and served as the senior U.S. Army Air Corps lieutenant. He and Lt. Hugh A. "Lefty" Parker were the only two air officers stationed there. They were later replaced by Capt. Mark A. Lewis and Lt. Robert L. Anderson. Their task was to train the Philippine Army air forces.

4. Jose Alejandrino joined the Philippine Revolutionary Army in 1895, rising to the rank of general. In 1899 he became acting secretary of war and also served as military governor of Pampanga Province. During the early years of American control, he served as city engineer of Manila. In 1923 he was appointed to the Philippine Senate and in 1934 served as a delegate to the Constitutional Convention. Alejandrino became MacArthur's nemesis, constantly writing letters to the editors of Philippine newspapers criticizing the mission's training and equipping of the Philippine Army. Finally, in 1937, MacArthur published in several newspapers a point-by-point rebuttal to Alejandrino's charges.

5. Sidney L. Huff, a retired naval officer and friend of Eisenhower, had met MacArthur in 1935 during shore leave in Manila. During that leave, he suffered a heart attack that forced his retirement from the navy. In 1936, MacArthur asked Huff to join his staff in Manila and develop an "Offshore Patrol," a proposed fleet of fifty torpedo boats. But Huff failed in his attempt to have the American Navy supply any of the craft; by 1941 the patrol consisted of two Thornycroft torpedo boats purchased from the British Navy and a single pilot model built by a Manila shipyard. See Sidney L. Huff and Joe A. Morris, *My Fifteen Years with General MacArthur* (New York: Paperback Library, 1964).

6. According to margin notes, Emily was in the Mayo Clinic.

111

AUGUST 25, 1937

The last week has been one of the most trying ones I've had on the P. I. There has been an unusually large number of difficult administrative problems to handle with the Army staff, (and incidentally I heard that the Pres. was astounded and furious at the size of our Budget). But the cause for special perturbation was the receipt by the Gen. of a letter from the Chief of Staff informing him that he would be relieved and ordered home on the October transport! The chief assistant to the Genl. in the ensuing conferences, proposals, speculations, arguments, etc., etc. [. . .] has become (or maybe always has been) a master bootlicker. From the start T.J. and I counselled moderation— and at least <u>initial</u> dependence on Mr. Quezon's efforts to have the order revoked. He agreed to send any radio proposed by the Gen. to accomplish such revocation, and we got up one worded as strongly as it possibly could be. We are informed that the Pres. secured the H.C.'s favorable endorsement to that radio. But we had no sooner submitted the draft of that radio to the Pres. when a hundred other schemes were proposed here and there to "help out". We wrote drafts (under instructions) of radios requesting retirement, of others protesting the "unjust and arbitrary procedure" of the W.D. while listening for hours on end to hypotheses and so called deductions as to what had occasioned the order. Gradually it percolated into the Gen's head that the theory lending the greatest hopes for a successful outcome (from his standpoint) was one that held the C. of S. solely and exclusively responsible for the action. The motivation was, under this theory, jealousy; fear of the growing stature of Gen. MacA as a world figure; egotism; revenge by the "Chaumont crowd",[1] and hopes of pleasing the "pacifistic, subversive element that surrounds the President". The defense T.J. and I put up was simply that we should give as much credit to the C of S for being an honorable person as we should to people like Murphy, McIntyre, Coy,[2] etc., etc. We emphasized that we'd done what we could, when we prepared the telegram for Mr. Quezon's signature. We insisted on waiting for an answer before making another move, since his wire was addressed to the President of the U.S. Finally the old habit of accusing every assistant who did not concur without reservation to hysterical theories and arguments with being a blockhead, an ingrate, a stupid dolt and so on manifested itself, so T.J. and I perforce stopped arguing. Finally the General shot off a "protest" wire to the C. of S.—and was answered promptly. The nature of the reply was that the <u>President</u> had decided, in view of world conditions, that a soldier of the General's reputation and abilities (and youth) should be in the U.S. His date of departure is put off until February.

I hope the subject will now cease to be a topic of conversation. I'm worn out!!

Every time one of these "tempests in a teapot" sweeps the office I find myself, sooner or later, bearing the brunt of the General's displeasure, <u>which always manifests itself against anyone who fails to agree en tote with his theories and hypotheses</u>, no matter how astounding they may be. These comic opera wars never center about any problem incident to the "job" we are on. They invariably involve something personal to the Gen.; I could be the fair-haired boy if I'd only yes, yes, yes!! That would be so easy, too!!

1. John Eisenhower states that "the 'Chaumont Crowd' derives its name from the location of Gen. John J. Pershing's headquarters during World War I. Pershing's staff, which included George C. Marshall, viewed MacArthur with ill-concealed distaste. However, MacArthur always overestimated the unanimity and intensity of their hostility."

2. Frank McIntyre (USMA, 1886) served in the Philippines from 1899 to 1902. In 1915 he was assigned to the Bureau of Insular Affairs, Department of the Army, where he served as chief of the bureau from 1912 to 1918. The Bureau of Insular Affairs was in the War Department until 1939, when it was transferred to the Department of the Interior. He retired from the army in 1929. It is possible, given McIntyre's long involvement in the Philippines, that even in retirement he had some influence with the War Department.

Wayne Coy was administrative assistant to the second Philippine high commissioner, Paul McNutt.

112   MacArthur Memorial Archives
                             Records of the Philippine Military Advisor

To James Ord

September 1, 1937

Dear Jim: There is much to tell you but, unfortunately, I am under heavy vows of secrecy with respect to some of the most interesting items. Consequently, here and there this letter will likely be rather incoherent, due to my veering away from subjects that are uppermost in my mind. I may as well start off by telling you that none of these things affect you adversely and so allay any trepidation that you may experience because of the mysterious atmosphere that always surrounds any attempt to tell everything possible without revealing so-called "secrets".[1]

The results of your work at home in permitting us to crystalize training and organization plans are quite noticeable. Naturally I am personally delighted and am in high hopes that upon your return we can definitely decide upon most details of armament and consequent organization. The only phase of your negotiations there that disturbs me is that applying to the deposit of bonds to assure payment on borrowed Ordnance.[2] If we are called upon to provide some definite financial security of this kind, I am afraid we will be at an impasse. However, you may have some really definite knowledge along this line. It was likewise a disappointment to learn that our supply of $8.00 ammunition is to be cut off.

It was quite a shock to hear, the other day, that the President is dismayed and astonished by the size of our Budget. He was recorded as being nonplussed in view of the definite promises made almost two years ago, and I gather that only the intervention of more immediate affairs has kept us from hearing about it in a big way. Naturally we will make such defense as we can on the basis of increased cost due to rising prices, emergency building, and stepping up of the whole development schedule. But we cannot dodge this fact: Our estimated expenditures for next year are P25,000,000. While this includes savings (which incidentally are not going to reach the P5,000,000. level we estimated) the cold truth is that this sum represents more nearly than does P16,000,000 the necessary annual expenditures of the next 5 years, if we are to maintain the plan on its present basis. After 1938 we will, of course, cut down drastically on our construction item. It will be a long time, however, before this will come down to an inconsequential amount, due to our needs for adequate warehouses, mobilization centers and general improvements. At the same time the items for Off-Shore Patrol, Air Corps, Armament, and ammunition must go up materially. Possibly you and I, two years ago, did not hold out as insistently as we should have for the P22,000,000 figure. In our own defense, however, we can remember that our studies and conclusions were academic ones and we had no means of demonstrating their accuracy.

We are making real progress in the overhauling of our supply arrangements. You know how terribly slow and difficult this has been. But I believe that now some glimmer of comprehension is beginning to seep through Army Headquarters concerning the necessity for systematic procedure, accurate accounting, and property responsibility.

You should not give another thought to the report you saw in the War Department alleging our unpopularity with certain elements of the Philippine Army.[3] Aside from some idle speculation as to how a salesman's report to his home office could have gotten into the files of the War Department, that item is as 5¢ worth of dog meat compared to some of the things that have been engaging my attention.

Naturally all of us are looking forward to your return. Almost every day I get inquiries about you at Malacañan and Army Headquarters, to say nothing of some of your old haunts in the city itself. Above all others, however, I am the one most interested. This is not only because of the extra work your absence throws on my shoulders, but principally because of the fact that I so often feel the need of discussing daily problems with you. As you must understand there is no one else with whom I can talk over many of the most perplexing subjects, and as a result I often find myself going around in circles in what I am pleased to call my reasoning processes.

The principal reason I have not written to you more frequently is that your peregrinations (look that one up) are such as to keep me constantly doubting where a letter could reach you. This one should reach Rochester along about the 10th and I am sure your last stop before flying to San Francisco will be at that place. Incidentally, I do not see how you can yet plan, with any assurance, on leaving the States on the 15th. To learn that you had to stay longer would be a bitter disappointment to me, both because it would indicate a slower recovery on Emily's part, and because also it would keep you away from here that much longer. However, I recall that when Mamie had her gall bladder removed she was desperately sick for three or four weeks and, as I remember, was not pronounced out of danger until about that time after the operation. I gather from your letter that Emily's operation involved both the gall bladder and the stomach. She will certainly be a very sick woman for some time. Concerning this subject, I simply want to tell you that if you decide at the last minute to send me a wire asking for further extension I am sure the General will approve it without protest. But if there should be any objection from any source I will go full out to your support and feel that I can guarantee approval. Naturally everything will begin to run more efficiently when you return. But you must be the sole judge of your responsibilities there and the need for your remaining longer. I definitely assure you that your place here is not being absorbed by anyone else and the integrity of your standing and prestige is not being impaired in any way. What I am trying to get over to you, Jim, is this. Assuming that your personal ambitions and interest dictate more or less permanent detail on this work, you should have the utmost confidence in the certainty of your retaining it so far as any influence or consideration from this end is concerned. From my standpoint and that of the Philippine Army you are badly needed, but we will limp along without you for as long as you feel it necessary to stay there. But I tell you now that when you arrive I am going to take myself about 10 days leave, even if I don't stir out of the hotel room during the whole of that period.

Please give Emily our love and best wishes. Mamie and I talk of her often and are hopeful that her operation will return her to a perfect state of health. Tell her to get to going and come on back here.

I apologize again for the rambling, stilted, and altogether unsatisfactory nature of this letter. If I have convinced you, however, that you have no need to worry about anything at this end (from this statement I except the stock market) and that all of us are deeply and sincerely appreciative of the work you have been doing in the States, then my message is complete.

I will possibly send you a radiogram or two before you leave the States. Otherwise, if you sail on the 15th, this will probably be the last word you have from me. As ever

1. This reference is to Eisenhower's private meetings with Quezon. He noted these meetings again later in the diaries. Quezon had come to mistrust MacArthur and would invite Eisenhower to the palace to visit discreetly without MacArthur's knowledge.

2. In his letter of August 10, Ord outlined a plan he had devised for funding additional procurement. It was apparent that the War Department would lend only a portion of the equipment needed and that the Philippine Assembly was unlikely to appropriate additional funds. Ord discovered that the Bureau of Insular Affairs had between $15 million and $21 million in Philippine funds in several accounts at the bureau. None of those funds were designated for any particular purpose, nor were they earning interest. Ord proposed to Eisenhower, apparently with the support of War Department officials, that these funds be invested in U.S. government bonds and the interest used as a fund to offset the costs of additional armament purchases. Ord to Eisenhower, August 10, 1937, Records of the Philippine Military Advisor, MacArthur Memorial Archives.

3. Ord wrote Eisenhower on August 17 that a report had been submitted to the War Department by a DuPont representative upon his return from a munitions sales trip to the Philippines. The DuPont representative asserted that several high-ranking Philippine Army officers resented the American Military Mission and felt it was totally unnecessary. The salesman recently had corresponded with Brig. Gen. Vicente Lim, Assistant Chief of Staff, Defense Plans Division. Ord and others in Washington suspected Lim had voiced the complaint. Ord to Eisenhower, August 17, 1937, Pre-pres. Papers.

113 MacArthur Memorial Archives
Records of the Philippine Military Advisor

MEMORANDUM FOR CAPTAIN BONNER FELLERS

SEPTEMBER 10, 1937

Will you please deliver to President Quezon the following message just received by radio from Colonel Ord:

"Horse that fulfills all requirements available here for approximately $1,000.00; one-half thoroughbred, 16 hands, 10 years old, chestnut; transportation by Army Transport authorized."[1]

This message was sent by Colonel Ord on August 23d, but due to an accident in the radio net was not received at this office until this morning. If the President can give you any reply to this message I will send a radio to Colonel Ord which he will receive upon his arrival in San Francisco.

1. Evidently Ord was trying to buy a horse for Quezon.

114

OCTOBER 1, 1937–OCTOBER 11, 1937

OCTOBER 1

The General, a few days ago, put in his application for retirement, effective Dec. 31. Possibly that will dispose of the question of his immediate future.[1]

1. In August, Chief of Staff Malin Craig had notified MacArthur that his tour of duty as military adviser would end after two years in the post and that he therefore would be brought back to the states to assume another command. Stunned, MacArthur wrote Craig, applying for retirement from the army rather than taking a subordinate command. Craig approved the request, setting December 31 as the date of his retirement. On that date Quezon issued an executive proclamation that retained MacArthur, now in retired status, as Philippine military adviser. Quezon also renewed MacArthur's rank as field marshal. See James, *Years of MacArthur*, 1:521–25.

OCTOBER 8

At 12:15 today the General had a conference (called a conference by courtesy. It was nothing but a monologue—since even when given "2 minutes" to present our views, we'd lose the floor and have to subside) in his office. Present, Ord, T.J., Fellers and myself. Fellers was unquestionably present to act as "reporter" of the conference, especially to be the messenger to Malacañan. There was no other excuse since he has not been associated with the work of executing the defense plan; which was the subject of the conference.

The occasion for the conference was a conversation the General had with the Pres. last evening. The Pres. showed him an estimate (prepared by Ord for the Pres. at the specific request of the latter) as to the total cost, up to 1946, of the military program that the General has laid down as our objective. This plan, as dictated to us by the General time and time again involves:

Annual training of 40,000 conscripts for 5½ mos. (3,000 to be trained for 11 mos).
Organization of 30 reserve and 1 regular division
Organization of an Air Force of approx. 50 fighting planes
Organization of an Off-Shore-Patrol—to be as strong as possible within a 10 year cost of 10,000,000 pesos.
School, supply, control and administrative elements necessitated by above.

The cost of this plan, taking into account our best information on prices to be charged us by the U.S. for various classes of equipment, for the years 1938–45 inclusive is estimated by Jimmy and me to be 178 million pesos, or roughly 50,000,000 more than the 16 million annual average would provide. This was the information furnished by Jimmy to the Pres. (including 32 million for 1936–37).

The General states that this information, if true, makes him out to be either a fool or a knave, since his earliest promise to Mr. Q. was "that for 160,000,000 pesos, distributed over a 10 year period, he would make the P.I. so secure from attack, that no nation would deliberately undertake the enterprise". He further says—now—that this 160 million program represents the only plan he has ever entertained for a moment. He <u>says</u>, now, that he has not deviated from that determination, and has not projected any plan that would contravene such a determination, for a single instant in the 2-year interval.

On June 15, 1936, I presented to the General what was intended to be a protest against the 30 Division program, a memorandum in which the <u>certain minimum</u> costs were estimated. A copy of this estimate is in the office files. It showed a <u>certain</u> deficit of 45,000,000 pesos and showed also that the estimates in it were generally far below what it was considered necessary to provide under the 30 Division plan. The General refused flatly to modify or restrict the objectives of his organizational plan as outlined at the beginning of today's entry in this book. He made some prophecies that additional money would be forthcoming, either in the form of gifts in kind from the U.S., or lump sums from various Commonwealth Credits in the U.S. But finally he said that failing such windfalls, he was prepared to raise the yearly "ante" and demand more money by the appropriation route. When I inquired—which I did—as to how he would make such action jibe with his 160 million peso promise, he replied that figure was just an approximation, and that it was understood by all that some changes would be necessary. He said also that we had plenty of reasons to advance for hiking the budget—World Conditions, possible early independence, etc., etc. (And this was long before the possibility of early independence was publicly mentioned by Pres. Q.)

So we proceeded on the 30 Division plan at the specific and unequivocal order of the Field Marshal. The occasion for bringing the estimate to his attention at that time was an effort on the part of Jim and myself to secure modification of the Marshal's order to call 20,000 conscripts for training on Jan. 1, 1937. The original plan, (finally pared down by arbitrary action to the 160 million basis) called for training only 3000 men on January 1, 1937. The new order called for extraordinary and unforeseen expenditures as explained in a prior note in this book.[1]

The General was adamant. He gave Jim and me a long lecture on "adequacy of security" as represented by numbers of "divisions" trained and ready. We urged a budgetary basis for all planning, and he grew furious, accusing us of "arguing technicalities" to defeat the conceptions of the high command!

Now—suddenly—when confronted definitely with the loss of the Pres.'s confidence because of the increased costs, he not only abandons this expanded plan, he deliberately states he never approved it, formulated it, or even suggested it except as an expression of his hopes and ambitions. He told the Pres. (he says) that all portions of the plan that exceed the 160 million limit are nothing but the products of Jimmy and myself—produced without approval from him.

Every scrap of auxiliary evidence, letters, partial plans presented to the Gen., requisitions, and the direct testimony of Jimmy, General Santos and myself furnish ample proof that he is again executing one of his amazing "about faces".

We (J. and I) thoroughly approve of modifying the plan. We've fought for and urged such downward revision as is necessary to get within reasonable range of the 110,000,000 for 2 years. But it is amazing, mystifying and completely irritating to see him take the position that he had never directed anything else. In the "conference" I challenged him to show that I'd done anything not calculated to further his plans. Also, I informed him that never had he asked me whether or not I considered his plan a good one in its possibilities for defense of these islands. It's not important what I think of his plan, but from any subordinate's standpoint it is important when a senior charges "substitution of policy"—and virtual sabotage. He repeated over and over again his "personal" confidence in us, and, in words, accepted much of the blame for the misunderstanding. He simply "shouted down" any real explanation of my attitude.

But it was not a misunderstanding!

It is a deliberate scuttling of one plan (and blaming Jimmy and me as the sole originators, advocates and apostles of that plan, which we actually opposed bitterly) while he <u>adopts</u> another one, which in its concrete expression, at least, I've never even heard of before.

He invited us to apply for relief if we wouldn't go along with the new plan.

I'm not so concerned in that part of it since it's <u>his</u> responsibility to decide upon the main features of our defensive system. But I've got to decide soon whether I can go much further with a person who, either consciously or unconsciously, deceives his boss, his subordinates and himself (probably) so incessantly as he does. I wonder whether he believes there is one atom of truth in his statements of this morning. I wonder whether egotism, exclusive devotion to one's own interests, (in this case a 66,000 peso salary, plus penthouse and expenses) can finally completely eliminate a person's perception of honesty, straightforwardness, and responsibility to the people for whom he is working.

When irritated at the Pres. I've heard him curse that worthy as a "conceited little monkey," and I've heard him, in turn, use even worse language with respect to every prominent officer in the U.S. Army, and officials in Washington. But sometimes I think that, in his mind, there is nothing ridiculous, absurd or even unusual in his attitude. He was raised in the conception of Douglas MacArthur superiority. Actually he has become only pathetic. The barest mention of his name in the gossip column of the poorest of our universally poor daily periodicals sends him into hysterical delight or deepest despair, depending upon its note of praise or condemnation. He gets frantic in the face of difficulty, even if the difficulty is only an imaginary one and displays an exaggeration of glee when he believes things are shaping up to glorify his name, or increase his income.

I shall never forget the time in Washington when receipt of instructions to report to the President,[2] led him to conclude, in the greatest seriousness, that he was to be invited to be the President's running mate in the succeeding election. It is this trait that seems to have destroyed his judgment and led him to surround himself with people [. . .] who simply bow down and worship.

For some months, I've remained on this job, not because of the Gen.—but in spite of him. I've got interested in this riddle of whether or not we can develop a W. D. and an army capable of running itself, and I prefer to dig away at it to being on a "mark time" basis somewhere else. But now I'm at a cross road. If the Marshal is to persist in his arbitrary methods, and is going to make things as unpleasant, if not impossible, as his today's homily indicated, then I'm for home. We should be able to get a better line on the situation within a few days! Right now I'm disgusted and in something of a temper, a bad state of mind in which to make any decisions.

There was some justification for his anger over the presentation of the 50,000,000 "deficit" estimate to Mr. Q. But in our defense it is to be said that we've literally begged him to arrange a weekly conference between the Pres. and himself. But in the past he's been too high ranking to do so. Now he thinks his job (and emoluments) are at stake— and maybe he'll do it. Thank God I scarcely know the little devil (Q.) so neither now nor in the future do I have to discuss anything with him.

In the meantime, "Quien soba".[3]

1. See the March 24, 1936, entry.
2. The reference to "the President" is to President Herbert Hoover. By late 1934, MacArthur was persona non grata at the White House, in large part because of his open support of Hoover's political philosophy. It is unlikely that MacArthur would have presumed President Roosevelt would have selected him, particularly by 1935, when Roosevelt would have been thinking earnestly about his running mate for 1936.
3. The correct Spanish is *Quien sabe.*

OCTOBER 11

These notes were originally started more as an "aide memoir"—and as a matter of possible future interest have obviously become necessary as a protection against changes in orders and directives. Changes in plans are of course always necessary when the period for their execution extends over a decade, and their details include all the activities, agencies and requirements of a national army. Changes are not bad in themselves, but when there is met a flat denial that the original plan ever existed it is best to keep in written form, some record of the principal features of the orders and directives a subordinate is following in his daily work. It is a terrible way in which to work—and feeling that it is necessary to observe such a practice carries an implication that "Someone is crazy." Maybe the keeping of notes will reveal whether or not it is I.

115

MacArthur Memorial Archives
Personal Correspondence of General Douglas MacArthur

TO GENERAL DOUGLAS MACARTHUR

OCTOBER 13, 1937

Memorandum to the Military Advisor[1]

Herewith the draft of the suggested message from the President to the National Assembly as requested by you. You will note that its length runs somewhat in excess of my estimate, but I believe that the three factors you desire presented as reasons for the increased budget cannot be adequately analyzed in a much shorter paper.

[Draft] Two years ago I presented to this assembly a bill providing for the National Defense of the Philippines. The essential objectives of the plan laid down in my message of November 25, 1935 were as follows:

First, that the system of National Defense actually provide security;

Second, that it be adjusted to our fiscal possibilities;

Third, that the development of our defense progress gradually, so that, while attaining fruition in 10 years, the increased costs incident to intensified effort would be avoided.

At that time the aggregate cost of the National Defense Plan, approved by this Assembly, was estimated at 160,000,000 pesos to be disbursed over a period of 10 years.

Since that date certain fundamental changes in general world conditions, as well as in our own special situation, have transpired which I feel compelled to place before you in order to determine at this time, the will of the nation as regards further development of our national defense.

The fundamental changes I refer to are three: the gradual and continuous decline of national security throughout the world, the necessity for accelerating the development of our national defense to correspond with a possibly shorter Commonwealth period, and finally the substantial increase, since 1935, in prices of all raw materials, fabrications and services.

The consequence of these changes has been a probable increase in the development cost of our National Defense by the substantial sum of P50,000,000 which in view of present necessities and probably future conditions must be added to the P160,000,000.00 originally estimated.

Specifically the collapse of all international efforts to provide for security through cooperative agreements and machinery, has imposed upon us the necessity not only to hasten our original program as regards our land defenses but to add to it at an earlier date the necessary proportion of the air force and the off-shore patrol. These elements must soon be made instruments of positive protection against the violation of our territorial waters. A second, and most important consequence has been the effect of measures adopted by great producing countries intended to insure their own neutrality in future conflicts. These measures have, and in time of war will, greatly curtail the possibility of securing in time of threatened emergency armaments from abroad; hence the necessity for building up at once a substantial reserve of such armaments as cannot be provided or produced by ourselves.

The possible curtailment of the Commonwealth period means that we must be prepared to stand alone, not in ten years, but much sooner. This in turn makes it mandatory that we train more men immediately than was contemplated under the original plan, and that we provide the mobilization centers and the equipment for the reserve units which these men compose, not proportionately over a period of 10 years, but in conformity with the quickened training program.

Finally there is the effect of increased prices. The average increase in costs of supplies currently used by the Army and purchased locally has increased substantially over the bases used for the detailed estimate of 1935. For example, in construction, costs have exceeded estimates by more than forty-four percent. In the case of weapons, aeroplanes, and all types of land, sea and air armaments the increase in prices, responding to the feverish demand for these in countries where defensive preparations have practically attained an emergency basis, is equally noticeable.

Obviously I may not with propriety disclose, in a public document, information concerning either the extent, or the detailed character, of our National Defense. However, these have been made available to the members of the responsible committee of this Assembly.

I could compare these increased costs, in proportion to our annual revenue, with similar statistics of other countries and our position would still be favorable in this regard. But this is not the point, the question that we must answer is; do we, or do we not, need to pursue, as a minimum objective, the defense policies represented in this essentially modest and reasonable program. If we do, let us determine here and now to procure that degree of security.

I assure you that the regular force, that is, the professional elements employed to train and encadre the National Defense, has been kept not only within the original estimated strength but has been materially reduced, both in regard to officers and to enlisted men. Furthermore, regardless of the aggregate authorized for the full development of our National Defense, the annual appropriations will be adjusted each year to the annual revenue, so that all other authorized government services and activities may develop in harmony with the growth of the population and the expansion of our culture.

In conclusion I must draw your attention to the increasing peacetime use of the military organization as a means of advancing national welfare.

The past two years experience has disclosed a most unfavorable domestic condition as regards the standards of literacy and of vocational efficiency as well as certain almost universal physical defects among our young men. More and more of the trainees' time, and of the government's funds are being devoted to improving and correcting these conditions. Results have been encouraging. Statistics that furnish indisputable proof of this progress will be made available to the committee.

With the development of engineer training through the cadres I anticipate the time when great economies and added efficiency may be realized in our necessary public works program.

A bill will soon be presented to you providing for a direct and extensive participation of the Army in a program for expanding the population and developing our resources in Mindanao.

Our National Defense is unique, in that it provides for development of the nation's resources, improvement of the individual citizen, consolidation of the race, and finally, defense of the things and of the rights that are ours.

It is for the continuance and development of the project in this sense that I request your consideration and approval of the resolution presented herewith.

1. Quezon evidently asked MacArthur to draft the president's remarks to the General Assembly. MacArthur in turn gave the task to Eisenhower.

116

Eisenhower Library
Philippine Diary

OCTOBER 15, 1937–DECEMBER 21, 1937

OCTOBER 15

Memorandum for the Military Adviser

With respect to the order designating me as Chief of Staff I request instructions as to the exact status of certain officers assigned or attached to the Defense Mission.

It is my understanding that Captain Davis is serving in a dual capacity. On the one hand he is assigned as Aide de Camp to the Military Adviser and on the other as Adjutant General and Administrative Officer of the Mission. With respect to him my supervisory responsibility extends only to the second of these categories of duties.

Two officers who have not formerly operated, so far as I know, as integral parts of the general and technical staff of the Military Adviser are Major Hutter and Captain Fellers. The former has been regarded by me as a special assistant or Aide of the Military Adviser, the latter as an Aide to President Quezon. In the absence of instructions to the contrary no change will be made in this understanding nor any attempt be made to use either of these officers in technical or General Staff assignments in furthering the work of the Mission.

It is my further understanding that all other officers assigned or attached or detailed to additional duty to the Mission, except for any re-detailed to the Bureau of Aeronautics or detailed to the Bureau of Public Works, fall under the normal supervising and direct influence of the Chief of Staff in carrying out the policies of the Military Adviser.

An expression of your approval of this memorandum, or instructions as to any modification desired, is requested.[1]

1. On October 12, MacArthur issued a general order appointing "Lt. Col. Dwight D. Eisenhower Senior Assistant to the Military Adviser, and as Chief of Staff to the Military Adviser to the Commonwealth of the Philippines." When his designation as senior assistant was announced, Eisenhower took the initiative to determine whom he commanded and in what respect. Evidently, because of the state of affairs within the office structure and MacArthur's circumstances as field marshal, Eisenhower felt it necessary to establish the "working order" of the office. MacArthur replied in a handwritten note at the bottom of the memorandum: "Approved. If any special work on the part of the officers mentioned in par. 3 is desired by you, they will be made available on your request. MacArthur." See Philippine Diary, October 15, 1937, Eisenhower Library.

OCTOBER 15 [SECOND ENTRY]

The other day we got the Gen.'s order for retirement. The Pres. of the U.S. sent him a flowery telegram which was, of course, promptly released to the press. His retirement, to take effect on Dec. 31, will leave him a free agent so now he can continue to live in the Penthouse, draw his munificent salary—do no work—and be protected against possible transfer to another station.

In the "conference" the other day the Gen. announced that hereafter the yearly budget would be:

Reg. Army	8,000,000	
Trainees	4,000,000	
Air Corps	1,000,000	
Off-Shore	500,000	
Reserve supplies	3,000,000	(To equip all Divs)
Construction	200,000	
Education & Incidentals	200,000	
	16,900,000	

From here on we are to plan on 15 Res. Divs. instead of 30 and are to get 20,500,000 (or total of 25,000,000, including savings) to run us in 1938.

OCTOBER 18

Jim is on a trip to Hong Kong. Was offered a free ride the other day on a plane chartered by the Chinese minister of Finance—Kung. Expect him back today!

We had considerable excitement recently due to forced landings by three of our airplanes while they were returning from a southern island trip. On eastern shore of Luzon they ran into the edge of a typhoon area, and, practically out of gas, each had to seek a spot to get down. One plane reported in by wire within an hour of landing; the occupants of another reached a telegraph station two days later; while the third, perched on a tiny islet that was completely isolated by weather, was unreported from Monday noon until Friday morning. Unfortunately this plane, piloted by Lt. Lee, had Gen. Santos as one of the passengers (Segundo was the other). As a result headlines and all types of newspaper publicity centered around Santos and, this apparently irritated the President no end, who doesn't like to see someone else's name in the public prints.

He has written a letter to Santos demanding a full report on the whole trip with "whys", "whats", "whos", and etc., etc. The letter was drafted by [. . .] who in his usual bootlicking way, made its language as bitter, sarcastic and nearly intolerable [. . .] The Pres. even stooped to calling in a newspaper owner, Romulo,[1] and inspiring an editorial of criticism against Santos. The whole incident is apparently to be used to relieve Santos, if possible, so they are working up an artificial sentiment of resentment toward him.

Actually the facts and reasons are simple.

The President wrote Santos a letter two months ago directing the destruction of all Moro cottas.[2] Santos got the original order considerably modified in favor of reason and moderation, but it was still sufficiently severe to arouse Moro antagonism and sporadic revolt. A few of them gathered in a cotta at Lanao and trouble started which constantly grew more serious. Calls for help came from the local constabulary and finally Santos conferred at length with MacA. It was agreed to send down additional land forces, to get three planes ready for tactical operation in case of necessity, and to have Santos go down by plane to make an extensive survey of the situation.

Gen. MacA. fully agreed that Santos should go. The reasons were several:

1. Santos is intimately acquainted with the country and the people.
2. It was necessary to get first-hand information concerning the seriousness of the situation.
3. It was obviously necessary to coordinate the plans and efforts of the army with those of the Governor-Commissioner of Mindanao, etc.

Gen. MacA. was the one who insisted that the planes, if they went, should be equipped for action. Jim and I have advised Santos to sit quietly, saying nothing except to answer the letter plainly, truthfully and without apology. He used his judgment and did the best he could.

I cannot believe anyone will try to carry the thing too far. But I notice the Gen. says the only error made in the whole incident was the "decision to return to Manila". This decision was, of course, Santos' own so if that was the only error, he alone bears the responsibility!!!

1. Romulo, noted author and journalist, served as vice president and publisher of People's Press, a newspaper chain. He worked on several Philippine newspapers and also served on the faculty of the University of the Philippines. In 1942 he won a Pulitzer Prize for his assessment of the military situation in the area surrounding the Philippines. During World War II he became an aide to General MacArthur on Corregidor. His radio broadcasts were known as the "Voice of Freedom." He returned to the Philippines in 1944 with MacArthur, as resident commissioner of the Philippines to the United States (1944–46). He then served as chief of the Philippine Mission to the United Nations (1946); president of the U.N. General Assembly (1949–50); Ambassador to the United States (1951); and on the U.N. Security Council (1956). In 1953 he ran for the presidency of the Philippines but withdrew to manage the campaign for the successful Ramón Magsaysay. Appointed president of the University of the Philippines in 1962, he resigned to serve as secretary of education under President Ferdinand Marcos.

2. The Moros (so named by the Spanish, who had expelled the Moors from their country) were Muslim Filipinos native to Mindanao and other southern islands who had been converted to Islam before Spain's seizure of the Philippines. From the sixteenth century onward they fought Spanish rule, allying at one time with the Dutch, who contested Spain for dominance in the archipelagos off southeast Asia. Spain's efforts to bring Catholicism to the islands was at the root of the Moro rebellion. Although Spain quelled the principal Moro opposition by conquering Jolo in 1850, groups of Moro guerrillas continued to harass not only Spanish authority but eventually American—and even Filipino—authority as well. *Cottas* were small fortresses, often with trapdoors underneath, used as bases from which the rebels harassed the Philippine Constabulary.

Today I'm starting on an inspection trip to the South. I'll see Dist. Commander at Iloilo, Cebu and Zamboanga. Will also visit Jolo. Mamie and Johnny are going along.

The other day Jim and I gave the General separate memo on the effect of his budgetary orders. That is, we attempted to translate financial limitations into limitations in activities. Jim softened his own opinions by estimating a possibility of cutting down on personnel "painlessly" and "gradually". I didn't. I put down in actual figures the extent of the lopping off, eliminating and discharging we'd have to do at an early date. Naturally these facts (and they are facts, as J. fully and completely agrees) were unpleasant, but the issue was ducked with the remark, to J., that my paper was a perfect example of a <u>poor</u> staff memo—since it showed how <u>not to do</u>!!! The truth, facts, hard facts, are the most unpopular items we deal with. We're like a bunch of skaters on thin ice, going faster and faster to keep from falling through, and always desperately looking for some lucky break that will carry us to firm footing. The "higher ups" apparently think they'll fool the public into believing we are not exceeding our budget because the Military Bill itself will carry only 16,900,000. The 5–6 millions of construction money we have to get this year and next are to be carried on "Public Works Appropriation," and we now take the attitude that we never, in our original calculations, intended to count construction as a military cost, when the Gen. said, for 160,000,000, spent over 10 years, he'd give this country the finest defense possessed by any of its size in the world!! Jim and I fought the 160,000,000 figure until we were told to keep still. We proved then that an army of, Regulars, 1000 Off. and 10,000 men, and Reserves, of an aggregate strength of 300,000 could not be developed and sustained on that amount. We begged and begged the Gen. to stick by the original plan, which would not have called 20,000 trainees for each half class until 1941. We argued that the cutting of our original estimates, (min. 220,000,000) had brought us to the danger line even without a single increase in expenditures, but we were over-ridden for "psychological reasons". Now—faced with the facts once more—the answer is again one with which we hope to fool someone—rather than one by which everyone could honestly and surely proceed to do the best we can!

The reason why a "phoney" decision may not get immediately found out is because the last assembly voted for us, for this coming year, 21,500,000 aside from 3,700,000 construction money. So, we can carry on this year at the present pace. But during the year we are to stop enlistments, discharge the lower classes of trainees, cut down on officers, and by every expedient presumably work down to a personnel strength in all categories that, by Jan. 1, 39, can be sustained on a 16,900,000 budget. To confuse someone, we'll call a number that we'll roughly refer to as 20,000 (the actual number will be 18,500) but by Feb. 1, we will, through discharges get down to 16,000. The hope is that no one will notice this. We won't get rid of officers, we'll just refrain from calling in those we bitterly need. We won't discharge enlisted men, we'll just refuse to make any original enlistments. These measures will not suffice to bring down costs to the indicated level, even if the General's hope is realized that no one will suspect we are not carrying on our military activities on the scale that he so freely and assiduously advertised 18 months ago.

Sooner or later there must be a day of reckoning. That, I suspect will come "sooner". This because of the fact that we must immediately prepare and submit the 1939 budget. In that document we must show how many men, officers and trainees are to be paid, and unless there is some more fancy confusing of the issue, the truth, or part of it, must come out!!!! We'll see.

From the beginning Jim and I have been practically isolated in thought, attitude, and intention. We did not want to come to the P.I. but were willing to do so because we thought we'd have a wonderful professional opportunity. Once on the job we've concerned ourselves with trying to develop for this gov't and country the best possible army with the means at hand. We have been beset on all sides by difficulties arising from personal ambition, personal glorification, personal self-ishness of the hot shot (66,000 pesos a year and a penthouse), etc., etc. When we have objected strenuously to measures which we believe un-wise such as the Field Marshal-ship; the 1937 calling of 20,000 trainees; the 1938 boosting of the budget; we've been finally told to shut up.

In spite of it all, I believe we've done fairly well under the conditions. But our work will be evaluated, not in the light of conditions as they are, but in that of conditions as the uninformed <u>think</u> they are.

117
NARA
Records of the Adjutant General's Office

To COMMANDING GENERAL, PHILIPPINE DEPARTMENT[1]

JANUARY 14, 1938

The recommendations of Major Prosser[2] as given in the basic com-munication have been made with a view of establishing an adequate inspection service for commercial airplanes in the Philippines. While obviously this duty will eventually fall on Filipinos it is equally appar-ent that a considerable period of training and of practical experience will be necessary before any of them can qualify for this highly tech-nical and important work. In the meantime the frequent replacement of the noncommissioned officers detailed from the American Army constitutes a serious handicap to development of efficiency in this ser-vice. It is therefore requested that Major Prosser's recommendations be approved.[3]

1. Lucius R. Holbrook.
2. This probably was Harvey W. Prosser, who joined the Aviation Section, Army Signal Corps, in 1917 and was commissioned in 1920.
3. According to the adjutant general records, the request was approved.

118

To Emily Ord

JANUARY 31, 1938[1]

Dearest Emily: I am sick in the hospital[2] but, even so, perhaps I can give you a few answers to the thousands of questions that must be torturing your mind in connection with Jimmy's tragic end. So far as possible, I will keep my personal feelings of bewilderment, loss and grief out of this letter so as to avoid beclouding facts—of which you must feel a burning need—by introduction of my own emotions.

For some days Jimmy had been counting on going to Baguio for a conference with the Commandant and staff of a new school we are just establishing there. To dovetail this visit with all his other work he finally decided to go up Sunday morning, hold the conference early Monday, and return to Manila before noon that day. He wanted to go reasonably early on Sunday as the Fairchilds (to whom you know he was devoted) were having some sort of anniversary that day, and he wanted very much to join them.

Yesterday, before leaving, he came to see me at the hospital. We talked of the projected trip, of his time of return, of his physical examination (just completed satisfactorily) and made a date for another meeting here at the hospital for today (Monday). He left me at about 8:50. He took off from the field in a BT at 9:10 and crashed at 10:15. The immediate scene of the accident was near the Fairchilds'[3] home in Baguio, not far from Mansion House. Jimmy had written a message to drop from the plane to the Fairchild family, asking them to send a car to the airport to pick him up. He instructed the pilot (Lieut. Cruz, a very fine flyer with whom many of us ride regularly) to fly low over the house so as to attract attention. They then circled back near the house once more, but Jimmy was anxious to drop the message right in the yard, so instead of letting it go he indicated his desire to go back over the house once more. In order to find out what was wanted the pilot throttled down the ship and turned his head to look back at the exact spot Jimmy wanted to cross. During this maneuver the ship lost some altitude, which may have been accentuated by down-drafts coming over the hills back of the house. The result was that when the pilot pushed open the throttle the ship stalled momentarily, and struck a tree on the hillside back of the house. Jimmy, naturally, was leaning as far out the side as possible in order to determine whether anyone was watching for the message he intended, almost immediately, to drop. So instead of being squarely in his seat, facing the front, the crash caught his body in a twisted, unprotected position and dashed him against the instrument board and fuselage. The pilot was practically unhurt, but Jimmy was injured internally—the end coming about two hours later in the Camp John Hay Hospital. Colonel Clarke and Dr. Walker were with him, and so far as I can learn from the meager reports, he regained partial consciousness for only an instant. He said nothing other than to ask them to watch his leg. Immediately upon receipt of the report we sent a rush telegram to some relatives of yours in Washington with whom Clays happen to be acquainted. This morning we have an answer to the effect that you were notified while at the Cocrofts in Fort Monroe.

From here on this letter will deal primarily with tentative plans for the future, and any feature of these may be somewhat modified before its execution through exchanges of radiograms between you and some of us here.

We plan a military funeral, with full honors. This information I asked TJ to send you this morning via radio so that we could observe your desires as to the church at which to hold the service. The necessary official things have been done through Boards and so on. Captain Clay has been appointed Summary Court to collect, inventory and safeguard all effects.

Ronnie Straight and Mr. Selph[4] have both come here, at my request, to give me some idea of the status of Jimmy's local investments. A copy of a will was found by Mr. Selph (we assume you have the original) which makes you and The Union Trust Co. of Washington, D.C., joint executors. Ronnie Straight informs me that as a result of a lot of hard work on Jimmy's part his stock prospects have just reached the point where the future holds real promise. Of course, I know that Jimmy had some dealings with Mr. Descals and Mr. Corea, to say nothing of Gordon MacKay[5] and others. These men I have not seen and can make no estimate of how things stand as a whole. But I rather believe that his Syndicate Investment and Mine Operations holdings (Ronnie Straight enterprises) represent the majority of his stock interests here, and I am hopeful that they will be not only reasonably easy to straighten out, but will yield you something decent as well.

All of us are desperately anxious to do anything and everything in our power that may, in some small way, ease your burdens. We are still suffering from shock, our minds are not functioning as efficiently as they might, but our hearts are with you—and with Tish and young Jim. Mamie and I in particular would like so much to help. So don't hesitate to radio us freely through the A.G.O.

The Clipper schedule has been badly disrupted lately. But I heard there's one due to leave here on the 3rd or 4th, so I'll send this to the office to get it typed (Otherwise you can't read it) and get it into the mail promptly.

With the deepest love and sympathy of the Eisenhower family, Devotedly

1. This was written the day after Ord's death in a plane accident. (See diary entry of February 15, 1938.) Ord's death greatly upset Eisenhower. He would speak many times later of Ord's outstanding service. Eisenhower wrote several letters about the accident to his friends and Ord's. In addition to those included here was one to Ord's sister, Mrs. E. T. Spencer, written on March 26, 1938 (Pre-pres. Papers). Most of his writings are similar in nature, explaining in great detail the cause of the accident and highly praising Ord.

A photostat of this letter was found in a file of early Eisenhower writings collected in the late 1960s by the Johns Hopkins University Eisenhower Papers Project. Unlike other items in the file, this document is not annotated with its source. It is possible that a former researcher with the project obtained the copy from one of Ord's relatives.

2. Eisenhower had been in Sternberg Hospital, Manila, from January 28 to February 2 with gastrointestinal distress. During the 1938 episode the acute attack was so severe that the surgeons were about to operate when the crisis resolved itself spontaneously.

3. The Fairchilds could have been either George H. Fairchild, president of Welch Fairchild, a sugar executive, or Kirby Fairchild, sales manager for Libby, McNeil and Libby (Philippines).

4. Ronnie Straight apparently was chief executive officer of Syndicate Investments of Manila.

Ewald E. Selph arrived in the Philippines in 1919, where he operated a successful law practice. He served as general counsel, American Chamber of Commerce of the Philippines, and was a prominent civic leader in Manila.

5. Ricardo Descals served as chief accountant, Campania General de Tabacos de Filipinas, and treasurer, Central Azucarera de Bais and Central Azucarera de Tarlac.

Gordon W. MacKay, a partner in MacKay and McCormick, stock and bond brokers, served on the board of directors of the Northern Mining and Development Company and as treasurer of the Manila Stock Exchange.

119

FEBRUARY 15, 1938[1]

On Sunday, Jan. 30, Jimmy Ord was killed in an airplane accident. I was in Sternberg Hosp. at the time, and Jim visited me about one hour before the crash, which occurred at Baguio. He was having his pilot maneuver low among the hills so he could drop a note to the Fairchilds, asking them to send a car for him to the airport. The pilot was uninjured in the crash. From testimony of the pilot, and from the two other officers who were in an accompanying plane, it is obvious that the accident was the result of a combination of unfortunate circumstances, rather than of any one particular thing.

The plane came in from Manila, flew over house, while J. pointed out its location to pilot. Pilot circled back, losing altitude, so J. could drop note. Pilot stayed on down hill side of house apparently not wanting to close in on hills too much. Jim leaned forward from his seat, tapping pilot on right shoulder (seen from accompanying plane and testified to by pilot) and pointing to right rear, toward the house. Obviously, in order to see what J. wanted the pilot dropped his right wing a bit, thus turning toward hills. He also looked back, and in doing so probably unconsciously pulled stick back a little, thus flattening glide and approaching a stall. Upon looking to front he saw trees ahead and his plane settling. Unquestionably he gave it the gun and pulled up the nose—a spin resulted.

The pilot was square in ship, Jim was leaning out as far as he could to right. As a consequence the left buckle of his belt broke and he was snapped against front of cockpit. Pilot was unhurt.

Jim had a world of friends here. The cathedral was crowded at the funeral; floral offerings filled the whole front of the church. Many, many people have lost a close companion and an intimate friend. I've lost this, also my right hand, and my partner on a tough job, who furnished most of the inspiration needed to keep me plugging away. With him gone much of the zest has departed from a job that we always tackled as a team, never as two individuals.

Office life has been hectic. I got out of the hospital in time for J's funeral and immediately plunged over my head into work. Some of it I'd kept up while in the hospital but new problems arose that were anything but easy.

Carry-over problems were:
Devising of plan for transferring Constab. to state police—in such a way as to save us (the Army) about 3,000,000 per year.

Development of recommendations on proposals to establish a commercial air ways system.

Preparation of lists of Res. Off. recommended for transfer to Regulars.

All of these were crowded with grief and hard, detailed work.

A new problem was the establishment of a workable basis for communications between this office and Dept. Hq. conforming to War Dept. instructions as to changes in administrative status of officers detailed to Commonwealth. This one would not have been so terribly difficult except for the attitude of the General. He was so fearful that the matter would so develop as to glorify my position as the senior officer (active) on duty with the Commonwealth that he found "sinister" motives in every solution proposed. Back and forth to Malacañan and to Dept. Hq. I went, then forth and back! Finally, I hope, the matter is settled and the Gen. satisfied! The position of the Dept. Staff has been entirely reasonable and sympathetic—but Gen. solves all difficulties from one viewpoint only—personal aggrandizement.

A few days ago Geo. Vargas told me that the Commonwealth Govt. wants to increase my per diem, in order to assure I was paid more than any other American Officer on duty with the Govt. (except of course the Gen.) and to recognize value of my two years service here. He proposed doubling my per diem, a most acceptable suggestion to me!! The Gen. made a counter proposal to raise me 5 pesos at end of 2½ years, then five more at end of 3½. He said that the 30 pesos per diem of a captain in the office could not be used as any standard of comparison as that was agreed to only on a "hold-up" deal. Actually he could have had no other reason than wanting to get rid of me—his fear that someone else might be recognized as a valuable man by governmental officials [. . . .] For the past few months the Gen. has missed no chance to insinuate things to me about Jim—and to Jim and TJ about me. Because he knows we <u>know</u> he had prevaricated in his administration of the defense plan, for the sole purpose of assuring his hold (as he estimated the situation) on 66,000 pesos <u>and</u> a penthouse, <u>and</u> all expenses, he has come to regard us as a menace to him and his soft berth. Actually we've done nothing to damage him. More than once, at Malacañan I've explained away some silly idea and tried to make him look good. The popular notion of his great ability as a soldier and leader, is, of course, not difficult to explain to those that know how war time citations were often secured. These, plus direct intervention of Sec. Baker to give him his first star (Regular) have been parlayed, with the help of a magnificent front both vocal and in appearances to a reputation of wisdom, brilliance and magnificent leadership.

1. Because of Eisenhower's stay in the hospital, he did not make his diary entry recounting Ord's death until nearly two weeks after the accident.

120

Eisenhower Library
Floyd L. Parks Papers

To Floyd Parks[1]

February 28, 1938

Dear Floyd: I heard just this morning that you are now aide to the Chief of Staff. It always delights me when I hear of any new assignment of yours that by its nature confirms my first impressions of twenty years ago as to your ability and personality. I have always considered it bad luck, on my part, that we were separated so soon after the war, and have since been denied opportunity to serve together. As aide to General Craig you are not only holding an important post, you are working for a leader from whom you will absorb a lot that will always stand you in good stead.

I am told that you are as baldheaded as I am. That scarcely seems possible, and must be akin to slander, because the flies have used my head as a skating rink for many years.

Recently I wrote a note to Colonel Eichelberger,[2] asking him to say "howdy" for me to old friends in the Department. But at that time I had no idea you were on duty there, or I would surely have mentioned you specially.

Drop me a line when you can, and pay my respects to your Chief.[3]
Cordially

1. Floyd Parks served in the Tank Corps under Eisenhower at Camp Colt. In 1938 he worked with the General Staff. His association with Eisenhower continued in World War II, when he served as Chief of Staff, Army Ground Forces (June 1942 to February 1943) and as assistant division commander, 69th Infantry Division. In August 1944 he was appointed Chief of Staff, and then commander, of the First Allied Airborne Army. He later commanded the U.S. sector, Berlin.

2. Robert Lawrence Eichelberger (USMA, 1909) served on the General Staff from 1921 to 1924 and from 1935 to 1938. From 1938 to 1940 he commanded the 30th Infantry at the Presidio and from 1940 to 1942 served as superintendent of West Point. In 1942 he assumed command of the 77th Infantry Division and later that year headed the I Corps in the New Britain, New Guinea, and Philippine reoccupation campaigns. He retired in 1948 as a lieutenant general.

3. On March 16, 1938, Parks wrote back to Eisenhower that he looked back on their

> association with great pleasure and have always been grateful to you for the wise counsel and advice which you always gave me, as well as for the many boosts and opportunities which came my way from your hands. I have told many people that I have served at a number of posts in the past twenty years and none of them had a better commanding officer or was better administered than Camp Colt, which you commanded. When I think of those days and how hard we all worked to put the tanks on the map, I feel very proud of the whole outfit. Some day maybe the gods of war will let me serve under you again. I have always hoped for such an assignment and perhaps it will be a reality. (Parks to Eisenhower, March 16, 1938, Parks Papers, Eisenhower Library).

APRIL 6

Following Jimmy's death the Gen. conceived the idea of using Fellers in an effort to <u>prove</u> that the Philippines can be defended on P16,000,000 per year generally along the lines of his 40,000 trainee program. So he took the 1938 budget and started cutting it, to produce a typical budget, at the same time that he did this he revived his advocacy of a large number of divisions—now using the number 90 to limit the ultimate 30-year objective. His statements about the Air Corps and the off-shore patrol are less definite; he contents himself with saying the former will receive 1,000,000 per year, the second, 750,000.

The Air Corps officials have worked out, in great detail, a cost estimate of producing by 1946 an Air Force of a total of 93 planes divided as follows:

Heavy Bombers	16
Light Bombers	13
Obs. or attack	26
Long Range Patrol	2
Transports	5
Pursuit	15
Primary Trainers	12
Basic Trainer	4

The cost of these airplanes alone, less spare parts, supplies, armament, etc., is <u>8,832,000</u> pesos. The Air Corps officials figure that other necessary expenditures, chargeable to Air Corps items of the budget (except that we might charge all armament and ammunition to ordnance) will run this cost to approx. 18,000,000 pesos. This does not count personnel costs, subsistence, trans., or any other item charged against general costs.

So we see that to obtain an Air Corps of only <u>72 tactical</u> ships (a much smaller force than the hypothetical one of 250 of which the Gen. has so often spoken) we must set aside 2,000,000 pesos a year for the next 9 years.

To get money for trainees, etc., etc. in the "typical budget" there has been cut also all such items as transportation, (including motors, animals, and all maintenance costs) Q.M. and other supplies, etc., etc. We are throwing out officers and using probationary 3rd Lts. because the latter are cheaper. We are stopping all enlistments in the Reg.

Force, although every station in the islands is crying for more men on a permanent basis.

When it came to the item we have heretofore carried as "mobilization equipment," we were arbitrarily ordered to cut it to P1,000,000 per year. Out of this we are to provide the equipment for 3 reserve divisions per year.

Although we allegedly train almost 40,000 per year only half is to be supplied with equipment. The original plan contemplated that when a man graduated from training camp he was to be provided with his individual set of clothing, arms and other equipment which would be fitted, packed and stored at the mob. center to which his reserve co. was assigned. Now we accept the idea that we can count upon only a certain percentage reporting when called, thus defeating any idea of fitting and storing individual sets. In other words, since the Gen. will not abandon the 40,000 trainee program, he has adopted a doctrine that we must pass this number through the camps in order to get 20,000 effective.

I suggested a return to our original plan, (Jim's and mine) of training only 20,000 yearly and making the camps of 10 months duration. This thought got no consideration. So we will continue to spend trainee money that should be saved for other purposes. Extra transportation, clothing and many other incidental expenses are involved, and individual efficiency is sacrificed.

Within the past few weeks I've had several talks with the President. I find that there are a number of things he wants to do, most of which strike me as being most sensible.
1. He wants to include in all R.O.T.C. courses a short tour of training in regular cadres. I wrote directives & etc., to accomplish.
2. He wants to place all trainee duty, beyond the normal 5½ months, on a voluntary basis but accepted my recommendation that in attempting this we should pay such individuals an extra 5 pesos per month. He has submitted an amendment to the Assembly on this.
3. He wants to separate the Constab. from the rest of the Army, carrying it on a separate budget, I wrote the bill & message to accomplish this. He has not yet sent it to assembly. This would be a fine thing for the Army!
4. He wants to place all officers transferred from Reserves to the Regulars on a probationary status for one year, giving them, in the meantime, a fixed place on the promotion list & the usual prerequisites, privileges & rights of Reg. Officers. I wrote an approval, in this concept, for the list of officers recently recommended for transfer. He has not yet acted on it. But he is quite right in assuming that determination of relative efficiency among these people is a most difficult thing to do.

Recently I have been nagging at Malacañan to get before the Assembly the many bills in which the Army is interested.

The Courts-Martial Bill

The list of Amendments to the N.D.C.[1]

Our arrangements do not work smoothly with Malacañan. The Gen. does not desire me to seek contacts with the Pres.—in fact has directed me to ignore the President's general invitation to "drop in on him often". But the Gen. himself won't do it—so things just hang fire!

1. Philippine National Defense Council.

Major R. K. Sutherland[1] reported for duty with us on March 27. He is an excellent officer & I expect him to take a huge burden off my shoulders. He is rapidly familiarizing himself with our problems and will be ready to go to work soon. We got him on my recommendation to Gen.

1. Richard K. Sutherland served in World War I, then held a number of posts with the War Department General Staff. He joined MacArthur's staff as a replacement for James Ord. MacArthur would appoint Sutherland chief of staff when Eisenhower returned to the states in December 1939. Sutherland would hold that position under MacArthur through World War II, advancing to the rank of lieutenant general. He retired in 1946.

This morning I intend flying to Baguio for a short visit with John. Mr. Vargas is going up & I'm taking advantage of the opportunity to get a ride.

Sutherland is absorbing budget & supply, with Harrison reporting to him as U.S. property officer & officer in direct contact with the Supply Services. I think the arrangement will work out fine. Dick Sutherland is an able, conscientious man, with plenty of sense. He'll keep his fingers in things. Right now he is working with Santos on plans for transfer of Constabulary to independent status.

I expect to leave on 4 months trip to States on July 26. Will visit: Chief of Ord., Chief of Staff, W.D., Adjutant General's office.

American Armament	- N.J.	
Stearman Aircraft	- Wichita	Shaeffer[1]
Beechcraft	- Wichita	Shaeffer
Remington Arms	- Conn.	Mr. Nelson
Benning	- Ga.	
Lockheed	- Calif.	

1. Julius Earl Schaefer (USMA, 1917), spelled with only one *f*, a native of Wichita, Kansas, knew Eisenhower casually at West Point. Schaefer was a plebe in 1914, Eisenhower's fourth year. Eisenhower's roommate, Paul Hodgson, was Schaefer's upperclassman mentor. In 1927 he joined the Stearman Aircraft Company, where two years later he became sales manager, a position he held until Boeing's absorption of Stearman in 1938. He then became general manager, Stearman Division, Boeing Aircraft. From 1941 to 1957 he served as vice president of Boeing and general manager of the Wichita Division. Schaefer may have offered Eisenhower a civilian job.

122   United States Military Academy Library
Sixty-Ninth Annual Report of the Association of Graduates[1]

JUNE 13TH, 1938

The most intimate of his associates in the final Philippine Tour was Lt. Colonel Dwight D. Eisenhower, who, like Colonel Ord, was assistant to the Military Adviser to the Philippine Commonwealth Government. He pictures those closing years and the ultimate tragedy as follows:[2]

General MacArthur and his staff arrived in the Philippines in late October, 1935, and, from the very beginning, Jimmy plunged into the new task with enthusiasm and energy. His linguistic ability, his magnetic personality, and his genuine liking for people soon made him a great favorite in all circles of Manila official and social life. I have heard many people say that in the two and a half years of Jimmy's sojourn in this city he made and held more friends than could be claimed by any other individual in the Islands.

So far as his duties were concerned Jimmy was an enthusiast. He worked all the time, at all hours, and was thoroughly convinced of the feasibility of developing, in ten years, a Philippine Army of respectable strength and efficiency. He often told me that he wanted to stay here until he could feel personally sure that the venture was to be a success.

In spite of heavy duties and responsibilities of an official nature, Jimmy always found time to engage in a variety of other activities. He interested himself in local business affairs and was a member of the Board of Directors of one or two Philippine Corporations. He belonged to practically every club in the city, his principal recreation being golf and riding.

Our work with the Philippine army required frequent trips to many sections of the islands. Because of the time consuming nature of ordinary transportation we got in the habit of using airplanes for these visits. His death occurred on this kind of a trip to Baguio. Jimmy decided suddenly to make the journey and to assure that an automobile would come to Baguio airport to pick him up, asked his pilot to fly over the house of a friend in the city so that he, Jimmy, could drop a note. The topography there is rather rough and in maneuvering to bring the plane directly over the house the pilot momentarily lost control and the ship crashed against the adjacent hillside. Two hours later Jimmy died of internal injuries.

It is quite impossible to give you an accurate description of the sense of shock that pervaded the city. Many oldtimers told me that his funeral was attended by the largest crowd that ever turned out in Manila on a similar occasion. So far as I am personally concerned, his loss was more than disastrous.

Even yet, three months after his death, I cannot fully realize that he is never again to come walking into the office with his cheery, "Top of the morning, Comra-a-ade!"

1. The opening paragraph was the introduction to Eisenhower's memorial of Ord.

2. Eisenhower was asked to write the memorial for the annual report of the Association of West Point Graduates. MacArthur, Quezon, and others also submitted memorials that were included in the publication. Eisenhower's handwritten draft is in the West Point archives. See *Sixty-Ninth Annual Report of the Association of Graduates of the United States Military Academy at West Point, New York, June 13, 1938* (Newburgh, N.Y.: Moore Printing, 1938), 276–77.

123   Eisenhower Library
                                                  Philippine Diary

JUNE 18, 1938

The General has been extraordinarily sympathetic, increasingly so, with my views, opinions, and personal situation. At one time it seemed almost impossible to discuss with him any point in which there was the slightest difference of opinion, but for the past few months this has not been so. He is willing to talk over things—and his answer is more often than not, "as to that I'll accept your judgment." It is difficult to believe that Jimmy's loss should have occasioned this change, but the fact is, that ever since then he has progressively grown more mellow, less arbitrary and less ready to allege sinister motive for every mere difference of opinion.

He has been particularly nice with respect to my trip to the States. Stated categorically that I deserved a rest—hoped I'd get a good one— was sorry that necessities of John's schooling would bring me back before I had a real chance to relax. Was delighted that the Govt. intends to give me a good travel allowance, and even stated, "Nothing that occurs around here with respect to you is to be considered a precedent.

In all respects you represent a special case, and it is my hope to keep you here a long time." The atmosphere has cleared to such an extent that this job, at long last, has become personally agreeable as well as professionally interesting.

I leave on <u>Coolidge</u>, June 26, with Mamie and John. Hooray!![1]

1. Eisenhower traveled to the United States to secure arms, ammunition, and matériel for the Philippine army.

CHAPTER SIX

From the Philippines to the War Department
June 26, 1938–December 12, 1941

Germany having invaded Poland, in September 1939 President Roosevelt supported a $552 million defense spending budget and two months later ended the arms embargo to the Allies. In January 1940—despite still-strong isolationism in the country—Congress approved a $3.46 billion defense bill and approved lend-lease to Great Britain.[1]

In the Far East, Japan's conflict with China and aggression in Indochina renewed concerns for the Philippines and raised again the possibility of a major conflict between the United States and Japan. Expansion of the war into Southeast Asia threatened, among other things, the American supply of raw rubber (though guayule rubber evidently never became an emergency source of rubber, Eisenhower's earlier inspection of the rubber shrubs in California and Mexico must have seemed fortuitous). Most planners considered the Philippines indefensible; the War Department paid scant attention to the work of the Military Mission. Not until early 1941 did the administration increase assistance to the Philippines. MacArthur unrealistically believed his forces could withstand any attack.

Isolated in the Philippines, Eisenhower expressed his concern that war was inevitable. He hoped that he would not sit it out in the states as he had done in World War I. Between late June and early November 1938, Eisenhower visited the United States to procure arms and munitions for the Commonwealth Army. He found—as had Ord on an earlier visit—the War Department's complacency toward the Philippine situation astonishing. Stopping briefly at Fort Lewis, Washington, to visit Maj. Mark Wayne Clark,[2] he voiced a wish to return to the United States, a wish that deepened when, disembarking at Manila, Eisenhower found that MacArthur had reorganized his staff and eliminated most of his duties as chief adviser. Frustration with his work and degenerating relations with MacArthur made Eisenhower increasingly impatient to leave. He, Clark, and Brig. Gen. James Ulio—a friend of both men who then served in the adjutant general's office—began searching for ways to obtain a posting for Eisenhower in the United States.

Meanwhile MacArthur's operational relations with the Philippine president had not improved and created major difficulties. Eisenhower's Philippine Diary registered not only his own professional dissatisfactions but also Quezon's growing trust in Eisenhower. The Philippine president came to rely more and more on his advice, often in a clandestine manner.

Eisenhower and his family finally returned home to the United States in December 1939. Shortly afterward, anguished at the money he had to spend on new uniforms, he wrote in his diary that perhaps the "only way out" was to retire. But, he wrote, "guess I am hardly ready to do that."[3] Fortunately, he wrote in jest. The service that followed at Fort Lewis, Washington, and Fort Sam Houston with the Third Army placed Eisenhower back in the mainstream of army life. His service as Gen. Walter Krueger's Chief of Staff during maneuvers late in the summer of 1941 focused attention on his abilities and won him his first general's star.

On December 12, 1941, the brigadier received a phone call ordering him to the War Department, then seemingly caught unprepared for total war. Emergency mobilization, procurement of matériel, and development of strategic plans all had to be accomplished virtually overnight. Eisenhower arrived in Washington on December 14 and soon reported to Gen. George C. Marshall as Deputy Chief of Staff in charge of the Pacific and Far East section, War Plans Division. As his first assignment he worked on plans for the relief of the Philippines and other Pacific islands. Eisenhower brought with him proven organizational, logistical, and strategic skills. The time was right for him.

1. On 1939–40 defense spending, see Allan R. Millett and Peter Maslowski, *For the Common Defense: A Military History of the United States of America* (New York: Free Press, 1984), 394–98.

2. Two years junior to Eisenhower at the academy, Clark (USMA, 1917), who would become a close friend and ally of Eisenhower, was a decorated World War I officer who had moved upward quickly in the army and for a brief period in 1941 outranked Eisenhower, receiving his first general's star about two months before his friend. Clark, whose friends knew him as Wayne, assisted Eisenhower in obtaining orders to leave the Philippines. They served together at Fort Lewis in 1940 and in the Louisiana Maneuvers of 1941. Clark later served in a variety of positions under Eisenhower in England and North Africa. Eisenhower appointed him to direct the Italian campaign as commanding general of the U.S. Fifth Army. In 1952 President Eisenhower relied on Clark, then Commander in Chief, United Nations Command, Far East, to end the Korean War stalemate.

3. Philippine Diary, January 25, 1940, Eisenhower Library.

JUNE 26, 1938–AUGUST 21, 1938

JUNE 26

Sailed from Manila on time, 5:00 P.M. Quarters 105–107. Sitting at Captain Ahlin's table. Deposited with purser, cash $360, traveler's checks, two packages, $3,000 and $1,010, also watch and chain.

JUNE 28

Docked at Hong Kong at 8:00 A.M. Went to Repulse Bay Hotel. One large room for the three of us. Exchange rate = 3.20 Mex. for $1.00 American. Forty Mexican dollars per day. Scheduled to leave here at 9:00 P.M., June 30.

JUNE 29

Bridge club—Bill Z.—Santos—Garcia—Lim—Segundo. Wrote notes to General MacA, Santos, Garcia, Lim, Segundo.

JUNE 30

Left Hong Kong 9:00 P.M., June 30. Have written to TJ.

JULY 4

Arrived Kobe, 1:00 P.M. Left Kobe, 10:00 P.M.

JULY 5

Arrived Yokohama, 5:45 P.M. Left Yokohama, 12:00 midnight.

JULY 13

Arrived Honolulu, 9:00 A.M. Left Honolulu, 6:00 P.M.
General Herron made available to us his private car and driver. We looked over Hickham Field, Pearl Harbor, new ordnance storage tunnels and visited spots of natural scenic beauty. Pali pass was particularly interesting.

JULY 17

Settled laundry bills on ship. Took receipt for ten dollars of my personal laundry, as it appears from regulations that I may be able to get that much back from government.

Landed at San Francisco at 3:00 P.M. Found there a radio from General MacA directing me to examine situation at Fort Mason with respect to shipments of rifles, gun slings, etc. Sent him a long radio on subject, copy of which is in my papers.[1]

Purchased tickets for Denver. My ticket and berth cost $51.95. Took receipt. Spent three dollars for baggage transfer (my own baggage), arranged by Colonel Hodgson while I was attending to business above described, so that receipt was not obtained. Have retained checks.

1. It is difficult to determine what MacArthur meant by the "situation" at Fort Mason. The July 24, 1938, diary entry suggests it may have involved the transfer of equipment from Fort Mason to the Philippines and the difficulties in locating shipping space.

Sent the general an air mail letter in further explanation of the Fort Mason situation. Last evening I sent him an amateur radio requesting he send a personal letter of appreciation to Colonel Harvey.

Wired Lieutenant Lee[1] to arrange conference at Wichita; commanding officer Picatinny Arsenal, to arrange visit at that arsenal. Personal wires to Colonel Dirst and my dad.

Received a radiogram from General MacA. regarding Fort Mason situation, with instructions to communicate with Colonel Harvey at once by telegraph. In compliance therewith I sent following by night letter: Colonel Harvey, Superintendent, Transportation Services, Ft. Mason. Radiogram from Manila states fifteen airplanes have been scheduled for shipment to Philippines on next voyage of the Meigs.[2] Otherwise only normal shipments apparently contemplated. To what extent will shipments of these airplanes offset your estimate of July eighteenth as to the availability of space on the next trip of the Meigs for transportation of Philippine Army equipment. If Philippine Army property is necessarily excluded from next trip of the Meigs because of airplane shipment what are present probabilities for the November voyage of Meigs. Will appreciate prompt telegraphic advice at seven fifty Lafayette street this city. Many thanks. Cost $1.35.

1. William L. Lee and Hugh "Lefty" Parker were the first two flying instructors with the Philippine Air Corps (1935–38). Lee had returned to the states by this time. The wire to Lee confirmed the meeting in Wichita with Stearman Aircraft. See July 24 entry, below.

2. The *Meigs* was one of four army transport ships that John Eisenhower can recall as having sailed to the Philippines. Each ship could make a round trip in three months, sailing to San Francisco, to New York via the Panama Canal, and back by the same route. Mrs. Eisenhower and John sailed to the Philippines on the army transport *Grant* in October 1936.

JULY 24

Received night letter (collect) from Colonel Harvey ($1.68) and immediately repeated the gist of it to signal officer, San Francisco, asking him to radio my message to the commanding general, Philippine Department, for General MacArthur ($1.35).

My message informed General MacA. that we would <u>probably</u> get <u>some</u> of our Fort Mason equipment on the August trip, but that Colonel Harvey could make no prophecy as to November possibilities.

Wire from Lee suggests conference at Wichita next Thursday or Friday, which is OK.

JULY 27

Last evening sent General MacA. clipper letter enclosing a message from Colonel Harvey regarding Fort Mason situation. <u>Unreceipted bill for stamp, fifty cents</u>.

This morning am taking off for Wichita, Kansas to talk to Stearman and Beechcraft people.

JULY 28, 29, 30

Made full inspection of airplane plants in Wichita. Arranged trip so as to cost government nothing except one-way ticket from Abilene-Denver, making rest of journey in private plane.

Beech[1] is confident his plane can be modified for military purposes. In fact he is now designing one for a South American government to use—somewhat bigger than present ship. Latest cost around fifty thousand dollars.

1—1100 bomb
2—600
8—100
3—300

Ample guns, etc. Speed 220, cruising, all other characteristics as to handling, etc., as good as present ship, of which eleven are in service. All reports good.

Lee and Parker much impressed.

1. Walter Beech, founder of Beech Aircraft, was anxious to enter into the military aircraft arena.

Sent General MacArthur long radio telling him of changed schedule because of Mamie's operation.[1] Also advised him to have Dick[2] go ahead with permanent program, reserving funds allotted to American armament items. Must write to Gen.—Beech—etc.

1. Although several historians have explained Mrs. Eisenhower's 1938 surgery as related to a gall bladder condition, she in fact had her gall bladder removed in 1933. According to Dr. Thomas Mattingly's medical history of Dwight D. Eisenhower, at the Eisenhower Library, Mamie's 1938 surgery was for the removal of a uterine fibroid tumor. Mamie Doud Eisenhower File, Thomas L. Mattingly Medical History of Dwight D. Eisenhower, Eisenhower Library. Eisenhower's letter to Ord dated September 1, 1937, below, supports Mattingly's assertion that her gall bladder surgery occurred prior to 1938.

2. The reference to "Dick" is to Richard Sutherland. Eisenhower often referred to him in this manner.

Wrote Mr. H.D. Fairweather, vice-president, Colt's Patent Firearms Company, Hartford, and Mr. Oliver E. Nelson, Winchester Repeating Arms Company, New Haven, explaining that my visit to their plants would be after September 1. I must ask the War Department for passes to visit Winchester and Colt plants. Wrote to Schaefer, J.E., Stearman Aircraft; Walter Beech, Beechcraft Company. In Beech Aircraft Company are Mr. Gates, sales; Mr. Wells, engineer; Mr. Rankin, pilot. Wrote to Parker.

Mamie went to hospital (Pueblo). Wrote Brent School,[1] American Armament, and Everett.

1. Brent School in the Philippines was attended by John Eisenhower. Eisenhower probably informed the school that John would be late returning for the next term.

American Armament Corporation, 6 East Forty-fifth Street, New York. (Plant at Rahway, N.J.)[1]

1. Eisenhower evidently entered the address of American Armament in his diary as a reminder. He had many contacts with this company.

Left Denver at 6:00 AM and headed north on York Street, which runs into main road to Cheyenne. Dad drove to Cheyenne without incident. Roads paved. Distance 104 miles. Time, two and a half hours.

Continued north and west from Cheyenne to Casper, 185 miles. Considerable portions of the road under repair, the rest rather rough gravel. Stopped for lunch under a cottonwood. Mother and Auntie fixed us a "swell" repast which we thoroughly enjoyed and saved some for next day.

Traveled west from Casper to Shoshoni, where we stopped at the Shawnee Hotel for the night. Rooms two dollars apiece. Supper and breakfast forty cents each per person.

Shoshoni is 390 miles from Denver. Reached it at 5:30 P.M.

The most interesting sights of the day were (1) Hell's Half Acre. About thirty to forty miles east of Shoshoni. It is a great sunken tract that was originally a volcano, then was filled with geysers, all now extinct. The solid salts from the geysers remain in all types of weird shapes. (2) The oil fields just west of Casper and the adjacent refineries. In one large tract there seems to be a well every 150 yards. Not many are pumping now. Very hot and dusty day.

1. Eisenhower took leave to make the trip with his in-laws. Mrs. Eisenhower remained in Denver, recuperating from her surgery. The diary of the Yellowstone trip was maintained by Eisenhower in a separate diary book, apparently to separate this narrative from his more "official" diary books.

Left Shoshoni at 6:15 and struck north through the Wind River Canyon. Reached Thermopolis at 7:15 (34 miles), and Dad got himself some breakfast, as we fared poorly at Shoshoni. He also got me some doughnuts.

We continued north to Greybull through a country not quite so barren as east of Shoshoni, and then turned west to Cody and then through a canyon to Shoshone Dam. Built 1910. Height 320 feet. Width at bottom 110; at top, 10. Built on an arch and dams up the Shoshone River to form a lake 10 miles long, 225 feet deep.

Ate lunch just above the dam. The road runs through tunnels in places.

We then entered a national forest and another canyon that continued practically to the entrance gate to the Park. It was a wooded rocky canyon, very pretty and interesting.

At the Park entrance we paid $3 and then came on about twenty-seven miles over a winding road under repair to Lake Lodge (Fishing

Bridge). $3.50 each for bed, breakfast, and supper. Tomorrow morning we expect to go fishing.

Both of us feel well, but as we don't go in much for the type of entertainment put on here for the guests, I suppose we'll just go to bed tonight. We will get supper, our first meal in the park, in twenty minutes, Hot dog!

AUGUST 13

Cold rainy day.

Intended going fishing at bridge, but about 9:45 A.M. started off on loop to see park. Saw Grand Canyon and falls of Yellowstone. Climbed down wooden steps into canyon twice—once 502 steps. Oh boy. Falls and canyon most beautiful sight I have seen. Canyon 1,200 feet deep, 2,000 feet across.

Continued north toward Twin Falls, 180-foot drop of small creek into Yellowstone River. Miserable road under repairs. Then went west to Mammoth, Paintpots, deposits from warm springs.

South along a valley of steaming springs and geysers, stopping tonight at Old Faithful Lodge.

Traveled about 105 miles today.

AUGUST 14 FRIDAY

Early this morning I made a trip to the principal geysers. Emerald Pool and Black Sand Pool were the most interesting I thought. At 8:20 we started for Thumb, about twenty miles. There we hired a guide and boat ($1.50 per hour) and went fishing. We trolled in lake with spinners. Each caught one nice trout (cutthroat).

At 12:00 we started home via south gate. Got into rain and, due to bad reports concerning roads to east and south, stopped at Jackson at 3:00 P.M. for the night. This is the famous Jackson Hole country and is bounded on the east by the Grand Teton Mountains. These peaks tower over the valley, no foothills intervening between them and the valley floor. We are stopping at a funny little hotel where both Wyoming United States senators are spending the night. Kendrick and Carey.[1]

1. Eisenhower was mistaken in his identification of the senators. Sen. Robert Carey had been defeated in 1936; however, this could still have been Carey referring to himself as "senator." Sen. Benjamin Kendrick served in the U.S. Senate from 1917 to 1933, when he died in office. The two Wyoming senators in 1938 were Joseph C. O'Mahoney and Henry Herman Schwartz.

Were ready to leave town at 6:00, but in order to get breakfast and get chains put on car (together with losing gas tank cap) it was 7:10 when we left. I drove 80 miles to Pinedale over a muddy winding road. Pinedale is 104 miles from Rock Springs, the nearest railroad. Dad drove to Rock Springs (100 miles) in 2 hours 10 minutes. We drove 410 miles today, although the first 78 miles took us three hours, and the last 20 took another hour.

Stopping at Laramie.

August 16

Up at 5:20. Left Laramie at 6:30, via Fort Collins. Home at 10:10 A.M. Total distance, 1,378 miles.

1st day[1]
6:00 AM start
Mileage 2800
Postage 1.00
gas full 20

Cheyenne	2902–13
Casper	3090–17
[undecipherable]	3190–11_
Yellowstone [Lake]	3430–12
[undecipherable]	3536–15
[undecipherable]	3569–15
[undecipherable]	3559–4½
Jackson	3460–5
Pinedale	3722–5
Rock Springs	3824–14
Rawlins	3931–10
Laramie	4048–10
Denver	4178–11
	140½

Qt. oil, Cheyenne
"   ", Lake
"   ", Rawlins

1. Eisenhower made these undated notes at the end of the diary. They are a record of miles traveled and gallons of gasoline used.

August 21

On August 18 I received (at Pueblo) written instructions to proceed on an emergency trip (by air) to the War Department to prevent adoption of policy that might limit our use of government property (United States) on loan basis.[1] Today I got reservations on UAL[2] and will be in Washington tomorrow night.

1. Eisenhower resumed writing in his regular diary book at this point, ending the Yellowstone trip account. The emergency trip to Washington probably was related to the old issue of War Department resistance to the Philippine Mission. Philippine Department Commander Lucius Holbrook had resisted full cooperation in the matter of transferring matériel to the Philippine Army, as in 1937, probably with support in the War Department from skeptics such as General Krueger, who felt the whole mission was a waste of time and money. However, according to Eisenhower's letter to MacArthur on August 23, 1938, perhaps the situation was beginning to change to one of more support, if not cooperation. See Eisenhower to MacArthur, August 23, 1938, Pre-presidential Papers.

2. "UAL" refers to United Airlines.

125

Eisenhower Library
Pre-presidential Papers

To General Douglas MacArthur

August 23, 1938

Dear General: Yesterday I sent you a radiogram through the War Department to give you prompt reassurance concerning the question of using War Department equipment in the Philippine Army. There is no intent on the part of the War Department to adopt a more restrictive attitude with respect to this question than has been applying in the past. In fact, G-4 showed me 2 communications directed to the Commanding General, Philippine Department, one dated September 29th of last year, the other February 7th, of this year. Both of these communications expressed War Department approval of the proposition that all property in the hands of the Philippine Army, kept on the Island of Luzon, would be deemed a part of the U. S. Army Reserve. They even went further than this. They stated that any property on hand in the Philippines, in excess of the calculated War Reserves might be disposed of as the Department Commander saw fit. In other words they felt the Commanding General there has authority to lend us this excess property for permanent use in other islands. Colonel Sparks[1] states that this includes not only small arms but any other types of weapons.

There is now a communication in the Department[2] from the Department Commander in the Philippines. It does not in any way recommend a restriction in the policies heretofore obtained. It is merely a requisition for some additional property over and above the calculated War Reserves. The letter also contains a request that the Department Commander be allowed to lend us this excess property for temporary training purposes on other islands. G-4 points out that this authority already exists, as indicated in the paragraph above, but he intends to reiterate it in unmistakable language. Moreover, G-4 tells me that he believes they will be able to ship to the Philippines the additional items called for in the requisition, except possibly for some of the machine guns. He is confident that the 16 field guns (2.95) and the 96 trench mortars enumerated on that requisition will be shipped.

I took up also with G-4 the question of authorized accessories for guns, since our authorization includes "weapons and accessories." He states that by this expression they mean every appliance necessary to insure the proper operation of the weapon, and therefore that all such things as battery commander's telescopes, fuse setters, etc., may properly be loaned with the guns.

I realize that the above does not agree with the impression Sutherland had gained as to the probable recommendations to be made by the Department Commander. Naturally, I think you should regard this information as confidential but I assure you it is absolutely correct. The communication from the Department Commander was dated August 8th. You will understand, I am sure, that my telegram of yesterday had to be worded so that it would not indicate the nature of the information I intended to furnish you. I had to guard against the possibility that any staff officer would obtain the impression that we were doing business in any way other than through normal channels.

I am preparing to depart immediately for Colorado where Mamie is still in the hospital. She is improving, however, and I am sure I will be back in Washington early in September. I have called on the Chief of Staff, The Adjutant General, the Chief of the Bureau of Insular Affairs, General Marshall in War Plans, General Tyner in G-4, and one or two others, including the Deputy Chief of Staff of course. All send you assurances of their very highest regard and their best wishes to yourself and family. I have encountered nothing but the most sympathetic attitude toward your task and your plans, and have discovered that every official quickly sees eye to eye with us, when there is explained to him the identity of interests between the United States and the Philippine Islands concerning the fundamentals of the defense plan. I am convinced that trips such as this one are well worthwhile because personnel in the Department changes and indoctrination must therefore be intermittently continued.

I have uncovered some very interesting information of a more technical nature. One of these items applies to the trench mortar which now may be manufactured and sold by the Ordnance Department. Arrangements to effect this have just been completed with Brandt. I will obtain more details on the matter when I return here in early September. There has also been developed a 60 mm mortar which I hope to see in operation before I return. It may be a splendid weapon for Infantry regiments in lieu of the heavier and more expensive 81 mm mortars. The latter weapon is of course the more suitable for the Mortar Battalion of our Artillery Regiment.

I have had great difficulty in attempting to get steamship reservations for my return to the Philippines. The best I can do to date is to get on the Empress of Canada sailing from Vancouver on October 14th. Even that ship is almost sold out and I have to accept very second-rate cabins.

I have had no word as to whether the gratuity for Mrs. Ord was voted by the Assembly. I would appreciate it if you would have T. J. send me a radio on this subject.[3]

With very best wishes to you, Jean and the baby, and to all members of the office, Cordially

1. From 1935 to 1939 Leonard Craig Sparks served with the General Staff Corps. He retired as a colonel in 1945.

2. This reference is to the U.S. War Department.

3. The reference to Ord's widow regarded an attempt to have a bill passed in the Philippine legislature to provide her with a stipend. During this time period, widows of U.S. Army personnel received very little compensation from the U.S. government.

126   Eisenhower Library
                                                                Philippine Diary

August 25, 1938–September 7, 1938

August 25

Returned from Washington this evening. Trip entirely successful. Contrary to impression in our office at Manila, General H.[1] has not sent any communication to Washington advocating limitations on his authority to lend us property. He has asked for additional property, which he wants to let us have for temporary use on other islands.

I contacted and had long talks with the chief of staff,[2] deputy chief of staff,[3] adjutant general,[4] War Plans Division,[5] G-4,[6] Chief of the Bureau of Insular Affairs,[7] Colonel Leonard C. Sparkes,[8] G-4 Division, executive officer.

Secretary of war and assistant secretary out of town.

1. "General H." is Gen. John H. Hughes, who assumed command of the U.S. Army's Philippine Department from General Holbrook in February 1938.

2. Gen. Malin Craig was still Chief of Staff.

3. Stanley Embick served with the War Department General Staff (1926–30). In 1935 he was first appointed Assistant Chief of Staff in charge of the War Plans Division and then as Deputy Chief of Staff. Embick retired in 1941 but returned to active duty, serving with several War Department defense boards before his permanent retirement in 1946.

4. Emory Sherwood Adams was appointed Adjutant General in 1938 and later promoted to major general. He retired in 1942 and was replaced by Eisenhower's friend, James Ulio.

5. George C. Marshall graduated from Virginia Military Institute in 1901. During World War I he became chief of staff of the VIII Corps. Assigned to the General Staff in July 1938, Marshall became Acting Chief of Staff in July 1939 and, in September of that year, Chief of Staff. He served as the chief military adviser to President Roosevelt during World War II and presided over the Combined Chiefs of Staff, directing the Allies' global strategy. After the war, President Harry Truman appointed him secretary of state. Marshall proposed the European Recovery Program, known popularly as the Marshall Plan. In 1950 he became Truman's secretary of defense.

6. Col. George Parker Tyner, serving as the G-4, was assigned as Assistant Chief of Staff for logistics in 1937, a position he held until his retirement in 1940.

7. Brig. Gen. Charles Burnett (USMA, 1907) headed the Bureau of Insular Affairs. He served in the Philippines as Pershing's aide-de-camp. A large portion of his career was in Asian service as U.S. military attaché in Tokyo (1919–22 and 1925–29).

8. The correct spelling is "Sparks."

AUGUST 26

Spent two dollars in air mail stamps for official letters to Manila.

SEPTEMBER 7

Left for Washington, stopping first at Leavenworth to go over school prospects. Exec. (Gilbreath) believes Villaluz, an instructor at the Philippine Military Academy, a better man than Garcia.

Arrived Washington thirteenth, called on all principal officials of department.

Wired General MacA. army directory OK. Merritt report? Had long conversations with Sparkes (G-4). We should request more ammunition at $8.50 price. 1906 can be obtained new at possibly $20 per. Ask for price in letter.

G-4 has approved shipment of sixteen 2.95s to Philippine Islands as well as a number of 3-inch mortars. Have been promised that G-4 will see how cheap ammunition for latter can be sold.

Ordnance can sell us 81-mm. and 60-mm. But some delay in these items will <u>probably</u> ensure better prices.

Talked to Air corps, Ordnance, Infantry, Adjutant General, etc.

Following sent special messages to General MacA.: Craig, Adams,

Embick, Tyner, Marshall, Lynch,[1] Arnold,[2] Westover[3] not in town (Hardenberg,[4] office of the chief infantry wants to be remembered to Hughes).

Not yet certain Lewis is going to Maxwell, but probabilities are affirmative. Air Corps is delighted to help us out.

Discussed our problems with Colonel Clarke[5] (Philippine Projects section, WPD, also Perkins),[6] Sparkes, Tyner, Marshall, Embick, Lynch, Booth[7] (ordnance), adjutant general.

The chief of staff is against the Oboza detail, but answer has not finally been determined.[8] Ordnance will give thorough test to Molex.[9] They are not hopeful, suspicious that this explosive is dangerous to handle.

1. Maj. Gen. George Arthur Lynch (USMA, 1903) held various positions with the General Staff Corps until 1934, when he became acting administrator of the National Recovery Administration. Lynch commanded the U.S. Army troops in China from 1935 to 1937. In 1937 he was appointed Chief of Infantry, holding that position until his retirement in 1941. His successor was Courtney Hodges.

2. General of the Army Henry H. "Hap" Arnold (USMA, 1907) served in the aeronautical division of the Signal Corps in 1911 where he received his pilot's training from Orville Wright. In September 1911, he flew in the first U. S. airmail service. During World War I he oversaw the army's aviation schools. In December 1935, he became Assistant Chief of Staff of the Air Corps, rising to major general and Chief of the Air Corps in 1938. Arnold managed to persuade the army and aircraft manufacturers to accelerate production of military aircraft well before entry into World War II. During the war Arnold served as commanding general of the Army Air Forces, as a member of the Allied Combined Chiefs. He created the Twentieth Air Force, which became the incubus for the independent U.S. Air Force when it was separated from the Army. Arnold retired in 1946 after turning over his command of the Army Air Forces to Gen. Carl Spatz.

3. Maj. Gen. Oscar Westover (USMA, 1906) commanded the Air Corps's Tactical School (1924–26), and in 1935 he was made Chief of the Air Corps. When Westover died in an airplane accident in California in 1938, his deputy, Hap Arnold, took over his position.

4. Col. Raymond W. Hardenbergh served during World War I. He retired in 1941.

5. George Sheppard Clarke served with the Philippine Constabulary from 1912 to 1916 and was an honor graduate of the Constabulary's officer's school in 1913. He retired in 1946 as a colonel.

6. Col. George Thompson Perkins (USMA, 1900) was assigned to the War Department General Staff (1925–29) and from 1932 to 1936 was G-4 with 3d Cavalry headquarters. He retired in 1945.

7. Lucien Dent Booth (USMA, 1907) served in both the chief of ordnance office and in the War Department (1919–40). He retired in 1943.

8. The reference to the "Oboza detail" pertains to training planned for Federico Oboza, who became Adjutant General of the Philippine Army in 1939.

MacArthur and Eisenhower may have considered detailing Oboza to the U.S. Army adjutant general's office in Washington, D.C., for training.

9. "Molex" refers to an experimental explosive.

127

To General Douglas MacArthur

September 16, 1938

Dear General: I have been carrying out a series of conferences with War Department officials. The subject of greatest interest has involved infantry mortars, both of the 81 mm. and of the new 60 mm. calibers. The story on these is about as follows:

The Brandt Company has now given authority to the Ordnance Department to sell mortars to us, subject, of course, to their manufacturing royalty which is only about $20 a weapon. This information was sent to you officially a day or so ago by War Department letter. In answer to an inquiry as to the prices of this weapon and its ammunition, you are going to be somewhat shocked when you learn of the price the Ordnance Department has placed upon this weapon, which is $1,525 without aiming circle, but including the sight and normal tool kits. As I recall, Brandt quoted us a price of about $1,310 on this weapon and, I believe, included the sight in that figure. Our office file will reveal the exact quotations. However, the Brandt price did not include importation duties which, without a change in the law, would run it up to at least as high as the price quoted by the Ordnance. The standard round of ammunition is quoted at $13.43 which again is somewhat higher than the Brandt prices, but subject also to the same observation concerning import duties.

However, the most serious aspect of the problem is that the Ordnance Department is not yet prepared to say that their ammunition is completely satisfactory. They have had considerable trouble in solving this problem and believe that they are just approaching its final solution. This indicates, however, that our immediate commitments should be very moderate in size. The Chief of the Ammunition Division in the Ordnance Department is confident that the price of the ammunition will fall very materially when once they achieve a production status. He believes that it can be produced for around $9 a round. It was hinted also that the price of the mortar may come down eventually since, to date, only a total of one hundred of them have been produced by the American Ordnance Department.

A development of the greatest interest to us in this connection is the purchase by the Ordnance Department, from Brandt, of the manufacturing rights on a 60 mm. mortar. This gun and ammunition, under Brandt quotations, run just about 50% of the 81 mm. prices, whereas its value as a purely infantry weapon is undoubtedly great. It has splendid accuracy with an extreme range of around 1,800 yards. It is much lighter than the 81 and, therefore, should be a better weapon for troops that are going to have only minimum amounts of transportation. The ammunition supply problem in actual operations should be far simpler. All of these reasons indicate the probable desirability of adopting the 60 mm. as our infantry mortar, while we include eight of the 81 mm.'s. in the Artillery Regiment, as originally planned.

The War Department is starting the manufacture of 476 of these mortars on July 1 of next year; and, if by that time the ammunition problem has been pretty well solved, we could tack on a reasonable order to the War Department project and secure them at the best available price.

Please tell T.J. that while the Adjutant General was agreeable to the detail of Oboza, the staff has found certain objections to the arrangement and I doubt that it can be approved. I will get the final answer before I leave here. The Adjutant General cheerfully agreed to placing your name on the mailing list for the Army Directory and promised to do his best to find you a copy of General Merritt's[1] report. Your letter with reference to disability allowance for the captain who served under you during the War I turned over to the World War Division in The Adjutant General's Office. They promised to do their very best in presenting his case.

Mamie has improved sufficiently to come East with me on this trip. She is still a semi-invalid and is confined to the house. It is fine for her mental attitude, however, as friends drop in on her daily.

I just received from Lloyd Lambert a telegram which stated that Andy[2] had died. This telegram contained no particulars nor any explanation, and his references to this tragedy were so casual as to make me think it must be a ghastly mistake. However, there is no mistaking the language and I, therefore, assume the news is correct. I cannot tell you how terribly shocked I am.

Sometime ago, I sent you a wire asking for such help as Mr. Vargas might be able to give me in securing better accommodations on the Empress of Japan. I made my reservations as quickly as the doctor assured me that Mamie would probably be able to travel by October 14, but was still not early enough to secure even one room that included a bath. This will be very severe on Mamie, as I imagine she will spend a considerable proportion of her time in her stateroom.[3]

This was the reason for asking for the assistance. I have so far heard nothing further from the steamship people, but I am still hopeful that I may work out a satisfactory arrangement.

I have two or three more conferences in the War Department, and will leave for New York City on the nineteenth. From my investigations in the War Department, I am somewhat doubtful of making any satisfactory arrangement with the American Armament Corporation (this is confidential for you and Colonel Sutherland only), but my trip up there should be profitable in contacting the Colt and Winchester people.

Mamie joins me in best wishes and cordial regards to you, to Jean and to the son and heir. Sincerely

P. S. Please tell Sutherland that from the reports I have picked up here Captain Garcia did not make as good an impression at Leavenworth as did Villaluz. Tell him also that a young lad named Pargas, who is soon returning to the Philippines, made an outstanding record at Fort Monroe. This information may be useful to him in making assignments.

1. Maj. Gen. Wesley Merritt commanded the American Army of Occupation dispatched by President McKinley in 1898 to seize Manila. Merritt negotiated a surrender of the Spanish forces and served for a short term as military governor of Manila. His report of the expedition to Secretary of War Russell A. Alger, written during his return by steamship from Manila, is presumably the document to which Eisenhower refers. See *Annual Report of the Secretary of War for 1899* (Washington, D.C.: Government Printing Office, 1899), 40–46.

2. Lloyd W. Lambert, a mining executive with Base Metals Corporation of America, managed the corporation's Philippine holdings, which included the Mapaso Exploration Company, Mother Lode Mines, Mountain Mines, and the Quartz Hill Mining Company. Eisenhower knew Lambert socially in Manila and apparently invested in several of Base Metals' Philippine enterprises. Lambert escaped Manila just before the Japanese occupation and returned to the states.

"Andy" was probably William Anderson of Manila, a friend of Lambert and Eisenhower. He served in the Spanish-American War both in Cuba and in the Philippines. He joined the Philippine civil service as an engineer. Later, he entered mineral exploration and founded the Leyte Asphalt and Mineral Oil Company, the Oriental Asphalt Company of Cebu, the Ambassador Gold Mining Company, and Fortuna Goldfield Mining Company. Evidence strongly suggesting it was Anderson can be found in a later letter to Mamie in which Lambert stated, "Andy Anderson is in the Presidio under a white marker." See Lloyd Lambert to Eisenhower, March 22, 1942, and Lambert to Mamie Eisenhower, September 16, 1942, Pre-pres. Papers, Eisenhower Library.

3. Eisenhower had a difficult time obtaining passage back to the Philippines. On September 20, 1938, an assistant in the military transportation bureau wrote Eisenhower that he could not obtain a room with bath on the SS *Empress of Japan*. Because of Mamie's ill health and traveling with young John, accommodations were of major concern. On September 24, the officer, Norman Randolph, informed Eisenhower that his "crack" transportation person had obtained a room with bath because

of a cancellation. See Randolph to Eisenhower, September 20, 24, 1938, Records of the War Department, NARA.

128   Eisenhower Library
                                                              Philippine Diary

Many conferences with Sparkes. G-4 has authorized shipment of guns and mortars. Question of ammunition comes up, since the department commanding officer feels it inadvisable to sell from stocks.

My solution is to defer purchase of mortars, buy now (for storage under facilities of commanding general, Philippine Department) about five years requirements in artillery ammunition. In this connection G-4 believes they have a few more million rounds of stuff they will sell at $8.50 per [round]. Also they are manufacturing a considerable amount of new 1906 caliber .30. We can purchase for $20–22 per thousand as compared to $30 per thousand for M1.

129   Eisenhower Library
                                                     Pre-presidential Papers
MEMORANDUM FOR COLONEL LEONARD T. GEROW[1]

SEPTEMBER 22, 1938

1. The questions propounded by Bratton[2] in his pencil memorandum to you are all susceptible of easy and fairly accurate reply. However, some of them can be answered fully only through somewhat lengthy explanation and such explanations I cannot give at the moment because of limited time. However, if Bratton will write to me at Manila, I will give him such amplification as he may desire. I am sorry that I did not meet him while I was in Washington.

(Note: I have numbered the questions given on the pencil draft and am returning it herewith. The numbers below correspond to those on the memorandum.)
(1) The Army consists of
a. Regulars
b. Trainees
c. Reserves (Graduated Trainees).

The regular contingent is small. At present it numbers about 620 officers and about 7300 enlisted men. Of these about 220 officers and something over 3,000 enlisted men are completely detached from the Army to form the constabulary. This is a police organization scattered in all islands and districts.

The remainder of the regular force is used as the instructional body for the trainees, to form the War Department and nuclei of services, schools, special units, and finally to establish a small contingent of constantly available military force. This permanent body when finally established in the strength desired will constitute the regular division stationed primarily in Luzon, but with contingents in Minandao and in the Visayas. The regular division will not, however, be composed completely of professional soldiers. It will be partly regular and partly trainee, roughly about 40% and 60% respectively. This particular group of trainees will serve one year with the colors and one-half of them will be returned to civil life each six months.

The trainees number about 20,000 men with the colors at any one time. The training period is roughly six months. Three thousand men of each group are carried over for an additional six months training to provide specialists and non-commissioned officers.

The reserves are only gradually coming into being. The whole reserve organization is divided into a ten divisional pattern and the Islands are divided into a corresponding number of districts. It is expected that the divisions will be produced at the rate of about one per district each three years so that at the end of ten years there will be approximately 30 divisions of reserves organized. This is the present tentative objective of General MacArthur's plan.

(2) The War Department is patterned roughly upon the American War Department. There is no Secretary of War, the Chief of Staff reporting directly to the President. General staff divisions, since the separation of the constabulary from the rest of the Army, are G-1 War Plans, G-2 Intelligence, Training and Operation, G-3 Personnel and Supply. In addition there is a section for handling provost marshal general affairs, namely registration, recruiting, and the like. This section is really a combined staff and operating section.

(3) The division is small, its total strength, officers and men, being about 7,250. The organization is roughly as follows:
Division Headquarters
3 Infantry Regiments
1 Complete Artillery Regiment
1 Engineers Battalion
1 Medical Service
1 Signal Company
1 Labor Battalion
Assignments to the reserve division exceed by approximately 50% the total authorized strength of the division, in order to provide the 100% turnout upon mobilization and to provide also a nucleus of a replacement depot in time of war.

The infantry regiment is composed of three rifle battalions and a special group. The rifle battalion each has 3 rifle companies and a small machine gun company. Each rifle company has a total strength of 110 men divided into three small rifle platoons and an automatic rifle section. The automatic rifle section has four guns. In the special battalion of the regiment is included (planned organization) 6 infantry mortars, and 2 - 50 caliber machine guns.

The artillery regiment as planned will consist of 3 battalions as follows:
1 battalion of 8 guns, either 2.95 or 75 m/m
A second battalion of 8 - 81 m/m mortars, modern type
Finally, 1 battalion of machine guns of which 4 guns will be 50 caliber and 4 guns 30 caliber.

(4) Independent commands at present consist of the military academy, the service school, the air corps, the garrison at Ft. Wint and two special schools for the advanced training of officer candidates. The strength organization and location of these comprise a subject too detailed to discuss at present. The following pertinent information is furnished on the air corps.

The air corps at present consists primarily of a training school. There are on hand at present about 13 planes primarily of training types, while 9 additional ships have already been purchased, of which 6 will have definite tactical value. To date all of the air corps has been located at Camp Murphy,[3] just outside of Manila, but with the arrival of the new ships the detachment of tactical planes will be attached to the Clark Field force of the American Army. Air corps training is proceeding satisfactorily under the direct supervision of two officers of the American Army Air Corps. Selected men are sent to the United States for training in the Army Air Corps schools.

(5) The Philippine Army technical and supply services are organized somewhat along the lines of the American services. Some of these are still very small, in fact are only just started. The quartermaster corps is the most highly organized and included in it is also the finance service. The engineers corps which has the function of construction in the Philippine Army, is well started and functioning reasonably satisfactorily. This applies also to the Ordnance Department, although the number of reasonably trained officers available for this duty is far too small. The Philippine Army, of course, attempts no design, manufacture or local production of technical matériel. So far as possible this is all bought from the American Army.

(6) About 100,000 men annually attain the age of 20 in the Philippines, at which age they are required to register for military service. Of this number somewhere between 35,000 and 40,000 are trained annually under the plan sketched above.

The individual is obligated to military service for 30 years, that is, from 21 to 51. The first reserve, however, comprises only those from

21 to 41 and it cannot yet be accurately estimated to what extent the second and third reserves can be maintained at any real military value, except as replacements for the first reserve. However, assuming availability of funds the 10 year cycle for production of divisions can be repeated three times under the law.

(7) The policy is to keep the armament of the Philippine Army on a simple basis, avoiding in so far as possible multiplicity of type. The basic arm is the Enfield rifle, procured from the American Army. Under purchases and loan agreements, a total of about 400,000 of these will eventually be available. The machine gun is the American type of Browning. The automatic rifle is the same as that used in the American army. The infantry mortar that is planned for eventual procurement is the new type of Brandt, probably both the 81 and the 60 m/m. The former will be used in the artillery battalion, the latter possibly in the infantry. All individual and organizational equipment is kept very simple. The normal uniform for the trainee is a short shirt, short trousers, regulation shoes and a helmet of special local manufacture, made from the bark of the coconut tree. Organizational equipment (company) is confined primarily to simple cooking utensils, a field desk, a small kit of common tools and two ————.[4] The same principle is observed in providing battalion and regimental equipment.

The question of transportation equipment requires a considerable explanation, which can be only outlined here. Since the objective of the plan is to train citizenry for local defense, each division is assumed to be in approximately the location it will be used in war. Its annual training periods will consist primarily in occupying and preparing the positions along the coast that the particular division is required to defend. In addition, however, to these coast defense divisions there will be a number assigned to GHQ reserve in each of the larger Islands. The former type of division is assigned no transportation at all in time of peace, and will necessarily rely upon that which can be secured locally in the event of mobilization (this may be modified to a slight extent in order to provide a small amount of artillery transportation). The second type of division, that is the one assigned to GHQ reserve, will be provided only that much of its transportation that can be classed as technical. This will apply particularly to the field artillery. For the rest of its transportation reliance will be placed upon existing transportation companies and local requisitions to secure the necessary mobility.

(8) Initially all training had to be almost exclusively infantry. This was because of the fact that facilities were not available for any other kind of instruction. With each half class, however, a greater segregation of trainees into specialized types of training has been possible. At present we are training infantry, field artillery, signal, medical, engi-

neers, in the training academies. In addition there are special stations at Camp Murphy and Fort Mint[5] respectively, where air corps and coast artillery personnel are being trained. The serious question of providing reserve officers for the large number of reserve units that will come into being has not been completely answered. However, ROTC units have been established in every secondary school of the Philippines (there may be one or two minor exceptions). Specialists, such as medical and signal officers are secured from members of these professions, and some reserve officers are secured by additional training given to men who have completed 11 months trainee instruction with the colors. Reserve units once formed are required to undergo at least 10 days training each year. This training cannot be by divisional organization until after January 1, 1940, by which time it is hoped that the first series of divisions will have attained at least skeletonized organization. It is certain that at that time assignments of enlisted men to divisions will have been completed.

I repeat my regret that this memorandum must be so sketchily and hastily done, however, I am sure that it will give Bratton something upon which to start and will suggest to him the definite questions that he may desire to send us in the Philippines. Please give it to him with this apology.

1. Gerow was Executive Officer, War Plans Division, War Department General Staff, at this time.

2. This reference is probably to Rufus Sumter Bratton (USMA, 1914). In 1932 he attended the Japanese General Staff College, then served two terms as assistant military attaché in Tokyo (1925–26 and 1931–33). Bratton retired in 1952 as a colonel.

3. Camp Murphy served as headquarters of the 1st Division, Philippine Regular Army. U.S. Army Air Corps personnel were stationed at Murphy.

4. Eisenhower left a blank space following "two."

5. "Fort Mint" apparently is a typographical error. Detachments of the 92d and 93d Coast Artillery, Philippine Department, U.S. Army, were posted at Fort Wint, Manila Bay. These units provided coast artillery training for the Philippine Army.

130   Eisenhower Library
                                               Philippine Diary

SEPTEMBER 23, 1938–SEPTEMBER 25, 1938
SEPTEMBER 23

Left Washington September 20. Sent radio to General MacA concerning all questions he had forwarded to me. Jim Ulio[1] is writing him a personal letter reference Merritt report.

Sent to Newark, $1.35. Receipt obtained.

Arranged for following trips:
1. Picatinny reference powder tests.
2. New Haven and Hartford—reference Winchester and Colt products.
3. Rahway, American Armament products. (Malcolm out of city for week.)

Flood conditions terrible. Communications will not be reestablished for some days to Hartford, consequently Connecticut trip had to be confined to Winchester plant at New Haven.

Cost of New Haven trip. Receipts not available, except for Pullman seat. All ticket inter-urban type, collected and no receipt given. See certificate and statement of witness.

We should carefully check net costs in ammunition from United States Ordnance and from Winchester, etc.

Mr. Nelson says we paid more for .22 ammunition than his company would charge us.

1. Ulio's relationship was very important to Eisenhower. John Eisenhower remembers that Ulio and Dwight Eisenhower often played golf at the Old Soldier's Home in Washington, D.C., in the 1930s.

Visit to American Armament and Rahway factory was instructive. Fine plant. Company apparently resented by certain people in United States Army. Took Colonel Hughes,[1] Ordnance, with me to inspect plant. Both much impressed. Did my best to unearth underlying cause of any antagonism to company.

The engineer (Brayton) acknowledged by all to be expert. Fifteen years with ordnance department. Unpopular.

All problems that have been bothering ordnance, such as fin assembly, capsule form, fuses (deformation of point), etc., have been attacked by company and a solution found. Have asked for latest prices, to compare in detail with ordnance department. Spent long time here.

Mamie accompanied me on trip east, but all expenses, of all kinds for her, were paid from personal funds. I habitually bought minimum accommodations for myself, no matter what I bought for her.

1. This reference is to Eisenhower's close friend, Everett S. Hughes.

To General Douglas MacArthur

SEPTEMBER 30, 1938

Dear General: We will soon be starting for Manila; we leave Denver on the 10th, catching the "Japan" on the 14th. I feel that my Washington trips were very successful, and I obtained much information on the mortar question. The story is too long to tell here, but I know you will be interested to hear it verbally. In the "equipment" end of my business I was disappointed in not getting to Hartford. I went to Connecticut and got caught in the middle of the great flood there. I finally gave up trying to see the Colt people when I received a telegram from a doctor in Colorado that Johnny might have to have an appendectomy before returning to P.I. I rushed back here and put him through the Fitzsimmons[1] clinic, learning that an operation was not necessary. We are of course greatly relieved, but I don't feel justified in going all the way back to Hartford just to see the one machine gun mount.

I'm enclosing an account of the Army-Wichita game.[2] I could not go up to see it as that day I had a date to inspect the Rahway factory of the American Armament. But I've arranged to have sent on to me all the dope possible on prospects for the fall, player assignments, etc. I'll bring it all with me if it comes through as I expect.

All the people I talked to in the W.D. feel that you are making much more progress out there than they originally believed possible. They have become convinced that you're doing a worthwhile job, and in a fine way.

Please give our best to the officer force—we'll be glad to see you all soon. Cordially

1. Fitzsimmons Army Hospital is located in Denver, Colorado.
2. Army's first football opponent in 1938 was Wichita Municipal University, Wichita, Kansas. Army won, thirty-two to zero.

132   Eisenhower Library
                                                    Philippine Diary

OCTOBER 8, 1938–DECEMBER 13, 1938

OCTOBER 8

Our scare over John's appendix was apparently useless. Fitzsimmons surgeons say there is no indication that operation is necessary. Repeated kidney tests show those organs normal.

Left Denver 5:45 P.M.

Arrived Portland at 7:30 A.M. on second morning. Left Portland one hour later, arriving Tacoma at 1:00 P.M. Spent day with Edgar[1] there, calling on General Sweeney[2] at Fort Lewis. Wayne Clark is on the general staff there. Also Hills in the Adjutant general's office wants to be remembered to Stuart -?-[3] Adjutant general's office at Ft. Stotsenburg.

1. Edgar Newton Eisenhower was the second oldest Eisenhower brother. Born in Hope, Kansas, in January 1889, Edgar as a boy was known as "Big Ike"; his smaller and younger brother Dwight was called "Little Ike." Edgar dropped out of school after the eighth grade to work at the creamery where his father was employed. He reentered school two years later and graduated from Abilene High School with Dwight in the class of 1909. Edgar received his LL.B. from the University of Michigan law school in 1914. He moved to Tacoma, Washington, in 1915 where as a tax and corporate attorney, he built a highly successful law practice. An avid golfer, Edgar won the Washington state seniors' championship four times and achieved a reputation as one of the best amateur golfers in the Pacific Northwest.

2. Maj. Gen. Walter Campbell Sweeney served in the Philippines from 1901 to 1911. In 1924 he became chief of the Army's Information Office. His relationship with Eisenhower continued when Eisenhower joined Sweeney's 3d Division at Fort Lewis.

3. The "-?-" is Eisenhower's.

Arrived at Vancouver, B.C. by ferry at 8:00 A.M., October 14, and sailed from Vancouver at 11:45 A.M., October 14, and from Victoria at 6:00 P.M.

Arrived Honolulu at 10:30 A.M., Oct 19. Sailed at 10:15 A.M., October 20.

Arrived Yokohama, 7:00 A.M. Left Yokohama, 3:00 P.M.

Arrived Kobe, 9:00 A.M. Left Kobe, 6:00 P.M.

Shanghai. Arrived 6:00 P.M.

Left Shanghai on November 2 at 1:30 P.M.

Arrived Hong Kong 8:00 A.M. Left Hong Kong 10:00 P.M.

Landed at Manila at 10:00 A.M. Paid table steward $10.00 and room steward $10.00 as personal tips for voyage from Vancouver. Both being Chinese, made no attempt to secure receipts.

Arrived in Manila from the States on Nov. 5, and found a vastly different situation, so far as it effects me and my work, than the one existing when I left on June 26.

First of all, the General has apparently been stricken with the same obsessions with respect to me that he suffered from in the case of Jimmy. He always bitterly resented J's popularity with Filipinos in general, and his intimacy with Malacañan in particular. So, while I was gone, he <u>reorganized</u> the office, so as to remove me completely in official affairs from Malacañan. Not content with this he re-arranged the office force so that I'm no longer his C. of S., but only another staff officer—he is theoretically the coordinator of the whole group. My section is plans, training, mobilization, education, etc.—the purpose being to keep me absorbed in academic work at my desk, and to rob me of any influence in the Army or at Malacañan. The only thing he forgets is that all of us are attached to Department Headquarters and whether he likes it or not the Senior Officer of the U.S. Army on duty with this group is compelled to make efficiency reports on the others [. . . .] While I was representing the office at Malacañan I kept him informed of everything pertaining to us. Now he gets only those things that are sent to him in letter form. Secretary Vargas is resentful of the change— but I told him it was a matter of indifference to me. I would make no move to recommend a change. Why the man should so patently exhibit a jealousy of a subordinate is beyond me. I guess it's because he is afraid a conviction will grow in the minds of local people that he personally is not so important to the Army and to the P.I. If this is his thought, he's taken the worst possible course, because when a subordinate maintains such contacts he can with propriety glorify the position, prestige and value of the Boss. He (if he has any modesty whatsoever, which I doubt) is handicapped in this direction. Administratively the new scheme is so clumsy as to require no comment.

Of course, he has accomplished one thing he wanted to do, that is, make certain that I'd get out as soon as I decently can. On the surface all is lovely. I will not give him the satisfaction of showing any resentment. But my usefulness is so curtailed as to rob the job of much of its interest, so I'm going at the earliest possible moment. If the d——fool had only sent his plan to me while I was in the States I would not have returned; but I guess he was afraid to do this for fear of the explanation he would have had to make at Malacañan. Sec. Vargas knows that I worked honestly, and with some effectiveness so it would have been embarrassing to the Gen. to show why I declined to come back. He did not have that much courage!

I regret the campaign I conducted everywhere in the States to make him appear a wise counsellor, an asset to the Philippines, and a splendid man in his present post.

The A.G. informed me I'd be expected to make up the 4 months & 10 days I was outside the Philippine Islands. This would bring my tour to a close in early March (1940) and I had originally intended asking to stay until end of June, that year, as John could finish school. Now, I'm going to try to beg off the extra four months and get out of here next October.

When the President & Mr. Vargas raised my allowance to 1000 per mo., and when they volunteered to give me air-conditioned rooms at the same price as the old ones, I see now that they convinced the Gen. he should get rid of me. It was in keeping with his hypocritive habits that these were the subjects concerning which he expressed so much personal satisfaction in the last interview I had with him just before I left for the U.S. But I must say it is almost incomprehensible that after 8 years of working for him, writing every word he publishes, keeping his secrets [. . .] he should suddenly turn on me, as he has all others who have ever been around him. He'd like to occupy a throne room surrounded by experts in flattery [. . . .]

So far as I'm personally concerned all this means nothing; as I have not and never have had any intention of remaining in the Philippine Islands beyond a definite, limited period. My fury is academic rather then practical and actual; [. . .] T. J. is no higher (apparently) in his estimation than I. His confidence in our integrity and gentlemanly instincts must be high, at that, because I cannot believe he'd deliberately make enemies of anyone that he'd fear might in the future reveal the true story of his black and tan affair;[1] [. . .] his speculations on his chances to be Vice-President of the U.S.; [. . .] his extravagant condemnations of Pres. of U.S. et al when he was summarily relieved before he reached San Francisco; his chiselling to increase the emoluments he's getting from the Phil. Govt; his abject fear that he'll do anything that might jeopardize his job (rather his salary of 66,000 and all expenses). Oh hell—what's the use! The point is he <u>knows</u> we won't tell these things!

Now that I've jotted all this down I hope that it never again comes, even momentarily, to my mind!

1. Eisenhower probably alluded to MacArthur's love affair with Isabel Cooper, a Eurasian Filipina he met in Manila in 1929. MacArthur, having recently been divorced from his first wife, Louise, brought Cooper back to the states with him in 1930. He provided her an apartment near his, and they carried on a furtive affair until early 1934. In May 1934, MacArthur sued columnists Drew Pearson and Robert Allen for their scathing attacks on him, particularly for his role in the Bonus March episode. Pearson and Allen countered by investigating MacArthur's past. They uncovered information about the affair and interviewed Cooper, who provided Pearson with MacArthur's love letters. When MacArthur was informed of this, he not only dropped the libel suit but also paid Cooper fifteen-thousand dollars to recover the letters. Eisenhower's letter to Everett Hughes of September 9, 1934, refers to this matter.

NOVEMBER 15

As a result of my inspection of American Armament Equipment, and of the information we've received from the U.S. Ord (Ord. mortars & amm.) will not be ready for sale for at least 1 more year at quantity production prices, since all technical problems are not yet licked. I came back here and suggested the purchase of about 6–12 A.A.[1] mortars with a thousand rounds or so of amm. to test out thoroughly this equipment. If satisfactory (and we have every reason to believe it should be) we'd have an additional source of supply in reserve, and would be able to secure items from the source offering the lowest price. Sutherland concurred in every respect except that he told me the Gen. wants to buy enough, at once, for 6 Divs. (48) and for 9 Divs. (72) if possible. Personally, I see no reason for going overboard this heavily on the A.A. mortar since eventually we count on using U.S. Ord. But OK!!

1. The "A.A." refers to the American Armament Company.

DECEMBER 12

I've played bridge recently with Pres. Q; once for a weekend on the Casiana; once for an afternoon at Malacañan. He's a peach of a player, but somewhat unorthodox in bidding.

Today I'm scheduled to give a talk to 31st Infantry officers on Philippine Defense Plan. It will be fun to address a bunch of people of my own kind.

The results of my trip to the States are very well outlined in the notebook I carried with me. For that reason I don't repeat them here.

How I wish poor old Jim were alive and here to go over things with me!

He'd be particularly astonished to find that, again, the 30 Division plan establishes the basis for all our work. No hint is ever given that it was once definitely and finally repudiated—that the Gen. shouted down in anger any suggestion that he had ever directed us to take 30 Divs. as an objective! He has completely forgotten that when, in a pinch, he momentarily had to look at <u>facts</u>, he hastily established 15 Divs. as the <u>limit</u> to which we'd aspire. Now the 30 Division plan is accepted, not only accepted, there's no suggestion of any other thought. Luckily, I'll be long gone before the Filipinos have the right to look about them and say, "Well, the time is up, <u>where</u> are the 30 Divs?" There will be no answer to that one; not for 160,000,000 pesos aggregate!!

To save money we've curtailed training plans and original concepts in every direction.

The Constabulary figure was finally fixed at 350 officers, 4500 enl. men. This leaves us (even counting provincials) with about 270 officers and 3000 enl. men. This number, the Gen. says, except for a special case here and there, is sufficient. We'll scuttle the Reg. Force, except in name. It will be just a number of <u>training cadres</u>!! This great reduction the Gen. justifies on the grounds that we no longer carry any responsibility to maintain a reserve force for maintenance of law & order!! If that was the only reason for a Reg. Force, it never was justified! We may as well establish the Constab. and let it alone! The Gen. decided to recall reservists for training only <u>every other year</u>!!

We're doing nothing about pre-military training except in the sketchiest way. Yet, in the beginning, when the Gen. still looked at some of these problems from a professional, no matter how warped, viewpoint, he justified the 5½ months training period <u>only</u> on the plea that each of them would undergo 10 years continuous training in schools; and would, after completion of trainee instruction, be called every year for unit training. But to preserve outward evidence of progress, which he thinks will get by with laymen who know nothing of efficiency, the Gen., as always, is willing to scuttle anything and everything real.

Will I be glad when I get out of this!!

DECEMBER 13

A small change in plan, that occurred while I was gone. Promises to involve a lot of administrative difficulty in the future.

Heretofore each infantry cadre has had in it both A.R.[1] and M.G.

413

sections. The proportion was such that each cadre would in 3 years produce 1 bn of inf; (riflemen, A.R. men and Machine gunners) and would provide for each the overages that would ensure 100% strength upon any recall to duty.

Average 130 men in cadre
220 men per year (allowing for 11 mos. men)
660 men in 3 years
Strength of Bn. (including Hdqs.) Approx. 450.

Each cadre had, as I remember, 19 A.R. men & 21 machine gunners.

This system permitted the <u>localization</u> of bns. with consequent minimizing of trans. costs; ease & rapidity of mobilization; and, in most sections, the unofficial get-togethers within bns that would do so much toward building esprit-de-corps.

Now they have segregated machine gun training by setting up special cadres for this work. The excuse given me is that, since we are now to call reservists for training by yearly classes, it is necessary to produce <u>full</u> companies each year. The machine gun cadre will thus produce 3 cos^2 in 3 years, or 3 machine gun cos. for a <u>regiment</u>. The ordinary cadre will, I suppose, produce approx. 2 cos. of infantry per year. Careful arrangements for assigning recruits each training course will be necessary, otherwise men belonging to a battalion machine gun co. will come from an area considerably removed from the remainder of the battalion.

In my opinion, someone did this that is either a poor exec—or doesn't know the background of study through which the whole proposition was originally processed.

1. "A.R." refers to automatic rifle.
2. Companies.

133   Eisenhower Library
Pre-presidential Papers, Family File

TO MILTON EISENHOWER

JANUARY 3, 1939

Dear Milton: Your letter of December 13 just arrived, and I'm dropping everything in order to get off a reply by the next clipper to leave here. In attempting to measure the attractiveness of the offer made you by Penn State, I am assuming that, by custom in United States Colleges, the summary or arbitrary removal from office of a College Dean is practically impossible.[1] In other words security—by which I mean your family's security—would be enhanced rather than diminished by the change. This is vastly important to a salaried man that has to think of a wife and two young children, and all observations I shall attempt to make below are dependent upon the validity of this basic assumption.

I am quoting a sentence from your letter. "Finally, I am not certain that I would be entirely happy in work that lacked the rigorous demands on many fronts that I encounter here."

I feel competent to enter a discussion on this point because of similar feelings of my own in the past, and some reflection on the results of my own decisions, that were based upon those feelings. The human machine wears out, although none of us ever applies this inescapable law to his own case. Deterioration and destruction are familiar phenomena, but the mind recoils from personal application of the logical conclusion. Signs of deterioration appear, just as they do in an automobile, in accordance with the speed of use. By tradition, when we speak of "burning up the road" we think of strong drink, weak women and raucous singing. Actually the speed that is most dangerous to the human is the speed that is involved in <u>driving, continuous mental endeavor</u>! Men of ability in the government service see so much to be done, they create or have created for them so many jobs that lazier men like to shunt from their own shoulders (except of course when it comes to collecting the glory for recognized accomplishment) that gradually the victim, which word I use advisedly, loses his sense of values, and with his needful governors failing him, he applies his mind, consciously and unconsciously, day and night, to important and intricate problems that march up ceaselessly, one after the other, for consideration.

In our younger days this is fine—we like it—we know with certainty that we are important to the organization we serve—and we thrive on the completion of each job, done to the full satisfaction of those around and above us. It can likewise be done and enjoyed by age with no great damage, but only where the conditions of service are such as to encourage, even force, increasing periods of enjoyable relaxation. To pursue further the automobile analogy; an old car must go for complete overhaul more frequently than the new one!

Most professional careers, even including the military, so arrange themselves that increasing opportunity to slow up in personal effort, to use the fruits of other men's work in arriving at decisions and judgments, come with advancing years. A disadvantage that I've always suspected to exist in your present job is that this general rule does not apply. Secretaries and Assistant Secretaries will continue to come and go—and the able, conscientious Bureau Director, capable of taking on his own shoulders the thousand and one recurring administrative, coordinating and miscellaneous jobs will be scarce as ever. In other words, you, because of your nature and your recognized abilities, will be on a steady, swift grind until you've definitely damaged your own capacity for enjoying life. When tires blow out or pistons freeze the car is no good to anyone—but these things are more readily repaired than a shattered nervous system, or a confirmed routine of activity that finally cannot be broken except at the acute distress and damage of the individual. When this occurs real unhappiness results—for only a man that is happy in his work can be happy in his home and with his friends. Which, incidentally, leads to the observation that Helen, in collaborating with you in solving your present problem, should do so with the purpose of insuring the suitability, congeniality and interest of your life-work.

All this to pose one single proposition! My conception of a worthwhile College Dean is a man that, as years go by, becomes a guide and inspiration to our youth, not through feverish activity and solution of involved administrative problems, but through the ripened viewpoint from which he sees youth's questions, and the high average of wisdom and leadership he uses in helping them solve their problems. His value derives from character, knowledge and personality—not from ceaseless expenditure of nervous energy. Of course I realize that in entering upon a new post of this kind, a season of intensive effort would be necessary. But if the picture presented in this paragraph is reasonably accurate, the new job would appear to be one in which the demands conform closely to the proper output of ripening ability, while in your present position, I feel, this characteristic is lacking, and you are in danger of becoming only an extremely useful tool! In other words, do we not have here a prospect for development, as opposed to possible stagnation?

This seemingly endless discussion of trite but nevertheless sound truisms may bore you, but if you've read to this point, you've at least been reminded of the most important point you and Helen must now consider, your future happiness in your work. Happiness in work means that its performer must know it to be worthwhile; suited to his temperament, and, finally, suited to his age, experience, and capacity for performance of a high order.

As to your house. On this point all I can give is my assurance that I understand, and sympathize with your reactions. It is a real home, instantly sensed by even a casual visitor. To sell it will be to lose something valuable from your life, because you two have put so much of yourselves into it. The money loss would not concern me much, but your abandonment of past plans and hopes and effort will cause even me a wrench, so I know what it must mean to you. Buy why not take a run up to Pennsylvania to determine whether the general setting and atmosphere is one to which you can transplant your ideas in home-building, even if you cannot take there your present shrubs, trees, stairways and vistas? The problem <u>might</u> solve itself through discovery of newly inspired anticipations.

One last thought occurs to me as very important. How about freedom in self-expression? The prohibitions, legal and ethical, surrounding the public servant might be largely removed in a position of the kind you are considering. If so I would regard this as a tremendous advantage. With your ability in composition, particularly in expository writing, and your wealth of experience in agricultural problems, you should have liberty and leisure to put down and publish what <u>you believe</u>, not what administration policy supports. With such opportunity presented you, I tell you, without flattery, that there is no reason you should not become a national figure in that field. You are honest, intelligent, natural, well informed, and you can express yourself clearly. Nothing else, it seems to me, is necessary particularly when the position you will occupy tends to make your words authoritative in the ears of the public.

Well, I've had my say. As you can see, I've argued myself into believing you should make the change, provided the various assumptions I've necessarily had to substitute for actual knowledge, are correct. At least Mamie and I want you and Helen to know we'll be thinking of you, and, in spite of your own doubts, we'll believe that whatever decision you make will be the right one. With best wishes for 1939 to you, Helen, Buddy and Mistress Ruth.

As ever

P.S. Mamie has read your letter and this reply. Her appended note gives her slant on the matter.[2]

1. Milton Eisenhower had been offered a deanship at Pennsylvania State University. He elected to remain in Washington with the Department of Agriculture. In 1950 he accepted the presidency of Penn State.

2. Milton Eisenhower's papers at the Eisenhower Library contain no letters dated prior to 1942 from Dwight or Mamie Eisenhower; presumably, the original of this letter and Mamie's note were destroyed or lost.

134

Eisenhower Library
Pre-presidential Papers, Speech File

JANUARY 6, 1939

Speech at Luncheon Honoring Generals Santos and Valdes

My distinguished guests: Our honor guests, this noon, have been the two senior officers of the Philippine Army practically from the date of its founding. No one could possibly be more familiar with the work they have done during the past three years, with the energy, the thought, the character, they have devoted to their duties, than myself. It is for this reason that I felt privileged to ask you to meet with me today in tribute to them, at the moment when one of them leaves the Army to assume another important position in the service of his people, while the other moves up to shoulder the responsibilities of the highest military post.

Recently, I attended a movie in which one obstreperous female character asserted, each time she opened her mouth, that she spoke for two million club-women of the United States. Unlike that person, I am not authorized to speak for any group or sect, for any military or civil organization, or even for any individual except only Ike Eisenhower. But to my own opinions as to the loyalty, abilities and worthwhile accomplishments of Generals Santos and Valdes in the Philippine Army, I can and do give the most emphatic expression. Confirmation of my convictions can be found in every district, every city, every barrio of the Philippines. Slow but steady development of a real defensive force, progress toward greater unification of a people through intermingling in training station, better physiques among the trainees, greater observance of rules of health and hygiene and, finally, a definitely enhancing appreciation of the requirements of democratic citizenship, are but a few of the accomplishments traceable wholly or in part to the gradual unfolding of the defense plan. In this process our honor guests have played important, untiring and effective parts.

My years of intimate contacts and personal friendship with these two men have been, for me, a real privilege and a source of inspiration. So it is with sincerity and earnestness that I congratulate the Mindanao re-settlement organization on its good fortune in obtaining General Santos as its Manager, and the Philippine Army in having General Valdes to serve as its Chief of Staff.

A moment ago I said that I spoke for no one except myself. Now I should like to modify that statement momentarily, and to this extent. If there is present any man that will not permit me to speak for him in wishing for General Santos and General Valdes a full measure of happiness in their new assignments, and unbroken continuation of their illustrious careers, then that man was invited here today by mistake. For I am determined that this thought shall be the sense of this meeting—enthusiastically adopted—by acclamation.

JANUARY 10, 1939–JANUARY 21, 1939
JANUARY 10

Recently I gave a luncheon for 40 people at the Manila Hotel in honor of Gen. Santos, retiring Chief of Staff, and of Gen. Valdes, newly appointed to that post. The circumstances under which the change was made, gave a popular impression that everyone, including this office, was trying to kick Santos out. My luncheon was given, in the hope that Santos could make some "face"—so dear to the Oriental—through the implication that his transfer to his new job was really a promotion! He's a much abler man than his successor, but he's a "tan"[1] and that condemns him the eyes of the Mestizo group,[2] and that group runs the P.I. Sec. Alunan is Santos' new boss.

1. The "tans" were full-blooded Malayan. Quezon, a mestizo with "markedly Castillian features," was accused of racial prejudice by political opponents. Theodore Friend, *Between Two Empires: The Ordeal of the Philippines, 1929–1946* (New Haven: Yale University Press, 1965), 121–22.
2. The mestizos were Malay-Spanish.

JANUARY 18

Major De Lalande, representative of Brant Co. (Paris) made another visit to Manila. He's frightened we are going to buy a small amount of mortar equipment from American Armament Co. He talked & talked so much that he has convinced me that his company really fears A. A. Co. as possible competitor. But he convinced the General that there might be some danger (just what I don't know) in buying an experimental lot of A.A. equipment so that deal is off; although only one month ago it had been determined here in office to buy more of the stuff than I recommended. We don't have policies, we just walk tight ropes! Anyway, we are apparently to wait some more to see whether the Assembly will pass our bill to remit customs duties. If they do then we'll buy, the General says, a number of mortars directly from Brant with necessary training ammunition; to carry training along until U.S. Ord. gets in position to manufacture both on quantity and reasonable price basis. In the long run this may prove to be the best plan—but 60 days ago we told Department Commander that we were placing an immediate order for from 48–72 modern mortars (I recommended 12). We made this statement on what Sutherland told me was the General's decision and with this understanding the Dept. C.O. authorized us to take 10 loaned mortars off Luzon for training use in South. Now we'll wait another couple months to see what Assembly is going to do.

I've been discussing lately, with Mamie, exactly what to do in the way of asking for a definite terminating date to my tour. When we were put on the foreign service roster (Jan. 1, 1938) our tours of duty were automatically extended to Oct. 20, 1938. After Jimmy's death the President asked me to extend beyond that time, which I finally agreed to do on two conditions; first that I'd get a trip home this last summer on Commonwealth business; second that some arrangement could be made whereby, with no increased cost to me I could have air-conditioned quarters at the hotel. He unhesitatingly agreed and further asked, "What can I do to induce you to stay even longer than one year after your return?" I replied that since my reasons were chiefly domestic the matter was not open to discussion. He accepted that but expressed emphatically and repeatedly at that conference (which included breakfast and the remainder of the morning until 11:30) his satisfaction with my work, and his anxiety to keep me. In the meantime Vargas had, as previously reported, and with the President's approval, raised my local allowance from 600 to 1000 pesos per mo.

The year I agreed to do is up in Oct. 1939. But now I find that the W.D. expects me to make up the 4 mos. & 11 days I was out of the Dept. during my trip to the States. That will interrupt John's schooling, so, what to do!! If I go in Oct. (assuming W.D. approved) John's school still presents a serious problem! If I ask to go back this July, I'm breaking faith with Malacañan, and will have to get personal approval from Mr. Q. (I rather suspect I could get such approval easily, since I'm no longer so useful to them in doing a bunch of work at the Executive Offices.) Surprisingly enough, the General suggested strongly that I ask the W.D. for nothing except a 3 mos. extension, so as to return home in July '40! I must decide soon!

136   Eisenhower Library
                                        Miscellaneous Manuscripts, 1972

To Hugh A. Parker[1]

Dear Lefty: Time marches on! In my turn I'm beginning to consider the detailed arrangements incident to leaving the Philippines, and, like everyone else, past, present and future I find that for this reason I'd prefer an earlier ship, while for that a later one would suit me much better. So far we've figured some on: July, 1939. October, 1939. March, 1940. July, 1940.

Mamie and I almost daily line up all four of these dates in a row, somewhat like the stakes on a polo field. Then we start bending exercises around and among them, and keep it up until exhaustion halts the performance; and then, the next day we repeat the process, and come to the same tired ending. But I'm still in hopes that sometime, somehow, we'll figure out the most convenient date of departure so that the W. D. can say, "Oh, that won't do at all!"

My flying is very intermittent these days, and it suffered considerably due to the long layoff while I was in the States. Jew Lewis[2] says that I did <u>not</u> fall off in coordination, or in general air work. But as far as I'm concerned I haven't had the same confidence in landings. Part of this is due, undoubtedly, to the fact that I transferred to the front seat just at the moment I left here last summer. I've never really gotten the same feeling for height and distance from the front seat as I acquired in the back, so that as I come in I always want to look over the side and get an additional check on my height, etc., etc.

I had an amusing time learning a slow roll because they just let me work it out myself. I'd be O.K. until the ship started to recover, then I'd go haywire and kick things around, and so find myself in an angling dive. Finally I found out that if I'd do quite a lot of letting alone at the right time, everything was swell—so then the boys gave me a passing mark on that. Even said I did it better than "these Filipino Instructors". Then (possibly for fear I'd get cocky) Jew took me on my first blind flying about a week ago! You will remember that you gave me a book on the stuff, and at that time I memorized the essential paragraphs. But Lordy, Lordy, it took me only about 4 minutes to get into a steep diving spiral. I tried everything I could think of except throwing the stick out of the cockpit, but it just wound up lighter and tighter. I've had 3 lessons now—and I've gotten to the point where I mess along in an approximate fashion—but, so far as I'm concerned, that's one feature of flying that is plain, hard work! Then this morning I flew a few minutes in formation!! That is, I was told that that was the idea when we took off. Great guns! Within two minutes I thought the leader (Andy) was just a jack-in-a-box, with a hellish disposition. He was everywhere except just in front of and outside my left wing tip—where he belonged! I was perfectly willing, even anxious for him to stay there, but the guy didn't even seem to realize what I expected of him. I was working the throttle like a slide trombone, but nuts; I need backing straps and a black snake!

But I have a lot of fun—and even better than that—I think I furnish a lot of fun for the others out at the field, because I often see them grinning at me.

One day I went out and no P.T.[3] was on the line. So I got Sales[4] to fly with me and took a new B.T.,[5] one of them with the supercharged engine. Take off was O.K. but boy, if Sales had just let me gone, I'd still be up. I'd head for the field and try to slow her down. It seemed to me that I had her nose in my lap but I'd scoot over the field at 90–100; and clear the ground by 6 feet—at the FAR end. Well, I finally made 2 landings, but I'm a PT boy—to heck with these other babies.

Right now we're wrangling with Stearman about the characteristics of their 76—maybe we'll switch over to Waco or Curtis for our basic combat types. We'd like to stick with Stearman but we're very disappointed in performance of the 6 new ships we bought.[6]

If you see any of my friends, like Bill Lee or Freddie Kimble or most any of the old devils that are losing teeth, hair and disposition—give them my best.

All of us are O.K. and the whole gang sends best regards. Mamie and I send love to Janet, and, as always, cordial regards to yourself. As ever

1. Parker was stationed at Barksdale Field, Louisiana, at this time.

2. Eisenhower referred to Capt. Charles W. ("Jew") Lewis, who had replaced William L. "Jerry" Lee as chief military adviser to the Philippine Air Corps.

3. The "P.T." referred to the Stearman-built PT-1, the basic aircraft used to train Philippine pilots.

4. Lt. Oscar Sales was a student flying instructor with the Philippine Air Corps.

5. The BT-1, a Stinson Reliant, had a longer range and often was used for official flights. Eisenhower received training in both aircraft, although his flight training in the BT-1 usually occurred during official inspection trips throughout the islands. An advantage of the BT-1 was that, unlike the PT-1, it had dual controls.

6. The approach of World War II led to explosive growth within the American aircraft industry along with attendant corporate reorganization. Boeing acquired Stearman and utilized its new Stearman Division exclusively to build trainers for the Army Air Corps; the parent company concentrated its production on the building of heavy bombers. Curtiss (Eisenhower incorrectly spelled the name) built many of the best American fighter aircraft, including the famous P-40 Warhawk. Eisenhower might have had in mind the Curtiss P-36C, unveiled in 1939. The Waco Aircraft Company dedicated its war production exclusively to building transport aircraft. See Frank J. Taylor and Lawton Wright, *Democracy's Air Arsenal* (New York: Duell, Sloan and Pearce, 1947); Enzo Angelucci, *The Rand McNally Encyclopedia of Military Aircraft, 1914–1980* (New York: Military Press, 1983); and Wesley Frank Craven and James Lea Cate, eds., *The Army Air Forces in World War II: Men and Planes* (Chicago: University of Chicago Press, 1955), 6:193–227.

137

MARCH 9, 1939–MARCH 18, 1939

MARCH 9

Last week the 1st Boeing clipper arrived in Manila, on the same day that the first unit of our Mosquito fleet, a 55-foot Thornycroft motor torpedo boat, reached here. One 65 foot boat is due to arrive in a couple of months.

General MacArthur has apparently been quite disturbed lately concerning the President's attitude toward the defense program. The General says that the President does not really believe in the plan, and is ready to sabotage it at the 1st opportunity. The two of them must have had a conversation within the past 2 or 3 weeks that did not sit so well with the General. One thing that upsets the General is the President's continuous efforts to re-enforce and improve the constabulary, even at the expense of the army. The General was not successful in getting the government to return to us sums spent on import duties, although it was suggested that we could obtain reimbursement in our next budget. Moreover, under agreement with Malacañan there is none included in the 1939 budget (6 mos. period to July 1) and in 1945 budget a proviso to effect that if there is a shortage of funds in the general treasury, constabulary expenses may be charged to the army. If this should happen we could not function! In any event it is obvious that General MacA. is fearful of what Pres. Q. may or may not do and, in our office conferences, constantly expresses dissatisfaction with the Pres. and criticizes many of his actions, whether or not these actions have any connection with the army.

One thing that the General talked about a lot was the President's action in getting P500,000 from the Assembly for "law enforcement". The excuse was the very serious labor unrest, accompanied by some disorder & lawlessness, that has lately been experienced in Bulacan, Pangasinan, etc. What the need for this money is, I don't know since the constabulary now has 350 officers and 4500 men and if these were properly employed, no additional help should be necessary. However, Gen. Francisco,[1] head of Constabulary is not too bright, and has probably dispersed his force so widely as to have no adequate reserves left. My own opinion that the P500,000 incident is merely the President's way of notifying the whole country that the whole govt. is back of him in keeping order etc. But the incident apparently stirred up the ire of the General who believes that the labor trouble was used only as an excuse by the Pres. in order to get in his hands a large sum of money that could be spent without supervision. ? ?[2]

More and more it becomes obvious that constructive action on this job has almost ceased. In the office itself the work is so uncoordinated that operation is difficult. I do not know, and cannot find out, how much money is available for important training and selected projects and much of our confusion arises from absence of intimate, daily, contacts with Malacañan. Further, since there is no head of this office—except the General—who is here only an hour a day—everyone does as he pleases, and no real coordinated progress is possible. I'm ready, more than ready, from a professional viewpoint, to go home. Interest has gone. I work on academic subjects, because I have no longer power or opportunity to start execution of needed projects. I hate confining work that shows no results—so, as soon as I can decently go—I'll simply Hooray!!

1. In his evaluation of officers for Quezon, Eisenhower wrote the following opinion of Francisco: "Honest but . . . of little creative ability. A satisfactory staff officer under a competent chief, but otherwise mediocre." See Memorandum on Philippine Officers, McCann Papers, Eisenhower Library.

2. The question marks are Eisenhower's.

A situation has arisen that looks desperately serious for the prospects of ultimate success in the MacA. defense plan. Our annual mobilization (for training purposes only) was limited by the General to 10 days for units comprising 1937 graduates only. Even with this limited number it looks as if we'd have plenty of trouble. About half the reserve officers so far contacted have said they cannot report for 10 days training, and because of our lack of reserve officers, we have not enough, in any event, to assign to T. of O. strength. We continue to suffer from the great error made in 1936 when it was decided to abandon a gradual process of development, beginning with officers, N.C.O.s,[1] and overhead, in favor of training hordes of draftees. We must swing back quickly and attempt to correct the error, or else.

The worst thing about the present situation is that it indicates a general indifference, if not antagonism, to the defense plan. An intensive, intelligent, educational program must be undertaken. This was urgently recommended to Gen. 3 yrs. ago—but he pooh-poohed the idea of its necessity.

I'm starting a campaign, using every available means to get this year's mobilization in shape, but it will be touch and go—and the long range problem will not be solved until we've shifted emphasis to the production of numbers of good reserve officers, & developed a real public opinion in support of the plan.

1. Noncommissioned officers.

138

Eisenhower Library
Pre-presidential Papers, Philippine Islands File

ADDRESS TO THE RESERVE OFFICERS' TRAINING CORPS[1]

MARCH 24, 1939

The Commonwealth Government is presently engaged in the development and utilization of its resources to meet the anticipated problems of future independence. In the fields of economics, politics, industry, social science, education and national security, great questions present themselves constantly for consideration, and the effects of answers developed today will extend indefinitely into the future. Among these questions none is clothed in greater significance than that of providing an adequate security, of developing the means and methods that will assure reasonable protection for the nation once it has been completely freed of all outside control, and, coincidentally, stripped of all outside support.

Military discussions need not, in these days, be prefaced with long and exhaustive arguments to prove a nation's need for defensive strength. World events, daily reported in our newspapers, continue to hammer home the deplorable fact that life, liberty and property are not safe in a defenseless nation when coveted by a more powerful neighbor. Indeed, this is not a newly discovered truth—two thousand years ago the greatest of all men said, "When a strong man, armed, keepeth his palace, his goods are in peace."

In the program adopted by the Philippines to meet its defensive requirements, the Reserve Officers' Training Corps is an indispensable feature. Consequently, in a very direct and important fashion, the destiny of an independent Philippines will be influenced and determined by the Reserve Officers' Training Corps of today and of tomorrow.

Because of the great significance to future Filipino welfare of this organization I feel particularly honored in the invitation to address you today. Entertaining such a conviction, I have not come here merely to offer you customary, though very sincere, congratulations upon the obvious perfection of your military ceremonies, nor upon the completion of another definite step in your academic and military education. Neither shall I attempt, in resounding generality, to expound upon those ennobling human sentiments and beautiful philosophies that are so frequently the subject of the commencement discourse. Rather, I am here to talk to you as one soldier to another on military matters that I am convinced will become of increasing importance to you and to your country as the years roll on.

As members of the Reserve Officers' Training Corps you are primarily citizens, and secondarily, soldiers. In the first of these capacities you enjoy all the rights and privileges of any other citizen; in the other you are compelled to forego such of those rights and privileges as involve participation in the political activities, decisions and policies of your nation. This distinction must be meticulously observed, because, in a democracy, the military is and must remain subordinate to civil power; the army is nothing but the servant, the tool, of civil government. Since this discussion is between soldiers, let us not concern ourselves with the wisdom of any political decision of the past or speculate on the possibility of significant political changes of the future. Rather, let us accept the political pattern as it now exists and as now projected by existing conventions, and confine ourselves to an investigation of our own duties, our own responsibilities and our own opportunities within this sphere.

The Philippine Defense plan was conceived in the purpose of providing maximum security at minimum financial cost. Of such dominating influence was, and is, the need for minimizing expense, that all thought of developing a strong professional army had to be flatly rejected. For this reason if for no other, the citizen-soldier must be the bulwark of Philippine defense! Lack of money with which to hire workmen for any task is not serious, provided we are ready, and able, to do the job ourselves. So long as there exists among a nation's citizens a common and flaming determination to protect themselves and their homes against any invasion by force, they can, in unified effort, develop a formidable defensive power. The Philippine Defense plan assumes that this spirit does exist and will continue to grow and flourish in these Islands.

As a consequence of these considerations and assumptions, the defense plan simply provides the machinery whereby the free citizens of this country may cooperate toward their own protection. They must be reasonably trained, properly equipped, well organized and efficiently led, so that they may be instantaneously ready in every province and barrio to line your beaches with the defensive fires that will beat back any attempted invasion. The plans attempt to provide, in detail, for satisfaction of these various requirements.

The function of the Reserve Officers' Training Corps, in this great program, is to develop commissioned officers for the citizen forces; that is, for the great bulk of the whole Army.

The officer is the keystone of the military arch. No army can carry out a difficult task, indeed it can scarcely perform the routine functions of peace without an efficient officer corps. Ragged armies, poorly equipped, badly outnumbered and half starved have, in the world's history, earned astounding victories when efficiently led. On the other hand, I know of no army in which the officer corps was rotten with corruption or professionally was inept, lazy and stupid, that has achieved decisive results, even over an inconsequential opponent.

You are a cross-section of the Philippines' finest young manhood, a cross-section that has been unusually favored in educational and cultural advantages, and possibly, also in economic standing. You are the men to whom others of your generation will naturally turn, in times of stress, for leadership. If, in that greatest of all crises, war, you are to be worthy of your birthright, and ready upon your country's call to lead men in battle, it means years of study and self-preparation.

There is no royal road to this goal—good blood and breeding may produce an excellent raw material, but only earnest and continued work can transform it into a useful lieutenant, an efficient captain, a capable general.[2] Successful defense of these Islands will never be possible unless you devote yourselves to this work, this study, this preparation, even while you are engaged in wresting a living from the world for yourselves and your dependents. Furthermore, you must do this without financial remuneration, your sole reward the sanctity of your firesides, the esteem of your countrymen and the approval of your own conscience.

Here, then, is the challenge to you as individuals and as an organization. Will you make of yourselves good officers? Between success and failure lies a vast gulf of personal and national possibilities—even perhaps the difference between virile independence and hopeless bondage.

The thorough training of an officer is an intricate process. On the physical side he must develop his stamina and strength, as well as a certain dexterity in those movements and exercises in which he, as a junior officer, is required to be an instructor. His mental training includes general, as well as a variety of technical subjects such as organization, armament, tactics, supply and logistics. He must specialize in aviation, infantry, artillery or another of the arms or services. He must develop his analytical powers, his judgment, his initiative. He must know something of practical or applied psychology, he must be a bit of a doctor, an engineer, something even of a butcher, a baker and a cook. On the moral side he must be fair and just, honest and straightforward; he must learn to make firm decisions and to accept responsibility for them without seeking to shift it either to superior or subordinate. He must understand men so that he may lead rather than merely command them; he must achieve self-confidence and courage, and, finally, he must be loyal—loyal to his Government, to his superiors, to himself and to his subordinates.

These qualifications may not be forced upon any individual. He may be assisted in their acquisition, he may be advised, he may be instructed, but in the final analysis, they come only of his own intense desire, his own straight-thinking and understanding, his own work, his own sweat!

The government provides you necessary equipment, it assigns instructors and it prescribes courses of training designed to teach you professional technique, and calculated to develop your powers of leadership. In the class room and on the drill ground the officer may learn much; but his natural field of instruction is on the march and in camp with his men. There he practices as he learns, and he learns with his mind, his muscles, and his heart. Never, so long as you are serious in your desire to develop yourself into a good officer, pass by an opportunity to go to the field with the men of your command. Every minute so spent will yield untold dividends if the time should come when the mobilization call is not for training, but for war.

Though by law you are obligated to such military service as your country may demand of you—your great President and your Government have not failed to realize that service performed only on a required basis cannot assure the ultimate safety of the Philippines. Woodrow Wilson once said "The highest form of efficiency is the spontaneous cooperation of a free people." The Philippine plan goes even farther than this. It says, in effect, "The defense of the Philippines is completely dependent upon the spontaneous cooperation of its citizens, the law is nothing more than the written expression of a universal purpose."

Your part, as the potential leaders in this cooperative enterprise, consequently requires more than routine work in the instructional courses laid out for you. These must be pursued thoroughly, willingly, even eagerly. The impulse for greater opportunity to learn should come from you—not from the Government. Never should we hear of a Filipino seeking to avoid military instruction, and if there should be any such, the contempt of his fellows should silence him forever. Moreover, you men, selected for training as leaders in time of war should also be the crusaders for and the shining examples of this cooperative spirit, in time of peace. Just as you have more than the average to lose in the event of national disaster, so should you, aside from nobler and more unselfish reasons, be most active in providing insurance against disaster. No physically fit young man in the universities and colleges of these Islands should permit himself to be excluded from the complete R.O.T.C. instruction. Let your actions prove to the country that the R.O.T.C. places pride of service above personal convenience, duty above immediate economic gain. When this organization, operating in this spirit, is graduating yearly into the Reserve ranks of the Army at least 2,000 young, eager, well-trained lieutenants, who, thereafter will pursue higher courses of instruction to the limit of their respective abilities, then the Reserve Officers' Training Corps will be doing its full duty to the nation.

No person familiar with the long record of this institution in contributing to Filipino progress and welfare, and with the reputation of its President and faculty for public spirited leadership, can doubt that, assembled on this campus, are all the ingredients necessary to success. The result is in your hands—and if you meet the issue with courage and determination, then each of you will be doing his part in assuring that the future of the Philippine Islands will be as a beautiful and enduring edifice, in which the Reserve Officers' Training Corps will be one of the principal supporting pillars.

1. Eisenhower delivered this address to the ROTC at commencement exercises at the University of the Philippines. The full document title is "Notes for Address by Lt. Col. D. D. Eisenhower, Commencement Exercises of the R.O.T.C., University of the Philippines, March 24, 1939."
2. Eisenhower may refer to the former practice in the Philippine Army of officers either purchasing their rank or inheriting it because of social status.

139
Eisenhower Library
Philippine Diary

APRIL 5, 1939–APRIL 17, 1939

APRIL 5

Several days ago the President called me personally to the phone, about 6:30 P.M., asking me to come immediately to Malacañan. This was on the evening of March 28. We had a 3 hour talk; Secretary Vargas was present. Many things were troubling him, and after making it clear to him that I recognized his right to question me, since he is the only chief I have on this job, except as he delegates his functions to another, I told him I would give him my personal convictions and any information I might have—on any military subject. He warned me that the conversation was to be considered secret.

He opened the talk by asking me whether or not it was improper for the G.S. (through its chief) making to him any recommendation it might choose to make on a military subject. I, of course, said "No—that one of the functions of the G.S. was to develop policy, and where these required such action, to submit them to him for approval." He then showed me a letter, written in the G.S. and apparently intended for his consideration. On this letter appeared an endorsement, signed by Sutherland, stating that the subject was one outside the purview of G.S. responsibility and would therefore be withdrawn from consideration by that body. I stalled a bit—and then told him, "Certain broad policies, it is assumed, have been permanently established by the highest general staff, namely the President himself in consultation with his Military Adviser. In such cases it was probably wise to prevent constant agitation of the question in the G.S., or elsewhere, as tending only to confuse, and, in any event, wasting time and effort."

He acknowledged some force to this argument but said, "But why am I denied an opportunity even to see the arguments on another side of that question?" I replied that that was a matter between him and his Mil. Adv.

He then asked me whether the production of a good officer corps was one of our real problems. The answer to that was obvious. Then he asked, "If that is so, why did we plunge into the mass training of enlisted reservists before we had the officers, at a time when we knew we did not have them, to do the job with reasonable efficiency?" To this I shot back, "Because you directed it, in the spring of 1936. The original plan contemplated the calling of only 3000 trainees in Jan., 1937, and, so Col. Ord & I were informed, you decided to raise this to 20,000, after consultation with the Mil. Adv." He replied that he had not made such a decision, and had been, from the start, opposed to the idea of rushing too rapidly into the training of enlisted reservists. I told him I could throw no more light on the subject, and that if he'd examine the records of 1936 he could easily substantiate my statements. One piece of direct evidence, I told him, was that for 1936 we had asked for only 350,000 pesos for construction, a sum which could not begin to supply the shelter and so on needed for 20,000 men. I informed him, further, that the reasons given to Col. Ord and me for this change was that he, the President, believed the psychological reaction of the people would be bad if only a small number of trainees was inducted promptly after the first registration of military manpower. He just said, "I never heard of such a thing."

Then he said, "If it is possible, I'm going to correct that mistake now! I'm going to call fewer trainees, and devote more money to officer development."

It then came out that his distrust of our present corps of officers was based on the results of several courts-martial. He considers, properly, that these courts have condoned offenses for which dismissal, and even prison sentences, would have been appropriate. He cited several instances.

I explained to the Pres., in detail, that I no longer was concerned in any personnel or administrative matter. I explained General MacA's famous "re-organization" order of Oct. 14, which relieved me as his C. of S., and placed in my hands only planning, training, etc. The President expressed great astonishment—and wanted to know why! I replied I did not know but it developed that one of his reasons for sending for me was because he assumed that due to my experience here, and so on, I was General MacA's chief assistant for all functions. I disabused his mind.

He speculated whether or not the decision to call 20,000 men in 1937 (total of 40,000 for the year) was based upon Gen's desire to be Field Marshal, with the resultant idea that it would be a good thing to get some soldiers under arms so the appointment would have some basis in logic. He said he bitterly opposed the appointment, although he did not say he opposed it openly to General MacA. He did say that the incident made his government look ridiculous!! I was astounded, since General MacA's account of the same affair was exactly the opposite already related, I think, in these notes. Somebody certainly has lied!!! The Gen. said he accepted the appointment with great reluctance, and only because refusal would have mortally offended the Pres.!! Wow!!

A dozen other related subjects were brought up and the Pres. discussed all in a manner that I thought showed a fine, thoughtful mind, and a much keener insight into some things of questionable validity than one would suppose if he listened only to the talk in this office.

I told the Pres. I wanted to go home. The matter was not discussed in detail, but he expressed the hope I'd stay until next year.

Secretary Vargas has called me on phone several times to ask about particular subjects and each time has told me he has been instructed by the President to have me re-detailed to Malacañan. (Contact duty requiring about 30 minutes per day.) I have told him time and again that I have no objection to doing the work, just as I have also told the President. But I've tried to make it clear to them that, for some reason, General MacA. planned otherwise, and my arbitrary detail by Presidential authority would make Gen. MacA furious. They, of course, want to keep on good terms with their Mil. Adv.; so the only way they can handle the matter is to get MacA approval. That, I doubt they can do—he thinks I'm likely to consider myself too important. I doubt that he even believes me when I say, the sooner I get out of here, the better I'll like it!

Well, we'll see what develops.

Made a trip to the Mountains Province Fri-Sat-Sunday.

Plane to Bagabag. Jitney through the rice terrace areas, plane from Naguilian. Johnny, Capt. Lewis & I on the trip.

Visited Banaue; Bontoc; Sagada (Mission) Sabantan; Mt. Data blocked there by landslide, back to Sabantan and over to Cervantes; then west to coast, down to Nagulian & home.

Rain made the narrow mountain trail treacherous, and caused many slides; all of us were jittery most of the time.

Terraces wonderful—worth the scares!

140

Eisenhower Library
Foltz Papers

To David and Ida Eisenhower[1]

APRIL 21, 1939

Johnny and I have just completed a trip to the "Bontoc" region of the Philippines, where tribes, called the Igorotes, still semi-barbaric in culture have, over a period of some three thousand years, developed a system of rice raising that involves the terracing of whole mountain sides. Rice is raised in paddies, or relatively small plots, that must be so constructed as to hold water to a depth of several inches. A typical mountain side, prepared for rice raising, therefore resembles a series of gigantic steps, the outside wall varying in depth from two to twenty feet, with the top perfectly level and about a foot lower than the water-proof retaining wall. The water is brought in by several methods, the first of course being by direct rainfall, which in some seasons of the year is extremely heavy. In certain cases, a spring will empty itself into the top terrace, and an opening in the outside wall of that terrace keeps the water at the desired level, and permits excess water to flow down into the next. This is repeated as long as the water lasts. In other cases, where a swift stream boils down the mountain side, a sufficient amount is merely taken off at each level, and where this fortunate condition exists, every inch of ground is cultivated, and the terraces are crowded together to take full advantage of the abundant water supply. Since many terraces have been constructed on barren, rocky, slopes, the topsoil has been brought in, often for a distance of miles, in baskets carried on the head. Often the slopes are incredibly steep, so that it makes the person raised on Kansas' flat prairies extremely tired and fatigued just to watch the Igorotes scampering up and down the mountain side.

Since, in the past, some of the tribes were very war-like (it is the country of the so-called head-hunters) the villages were ordinarily built on small steep, promontories, which could be easily defended. From these villages the people have to go daily to care for the rice, maintain the terraces, regulate the water and so on. In the circumstances just going to and coming from work would completely exhaust the average American and leave him unfit for any productive labor.

In some instances a mountain side may be suited to raising of rice except for lack of water. Where a sizeable stream runs through the valley this problem has been partially solved through the construction of irrigation systems. Since the country is mountainous the streams ordinarily have a considerable fall, or drop per mile, so, by topping the river a sufficient distance up-stream from the area to be cultivated, it is possible, of course, to bring the water down in a ditch paralleling the stream to the desired spot. But to carry out this simple idea has involved an amount of labor, all of it performed by hand and with only the crudest of tools, that no other people would even have undertaken. We followed one such ditch for several miles, certainly no less than five. Every foot of it was cut out of solid rock, and often, because of the configuration of the mountain sides, tunnels had to be dug through projecting points. On top of all these difficulties was the additional one of getting across the tributaries cutting into the main stream. Whenever these entered, the ditch had to be carried all the way up to the headwaters of the tributary, adding miles to the required construction.

All in all, a visit to the region leaves one well convinced that the rice terraces of the Bontocs deserve to rank, as they do, with the special wonders of man's accomplishments in this world. Moreover, there is no room left for doubting the archaeologists' contention that the terraces were begun at approximately the time of Moses.

The region is difficult of access. The mountain roads, or tracks, are so narrow that one-way traffic, controlled by gates, is compulsory. It is normal to be riding along a narrow winding shelf road, with hundreds of feet of over-hanging boulders and rocks on one side, and a seemingly bottomless abyss on the other. The roads have steep grades and during wet weather, which we had, the frequent slides across the road render it slippery and exceedingly treacherous. We were blocked at one spot by a land slide that was more than one hundred feet in length, and as many deep. A huge pine tree, certainly 50–75 years old, was carried down with the slide and sprawled drunkenly across the road. Luckily we were a few minutes behind its occurrence, and so, instead of being tossed over a sheer drop of some two thousand feet, we had merely to back carefully, I don't know how far, until we found a spot that permitted us cautiously and laboriously, but successfully, to turn around. Then we had to travel an extra hundred miles to get out of the mountains.

When I started this letter, I had no idea of including in it such a lengthy and wordy description of our trip. But since I have done so, I'll try to get one or two prints of pictures Johnny took in the region. They should tell you the story much better than I can.

All of us send love and best wishes to you two. Devotedly your son

1. Mamie Eisenhower sent a copy of this letter to her parents on this date. She wrote on the letter, "This is a letter Ike wrote his Dad and Mother, it was such a good description of their trip he had it mimeographed for you to read."

141   The Citadel Archives
                                                 Mark Wayne Clark Collection

To Mark Clark

May 27, 1939

Dear Wayne:[1] I've just received W. D. orders assigning me to the 15th Infantry at Lewis.[2] I'm delighted with the detail, although there are still some points to iron out administratively before the orders become effective. Apparently my present tour would, if handled according to accepted routine, be terminated next March. The orders read about as follows: "Colonel Eisenhower's foreign service tour is shortened to August provided all authorities in the Philippines concur. Otherwise tour shortened to November". I have a hunch that the Commonwealth officials are going to ask for some postponement of effective date but I've already told them that I consider myself lucky to get Ft. Lewis and the 15th, and don't want to take chances. All in all I don't know what to count on as yet, but I should know in a few days.

While the powers-that-be are figuring out that part of it, I thought I'd get off some questions to you. To begin:

How about school for my son, who will be in his senior year in high school next year? I heard that the officers of the 15th have no quarters on the post. Is this true? I heard also that a lot of construction is going on at Lewis. Does the program include quarters for officers of 15th? If so, when will they be completed? How much longer are you due to be at Lewis? Is it easy to bring uniforms in that sector? (After four years in the P.I. I do not own a presentable States uniform.) Has a Colonel been assigned to the Regiment? Our last information is that Col. McAndrew[3] has gone, but we have heard nothing about a successor.

Give me any other dope you think I ought to have.

Please pay my respects to General Sweeney. He knows, without my saying it, that I'm looking forward with real pleasure to service under him. I've met Fred Walker,[4] and although he probably won't remember me, give him friendly greetings from me when you see him.

I'll deeply appreciate on a return airmail answer to my questions, and promise to buy you a drink next fall, in payment for the clipper stamp you'll have to put on the letter.

With warm regards, Cordially

1. Clark's close friends always addressed him as "Wayne."

2. The orders to leave were a direct result of the efforts of Clark and James Ulio. See Daniel D. Holt, "An Unlikely Partnership and Service: Dwight D. Eisenhower, Mark W. Clark, and the Philippines," *Kansas History* 13 (autumn 1990): 158–59; and Clark to Eisenhower, May 27, 1939, Mark Wayne Clark Collection, The Citadel Archives.

3. Joseph A. McAndrew (USMA, 1903) commanded the 15th Infantry Regiment in China (1937–39). He retired in 1944.

4. During World War II, Maj. Gen. Fred L. Walker commanded the 36th Infantry Division in the Italian campaign through its march into Rome on June 5, 1944. He became a bitter antagonist to Mark Clark after World War II because of the tremendous casualties suffered by the 36th Division during the Rapido River crossing in Italy. Walker retired in 1946.

142

The Citadel Archives
Mark Wayne Clark Collection

TO MAJOR MARK CLARK

JUNE 7, 1939[1]

Is there a Tacoma boarding school of excellent high school standing where my son could enter in September pending my later arrival. Please rush radio reply

1. This telegram was sent to Clark at Fort Lewis.

143

The Citadel Archives
Mark Wayne Clark Collection

TO MAJOR MARK CLARK

JUNE 22, 1939

Dear Wayne: Thank you very much for your clipper letter. My original orders for Ft. Lewis indicated an effective date of next November, but stated that if all authorities here should agree, I might leave in August. This last provision was on my own request, so that my son's schooling might not be interrupted. However, the Commonwealth authorities here are very reluctant to let me go in August, in fact they brought some pressure on me to stay another complete year. Since the local government has been more than considerate to me during my whole tour here I did not feel justified in insisting upon my desire to leave in August; but did inform them that I must go before the end of this year.

In these circumstances it seemed to me that the only thing to do was to send my son John on ahead so that he could enter school in September. I now find that neither he nor his mother consider this a good plan, both of them insisting that he is to stay until the three of us can come together. Since this dovetails with my own inclination, even though it violates the dictates of good judgment, I suppose it is the program we shall follow.

Reports have reached Mamie (my wife) to the effect that servants are almost impossible to secure in that region. She hears also that when one is sufficiently fortunate to secure a servant their wages are extraordinarily high, and union hours must be observed. Can you give me any information on this point?

I sincerely hope that a house will be available by the time I report to the post, since, if possible, we expect to enjoy lengthy visits from both our families.

I shall soon write to the Quartermaster General concerning the shipment of my property, which is now stored on the East Coast. Some of it is in cold storage in Washington, D.C., the remainder is in a government warehouse. I am anxious to have it reach Ft. Lewis before I arrive and feel certain there will be no difficulty about its proper care and storage while there. Is there anything I need to know on this point before writing an official letter to the Quartermaster General?

I can scarcely tell you how delighted I am that you have another year and a half to serve at Ft. Lewis. I do not worry much about other conditions of Army service, but I do like to be at a place where I have a fine friend.

Once again I engage myself to purchase a drink for every airmail stamp you use on me, and when I say "a drink" I naturally include Mrs. Clark.

Thanks for your advice as to uniforms; I will not attempt to procure any until I arrive at Ft. Lewis.

It is disappointing to learn that General Sweeney will probably leave the post about the time that I arrive. However, he will make one swell CORPS AREA COMMANDER, and undoubtedly will have to make frequent official inspections of his old station.

With cordial regards, and sincere appreciation of your kindness and help. As ever

When you see my brother,[1] if ever, tell him I received his radio but that my son will not come home ahead of me. You will probably wonder why the words Corps Area Commander are capitalized and underlined. The story behind that is simple, but typical of the service we get out of Filipino stenographers. I wrote this letter in long hand, and, inadvertently put <u>Department</u> Commander instead of Corps Area. Then I made a slight botch of correcting the mistake, and finally printed the words, as you see them above, so there could be no mistake. The crossing out of the original words was taken by the copyist as underlining. Of course he does not <u>ask</u> me about it. That would have meant loss of face.

1. Eisenhower's brother, Edgar, lived in Tacoma, Washington.

144   The Citadel Archives
                                  Mark Wayne Clark Collection

To Major Mark Clark

JUNE 28, 1939

Dear Wayne: Thanks a lot for the Fort Lewis Army Day Program, which just arrived. Naturally, it is full of interest for me and my family. Not long ago we saw, in a local movie, some shots showing maneuvers of your Tank Company on Army Day.

The other day I received a note from Jimmy Ulio (Executive in office of T.A.G.), telling me that, according to the Chief of Infantry, I was set up on next year's slate as second ranking officer in the 15th. This is of no special importance, I suppose, except that I thought it might have some bearing on the possibility of my obtaining a house, rather than an apartment. What do you think?

Mamie and I are truly grateful for your kind offer to take us in your home during the "settling" period. We'll hope to avoid any such imposition on your hospitality, but whether or not we have to park on you a day or so, we will always appreciate your invitation.

I'll have to buy a new car when I come home; it will be one of the Plymouth-Ford-Chevrolet variety. But we may bring along, also, an old Plymouth we have, for Mamie to run about the post only. I got the impression, last October, that the post, proper, covers quite a lot of territory, and her little tin can might come in handy for going to the Commissary, Post Exchange, ladies' bridge clubs, and what not. The Q. M. will [ship] it to San Francisco, and all I'd have to do is pay the freight to Ft. Lewis, which, I think, couldn't be more than thirty or forty dollars.

I don't expect you to answer all my letters to you. We're just getting so pepped up as the time slowly approaches for us to come there, that ideas connected with our transfer pop into my head and I grab a moment to dash off a line to you. Be patient with me and maybe I'll wear myself down.

With kind remembrances to the General, and cordial regards to yourself, Faithfully

JULY 16, 1939–JULY 20, 1939

JULY 16

Have brought home a typewriter with the idea of using it hereafter in letter writing and in making these notes. Dictation to Filipino stenographers is not only frequently irritating and patience trying; it often prevents a free expression of opinion because so many subjects seem to involve evaluation of racial characteristics. For a long time I've been trying to jot down an occasional note in longhand, but when I found the other day that in certain cases I could not decipher my own writing I decided the time had come to do something about it.

During May so many difficulties arose involving misunderstandings with, or at least, lack of effective contacts with Malacañan, that Secretary Vargas finally took the bull by the horns and insisted that I undertake my old liaison job. So now I go there every day.

While I doubt that we can ever again get things running in their old time smoothness, we are at least spared many embarrassments and irritations that were habitual when our contacts with that office consisted only in seeing the papers that were sent to our office daily through a junior clerk.

A couple of weeks ago the General published a statement setting forth his views with respect to the "Jap" menace to the Philippines. So far as anyone could see there was no excuse for the outbreak except that Gov. McNutt[1] had said, in support of his contention that the U.S. should hold on [to] the Islands, that upon independence they would immediately fall prey to the military might of the Japs. The General not only argued that the defenses of the islands would be effective; he rather pooh-poohed the possibility of a Japanese aggression in this region. TJ and I, as usual, recommended against breaking into print; and, as usual to no effect. Locally we have seen but one American newspaper comment on the statement. The N.Y. Tribune ridiculed it. When he was insisting that the statement HAD to be published the General discounted the idea that the possibility of antagonizing Mr. McNutt would have any effect on his acknowledged political ambitions because he had decided that the High Commissioner was not going anywhere, and, he concluded, the statement would be acclaimed locally among the politicians; renewing his own popularity and cementing his hold upon his job.

A week after the above incident the news came out that Gov. McNutt had accepted an important political job at home under the auspices of the New Deal. This act, in the General's opinion, immeasurably strengthened the Gov's political standing, so, post-haste he got off a flowery letter of congratulations, hoping desperately the Gov. would not read anything personal in his argumentive statement of a week earlier.

Two days ago the evening broadcast contained an item to the effect that Congressman Kennedy[2] was recommending to Pres. Roosevelt the appointment of the Gen. as High Commissioner. Burning to secure some political job that would restore the power, prestige and face that he has lost during the past four years through ego, laziness and stupidity the Gen. immediately undertook, characteristically, some of the machinations that he conceives to be clever. He wired Steve Early, Congressman Van Zandt[3] and Simpson, a newspaper man, asking their support.

Since the wires went through the department (by no chance would he spend the money for commercial dispatch) every officer of the Dept. Staff will immediately know that he is in the position of importuning for a job. Assuming that he will not get it, although it is perfectly true that four years ago the Pres. announced to him an intention of making the appointment at that time, there will be an additional number of people here who will feel entitled to sneer at his connivings, and will read, between the lines, that he is getting fearful and discontented in his present job. It's his business, exclusively, but I get exceedingly tired of defending him in front of personal critics for words and deeds that I consider as stupid as they do. Ho-hum.

One reason that the Military Adviser's post has lost for him some of its former attractiveness is continued proof that he is losing influence and prestige, that no longer may he announce an arbitrary decision and see it accepted as the law of the Medes and Persians by the President and the Army. Almost four years ago poor old Jim and I tried to make him see that the price of staying at the top of the heap was eternal watchfulness and, above all, so conducting himself and his job as to inspire confidence and a <u>dependence upon him</u> for important information and decisions. We begged him to arrange a weekly meeting with the President, so that there would not grow up a tendency on the part of the President to depend upon others. He ridiculed us. He was then riding so high that his favorite description of himself was the "Elder Statesman". He informed us that it was not in keeping with the dignity of his position for him to report once a week to Malacañan.

While I was home last summer the Scout question came to the fore once more, and the General's decisions and attitude were so unsatisfactory to the Scouts that many of them left us and went back to the American Army. At that time he succeeded in working up the President to the point where the latter believed in a "scout cabal seeking the eventual seizure of the government a la Cuba!" So—with a supposedly decisive victory, one that clearly re-established his power and prestige, the General felt that all was clear on his horizon. But the Scouts did not quit . . . [4] As time went on they kept dinning away until the Pres. got another slant on the whole affair. Finally in a public speech, that is, it was public so far as the officers of the Army were concerned, the Pres. announced that he was misinformed as to the fact at the time he expressed a desire to get rid of the Scouts, that he had acted hastily, that he regretted his statements and decisions of that time and that he would seek to correct them. The General was present when all this was said, and I think it was really the first time that he clearly realized how far we had come from the days when the merest expression of his "professional opinion" served to enlist enthusiastic and universal support for any and all of his schemes.

Of course, to those of us that were close to events, and not concerned with our own future fortunes, nor blinded by illusions of glittering grandeur the trend had been plainly visible for months. But such indications as had come to the Gen. previously had, in his opinion, been discernable to no one else, consequently he had, he thought, lost no FACE. For a man of his type the answer was to ignore them. This he did . . . . . but now, under the lash of practically public repudiation on a particular incident, he writhes. Just as, in his own mind, he was formerly higher in public prestige and official position than he was in reality (although lord knows he was high enough) so now he really believes himself to be closer to disaster than he is. Mr Q. is not going to let him go . . . . he cannot afford to except as a voluntary act on the part of the Gen. or as a result of almost open insubordination. He, the Pres., has too often tied his administration and his govt. to the PLANS and ADVICE of the Gen., and done this publicly and emphatically, to cut him suddenly adrift.

And that is enough of all that.

A few weeks ago I received WD orders to go to Ft. Lewis upon expiration of my tour. The question of the official terminating date was taken directly to the CoS by the AG, according to personal advices from Jim Ulio, and it was decided to shorten my tour to November at the latest. I was further authorized, if I could arrange with local officials, to come home in August. All this came about as a result of letters I wrote to Jim Ulio, because for many reasons Mamie and I were looking with longing eyes to our return date.[5] It turned out to be impracticable to get away in August, but we are going in November.

John's schooling presented a problem, but we finally agreed to keep him right here and bring him home with us in the fall.

We are delighted with the Ft. Lewis prospect. We believe we'll like the place thoroughly. Be a little tough to give up 500 dollars a month . . . . . but that had to end soon anyway.

1. Paul V. McNutt was the second high commissioner to the Philippines, succeeding Frank Murphy in 1937.

2. Congressman Martin Kennedy, a New York Democrat, was appointed to the Seventy-first Congress in 1930 to fill a vacancy. He then was reelected, serving from 1931 to 1945.

3. James Van Zandt served in the U.S. House of Representatives from 1939 to 1943 and from 1947 to 1963. A naval veteran of World War I, World War II, and the Korean War, Republican Van Zandt served on the House Armed Services Committee, eventually becoming the ranking Republican member during Eisenhower's presidency. Van Zandt had been an active supporter of MacArthur for president.

4. The ellipses in this letter are Eisenhower's. Apparently, when he used a typewriter he substituted ellipses for dashes. He used this method in all typewritten entries.

5. Ulio and Mark Clark assisted Eisenhower with his arrangements to transfer to Fort Lewis. Clark and his wife obtained quarters (the Clarks even sent the window measurements so Mamie could make curtains for the windows before they left the Philippines) and made the arrangements for the Eisenhower family's arrival. See Holt, "An Unlikely Partnership," 161–62.

JULY 20

I took my exams. early this month for "private airplane pilot," under both the American & Philippine Bureaus. Passed successfully. So now I'm a licensed pilot. While I'll never be good, and after going to states perhaps I'll never get a chance to handle a stick—still I've realized one ambition. I have about 180 hours pilot time; and some 140 observer time in the air.

[1939]

FLEDGLING AT FIFTY[1]

It all started one afternoon as we were droning along, 5,000 feet up, off the farthest tip of the Sulu Archipelago. The tropical sun was already slanting down over the coast of Borneo, just a faint dark break on the shimmering horizon, and we were lazily wondering whether we'd make it to Zamboanga for the night, and whether we'd prefer the hard but clean comfort of the barracks over the inescapable threat of dysentery implicit in the ever-ready hospitality of our friend, the Governor, if we had to stay in Jolo.

"The truth is, Colonel," said Bill, the pilot, "I get so tired and bored pushing this bus up and down these islands, I find myself wondering whether to fall asleep over the wheel or to step out and see whether that gang at the field re-packed this chute properly this month." Then it happened. "Well," there popped out from somewhere inside me, "why don't you crawl back there in the rear seats and take a snooze? I'll keep her nose pointed in the right direction, and will let you know

441

if anything looks off-color to me." "Just what I'll do," he instantly replied, "we're still an hour from Jolo, and we don't even have to decide what to do until we get there."

Sheer panic crawled up and down my spine, shook my knees and, worst of all, paralyzed my tongue as he nonchalantly began unbuckling belt and harness and lunging around in his seat preparatory to the move. "My Lord," I thought, "does the fool really believe I can fly this thing?" Rapidly I tried to recall what he had said to me during the few times I had rather fearfully grasped the wheel while he consulted his maps or filled and lighted his pipe. "Surely he must know" it ran through my befuddled head, "that I don't know a cockeyed thing about an airplane." My deepest fear was that he was woefully, dangerously, ignorant on the point, never realizing for a moment that any experienced pilot, after taking a tyro for only a sightseeing hop, to say nothing of flying him around for weeks, as Bill had me, will not only be perfectly cognizant of his ignorance of aviation, he will tag, within a matter of minutes, the total time he has spent in the air.

If only I could have known all that as the Stinson began a series of lurchings and wallowings as Bill pushed his 209 pounds of bulk and contently snuggled down for his siesta. I knew nothing; only that responsibility had jumped down on me with overpowering suddenness, and that safety of life and limb now depended upon my success in keeping that crate on an even keel and some distance, at least, above the waves of the Sulu Sea, which for some reason no longer seemed to me so peaceful looking and so beautiful as they had, just a few seconds before, when I still trusted the altimeter evidence that they were a mile below.

Not until long afterward did Bill tell me that he had deliberately planned the incident; that he watched me like a hawk—like a flying instructor—as I grimly gripped the wheel, tried to fix my gaze on compass, altimeter and tachometer, and fearfully tried the rudder pedal, in some vague notion that I ought to know how to handle them, just in case. And he told me more than what I did, and how my staring eye would scarcely concede a wink to the glare of the sun on the scattered clouds in front; he read my mind like you are reading this printed page. He knew that I was testing, millimeter by millimeter, the several controls that I had so often seen him toss or kick around like the tag end of a cigarette, or like a slipper discarded for the night. He knew how desperately I wanted to do the thing correctly, and how I calculated for minutes in an effort to determine, in advance, which way the compass would turn if I should move the wheel to the right.

At 5000 feet even the tropics are comfortably cool, but very soon I ventured one hand off the controls long enough to slide open a ventilator. Bill knew, but I didn't, that I was tense as a fiddle string, that only a cough in the humming motor, or a hawk floating close up into my staring vision, was needed to send me into hysterical action, probably pulling the faithful plane into a whip stall and bringing Bill jumping to the rescue. How often since, as he has chortled over the agonizing beginnings of my "flying training" have I wished that I could have, purposely, done just that!

As, gradually, the sensible behavior of the plane rescued me from the more acute stages of panic, it occurred to me that there were a few other gadgets on the instrument board, probably deserving of such momentary attention as a busy man could give them. Vaguely and fearfully at first, but finally with some greater degree of concentration, I made a survey. Here was one that said "Air Speed". I wasn't greatly interested. Another said "Oil", still another "Temperature", and yet another "Tachometer". None of these suggested to me anything I ought to do, but eventually my attention centered on one that was marked, "Rate of Climb". The needle there seemed in rather odd position. Why shouldn't the thing be level. In fact I'm sure, something kept saying to me that that thing was usually pointing straight across when Bill was flying this machine. I must be climbing some. Consult the altimeter, I know where that is. Let's see. The little hand is close to six. Golly, I must be around six thousand feet. The big one says four, but it's moving slowly—yes it's going toward five. Good Grief, I'm 1500 feet higher than when I took over this job. Well, I'll push on the wheel a bit. A little harder. Still more. Why in the name of all that's holy doesn't that needle start down a bit. Push. More yet. Say, do you have to keep shoving like this all the time you are flying one of these things. Anyway that needle is at last level, now keep it there. No, there it goes again. Push some more; boy, this is anything but fun. Then a yawny drawl from the back seat, "Say, Colonel, my coming back here has probably made her tail heavy; if she's hard to fly level, move your stabilizer a bit." What a help! Where is the stabilizer? Which way do you move it? How much? Thank the gods, the voice goes on, "It's that handle above your head. Turn it clockwise to pull the nose down."

A hasty look. Yes, there it is all right. Now not too fast. Clockwise is to the right; that's easy. I've got it pretty well located, so I can reach up there with my left hand without risking taking my eyes off their job. Now, we'll take this easy and get it right. Move it just a trifle, say a quarter of an inch. Well, I'm still shoving, and my right arm is getting darn tired. Try again with another quarter. Still no results. A real yank this time, maybe a whole inch. Wonder if the thing is working. Take a look around. Altitude, 6700 feet. Still climbing? Yes, the needle is up again, and oh, my arm. Boy, I'll move that thing this time, the handle is pointing straight ahead, I'll get it all the way round to point at me. Now . . . what! still not enough. Well watch this; a whole turn; golly, I'm reckless! Ah, a blessed easing on my arm, look! I've got that blankety blank needle almost to where it belongs, and a few more taps, this way, that way, and it's perfect. I'm really picking this business up remarkably fast; I'll bet that if I had started a little younger I could be a crack pilot by this time. Look at that needle, oh boy, oh boy. "Say Colonel," from the rear, "I think your right wing is down a little, you're turning that way." Right wing down, turn the wheel to the left, that's the dope. Now take a look at the compass. Let me see. My course was 85, I remember that. What is this? One hundred, no, one hundred fifteen. Now to get her back. More work, more to the left. . . . push the rudder and turn the wheel. Whoops, pull her back. Holy Moses! I was really turning her that time. Now go EASY. I do. And I pull the ventilator back a bit more. But then I'm getting so much noise I might not hear Bill if he wanted to talk to me again. Better sweat. I do. There she is. 85. Fine, hold her there. Ah, boy I'm really learning. There I had her off course, and I darn near put her on her back and now here I am flying along just as ordered. Handled her like a veteran.

Hey! there's that needle. Down now, pull back a little! Altimeter? 6000 feet. My Lord, a little more and I'd been diving into the sea!

1. Although Eisenhower did not date his account, it seemed logical to include it after the July 20 entry even though the events described took place earlier and the narrative itself may have been written later—perhaps after his return to the states. "Bill" was almost surely William Lecel Lee. As Lee left the Philippines on May 19, 1938, the trip Eisenhower described must have taken place before that date. When he titled the story "Fledgling at Fifty," Eisenhower presumably rounded off his age for the sake of alliteration.

146   Eisenhower Library
                                              Pre-presidential Papers

To General Malin Craig[1]

August 3, 1939

Dear General Craig: It has, of course, long been a matter of common knowledge in the Army that you are to retire from active service at the end of this month. Yet it was with a feeling almost of shock, and certainly of distinct personal loss, that I read in War Department orders, recently arriving in Manila, official notification to that effect.

Retirement of a high ranking Army officer does, however, confer upon juniors in the service a particular privilege previously denied them. This privilege is that of expressing to the senior sentiments of admiration and esteem with the assured feeling that their timing will eliminate any suspicion of self-seeking, and so evidence their complete sincerity.

With this somewhat laborious preamble, I want to tell you that, for many years, you have been, for me, one of those officers whose careers and accomplishments have justified the great pride I take in the military service.

Most of the Army, I believe, associates your name intimately with those of Generals Fox Conner, Heintzleman, Collins, Drum, Marshall, W. D. Connor, Simonds, and others that, regardless of pronounced individualism in personalities and methods, have come to be regarded collectively as the brains and the backbone of the A. E. F. and of our post-war Army. I count myself more than fortunate to have served under some of them closely and directly, and to have known, personally, most of the others.

In this brilliant group, you occupy, in my mind, a very special place, not only because, as Chief of Staff, you fearlessly and effectively advanced principles and doctrines that I have heard most of the others actively support, but because also, you have seemed to me to typify that group's hatred of pose and pomposity, its generosity to subordinates and its unswerving devotion to the Army rather than to self.

Holding such convictions, I know you will understand the sincerity of my regret that time has marked you for retirement. But I am sure that you have stored up, during your many years of active service, a thousand intentions involving interesting things to do upon your release from active service, and Mamie and I wish for you and yours many happy years in which to do them. Very sincerely

1. Malin Craig technically served as Chief of Staff at this time, holding the title through August 31. George C. Marshall, whom President Roosevelt had appointed in April as Craig's successor, had assumed all the duties and responsibilities of the position on July 1. Officially, Marshall became Army Chief of Staff on September 1. He held that position throughout World War II.

147   Eisenhower Library
                                                              Philippine Diary

September 3, 1939

This evening we have been listening to broadcasts of Chamberlain's speech stating that Great Britain was at war with Germany. After months and months of feverish effort to appease and placate the madman that is governing Germany the British and French seem to be driven into a corner out of which they can work their way only by fighting. It's a sad day for Europe and for the whole civilized world, though for a long time it has seemed ridiculous to refer to the world as civilized. If the war, which now seems to be upon us, is as long drawn out and disastrous, as bloody and as costly as was the so-called World War, then I believe that the remnants of nations emerging from it will be scarcely recognizable as the ones that entered it. Communism and anarchy are apt to spread rapidly, while crime and disorder, loss of personal liberties, and abject poverty will curse the areas that witness any amount of fighting. It doesn't seem possible that people that proudly refer to themselves as intelligent could let the situation come about. Hundreds of millions will suffer privations and starvation, millions will be killed and wounded because one man so wills it. He is a power-drunk egocentric, but even so he would still not do this if he were sane. He is one of the criminally insane, but unfortunately he is the absolute ruler of 89,000,000 people. And by his personal magnetism, which he must have, he has converted a large proportion of those millions to his insane schemes and to blind acceptance of his leadership. Unless he is successful in overcoming the whole world by brute force the final result will be that Germany will have to be dismembered and destroyed.

I have had some degree of admiration for Mussolini, none, ever, for Hitler. The former has made some tragic, stupid, mistakes. But he at least has seemed able as an administrator, and for a dictator, has abstained from the use of the "blood purge" in maintaining himself in power. Hitler's record with the Jews, his rape of Austria, of the Czechs, the Slovaks and now the Poles is as black as that of any barbarian of the Dark Ages.

A big question of the moment is, "What will Italy do?" Personally, I'm going out on a limb and answer that Mussolini will not go into the war on the side of Germany. One big reason for this conclusion [is] that the Italian is smart enough to know what would happen to him after a victory by Hitler and his allies. They'd all take orders from the maniac . . . . . No master of Europe can have an equal partner. If Mussolini does not fight with Hitler, what will he do? The answer to that is, "For the present, nothing." My guess, and god knows I do not pose as one of these all-seeing persons that utter prophecies with the confidence of a new Delphic oracle, is that the Duce will hang back as long as he can, preferably until both sides are near exhaustion then . . . . attempt to use his own forces to settle the outcome and, if possible, make himself the strong man of Europe.

It is my guess that only a wide spread conviction or sub-conscious feeling that our own eventual safety demanded active intervention will ever get us actively engaged, unless we are attacked.

This crisis has made me more than ever anxious to get home.

I want to be back with my own army to watch and be a part of our own development and preparations; also to keep in closer touch with the daily record of the war as it is made. We're too far away in Manila; our papers are not particularly informative and short-wave radio is not yet an adequate system of broadcasting information.

148

The Citadel Archives
Mark Wayne Clark Collection

To MAJOR MARK CLARK

SEPTEMBER 23, 1939

Dear Wayne: My sailing date is now only about two and one-half months away. Sometime ago I sent an official communication to the War Department asking that my household goods, stored at New Cumberland, Pennsylvania, be shipped to Ft. Lewis, c/o Quartermaster. I don't know exactly when they will arrive there but, as I recall, I requested that they make the shipment as early as possible, so, if you will be on the look out for them on and after December 1st, I will appreciate it deeply.

As the time draws near for us to leave the Philippines I cannot tell you how anxiously we are looking forward to our return to the States and to service with a Regular Army officer. I feel like a boy who has been promised an electric train for Christmas.[1]

I have been watching the Army orders for notice of an assignment of a Colonel to the 15th Infantry. So far I have seen nothing but it occurs to me that Fred Walker may have been promoted by this time, and if so, they may give him the regiment. In my opinion that would be a swell arrangement. While I have not had the opportunity of serving intimately with him he has certainly a grand reputation in the Dough Boys.[2]

As soon as it is possible to determine exactly the type of quarters to which I will be assigned I wonder whether you would drop me an air-mail note. As I told you before, I am extremely anxious to get a house, and earnestly hope that by the time we arrive there the building program will be far enough advanced so that I can realize this ambition.

Like everyone else, we are engrossed, daily, with the war news. At this moment, however, we are lost to determine whether there is actually a war on between Germany and the Allies, or whether there is merely an armed truce while everyone gets ready to spring some new idea of action upon the world. It is most certainly a puzzling situation to me. I am writing a short note to General Sweeney by this same mail. If he has already left Ft. Lewis, please re-address the letter to his new station.

With cordial regards to yourself, Very sincerely

P.S. Mamie (Mrs. Ike) has just asked me to find out, if possible, the number of windows in dining room, bedrooms, kitchen, etc. in the type of house we MAY get. Would you have a soldier count them? I think she wants to buy some material.

1. Although Clark and Ulio had made the arrangements for Eisenhower's orders to leave, MacArthur appreciated Eisenhower's ability and tried to delay his departure. It is also possible that Quezon, who fully recognized Eisenhower's abilities, wanted him to stay as well. See Clark to Eisenhower, July 11, 1939, and October 10, 1939, Mark Wayne Clark Collection.

2. "Dough Boys" was the popular name for American soldiers in World War I.

149   The Citadel Archives
                                  Mark Wayne Clark Collection

To GENERAL WALTER C. SWEENEY

SEPT. 27, 1939

Dear General: While I am delighted to learn that you are to command the 9th Corps and presumably, therefore, will get your third star. I am deeply disappointed that you will not be at Ft. Lewis after I arrive there about the first of the year. One of the reasons I was so pleased with my assignment to that station was the prospect of serving under your relatively close command. I hope that, when you go to San Francisco, inspectional duties will bring you often to your old station.

So far, the events of the European war have failed to make a great deal of sense, as far as I am concerned. Quite evidently the Allies are playing a waiting game in the hope that something will happen to weaken the German stand and position, but it is difficult to see, for me at least, just what they expect to see happen. And, out here, no one will even guess at Russia's basic intentions.

In the Philippines we have had several noticeable consequences of the declaration of a major war. Freight rates have gone up, general prices have done likewise, fewer ships come into port, and the Canadian Pacific Line has had its vessels painted to render them less conspicuous at sea. Since, in Manila, we have consulates of all the warring nations it is the part of wisdom to be very discreet and silent on war subjects. Not long ago I had quite a talk with a French reservist. He said that many French officers believe the Germans intend attacking through Switzerland.

When I arrive in San Francisco I shall, if time permits call at your office to pay my respects. With personal regards, Sincerely

150

To Leonard T. Gerow[1]

October 11, 1939

Dear Gee: Your note arrived a day or so ago, and naturally received the concentrated attention of the Eisenhower family. Entirely aside from the news of what you were doing officially, something on which we had been speculating a lot, we were delighted to have the first-hand account of your marriage.[2] I cannot tell you how happy we are for you. We are sorry only that your station for some time to come is apparently to be Ft. Benning, while we go to the opposite corner of the United States.

If my imagination is operating with only passable accuracy, your job in San Antonio must have been full of interest. From your note I assume that you will be returning to Benning in the next month or so. If the clean-up process should require longer, say until January, it would be a pious idea for you to take a long leave and make a leisurely tour of the U.S., stopping for a long visit with us at Lewis.

The war has me completely bewildered. For the moment it appears that the struggle is to be economic in nature. The Allies apparently believe that with control of the seas they will finally force Germany, in spite of her access to all southeast Europe and Russia, to break down. Certainly it seems obvious that neither side desires to undertake attacks against heavily fortified lines. If fortification, with modern weapons, has given to the defensive form of combat such a terrific advantage over the offensive, we've swung back to the late middle ages, when any army in a fortified camp was perfectly safe from molestation. If we assume that no violations of the flanking neutrals will occur, and further that in the air, as on the ground, virtual stagnation is to occur, what, will you tell me, is the answer?

With the world's attention centered on Europe I suppose that a rather significant tactical incident in China has gone almost unnoticed. A heavy Jap drive on Changsha got started in fine style, began running into increasing resistance, and finally, by Jap admission, was driven back to its starting areas. The Japs, of course, put the best face possible on the matter, saying that the mission was only to forestall a Chinese offensive. The Chinese Army seems to be fighting as well as ever, in spite of discouraging handicaps. This war in the East is as hard to understand as the European struggle.[3]

We read in our meager dispatches much about the rejuvenation and building up of the American Army. The statement appeared recently that by next year we'd attain authorized strength in the Regular component. If we get 280,000 men, are we to have authorized strength in officers? If so, are we to keep prevailing percentages in the field grades? Is the War Department going to renew its effort to secure age-in-grade retirement?

I know that, while you are busy on your report, you'll have no chance to answer all these questions. But after a while, maybe you'll find time to undertake the education of a poor, ignorant, farmer boy, and when you do, I want you to have some idea of the gigantic size of the job.

Mamie is counting the days until December 13th. She really wants to come home—that's one point on which I have no remotest doubt or question. And as the time draws near, I must say I begin to share her impatience.

Our best to you both—As ever

1. Gerow was serving with the 2d Division, Fort Sam Houston, Texas, at this time.

2. Gerow, whose first wife, Kathryn, died in 1935, married Mary Louise Kennedy in July 1939.

3. The Japanese army had overrun Manchuria in 1931, and in 1932 Tokyo recognized the puppet Manchurian state of Manchuko. In 1933 and 1934 the Japanese seized portions of Inner Mongolia and northern China near Peking. In July and August 1937 heavy fighting broke out between the occupying Japanese Army and Chiang Kai-shek's Nationalist Army. By the end of the year Shanghai and the capital, Nanking, had fallen. In 1938 the Japanese captured Hankow, Canton, and Inner Mongolia and seized control of China's principal cities, half the country's area and well over half its population. Chiang and his Nationalist Army fled to Chungking in western China, where they set up a base for counterattack. One of Chiang's greatest victories in 1939 was his successful defense of Changsha in Hunan Province. Japan attacked Changsha again in September 1941 and January 1942 but both times was repulsed with heavy losses. It was not until June 1944 that the Japanese finally drove the Nationalists from the city. See Edwin O. Reischauer, *Japan: The Story of a Nation* (New York: Knopf, 1970), 190–91, 204–5; Marcel Baudot, Henri Bernard, Hendrik Brugmans, Michael R. D. Foot, and Hans-Adolf Jacobson, eds., *The Historical Encyclopedia of World War II* (New York: Facts on File, 1980), 84–87; and Robert Goralski, *World War II Almanac: 1931–1945* (New York: Bonanza, 1981), 96–97, 175–76, 196.

151

The Citadel Archives
Mark Wayne Clark Collection

To Major Mark Clark

October 11, 1939

Dear Wayne: Through the Quartermaster Department I've requested that my household goods, now stored at New Cumberland depot, be shipped to Lewis, to arrive about December 1. I've also requested the Fidelity Storage Company, in Washington, D.C., to make a private shipment, to arrive about the same time. Both are to be sent in care of Post Quartermaster, and I wonder whether you'll ask him to keep you informed as to their arrival, etc. The commercial shipment is to be prepaid, by a friend in Washington.

I saw W.D. orders the other day, detailing Col. Walker to the G.S., so of course, someone else will be the Commanding Officer of the 15th. I had assumed that he was close to his full Colonelcy, and would probably be assigned to command the regiment.

We have just two months more in the Philippines. We're getting to the point we can hardly wait for December 13.

If General Sweeney is still at Lewis, please pay my respects to him.

With cordial regards to yourself, and many thanks for all the trouble I cause you, As ever

P.S. Is there any definite dope yet on my quarters?[1]

1. By this time, Clark had made arrangements for living quarters, John's schooling, and a car. See Holt, "An Unlikely Partnership," 161.

152

The Citadel Archives
Mark Wayne Clark Collection

To Major Mark Clark

October 25, 1939

Dear Wayne: Again I am indebted to you for a very informative and fine letter. Mamie asks particularly that you thank Mrs. Clark for all the trouble she took in getting the information on the windows.

I think that the shipments of household effects (one governmental, the other commercial) can scarcely reach Lewis before Nov. 15 to Dec. 1. But you never can tell, so my purpose in asking you to be on the lookout was merely to make sure that things would not be lost.

Such property as I have here, including an old rattle trap of a car, will be shipped commercially by the Commonwealth Government, arriving at Seattle about Dec. 26. I'll send you all the necessary papers at the proper time, so that the Post Quartermaster can send a truck and collect the plunder. I still expect to arrive about Jan. 2–3.

I am glad the prospects as to quarters are no worse. We've set our hearts on living on an Army Post. We've been occupying civilian quarters most of our married life and it has been a happy thought to believe we're coming back, on an intimate basis, with our own people.

The information about the training and Divisional programs was most interesting. I'm ready for anything! Field, garrison, wilderness, let them send the outfit wherever they please. I'll be happy as long as I can go with a regular unit.

I saw in recent orders that Jesse Ladd[1] is coming to the 15th. He's an old friend of mine, and I'll enjoy service with him.

Please remember me kindly to General Sweeney. Again, many thanks to you and Mrs. Clark. Cordially

P.S. One month and eighteen days more in the P.I.!!!!

1. Jesse A. Ladd (USMA, 1911) attended the Command and General Staff School with Eisenhower in 1926. He assumed command of U.S. Troops, Alaska, in 1941 and, in May 1945, of the 9th Infantry Division on occupation duty in Europe. He retired as a brigadier general in 1948.

153 Eisenhower Library
Thomas Jefferson Davis Papers

To Major T. J. Davis

December 6, 1939

My dear Major Davis: Though, because of our close personal relations, you are well aware of my very high opinion of your soldierly qualifications, I should like, in terminating my duties as Senior Assistant to the Military Adviser of the Philippines, to leave with you a somewhat formal expression of these sentiments.

For nine years I have served in intimate association with you. Throughout those years you have unfailingly demonstrated a thorough knowledge of Army Administration, real executive ability in applying that knowledge, and a splendid personality that makes cooperative effort with you a pleasure. I have noted with particular interest that, no matter how trying or difficult the circumstances, your tact, your judgment and your solid common sense have been equal to any contingency. Your past record and my personal knowledge of your abilities justify my confident prediction of a brilliant future for you.

I genuinely regret that our official association is now to end, and it is my earnest hope that Army life will soon again bring us together.

With cordial personal regard, Sincerely[1]

1. Davis left MacArthur's staff in 1941 for an assignment with the Adjutant General. He rejoined Eisenhower in 1942 when Eisenhower selected him to be his adjutant at Allied Force Headquarters in the North African Theater of Operations. In 1944 he became adjutant for Supreme Headquarters, Allied Expeditionary Forces,

under command of Eisenhower. Davis retired from the army in 1946 as a brigadier general.

154

NOVEMBER 15, 1939–DECEMBER 14, 1939
NOVEMBER 15

The typewriter is too intricate for me.

The date of our going has been definitely fixed as Dec. 13, sailing on the SS <u>Pres. Cleveland</u>. Our freight will go on the S.S. "Capillo", direct to Seattle. We should reach Ft. Lewis about Jan. 7.

I have been trying to turn over all work to others in the office, especially since the arrival of two new assistants from the States; Lt. Col. Richard Marshall, Q.M.C., and Maj. Tom Dunckel, F.A.[1] Both seem to be very able, and I believe that Dunckel is outstanding! My efforts to free myself of official tasks, in order that I can take care of personal affairs, have been futile. The Gen. seems to find more and more things he wants me to do personally. While at Malacañan there have been a hundred odd jobs to complete. General MacA. has been particularly pleasant. I've written several statements for him, including a 13-minute speech that was recorded for possible future use, by the NBC, and he's been lavish in his praise of them. Actually they are the same old platitudes on Phil. defense, dressed up in only slightly new language. But so long as any sentence puts a good face on his "plan," or uses resounding language in support of his views, it is perfect, so far as he is concerned. His consuming desire for favorable publicity is going to give him a hard bump some day—or I miss my guess.

The President, and his Malacañan assistants <u>appear</u> to be genuinely sorry that I am going. I hope they are sincere, but the Malay mind is still a sealed book to me. They may be secretly delighted. However, I'm tempted to believe them, if for no other reason than the number of times my advice has been sought lately—often on subjects that are not connected with the Army.

Recently a Department of National Defense was established. There were certain ridiculous aspects, or at least amusing, to this incident. I'm not sure I've ever entered in these sketchy notes anything at all on this subject so I'll outline the development.

A couple of years ago the President first expressed an intention of establishing such a department. Upon hearing of this the Gen. was greatly disturbed, because he feared that a Sec. of Nat. Defense would tend to supplant him as the Chief Military Official in the govt. and so lessen his prestige and endanger his job. In fact, when the rumor first made its appearance the General flatly stated to the office gang, "If a Sec. of Nat. Def. is appointed, I will immediately resign." He sought an interview with the President and, at that time, succeeded in having the matter dropped.

However, in the summer sessions of the Assembly in 1938 (I was in States) (or possibly the actual passing of the law was in the fall of 1938) the President authorized the enactment of a law establishing two Departments—Public Health and Defense. It was provided that both should be set up before the end of the President's term, in 1941. The General felt temporarily safe, since he said he had the promise of Malacañan that no action would be taken on the Defense Dept. until the summer of 1941.

When I returned from the States I heard immediately that the President's mind was made up and that he was soon going to select a Secretary and appoint him. I reported this to the General and advised him that if he still felt so strongly about the matter he should exert himself without delay before further publicity was given to the matter, and especially before any individual was notified as to his impending selection. He pooh-poohed the accuracy of my information saying he had the situation under full control.

When I resumed my former duties at Malacañan, about May 1, 1939, I constantly ran into evidence that something was going to be done along this line. I brought it again and again to the Gen.'s attention, but for the first time he refused to show fright in the face of unpleasant news. He just didn't believe it.

Suddenly the Pres. made a public announcement of what he had in mind, and the Gen. raged to us in the office. He said he'd dissolve the mission and didn't like it at all when I reminded him there was no mission; that he was a retired officer working for Manuel Quezon, and the rest of us were officers attached to the Dept. Commander's staff, and loaned by the U.S. Govt. to the Pres. of the Commonwealth. He then pointedly requested me (and later Sutherland) to go with him to the Pres. to protest against the announced intention. I told him that, of course, I'd go with him, but that my comments (if called upon) would be confined to expressing a conviction as to the uselessness of the office, but that personally I had nothing otherwise against it. Certainly, I told him, it doesn't affect the work I do for the Commonwealth, one way or the other. I further advised him that since his objections were personal, based upon his prestige, face and desires, that he should seek a personal, confidential conference with the Pres., to have the matter out. This he decided to do.

He immediately called up for a date with the Pres. but received a very evasive reply from the aide. That afternoon he couldn't stand it longer so he took poor old Hutter and went to Malacañan. He went at an hour when he could find no one on the job, but he sent Hutter, who is an habitué of the Palace, on a detailed search. Hutter found the Pres. asleep and when this invasion of his privacy was later reported to Q. by underlings he got furious.

However, the Gen. hung around until finally he got an appointment and, according to him, had a most satisfactory talk.

We heard no more about the matter for some little time, but suddenly, another definite, and public, announcement was made by Q. in which he even named the man he was going to make Sec. of Nat. Defense (Sison).

Seeing he was licked the General now executed another of his amazing "about faces." He simply sat down and wrote a memo to the Pres., a long memo, <u>urging</u> the setting up of the Dept. of Nat. Defense. Soon the appointment was made, and on the surface, all was lovely. The moral is—they can't make him give up that job, no matter what they do!!

Dozens of entertainments in the nature of despedidas[2] have been arranged for Mamie and me. It's all very gratifying, but is likely to be hard on Mamie, who cannot stand much running around.

More gratifying is a message from Mr. Vargas, to the effect that, with the authority of the President, he is arranging a bonus for me upon departure, equal to two months pay (not including my hotel allowances). That is most pleasing, not only to the pocketbook, but as evidence that the govt. really regrets my departure. In this connection the Gen., in spite of our many dirty fights, has expressed the same views. But when I remember his parting conversation just before I went to the States in '38, and what he <u>tried</u> to do to me while I was gone, I simply cannot believe him.

I'm leaving in a day or two for a last inspection trip to the south. Andy and I are going in the Beechcraft.

1. Richard J. Marshall first met General MacArthur during his tenure as Assistant Quartermaster of the Philippine Department (1929–30). In 1939 he oversaw Philippine Army procurement, developed an economic mobilization plan for the islands, and created a Philippine army services of supply. Marshall remained with MacArthur as his Deputy Chief of Staff throughout the war in the Pacific, succeeding Richard Sutherland as Chief of Staff in 1945, a position he held during the occupation of Japan.

"Tom" presumably was the nickname for William C. Dunckel. Dunckel served most of his career in the field artillery. He retired in October 1945. The "F.A." is the abbreviation for field artillery.

2. A *despedida* is a farewell party or celebration.

We sailed yesterday on the S.S. Cleveland, via Hong Kong–Shang-hai–Kobe–Yokohama–Honolulu–San Francisco. In Shanghai we are doing some shopping, principally with respect to fur coats, of which Mamie has ordered two. I hope she gets some use out of them.

There were many despedidas. Gen. and Mrs. Valdes gave us a nice dinner; Oak room of Hotel. The Air Corps gave me a luncheon, an aerial review and a present of a desk set, including two Shaeffer pens. Sec. Vargas gave us a dinner, with a present to Mamie of a full luncheon set in Piña. The P. A. gave a review for me (the Camp Murphy command) after which Capinpin[1] and his officers presented me with a Hamilton watch. The President gave us a very large, official luncheon at Malacañan. That was the day before we left, and the climax of the whole round of parties. At the boat were many friends, both American and Filipino. Gifts included lots of flowers, champagnes, whiskies, books, etc. etc. The P.A. Band played on the pier until we were through the breakwater. Coupled with all this were many speeches, flattering comments, etc., including a newspaper editorial, so that all in all we not only felt we had made many fine friends, we were made to feel that our going was sincerely regretted in Manila.[2]

As a final gesture, Sec. Vargas told me that, with the approval of the President, he was giving me a bonus of two months per diems (not including hotel allowance). This will be $1000.00—which will be a real help when we start buying uniforms, auto, etc., etc. We have succeeded in building up our Riggs Acct. to approx. 10,000.00

So now we go back to the American Army—and I'm looking forward with the keenest anticipation to service in a regiment.

1. Col. Mateo M. Capinpin served as Chief of Staff of the 1st Division, Philippine Army. In his memorandum to Quezon on army personnel, Eisenhower described Capinpin as "a simple, straight-forward soldier who is singularly free of any tendency to seek advancement through favoritism or political maneuvering. He is at his best as a troop commander . . . loyal, hard working and honest." Memorandum to Quezon, Eisenhower Library.

2. John Eisenhower states that among the friends at the boat were Gen. and Mrs. Douglas MacArthur. Contemporary photographs also show that MacArthur attended all the farewell functions. In addition, John Eisenhower noted that his years in the Philippines were "among the happiest of my life." See John S. D. Eisenhower, *Strictly Personal* (New York: Doubleday, 1974), 6, 17.

To Jorge Vargas, Secretary to President Quezon

Dear Jorge: In a separate paper I sent you a draft of the report on the Philippine Army, as agreed upon before I left Manila. I promised, also, to submit brief personal estimates, on a confidential basis, of the abilities and qualifications of various officers of the army. Since it is possible that you, or His Excellency, may want to discuss portions of the main report with others, I deemed it best to separate the two papers and submit them individually. I particularly request that the opinions expressed in this paper be communicated to no one except yourself and His Excellency.[1]

I have mentioned only those officers with whom or with whose work I am reasonably well acquainted, and only those that, because of special qualifications, or notable lack of qualifications, are somewhat outside the average class.

As suggested in the letter accompanying the general report, I will be more than glad, at any time, to expand upon the comments included in this paper. All you have to do is to let me know what is wanted, and I shall do my best to answer promptly and accurately.

As in the other case, I shall have to ask you to get the final typing done. But in this instance please have your own confidential stenographer do the work, so that the paper does not get into circulation in the stenographic and records divisions of the office. You understand that, personally, I like every one of the individuals named, and where I am compelled to make some adverse comment with respect to efficiency, I do not desire that such comment become public property. I know you will appreciate my feelings in the matter.

With cordial regard to you and the family, in which Mamie joins me, Sincerely

1. On December 9, Vargas wrote Eisenhower: "His Excellency, the President, desires that you prepare and submit to him such observations and recommendations with respect to the development of the National Defense program in general and the Philippine Army, in particular. . . . In view of your early departure from Manila, it is desired you report by mail . . . not later than February 14, 1940." Vargas to Eisenhower, December 9, 1939, Pre-pres. Papers. A synopsis of the draft report follows in the next entry. The full report is located at the August 8, 1940, entry. Eisenhower was very aware of the personality and political conflicts and wished to ensure that the report would only be read on a need-to-know basis.

Eisenhower also refers to the undated draft memorandum on Philippine officers explained in note 10 to diary entry December 27, 1935.

156

To Jorge Vargas

DECEMBER 30, 1939

Dear Jorge: Herewith a draft of the report on the Philippine Army, which I have been working on steadily since leaving Manila. I am compelled to send it back to your office for typing, since there is no stenographer on the ship, and if I should carry the draft with me to my new station I cannot even guess as to the date I would be able to return it.

After the paper has been completed, you can, of course, make such use of it as you may desire. I suggest, however, that if anyone other than yourself and his Excellency is to read it, that it be referred to General MacArthur, who may not agree with some of the observations made.

I will be delighted to answer any questions that may occur to you in connection with any of the statements I have made. Just drop a note to me at Ft. Lewis, and I'll be glad to clarify anything I can. Or if there should be any particular subject that I have failed to discuss, and concerning which you, or His Excellency, would like my opinion, please feel perfectly free to call upon me.

We've had a typical winter crossing. Not particularly stormy, but usually blustery and unpleasant. Johnny and I have been well, but Mrs. Ike has had a very bad cold ever since we cleared Shanghai.

Please pay my respects to His Excellency, and with the best wishes of the Eisenhower tribe to you and yours, Cordially

P.S. I've typed this myself via the hunt and hope system, so please don't be too critical of errors.[1]

In addition, I have summarized, in the following paragraph, the highlights of this report. They are:

I. THE DEFENSE PLAN, in its essentials, is satisfactory and peculiarly applicable to the requirements of Philippine Security. If the plan continues to develop on the present basis of appropriations and objectives,

A sufficient number of trainees will eventually be passed through the training cadres.

Equipment for the First Reserve will be satisfactory and adequate— but the second reserve will probably be woefully deficient in this regard,

Special items of importance (anti-aircraft matériel, planes, patrol boats, gas-defense equipment and special types of vehicles) will be lacking throughout, either in quantity or entirely.

General efficiency in the officers corps (both Regular and Reserve) will not develop with sufficient rapidity unless corrective measures are initiated. More money and attention are needed to place this on an entirely satisfactory basis.

Adequate reserve stocks in supplies and equipment will not be on hand. This is a vital matter and is principally a matter of more money. In certain of the non-technical items required by the nation in emergency, such as food-stuffs, textiles and building materials, deficiencies can be partially supplied by industrial development. Ammunition and technical items must be purchased and stored before the beginning of any emergency.

II. THE GENERAL ORGANIZATION of the Army is satisfactory for training, tactical and administrative purposes. Improvements in details should come about gradually, as need for change is demonstrated. The time and attention of the Army should not be consumed in profitless discussion and debate on these matters, which, in the normal case are of academic rather than practical importance.

III. TRAINING is, in the average case, somewhat below satisfactory. Proper corrective measures involve:

Obtaining good district commanders.

Finding and retaining good cadre commanders.

More intensive work on the part of Army Hqrs.

Improvement of training facilities, particularly target ranges.

IV. APPROPRIATIONS are too low to permit desirable progress in training, organization and procurement. They should properly be increased by 10% at once and, about 1933–4 should go up by 33%. Such increases would permit the immediate institution of a more thorough system of public school and college instruction; they would allow the maintenance of more officers on an active duty status; they would finance a better and more comprehensive system of reserve unit training; they would make possible a beginning in the development of anti-aircraft organizations for the Manila area; they will meet the added costs (in 1943–4) involved in the development of regular coast artillery units, and, finally, about that time, will finance the accumulation of reserve stocks in ammunition and many important items of technical equipment.

V. PERSONNEL is, to date, below desirable standards in professional qualifications and, except for trainees, in numbers. More officers are needed on active duty so as to speed up the training and development of unit commanders and staffs. The Regular enlisted corps should be weeded out, improved in quality, and strengthened. The Army's system of eliminating worthless officers <u>must</u> operate more speedily and intensively. VI. MISCELLANEOUS, The principle of decentralization of authority and responsibility should be more faithfully followed in all echelons. Repeated failures should result in the relief of offending subordinates, but they should not lead higher authority into the fundamental error of <u>operating</u> from the top. The high command should establish policy——each succeeding subordinate in the hierarchy of command must be taught to carry his own responsibilities in the execution of those policies. There must be only one channel of official communication between the High Command and the Army, namely via the Secretary of Nat. Defense and the Chief of Staff.

The Office of the Military Adviser will continue, for at least the next 7 years, to be of the utmost value to the Commonwealth.

1. The Eisenhower Library has an original annotated draft of this letter that includes a handwritten note at the bottom that reads, "Please tell the typist to get the carbon back to me as soon as possible, so that if any errors have been made, I can send you a final corrected reply." Marcos G. Soliman Collection, Eisenhower Library.

157   Eisenhower Library
                                                           Philippine Diary[1]

JANUARY 25, 1940

San Francisco

Twelve hours before landing at this port I received a radio directing me to report to Fourth Army Hdqrs, located here, for temporary duty.[2] At first I thought it was the old, old story, and that once more I was to start a tour of "staff" duty instead of getting to troops. But General DeWitt assured me the detail was purely temporary. His hdqrs. had a rush job and needed someone to do some pick and shovel work during the month of January. Feb. 1 we proceed to Ft. Lewis, get settled there, and then I take off for Monterey, where the 15th Inf., along with the rest of the 3rd Div. is in training camp.

We had a slow, uninteresting trip across the Pacific. Capt. Henry Nelson was nice to us, we met a fine couple, Mr. & Mrs. William Boyd, Chicago, Tucson & Florida. Also met a gang of young men of whom our favorites were William Holloway, Texarkana; and "Heavy" Claunch, a fine chap from Texas.

We bought the fur coats in Shanghai and Mamie has used one, two or three times here. I hope that this time her purchases really prove useful; sometimes they're just extra freight. She also bought some cultured pearls; 2 strings.

I'm busy buying uniforms in my odd moments. It grinds my soul to put out the money I have to spend—but there's no way out unless I retire. Guess I'm hardly ready to do that![3]

But—1 blue suit and cap and belt—$154.00

1 O.D. suit and cap and shoes—$100.00

Thank the Lord I have a cape (blue). Also I can have my special field dress coat remodelled a bit and, with a new vest and new pair of trousers, I can get by, I hope. Field stuff, such as sleeping bags, shoes, leggings, etc., will run 50–75 bucks. Ouch!!

1. Even though Eisenhower was now in the states, this entry was filed with the Philippine Diary.

2. Upon arriving in the States, Eisenhower was first assigned to temporary duty with the IX Corps Area Headquarters at the Presidio, San Francisco. His principal task at the Presidio was to plan for the mobilization of all Corps Area Regular Army and National Guard troops, including their supplies, and arrange transportation to two sites in California, which were to be used for large-scale training exercises. As the Eisenhowers previously had enrolled John in a high school near Fort Lewis, they sent their son ahead to live with his Uncle Edgar in Tacoma until they could join him in early February.

3. Several times during his army career Eisenhower was tempted by offers of lucrative jobs, some of which would have assured him financial security for life. He turned down the offers, because, as he said, "I had become so committed to my profession." Dwight D. Eisenhower, *At Ease: Stories I Tell to Friends* (Garden City, N.Y.: Doubleday, 1967), 229–30.

158   James S. Copley Library[1]

To MAMIE EISENHOWER

[APRIL 1940][2]

Darling: It's been many days since a letter arrived from you—but the inference is that you are both O.K.—and I can well imagine that there are many things, other than writing, to do. We're on a problem today; but I got a half an hour vacation while I'm waiting at the regiment to pick up another officer. The 15th is at San Luis Obispo,[3] as I told you, I had to stay back for this umpiring work. I'm living in the field steadily until next Wednesday. Then I get a few days breathing space, then five days more. Anyway, all I'm trying to say is that time is not hanging heavily on my hands.

I'm enclosing a statement of John's qualifications etc, made up by Milton and me, between us. I expect to mail copies to person's that I want to get endorsements from, if necessary. [marginal note] The reason the statement talks so much about the Eisenhowers, is because we must establish John's claim to Kansas connections.

Tell Johnny to write Milton a note at once, since I'm too rushed to do so at this moment. Acknowledge his nice invitation (see letter attached), but tell him (Milton) that if J. goes to Millard[4] he is required to be a boarder. However, he can have week ends off, and I should think he'd be <u>glad</u> to spend those with Milton.

Tell J. to let me know how his pictures came out.

Lots of love to you both, I certainly do miss you. As ever, Your devoted Lover

1. Permission to reproduce or quote this letter must be in writing from the James S. Copley Library, La Jolla, California.

2. Based on incoming correspondence and the letters included here sent later in April on this subject, it is obvious this letter was written the early part of April.

3. Eisenhower, Executive Officer with the 15th Infantry Regiment, Fort Lewis, had drawn a temporary assignment to referee Fourth Army field maneuvers in California. Although his regiment had been sent to a maneuver area in southern California, Eisenhower was based during this period at Camp (later Fort) Ord, south of San Francisco.

4. Milton, in his letter, had offered to house John if he were to attend the Millard preparatory academy in Washington, D.C.

159   Wichita State University Archives, Special Collections
William M. Jardine Papers

To WILLIAM JARDINE[1]

APRIL 26TH, 1940

Dear Doctor Jardine: My brother Milton has just forwarded to me, copies of the splendid letters you wrote to Senators Capper and Reed in support of my son's candidacy for an appointment to West Point. It is difficult indeed to find words in which to express, adequately, my appreciation, not only of your promptitude in responding to my brother's request, but of the forcefulness and very flattering nature of the sentiments voiced in your letters.

I earnestly hope that John may realize his ambition to enter West Point. If he does, he will be permanently indebted to you for practical and powerful assistance. But even if circumstances should compel him to enter some other field of service, I assure you that he and I, as well as Milton and all the other Eisenhowers, will always take a deep pride in your high opinion of my parents and their sons, and will be grateful to you for your readiness to express it.

Very sincerely yours

1. Eisenhower's letter was written from Fort Ord, California, where the 15th In-

fantry Regiment was participating in field maneuvers. He served as the Executive Officer of the 15th. William M. Jardine, a well-known educator in agronomy, served as dean of agriculture, from 1913 to 1918, and from 1918 to 1925 as president of Kansas State Agricultural College. From 1925 to 1929 he was President Coolidge's secretary of agriculture. Appointed president of the Municipal University of Wichita in 1933, he held that position until 1949. Jardine and Milton Eisenhower had a long association together, first during Jardine's presidency at Kansas State University when Milton was one of the brightest student leaders on campus, then at the Department of Agriculture, where Jardine secured for Milton a position as his assistant. See Steve Neal, *The Eisenhowers: Reluctant Dynasty* (Garden City, N.Y.: Doubleday, 1978), 54–59.

160

To Brigadier General Thomas A. Terry[1]

MAY 1, 1940

Dear Tom: With the bases loaded you certainly put the ball out of the park! And from out here in the bleachers I'm still yelling, although the great event is now several days old. I'm so d— glad about it that such ordinary words as congratulations and so on don't help; nothing fits but wowie! wow-e-e!! Maybe zowie is even better.

Of course I knew that, short of an unforeseen cataclysm, the promotion would come to you soon—but there's always a period of suspense between the moment you take a healthy cut at the ball and the one when you see it clear the fence.

As soon as you get orders, tell me what your first command as a general officer is to be.

Here in Ord I've been having a grand time in a succession of field exercises and maneuvers. I've had to serve as Chief Umpire for the Division, but in spite of that have managed to stick pretty close to the regiment. I'm Executive Officer, but believe that, soon, I'll also have a battalion of my own. I hope so!

Mamie and I have been trying to get a West Point appointment for Johnny, but I guess he'll have to take his chances in the Presidential competitive. I'll send him on to Millard's this summer, and give him every chance. He <u>may</u> make it; but it's a tough assignment.[2]

When we go north we go by trucks, and do not get into San Francisco. But I still hope that you and Ruby make up your minds to visit us at Lewis this summer.

Lots of love to you both, and when I see you I'll buy the champagne to drink to your next star. As ever

1. Eisenhower's letter referred to the announcement that Thomas A. Terry (USMA, 1908) was to be promoted to brigadier general, effective September 1, 1940. Terry retired from the army as a major general.

2. By the end of the semester at Millard's, however, John had secured an appointment to West Point and left the school. He returned to Fort Lewis at Christmas. On July 1, 1941, John arrived at West Point to begin his plebe year. See Eisenhower, *Strictly Personal*, 32–34.

161

Eisenhower Library
Pre-presidential Papers

TO BRIGADIER GENERAL COURTNEY HODGES[1]

MAY 1, 1940

Dear General: I cannot tell you what a thrill it was to read in the bulletin the other day that you had received your promotion. To say that I'm delighted is just understatement. I congratulate you sincerely, and the army even more sincerely. I wonder what your first command as a general officer is to be!

Here at Camp Ord I've been having a grand time in a succession of field exercises and maneuvers. We break up camp and start for home stations on the 15th, but in the meantime have one more big maneuver covering five days and a lot of ground. I'm Executive Officer for the 15th Infantry (Jesse Ladd Commanding), though right now I'm the Chief Umpire for the division in it's field maneuvers. Our permanent station is Fort Lewis, Washington, where Mamie and I arrived on February 1st, after leaving Manila on December 13th. Give my best regards to Barney and Mrs. Barney when you see them, and, with warm regards to you and Mrs. Hodges. Here's to your next star! Cordially

1. Hodges was Commandant of the Infantry School, Fort Benning, Georgia, at this time.

162

James S. Copley Library[1]

TO JOHN S. D. EISENHOWER

MAY 10, 1940

Dear Johnny: Some time ago I wrote to the Adjutant General, asking for a Presidential appointment for you and another letter requesting a list of prospective vacancies for 1941. The answers are supposed to come to Lewis. If they do, hold on to them and do not forward here. But I would like to know whether or not they've arrived, because I wrote the letters some time ago. Incidentally, please ask Mamie to forward <u>no more mail</u> to me here.

I'm delighted to know you have your own opinions, deliberately arrived at, concerning such matters as the Far Eastern and the European struggles. However, I'd like to point out that our information concerning basic, rather than apparent, causes of these wars is most untrustworthy; so none of us can be certain that his conclusions are sound. In such cases it is more than ever necessary to combat the natural tendency to permit impulse and sentiment and prejudice to color our judgements. A lawyer can make out a plausible sounding case for either side of <u>any</u> question; but we're not lawyers pleading a case at the bar.

If you feel no kinship to, nor any sympathy for, the British, that's a matter of sentiment; and as such it's a settled matter so far as you are concerned. But as you expect others to respect your sentiments, you, likewise should not jeer at theirs.

Then again, you list the chemicals and elements of which man is made. I was quite astonished just to read the list of them. But that isn't the final answer! Suppose you take the same list and mix them together as you will; can you produce a young man, 17 years old, capable of thinking, laughing, working, struggling to realize ambitions—in short, of living? Is not a dog composed of approximately the same elements? Yet do you think that, in the higher manifestation of their accomplishments that man and the dog are to be compared? I'll admit, when I see thing like are now going on in the world, that my respect for dogs as compared to man goes soaring to new heights, but dogs have not produced a Mona Lisa, a Taj Mahal, a Lincoln Memorial or a Notre Dame. The plays of Shakespeare, the Bible, the Gettysburg Address and Gray's Elegy are <u>not</u> merely mixtures of natural elements. So, take all these things into consideration when you begin to consider the question of mans origin, his mission and his destiny.

Don't worry because age and maturity look at many things from a viewpoint that seems to you unsound. Youth has done that, always. One of the things that makes life so intriguing is the superiority of every age. At 20 one wonders why the rest of the world doesn't get out of the way and permit the wisdom of 20 to run things; at fifty he feels exactly the same except that he adds 30 years to the ideal age. Having almost arrived at this latter age I can realize how true this is—but I can realize too that my ideas differ radically from those I held at 20. The conclusion is inescapable that one was, or is, wrong!

So be self-confident; when your own conscience tells you you've studied a matter out honestly and well, stick by your conclusions, and if necessary to act on them, do so fearlessly. But merely because one has an opinion, he doesn't have to shout it from the housetops, if nothing is to be gained for himself, or more importantly, for mankind, by so doing. And above all, we must not be arbitrary and intolerant, for as surely as you find, as you will, that many of your ideas of ten years hence will be almost diametrically opposed to some you hold now, you will come to realize that, after all, even such smart fellows as you and I can be wrong; the other fellow might be right. Tolerance and a sense of humor are, I sometimes think, the two commodities the world is now needing most.

I'm sorry the tennis boys are giving you the run around. But sooner or later one or more will have to meet you, so be ready for that day. Don't get discouraged, and don't get bitter and angry. For anger, discouragement, fear and all such emotions serve only to defeat the person that feels them. Again, don't forget a sense of humor.

Well, I didn't mean to grow garrulous, I'll be seeing you soon, and we'll have a long talk at our leisure. As ever, your devoted Dad

1. Permission to reproduce or quote this letter must be in writing from the James S. Copley Library, La Jolla, California.

163   Eisenhower Library
                                                      Pre-Presidential Papers

To Lieutenant Colonel Omar N. Bradley[1]

July 1, 1940

Dear Omar: Ike Eisenhower, 15th Infantry, speaking; looking for a bit of information. This is it:

The 15th Infantry, like other regiments, has had a quota of Thomason Act officers, and, according to instructions, we recommended, last spring, a certain percentage of them for permanent commission.[2] In the course of time, orders arrived (from Corps Area or W.D., I don't know which) directing the physical examination of a few of those that had been recommended on the basis of efficiency.

Just the other day telegraphic appointments came in for about half of those that had been physically examined.

In our regimental list two, named Natzel[3] and Hilpert,[4] were commissioned, while three, Cassidy, Soderquist and Pepke[5] (this man formerly in 4th Infantry) were omitted. Now the question is this: Is there any hope that any more of last years Thomason Act officers will receive permanent commissions? We think a lot of the three boys named above, and would like to hold out to them some hope, if there is any. Could you give me the dope on this? I'll appreciate it.

I realize that detailed personnel matters, such as involved in this question, are probably far out of your particular line. But I figured I could impose upon old friendship—trusting that you'll have to do nothing more than grab a phone and ask the man who knows about such things.

I've been with this regiment about five months, and am having the time of my life. Like everyone else in the army, we're up to our necks in work and in problems, big and little. But this work is fun! Since I have a peach of a colonel (Jesse Ladd) I could not conceive of a better job; except, of course, having one's own regiment, which is out of the question because of rank. I'm regimental executive, command the 1st Battalion, and run a school four afternoons per week. I hope the students don't know it, but I learn more than they do.

Best of luck—and thanks a lot for any trouble my request may cause you. As ever

1. Bradley was on the General Staff at the War Department. Omar N. Bradley graduated with Eisenhower in the West Point class of 1915. He served in various posts throughout the United States until 1919, then spent most of the pre–World War II years as either a student or an instructor at army schools. He served on the General Staff of the War Department from 1938 to 1941. In early 1943, Bradley was ordered to North Africa, where he served as an aide to Eisenhower for several months before being assigned to command the II Corps in the North Africa and Sicily campaigns. In late 1943, Bradley participated in the planning for Operation Overlord, and in January 1944 he received command of the First Army that landed at Omaha and Utah beaches on D-Day, June 6. He then commanded the Twelfth Army Group and received his fourth star shortly before the end of the war in Europe. After the war he directed the Veterans Administration until 1948, when he succeeded Eisenhower as Army Chief of Staff. In August 1949, Bradley became the first permanent chairman of the new Joint Chiefs of Staff. He received his fifth star in September 1950 and retired in 1953. Bradley died April 8, 1981.

2. Eisenhower referred to legislation introduced by Texas congressman Robert E. Thomason. The legislation prescribed how reserve officers could obtain regular army commissions through a reserve training program. Thomason served on the military appropriations committee in 1937 and 1941.

3. Robert J. Natzel received a second lieutenant's commission in the Infantry Reserve in 1939, then on June 1, 1940, a commission in the Regular Army through the "Thomason Act" provisions.

4. Robert C. Hilpert also received a reserve commission in 1939 under the same Thomason provisions. Hilpert retired from the army in 1946 with the permanent rank of major.

5. Donn R. Pepke received a second lieutenant's commission in the Regular Army in 1942.

To Manuel Quezon

                                                   August 8, 1940[1]

Memorandum for His Excellency, the President of the Philippines
(Thru the Honorable, the Secretary to the President).

This memorandum is submitted in accordance with a request made
upon me by the Secretary to the President, prior to my departure from
Manila. It consists in a resume of <u>personal</u> observations and convictions with respect to the Philippine Army and the Defense Plan, based
upon more than four years service, in a military capacity, with the
Commonwealth Government.

I have taken advantage of your familiarity with fundamental features of the defense plan to omit, in the interests of brevity, many long
explanations that would, in other circumstances, be necessary.

For your convenience, I have arranged the memorandum under
the following headings:

    I. Fundamentals of plan.

    II. Organization.

    III. Training.

    IV. Finances.

    V. Personnel.

    VI. Miscellaneous.

In addition, I am summarizing, in the paragraphs immediately following, the highlights of this report . . . .[2]

DETAILS OF REPORT

I. <u>FUNDAMENTALS OF PHILIPPINE DEFENSE PLAN</u>.

The basic system of military preparation prescribed by the National Defense Act is the only one that can provide the country with a respectable defense. This system declares that all the people must cooperate, without financial remuneration and purely as a civic duty, in
the enterprise.

The plan itself is merely a detailing of the necessary rules, procurement schedules, organizational schemes and basic methods
whereby this cooperation may become effective.

<u>Necessary Assumption as to Nature of Potential Attack</u>.—ALL
PROSPECTS OF SUCCESSFUL DEFENSE, CONDUCTED BY THE PHILIPPINES
WITHOUT ALLIES, ARE NECESSARILY BASED UPON THE FOLLOWING
STRATEGIC ASSUMPTION:

Any attack against the Philippines will not represent an onslaught
by the full naval, military and economic might of a great empire, but

rather an expedition definitely limited as to size, which will hope, through surprise, rapidity and efficiency to overpower defenses in a particular locality, seize vital portions of the Islands, take over normal governmental and industrial activity, and dictate a peace from that position.[3]

This assumption is one that is not susceptible of proof. Moreover, any conclusions reached with respect to it involve familiarity with international conditions and surveys of all possible opponents; their national policies, racial habits, their potential enemies, material resources and so on. My own beliefs on this particular point are immaterial, and, for this reason, I do not discuss further the validity of the assumption in this paper; it is merely set down as the foundation on which must be built all calculations for successful defense.

However, one single observation, with respect to it, is made. Even if mature reflection should fail to inspire any confidence in the correctness of the assumption, yet sovereignty is inherently responsible for its own preservation, that is, for national security—fear of possible failure should therefore serve only to spur the government on to greater effort. To give up, supinely, is unthinkable.

With this assumption always understood, the essentials of successful Philippine defense are:

a. Adequate numbers in the defensive force, trained and instantaneously ready for mobilization in every portion of the Islands.

b. Adequate equipment, of reasonable efficiency.

c. Qualified leadership.

d. Solidarity of purpose.

e. Sufficient reserves, in supplies, for both the Army and the civil population.

With respect to the first essential, numbers and mobilization readiness.—There is one line, and one only, at which the defending forces will enjoy a tremendous advantage over any attack by land. That line is the beach. Successful penetration of a defended beach is the most difficult operation in warfare.

If any attacking force ever succeeds in lodging itself firmly in a vital area of the Islands, particularly on Luzon, 90% of the prior advantage of the defender will disappear. Behind the protective lines established by such attacking force, more and more strength can be brought in, by echelon, until with superior armaments and with naval and other support, the whole will be strong enough to crush the defending army.

The enemy must be repulsed at the Beach.

No matter how efficient a small defensive force (15–20,000) might be, it cannot cover all beaches, not even in the limited Lingayen—Manila—Batangas area. To take advantage, then, of its one tremendous asset, which is a surrounding shore-line, <u>the Philippine Army must have the numbers to defend all sensitive beaches</u>.

Exact determination of these numbers presents another question that cannot be answered categorically. The top limit available is that represented by a completely militarized nation, the aim of the so-called Swiss system. Experience seems to show that about 80,000 <u>able bodied</u> male Filipinos annually reach military age, and if this number were multiplied by 30 (to include all men from 21 to 50) we would have, less natural attrition, a potential army of more than 2,000,000. If, in emergency, that many well armed, organized, supplied and trained citizen-soldiers could be ready to defend the shore-line, the conquest of the Philippines, <u>by land attack</u>, would be impossible for any single nation.

In practice, of course, actual limits are set by other considerations. An important one is cost. With a definite ceiling on appropriations, decision must be made as to the most efficient distribution of money available, manifestly all of it cannot be devoted to personnel training alone. The current plan visualizes a maximum army, in 30 years, of 90 divisions or approximately 650,000 men in the field forces. However, the plan is quite indefinite as to the degree of efficiency that can be sustained in the 2nd and 3rd Reserves, particularly with respect to the amount of equipment and annual training that can be given them. <u>So the plan presently emphasizes the formation of 30 divisions, (some 220,000 men) in the 1st Reserve</u>, and during the first ten years. This will provide about 100,000 for Luzon, 25,000 for Mindanao and 95,000 for the Visayas.

When there is considered the tremendous stretches of exposed areas in these regions, it becomes apparent that the numerical objective is a modest one. <u>Prudence demands the utmost in effort to develop and sustain the 2nd Reserve on the same footing as to effectiveness as the first Reserve</u>. In other words the figures just given should be doubled by 1956; not merely on paper, but in efficient divisions. A larger annual contingent of trainees is <u>not</u> needed but plans should definitely contemplate the continued training and effectiveness of reserve units throughout the period of 2nd Reserve Service. This will require, particularly between 1946–1956, more money than is presently being appropriated; but it will be less expensive than to attempt to enlarge the reserve force by increasing the number of trainees and allowing their effectiveness to deteriorate after 10 years' service.

Not only are numbers required; if beaches are to be secure, these numbers must be available, with a minimum of delay, for actual operations. Consequently a second indispensable feature of the defense plan is its provisions for rapid mobilization in emergency. Numbers and availability are equally important, and no future considerations of any kind should ever be permitted to reduce either of these factors below a safe level. This point is so obvious as to require further discussion.

The next essential is adequate equipment, of reasonable efficiency.

The equipment needed is that which is peculiarly effective in defending beaches. Intensive small arms fire is indicated. Rifles, automatics and machine guns are needed in great numbers. There is no need for many of the highly technical and expensive items required for clashes between major armies in the open field, but available resources should be devoted, in this regard, to infantry weapons, to light artillery, and to necessary air and marine supporting elements. An exception is noted in favor of the fixed defenses of Manila and Subic Bays. Later, also, submarine mines to block sea passage, artillery to cover the areas where mines are planted, and anti-aircraft equipment will be most desirable.

Some questions have been raised with respect to the efficacy of the rifles secured, after long negotiation, from the American Government. This is one item in the whole development of which the wisdom is not open to question by anyone acquainted with the facts.

These weapons are, ballistically, equal to any other military rifle now in general use in the world. They are rugged, durable and efficient. Even if, in final negotiation, their list price of about 17 pesos should have to be paid in full, their purchase would still be wise. A minor difficulty encountered with this weapon has been some trouble with the extractor, due to a defect in the manufacturing process. New stocks of this particular part, available at reasonable prices, assure the Philippine Army of a good weapon, at a fraction of the price that would have to be paid for any other. Hundreds of thousands of these rifles now form part of the U.S. Army reserves, and they are identical in type to the standard issue of the British Army. Any criticisms of the defense plan that are based upon alleged unsuitability of the Enfield rifle are not only invalid, they should serve to establish the lack of vision, or the faulty judgment, of the person making them. If the entire citizen Army attains an efficiency comparable to that of its rifle, the Philippines will have nothing to fear.

Under present allotments of annual funds, machine guns, mortars and necessary field pieces will be secured in minimum necessary quantities for the 1st Reserve.

The Off-Shore Patrol and the Air Corps require special, and relatively expensive, equipment. These two services are essential to the defense. They contain a definite threat to hostile shipping in these waters, and their combat power is tremendous, particularly against troops attempting to land on these shores.

With funds provided as at present, neither service will be as strong as I believe to be desirable and necessary.

My conviction is that the minimum strength that should be provided in these two services is:

60 Bombing planes (2 engine) with necessary supporting elements of pursuit, attack and observation; a total of about 130–150 tactical airplanes. The present program calls for about 75.

60 motor torpedo boats. The present program calls for about 25.

Another item of special equipment to be considered is anti-aircraft material. For some years to come there will be relatively few profitable targets in the Philippines for raiding air forces. But Manila, with its docks, its warehouses, its governmental activities and its industries and crowded areas will be a fine objective for this kind of attack. Ground defenses should be supplied to supplement the efforts of the Philippine Air Corps. This equipment is expensive, but, in emergency, at least 2–3 efficient regiments should be available in the Manila district, exclusive of any stationed on Corregidor or at military air-fields. Moreover, it should be noted that long and intensive training is necessary for the effective use of this materiél. If the project is to be undertaken, a start should be made by 1941, at the latest.

Other desirable items of special equipment are mines and gas-defense materiél.

<u>Leadership</u>.—Leadership is an indispensable feature of any successful army. By this term is not meant merely a satisfactory General-in-Chief; it means that <u>officers, in all echelons, must be available and qualified to handle their commands</u>.

Since the Philippine Army must be essentially civilian, this requirement throws predominant importance on the problem of <u>developing and maintaining reserve officers</u>. They must be basically well trained, and must thereafter be progressively developed as long as they stay in the reserve. The universities must perform the first part of this essential work. The program of R.O.T.C. instruction must be placed on an efficient basis <u>now</u>, and the yearly training of reserve officers, through practice mobilizations, must be thorough and progressive.

The R.O.T.C. course should be three years of compulsory training. This has already been agreed to, in principle, by all concerned, and there appears to be no legitimate excuse for failure to start the system, now.

No graduating certificate should be obtainable by an able bodied male student, unless he is also a graduate of the R.O.T.C. Moreover, any young man who, after graduation, fails to carry out his duties as a Reserve officer, should be subject to punishment by law, and should not be eligible for employment by any governmental or quasi-governmental organization. If the educated, favored classes do not support the government in this vast and vital undertaking it is certain to be a dismal failure.

One of the fundamental missions of the Philippine college and university system must be to inculcate in all students a thorough appreciation of these axioms, and an earnest desire to serve the nation through self-preparation for leadership of military units.

Regular officers must, of course, be maintained in sufficient numbers to carry on instruction, perform necessary overhead, and to provide key men for staff and command positions in war. The development of individuals qualified for all these tasks is a prerequisite to success, and the plan has not, as yet, been able to put into practice methods calculated to produce a well-rounded corps of the necessary qualifications. This, however, is a slow process at best, and only time, supplemented by wise policy can correct the defect.

The Military Academy is doing a wonderful work; it is a certain future source of splendid 3rd lieutenants. The further development of these fine youngsters along correct lines must be provided for through efficient schools, through logical assignments to duty, through removing the worthless type of seniors from controlling positions, and by practice in troop leading. This subject is mentioned again under "training."

A considerable criticism has been voiced, perhaps with some justice, as to the efficiency of officers heretofore available for duty, and as to the failure of the plan to anticipate this difficulty and prevent its occurrence.

In undertaking any great organizational effort it is an axiom that the development of leadership, in all units, should keep a step ahead of mass operation. Otherwise inefficiency and waste are unavoidable.

In 1935 it was initially planned to follow a development procedure that would center attention, for the first few years, on the production of officers and enlisted instructors, with the trainee contingent large enough only to provide a practical field in which leaders could become experienced, and from which selected men could be chosen as non-commissioned officers. For two reasons this plan was abandoned, by orders of the High Command, in the early summer of 1936.

The first of these reasons involved calculations as to the size of the defensive force to be produced, and the time available for its production. To meet the announced requirement of numbers some 300,000 men would have to pass through the training cadres in 10 years. To postpone initiation of the general enlisted program would require, later, a much larger plant than if a schedule of about 30,000 men per year should be started at once.

The second reason involved national psychology. In the spring of 1936 about 150,000 young men registered for military service. This fact was widely publicized and the fear was born that if, after this magnificent response, only 3,000 men, as originally planned, should be called to duty on the first of the succeeding year, a let-down or a feeling of deflation and disappointment would be noticeable throughout the nation.

The High Command therefore ordered a concentration of 20,000 trainees, in cadres, on January 1, 1937, and this order necessitated, thereafter, a parallel rather than a sequential development of qualified leadership and required masses. With this handicap, it is true that leadership has not been, on the average, satisfactory in efficiency. But regardless of handicaps and excuses, there exists no reason why the quality of the leadership in all units should not steadily increase, provided only that the General Staff give to this matter the thought and attention that it deserves.

An essential ingredient of good leadership is morale.

Morale is born of loyalty, patriotism, discipline and efficiency, all of which breed confidence in self and in comrades. Most of all morale is promoted by unity,—unity in service to the country and in the determination to attain the objective of national security. Morale is at one and the same time the strongest, and the most delicate of growths. It withstands shocks, even disasters of the battlefield, but can be destroyed utterly by favoritism, neglect or injustice. To foster a proper morale in the Army is an undertaking worthy of the incessant effort of His Excellency, himself.

The Army should not be coddled or babied, for that does not produce morale, it merely condones and encourages inefficiency. But the Army should be taught to respect itself, and to render a quality of service that will <u>command</u> respect throughout the nation. Thus the population will come to look upon the uniform as the badge of loyalty, of duty and of efficiency, and this feeling will be reflected, inescapably, in still higher performance in the Army.

There must constantly be demanded of the Army, individually and collectively, an unswerving devotion to duty, a constantly increasing professional efficiency and the highest standards of discipline and loyalty. Then, reward the Army with just appreciation of merit and performance, frown upon all injustice or favoritism in its administration, and there will be produced a real morale. When this is done the Army will have real leadership, throughout its organization.

<u>Solidarity of Purpose</u>.—The solidarity of purpose, above listed as an essential factor in developing a successful defense, is not only the most important feature of the whole problem, its production is peculiarly the function of the High Command, which must use every available agency and method to attain this end.

Education, propaganda, the full persuasive power and influence of all governmental agencies, rewards, punishment for the recalcitrant; everything should be used to produce unity of purpose and a flaming desire to do the job. The Philippines is building an army without financial reward for the individual; so the only inducement to effort must come from patriotic incentive, universally felt. Integration of 16,000,000 people in this single idea of unity is necessary.

Of all places where this idea must be unfailingly exemplified, the Army is the first. Disunion, born of efforts to advance personal interests, to gain favor with the highest authorities, to advocate, irregularly, pet theories that are relatively unimportant to the whole, personal jealousies; all these must be ruthlessly stamped out, whenever and wherever found.

The Secretary of National Defense should enjoy the full confidence of the President, and he should be held rigidly responsible for results. The single avenue of communication from His Excellency to the Army should be through the Secretary of National Defense. In the same way the Chief of Staff should enjoy the confidence of the Secretary of National Defense, and the Chief of Staff should be left free to assign <u>his</u> subordinates as he desires. Moreover, the Chief of Staff should know, and <u>the Army should know, that any attempt to short circuit the Chief of Staff, or the Secretary of National Defense, in placing a military question before higher authority, will result, always, in the instantaneous relief of the offender</u>.

If the Chief of Staff does not have this recognized control within his own military family, he cannot, in justice, be held responsible for results.

If there is allowed to grow up a belief that any favored individual can, by back door methods, obtain the ear of higher authority, or if any person in the Army is permitted to believe that he owes his assignment to anyone superior to the Chief of Staff, and therefore cannot be relieved by the Chief of Staff, then organizational procedure, discipline, and loyalty disappear, and the Army should be disbanded.

Trust the Chief of Staff, or fire him.

In like manner, every commander in the Army must be held responsible for all activities and personnel under him, and must have the necessary legal and delegated authority to meet those responsibilities.

Violation of these principles breeds disloyalty; and any individual that becomes faithless to one authority will, finally, become faithless to all. The Army will become a debating society, in which the various teams will be inspired by one motive only—advancement of self-interest.

Observance of these rules does not impose a bar to initiative, or a gag upon honest opinions. Subordination is indispensable in an Army; but subordination is not servility! The Command and Staff processes of a well run army provide ample encouragement for new ideas and progressive thought.

In this connection—it is entirely proper, and sometimes highly desirable, for higher authority, even including the Commander-in-Chief, to require that all basic staff studies made on a particular subject, accompany the recommendations submitted on that subject. In all such cases the complete study, including all minority or differing opinions are to be submitted, and without prejudice to the officers responsible for such differing opinions. This practice is a part of proper staff procedure, and in no wise constitutes a violation of the principle of unity of command, which is the essential under discussion.

When the necessary solidarity has been achieved in the Army, the victory will be more than half won, for this accomplishment will unfailingly inspire a similar attitude among the civil population. Thereafter, the two elements, civil and military, will act and re-act upon each other so that the beneficial results will be astonishing.

To sum up: In the Army there must be no toleration of whining, of defeatism, of laziness, of ineptitude, and above all, of favoritism or of any kind of disloyalty. These are the characteristics of dis-union, the antithesis of military efficiency.

The thing sought is the instantaneous, effective and loyal responsiveness of the whole Army to the will of the Commander-in-Chief. This means that the whole must be unified; and to achieve this unity the system of command and staff has been set up to transmit the Commander-in-Chief's orders, without delay, to the last private in the ranks. The Army must learn to look to that system, that is, each individual to his next official superior, as the only source of orders and leadership. To use any other method, except in temporary emergency, is to destroy solidarity—and without solidarity there is no army.

I have written earnestly and at length upon this subject and that of morale, not only because of their intrinsic importance, but because also, in a new army, where the High Command sees so much to be done, and done quickly, the temptation is always present to ignore the hierarchy of command. Even though, in particular instances, a specific problem might thus be more expeditiously handled in the long run, such practices will ruin the army.

War Reserve Equipment.—Adequate reserve supplies and equipment are necessary. This subject is of particular importance in the Philippines, where any attack must automatically cut off all imports.

The item of ammunition is of transcendent importance, because it cannot, under existing circumstances, be made in the Islands. But all supplies, essential to the maintenance of the Army and the civil population must likewise be provided for. Increased production of food-stuffs, textiles, building materials and other necessaries, will have a most advantageous effect on the emergency strength of the nation, but for all technical items there must be ample stocks on hand to meet probable needs.

The equipment and supplies that may probably be left here by the U.S. Army in 1946 will partially fill the gap now existing, but only partially. Before 1946 accumulation of these essentials must begin on a basis that will demand increased annual expenditure. It would be futile, here, to make a guess as to the amount involved, since such an estimate must be based upon the most exhaustive analyses. However, some idea of the costs can be gathered from a few simple examples.

Rifle ammunition, delivered, costs P66 per thousand rounds. If we assume that for every active rifle intended for the fighting forces we should have a minimum of only 1,000 rounds of ammunition in storage for emergency, the cost will be P66 per rifle. Assume further that in the completed army there would be only 100,000 men armed with the rifle (a total procurement of about 400,000 has been arranged for) and the reserve ammunition requirement for this one weapon becomes 100,000,000 rounds, costing P6,600,000.00. It is safe to estimate that automatic rifle and machine gun requirements (30 caliber) will be almost as much; so that minimum estimates for 30 caliber ammunition alone run to some P13,000,000.00. In the same way assume a reserve of only 1,000 rounds per infantry mortar. This involves about P24,000.00 for each gun, or for the 780 mortars planned for the first reserve alone, about P18,700,000.00.

For each type and kind of weapon in the army these reserves must be provided, else the weapon itself will represent only wasted money.

Further complicating the problem is the fact that ammunition is a perishable commodity, the life of the best being about 20 years in tropical climates. This adds to the cost of maintaining reserve stocks, because the amounts required will normally exceed 20 times the annual training allowances.

To reiterate: While numerical strength in the Army is essential, that strength will be useless without adequate stocks of armament and ammunition. At the risk of dwelling on the obvious it is repeated, therefore, that unless future plans make ample provision for a sufficient reserve of these expensive items, the defense of an independent Philippines will never be possible, if attacked.

II. ORGANIZATION.

The Army is physically organized so as to produce annually the individuals necessary to build up the enlisted strength of the reserve divisions deemed essential to security. This strength, heretofore discussed, is, in the opinion of the Military Adviser:

1st Reserve — 30 Divisions
2nd Reserve — 30   "
3rd Reserve — 30   "

Because of your familiarity with the outlines of the existing organization, I will refer to it only in specific comments, and will not include general explanations.

a̲. The cadre organization was made the subject of long and exhaustive study in the latter part of 1939. The officers making that study reached certain conclusions which were reported to you in detail by General MacArthur. I have nothing to add to what was said in that report, in which it was declared possible and desirable to effect some improvements in cadre organization, but that these were not revolutionary in character, and, in any event, could not be expected to have any drastic results upon the working out of the whole plan.

b̲. The organization for the production of reserve officers is very faulty. Immediate correction is needed, and the Secretary of Public Instruction should receive definite orders to cooperate, at once, with Army Headquarters so as to make a three-year course in the R.O.T.C. a pre-requisite to graduation; to increase the efficiency of military instruction in schools and colleges; and to intensify indoctrination of all students, everywhere, in the basic purposes and the necessity of public spirited service in the building up of national security.

c̲. The general administrative organization of the Army is satisfactory. It will be progressively improved in details, but academic discussions and furious debate in support of some particular change are not only of no benefit, they are harmful. The effort of the Army should be devoted, not to futile debate, but to perfection of training, to raising the efficiency of the reserves, improving instruction in schools and colleges, preaching loyalty, finding means and methods of changing gradually where change is indicated, but, above all, to make the essentials of the defense plan work successfully. These are the things that must be demanded of all the army, every day!

The difference between success and failure is ordinarily found in the amount of coordinated work and sweat that is applied toward a principal objective. Only the academician insists that in some detail of organization is this difference to be found. For army officers to consume their own time and that of higher officials in quarrels about details of organization is criminal—it shows that all sense of relative values has been lost, and, as a consequence, that attainment of important objectives has been sacrificed to indulge ego.

It is repeated that many details of the present organization are faulty. But improvements must come gradually,—as the result of intelligent, loyal effort on the part of the staff. If these subjects are brought up in such a way as to clothe them with an unjustified importance, and to hint at a necessity for revolutionary and drastic revision, then all progress stops. The training branch does not know what to plan for; the supply services do not know what to buy, or where to put things after they are bought; the high command becomes paralyzed. Money and time are wasted, two commodities in which we are now too deficient.

d. Reserves.—An important phase of organization applies to the Reserve. In these units resides the hope of successful defense, and no detail of their efficiency should be neglected.

Once the man has gone through the training cadre he becomes an asset to be carefully guarded and maintained. The policies of the government should lend every aid to the reservist in providing for his economic stability. A tramp cannot be considered available as a good soldier.

The civil and unclassified service lists of the Insular, Provincial and Municipal governments should give preference to the reservist. Every opportunity should be sought to identify him with the other members of his own military unit through holiday parades, fiestas, etc., and, finally, all units must be called out for active service (2 weeks) at least 2 years out of each 3. This schedule can be reached in 1946 and thereafter must be maintained.

Specific comments applicable to the principal features of the existing organization are as follows:

The General Staff—

Organization satisfactory. It is not yet strong enough in personnel or in ability to discharge its duties to its own or the government's satisfaction. However, nothing is to be gained by revision in nomenclature or distribution of functions, and any recommendations looking toward that end can be nothing but the results of misconceptions or ignorance.

The General Staff is the Chief of Staff's assisting and advisory body. His deliberate opinion as to the assignment of assistants therein should be controlling, and he has already approved the existing set-up.

The Services (Adjutant General, Judge Advocate General, Quartermaster, Ordnance, Signal, Medical, Engineer)—

All organized on satisfactory lines, but each can be greatly improved by more intensive effort. The Supply Services, through the District Depots, are now in position to store and distribute items as needed by the current army, but the whole system must be greatly expanded to be ready for emergency needs.

The Quartermaster, Engineer and Ordnance Services deserve special mention as having made more definite progress than average. Their methods of procurement, supply and administration are improving daily. The reason is, that the officers in charge of these services have demanded greater application to duty, more work and sweat, than have the others. These officers are:

Colonel Aguilar, Quartermaster
Captain Cunanan, Ordnance
Captain Torres
　　　　　—Engineers
Captain Jimenez

I believe the same remarks can soon be made with respect to the Judge Advocate General, for Colonel Torres gives every indication that he will lead that corps properly, and will fully meet the high expectations of His Excellency in selecting him for this important post.

District Commanders—

Most of our District Commanders have failed to meet their responsibilities in the way that should be expected. It is true that they've had unusual difficulties, but, even so, their performance has been disappointing. The several district headquarters are so vitally important to the whole organization that I believe we should seek out and place our best officers in charge of them, and where relative rank interferes, I would take the senior out of the way by giving him an inconsequential job—until the Army can get rid of him.

We are now in a stage of development where the important thing is to get something done; operation, for the next two or three years, is far more important than planning. The essentials of the preparatory system are established; effort must now be devoted to making them work. In two or three years planning will again come to the fore, based upon operating experience and in anticipation of the critical task of actually starting the taking over of facilities and functions from the United States Army. But unless we now get good officers in operating capacities we will not know whether a discovered fault is traceable to an undesirable feature of the system or merely to inefficient personnel. It is not too much to say that, so far as the immediate good of the Army is concerned, priority in assignment of the best officers should go to command and operating positions, including the District Headquarters, even at the expense of taking officers from the General Staff.

To be more specific, in my opinion the Chief of Staff would now be making a better use of his available personnel if he should shift it somewhat as follows:

Retain in their present positions the Commanders of the 1st, 3rd and 9th Districts. These are all Majors, of whom the one in the 3rd, Major Dumlao, seems to be doing particularly well.

Get rid of all other District Commanders, transferring to Constabulary all that are desired by that service, instituting retiring proceedings with respect to the remainder.

Assign to these 7 Districts the following:

Col. Capinpin—This officer should be given the 4th District, retaining his control of, and his office at, Camp Murphy. He is capable of handling the expanded job efficiently.

Col. Garcia—5th District. We have a number of officers, graduates of Leavenworth, who could carry on satisfactorily the duties of his present post, while he, because of his experience, should make an excellent District Commander. Major Gomez, a quiet, studious type, would undoubtedly make a good G-3.

Majors Moran, Garcia, Caluya, and the best available others, should be given the 2nd, 6th, 7th, 8th and 10th Districts. (When Col. Stevens returns he should probably go back to the 10th.) [4]

These officers are now, in general, acting as District Executives, and it is to be expected that their commanders will make good use of them. But all are mature, experienced men, and should bear direct responsibility, untrammelled by a local senior who is worthless. Major Caluya is now commanding Parang, and should retain that control while commanding the 10th District.

All the officers named are my good friends, and I do not want to be understood as criticizing them in their present position—I merely desire to show where I think the Army's good would be served by some changes in assignment. I realize also that these are not matters for Executive intervention—they pertain to a responsibility that should be discharged by the Chief of Staff. But it has been my purpose, through these specific comments, to emphasize my conviction with respect to the importance of the District Command in the success of the Philippine Army.

Cadres—

Fully discussed in the long report already submitted to His Excellency by General MacArthur, and above referred to.

Schools—

I have nothing to suggest with respect to the Philippine Military Academy. It is one activity that has, in its progress, exceeded my expectations. (This is likewise true of Camp Dau, Camp Murphy, the Air Corps, Ft. Wint, and Ft. McKinley.)

The Service School for officers (under Major Hill) is doing exceptionally good work. Its only real weakness is that, due to lack of money to maintain more officers in the Army, no resident students, except for a few reservists, can be detailed there. All its work is done by correspondence. As soon as possible it should be established in the normal pattern; which statement applies also to schools for the arms and services. The effects of Major Hill's work, even with this handicap, are already apparent. The same methods should be put into operation by the Chiefs of all technical services for the education of their own Regular and Reserve officers, pending the establishment of formal schools. Camp Dau should do the same for officers of the Field Artillery.

Air Corps and Off-Shore Patrol—

These services, particularly the first named, are developing satisfactorily, and as rapidly as available funds will permit. Their need for extra funds will become acute in the latter part of the Commonwealth period, when it becomes necessary to obtain desirable strength in tactical equipment.

The Air Corps is being run so well, and to such good effect, that it could well serve as a model for most other units in the Army.

III. TRAINING.

Not enough work has been done by any echelon of the Army to improve training in all its phases. Here is where intensification of effort yields sure and important results.

Some few places have been specially favored, either in the presence of a commanding officer of exceptional qualifications or through the close cooperation of American Army personnel. These are Camp Murphy, McKinley, Dau, Wint and the Philippine Military Academy and the General Service School. At these the training is reasonably efficient.

But in the normal cadre, as well as in colleges, high schools and elementary schools there must be a greater application of training effort. Good officers must be encouraged and promoted—the bad must be eliminated.

The training division of the General Staff has been engaged in too many activities tending to distract it from its main mission. In some respects this distraction has been unavoidable, but in others it has been inexcusable. For example, the head of the training division was required to devote practically his full time for 2 months, in 1939, to investigating race-track irregularities. No matter how necessary that investigation, it was not as important as training the Army. In other ways this officer's attention has been unnecessarily taken away from a task whose scope and importance is sufficient to challenge the full abilities of the ablest soldier in the world.

In a lesser degree this has been our experience throughout the Army. Too many things are allowed to interfere with training. This must stop. The Army must train first—do all other things second, if at all.

With rare exceptions training in cadres has been far from satisfactory. Poor officers, meager facilities and faulty supervision have been responsible. One glaring defect is in shooting—this must be improved, markedly, and at once. Each trainee should shoot during his course of instruction, and under competent direction, at least 100 rounds of 22 calibre, and at least 40 of the 30 calibre.

In some places, like Davao, Camp Keithley, Bontoc, Batangas, Lipa and others it has been conclusively proved that cadre training can be satisfactory. The job is to raise all stations to similar standards.

IV. FINANCES.

This subject is important but delicate. More money is desperately needed, but whether it can be provided without wrecking the very thing it is appropriated to secure, the stability and security of the nation, is a subject for statesmen, not soldiers.[5]

I point out certain deficiencies that can be made good only with more money.

a. Present appropriations will not provide, by 1946, the numbers of airplanes that should, in my opinion, be maintained.

b. They will not provide, in the same period, the number of patrol boats that should be on hand.

c. Present financial plans make no provision for necessary reserve stocks of ammunition, and for many important items of armament. As pointed out above, this defect, unless corrected, will be fatal.

d. They do not permit a sufficiently frequent and comprehensive training of reservists.

e. They do not permit highly desirable increases in the professional force to take proper care of mobilization property, and to detach a larger number for attendance at professional schools.

f. They do not permit of the institution of measures in schools and colleges, deemed necessary to the development of a thoroughly efficient Reserve Officers Corps.

g. When the time comes to take over fixed defenses, deficiencies in these appropriations will be even more marked.

My own conviction is that, at present, reasonable efficiency cannot be accomplished with less than about 18,000,000 yearly, which, about 1943–44 should be stepped up to 22,000,000, and thereafter maintained at that level. It is true that this statement represents only an educational guess, but this much is obvious. We are now using up, on necessary activities, about 16,500,000 per year. Consider the things just named as deficiencies, and it becomes apparent that the development and maintenance of 30 efficient divisions and necessary auxiliaries to say nothing of any portion of the 2nd or 3rd Reserve, will require more money.

At present the Army is like an individual that is living on a diet sufficient for existence, but which is so poor in vitamins and nutriment that he gains no vitality and energy for truly efficient work. Only a little more expenditure is needed to make his diet fully satisfactory.

2,000,000 pesos extra per year, now, would result in a 50% increase in efficiency and in defensive assets.

I realize that in the unequivocal statement of this conclusion I may be speaking in ignorance of particular phases of the plan, as yet undisclosed to me. No matter what any such may be I still believe that the essentials of Philippine Defense, namely,

Requisite numbers,

Adequate initial and reserve training,

Sufficient armament,

Adequate reserve stocks, particularly in ammunition,

cannot be produced on 16 million pesos per year.

V. PERSONNEL.

In personnel, serious deficiencies have been encountered, both in quantity and quality. Appropriations limit the number of officers on active duty, including both regular and reserve, to about 1050, whereas there should be authorized no less than 1500. The latter number would permit the strengthening of staff; provide quotas for schools, and would establish a greater number of vacancies through which reserve officers could be passed, to insure their practical training. For this last reason, the Regular Corps should never become large enough to fill all active duty positions. That would be a serious error.

The Regular enlisted corps must be improved, both in quantity and in quality. Instruction by enlisted men has been, on the average, far below satisfactory. Quality can be improved by weeding out the unfit and enlisting well trained men out of the cadres. The need for greater strength becomes obvious when it is realized that at every mobilization center there should be four regulars, at least, for every reserve battalion assigned to that center. This requirement is over and above present uses.

The common tao, under a reasonably able instructor, readily becomes a good soldier. If we succeed in establishing Regular and Reserve Corps of efficient officers, in adequate numbers, and maintaining a proper schedule of reserve training, there need be no fear on this particular score.

The older Constabulary officers, with occasional exceptions, have not made good officers in the Army. Old methods, old routine and old habits have not fitted into the new requirements, and many of these individuals have become too set in their ways, too inflexible, possibly just too old, to change. This applies to American and Filipino alike. Many of the younger Constabulary officers are improving and will be satisfactory; among the older ones it is the exception that can carry on effectively in the Army.

The Scout officer is on the average, of satisfactory efficiency along the lines in which he worked in the American Army. In experience and training, however, most of them have pursued rather narrow channels, and none of them has had opportunity to serve in positions close to the high command, where special technique and broad outlook are mandatory. It is to be expected that time will cure this defect. We have but few Scouts; their importance comes from the fact that because of their assimilated rank they occupy, without exception, positions of real responsibility.

One of their weaknesses, from the standpoint of the whole Army, has been that, for years, they have maintained among themselves a tight social and personal organization. There was nothing wrong in this, but it has had the effect of making them a clique, and it is difficult for the individual, now, to forget this bond and to merge himself unreservedly into the interests and tasks of the Philippine Army.

All of these men take a justifiable pride in their records and in their military experience. Frequently, however, this is carried too far, so that they act on the theory that unless a Filipino has been a Scout, he cannot be a good soldier and officer. They frequently are tempted, therefore, to be-little the abilities of others, and this habit does not promote in the Army the one characteristic which they, as professional soldiers, should know is the <u>sine qua non</u> to success, unity. Among most of them this habit is less noticeable than it was four years ago, but unfortunately, it is not yet eradicated.

Most of them have an unusual degree of personal ambition. This trait, admirable when present in reasonable degree, tends to bias judgment and discolor decision when it becomes unduly pronounced.

Officers absorbed into the Regular Force through the Reserve Corps, are, in general, an efficient group. This is because they were selected only after a long period of probation, and represent the cream of hundreds of applicants. Moreover, in addition to present efficiency, they were judged upon the basis of potential capacity and value. About 150 of these have now been taken into the Army, and, because of the fact that next year the Military Academy will begin to turn out about 75 third lieutenants per year, it is not to be expected that many more reserve officers will be taken into the line of the Regular Army. In the Medical and Chaplain's Corps, the Reserves, of course, continue as the source of supply.

The Philippine Military Academy provides the real hope for future efficiency in the Regular officer corps. This statement does not deprecate the outstanding efficiency of a few of the older men now in the Army; but, as pointed out before, the need is for a high level of efficiency among the whole corps.

These boys undergo, in their formative years, a course of training that stresses loyalty, duty, patriotism, and the highest standards of personal character. Colonel Martelino has done a masterly piece of work; and its results will be felt for all time in this country.

It is essential that, with the start these young men have, they do not drift, under inept leadership, into habits incompatible with efficiency. Here is another reason that the position of District Commander looms so importantly; he is close enough to junior officers to watch over and guide their development. This is another reason, too, for vitalizing the processes for eliminating worthless individuals. We have been too dilatory in getting rid of men that are not only of no value, but whose presence is damaging to progress.

VI. <u>MISCELLANEOUS</u>.

a. Secretary of National Defense—

(Note: In discussing this subject, I refer only to the office, not to any personality or incumbent.)

To the Secretary should be delegated, by His Excellency, every vestige of authority and responsibility that is possible under a liberal interpretation of the law. (<u>Note</u>: If the law prevents desirable delegation—then it should be amended.)

In the U.S. Government, not more than one military communication normally goes to the White House in a week—but if anything goes wrong the Secretary of War is on the carpet immediately.

When the Department of National Defense was about to be established, I wrote a draft of a letter of instructions which was intended to accomplish the necessary delegation of authority, but that letter was never issued. A similar one should be written—otherwise the Secretary of National Defense may become a figurehead, will pass his problems on to Malacañan, and so instead of becoming a valuable assistant to His Excellency, will be merely an additional, and useless, link in the chain of correspondence and command.

The responsibilities and authority of this office should <u>compel</u> its head to familiarize himself with every essential feature of the Army, and he should have to guide every activity, under his delegated authority, in accordance with the policies announced to him by His Excellency. I am against figureheads, not because I object to them <u>per se,</u> but because their presence slows up action and does not relieve superior authority of any work or worry.

b. American Schools

Training of officers in American Military Schools should be continued as long and as comprehensively as possible. Occasionally the individual gains nothing but an exaggerated ego—but in the average case he gains new viewpoints, wider understanding of his profession, and appreciation of high standards in performance.

c. Barrack Construction for R.O.T.C.

This project should be undertaken on an experimental basis. It should be tried at one school for the 3rd (last) year R.O.T.C. students. Note results, and if successful, establish the system gradually at all. Its accomplishment must not take money from other essential activities.

d. Illiteracy Training.

This fine by-product of the cadre system should receive more attention. It is sadly neglected at most places.

e. Every man that graduates satisfactorily from a cadre should carry a note testifying as to his honesty, willingness to work, special qualifications, etc. Any chronic offender in a cadre should not be given such a letter, and we should start to build up, throughout all employers in the Philippines, a desire to get hold of good reservists.

f. Continued emphasis should be placed upon the task of perfecting the Army's system of courts-martial and improving the operation of the system. The Chief of Staff should, in every way, encourage the Judge Advocate General in this necessary effort.

THE OFFICE OF THE MILITARY ADVISER

This office, although not a part of the hierarchy of command in the Army, exercises a definite influence because of the closeness of the official relationship between the head of the office and His Excellency. Moreover, since the Military Adviser was the author of the fundamentals of the Defense Plan, interpretations of its intent and objectives are naturally referred to him. In practice, the value of the office has been well established along several lines.

First of all it provides for the Philippine Army a broadened viewpoint and experience in higher organization and in war-planning, that are not otherwise available. Next, it seems as a balance wheel, a steadying influence in the organization. More important, it establishes a perfect connecting link between the new Army and the American War Department; a liaison service that is absolutely essential to current progress. In addition, the office provides professional and technical advice that, under present conditions, are indispensable.

In certain of these lines the importance of the office should begin, now, to diminish, in exact step with increasing professional capacity and experience in the Philippine Army. Unless this progress is evident in the Army, then the Military Adviser's Office is not functioning efficiently, because its mission is not to run the Army, but to teach the Army to run itself.

But in one direction, the importance of the office will constantly increase up to, and possibly for a year or two after, the realization of Philippine Independence. This involves its function of serving as go-between for the American and Philippine Armies. With the approval of independence more and more problems requiring the close cooperation of the two armies will arise. Some of the anticipated problems are as follows:

Transfer of military reservations.

Transfer of harbor defenses.

Negotiations involving the acquisition of stocks of equipment and supplies that will, probably, be obtainable from the American Army on an advantageous basis.

Use of personnel from the disbanded Scout organization, etc., etc.

The suitability of the Mission for these tasks is too apparent to require discussion.

<u>CONCLUSION</u>

In four years the Army has made a good organizational start. What is needed is work—intelligent and intensive work by all concerned, each in his own sphere.

Clean cut administration through established channels of communication and authority must be relied upon, together with ceaseless indoctrination and education, to achieve that unity of purpose and effort, both in the civil and military population, is indispensable to success.

Sober analysis of progress and of current objectives discloses a number of important deficiencies in the security organization that is to be anticipated on a financial basis of 16,000,000 pesos annually. Timely steps must be taken to correct these; and such correction will cost more money. Examples are given in the section entitled "Finances".[6]

1. On June 16, 1960, Jorge Vargas, former secretary to President Quezon, attended a dinner President Eisenhower gave for high Philippine officials at the American Embassy in Manila. Although Vargas held no office at the time, he apparently was invited because of his long association with Eisenhower. At some point during the evening Vargas handed Eisenhower the final copy of the December 1939 report on the defense plan, referred to in Eisenhower's letter of December 30, 1939. The copy given to Eisenhower was dated August 8, 1940. Because that is the date on the document, it is included at this location in the chronology; however, it evidently required of Vargas and his staff seven months to prepare and submit a clean draft to Quezon, therefore the August 8 date. It is obvious that changes took place in Eisenhower's draft (see note 1, December 30, 1939, entry). The whereabouts of the original December 1939 draft prepared by Eisenhower is unknown. Nevertheless, the summary, which begins with section 1 of the report, is so faithful to the wording of the summary Eisenhower added to his December 30 letter that the full report included here is probably changed very little from Eisenhower's draft. After returning to Washington, Eisenhower copied the report and returned the original to Vargas. The document included here is the copy Eisenhower's staff retained.

2. The summary Eisenhower prepared and sent Vargas on December 30, 1939, has been deleted from this document. It is included word for word in the December 30 document.

3. Eisenhower's assumption proved to be correct. Beginning December 10, 1941, the Japanese made several small amphibious landings at vital points in the Philippines. But a large force, consisting of forty-three thousand troops, landed on the Lingayen coast on December 22 and within ten days took Manila and the surrounding area. From that base, Japanese forces pursued MacArthur and the remnants of the Philippine and American armies overland into the Bataan Peninsula, where the defending forces finally surrendered. See Louis Morton, *The Fall of the Philippines* (Washington, D.C.: Office of the Chief of Military History, 1953), 122–44.

4. Major Garcia was probably Ricardo Garcia, who had been serving under the other Garcia with G-3, Personnel and Logistics, Philippine Army. Luther R. Stevens, an American army officer, commanded the Philippine Constabulary, District of Southern Mindanao. At the time of the Japanese invasion, Stevens, by then a brigadier general, commanded the Philippine Scout 91st Division, which withdrew with the main forces to Bataan.

5. Eisenhower believed that any nation that risked bankrupting its economy in order to build unchallengeable military strength would, itself, pose the gravest threat to its security. This concept would prove central to his role as commander in chief during his presidency, when time and again he infuriated military service heads by cutting their budgetary requests because he believed fiscal solvency was of paramount importance.

6. In 1942, president-in-exile Quezon asked Eisenhower to write a memorandum that summarized the mission to the Philippines. The report can be found in Louis Morton, "The Philippine Army, 1935–1939: Eisenhower's Memorandum to Quezon," *Military Affairs* 12 (summer 1948): 103–7. The original document is in the Plans and Operations Division Files, Records of the War Department General and Special Staffs, NARA.

165

Eisenhower Library
Pre-presidential Papers

To Colonel Leonard T. Gerow[1]

August 23, 1940

Dear Gee: General and Mrs. Gasser[2] have been up in this section for some three weeks. Last night the four of us had family dinner, and, naturally, you were the subject of much of our conversation. This reminded me that you've owed me a letter for so long I can't even remember whether it's the other way round—so I'll send such news as I have to you via the indirect method of scribbling it first and then getting hold of someone to convert my scrawl into a legible document.

We've just returned from maneuvers. For four days and nights we attacked through country that is mainly so-called cutover. Actually it would have made good stage-setting for a play in Hades. Stumps, slashings, fallen logs, tangled brush, holes, hummocks and hills! While I am Regimental Executive, I asked for, and got, command of a battalion—and we certainly went places and did things.

489

Certain things stood out:

<u>a</u>. The Infantry Regiment needs more transportation; roughly one more 1½ ton truck per rifle company, two 1½ ton trucks in the Regimental Headquarters Company (in place of ½ tons) and about three more in the Service Company.

<u>b</u>. On the other hand the methods of using foot troops and trucks on a single, rather poor road, especially when all other elements of the combat team are following closely, have <u>not</u> been perfected.

<u>c</u>. In difficult country the battalion communications, particularly when the battalion is allotted a considerable frontage, are inadequate. This was noticed particularly in our maneuvers because of lack of experienced officers. In my battalion, aside from myself, there are two 1st Lieutenants, Regular Army, two 2nd Lieutenants, Regular Army, and the rest Tommys.[3] My staff was one Tommy 2nd Lieutenant. Maintenance of control is a real job! Mighty close to an impossible one!

As yet we've received no light machine guns nor BAR's 1918-A-2's, nor any 60mm Mortars. Finally, the regiment was some four hundred men short of authorized strength.

In general, that's the alibi side of the picture. For the rest we really learned a lot, shook down our organization and on top of it all, had a lot of fun. I froze at night, never had, in any one stretch more than 1¾ hours sleep, and at times was really fagged out—but I had a severe time.

I haven't been watching the promotions, but assume you have either gotten your eagles, or will have them in a week or so. I hope the W.D. is smart enough to pass you a star at its first opportunity.

Johnny is going to school at Millard's, in Washington; Mamie and I are living here alone. Both of us are well and send our very best to you and to Mrs. Gee, whom we are still hoping to meet, soon! As ever

---

1. Eisenhower was at Fort Lewis at this time, and Gerow was Acting Assistant Commandant, the Infantry School, at Fort Benning. In December 1940, Gerow became Chief of the War Plans Division.

2. Lorenzo D. Gasser, Acting Deputy Chief of Staff, became Assistant Chief of Staff in 1936. He retired in 1945 as a major general.

3. This reference is to the so-called Thomason Act officers.

To Colonel George S. Patton Jr.[1]

Dear George: Thanks a lot for your recent note; I am flattered by your suggestion that I come to your outfit.[2] It would be great to be in the tanks once more, and even better to be associated with you again.

Since you did not specify the capacity in which I might serve in the armored division, maybe I should tell you that by requirement of law and by preference, I'm at long last doing "command duty". It's not only that, like yourself, I like to work with soldiers, but I'm weary of desk duty. I suppose it's too much to hope that I could have a regiment in your division, because I'm still almost three years away from my colonelcy. But <u>I think</u> I could do a damn good job of commanding a regiment and I hear that Douglas Greene,[3] who won't get his colonelcy for some time yet, has one of the armored regiments. Explain that one to me!!

Anyway, if there's a chance of that kind of an assignment, I'd be for it 100%. Will you write me again about it, so that I may know what you had in mind?

I had not heard before that you were in Benning; thought you were still commanding Myers. I've been back in the U.S. since January, and have had a swell time in the 15th Infantry. I command the 1st Battalion, am Regimental Executive and have odd jobs of various kinds. I've studied every M.I.D.[4] Report coming out of this war, and to make sure that I study them well, I prepare lectures on them.

Suppose I told you long ago that I qualified as a private pilot under the U.S. Bureau a year or so ago—but I've had to give up flying. I can't afford to get the kind of machine necessary to do the flying I like to do—so that's that!

Give our best to Bee.[5] Mamie and I are alone now, because John is in Millard's struggling to make the grade on the Presidential Competitives for West Point next spring.

Thanks again for your thought of me. As ever

1. Patton commanded the 2d Armored Brigade at Fort Benning.
2. The "note" to Eisenhower is not available. Patton had asked Eisenhower to join him at Benning, in part, probably, because of Eisenhower's continuing wish to be placed in a tank command.
3. Douglass T. Greene, a classmate of Eisenhower's at the USMA, served as a professor of military science and tactics at the Drexel Institute of Technology from 1934

to 1940. Eisenhower was correct: Greene would not become a colonel until July 1942. Greene retired in 1946 as a major general.

    4. Military Intelligence Division.

    5. Patton's wife, Beatrice Ayer Patton.

167

To MARK CLARK[1]

SEPTEMBER 17, 1940

Dear Wayne: This is one of Fort Lewis' cold, dark days—windy but no rain. Wait a minute, I'm wrong, its coming down now! I'm hugging the radiator in my office, whereas yesterday I was opening up everything in search of a cooling breeze.

Your notation to look up page 25, FM 30-20,[2] reminds me of the high school gag we used to have; give a guy a reference, which referred him to another; repeat and repeat until the dope was dizzy—at which point he'd find some very unflattering remark concerning people that look up references. In other words the only thing of any possible significance I can find on the page is "See appendix" and "FM 5-245".[3] Otherwise I learn that maps <u>are</u> classified and that some maps can be made in the field. All of which would indicate that my edition of FM 30-20 is not the same as yours.

However, on page <u>21</u> I find a reproduction of an oblique you used at Ord—so with my uncanny intuition and sparkling intelligence I make the amazing deduction that you merely couldn't distinguish between paragraph and page numbering! (Compare numbers at top and bottom of page!) But, after all, why should a G.H.Q. brass hat give a damn about details?[4]

Well, in looking at the picture I'm reminded of a statement I read in a German criticism of the French Army (one of our M.I.D. Reports). It said "They were too slow in issuing orders; they even used overlays". I agree heartily with the criticism, and I think your initiation of the use of the oblique photo as an operation map accompanying a <u>verbal</u> order was a real contribution to decent staff procedure. You'll remember how, at Ord, I always yelped about overlays; but I think obliques are the tops!

I am hopeful you can make the trip out here. There's lots of things to talk about—professional and personal; and a lot of scotch that needs a bit of expert attention.

What you say about General McNair agrees exactly with what I've always heard about him. General Moseley (who in spite of his retired activities was a shrewd judge of officers)[5] often told me that General McNair was the soldier of his time in the Army. He (Moseley) said that General McNair had everything. I am deeply regretful I never had a chance to meet him; but when he visited our C.P. during the recent maneuvers I just couldn't take a minute off; not even if at that moment old Gabriel had blown his trumpet.

Sorry about your furniture. I told Mamie and she said to tell you she was weeping with you. And we're anxious to know how Renie's mother is getting along. Give my best to Charley Gerhardt, and, with warm regards to you and Renie, and the children. As ever

1. Clark, now a lieutenant colonel, was living in post housing at Fort Humphreys, home of the Army War College. Although George Marshall had requested Clark's assignment to the War College faculty, he had done so as an administrative ploy to get the talented Clark near him for a more important assignment. On the day Clark and his wife arrived in Washington, Marshall had him transferred immediately from the War College to the staff of General Headquarters. There he served as principal assistant to Maj. Gen. Leslie McNair, who had been tasked by Marshall with organizing and training all army field forces for the coming war. Clark, noted for his skill in troop training, was a logical choice as McNair's assistant. Clark would employ his ready access to the Army's Chief of Staff to bring to Marshall's attention, repeatedly, Eisenhower's name and growing reputation. The reference in the letter to furniture relates to damage during the Clarks' move to the War College. See Martin Blumenson, *Mark Clark* (New York: Congdon and Weed, 1984), 36–51; for further discussions on this matter, see Holt, "An Unlikely Partnership."

2. FM 30-20 refers to the *Basic Manual: Military Intelligence, Military Maps* (Washington, D.C.: Government Printing Office, 1940).

3. As a joke, Eisenhower referred to a footnote at the bottom of page 25 that simply reads, "See Appendix." The reference to "FM 5-235" should have been to training manual "TM5 245."

4. Page 21 of FM 30-20 refers to an "oblique photograph used as map substitute to accompany oral field orders."

5. After his retirement from the army in 1938, Moseley became an outspoken critic of Roosevelt and the New Deal. He not only published his reactionary views, which included a strain of anti-Semitism, but also affiliated with such demagogic right-wing radicals as Gerald L. K. Smith.

168   Eisenhower Library
                                                          Fort Lewis Diary[1]

SEPTEMBER 26, 1940–OCTOBER 26, 1940

SEPTEMBER 26

During the war of 1917–1918 many interesting things happened to me that later slipped from my memory. That experience suggested that when a new emergency arose, if ever, I'd try to keep a brief diary, so as to have a day-by-day account of outstanding events. This is the beginning of such an effort.

Right now the so-called "Battle of London" is progressing. It is a German bombardment of England, by air, apparently conducted with two main objects:

(1) To cut off British imports.
(2) To cause such damage to England's morale, material resources, industries and military forces, that an invasion by sea will be feasible.

England seems to be standing up better than had been anticipated. Hitler occupied Austria & Czechoslovakia without fighting. Then he conquered Poland, Denmark, Norway, Holland, Belgium & France by force of arms. He's now turning against England the full resources of all these countries; to say nothing of the strength of his ally, Mussolini.

During the summer & early fall, the United States at last began to awaken to their own peril. A few days ago the Congress, at last, passed a conscript law, and their training should begin sometime in November. The program will not be in full swing until Jan. 15, at the earliest—possibly not until March.

In the regiment, now of an authorized strength of 2961, plus band, we are short:
About 1300 men
all 60mm mortars
all eight m.g.
all modified BAR (1918-A-2)
1/2 our 50 cals
1/2 our 81mm mortars
1/2 our 37mm guns
about 1/5 of our necessary housing
    Bn parade—5:30 today

Training effort directed toward producing a fine corps of instructors (all men now present) in all weapons, methods and practices, before arrival of conscripts, or any other large contingent of recruits.

The 41st Div. is now mobilizing at Camp Murray. Been coming in for a week.

On Fri, afternoon, Sept. 27, Gen. Thompson[2] sent for me and told me he wanted me to go on duty as Post Executive. This I immediately did—but behind it lies somewhat of a story, which I will try to highlight.

Upon my returning from the P.I. in Jan. '40 I was placed on G.S. at 4th Army Staff at San Francisco for 1 mo. At that time I told Gen. De-Witt, the Army Commander that I had only one ambition—to serve with a Reg. Inf. Regiment. I gave him my reasons, and he agreed with them saying that he'd keep me only a month and see that I got to my regiment immediately thereafter.

From the moment I actually joined my reg (at Ord on Feb 17) it has been a constant battle to stay with the outfit.

A month ago Gen. Thompson called me in to discuss the possibility of my serving as his Ch. of S., if he got command of a Corps. This I could not refuse and said O.K.

Later, just a few days ago, he found a need for additional staff officers around Post Hq and apparently still thinking he might be named a Corps C.G. told me to act as Post Ex. pending the establishment of such corps.

Now it turns out that he is <u>not</u> to get the Corps., and I'm still hung up with the Post Ex. job. But he's promised to see that I get back to my outfit before he relinquishes command. Maj. Gen. Joyce[3] is to command this corps.

1. This is the first entry of the very brief Fort Lewis Diary.

2. Maj. Gen. Charles Fullington Thompson (USMA, 1904) commanded the 3d Division at Fort Lewis (1940–41). Eisenhower served as his Chief of Staff from November 30, 1940, to March 3, 1941. He retired in 1945.

3. Maj. Gen. Kenyon Joyce commanded the IX Army Corps at Fort Lewis (1940–42). Eisenhower served as his Chief of Staff from March 4 to June 24, 1941.

OCTOBER 7

Now let's see, where was, and am, I?

On Oct. 3 an inspecting group from G.H.Q. headed by Gen. Mc-Nair,[1] dropped in on us and remained until Oct. 5. Just before the group arrived we received the W.D. & Corps area training schedule. In the W.D. it was written to apply to N.G. & newly formed units; the Corps area made it also applicable to Reg. Army units. It prescribed a cycle of training (basic) that, on a 44 hour a week program is to be completed in 13 weeks. Presumably it was to go into effect on Oct. 1 and since we didn't receive it until Sept. 29, a lot of rushing around & many general conferences became necessary.

The G.H.Q. crowd gave certain interpretations that made the application of the schedule to Reg. Army troops (many of which have just completed definite portions of the prescribed subjects) entirely logical.

Gen. Thompson is still adhering to his 7½ hr. daily schedule instead of the 8 hours contemplated in the program.
Mickle[2] and I thought this a mistake and said so, but it is still going on.

1. Lt. Gen. Leslie J. McNair (USMA, 1904) served with the General Staff during World War I. During the first two years of World War II, he remained in Washington, where he continued to direct the Army's troop mobilization and training program. Shortly before the Normandy invasion, he was sent to England to command the First Army Group, a nonexistent diversionary force. In July 1944, while observing action at the front lines, he was killed by an Allied "short" round.

2. Brig. Gen. Gerald St. Claire Mickle (USMA, 1919) served in World War I as Chief of Staff, Amphibious Corps, Atlantic Fleet, and as assistant commanding general, 75th Division. In 1945 he became commanding general of the 101st Airborne Division. Mickle retired in 1946.

Gen. Joyce phoned yesterday. He expects to arrive here about the 27th. Wants quarters on the post with his hqrs located elsewhere. In that way he won't have to take over the job of commanding the post. I hope to get back to the reg. before he gets here because he might just say "stay right there." Nix.

Gen. Joyce arrived here 2 days ago, and I'm still on same job. In fact he has asked for me for his corps staff—G-3, I think. I'm sure the A.G. will turn it down. I devoutly hope so because I have only two (alternative) ambitions—one is to be in the 15th—the other to command a new armored regiment.

169

Eisenhower Library
Pre-presidential Papers

TO LIEUTENANT COLONEL MARK CLARK

OCTOBER 31, 1940

Dear Wayne: First, I will answer some of the questions in your letter of October 29th, which arrived at my desk about five minutes ago. Our temporary set-up here at Lewis is as follows:

General Joyce did not assume command of the reservation nor has he taken over responsibility for any of the major construction and administrative problems. He has established a very temporary headquarters on the second floor of the Post Headquarters building (the permanent headquarters) and is organizing his Corps staff so as to begin his supervision of training, organization, and operation.

The reservation remains divided into two parts, that pertaining to the Fort Lewis garrison, and that pertaining to the 41st Division. General Thompson retains command of Fort Lewis and the 3rd Division, and General White[1] retains command in the 41st area.

General Thompson, however, is responsible also for all construction in all parts of the reservation so that, in effect, the situation is exactly as it was when you were here, except that General Joyce exercises command for training purposes over the whole 9th Corps.

We have been informed that a Colonel of the Regular Army is soon to be ordered here to take command of the "Station Complement". So long as the War Department does not put into effect the complete separation of administrative and training functions, I assume that this Colonel will be, in addition to the Commanding Officer of the Station Complement, the Administrative Executive for General Thompson. In line, then, with War Department instructions, General Thompson will delegate to that officer full administrative responsibility and will, himself, merely outline the broader policies to be followed.

Recommendations for the location of the Corps Headquarters building have already been sent through channels. This recommendation involves a location some 100 yards southwest of this headquarters building on the grassy triangle facing the commissary.

We made quite a survey of the whole countryside, looking for a suitable place to lease. None that we could find proved to be adequate. Hence the solution that I have outlined above. When final word is received here on the location of the Corps Headquarters, I will drop you a note.

I thought I made it clear, in one of my notes to you, that I was quite keen to get a command in the Armored Corps. As you know, George Patton rather expects to get one of the new divisions that are to be organized next year. When he wrote to me, he thought such organization would take place in January, but I now hear that it is deferred until June. In any event, that is exactly the thing I would like to do and I am sure that George Patton intends to ask for me in that capacity. The only difficulty that I can anticipate is that the War Department, because of my somewhat junior rank or for some other reason, may turn him down. In the meantime, I am delighted that they are not going to yank me out of the 15th Infantry on any excuse whatsoever. In the note to you the other day, I asked you to confirm once more, with the Chief of Infantry, the intention of that office to let me alone so that I would be available for the Armored force when the time comes. In the light of what you tell me now, I see that it was unnecessary to make that request of you. However, it is perfectly okay with me if the personnel section in that office is aware of the fact that I have an ambition to command one of the next armored regiments to be formed. They will probably think me a conceited individual, but I see no objection to setting your sights high. Actually, of course, I will be delighted to serve in the Armored Corps in almost any capacity, but I do hope to avoid Staff and to stay on troop duty for some time to come. And since I notice that in the original assignments they gave one of the armored regiments to a Lieutenant Colonel, I will hope that they might think that much of me also.[2]

Give my love to Renie and the youngsters, and with cordial regards to yourself

1. George A. White founded the *American Legion* magazine in 1919, serving as its first editor. When his guard unit was activated in September 1940, he served as its commander. White died on November 23, 1941.

2. Eisenhower sought Clark's assistance for a troop command in a letter of November 28. Clark responded by discussing with Gerow Eisenhower's wish to be left alone by the War Plans Division. Eisenhower was left temporarily alone. After the United States entered World War II, Clark was the person to recommend that Eisenhower be ordered to the War Department. See Holt, "An Unlikely Partnership," 162–63; Stephen E. Ambrose, *Eisenhower: Soldier, General of the Army, President-Elect, 1890–1952* (New York: Simon and Schuster, 1983), 125–26; Eisenhower, *At Ease*, 237–39; and Blumenson, *Mark Clark*, 49–50.

170

Eisenhower Library
Pre-presidential Papers

To Major T. J. Davis[1]

October 31, 1940

Dear T. J.: I don't know whether you are acquainted with the winter climate of the great Northwest, but one of its characteristics is [the] long, rainy and dark afternoon and evening that must necessarily be spent indoors. This feature of our winter makes us particularly sensitive to all suggestions that seem to have a definite value in producing and maintaining a morale and contentment, particularly among enlisted men.

This afternoon there came to my desk (I am temporarily acting as Post Executive for General Thompson) a request from an organization for some musical instruments. It is a new unit and therefore without funds of its own with which to buy the instruments desired. The Commanding Officer reports that there are some very good musicians in the outfit, who are voluntarily devoting their time to practice, and that the men, particularly the recruits, take a tremendous interest in the effort.

I have searched the Regulations and asked the local Quartermaster concerning the prospects for obtaining instruments through normal channels of supply and have encountered nothing whatsoever that I can class as encouraging. While pondering the matter I happened to remember that you are in the Morale Division of the Adjutant General's office, and the hope was born that you might be in a position to do something about the matter. In the particular instance, at least, there is no desire to build up a big military band. Rather, the effort is to produce a small orchestra that could provide entertainment for the men during the evenings and, when the organization can arrange a dance of its own, to furnish the music. A couple of saxophones, a trumpet or two, drums, something called a sousaphone, and possibly a clarinet would certainly be all that would be needed. At least such an assembly of instruments would furnish the backbone of the equipment required and the rest could be secured by contribution, and so on.

Would you nose around in your inimitable way to find out whether or not such a thing could be put over? It might be done either through a supply in kind of orchestral instruments to regiments and separate battalions, or through a grant of recreational and entertainment money to posts, out of which such things could be bought.

I must confess that I write this letter with only a modicum of hope that anything can be done about it, but it struck me as such a worthy project that I didn't want to deny you a chance to work on it a bit.

I haven't had a letter from you in many weeks. I sent you a message by Huntington Hills[2] when he was here on a trip. For the life of me I cannot see why you don't make a similar trip to the outlying stations. I have plenty of room in my house for you and for Nina too, if she can come along.

My ambition is to go, eventually, to the armored outfit. George Patton has told me that at least two new armored divisions are to be formed early next year, and if he is assigned in command of one of them he intends to ask for me, possibly as one of his regimental commanders. That would be a swell job and I only hope that the War Department won't consider me too junior in rank to get a regiment. I realize that I am quite conceited to entertain the idea, but I have noticed that in certain instances regimental commanders have been given to Lieutenant Colonels. It is always possible, therefore, that the War Department might be charitably inclined in my case.

Mamie and I are well, and our reports from John's school are to the effect that he is getting along splendidly in his studies. If you hear of any Congressional or Senatorial appointment lying around loose, for goodness sake grab it off, because John could certainly use it next spring. With cordial regard

1. Davis was in the office of the adjutant general.
2. Jedediah Huntington Hills joined the adjutant general's department in 1922, where he remained until his retirement in 1952 as a colonel.

To Milton Eisenhower[1]

Dear Milton: [. . .][2] I anticipated a very much closer race than we had on November 5th. While I was never of the opinion that Mr. Willkie[3] had anything but an outside chance, I felt confident that he would run stronger in Pennsylvania, Ohio and Indiana than he did. We had arranged quite an election-night party with a great system for getting and distributing returns as they came in; but victory was conceded to the Democrats at such an early hour (Pacific Coast Time) that the whole effort fell rather flat. I sincerely trust that the Democrats and Republicans will soon get on friendly terms because if this country needs anything at all at this time it is unification.

1. Milton was at the U.S. Department of Agriculture.

2. A long discourse on John Eisenhower's appointment to West Point has been deleted.

3. Eisenhower referred to the 1940 presidential election. Wendell L. Willkie, a Democrat, became disillusioned with Roosevelt's New Deal and joined the Republican party. In 1940 he ran as a maverick outsider for the party's presidential nomination and won. He criticized the New Deal but supported Roosevelt's internationalist foreign policy. Although he lost the election, he continued to support Roosevelt's foreign policy, and the president appointed him as his personal emissary to England, Russia, and the Far East (1941–42). Willkie died on October 8, 1944.

A hectic day.

Mamie's birthday, but she is not well. At 9:00 a.m. a wire arrived from John saying he'd won Sen. Capper's principal appointment. That's a great load off our minds with nothing to worry about now except his phys. condition.

Had a letter from T.J. He says I was turned down as C. of S. of Gen. Krueger's[1] corps, who had asked for me, on the grounds that I was too junior in rank.

God knows I've told everyone I want to stay with troops but it never occurred to me the W.D. would have to give such a reason.

1. Gen. Walter Krueger held several important staff positions in the War Plans Division. From 1938 to 1939 he commanded the 16th Infantry Brigade and from 1939 to 1940 the 2d Division at Fort Sam Houston. Krueger commanded the VIII Corps in 1940 and from 1941 to 1943 the Third Army under Eisenhower. His final command was with the Sixth Army in the Southwest Pacific Theater and the occupation of Japan. Krueger retired in 1946.

173

Eisenhower Library
Pre-presidential Papers

To THOMAS JEFFERSON DAVIS

NOVEMBER 14, 1940

Dear T. J.: Thank you very much for your prompt reply to my letter. I did not know whether or not anything could be done about the procurement of musical instruments as recreational facilities for the various units, but I thought it might well be worthwhile making the suggestion. In this connection, an official letter went forward the other day on the subject of recreational facilities, in which it was recommended that a set of instruments be provided at the rate of one set per each Service Club established at Posts. So I imagine that sooner or later the matter will get to the War Department on an official basis.

The other day I had a letter from Matt Capinpin. He was still on the same old job at Camp Murphy, and told me that quite a number of changes had been made in the Philippine General Staff. Garcia has been sent to command the Military Academy and Segundo has been sent south to command Parang. The other Martelino has been brought to the War Department, as well as some other officer that Matt did not name. He told me that the rumored reason for the change was that the President was sick and tired of the battling and bickering around headquarters. He did not mention any member of the Mission. With regard to that incident in my life, I feel exactly as you do and I have always been particularly resentful of the treatment accorded you, because of the great personal and unofficial services you rendered so loyally and so effectively to the General.[1]

I was highly interested in the gossip you gave me concerning the request made for me by General Krueger. I have consistently told all my friends in Washington that I was very desirous of remaining on troop duty, and did not desire staff duty at this time; consequently, the War Department's answer in this particular case was exactly in line with my own desires. The only job that would really tempt me to leave the 15th Infantry, willingly, would be to obtain command of an Armored regiment. In view of the fact that the War Department thinks I am too junior to be a Chief of Staff of the Corps, it seems evident that they will consider me too junior for commanding a regiment. Therefore, I want to stay right in the 15th Infantry.

It strikes me that this business of being so particular about the details of rank is, to say the least, somewhat amusing under existing circumstances. When a man has reached the age of fifty years, has been graduated more than twenty-five, and is some two and one-half years away from his eagles, it seems that the matter of rank could be so adjusted that the War Department could put a man wherever they want to.

If I knew for sure that General Krueger had made the particular request you told me about, I would write him a letter of thanks, because I am deeply appreciative of such a compliment. It has always seemed to me that my friends have built up for me a much brighter reputation than I remotely deserve; but it does make a fellow feel fine to know that, as a result of his friends' propaganda, such requests as this one are made upon the War Department.

Give my best love to Nina and, as always, warmest regards to yourself.

1. Apparently Quezon had directed that the Philippine Army General Staff should be reorganized, as Col. Rafael L. Garcia had been serving as Assistant Chief of Staff for Supply and Personnel and Col. Fidel V. Segundo as Assistant Chief of Staff, Intelligence, Operations, and Training. Demotions may have been involved, as Garcia's predecessor at the Philippine Military Academy had held only the rank of captain, and Segundo's provincial command with the Philippine Constabulary in Parang, Sulu Province, ordinarily carried with it the rank of major. Because Capt. Pastor Martelino had been serving as Superintendent of the Military Academy before Garcia's transfer to that post, it would seem logical that he had been assigned to the General Staff. Eisenhower's reference to "the other" Martelino, however, suggests that he might have meant Lt. Leopoldo C. Martelino, who had been serving as superintendent of the property and finance office at the Reserve Officers' Training School, Baguio. "General" here refers to MacArthur's U.S. Army rank.

174   Eisenhower Library
Pre-presidential Papers

To Brigadier General George S. Patton Jr.

NOVEMBER 16, 1940

Dear George: I have already sent in a letter similar to the one you suggested. Max Lough,[1] a friend of mine, is head of the personnel section in the Office of the Chief of Infantry, so I wrote him the whole story a couple of weeks ago.

Day before yesterday I had a letter from a friend in the A. G. office at Washington. He told me that one of the new Corps Commanders, down South, had asked for me as his C. of S., but that it was turned down because I was so junior in rank. The only significance of the incident is that, regardless of the source of any request I am probably to be allowed to stay with troops. So I ought to be available and eligible for transfer when the time comes, whereas, if I should get tangled up in one of these staff jobs, they would simply say "<u>not available</u>"!

Just had news from Washington that my son John won a West Point appointment in a competitive examination held by Senator Capper; John had an average of 92%.

Good luck, and maybe I'll be seeing you in the spring.
Yours

1. Max S. Lough received his promotion to colonel in September 1940, shortly before Eisenhower wrote to him at the War Department. Lough became a brigadier general in 1941 when, in December of that year, he succeeded Jonathan Wainwright as commander of the army's Philippine Division. He was in the Bataan Death March and was brutally beaten by the Japanese.

175

Eisenhower Library
Pre-presidential Papers

To Leonard T. Gerow[1]

November 18, 1940

Dear Gee: Your telegram, arriving this morning, sent me into a tail spin.[2] I am going to tell you the whole story and then if you decide that I should come to the War Plans Division, all you have to do is have the orders issued without any further reference to me.

In the first place, I want to make it clear that I am, and have always been, very serious in my belief that the individual's preferences and desires should have little, if any, weight in determining his assignment, when superior authority is making a decision in the matter. So all the rest of this is because, by implication, you asked for it!

With this somewhat pompous-sounding preamble, here goes.

There is no other individual that ranks with yourself so far as my personal choice of commanders is concerned. You have known this for so many years that it seems redundant to repeat it. I have never been so flattered in my life as by the inclusion, in your telegram, of the word "need", as you used it.

Next, I have, in the few short months I have been allowed to serve with troops, completely reassured myself that I am capable of handling command jobs. I feel confident that my superiors' reports have and will show this, and certainly I have had nothing but the most splendid cooperation and loyalty from those who have served under me. But in this Army, today, such self-confidence (or egotism if you choose to call it that) does not appear to be sufficient when some of the ritualistic-minded people begin to scrutinize the record. They simply say, "He has had only 6 months actual duty with troops since 1922. He cannot possibly be given a regiment or what have you."

As I wrote you when you were at Benning, I have resisted every suggestion that I leave troops, not so particularly because I felt that after so many years of Staff duty I was entitled to my own turn at the more fascinating work of handling soldiers, but also in conformity with the War Department policy that requires a certain proportion of troop duty in order for a man to be considered a capable and rounded officer. In correspondence with friends in Washington, I have consistently indicated my desire to stay with troops, either with the 15th, or, if possible, in command of one of the mechanized units to be organized in the spring.

At various times I have had informal reports from Washington, to the effect that I had been requested for positions on certain Corps and Division staffs. My informants[3] have told me that in each such instance the War Department (Chief of Infantry) has declined to give favorable consideration, on the ground that I needed duty with troops. In one instance, where I am told a Corps Commander (believed to be General Krueger) asked for me as his Chief of Staff, the answer was that I was too junior in rank for that post. I suppose that you have informally investigated the attitude of the Chief of Infantry and The Adjutant General, or possibly even of the Chief of Staff, toward assigning me to the W.D.G.S. and are, therefore, sure that if you put in the request it will be approved. Incidentally, another question interjects itself and that is the one concerning the provisions of law affecting eligibility for the General Staff. Naturally, if a fellow is going to serve in a General Staff position, he would like to get official credit for doing so, and unless the Department has waived normal eligibility rules for the period of the emergency, it might be impossible to have me assigned. Again, however, I presume that you have investigated this particular point.

All the above seems to be a lot of beating the devil around the bush. However, it is almost necessary to recite these things to you so that you can understand the reasons for the somewhat confused state of mind in which I now find myself. Oh yes! Another thing I should probably tell you is that General Thompson is merely waiting favorable action on a recommendation of his, regarding a new assignment for his present Division Chief of Staff, before putting my name before the War Department to fill that position. I believe, however, that particular request has not yet gone forward, as I am sure he is awaiting the result of his first recommendation.

To summarize, then, my ideas on the matter:

For both Mamie and me the thought of renewing our old close companionship with you is a delightful prospect.

From the official angle, assuming that all the obvious objections to my present assignment to the General Staff have been eliminated, I would like, before the matter is officially consummated, for those in authority to know that I have earnestly tried for many years to get an assignment to troops and to serve at least a normal tour with them. Unfortunately, General MacArthur would never allow those requests to be made of record. I know that General Marshall, in person, is not concerned with the assignment of such small fry as myself; but I would like to see the matter so handled that not only is the attention of the Chief of Infantry and The Adjutant General, but, if possible, even that of the Chief of Staff attracted to the above facts. Particularly, I would like to see it clearly noted in the official records. I think it's just a matter of pride, but I don't want to be considered, on the basis of records, as unfit for duty with troops.

But, if you're satisfied that the matter is understood by all, as I've roughly indicated, go ahead!

Finally, if I am ordered to Washington, I would like to have the orders framed, if possible, so as to order me and my household goods there by rail. This would allow me to make a short visit with both Mamie's and my family on the way to my new station. I would need, of course, about 10 days' leave on the way.

I hope that all of this does not sound too demanding or unreasonable. I do not need to tell you what whatever I am told to do will be done as well as I know how to do it, but since your radio seemed to request my complete reactions to your suggestion, I have tried to put them before you fully and frankly. Please send me advance notice, by radio, of the final decision.

P.S.: By the way, if you are living in an apartment house in Washington, would there be any chance for Mamie and me to get into the same building? And if war starts, I expect to see you raise the roof to get a command, and I go along!

1. Gerow was deputy director of the War Plans Division.

2. The telegram read: "I need you in War Plans Division. Do you seriously object to being detailed on the War Dept. General Staff and assigned here. Please reply immediately." See Kevin McCann, *Man from Abilene* (Garden City, N.Y.: Doubleday, 1952), 24. On November 23, Eisenhower received Gerow's reply, in which he withdrew the offer. See McCann, *Man from Abilene*, 29; and Eisenhower to Gerow, November 25, 1940, Pre-pres. Papers.

3. The reference to "informants" is probably an allusion to Davis, Ulio, and Clark.

176

NOVEMBER 20, 1940

Things have been popping! Gen DeWitt and some of his staff officers arrived here on the 18th. The principal purpose of his short stop here seems to have been to knock over the somewhat elaborate "Post" staff, organization, and to force administration into the hands of an "Executive." All W.D. instructions of the past 2 months have clearly indicated this purpose, but Gen. T.[1] felt he could not do it because of the great importance of housing, hospitalization, etc., etc., for conscripts. Gen. DeWitt finally got impatient with lack of progress in this direction & <u>ordered</u> immediate compliance.

As a result, Col. Glass[2] has been set up as Post Exec.

Telephonic request was made on W.D. to assign me as Div. C. of S. Gee wired from Washington to find out whether or not I'd come to W.P.D. In the meantime I'm sitting on the lid at Post Hq. now as asst. to Col. Glass. I'd like to stay with my regiment—but it looks like I were sunk.

1. "T." is no doubt General Hugh Thompson.
2. Col. Ralph Glass (USMA, 1904) became chief of staff with the 3d Division in 1939, a position he held until he was succeeded by Eisenhower in November 1940. Glass retired in 1944.

177

TO LEONARD T. GEROW

NOVEMBER 25, 1940

Dear Gee: Thanks a lot for your radio.[1] Since the only point my letter raised involved "troop duty", I first assumed that the assignment fell through because you found that the W.D. took the attitude that I needed longer service in a regiment, which, of course, I do under existing policy. Yet when your message went on to say, "consideration of General Thompson's request", I had a sinking feeling. I'd hate to think that, in trying to explain to you a situation that has been tossed in my teeth more than once, all I accomplished was to pass up something I

<u>wanted</u> to do, in favor of something I thought I <u>ought</u> to do, and then to find myself not even doing the latter. But the next day or so should tell the story. Anyway, I'm grateful for your consideration.

For the past two weeks I've been suffering with the "shingles". Don't laugh; it's one of the most painful things you ever heard of. The doctors tried to put me to bed, but I found I was less miserable with something to occupy my time and mind, and so have kept going. I think I'm over the worst of it now—and I most certainly don't want the disease again.

For a long time I've been convinced that we will eventually be in this war. I can't see any other answer; and I don't believe that it will be a question of anyone "leading" us into it. In the long run, I think, the public will get infuriated at the necessity of building, spending and defending against a threat, and will get in the frame of mind that it will be better, cheaper and quicker to <u>remove</u> the threat.

General Stone[2] was in my office yesterday morning. We had a long talk, principally about you and another favorite subject of his, Panama. He's just as devoted to you as ever. Looks fine and apparently is very happy and contented.

I don't suppose I've told you that for the past six weeks I've been serving as General Thompson's "Executive". He was getting snowed under with his division and with the additional job of reorganizing command and administrative systems, to say nothing of facilities for an eventual garrison of some 45,000 men. So, "in addition to other duties" I was assigned as Executive, to serve as such until a Regular officer should be assigned here to the Post Complement. That officer, Colonel Glass, who was C. of S., 3rd Div., is now assigned, so in a day or so I go back to my regiment, unless I go to Div. Hq. as C of S.

Actually, Gee, the job of staying with a regiment is a damn near hopeless one. I landed at San Francisco on Jan. 6, hurrying to join the 15th before it sailed for Monterey on landing exercises. At the dock I was met and told to go to 4th Army staff for one month—which I did. I then joined the regiment and within a month I was battling to keep from going with the Navy on a two months' cruise. Finally, General De-Witt let me off that and General Sweeney immediately made me the "Chief Umpire" for all divisional maneuvers at Camp Ord. That took another month. Then two suggestions were made. One that I be Deputy Chief Umpire for 4th Army maneuvers, in August, the other that I be President of Rents & Claims Board for the same operation. I talked myself out of both those. Then, at the end of September, I was put on this job! So there you are. I've enjoyed the regimental "intervals", particularly the 4th Army maneuvers, where I had my own battalion.

On top of everything else, it now turns out that Mamie, who wouldn't even give me a hint at what she wanted to do, is broken hearted over not going to Washington!

Well, I'll be seeing you, As ever

P.S. Serving on the G.H.Q. staff is one of the finest officers in our Army, Lt. Col. Wayne Clark. When you get a chance, get hold of him and have a half-hour's talk.[3]

1. Gerow telegraphed Eisenhower: "After careful consideration of contents of your letter and the wishes of General Thompson as indicated to G-1 I have withdrawn my request for your detail to War Plans Divn. Will write details later. Regret our service together must be postponed." Gerow to Eisenhower, November 18, 1940, Pre-pres. Papers.

2. David L. Stone (USMA, 1898) commanded the 3d Infantry Division at Fort Lewis (1935–36). Stone retired in 1940 as a major general.

3. Eisenhower was repaying Clark's many favors by highly recommending him. Clark was assigned to War Plans and after Pearl Harbor recommended Eisenhower be brought immediately to the War Department. In March 1942, Eisenhower requested that Clark be his Chief of Staff. See Holt, "An Unlikely Partnership," 163.

178

To Everett Hughes[1]

November 26, 1940

Dear Everett: Between the hourly cyclones in this office, I'll try to get down on a scratch pad some of the things I'd like to talk to you about, then I'll get someone to decode my notes and translate them into a readable message.

The reason I didn't write to you about Ord. Dept. promotions was because I was infuriated. I felt that anything I'd say would only serve to disturb the philosophic calm with which you always contemplate such things. Of course I don't know the details of the situation, but I can make some damn shrewd guesses. But long and bitter wars have a habit of sending to the bone pile those that have had time to indulge in petty jealousies, personal animosities and the like; it brings to the top the fellow who thinks more of his job than of his own promotion prospects. When your turn comes, it will be because they have to have you![2]

We may not be at war now—I'll argue the question though if you'd like—but how can we eventually avoid it? What possibility is there of a European peace that will remove the threat that is now urging us to such great expenditures in money, time, resources and effort? So, if we have to keep on spending and working just to protect against a threat, how long will it be before public opinion decides that it will eventually be cheaper, both in money and in every other way, to re-move the threat? It is my belief that we're going to fight, and no one is going to "lead" us into it. The American population, once it gets truly irritated, is a self-confident, reckless, fast-moving avalanche; it is some-one's job to keep that irritation from becoming too acute before the country can be ready to deliver something like its sustainable output of destructive force. And it is our job to speed up the preparatory forces!

I was never more serious in my life than I am about the need for each of us, particularly in the Regular Army, to do his own chore intelligently and energetically. The thing that worries me most is the seeming lassitude, and the apparent indifference to the existing international situation, that is displayed by so many of our officers. Training programs are scanned carefully and fearfully to see whether they demand more hours; whether their execution is going to cause us some inconvenience! Jesus wept—if ever we are to prove that we're worth the salaries the government has been paying us all these years—now is the time!

For the past few weeks I've been pinch-hitting as Post Executive. Requests for leave come to my desk, many of them not even pretending to give an emergency reason, but indicating that the individual considers himself entitled to it. I believe in morale—nothing is more important to us now; but morale that is purchased with favors will be less steadfast in adversity than would a light o' love after she found out you didn't have two bucks. We should speed up, all of us! Your comment on the French debacle was apropos. Inaction destroyed them, and we should build morale by the intensity and effectiveness of our effort. The sooner the weaklings in the officers' corps (and I don't mean the physical cripples) fall out and disappear, the better.

When I began to express such thoughts, last March, there was a certain bunch that somewhat sarcastically referred to the "alarmists" in the regiment. But my battalion caught on to the idea, and I was fully repaid when in the August maneuvers my youngsters (no other officers in the battalion above lieutenant) kept on going and delivering handsomely after five days of almost no sleep! I was certainly proud of that gang.

By golly, if I don't get off the subject of the Regular Army's job, I'll get really started, and this is no time to begin a serial on ideas that you've probably considered a lot more profoundly than I have.

Ordnance supply is something that we know little about at remote stations such as this. Naturally we wonder when we're to get our complements of 60 m.m. mortars, light machine guns, B.A.R.[3] (1918-A-2), 81 m.m.'s, .50 cal. machine guns, etc. In certain instances we have small numbers of these, but in others, none. Since our training programs, prescribed by the W.D. are based upon the possession of these weapons, we've been hopeful that soon we'd have the works. Our Post and Division Ordnance Officer, Lt. Col. Luse,[4] is a fine chap, and, apparently, is doing all that can be done locally to keep us in ammunition, etc. etc.

The future synchronization of the training program as between readiness of cadres and arrival of increments of trainees is something that I have not yet seen explained. For example, the N.G. was called up last September for one year. It is to be filled up with trainees in January, who are also due for one year's training. What happens next September? Again, after the January crowd comes in, future increments are scheduled to go first to Replacement Centers for three months. Will there be an overlap of three months in calling succeeding classes, or, if not, what do regular and other cadres do during the three months period?

These are some of the questions that I wrestled with in the P.I. for four years, and none of them is easy to answer. I assume the W.D. has ready partial solutions, at least, but nothing yet has percolated down to us.

From my personal viewpoint I'm sure of one thing! Nothing can kill my own enthusiasm for the job at hand. I realize that no one gives much of a hoot what I think or do, except myself but I'm getting a great kick out of plugging away. My view may be "worm's-eye", and my efforts may be little above the futile, but I like to keep peering ahead as far as I can, and I like to work. So I'm having a fine time!

I had a recent message from Gee. He suggested that I might come to W.P.D., but after I pointed out how little troop duty I'd had, he withdrew the request. I want to be considered fit and qualified to command a unit, and under our system, that means that one must have so many months of troop duty on the official record! So, though I'm conceited enough to believe that not only during the past few months, but in the World War as well, I've demonstrated an ability to "command," I'm delighted to stay with troops for two reasons. (1), I like it. (2), I want to convince the most ritualistic-minded guy in the whole d—— Army that I get along with John Soldier.[5]

Lots of love to Kate, and, as always, my best to you—as ever

1. Hughes was chief, Equipment Division, Office of Ordnance, War Department.

2. Evidently Hughes was passed over for promotion.

3. Browning automatic rifle.

4. Arthur H. Luse was assigned to the Ordnance Department in 1921, where he spent the remainder of his army career. He retired as a colonel in 1948.

5. Eisenhower referred to his "commands" at Camps Colt and Meade during World War I.

To Lieutenant Colonel Mark Clark

November 28, 1940

Dear Wayne: Not long ago, we had a letter from John, in which he told us of having dinner at your house. He said he particularly liked to come to see your family because he felt so much at home. You know how much Mamie and I appreciate the fine way you have treated our one and only child.

As you know, he has now a principal appointment to West Point, having won the competitive examination given by Senator Capper. He may come home after Christmas and pass up the second part of the Millard course. It would be lots of fun to have him around for six months before he finally enters the Point, and such a visit ought to give him the best kind of opportunity to be in good physical shape when he takes the examination.

Since I last wrote to you there arose two different possibilities involving a change of assignment for me. General Gerow, Chief of the War Plans Division, in Washington, suggested that I come to his division. I told him about the struggle I had to get in some troop duty and so he withdrew the request. It later developed that Mamie was very anxious to go to Washington and was almost broken-hearted when the thing fell through. I didn't know this in advance or I possibly might have given up my struggle to stay with the regiment.

The other suggestion made was that I become Chief of Staff of the Third Division. Colonel Glass was relieved from that post and made Executive Officer of Fort Lewis. In working out that arrangement, General Thompson requested the War Department to assign me as Chief of Staff. While no final answer has been received here, I am of the opinion that the War Department did not consider it favorably; otherwise we should have had an answer long before this.

I have one ulterior motive in struggling to stay with troops, which is my hope that I may get one of the armored regiments next spring. I realize this is a very slim possibility and am not counting on it at all, but I still think that it is a good thing for me to get in at least one year of regimental duty. That year, including all temporary special duty assignments, will not be up until the middle of February.

A friend in Washington wrote me a curious story not long ago. He said that a corps commander, down South, had asked for me as his Chief of Staff, but that the War Dept. had turned down the request on the ground that I was too junior in rank for such a position.[1] I can see a dozen reasons why the War Department might not want to approve such a request, but in these times it does seem a bit odd to insist on the details of rank in such a connection.

I wonder whether or not you people are completely satisfied with the new organizational setup. As I understood the fundamentals of the plan, it was to relieve tactical troops of all administrative responsibilities, and to set up higher staffs that were concerned only with training and organization. If this is correct, it would seem to me logical for the Corps Headquarters to organize somewhat along the lines that G.H.Q. has done. By this I mean that instead of setting up, in ritualistic fashion, each section of the General Staff, it would be far better to concentrate in the G-3 section and then to use the tactical staff officers as advisers and assistants to that section. Unless this is done, the G-3 division of Corps Headquarters does not become strong enough in personnel to absorb all the functions of planning, producing programs, and supervising all training activities.

These are just some random thoughts given to you personally.

The weather is of the usual saturated variety but, at that, is not as bad as it was last January when I was here for a few days.

Give my love to Renie and the children and remember me to your gang in G.H.Q., and pay my respects to the General.

1. Eisenhower may have referred to Walter Krueger, who was stationed at Fort Sam Houston. Eisenhower's letter to Gerow of November 18, 1940, mentions Krueger by name on the same subject.

180 MacArthur Memorial Archives
Personal Correspondence of General Douglas MacArthur

To General Douglas MacArthur

December 11, 1940

Dear General: A very Merry Christmas to you and yours, and may 1941 be the finest year you've yet lived. Mamie and I hope that you, Jean and young Arthur are all well and happy.

It did not take me long to find out, after I came home, that it is well nigh impossible for a field officer who has been through the schools to remain quietly with troops these days. When I hit the dock at San Francisco I caught a month D. S.[1] on secret work in 4th Army Headquarters. Then, after serving two months with the 15th Infantry, I had to make a personal appeal to the Army Commander to get out of a long training cruise with the Navy, and having been excused from that, I served as Chief Umpire of the Division during a month of maneuvers.

That was at Camp Ord, in California.

After we came back here, a number of suggestions, some of them official in character, were made that I go on Staff duty, but I declined on the plea that I'd been with troops only four months. However, in September I received a local order to serve as Post Executive during our great building and expansion boom. While on that job, General Krueger asked the War Department to detail me as his Corps C. of S., just after the War Department had sent me a wire saying it was contemplated assigning me to Washington in War Plans Division. Again I repeated my sob story, and, when both those projects were dropped, thought I was in the clear. But then along came another request, and this one was approved; so now I'm Chief of Staff, 3d Division, with station at Fort Lewis.

My case is not particularly unusual. Other officers of my acquaintanceship that thought they'd settled down to a normal tour of troop duty have had the same experience. Details to Staffs, to schools, to special tasks of all kinds are daily occurrences. I'm luckier than most in that I don't have to pack up and move.

The entire administrative system of the Army, in the U. S., has been radically changed. The purpose is to free combat troops from Zone of Interior duties. Station complements are gradually being built up, and post headquarters is an entirely separate entity from tactical headquarters.

Combat troops report through tactical Divisions, Corps, Armies to G.H.Q., while post complements report through Corps Area headquarters to the War Department. All this causes some confusion, particularly because station complements, so far, have had to be largely obtained by detachments from tactical troops; but the purpose is good, and in the end the effect will be the same.

At this post we have two Divisions and Corps Troops, with an eventual strength of about 50,000. We should reach this strength about next April 1st.

Johnnie won, in a competitive examination, Senator Capper's principal appointment to West Point. If he has no trouble with his eyes he will enter next June.

So far as the U. S. is concerned, the guns, of course, are not yet roaring. But how long they can keep silent becomes more of a guess, it seems to me, with every day that passes. Once they really open up I'll expect to see you in the thick of it.[2]
Sincerely

1. Detached service.

2. Eisenhower and MacArthur truly experienced a love-hate relationship. Eisenhower regularly sent birthday greetings to MacArthur in the 1940s, and although he

ceased doing this annually after 1950, he wrote a lengthy note on MacArthur's eight-
ieth birthday in 1960. More importantly, however, in letters Eisenhower wrote to
MacArthur in 1948 and 1951 he strongly disputed press stories that the two military
heroes were profoundly estranged. Eisenhower wrote on December 7, 1948, "Another reason for writing is because of the efforts that some of our cheaper type of
columnists have been making to prove that you and I have always been deadly enemies. . . . In a recent press conference I emphatically denied all this. I told them that
the last person I saw in the Philippines in 1940 was you and that you were the first
person I met when I reached Japan in 1946 and that I hoped you treasured our old
friendship as much as I do." Eisenhower to MacArthur, December 7, 1948, and May
15, 1951, Pre-pres. Papers, Eisenhower Library; and Eisenhower to MacArthur, January 26, 1960, President's Personal File, White House Central Files, Eisenhower Library.

181   Eisenhower Library
                                   Miscellaneous Manuscripts, 1972

To Hugh A. Parker[1]

FEBRUARY 8, 1941

Dear Lefty and Janet: Either I wrote to you at Christmas time, or I did
not. Yesterday, had I been required to take oath on the matter, I'd have
sworn that I sent letters to you, as well as to Jew, Andy and Jerry. But
this morning I found in my desk a draft of a letter I'd written to you,
so now I have the uncomfortable feeling that I don't know whether I
did or I didn't. If the first, you can chuck this away without reading further; if the second, I'm just making good on an intention I've had for
a long time.

Out here in the West we've had two major crackups lately, one of
them occurring just a few miles south of here. That one appeared
easily explainable but that four motor job, on an ordinary flight from
Sacramento to Denver, apparently blew to pieces in mid-air. That's not
so good!

Right now, I'm Chief of Staff, 3rd Division. I've had a dozen different jobs since returning from Manila, and while, in the ordinary run
of events, an assignment of this kind should hold good for a year or
so—these are not normal times, so I don't know when I'll get orders
to move on. Of one thing I'm certain: I'm weary of these eternal staff
details. I'd like to get a command of my own, even if just a squad.

When I was writing to all the gang at Christmas time, I put down, in
a separate paper, a short account of the family's doings since leaving
Manila. I'll enclose a copy, because, though it's now two months old,
it still covers our principal doings of the past year or so.

Mamie, Johnny and I send our best to you two and the new Lefty.

The latest Blue Book gives your address as Barksdale Field, but a letter from one of the gang said you had transferred to Savannah. I'll address this to the latter place, and, if you don't receive it, send me a wire! As ever

[ENCLOSURE] DECEMBER 13, 1939—DECEMBER 13, 1940[2]

The former date is the one on which the Eisenhowers left Manila, the latter is today.

We took passage on the Cleveland, and Andy flew out in a pursuit ship to swoop and scoot around us as we left the breakwater. Another couple on board, attracted to the top deck by his antics, became our real friends of the voyage; and have since visited us. It was a swell good-bye!

We made the usual trip along the Asiatic Coast. Shopped in Hong Kong, got tight in Shanghai (Only one of us), disgusted in Kobe, more so in Yokohoma, and so hit Honolulu. Had a swell day there—and then the regular family fight started over interpretations of customs declarations. As we knew from many identical experiences, it was all useless; the Customs people took a general look at us and then started pasting stamps on everything in sight!

All that was swell; we had our reservations to Ft. Lewis and were hustling off the dock when a very military looking sergeant came down the line paging Colonel Eisenhower, in a voice that indicated he thought I was still in Hawaii. Upon acknowledging, unwillingly, my identity, (I could smell trouble) I was handed an order to report to 4th Army Headquarters for temporary duty. That order blew up a sizeable typhoon in the family. Finally we decided to send John on to Tacoma to enter school; and Mamie and I went to a hotel. There we lived for a month, when I was released from that job, and came on to Lewis. After a week of settling a house, I took off for Camp Ord, where I remained until May 15.

About the time I got home, John was graduating from high school and shortly after that we entered him in Millard's School, Washington, D. C. Mamie and I went as far as Denver with him, and then came on back here. I had a dozen jobs, finally landing in the one I now occupy, Chief of Staff, 3d Division. I'd been ducking Staff positions for some time, but finally the War Department failed to listen to my sob story. So again I'm looking down a pen instead of a gun.

In the meantime Johnny won, in a competitive exam, Senator Capper's principal appointment to West Point, and is coming home after Christmas to rest up before the final exam in March.

Mamie doesn't think too highly of the Great Northwest, but is so glad to be out of Manila that she takes most things, including servant trouble and shopping difficulties, without too much concern.

All of us remain in reasonable health, except for an attack of "shingles" visited on me for my sins. It couldn't be anything else, because it's the god-awfulest disease I ever heard of. But now I'm mostly well. And, that's all, folks!

1. Parker was stationed at Savannah, Georgia.

2. This document is the earlier draft Eisenhower found in his desk drawer. He included the draft, dated "December 13, 1939–December 12, 1940," in his letter to Parker. It is included here with the letter of transmittal as one document.

182

Eisenhower Library
Fort Lewis Diary

MARCH 3, 1941–APRIL 18, 1941
MARCH 3

In late November, I was made Div. C. of S. Today I received orders detailing me as Corps C.S., IX Corps. Gen. Joyce Commander.

In Jan. made a trip to Vancouver and Presidio on Bn tests. Gen. T., Gen. Ridley, Magruder[1] and I made up party. We stayed at Hotel Bellevue, San Francisco. Manager—Frank N. Harper.

1. Maj. Gen. Clarence S. Ridley (USMA, 1905) served as a military aide to the president of the United States from 1917 to 1921 and, from 1936 to 1940, as governor of the Canal Zone. Ridley retired in 1947.

The Magruder mentioned is probably Marshall Magruder, who was stationed at Camp Roberts, California (1940–41).

MARCH 12

Read radio from W.D. appointing me a temp. Colonel in Army of U.S., rank from Mar. 6.

APRIL 4

Have been in our new HQ bldg about 2 weeks. Have requested W.D. to authorize it's expansion, it's too small.

Plan to leave here on May 19 for Jolon.[1] Return here by July 10. Corps, less troops undergoing MTP training, will make the trip. Maximum possible on trucks, freight and balance of men via rail. Corps maneuvers at Jolon; Army maneuvers here in August. Finding this job most intriguing and interesting, with Gen J.[2] a swell commander & fine person to work for.

1. The maneuvers were held at the Hunter Liggett Military Reservation located near Jolon, California. The Liggett Reservation area was purchased from the estate

of William Randolph Hearst in late 1940 and was located only a quarter mile from the old Mission San Antonio de Padua on El Camino Real.

2. Kenyon Joyce.

CPX's for 3rd & 41st Divs. this week worked out very satisfactorily for 3rd Div. 41st was, by comparison, rather lazy & indecisive in its actions.

Income tax report for 1940 mailed on Feb, 25, '41 to Collector of Revenue, Balt. Md. Total amount $111.74. Check No. 253 for full amount (Ft. Lewis Branch, National Bank of Washington).

Registered Letter[2]

June 1st Received 55.20 Travel money for trip to Cal. Required to live separately—Costs 10.00 accommodations
35.00 Board
Received 45.00 Mindanao, dividend
Statement of Income, aside from salary-
Travel money—Feb 1st—for 2 weeks trip to Vancouver Barracks & San Francisco—Total 90.90
Expenses—Pullmans 12.50
Hotels 20.00
Meals 30.00
Trips 10.00
        72.50
Dividends—from Mindanao received in 1940, and included in income report for that year 92.00

1. This is the final entry of the Fort Lewis Diary, the last of the pre–World War II diaries. The diary abruptly ended on April 18, 1941, and Eisenhower did not again keep a diary until 1942.

2. Eisenhower added this brief financial statement in the diary on June 1.

183

Eisenhower Library
Pre-presidential Papers

NOTES FOR COLONEL CHARLES H. CORLETT[1]

JUNE, 1941

1. The Commanding General's method of operation is to announce policies and major decisions in definite terms and then to require his Chief of Staff to see to their execution, through established agencies. General Joyce observes this method meticulously, and expects his Chief of Staff to take all necessary steps within the limits of his

policies and directives to see that orders are carried out. The Chief of Staff for General Joyce, has, within his own proper sphere, complete authority and independence of action. Daily you will find that the General spends long periods with the troops. He can do this in the confidence that his Chief of Staff will carry on, in the method above indicated.

2. General Joyce does not read long directives, regulations and circulars. He expects his Chief of Staff to absorb the essentials of such documents and to keep him informed thereon. All occurrences and incidents of the day, throughout the Corps, must likewise be reported to him. In the field as well as in garrison a brief blotter should be kept which will serve you as an aide memoire, in assuring that you overlook no item.

3. The General's own immediate group consists of himself, the Chief of Staff, the Aides (including Major Wyman)[2] and his pilot, two master sergeants, his personal orderlies and chauffeur, mess personnel and a few others. All these officers are top-flight—you need have no hesitancy in discussing, in their presence, any subjects of general interest to the command.

4. Major Wyman occupies a particular status. He is the G-1 of the Corps and in periods of stress has acted also as an Assistant G-3. In addition he was, until very recently, General Joyce's Aide, and the General continues to depend upon him in a number of ways, both personal and official. Sometime ago the General approved a proposal (and orders were issued) detailing Wyman as "Acting Secretary of the General Staff." You will find it absolutely essential to have an officer acting as such both in the field and in the garrison. Major Wyman is "Superior" in every detail, and the only available man who is qualified to perform this duty. Since his G-1 duties will keep him busy only part of the time, he will not only be able to serve as Acting <u>Secretary</u>, but this particular assignment will logically keep him as one of the General's immediate group. With this purpose I am sure the General will concur.

5. The Judge Advocate, now located at the rear echelon, has very good tactical judgment. I suggest his use, in maneuvers, as a liaison officer to Army.

6. A short directive to the various staff sections in which we have attempted to incorporate the lessons learned during the recent Command Post Exercise, has just been prepared. Its purpose is to accomplish a streamlining of the forward Command Post and improvements in its functioning. It will be in effect a revision and extension of the existing "Staff procedure, IX Army Corps."

7. In the field I have found it profitable to hold one staff conference a day at which all general staff sections and all special staff sections are represented. In addition a smaller conference at which G-2, G-3, and G-4 are present is frequently necessary, particularly just after the General has announced a major decision.

8. The only source of censure or praise for an individual or unit within the Corps is the General himself. (This, of course, does not limit your own methods of controlling your own immediate assistants.)

9. The General is a perfectionist. Sloppy staff work is anathema to him.

10. You will find that all members of the group of persons surrounding you—commissioned and enlisted—are constantly looking for ways in which to make your work less burdensome. They are loyal, cheerful, full of initiative, and you should not hesitate to use them. They like it. Captain Curtis,[3] as the General's Aide, has the sole duty of meeting the Commanding General's requirements. But he is frequently available to assist you in innumerable ways and his ability is such that you will find many important tasks for him. He has a flair for writing straightforward, direct English; something that as a Chief of Staff, you will find a valuable asset. Captain Curtis is, in addition to other duties, detailed as an Assistant G-3.

11. Some of the work coming from the Staff Sections will be incomplete, at least to the extent that the "action recommended" will not be couched in satisfactory phraseology. It is useless to send such a piece of work back to the responsible section. You will have to put it in usable form. (Here is one place where a capable "Secretary of the General Staff" will be most valuable.) The General does not like pompous, pretentious expressions. Be chary with adjectives and adverbs.

12. In Fort Lewis, be sure to cultivate the closest possible relationship with Colonel Glass. Cooperation between Corps and Post is <u>constantly</u> necessary. Take up all matters in this category directly with Colonel Glass on an informal, friendly basis. He will go to any limit to meet General Joyce's desires when he is approached in this way.

13. In 4th Army, deal with Colonel Bradley.[4] He is now Deputy Chief of Staff, so all subjects come within the purview of his responsibility and interest. Don't hesitate to use the phone to reach him. He seeks opportunities to assist you. The others in the Army Staff are also cooperative.

14. If the Staff re-arrangement, as recommended by the Commanding General, is approved, Colonel Truscott[5] will become G-3, but will be short one Regular Army assistant. An available man <u>must</u> be found at once. You need a top-flight doughboy, because Truscott is Cavalry, and Barney is Artillery. In this connection, the Staff's operations plans and proposals should always be developed along <u>sound</u>, <u>methodical</u> lines. The General feels perfectly competent to introduce into tactical plans any degree of the bizarre, the unusual or the startling that may be appropriate.

15. The heads of all the General Staff and Special Staff sections are competent men. Each will do his work well. Moreover, the progress re-

alized in developing a smooth coordination among them has been more than considerable. But I recommend your constant attention to this objective. In addition, you should <u>insist</u> upon the <u>constant training</u> of all subordinates (Regular, National Guard and Reserve) in every section. We must realize, I think, that further dilution is coming, and we must pass up no opportunity to prepare ourselves to carry on with fewer Regulars.

16. Subjects in which the Commanding General is always and earnestly interested:

a. (Uniforms) (Saluting) (General conduct in public) These subjects are important to him as outward signs of a real discipline; and he insists that our big job is to inculcate in all ranks a conception and practice of fundamentals discipline. I advise you to keep thinking every moment of this basically important subject.

b. Smooth staff operation. This I have already mentioned.

c. <u>Basic and small unit training</u>. Re-read his "Tactical Doctrine."

d. Logistics and signal communications. (I have come to the conclusion that we should provide an intra-staff communication system, entirely separate from the switchboard for outside communication.)

e. Teamwork throughout the IX Army Corps.

1. Corlett became Chief of Staff, IX Corps, Fort Lewis, when Eisenhower left on June 24, 1941, to become Chief of Staff, Third Army, San Antonio.

2. Willard G. Wyman (USMA, 1919) served as assistant commanding general, 1st Infantry Division, 1943–44.

3. James O. "Jimmie" Curtis Jr. (USMA, 1930) had a long, closely associated service with Eisenhower. He served with the Allied Force Headquarters, Mediterranean Theater, 1942–43; 1st Infantry Division, Mediterranean Theater of Operations, 1943; with the Chief of Staff, Supreme Allied Commander, 1944; and as Assistant Chief of Staff, XX Corps, ETO, 1945. He was commanding officer, 3d Armored Cavalry Regiment, 1951–52; Chief of Staff, 40th Division, Korea, 1953–54; and staff secretary, Supreme Headquarters Allied Powers Europe, 1957–60. He retired as a brigadier general in 1960.

4. James L. Bradley (USMA, 1914) commanded the 96th Division (1942) in the South Pacific Theater. He retired in 1947 as a major general.

5. Lucian K. Truscott Jr. was commissioned in 1917. In 1941 he began what would be a long association with Eisenhower when he was assigned to the staff of the IX Corps, Fort Lewis. Promoted to brigadier general in May 1942, he served with the allied combined staff, organized a brigade of Army Rangers, and participated in the raid on Dieppe. He participated in the invasion of North Africa (1942), then commanded the 3d Infantry Division in Sicily and Italy. He assumed command of the VI Corps in February 1944, participating in the drive to Rome and the Allied landings in southern France. As a lieutenant general he became commander of the Fifth Army, part of Gen. Mark Clark's Fifteenth Army Group. He retired in 1947.

To the Quartermaster General, War Department

JUNE 26, 1941

SUBJECT: Jacket, Field.
TO: The Quartermaster General, War Department, Washington, D.C. (Attention Colonel R. M. Littlejohn.)[1]

1. Replying to your letter of May 24, 1941, [. . .][2] the following report is submitted.

The field jacket forwarded to me for test has been worn constantly in maneuver and field exercise since its receipt. No recommendations for improvement in pattern or materials are submitted, since, from these standpoints, it was proved eminently satisfactory.

Because of the nature of the garment, the collar fits closely to the back of the neck, against the skin of the wearer. This results in a collection of perspiration and dust, which soon creates a grimy and unsightly appearance. Since the jacket must be worn for protracted periods in the field, it is not feasible to send it frequently to a cleaning establishment. It is therefore suggested that the collar might be covered with a shield, fastened on with snaps, and made of the same material as the outer cloth of the jacket. This could be removed occasionally, washed, and replaced, and so keep the jacket in satisfactory wearing condition for long periods in the field. It is believed moreover, that signs of wear will occur first in the collar, and the shield would have the effect of prolonging the life of the whole garment.

2. This jacket fills a long felt want in the Army's field uniform with or without any change, such as that suggested, it should be retained as an item of issue.

1. Robert McG. Littlejohn (USMA, 1912) served in World War I. In 1920 he transferred to the Quartermaster Corps, where he spent the remainder of his army career. He served with the War Department General Staff from 1930 to 1934, while Eisenhower was also with the General Staff. In 1939 he served as Quartermaster of the Philippine Department. He retired in 1946.
2. A long series of file reference numbers have been deleted.

To Major Willard Wyman

July 9, 1941

Dear Bill: I thoroughly enjoyed your excellent description of the final maneuver at Jolon. If the staff and others carefully analyzed the General's basic plan, they should have learned well, one valuable lesson. This is that if superior forces are used to put early, constant and severe pressure on an opponent, he will have no opportunity to chase about the country-side capturing command posts, driving in flanks, destroying bases and otherwise making himself a scourge by day, and a terror by night. Grant learned early in his career one great truth, one that, possibly more than any other, accounted for his later successes. This was, "The other fellow is just as scared as I am". McClellan, mentally a far abler man, was ruined because he could not grasp this simple idea.

My experiences of the past week, and more, have completed my conviction that you fellows, in that headquarters, are among the most fortunate in the Army today. You have a group of able, loyal, serious soldiers in both the General, and Technical staff divisions, and they are a happy official family. You have a big job, chock-full of professional interest, and you have a real leader at the head. Could a soldier want more?

I know, of course, that all of you recognize these obvious facts, but sometimes a man is not definitely conscious of his own good fortune until another suggests it to him.

Our G-1 is a man named Coiner,[1] of the Cavalry, I think. G-2 is a Lt. Col. J. K. Boles,[2] who for some reason has been jumped in the promotions to Colonel. G-3 is Lt. Col. Barker,[3] and G-4, Lt. Col. Lutes.[4] The Adjutant is Lt. Colonel Rawls.[5]

We move to Louisiana about August 5–8. We conduct Corps maneuvers until September 1. Then we have a short Army C.P.X., followed by a very large maneuver (2 Corps against 1), and finally, on September 15, begin Army against Army. We have to whittle the estimated costs, so the exact determination of participating units is yet to be made. I have a very difficult job ahead, and unfortunately, the decks are not yet completely clear for beginning the effort. But we'll manage somehow!

I hope that some of you in the IX Corps Staff come down here during September. Especially I hope that the General, with Jimmy, Chandler[6] and yourself can find the opportunity and the inclination to do so. Such a re-union would be delightful, for me.

Remember me to all the gang. There's no use in naming them all; just start at one end of the building and go right on through. But, particularly, pay my respects to the General, and tell Jimmy I'd like a report on Chandlers weight at the end of the "forced-feeding" campaign. . . . As ever

1. Benjamin H. Coiner achieved the rank of lieutenant colonel in 1938. He retired in 1949 with the permanent rank of colonel.

2. John K. Boles served in World War I. He retired in 1947 as a colonel.

3. "Lt. Col. Barker" could have been any one of the following: Ernest S. Barker, George R. Barker, Maurice E. Barker, or Ray W. Barker, all of whom held the rank of lieutenant colonel at this time.

4. As a brigadier general in 1941, Leroy Lutes distinguished himself by his able handling of logistics for the Third Army during the Louisiana Maneuvers. In 1942 he was named director of operations, Headquarters, Army Services of Supply. He retired in 1952.

5. Walter O. Rawls was assigned to the adjutant general's department in 1934, where he remained until his retirement in 1946.

6. The "General" to whom Eisenhower refers was IX Corps commander Kenyon Joyce. "Jimmy" Curtis served at the time as aide-de-camp to General Joyce.

Charles G. "Tex" Chandler Jr. received a commission in the Air Reserves on May 25, 1939, and entered the Army Air Corps on August 15, 1939. Chandler may have been serving at this time as General Joyce's personal pilot.

186

To Fort Lewis Post Quartermaster, Attention: Lieutenant McClain

JULY 17, 1941

Dear Lt. McClain: The Argonne Van and Storage Company finally reached here with my property on July 15. My household effects had been reloaded two or three times and a considerable damage resulted. The following action was taken:

a. In company with the driver of the van, I inspected the property and made a list of that damaged, lost, or broken. Duplicate lists were prepared of these defects, and I required the driver to sign them along with myself.

b. When I signed delivery papers carried by the driver, I noted on each set the following: "Exceptions noted on signed sheets attached hereto, copies of which are in my possession."

c. I informed the driver as soon as the Argonne Van and Storage Company completed the substantial repair of damaged furniture, I would notify you promptly so that their contract with the Post Quartermaster, Fort Lewis, could be promptly settled.

When delivered, there was no tail load.

I informed you in a recent letter, provided my goods were delivered in good condition, I was willing to pay through you to the company a maximum of $75.00 over and above the sum paid by the Quartermaster to the Van Company. The goods were not delivered in good condition, and some of the damage incurred cannot possibly be corrected. For example, a couple of articles of valuable china were broken, and I know of no place in this country where they can be secured. Likewise, certain new items of valuable furniture had spots on their upholstery completely worn through, and the material for the repair is now unobtainable.

The owner and manager of the van company is completely aware of some of this damage. The driver informs me that he personally supervised the repacking of my furniture in San Francisco and merely informed the driver that all the damage would be corrected.

On top of all this the contract called for the shipment to begin no later than June 24. It was not delivered here until July 15. This represents inexcusable delay on the part of the van company.

In view of all the above, I feel strongly that the company should not be paid any amount over and above the original contract price, and that the entire payment should be withheld until repairs, so far as they are possible to make have been accomplished to my satisfaction.

I enclose a copy of the listed defects merely for your information.

Please advise me further with respect to this whole affair in the event the procedure I have outlined above is irregular, or illogical.[1] With best personal regards. Very truly yours

Property of Colonel Eisenhower

From: Ft. Lewis, Washington, To: Fort Sam Houston, Texas

Small Buffett: Small scar on legs

Octagon Shape table: " "

Chaise Lounge: Torn Uphl on left side and legs scarred

Large Canvas Picture : O.K.

"   "   "   : "

"   "   "   : Scar on frame left side

Foot stool: Scar on leg

1-chair cushion, for chair: O.K.

Metal upl bench: Top M/Scarred

Bundle, Bedding: O.K.

Trunk, P.E.: Lock O.K.

Box Spring: O.K.

Nite table: Chipped on right front leg.

K- Stool: scarred on two legs.

Nite stand: O.K.
Bath room scale: O.K.
Electric Heater: O.K.
Picture (Lady) (Medium size): O.K.
Kitchen garbage can: O.K.
Mirror (medium size): O.K.
¾ Bed spring : O.K.
¾ "   "   : O.K.
Carton, (Miscl): O.K.
Carton (Miscl): O.K.
Folding card table: O.K.
Large Mattress: O.K.
Chinese Folding Screen: M/Scarred on frame
Bed Base (Large): O.K.
Lawn Chair (Metal): Seat scarred
Carton, Miscl: O.K.
Book case (No Shelfs): M/S
Gun Chest (Not Locked): M/Scarred
Ironing Board: O.K.
Walking Cane: O.K.
¾ Mattress: O.K.
Trunk, (Lock O.K.): O.K.
4-Book Case Shelfs: M/Scarred
Vacuum Cleaner: O.K.
Metal Stand: O.K.
1-Large Bed end (wooden): M/Scarred
1- "   "   " (wooden): "   "
1¾ Bed end (wooden):   "   "
Small Mirror: O.K.
Picture, (Lady): O.K.
Steel Clothes hamper and contents: O.K.
Carpet Sweeper: M/Scarred
Clothes rack: "
Bundle, 1-mop 1-brush 1-brush, handle: O.K.
Library Table: M/Scarred
Folding Mirror: "
Box, & Contents: O.K.
China Closet, glass front: Right Side scarred & Top (Deep)
Brass Round table base: O.K.
Buffett: Whole top and sides scarred bad.
Dresser Base: M/Scarred
Chinese Screen (Folding): M/S
Oval Shape Picture: O.K.
Drop leaf table (Small): Top chipped on side

O/S Chair (No Cushion): O.K.
O/S Arm Chair "   "   : O.K.
Folding table (Flower decoration top): Top scarred
Box, Miscl: O.K.
Large Bed side table: Top unscrewed (M/S)
Box, Books: No Lid.
Metal Chair (Lawn): M/S
Large Rug: Worn
Settee (No Cushions): R-R Leg Chipped
3 Piano Legs and foot piece: M/S
¾ Mattress: Worn-Soiled
2-Pillows: O.K.
Settee (No Cushions): O.K.
S.B. Chair Upl Seat and Back : O.K.
S.B.   "   "   "   "   " : O.K.
¾ Bed end : M/Scarred
¾   "   " : "   "
¾   "   " : "   "
Large Mattress: Soiled & Worn
2-Bed Rails: M/Scarred
Bundle, rug and pad: O.K.
      "   Large Rug (Blue)
2-Rails: M/Scarred
2-   " : M/Scarred
1 Medium rug: Soiled and worn
1-Long rug: "   "   "
1-Runner rug: "   "   "
2-Medium rugs: "   "   "
1 Large Rug: "   "   "
Marble top smoking stand: O.K.
2-small rugs and 1 cushion: Soiled and worn
Drapery: "   "   "
1 small rug: "   "   "
Leather mattress: "   "   "
1 small rug: "   "   "
Writing desk: M/S all around
Chest of drawer: O.K.
     "   "   ": M/S, Lid broken on left top drawer
Small drop leaf table: Crack on top (Old)
Carton and contents: O.K.
S.B. Antique Straw bottom chair: O.K.
Antique S.B. Chair Upl Seat: M/Scarred
Arm Chair Upl seat: "
S.B. K-Chair: "

Large bed spring: O.K.
Book shelf: M/Scarred & Scratch
Chair S.B. Upl seat and bottom: M/Scarred
Box, Miscl: O.K.
    ″   ″ : O.K.
    ″   ″ : O.K.
Desk- Bed Antique: O.K.
Blanket & Cushion: ″
Barrel, China ware: ″
Barrel Miscl: ″
Wash board and Carton: M/Scarred
Barrel China and Dishes: O.K.
S.B. Chair, Upl seat and back: O.K.
Bed room chair & Cover: Legs scarred
Box, Miscl: O.K.
Small Table Top: O.K.
Rug holder: O.K.
Serving table Small: O.K.
Metal floor lamp: O.K.
   ″   ″   ″ : O.K.
Table base: O.K.
Table Lamp Metal: O.K.
   ″   ″   ″ : O.K.
Box Miscl: M/Scarred
End Table: O.K.
Chinese Hat: O.K.
Bed stand: O.K.
Bed stand: O.K.
Carton, Bedding: O.K.
Bag Cellophane, Clothing (Uniforms): O.K.
  ″   ″   ″   ″ : O.K.
Cushion: O.K.
Nest of tables (4): O.K.
S.B. Chair Upl Seat: Loose Joints
Carton, Miscl: O.K.
2 Cushions: O.K.
1 cushion: O.K.
Silver Chest and Silver Not Locked: O.K.
Carton, Miscl: O.K.
Carton,   ″ : O.K.
Smoke stand Metal: O.K.
Smoke Stand Metal: ″
Suit Case: ″
Wicker Basket and contents: O.K.

Carton, Miscl: ″
Table, Radio (Philco): M/S
Two table leafs and cushion: Gd
3- Waste paper baskets and 1- straw mat: O.K.
Carton, Miscl: O.K.
Cushion: O.K.
Bread box, Metal: O.K.
Portable Radio: O.K.
Dining Table: O.K.
Folding Tray Shelf: O.K.
Bundle Drapes: Soiled & Worn
2- Cushions: O.K.
1- Large rug and pad: Soiled and worn
1- large rug: ″   ″   ″
Cushion and bundle: O.K.
2 Small Rugs: Soiled and worn
2 Medium Rugs: ″   ″   ″
1 Down Pillow: soiled.
Canvas Case: O.K.
Suit Case: O.K.
Bundle Miscl: O.K.
1- Typewriter: O.K.
1- large rug and pad: O.K.
Carton, Miscl: O.K.
2- medium rugs: O.K.
1 large rug: O.K.
Bundle, Drapers: O.K.
Trunk P.E. Lock O.K.: O.K.
Bundle, Rug and Pad: Soiled
Chest of drawer: M/Scarred, right rear leg broken, <u>off</u>
Barrel, Miscl: O.K.
Barrel, clothing and earthenware: O.K.
Camphor Chest P.E. Lock O.K.: O.K. M/S
Barrel, China: O.K.
Barrel, China: O.K.
Box, K- Ware: O.K.
Box, Miscl.: O.K.
Box   ″   : O.K.
Box   ″   : O.K.
Box   ″   : O.K.
Crate, and contents: O.K.
Box, Books, No Lid: Bottom Broken
   ″   ″   ″   ″   : O.K.
S.B. Chair & Cushion: O.K.

Bed room Upl Chair: "
Arm Bed room chair, deep scar on right leg: M/Scarred
Arm Chair, Upl Seat and back: Chipped on right leg
Suit case and contents, lock O.K.
Bed room Uphl chair: Uphl torn on right arm
Trunk, and contents, lock O.K.
Bed room Uphl chair: Uphl torn on right arm
Small Trunk No Lock (M-T.)
Trunk and Content Lock O.K.
Barrel, China: O.K.
Rocker, straw bottom: Scarred on both rockers
Bed roll: O.K.
Waste Paper basket and two rubber mats: O.K.
12 rug pads: O.K.
Ironing Board: Soiled
Box K-Ware: O.K.
Box, Miscl: O.K.
S.B. Chair, Straw bottom M/S: Loose joints
Piano: O.K.

1. Correspondence on this matter continued for several weeks. It is interesting to
note the range of household items the Eisenhowers owned—including a piano—considering their many moves throughout the United States, Panama, France, and the
Philippines. One of the beds listed is probably the spool bed from the Eisenhower family home in Abilene which Eisenhower and Mamie kept with them throughout their
lives, including during their time in the White House. The bed is still in the family.

187   Virginia Military Institute Archives
                                    Leonard T. Gerow Collection

To Brigadier General Leonard T. Gerow

JULY 18, 1941

Dear Gee: Wayne Clark, here the other day on an inspection trip, told
me you were fully recovered in health. That is such good news that I
couldn't help dropping other things long enough to say "Bonzai."
    Since last I wrote you things have happened to me—as possibly Ham
has told you. I was in the middle of maneuvers at Jolon, California, and
expecting a report from one of the divisions when we were told Gen.
Joyce was wanted on the phone. In a few minutes he called me over
and said, "You start packing; you go to Lewis for orders, which will direct you to go to San Antonio as Chief of Staff, Third Army."[1]
    My packing and shipping troubles were a bit worse than usual, but

here we are! The change here is not completely accomplished, but since yesterday morning I am "acting", and soon all the official details will be accomplished.

Our staff job in getting ready for the maneuvers in August–September is a big one.[2] We have some good men—others not so hot. Since none of us has ever functioned on an Army Staff in such large maneuvers, we are having some difficulty in deciding just how many individuals are needed in each section. The average section head, of course, wants enough people so that he can be prepared for anything; I'm trying to find out what would constitute a reasonable employment, and stick to that. Moreover, since our only source of experienced officers is the troop units, every time we take a good man we hurt an organization. This morning I'm having each section in to see if they can prove their respective cases.

The "shake up" reported in yesterdays paper was really nothing more than a "shuffle." I'm glad to see certain of the changes. We need "Can Do" soldiers in high places—badly.

General Krueger is, in addition to commanding the Third Army, in charge of a Defense Command. We have one staff officer in that section—and while I've had no chance to study the set-up, I assume his work will tie-in, some way, under W. P. D. I'm going to get hold of him soon, and see what he knows about it.

I think you saw Johnny when he went through Washington. So far, he's written one letter, reporting that in his company he's fourth highest in <u>demerits</u>. Can't you just see that long, awkward, drink of water trying to fold his handkerchiefs into a perfect stack, etc., etc.? "But," he said, "I'm getting the hang of things now, and won't pull so many boners in the future."

Mamie is well—though the heat saps her energy, of which she has only a fair share at any time. We are in a set of quarters on the Artillery Post, but may, soon, move into another. We'd like a bigger and better house, but dread the thought of moving again.

Our salutations to Mary Louise, and, as always, best of luck to you. As ever,

I wrote this in long hand, and sent to a new clerk for typing. Apparently he has some trouble reading my handwriting, which astounds me!

---

1. Eisenhower had been assigned as Deputy Chief of Staff, Third Army, San Antonio, Texas. While this position was staff duty, it was with a troop command. This provided the opportunity to command troops at the staff level in the forthcoming Louisiana Maneuvers. Eisenhower had turned down a transfer as recently as January 9, 1941, telling Gerow that for "family reasons [I] consider it unwise to leave Lewis in near future" (Eisenhower to Gerow, January 9, 1941, Virginia Military Institute Archives).

2. The 1941 Louisiana Maneuvers were ordered by Chief of Staff George C. Marshall to prepare the army for probable U.S. involvement in the war against the Axis. They also were designed to weed out National Guard and army officers who were less than competent. The maneuvers, which took place in August and September, pitted the Second Army against the Third in a mock battle in which the 180,000-man Second was to defend territory against the "invading" 240,000-man Third. Eisenhower served as chief of staff for Third Army commander Walter Krueger. Important lessons learned during the maneuvers led to improvements in troop training, supply and transportation, doctrine, and general administration. Because the American press assigned a large corps of reporters to cover the maneuvers, newspapers carried detailed accounts of the war games. Drew Pearson and Robert S. Allen, in their syndicated column, *Washington Merry-Go-Round*, brought Colonel Eisenhower's name to the nation's attention for the first time in a highly laudatory article. See Christopher R. Gabel, *The U.S. Army GHQ Maneuvers of 1941* (Washington, D.C.: U.S. Army Center of Military History, 1991).

188

Eisenhower Library
Pre-presidential Papers, Family File

To John S. D. Eisenhower

July 24, 1941

Dear Johnny: Two of the letters you wrote were apparently held a long time in the local post-office, because they were addressed merely "Ft. Sam Houston." The ones you wrote July 4th, and July 14, were delivered only yesterday. The best way to address them is "Quarters 221, Artillery Post, Ft. Sam Houston, Texas." Of course, if ever you want to write a confidential letter to me, you should write to "Headquarters Third Army, Smith-Young Tower, San Antonio, Texas.

I can well understand how you are having trouble with demerits. But don't give up and you'll soon be straightened out. I had a couple of class mates that got a few slugs to start with and made up their minds it was rather "smart" to have a lot of them; and they got plenty. After demerits really begin to be made of record, which as I remember was after the first month, when I was a cadet, they definitely count against your final class standing.[1]

Undoubtedly, as you've grown accustomed to the place you are not getting so exhausted physically. The work is gruelling, but you are pretty tough, physically, and it's just a question of getting used to the routine.

Did you ever make the awkward squad? Or report to the head of the beast detail after supper and catch on how's bracing.[2] I can still remember a couple of those sessions! The green tie stunt was a honey. I can almost hear what they said to you on that one.

531

We're having some difficulty getting used to Texas heat, but it's not so severe as I remembered it. They tell me that when I go to the Louisiana maneuvers I'll find out what disagreeable weather is. But I figure I can take it.

The War Department has not yet gotten to my case. But it appears that, eventually, everything will work out according to plan. Certainly I'm not worrying about it.

Do you have a room-mate? Your letters intimate that you're living alone—and if you are, what is the reason?

Good luck—keep on the beam and try to get an occasional laugh.

1. Dwight Eisenhower had somewhat of a reputation for demerits at West Point where, in discipline, he finished 125th in his graduating class of 162. See Eisenhower, *At Ease*, 7–12.

2. The "Beast Detail" was comprised of upperclassmen cadets who made a practice of harassing plebes. Bracing was the art of an exaggerated position of attention.

189   Eisenhower Library
                                  Pre-presidential Papers

To General Kenyon Joyce

July 25, 1941

Dear General: The opening date of maneuvers is rushing toward us, and with each passing day it seems we discover new problems that must be solved before the shooting starts. This Army of eleven divisions stretches from Arizona to Florida, and concentration plans are not easy to perfect. But I'm hopeful that we'll get the job done passably well.

The head-lined drastic "shake-up" in high commanders turned out to be little more than a gentle nudge. A few traded jobs and a few others got up into the charmed two-star circle. You are getting a commander for the Third Division who appeals to me as a top-notcher. He has both feet on the ground, is energetic, and from what I've seen, a yes-sir soldier. I like him very much.[1]

You must know how deeply I appreciate the generosity of your final report on me. I sincerely hope that others besides the clerks and Adjutant Generals in the War Department see it, not only because of what you said, but more particularly because you said it.

Last Monday we received an order here approving my predecessor's application for retirement, placing him on leave status and vacating his temporary commission as brigadier. That made me Acting Chief of Staff, and that is the way the matter still stands.

I have just read the critique on the final maneuver at Jolon. Some of the criticisms were, of course, obvious ones, and could and would be made about any troops in the service. But I noted with particular satisfaction the admission that the division were away the best so far seen, and that the Corps Headquarters functioned efficiently. Two points only made me gnash my teeth a bit. The statement was made that the artillery-marking teams were the least efficient of any that had come to the notice of General Headquarters, and the Corps Headquarters was accused of writing voluminous, ponderous orders.

In the first of these criticisms there is little excuse if everyone has played the game. Unless instructions have been disobeyed, the same teams should have been operating the sets that started on them several months ago, and under the supervision of Colonel Vanderveer[2] and the signal officer (intensified after the execution of D-3 by the 41st Division) these teams should have become well nigh perfect in technique.

As for "voluminous" orders, I cannot see why the G-3 section should have again succumbed to that temptation. I went over that with them after the C.P.X., and pointed out that the mere demand of a higher headquarters for a number of copies should not be allowed to interfere with efficiency in the issuance of orders. Copies can be made and submitted, <u>after</u> the fragmentary orders are out.

But all in all the reports indicate clearly that your command did a fine job, and when you stop to consider what you started with only last fall, you must have a feeling of intense satisfaction. Part of the GHQ crowd was here a week ago, and my conversations with them were definitely on the pleasant side, since they agreed that you had developed the IX Army Corps into a gang of first class fighting men.

So far, I've seen no orders detailing you a new Chief of Staff. I hope when one is assigned you'll let me know, because of my real interest in his identity.

I hope you'll find an opportunity to give my best to Bill, Jimmy and our favorite trenchermen. I miss them! Sincerely

1. Eisenhower referred to the appointment of Brig. Gen. Charles P. Hall as commander of the 3d Division in August.

2. Harold C. Vanderveer was a classmate of Eisenhower's at the Command and General Staff School in 1926. After the Louisiana Maneuvers he transferred to the 38th Infantry Division at Fort Shelby, Mississippi. Vanderveer retired in 1949 as a brigadier general.

To Wade Haislip[1]

JULY 28, 1941

Dear Ham: Last night's paper carried the news of General MacArthur's appointment to command all Philippine Forces. He will soon be attempting to build up a big staff of his own choosing.

In many ways I was always a thorn in his side—I hope and believe he'll never even consider submitting my name as one of his prospective assistants. However, no one can ever tell which way he is going to jump, and it would not surprise me in the slightest to learn that he had turned in my name to the Department.

In any such unlikely event I want you to argue and prove that I'm positively indispensable here.

To begin with, I do not believe that the shooting is going to start out there.

Secondly—I don't want to get stagnated in a secondary theater, nor so far away from where the final, decisive action must take place if we really get into a big affair.

Thirdly—I worked for him long enough! I put in four hard years out there, to say nothing of the War Department tour. If General MacArthur keeps Sutherland, he'll never mention my name, because my opinion of that buckeroo went lower and lower the longer I knew him, and both of them were aware of that fact!

Once the Department gets around to confirming my position in the Third Army, I'll feel safe—but none of us can do anything about that! I still laugh when I recall how terribly impressed all of us became, in California, with the necessity for my rushing down here to be Chief of Staff—without delay! In the meantime, don't send me back to gugu land, no matter how wonderful the possibilities may appear to be.

When I talked to you the other day, I had scarcely left the phone when in came a radio turning us down on all three of our men. The Adjutant General named us a couple of "availables" and we countered with a still longer list of recommendations. However, we said that we'd take one of their boys, if ours could not be made available. So that will work out—I hope.

As ever. P. S. I'm not a Filipino

1. Wade "Ham" Haislip had been appointed Assistant Chief of Staff, G-1, Personnel and Administrative Division, on the War Department General Staff and promoted to brigadier general.

To Arthur Eisenhower

July 28, 1941

Dear Arthur: Thanks for the news from home. I doubt that we can ever expect to have any particularly encouraging news about dad.[1] But he's astoundingly better than he was when I arrived home last May. The doctor had practically given up. I rarely get any information. Naomi[2] is too busy to write; it's too difficult for mother to do so, and Roy is not well.

I'm not surprised at Naomi's difficulty with military titles; in fact she's invented a new one, according to your letter. You are correct in your assumption that I am a colonel. My transfer to this station and job is supposed to carry with it another promotion, but that has not yet been accomplished. But it will be along in due course.

Hated to leave the North West. That's a real country. In a week or so I go on a seven weeks maneuver in Louisiana, to live with the mosquitoes and ticks. You'll read about it in your papers—it's to be the most ambitious maneuver ever held in this country. I'll be Chief of Staff of the larger Army, the Third.

When you write, please use the address as given on the letter head. Affectionately your brother

1. "Dad" in this case refers to Eisenhower's father, David.
2. Naomi Engle, a friend of the Eisenhower family, assisted Ida Eisenhower in caring for her ill husband. After David's death in March 1942, Milton Eisenhower retained Engle as a live-in companion and secretary for the elderly Ida, whose health was failing. Initially, Eisenhower appreciated Engle's attention to his mother's needs as well as Engle's periodic letters reporting on Ida's health. But in 1944, the Eisenhower brothers learned that Engle, a Jehovah's Witness, had been exploiting her relationship with Ida. Engle not only had taken Ida with her to a state Witnesses' convention in Wichita but also had forged a letter from Ida to a young soldier, in which Ida expounded upon her Jehovah's Witness faith. The Witnesses were pacifists and male Witnesses had claimed exemption from military service owing to conscientious objection. The letter, published in a newspaper, dismayed the brothers, who soon thereafter replaced Engle with Trula Robinson. See Dwight D. Eisenhower to Milton Eisenhower, September 10, 1942, Family File, Pre-pres. Papers; Eisenhower to Engle, April 3, 1943, Pre-pres. Papers; Home and Family Restricted Material, undated, Documentary Histories Series, J. Earl Endacott Records, Eisenhower Library.

To KENYON JOYCE

JULY 30, 1941

Dear General: Last evening we had dinner with Hal Mangum,[1] and I promised him to write a note to you this morning, giving you his greetings and best wishes. Following his terrible accident of a year and a half ago, he allowed himself to get too heavy, and finally contracted some heart trouble. He is now reducing, supposedly, and is taking Digitalis and resting. He stays close to his rooms in the St. Anthony Hotel, and is obviously lonesome. But he is as interesting as ever; we had a most enjoyable evening. He said he was going to devote some time to studying how to get you down here!

The Philippine situation is a curious one. That may be the place where the shooting starts; but even so, I don't see how it can ever be anything but a secondary theater.[2]

Present circumstances would make it appear that the Department was merely indulging in a practical joke when my transfer was ordered and a promotion promised. I think, however, that there is just a certain ritual to follow in Washington, as well as a great preoccupation in important matters, and that, in due course, they'll get around to my case. In the meantime, this is most certainly a busy spot.

Knowing of my intention to write, Mamie asked me to include her best wishes with my own to you and Mrs. Joyce. Cordially

1. Hal Mangum, a wealthy San Antonio businessman with extensive ranch holdings in Mexico, may have met Eisenhower through his in-laws, John and Elivera Doud, who wintered for many years in San Antonio. Mangum maintained a regular correspondence with Eisenhower until his death on August 3, 1950. See Mangum File, Pre-pres. Papers, Eisenhower Library.

2. At the War Department in 1942, Eisenhower worked on the overall strategic plan for World War II. Eisenhower firmly believed, along with Marshall and Roosevelt, that the war in Europe must receive the major attention. This "Germany first" strategy was accepted.

To Wade Haislip[1]

[August, 1941][2]

Dear Ham: I've already started the machinery to moving to find out about Major Malin Craig.[3] His outfit did not come into the maneuver area and it may take me a little time. However, if there's nothing to prevent, I'll see that he gets his chance, as soon as possible.

When you want to get rid of that man Byers,[4] send him along to us. I liked his style.

As to the Philippine set-up, I'm happy that the "Field Marshal" didn't recall my name. While I felt reasonably certain he would not make a request for me, I didn't want to take chances. But I do wonder how come they can make his C. of S. so darn quickly. They've succeeded in doing nothing with my case an awful long time—maybe it just seems long to me.[5]

I cannot remember whether or not I owe Gee a letter. I always try to keep up at least a sketchy correspondence with my old friends, even in the field.

We're certainly hitting the ball. My own hours are from 6:00 AM to 11:00 PM, every day. The others on the staff have, on a staggered arrangement fully as long a day. The General keeps worse hours than any of the rest of us. Darned if I know how he keeps up! We've been here just two weeks; but at that it's worse, so far as "drive" is concerned, than when we're at San Antonio. We do have our Sundays off there.

You'd not recognize the San Antonio of our 19th Infantry days. If you haven't been down this way in a long time, you should come, just to see the changes.

I'll drop you a note when I get the final dope on Craig.
As ever

1. Haislip was still on the War Department General Staff.

2. This letter from Camp Polk, Louisiana, was probably written during August 1941, at the beginning of the Louisiana Maneuvers.

3. Maj. Malin Craig Jr., son of Chief of Staff Malin Craig.

4. Clovis E. Byers (USMA, 1920) served during World War II as Chief of Staff of the 77th Infantry Division, I Corps, and the Eighth Army. He retired in 1959 as a lieutenant general.

5. Eisenhower is probably referring to his letter of July 28, 1941, to Haislip. His reference that MacArthur "didn't recall my name" was a satirical comment directed at MacArthur's choice of Richard Sutherland for that post in the Philippines. Sutherland's appointment was accomplished very quickly, which disgusted Eisenhower.

194

TO LEONARD GEROW

AUGUST 5, 1941

Dear Gee: I thoroughly enjoyed your note; it's particularly nice to know that you're safely over your shoulder trouble.

Next Monday I go to Louisiana and stay there until September 30. All the old-timers here say that we are going into a God-awful spot, to live with mud, malaria, mosquitoes and misery. But I like to go to the field, so I'm not much concerned about it.

Mamie is still wondering whether to go to Denver during maneuvers, or to stay here. She has just acquired a new pair of blacks in the house, so she may feel she has to stay here and watch and train them. For the present we are living in the Artillery Post, on New Braunfels Avenue. The place is noisy, and the house is small. So we are rather avoiding settling too firmly, believing something a bit more desirable will become available.

I had a note from Fort Lewis saying that inquiries from the War Department had reached there concerning availability of Major W. G. Wyman for W.P.D. While his preference is probably to stay at Lewis, I want to tell you he is tops. During the three months we worked together closely, I considered him a cold wax.

Give my best to Ham and any other friends, and, of course, love from us both to Mary Louise. As ever

195

TO COLONEL AUGUSTUS F. DANNEMILLER[1]

AUGUST 12, 1941

Dear Colonel Dannemiller: The dates indicated in your letter of August 8th for the Corps versus Corps maneuvers are correct. As to the best time to be present, I believe that the first exercise, beginning on August 17th will be the more interesting.[2] The second exercise has not been written completely due to the fact that it is impossible to tell at the present time just where the first exercise will end. In this first exercise, two fairly balanced corps, over one hundred miles apart, each with an offensive mission, will advance toward each other.

Upon completion of the Corps versus Corps maneuvers, on August

28th, the Army will participate in a C.P.X. which will be completed on September 2d.

Immediately after this CPX, troops will be concentrated for another series of maneuvers in which the Army, consisting of two corps, will operate against its own IV Army Corps. The first of these two exercises will take place on September 5–6, and the second exercise on September 9–10. Both of these maneuvers should be worth attending.

To avoid useless administrative marches, we are attempting, within limits, to start each succeeding exercise with troops in the general positions in which they concluded the prior one. For this reason, general situations and preliminary orders have not been drawn up in their entirety. For your information, I inclose such as are now available.

With warm personal regards, Sincerely yours

1. Eisenhower wrote to Dannemiller from Lake Charles, Louisiana. Dannemiller served with the General Staff Corps from 1935 to 1939 and on January 2, 1941 transferred to the Office of the Inspector General. He retired from the army in January 1944, with the rank of colonel.

2. Dannemiller observed the Louisiana Maneuvers operation on behalf of the inspector general's office. The letter was obviously written to establish a beneficial time for his visit.

196

To Wade Haislip

August 27, 1941[1]

Dear Ham: Major Malin Craig, Jr., is detailed to attend the next Leavenworth course. Its opening has been postponed from September 20 to October 4. I thought you might like to know this at once, so that when you again see General Craig you can tell him.

Incidentally this was not arranged by arbitrary action in this headquarters; the Corps Commander had already selected him on his own merits. I think the General might like to know this also.

If you are counting on coming down for our September battles, please give me a bit of notice so I can have you met with the proper pomp and ceremony. Maybe that part of it won't be so much, but at least you will get a very warm welcome when you get to headquarters. Give my love to Alice. As ever

1. The letter was postmarked at Camp Polk, Louisiana.

To Rupert Hughes[1]

August 27, 1941

Dear Mr. Hughes: I am sending this note through "Esquire," because I do not recall your Southern California address.

You've written a Philippic; I wish every person in the world, including those under Hitler's heel, could read it.[2]

I have a private resentment for one statement in your article; "referred it to a staff officer, who advised against it—being a staff officer".[3] The dig reflects a rather popular impression I think, but if we could be together again in a field mess, as we were at Jolon, I think I could easily convince you that the impression is erroneous. (But I still like the article.)

Are you going to be one of the "War" correspondents, covering our September 15–30 battles here? If you're allergic to red bugs, ticks, heat and humidity, I advise against it, even though I'd consider it a real opportunity to see you again. The Press Relations Bureau is accrediting quite a number of press representatives to each of the opposing armies, and I thought that possibly, because of your interest in things military, you had told them you would like to attend.

I left General Joyce—most reluctantly—shortly after the end of your visit. I'm Chief of <u>Staff</u>, Third Army; which, of course, explains the plaint, made earlier in this letter.

With best wishes and warm personal regard, Very sincerely

1. Rupert Hughes, a prolific author, playwright, songwriter, radio commentator, and motion picture producer, assisted in the formation of the California National Guard (1940), in which he served until 1943.

2. Eisenhower read an article in *Esquire,* the popular men's magazine of the time, written by Hughes. The article ("The End of Hitler," 16 (September 1941): 27–29) concerned the possibility that Hitler would die in 1941, as predicted by the fuhrer's astrologer, and what would happen if he did. Hughes wrote that "no punishment could ever fit his crimes but it's sweet to recall unhappy deaths of other conquerors, greater men than he." Hughes then proceeded to examine what had happened after the deaths of Alexander the Great, Charlemagne, Napoleon, and many others. Some, he wrote, faded from history, while the death of others brought lasting fame or infamy, peace or more war. His dream for Hitler was that "I might live to see, and Hitler might live to furnish, a newsreel or photograph showing him on his knees scrubbing some filthy pavements while ancient rabbis pour lye on his wrists."

3. Eisenhower's statement refers to Hughes' story of Robert Fulton offering to Napoleon his new invention, the steamship, as a new weapon of war. Hughes wrote

"Napoleon thought it an interesting idea and referred it to a staff officer, who advised against it—being a staff officer." Napoleon's new naval fleet shortly thereafter was destroyed by Admiral Nelson at the Battle of Trafalgar.

198

GENERAL GEORGE V. H. MOSELEY[1]

AUGUST 28, 1941

Dear General: Receipt of your letter, forwarded here from Fort Sam Houston, made one bright spot in a very busy and difficult day. We have been in Louisiana for something more than two weeks, and have had a number of maneuvers involving Corps versus Corps. One was completed yesterday, with this morning devoted to the critique. The critique days are always nightmares for the staff.

You cannot know how much I appreciate the good wishes you send me—and I constantly recall my association with you as a very wonderful personal opportunity, and your good opinion means a lot to me.

I suppose you know that Gerow is head of War Plans and Haislip head of G-1 Division, W. D. G. S. Both are Brigadier Generals. My own promotion, presumably on the way—but certainly the War Department has taken a long time getting to it. I was Chief of Staff for General Joyce in the IX Corps, and thoroughly enjoying the job, when I was rushed down here to take over the job of Chief of Staff for the Third Army. It's a big job; none of us now on these staffs has ever before had a similar experience. The World War "G-S"[2] of all echelons above the Division have largely passed out of the service. Luckily I've spent most of my life in large headquarters, so am not overpowered by the mass of details.

Unquestionably General MacArthur is congratulating himself on his new assignment. He had largely exhausted the possibilities of his former position but he has clearly landed, once again, on his feet![3]

Mamie is fine. She is in San Antonio; John has just entered West Point. I think he is having tough sledding with the demerits, but otherwise he considers the place all that it has been in his life-long dreams. He is 6 feet, 1 inch tall, and weighs only 150 pounds.

I must apologize for the disjointed character of this letter. My office seems to provide the only "cracker-barrel" in this army. Everyone comes in here to discuss his troubles, and I'm often astonished how much better they seem to work after they have had a chance to recite their woes.

I'll hand this terrible scribble to my sergeant to put it in legible form for you.

Thank you again for your letter. With warmest personal regard, Cordially

1. Moseley retired in 1938.

2. The "G.S." referred to general staff officers from the World War I era.

3. Eisenhower's comment is directed to MacArthur's July 26 appointment as commanding general, U.S. Army Forces in the Far East (USAFFE).

199   Eisenhower Library
                                            Pre-presidential Papers

To Lieutenant Colonel Hubert W. Beyette[1]

September 4, 1941

Dear Hubert: The Third Army's control of the field maneuvers will terminate on September 9. Up until that moment, it is easy enough for this Headquarters to arrange for any tour you might wish to take through the area. You would simply report to the Public Relations Bureau here at Lake Charles, and you could start rolling.

Between September 9 and 17, no actual field maneuver will be in progress, but heavy troop movements will be taking place in order to get all organizations in position to begin the big battle starting about September 17. So far as supply methods are concerned, this period should prove only slightly less interesting than one of the actual maneuvers. I am somewhat doubtful as to the exact procedure that will obtain after September 17, under the authority of GHQ. However, I am of the opinion that all that will be necessary is for you to report into Camp Polk, near Leesville, and go to the Visitors Bureau. That Bureau will give you all the credentials and markings for yourself and car that are necessary in the maneuver area.

My own opinion is that the most interesting period for your visit would be the 17th and 18th of September. I would arrive at Camp Polk on the evening of the 16th, get myself all set, as described above, and spend the two following days going over the maneuver area. By all means you should come to Third Army Headquarters and let our G-4 explain the complete workings of the supply system.

I realize that this is not much of a letter but assure you that I am never caught up on my work, and I feel some guilt every time I take a minute off.

Give my love to Dannie and the girls, and with warm regards to yourself. As ever

1. Eisenhower sent the letter from the maneuver headquarters in Lake Charles, Louisiana. At this time, Beyette, who served with Eisenhower on the American Battle Monuments team in France, was with the Quartermaster Corps at Fort Sam Houston.

200
Eisenhower Library
Pre-presidential Papers

To Major General Kenyon Joyce

September 15, 1941

Dear General: Our big war started this morning.[1] The customary lull in the flow of early reports has set in, and I should have a few minutes in which to answer your deeply appreciated letter. We have three Corps in line; all attacking to the northward from the Lake Charles area, with the Cavalry Division (56th Cavalry Brigade attached, and with an anti-tank <u>Group</u> on call) is covering our left on the west bank of the Sabine. Opposing forces line up as follows:

	Blue (Us)	Red
Infantry Divisions	9	5
Cavalry Divisions	1	1
Armored Divisions	0	2
Air Corps	(About equal - some 330 combat planes per side.)	
Anti-tank <u>Groups</u>	3	0

The weather has closed in so much that air operations are almost out of the question, but operations early this morning were quite productive of results, both as to information and tactical effect. We've located at least a large part of the hostile mechanization, and if we can stymie it in the swamps and batter it to pieces with our A.-T. Groups,[2] those Reds[3] are going to be on the run by day after tomorrow. If the hostile tanks can preserve their freedom of action, the battle will probably become a confused dog fight. Maybe we're just over-confident, but we <u>think</u> we can take care of ourselves. Anyway, we're attacking all along the line.

Our <u>effective</u> strength this morning is about 220,000.

As you can well imagine, we've had a visitation of brass hats. Of them all, none has been so welcome, from my standpoint, as the group from the West Coast. I've seen Truscott, Nicholas, Lehman and Major Howard[4] (3d Division). Had nice talks with each, and was especially delighted to have, from Truscott, the message you sent. I regret that your own schedule would not permit you to come down, even if these things are just an old story to you. Your presence would have made my

543

"old home week" complete! I saw General DeWitt and Colonel Bradley last evening.

We've started _real_ reclassification proceedings. So far, one Major General and one Brigadier are, along with a flock of lesser fry, awaiting results! A lot more must go, in my humble opinion.

We hear that General Marshall is due here tomorrow. It may be that he will take the trouble to tell General Krueger the whys of the promotion difficulty in my case. Certainly, the implication of the present imbroglio is that I, along with a generally acknowledged incompetent, cannot be promoted. Though I always make allowances for my own egotism, I still hope that my friends will differentiate as to reason, even where circumstances _appear_ identical.

I phoned Mamie a couple of days ago and found her in fine fettle. Her mother, sister with female infant,[5] and Mrs. Grunert and daughter were all visiting her. With such a houseful of women, I can well imagine that there are only shreds of reputation left among their combined list of acquaintances.

General Krueger and I often talk of you. Whenever the question of cavalry arises, he cites your handling of the 1st Division in maneuvers last year. So after he gets all done, I tell him how you handle a Corps. And by the way; all the GHQ gang from General McNair on down, gives you and your command the "well done" with oak leaf cluster for your recent maneuvers. It's all music to my ears.

Tell Jimmie[6] I just received, within the hour, his very fine letter. I thank him and will soon answer. I've told the Publicity boy to send him the picture he wanted. While it will contribute nothing to ornamentation, I'll be proud to have it hang in the Chief of Staff Office, IX Army Corps.

With warmest regards to you and Mrs. Joyce, Sincerely

1. This referred to the first major "battle" of the maneuvers.

2. "A.-T." refers to antitank groups.

3. The "Reds" were Gen. Ben Lear's Second Army, which opposed Krueger's Third Army, the "Blues."

4. This probably was Richard U. Nicholas (USMA, 1913). In 1941 he served at Fort Lewis as chief engineer of the IX Corps. He retired as a major general in 1945.

Raymond G. Lehman commanded the 93d Infantry Division in the Southwest Pacific in 1943–44. Lehman retired in 1945 as a major general.

Edwin B. Howard (USMA, 1923) served with the 15th Infantry Regiment from 1938 to 1941, then with II Corps. From 1943 to 1945 he served with the Fifth Army. He retired from the army in 1954 as a brigadier general.

5. The sister was Mabel Frances, who had divorced her first husband, Richard Gill, and in July 1940 married Gordon G. Moore Jr.

6. James "Jimmie" Curtis.

To Brigadier General Leonard T. Gerow[1]

September 25, 1941

Dear Gee: Yesterday while talking to Ham over the phone, I learned that you were again in Walter Reed, this time as a result of an accident. He said that you had injured your back, and that the doctors had you flat on a board. I had that same treatment once and I know what distress it means for the first few days. I cannot begin to tell you how badly I feel about your bad luck. I know, though, that you won't let the thing get you down, and that very soon you will be up and at 'em again.

General Krueger and I often talk about you. Particularly we spoke about the prospect of having you as one of the Corps Commanders in this Army. I suppose the Department will require you to command a division for a short time before you can be assigned a Corps, but so far as I am concerned, I wish you were doing so right now.

There is a tremendous job facing every senior commander in this Army. The nervous energy and drive that are required in bringing a large unit along toward high training standards is tremendous; only people who are highly trained professionally and who have an inexhaustible supply of determination can get away with it. It is only rarely that the necessary qualifications are combined in one person. Some of them have plenty of drive but are totally unacquainted with training standards and methods in the smaller units, while others are technically proficient but have not the iron in their souls to perform the job.

One of the things that is causing the greatest trouble is that of eliminating unfit officers, of all grades and of all components. It is a hard thing to do, and in many cases it is too hard for some of the people in charge. But it is a job that has got to be done.

The last year has made a tremendous difference in the physical stamina of the men and in their ability to take care of themselves. Just before we started the problem in which we are now engaged, the tail end of a hurricane visited this section of the country and the Army got a good drenching. Yet when the problem started at noon yesterday, everybody was full of vim and ready to go. I do not know how long this problem will last but I can assure you that in Armies of about a quarter of a million you don't do things in a hurry. You have to take time to unwind things, even for minor changes in plans and orders.

I had a long letter from Johnnie. He is in rather good spirits and except for demerits is apparently doing well enough at West Point. Occasionally he gets down in the mouth but, as you know, at his age that is a normal practice.

Mamie is in Fort Sam Houston. For the past month she has had a succession of house guests including some of her own family and Florence Grunert and daughter. I am certainly looking forward to getting back home again, which I shall do in about two weeks—maybe, that is.

I wonder if you heard a story that is going the rounds about some of the "Simulated" things that are part of peace-time maneuvers. A corporal brought his squad up to a bridge and marched across it. An umpire yelled at him "Hey, don't you see that that bridge is destroyed?" The corporal answered "Of course I can see it's destroyed, can't you see I'm swimming?"

Stories such as the above float around and give us an occasional smile in spite of all the strain that goes with a job such as this. Handling an Army staff that has had very little chance to whip itself together has its tough points, in spite of which I am having a good time. But I would like a command of my own.

Give my best to Mary Louise and to any of our friends whom you may see. As ever

1. Eisenhower wrote this letter from Third Army Headquarters, now in Eunice, Louisiana. Gerow was in Walter Reed General Hospital, Washington, D.C.

202   Eisenhower Library
                                               Pre-presidential Papers

To James O. Curtis[1]

October 2, 1941

Dear Jimmy: I've owed you a letter for some time, but when your congratulatory wire arrived, I vowed I'd do something about it before leaving this area. Naturally, I'm delighted to get the star, but the nicest part of all, I've quickly discovered, is to be assured by good friends that the War Department was not too d—— dumb in making the selection.[2] Of course, others can say that friends are prejudiced, but my reply is, "I don't give a hoot if they are, so long as they're the kind of people that my friends are."

The maneuvers have really been big, as I'm sure Truscott, Lehman, Nicholas and Howard will tell you. We're on the home stretch and if no catastrophe hits us in the next 48 hours, I'm going to do a lot of cheering—in spite of serious defects that cursed us throughout the performance. When I can get some time, I'll try to write you a full account. Thanks again to you and Millie. Pay my respects to the General and remember me to our Texan friend and all the gang. As ever

P. S. I've heard a lot of fine things about your maneuvers in the Northwest. The IX Corps made a ten strike, as, of course, you and I knew it would!

1. Eisenhower sent this letter from San Antonio. Curtis was serving at Fort Lewis.

2. Eisenhower received his promotion to brigadier general on October 3, 1941. The story is told that when Mark Clark read the promotion list to the group of officers slated for promotion, including Eisenhower, he intentionally omitted Eisenhower's name. After a brief pause he then announced Eisenhower's promotion. See Blumenson, *Mark Clark,* 73–74.

203

To Leonard T. Gerow

October 4, 1941

Dear Gee: Your wire of congratulations reached me within a matter of hours after I had received notice of my promotion.[1]

Things are moving so rapidly these days that I get almost dizzy trying to keep up with the parade. One thing is certain—when they get clear down to my place on the list, they are passing out stars with considerable abandon. Nevertheless, I am glad to get it if for no other reason than I get some word from you as a result. My latest news of you is that you are out of the hospital, and that your injury is not as serious as first feared. I am thankful for that.

Mamie's parents are visiting us, and all join me in sending you our best. As ever

1. Eisenhower received many congratulatory notes on his promotion to brigadier general. Only a select few are included, to represent those received.

204

To Colonel Norman Randolph[1]

October 6, 1941

Dear Norm: It was thoughtful of you and Dorothy to wire me congratulations on my promotion, and I want you to know how deeply I appreciate it.

While I feel that when the War Department hands me a star, it must be getting rather reckless in the way it is making distribution, still, I'm glad to be so lucky. I know that, in short order, I'll be sending you similar congratulations, the sooner the better! Mamie joins me in love to you both.

As ever

P.S. Your letter of the 1st arrived just as I was ready to sign the above. Of one thing I'm certain, we'll be delighted to have you in this Army.[2] I've been rather expecting that the War Department would get around to making Robertson[3] (9th Inf.) a B.G. He's good—and though I hear that he has something of a name as a grouser, he's still <u>good</u>! But I'll see that your end of this thing is so presented to General Krueger that if any hole occurs at the right time, you'll go right in. And I repeat, even if that particular vacancy doesn't occur, for God's sake don't stay away from the Third Army. We need top notchers so badly we cry every day about it. In the meantime, I'll try to keep you informed!

P.P.S. I don't give a hoot who gets credit for anything in the P. I. I got out <u>clean</u>—and that's that! Again love to Dorothy.

1. Norman Randolph served with Chief of Infantry Courtney Hodges. He graduated with Eisenhower's West Point class of 1915. He retired at the end of World War II with the rank of brigadier general.

2. There is no evidence that Randolph was assigned to the Third Army.

3. Walter M. Robertson (USMA, 1912) served in the Philippines, with the War Department, and the General Staff Corps. Robertson assumed command of the 2d Infantry Division on May 9, 1942. He retired in 1950 as a major general.

205
Eisenhower Library
Pre-presidential Papers, Family File

To Mr. and Mrs. Edgar Eisenhower and Janis[1]

October 7, 1941

Dear Bernice, Janis and Edgar: Thanks a lot, not only for the telegram but for Ed's long letter, the surprise of which was practically overwhelming. I do not know whether Mamie has answered Bernice's letter written from Abilene, but I have my doubts, because Mamie has (a) had a houseful of visitors for 2 months, (b) moved from one house to another, and (c) lost her servants. The visitors were mostly members of her family (her dad and mother are still here). The new house is as big as American Lake, and the servants weren't worth a hoot, anyway.

I was delighted to have definite news from home. It is difficult to keep up with dad's and Mother's actual condition, because neither writes any more and Roy's letters are not only infrequent, but are about six lines long. So far as I can see, from your letters, both dad and mother are much as they were four months ago, when I was home.

We had some real maneuvers in Louisiana. We got through them O.K. and now most of the troops are home again. I came back to San Antonio on October 3. But I have a lot of travelling to do in the next few weeks. Much to Mamie's disgust!

The Russians are still hanging on. I devoutly hope they can continue to do so. Someone has got to help wear out that so and so of a Hitler and his army, and it doesn't look as if the British were accomplishing too much.

Thanks again for the congratulations. It was nice to be promoted, but it doesn't seem to make my work any easier. As ever

1. Janis is the daughter of Edgar and Bernice Eisenhower.

206

To Colonel Joseph Sullivan[1]

October 7, 1941

Dear Sullys: Your telegram was read with great hilarity by the Doud-Eisenhower tribe (Mamie's folks are here for a short visit). Mamie allows that there's more truth than poetry in this doubt about her living with me. She has found out that I don't get a red cent with all this new glory—but she has to dole out to tailors some hundred and fifty bucks just to change over uniforms. She's been slightly punch-drunk ever since learning all this.

It's too bad that Sully has to go to the P.I., not because it's not a good station, but it's h—— to be separated so long from families. I was out there a year alone, and I did <u>not</u> like it. Anyway, good luck to you, and thanks a million for your wire. We truly appreciate your thoughtfulness.

1. Joseph P. Sullivan (USMA, 1917) served as the quartermaster at Fort Lewis. From 1942 to 1945 he was Quartermaster of the Fifth Army. He retired as a major general in 1953.

To Lieutenant Colonel Mark Clark[1]

OCTOBER 7, 1941

Dear Wayne: All major units are at home stations, or practically so and, thank the Gods of War, we had no tie-ups in getting them there! It's now time for those double scotches, so you'd better come down to this sector for a day or so.

The re-classification business goes awfully slowly, but we're doing the best we can, and unless a hurricane or a bomb shell hits us we're going to have a new first team on this club, ere long.

I wonder whether or not you can yet predict the probable future station of the 104th Anti-tank Battalion—now assigned to one of the Anti-Tank Groups in Carolina. If, at any time, it should become apparent to you that the battalion will <u>not</u> come back to Fort Sam Houston, <u>let me know by radio</u>. We need the barracks it used to occupy.

Orders were issued to send you Porter;[2] also the Artillery Officer was changed according to your request. I hope that gang works out well!

The Second Division is giving me a guard of honor. I'm completely overcome, particularly because of the cordiality of the invitation, even after I demurred. I've always been on the other end of such things, and I hope to heck I don't fall over my own feet! But durned if the prospect doesn't scare me more than would an order to go charge Hitler's legions!

Love to Renie and regards to the gang! As ever. . . .

1. On June 18, 1941, Clark received appointment as Assistant Chief of Staff, Operations and Training Division (G-3), War Department General Staff.

2. The army *Register* lists six Porters who held the rank of lieutenant colonel. Eisenhower is possibly referring to Ray E. Porter, who in 1940 served with the General Staff Corps. Early in 1945 he commanded the 75th Infantry Division in the Ardennes counteroffensive and in the unit's drive across the Rhine into Germany. He retired from the army in 1953 with the rank of major general.

208

To JOHN S. D. EISENHOWER[1]

OCTOBER 9, 1941

Dear Johnny: I seem to be as busy as ever! When I was a teniente,[2] I was foolish enough to think that when I became a major, or higher, I'd have someone else to do my work for me. It's now late in the evening, and I'm literally stealing a few minutes from a piled up desk to dash off a note—just to say we're O.K. Tomorrow morning one of the men will type this and I'll send it off then.

A battalion of the 2nd Division is giving me a "guard of honor" tomorrow at 11:15. It's mighty nice of them, but to tell the truth, I shouldn't go! It will take me away for 1½ hours.

It's easy to see you're settling down into cadet life. There's no question but that you will profit from the training, and, in turn, will be a credit to the institution. No one need fear that you'll ever do anything to bring discredit on the position or uniform of a real cadet. I hope your son, if the gods give you one, goes there too!

Well, old top, don't forget to send me your grades and standings from time to time. Except in English and a few minor subjects, they will always over-shadow the ones I accumulated thirty years ago.

All of us are well. Mamie will be sending some boodle soon.
As ever

1. John Eisenhower, in his plebe year at West Point, served in A Company.
2. *Teniente* is Spanish for lieutenant.

209

To DANIEL W. KENT[1]

OCTOBER 9, 1941

Dear Dan: Thank you very much for your nice note of congratulations.

What you had to say about the circumstances under which you left the Third Division something over a year ago completely astonished me. In fact, I cannot figure out exactly what you are talking about, because there is no slightest excuse for anyone intimating that your leaving of the 15th Infantry resulted from any action of Colonel Ladd. Some of the exact circumstances have become hazy in my memory.

Unless I am mistaken, you received tentative orders to go to Panama, and we protested them on the basis of the short time you had been in the United States. A little later we got orders for you to go to the CCC, and I definitely remember that I took this matter up verbally with some of the staff officers at Corps Area Headquarters. To save me, I cannot figure out any slightest circumstances connected with your going away that could have given anyone an excuse for making derogatory remarks with respect to you and your standing in the Regiment. At that particular time I was not in Division Headquarters, but all the officers up there were friends of mine, and I am certain that had there been any thought of "railroading" one of them would have talked the matter over with me informally even if they did not choose to take it up with Colonel Ladd officially.[2]

To tell you the truth, I have the definite impression that some gossip thinks he is being funny at your expense.

I know that your reputation with the Colonel as well as with the other senior officers of the 15th Infantry was that of a hard-working, well trained, experienced officer of unquestioned loyalty and integrity. In all the time I served at Fort Lewis, I never heard a single derogatory opinion expressed concerning you, and I know beyond doubt that I would have heard them had they been made by any responsible person.

So far as I am concerned, you may show this letter to anyone you please. Moreover, in writing to one or two other officers at Fort Lewis, I will express similar views. We are far too short on experienced, efficient officers to stand for our good ones becoming the victims of any kind of irresponsible gossip.

Give our love to Crys and, of course, best regards to yourself. Cordially

1. Eisenhower apparently met Daniel W. Kent at Fort Lewis in 1940 while the latter was with the 15th Regiment. Shortly thereafter, Kent was assigned to Civilian Conservation Corps duty in Boise, Idaho.

2. When Kent returned to Fort Lewis in the fall of 1941, he was told by a fellow officer that the CCC detail had been a form of "blacklisting" and that he had little future with the army officer corps. During World War II, Kent did receive further promotions, retiring with the rank of colonel. See Kent to Eisenhower, October 6, 1941, and June 23, 1946, Pre-pres. Papers.

210

To Frederick H. Payne[1]

Dear Mr. Secretary: Thanks so much for your fine letter and words of congratulations. Letters from old friends are one of the best parts of a promotion.

We did have a few headaches in 1930–33, but I hope that some of the people that took up that work where you left off, have been able to profit a little from those headaches.

I, too, hope our paths will soon cross, but in the meantime, I know that you are doing an outstanding job in your present, important position.

Again, my sincere thanks for your good wishes, and please remember me kindly to Mrs. Payne and the children.

Sincerely yours

1. In 1940, former Assistant Secretary of War Payne retired as chairman of the board of the Greenfield (Massachusetts) Tap and Die Company. A colonel in the Reserve Officer Corps, Payne was appointed assistant chief, Springfield Ordnance District, in 1940, a position he held throughout the war.

211

To John Boettiger[1]

OCTOBER 10, 1941

Dear John: One of the nicest things about this promotion was that news of it jolted you into writing me a note. It was fine to hear from you. Incidentally, you probably suspect me of "bribing" the Merry-Go-Round columnists.

I simply cannot tell you how much Mamie and I miss the Northwest. When it came time to move, we found the region and its people had gotten into our blood. We get home sick for Fort Lewis.

A couple of days ago Captain Elliot Roosevelt[2] came into our office and chatted with General Krueger and me for quite a while. He's had some intensely interesting experiences—hope you get a chance to talk to him soon about Iceland, England, etc.

Mamie joins me in kindest regards to you, Anna and the children. Sincerely

1. John Boettiger worked with various Chicago newspapers, including ten years with the *Tribune* (1924–34). In 1934 he left Chicago to become assistant to the president of the Motion Picture Producers and Distributors of America. In 1936 he became publisher of the Seattle *Post-Intelligencer*.
2. Elliot Roosevelt, son of President Franklin D. Roosevelt.

212   Eisenhower Library
                                                        Pre-presidential Papers

To Edward E. Hazlett[1]

OCTOBER 11, 1941

Dear Swede: Of all the things that have happened to me incidental to my promotion, none has been nicer than the receipt of your very fine letter. I truly appreciate it.

I am happy to know that in spite of the affliction of a defective "pump" you are engaged in work that is not only necessary, but which is an integral part of our effort to re-arm. While it is naturally a disappointment to you that you cannot be taking part in the more strenuous phases of naval activity, it must be a source of great satisfaction to know that you are doing something well that must be done. In the Army our biggest job is the production of young leaders. To it we give more concern than to any other single thing. Anyone who has studied this defense problem seriously will readily see that your job is one of vital, even if indirectly important, to [a] final solution. On top of all this, you must be developing into a bang-up "prof" when they have already made you the Executive of the department.

Both last summer and this I made very short visits to Abilene. My Father and Mother are both still living there, although both are getting feeble. During each visit, I have had a chance to call on most of our old friends, notably Mr. Harger, Charlie Case, Art Hart, Reynold Rogers, the Sterl Brothers and Henry Giles. I mustn't forget Joner Calahan.[2] All of them seem to be going their accustomed ways with very little noticeable change either in themselves or in the town.

You are quite right in your thought that you are responsible for my being in the Military Service. As you well know, it was only through you that I ever heard of the Government Academies. To the fact that you were well acquainted with the methods for entering the Academies and my good fortune that you were my friend, I owe a lifetime of real enjoyment and interesting work. Incidentally, every time I go home I remind all and sundry of this.

Mamie and I send our very best to you both. I will try to do my part in seeing that our correspondence is not interrupted by another three year lapse. As ever

1. Edward Everett Hazlett Jr., born on February 2, 1892, into the home of a prosperous Abilene, Kansas, physician, played a critical role in Eisenhower's life. Hazlett, born on the "right side of the tracks," did not attend Abilene High School after his freshman year. He graduated in 1910 from a Wisconsin military preparatory school. Having failed one portion of the Annapolis entrance examination, he returned home for a year in order to study for the 1911 Naval Academy tests. Eisenhower, who had graduated in 1909 from Abilene High, struck up an acquaintance with Hazlett in the summer of 1910 that led to a close bond between the two young men. Hazlett persuaded Eisenhower to abandon his plan to follow his brother Edgar to the University of Michigan and to instead pursue an appointment to the Naval Academy. Although circumstances prevented Eisenhower from getting an Annapolis appointment, he did receive Kansas senator Bristow's appointment to West Point. Hazlett retired early from the navy because of chronic illness, but he and Eisenhower maintained an intimate correspondence until Hazlett's death in 1958. Eisenhower's lengthy, frank letters to his old friend about government policy, politics, and personal matters indicate that Eisenhower trusted Hazlett so implicitly that he felt free to discuss even the most sensitive matters with him. See Eisenhower, *At Ease*, 104–6; and Robert Griffith, ed., *Ike's Letters to a Friend* (Lawrence: University Press of Kansas, 1984).

2. Although a number of Harts lived in Abilene, no Arthur Hart is identifiable. Eisenhower might have meant Arthur Hurd, a friend and prominent Abilene attorney. Reynolds Rogers, another friend, was an Abilene banker, and Oscar and William Sterl were proprietors of Abilene's largest men's clothing store. Henry Giles, who had worked for his family's lumber company in Abilene, had retired by 1941. Joner Callahan was proprietor of the town's Tip-Top cafe, where Eisenhower met with his old friends during his infrequent visits to his home town. See Kenneth S. Davis, *Soldier of Democracy* (Garden City, N.Y.: Doubleday, 1945), 117, 155, 215, 251.

213
Eisenhower Library
Pre-presidential Papers

To Major Willard Wyman

OCTOBER 16, 1941

Dear Bill: You realize, of course, that I swelled all out of shape when I read your letter. I've never had finer things said about me by one whose opinion I respected more. Thanks a lot. . . .

Ask Ethel, as my press-agent, whether she was responsible for the things the Washington Merry-Go-Round had to say about me? It was quite astonishing that the authors of the column picked up roses instead of brick-bats when they started throwing in the Army's direction.

If the Wyoming[1] is like it was 10 years ago, you'll like the place. We did, very much. I hope, too, that you like your work in the W. P. D. You are under one of the finest officers this Army has produced, he is top flight! I'd like to see him get a division (better still a corps) in this Army. Give him my best regards.[2]

Which reminds me! I've heard that some new policies, soon to be put into effect will remove some of the younger men from the G. S. in Washington and send them to the field forces. Is there the slightest chance of your being included in that category? Golly, I'd like to slam in a request for you. We've got a vacancy right this red-hot minute! Cordially

1. The Wyoming apartments in Washington, D.C., at 2022 Columbia Road, was a favorite location for many army officers.
2. Eisenhower referred to Gerow. Wyman mentioned in his letter that he and his wife "called at General Gerow's last night." See Wyman to Eisenhower, September 30, 1941, Pre-pres. Papers.

214

To Joel F. Carlson[1]

October 24, 1941

Dear Unc: Thanks a lot for your fine letter of congratulations. I truly appreciate your thoughtfulness.

I was quite interested in your account of the National Guardsman's growls. I don't know, of course, just what his "peeve" is, but I can tell you this: In higher headquarters everyone is searching for officers who can deliver the goods—and no questions are asked as to whether the man is Regular, Reserve or National Guard! In fact we are issuing, today, an order bringing into our headquarters in a position of great importance and responsibility, a National Guard officer. On this staff we must have 15 to 20 Reserve and National Guard officers, and we most certainly would not take them in if we were "agin" them. There is too great a need for qualified officers for us to worry whether or not a man is a Regular.[2]

It is, of course, difficult for most people to understand that long years of study, reflection and <u>practice</u> are required for the production of a good officer in the senior grades—that is, above lieutenant. The popular idea is that an officer leans back in a swivel chair (or in his auto) and shouts an order; whereupon everything is supposed to begin clicking like a well-oiled machine.

Suppose that were true!

Who developed the machine that starts clicking so perfectly? It had to be the officer! This particular machine has to be able to march and maneuver and to attack and defend with a multitude of different types of weapons. It has to eat; it uses prodigious quantities of ammunition; it has to care for its own sick and wounded and it has to do all these things in rain, sunshine, mud, darkness, woods, mountains—in every condition of climate and terrain.

Take a small unit in attack; say a company. To capture a particular hill there are a dozen possible methods, not only as to general outline, but in the detailed movements of individual men. If done properly we will get the hill with a loss of 5–10 men; if we blunder we won't take the hill and we'll lose 30–40. Every man in the company must know his own weapon perfectly; he must have practiced, time and again, the correct methods of moving toward his objective and coordinating those movements with every other individual in his own small unit.

As he goes forward he runs out of ammunition—someone must put more in his hands! He gets hungry, someone must bring him his food. How to do these things without losing any of the power or momentum of the attack? I've actually seen, in maneuvers, poorly trained officers stop a platoon in attack and assemble it in a sheltered place to feed it!

Now, I've brought up only a few of the problems that the Captain of this particular company has had to solve long before he came onto the battle or maneuver field! There are a thousand other problems, not the least of which has been the acquisition of knowledge and methods on his own part, that is, self-education, for this terrific task.

The higher you go in the military scale the greater and more complex the problems of leadership, tactics, supply and care of the command. To the professional soldier it seems amazing that our people expect the average man to step out of a lawyer's office and, on the basis of a few days yearly training, solve these problems satisfactorily. They are complex and difficult and the cost of blunders is disastrous loss of life. All we (professional soldiers) want is efficiency; and all too frequently we find individuals among our own ranks who fail to come up to the mark! We can get rid of Regulars easily, for who cares what happens to a professional soldier. But the point is that we need efficiency in every position, and efficiency requires character, personality, knowledge and earnest study and practice.

So, in my opinion, the officer of whom you speak is merely exhibiting a woeful lack of knowledge of the Army's stupendous responsibilities when he made such laborious distinction between Regular and

National Guard. He should talk about those that <u>can</u> do the job and those that <u>cannot</u>! And he should show his listeners that they should <u>demand</u> efficiency; the safety of the country, and the lives of their sons and brothers are possibly going to be at stake! So let's stop talking of classes and of castes. We must see what the job is, and we must insist on getting people who can do it, and we shouldn't give a hoot whether he is Regular or National Guard. He merely must do the job <u>right</u>—or get out! We cannot safely tolerate ineptitude, ignorance, inexperience.

I didn't mean to make a speech! But when I get started on this subject I can scarcely stop; the need is so great in every position from 2nd lieutenant to general for moral courage, military efficiency, and self-sacrifice. And far too often, these are hard to find. Cordial regards to you both, As ever

1. Joel Carlson of Boone, Iowa, Mamie's uncle.
2. Carlson's letter to Eisenhower of October 21 does not mention the National Guard complaint. Evidently, there must have been an enclosure in the letter that was not retained in the Eisenhower files. See Joel F. Carlson to Eisenhower, October 21, 1941, Pre-pres. Papers.

215   Eisenhower Library
                                          Pre-presidential Papers

To Brigadier General Wade Haislip

November 12, 1941

Dear Ham: I am writing to you about Lieutenant Colonel P. A. Hodgson[1] who has already appeared before a retiring board and who is to be retired for physical disability in February.

It is my understanding that retired officers may be assigned to duty in corps area service command as long as they are not overage.

Sonny Nulsen,[2] Post Commander at Fort Sam Houston, would be delighted to have Hodgson as his executive since he has already been informed that he is to lose his active duty regular now assigned to that post. This man is Lieutenant Colonel Patrick Hurley[3] of the Infantry.

Hodgson is now on leave and his property is at Fort Leavenworth where he has been stationed for the last three years. Assuming that the War Department policies will permit the employment of officers retired for physical defects on corps area service command duties, I would like to know what to tell Hodgson as to the method of procedure.

He is still, technically, an active duty officer. However, he could be assigned <u>now</u> to the Corps Area Service Command, Fort Sam Houston. His property could be shipped down here and he could start functioning at once. Then when Colonel Hurley is relieved there would be no break in continuity of administration.

If such assignment would be contrary to War Department policy then it might be possible for Hodgson to ask for immediate retirement, merely giving up his leave. This would make no difference at all to him because he is ready to go to work. In this case he would simply designate San Antonio as his home and his property would automatically be shipped here.

This subject has not yet been discussed with the Corps Area Commander. Naturally, however, Nulsen's application for Hodgson's assignment would be forwarded through General Donovan,[4] who, I assume would approve of the detail. My immediate purpose is to find out what are War Department policies with respect to the employment of retired officers of his classification and would be able to advise him what to do. He and his wife are now our house guests but are looking for a furnished apartment for the time being. Hodgson was my roommate for four years at West Point but entirely aside from personal feelings in the matter I consider him a most able administrator and fully capable of doing a swell job as executive at Fort Sam Houston. The employment would be a godsend to him because in spite of his arthritic condition which makes him look almost hunchbacked he cannot stand idleness. I will be deeply appreciative if you will have one of your bright boys give me whatever information on this subject that will be useful. I will be grateful too if you will have your assistant send me an answer by Air Mail, Special Delivery.

We are looking forward to your next visit. You did us both a world of good. Cordially

1. Hodgson was Eisenhower's roommate at West Point.

2. Charles K. Nulsen (USMA, 1908) served as commanding officer of the 23d Infantry (1940–41). He retired as a brigadier general in 1943.

3. Patrick James Hurley (not to be confused with Patrick Jay Hurley, Hoover's secretary of war), served with the General Staff Corps. He retired in 1948.

4. Richard Donovan (USMA, 1908) was assigned to the General Staff Corps in 1937, where he remained until his assignment in 1940 as commanding officer of the 8th Service Command.

TO COLONEL HARVEY PROSSER[1]

DECEMBER 4, 1941

Dear Colonel Prosser: I am happy to accept your invitation to be present at the review and graduation of the Kelly Field Cadets on December 12. I shall be accompanied by 1st Lieutenant Lee, of this headquarters, and will arrive at your station slightly before 9:00 a.m.[2]

I assume that the uniform for the occasion is the usual O.D.
Cordially

1. Col. Harvey Prosser commanded the Air Corps Advanced Flying School, Kelly Field, Texas.
2. Eisenhower accepted the invitation to speak at the graduation exercises of the Kelly Field cadets. Document 218, although dated December 12, 1941, the date the speech was to be given, is the first draft. Document 219, again dated December 12, is the final draft of the speech but was written after the attack on Pearl Harbor.

217   Eisenhower Library
Leroy Lutes Papers

TO BRIGADIER GENERAL LEROY LUTES

DECEMBER 5, 1941

Dear Roy: Thanks very much for your note of the 3rd. I am happy indeed to get some idea of your new job and its problems.

I am envious of the standards your brigade has already obtained in motor maintenance. I am going to send Murray out to inspect all the motor transportation belonging to the Headquarters Detachment and Company on Saturday morning and see how we come out. If the results are not too terrible, I will send you a note.

The tentacles of the story back of your promotion are too many and in some cases too tenuous to justify an attempt at complete description. However, you will recall that G-1[1] of the War Department visited us at Lake Charles. In fact, he occupied your room for the night he was there. Your name was brought to his attention in many favorable ways, with the chief one, of course, involving your G-4 work in the maneuvers. It appears that he had heard favorable comments also at GHQ concerning the supply system of the Third Army, and the result was that when he went back to Washington he repeated the story in the highest places. The matter, according to my best information, was never referred to anyone else, but was consummated at that red hot moment. So there you are with a brigade on your hands, and I hope that on that job you will continue to enhance your enviable reputation. One thing is certain, if we could evolve a vacancy for a brigadier general, Coast Artillery Corps, I am certain the General would start a campaign to get you.

Things rock along in the office in their accustomed way. I am making a drive to compel all chiefs of sections to complete their organization and to get all their operations reduced to a workable system. Due to maneuvers and the necessity of attaching rather than assigning personnel, we have lived too much on a hand to mouth basis. I am going to get this outfit organized if I have to start shooting from the hip.

I am planning a short Christmas leave with the intention of running up to West Point, with Mamie, to see our son. I expect to be back here by January 5.

Best of luck to you and I am sorry that I cannot give you <u>exact</u> information on your promotion. I repeat though that you are perfectly safe in assuming that General Krueger's oft repeated commendations of your work, expressed to the highest authorities, had a lot to do with it.[2] With cordial regards. As ever

1. The G-1 was Eisenhower's friend Wade Haislip.
2. Eisenhower would not be able to visit West Point because of the United States' entry into World War II.

218   Eisenhower Library
                                                        Pre-presidential Papers

To Graduates at Kelly Field, Texas

December 12, 1941[1]

Col. Prosser—Ladies and gentlemen:

I am highly honored in having been invited to welcome this class into the commissioned ranks of the army. This day is an important one to each of you; it is like wise important to our government and our army, because it witnesses an appreciable re-inforcement in our flying personnel, and marks another definite step toward attainment of the country's objective in military preparation.

That preparation involves much more than mere numbers in technically trained personnel, more than guns, planes, tanks, ammunition and adequate supply. It requires, as its first essential, a spiritual unity— a devotion of self to a common cause, that alone can weld this nation into a gigantic force sufficiently formidable to command respect throughout the world. This requirement for unified purpose and effort is not limited to the fighting services—it comprehends every man, woman and child, every dollar and every material asset throughout the length and breadth of this great land. For we must remember that, in modern war, armies and navies are directly dependent for their [operations] and maintenance upon an efficient industry and a loyal population. More than this, when a nation resorts to force to insure the execution of policies that it considers vital to its prosperity or to its safety, there is brought into play not only the power of bomb and shell and bayonet, but a myriad of other forces that find their source in the nation's industries, its economy, its foreign trade, its political concepts, and in its moral fibre. The war machine is a vastly complex mechanism through which must be generated and coordinated the maximum power of a whole nation. Manifestly this effort must be unified if it is to be successful.

If we should go to a football game and find one team torn by open discord, with its half-backs trying to snatch the ball from each other in every play, with blockers tackling their own men, with the guards refusing to play unless guaranteed a proper share in the headlines, and the ends calling all the others a bunch of cowardly quitters, we would not only consider the whole performance highly ridiculous, but there'd be little doubt in our minds of the game's outcome. Yet the grim game of war demands a team-work, a perfection of coordination that is typified in the play of a championship club. And the stakes are not a mythical annual championship—they are liberty against slavery; happiness against degradation; life against death.

In military dictatorships the required unity of effort is always insured by the authority resting in one man's hands. Every individual must conform to the dictator's orders, the alternative is the firing squad. So, from the beginning, the necessary mechanical coordination is automatic.

In democracy this result is achieved more slowly. The overwhelming majority of its citizens must first come to realize that a common danger threatens, that collective and individual self-preservation demands the submission of self-interest to the nation's welfare. Because this realization and this unification come about so slowly, often only after disaster and loss of battles have rudely awakened a population, democracy is frequently condemned by unthinking critics as the least efficient form of government. Such criticism deals with the obvious factors only, it fails to throw into the balance the moral fibre, the staying qualities of a population. A Democracy resorts to war only when the vast majority of its people become convinced that there is no other way out. The crisis they have entered is of their own choosing, and

562

in the long, cruel ordeal of war this difference is likely to become decisive. The unification and coordination achieved in this way is lasting. The people work together because they have a common belief in the justice of their cause and a common readiness to sacrifice for attainment of national success. It was in appreciation of the great strength arising from this truth that Woodrow Wilson said "The highest form of efficiency is the spontaneous cooperation of a free people."

Whether or not our own country is to be plunged into war none of us can say. But the necessity for this nation to prepare against the danger of such a catastrophe we all recognize. We are pouring into the effort prodigious sums of money, and the flower of our manhood.

Each of you in this graduating class is now assuming an important position in this great national effort. It is particularly incumbent upon the man that holds his government's military commission to devote himself unstintedly to his assigned tasks. You will probably specialize in pursuit, or bomber flying, in navigation, engineering or technology. Your graduation from this school is proof enough that you have every physical and mental qualification to guarantee success in all these tasks. But success in any or all of these is not enough.

Each of you has become a public character, and your deeds, your conduct and your words will have, for your acquaintances in civil life, a greater weight and influence than ever before. In the Army you are an official upon whom will be thrown increasing responsibilities, and under whose care will come increasingly large numbers of men and materials. So both within the Army and without your opportunities to assist toward attainment of unity will be very real and will become constantly greater.

Progress is mandatory! New blood, bold ideas, youthful energy! These insure that we shall continue to forge ahead and not fall victim to the decay of laziness, age and conservatism.

But progress is not furthered by internal strife.

1. See note 2, December 4 entry.

219   Eisenhower Library
                                                    Pre-presidential Papers

To Kelly Field Graduates

December 12, 1941[1]

Today the members of this graduating class take their place among the commissioned ranks of the Army. I am highly honored in the opportunity to bid you welcome to the long unbroken chain of American Army officers that extends back to General George Washington and the first days of our Republic. You become, today, one of the sturdy links in that chain, links that will—God willing—each joined firmly to its neighbors stretch on and on into the dim and distant future!

But it is with deeper feelings than those of mere comradeship, deeper than those of mere fraternal friendship that I welcome you as lieutenants in the Army. You are a very real and significant reinforcement to a vital section of this nations defense forces. You come into the fighting ranks of the Army when its need was never greater.

Within the past few days our beloved country has found itself involved, with bewildering speed, in a war against the most powerful combination of ruthless military force ever known upon this planet. Once again America's call has gone out to all her sons to rally to the common defense. They are answering by the thousands. There is no need for us to concern ourselves with the basic patriotism of our young men. But patriotism, though indispensable, is not enough! Love of country can not, alone, produce the skill, the hardihood, the training and the techniques that are necessary to the modern day warrior. The raw recruit, no matter how brave, is not yet an efficient fighting man. But you men have met the high standards in discipline, in morale, in courage and in professional attainments, for which the name "Kelly Field" has always stood!

You have, of course, many hours of study, many hours of flying, yet to accomplish before your names will stand with those of your illustrious predecessors who have written the aviation history of our country. But you are ready, now, to take your places as efficient lieutenants in the Army of the United States and what we need—now—is efficient lieutenants.

The lieutenant is the commissioned officer closest to the enlisted man. The lieutenant is the only officer charged with direct training of the individual fighting man, all other officers are charged, normally, with training junior officers. On the lieutenant falls the burden of producing the small fighting units that, in the main, make up the army, no matter how large.

It is the lieutenant's privilege to live close to his men, to be their example in conduct, in courage, and in devotion to duty. He is in position to learn them intimately, to help them when in trouble, often to keep them out of trouble. No matter how young he may be nor how old and hard boiled his men he must become their counsellor, their leader, their friend, their old-man. This opportunity—that of becoming a real leader of fighting men—is one that you are yet to master. It is the part of soldiering that challenges the best that's in the officer, and its the one part in which he must not fail! To gain the respect, the esteem, the affection, the readiness to follow into danger, the unswerving and undying loyalty of the American enlisted man. That is the privilege and the opportunity of the lieutenant, and it is his high and almost divine duty. It is the challenge to his talents, his patriotism, his very soul!

1. Eisenhower expected to give this graduation address at Kelly Field on December 12, 1941, but was unable to do so. A War Department telegram dated December 12 ordered him to Washington by December 14, and Eisenhower recalled that when the telegram arrived he immediately boarded a plane for the East Coast. Weather forced it down in Dallas; he reached Washington by rail on the 14th (Circular Diary, McCann Papers, January 1, 1942, and Emory Adams to Commanding General, Third Army, December 12, 1941, both in Eisenhower Library, and *At Ease*, 245).

Ann Hussey and SSgt. Shawn Bohannon, historical office staff at Kelly Field, searched the post adjutant general's diaries for December 12, 1941, and Eisenhower was not listed as a guest. The San Antonio *Express-News* newspaper on December 13, 1941, reported that Col. Charles Hutter, Army liaison officer with the American Medical Association, delivered the graduation address to class 41-I on that date. Hutter did not use Eisenhower's speech.

Even though Eisenhower did not deliver the speech, the prepared text clearly testifies to his own sense of duty at the time the United States entered World War II and his talent for patriotic inspiration. Reminiscent of his "Our Flag" message at Camp Colt in 1918 and a forecast of his Order of the Day just before the Normandy landings in June 1944, this speech grows out of Eisenhower's traditional values, sense of discipline, and remarkable ability to challenge and draw the best from soldiers who also were free citizens. For the Normandy address, see Alfred D. Chandler Jr., ed., *The Papers of Dwight D. Eisenhower: The War Years* (5 vols.; Baltimore: Johns Hopkins Press, 1970), 3:1913, and "Order of the Day, June 6, 1944," Subject File, Prepres. Papers, Eisenhower Library.

INDEX

Abbott, Oscar B., 278–79
Aberdeen Proving Ground, Md., 175, 260
Abilene, Kans., 1, 4–9, 281–82, 554–55
Adams, Charles Francis, 169–70, 219
Adamson, Godfrey Douglas, 108
"Address to the R.O.T.C., University of the Philippines" (E. speech, 1939), 425–29
Agricultural Adjustment Act, 255–57
Agriculture, Department of, 113–14, 169
Aguilar, Miguel, 306, 346–47, 480
Air mail service, U.S., 265–66
Aishton, R. H., 186, 188, 198
Aitchison, Clyde B., 198, 201
Alejandrino, Jose, 352, 354
Allen, Robert H., 202
Allen, Robert S., 268–69, 412, 531
American Armament Corp., 390, 407, 412, 419
American Armies and Battlefields in Europe (American Battle Monuments Commission, 1929), 102, 104–6
American Battle Monuments Commission: E. service with, 58–61, 79–84, 99, 202; staffing of, 79–80, 105; U.S. Navy role, 80–82, 104, 107–8
American Federation of Labor (AFL), 165, 194, 197, 201
American Legion, 163–64, 168, 194–95
American Peace Society, 192, 200
American Rubber Producers, Inc. *See* Intercontinental Rubber Co.
Anderson, William, 400–401
Armor. *See* tanks
Army Air Corps, 264–66, 398, 561–65
Army Industrial College, student selection policy, 178–79, 202–3
Army-Navy Munitions Board, 184–85
Army War College, 59, 147, 179, 231–32
Arnold, Henry Harley "Hap," 398
Ayres, Leonard Porter, 168–69, 194

Babson, Roger, 248–49
Baguio, Philippine Islands, 300–301, 305, 373
Baker, Newton D., 165, 168, 191–92, 194, 197
Ballantine, Arthur Atwood, 198, 201
Bank Holiday, 1933, 249
Bartlett, John H., 246
Baruch, Bernard, 100–101, 163, 165, 168, 186–87, 194–97, 220
Bataan Peninsula, 489
Beech, Walter, 389–90
Beech Aircraft Co., 389–90
Beyette, Hubert Ward, 80, 542–43
Black, Forest Revere. *See* "Profits of War, The"
Black, Herbert A., 159, 262–63
Black, Hugo, 265
Boettiger, John, 553–54
Boles, John K., 522–23
Bolton, Chester Castle, 260
Bomar, Ernest C., 175, 277, 330
Bonham, Francis G., 278–79
Bontoc region, Philippine Islands, described by E., 432–33
Bonus March, 1932, chief of staff report on (written by E.), 233–47
Booth, Lucien Dent, 398
Boy Scouts, in Philippine Islands, 337
Bradley, James L., 519–20
Bradley, Omar Nelson, 103, 466–67
Brandt Co. (mortar manufacturer), 327, 395, 399–400
Bratton, Rufus Sumter, 402, 406
Brees, H. J., 58
Brent School, Philippine Islands, 60, 301, 333, 390
Brett, Sereno, 24
Bridges, Charles Higbee, 214–15

"Brief History of Planning for Procurement and Industrial Mobilization" (Industrial War College paper by E., 1931), 176–88

Bristow, Joseph L., nomination of E. to USMA, 8–9

Brookins, Homer DeWilton, 165

Brown, John Edward, 143

Bump, Arthur Leroy, 143

Bureau of Insular Affairs, 340, 359

Burnett, Charles, 396–97

Byers, Clovis E., 537

Cahill, Howard F. K., 104–6, 109–10

Call, Arthur Dearing, 192, 200

Callahan, Joner, 554–55

Callan, Robert Emmet, 225, 231

Camp Colt, Pa., report on, by E. (1920), 25–28

Camp Dix, N.J., 34, 175

Camp Gaillard, Canal Zone, 43

Camp John Hay, Philippine Islands, 300–302

Camp Keithly, Philippine Islands, 300

Camp Meade, Md. See Fort Meade

Camp Murphy, Philippine Islands, 296, 300, 311, 326, 404, 406, 456, 501

Camp Murray, Wash., 494

Camp Ord, Calif., 462–64

Camp Perry, Ohio, 142–43

Camp Polk, La., 537, 542

Capinpin, Mateo M., 456, 481

Capper, Arthur, 462, 500–501, 503

Carlson, Eda (Mrs. Joel), 180–81, 201–2, 208–9, 282

Carlson, Joel (Mamie's uncle), 170, 208–9, 556–58

Carnahan, George Holmes, 113–14, 125

Carr, Irving J., 146, 180

Catorce, Mexico, guayule rubber factory, 123–25

Cebu, Philippine Islands, 296, 370

Cedral, Mexico, guayule rubber factory, 123

Chandler, Charles G., Jr., 522–23

Chief of Staff, U.S. Army. See Craig, Malin, Sr.; MacArthur, Douglas

China, Japanese invasion of, 449–50

Citizens Military Training Camps, 67, 78–79

Civil Works Administration, 255–56

Civilian Conservation Corps (CCC), 211, 252–53, 552

Clark, Mark Wayne: E. letters to, 434–37, 447, 450–52, 492–93, 511–12, 550; Fort Lewis service and E., 385–86, 508

Clark Field, Philippine Islands, 328, 404

Clarke, George Sheppard, 398

Coffin, Howard, 186, 197, 200, 228

Coiner, Benjamin H., 522–23

Collins, Edgar Thomas, 225, 231

Collins, Ross Alexander, 169–70, 219, 257–58, 260–61

Colt's Patent Firearms Co., 390

Command and General Staff School (College), Fort Leavenworth, Kans., 2–3, 42–59, 214, 335, 340, 397

Commerce, Department of, 113, 169

Committee of the Nation, 262

Conklin, John French, 275–76

Conner, Fox: E. evaluation of, 226–27, 445; E. letter to, 267–68; influence on E., 2–3

Connor, William Durward, 213–14, 227, 232, 445

Continental Mexican Rubber Co. See Intercontinental Rubber Co.

Cooper, Isabel, relationship to MacArthur, 411–12

Cordon (linear) defense for Philippine Islands, 298

Corlett, Charles H., IX Corps operations and staff, Fort Lewis, 1941, 517–20

Covell, William E. R., 278–79

Coward, Jacob M., 269–70

Cox, Richard Ferguson, 161–62

Coy, Wayne, 355–56

Craig, Malin, Jr., 537

Craig, Malin, Sr., 277, 283–85, 342, 360, 396–97, 444–45

Crane, John Alden, 161–62

Crea, Harry Bowers, 261

Croft, Edward, 260–61

Crowell, Benedict, 142–43, 165, 198

Cunanan, Hugo V., 347, 349, 480

Curtis, James O., Jr., 519–20, 522–23, 544, 546–47

Dannemiller, Augustus F., 538–39
Davis, Thomas Jefferson, 214–15, 253, 293, 306–7, 327–28, 330, 342–43, 352, 355, 360, 367, 377, 400, 411, 431, 438, 452–53, 498–502
Davison, Frederick Trubee, 225, 231
Delafield, John Ross, 165, 168
Democratic Party. *See* "Student in Politics, The"
Dern, George H., 227, 232, 284, 286
Descals, Ricardo, 374–75
Detzer, Dorothy, 192–93
DeWitt, John Lesesne, 257–58, 308, 337, 460, 506–7
Dilley, Tex., guayule rubber operations at, 125
Donovan, Richard, 559
Doud, Elivera Mathilda Carlson (mother-in-law), E. letters to, 83–84, 157–59, 189–90, 201–2, 207–9, 281–82
Doud, John Sheldon (father-in-law), E. letters to, 83–84, 201–2, 212–13, 333–34
Douglas, Lewis William, 270–71
Drum, Hugh Aloysius, 227, 232, 445
Dumlao, Amando, 346, 349
Dunckel, William C., 453, 455

Early, Stephen, 268–69
Eichelberger, Robert Lawrence, 378
Eisenhower, Arthur B. (brother), 4, 5, 535
Eisenhower, David (father), E. letters to and about, 432–33, 535, 548–49
Eisenhower, Doud Dwight "Icky" (son), 13–16, 35
Eisenhower, Dwight David: Army duty stations, xxiii–xiv; aviation interests, 12, 421–22, 441–44, 491; boyhood, 1, 115; diaries: —Chief of Staff (1929–34), 102–14, 125–279; —Fort Lewis (1940–41), 493–517; —Gruber-Eisenhower (1929), 84–97; —Guayule (1930), 114–25; —Philippines (1935–40), 286–461; family matters, 10–16, 189–90, 201–2, 348, 390; medical history, 115–16, 170, 276–77, 373, 375; personal property, 145, 450–51, 460–61, 523–29; as USMA cadet, 531–32; USMA entrance, 1, 8–9, 554–55. *See also* MacArthur, Douglas;

Philippine Army; Quezon, Manuel; War Department; War Policies Commission
Eisenhower, Earl Dewey (brother), 158–59
Eisenhower, Edgar Newton (brother), 1, 159, 266–67, 409, 436, 461, 548–49
Eisenhower, Helen Eakin (Mrs. Milton S.), 208–9, 268
Eisenhower, Ida Stover (mother), E. letters to and about, 432–33, 548–49
Eisenhower, John Sheldon Doud (son): appointment to USMA, 462, 500, 503, 511; boyhood, 60, 84, 105, 107, 157–58, 189, 201, 208, 281–82, 301, 333–34, 370, 383–84, 401, 408, 420, 431, 456, 460–63; comment on Eisenhower-MacArthur relations, xxvi–xxvii; letters from E., 464–66, 551; as USMA cadet, 530–32, 541, 545–46, 551
Eisenhower, Mamie Doud (wife), 10–16, 189–90, 282, 329, 332–34, 370, 384, 390, 400–401, 417, 436–37, 441, 448, 451, 455–56, 460–62, 500, 511, 530, 538, 546, 548–49
Eisenhower, Milton S. (brother), 4, 59, 208–9, 268, 414–17, 461–63, 500, 535
Eisenhower, Milton S., Jr., "Buddy," 268
Eisenhower, Roy J. (brother), 5, 535
El Paso, Tex., 118–20
Embick, Stanley, 396–97
Engle, Naomi, 535
"Enlisted Reserve for the Regular Army, An" (E. study for War College, 1928), 62–79
Erie Ordnance Depot, Ohio, 143
European War (1939–41), E. evaluations of, 445–48, 508–9, 513, 536, 549

Fairchild, George H., 373, 375
Fairchild, Kirby, 373, 375
Fairweather, H. D., 390
Farnsworth, Charles S., 43
Fellers, Bonner, 346, 349, 360, 367, 379
Ferguson, Harley Bascom, 178–80, 182–83, 188
Ferrell, Robert, publication of E. diaries, ix, 311
Ferris, Benjamin Greeley, 261
Fitzsimmons Army Hospital, Colo., 408

"Fledgling at Fifty" (E. essay on flying solo), 441–44

Fleming, Philip Bracken, 213–14

Ford, Henry, 229, 254

Fort Benning, Ga., 34, 43, 59, 175, 449

Fort Bliss, Tex., 119–20

Fort Howard, Md., 237

Fort Humphreys, Va., 237, 493

Fort Leavenworth, Kans., 2–3, 42–59, 214, 335, 340, 397

Fort Lewis, Wash., 385–86, 409, 434–37, 451–53, 551–53

Fort Logan, Colo., 2, 43

Fort McKinley, Philippine Islands, 326, 328, 337

Fort Mason, Calif., 388–89

Fort Meade, Md., 28, 34, 42–43, 175, 237

Fort Myer, Va., 237

Fort Oglethorpe, Ga., 13–16

Fort Ord, Calif. *See* Camp Ord

Fort Sam Houston, Tex., 11, 111, 213, 529–31, 538, 543, 558–59

Fort Stotsenburg, Philippine Islands, 326, 328

Fort Washington, Md., 214–15, 237

Fort Wint, Philippine Islands, 406

Francisco, Guillermo, 296, 299, 306, 423–24

"Fundamentals of Industrial Mobilization" (E.'s draft of *Army Ordnance* article, 1930), 138–42

Fuqua, Stephen O., 207

Garcia, Raphael L., 338–39, 341, 481, 489, 501–2

Garcia, Ricardo, 481, 489

Gasser, Lorenzo D., 489–90

Gerow, Kathryn, 103, 158, 228, 232, 280–81

Gerow, Leonard Townsend "Gee": E. letters and memoranda to, 402–6, 449–50, 489–90, 503–8, 529–31, 538, 545–47; E. service with, 103, 111, 228, 269

Gerow, Mary Louise Kennedy, 449–50

Gifford, Walter Sherman, 186, 188, 194, 197

Giles, Henry, 554–55

Gill, Mabel Frances Doud "Mike" (Mamie's sister), 125, 208–9, 544

Glass, Ralph, 506–7, 511

Glassford, Pelham D., 239–40, 247

Gold standard, 251

Gold Star Mothers, 258

Gompers, Samuel, 201

Great Depression: E. comment on, 211, 247–49; effect on U.S. Army, 99, 224, 250–53

Green, William, 165, 194, 197, 201

Greene, Douglass T., 491–92

Greenwell, Samuel Alexander, 270–71

Griswold, Augustus H., 194, 200

Gruber, William, European tour with E.s 1929, 60, 84–97

Grunert, George, 336–37

Guayule rubber industry: in California, 116–18, 129–31; E. inspection trip (1930), 114–37, 385; E. report to assistant secretary of war on (1930), 126–37; in Mexico, 121–25, 127–28; in Texas, 125

Guide to the American Battlefields in France (1927), 102

Hadley, Lindley Hoag, 163–64, 204, 215–16, 219

Hagan, Harry Edgar, 143–44

Haislip, Wade Hampton "Ham," 111, 269, 534, 537, 558–61

Hall, Charles P., 532–33

Hardenbergh, Raymond W., 398

Harding, Gladys, 11

Harger, Charles M., 554

Hartrick, Guy R., 146–47

Harts, William Wright, 80

Hasson, John Patrick, 143–44

Hawaii, military installations, 387

Hazlett, Edward Everett, Jr., "Swede," 554–55

Heintzelman, Stuart, 214, 445

Hickham, Horace Meek, 161–62

Hills, Jedediah Huntington, 499

Hilpert, Robert C., 466–67

Hitler, Adolf, E. comment on, 445–46, 494

Hobbs, Leland Stanford, 260–61

Hodges, Courtney, 336–37, 464

Hodges, John Neal, 146–47
Hodgson, Paul Alfred, 208–9, 558–59
Holbrook, Lucius R., 342, 372, 394, 396
Honan, John James, 270–71
Hoover, Herbert, 99, 265, 363–64
Hopkins, Harry, 256
Horkan, George, 60–61, 79–80, 201–2
Horkan, George, Jr., "Bo," 60, 201–2
Horkan, Mary, 201–2
Howard, Edwin B., 543–44
Howard, Roy Wilson, 329
Howland, Charles Roscoe, 207
Hudson, Paul R., 143
Huff, Sidney L., 353–54
Hughes, Everett S., 161–62, 259–60,
    272–74, 407, 508–10
Hughes, John H., 396
Hughes, Rupert, 540–41
Hunt, Percy Emery, 106–8
Hunter Liggett Military Reservation,
    Calif., 1941 maneuvers, 516, 532–33
Hurd, Arthur, 328–29, 555
Hurd, Bruce, 328
Hurley, Patrick James, 558–59
Hurley, Patrick Joseph (secretary of war),
    xxvi, 112–13, 162, 205, 216, 218, 228–29,
    237, 287
Hutter, Howard Joseph, 293, 298, 330,
    339, 367
Hyde, Arthur M., 169–70, 219

Ickes, Harold, 229, 232, 254–55
Igorotes tribes, agricultural practices. *See*
    Bontoc region
Industrial Mobilization Plan, 145, 188
Intercontinental Rubber Company: in Cal-
    ifornia, 116–18; E. contact with, 114–37;
    E. report on, 1930, 126–37; in Mexico,
    121–25; in Texas, 125
Isolationism, U.S., 283

Jackson, Nettie Stover (cousin), 4
Japan: China invasion by, 449–50; Philip-
    pine Islands invasion by, 489; U.S. rela-
    tions with, 438–39
Jardine, William M., 462–63
Jehovah's Witnesses, 535

Johnson, Hugh Samuel, 229–30, 232,
    255
Johnson, Royal Cleaves, 194, 200
Jolon, Calif. *See* Hunter Liggett Military
    Reservation
Jones Act (Philippines, 1916), 291–93
Joyce, Kenyon, 495–97, 516–20, 522–23,
    529, 532–33, 536, 543–44

Kelly Field, Tex., 560; speeches to be deliv-
    ered at, 561–65
Kennedy, Martin, 439, 441
Kent, Daniel W., 551–52
Kilbourne, Charles Evans, 225, 231
Kimble, Frederick von Harten, 170–71
Kirby-Smith, Selden, 122–23
Kroner, Hayes A., 146–47
Krueger, Walter, 354, 386, 394, 500–502,
    512, 530, 544, 561

Ladd, Jesse A., 452, 467, 551–52
LaGuardia, Fiorello, 190, 193, 200
Lake Charles, La., 539, 542–43
Lambert, Lloyd W., 400–401
Lamont, Robert P., 169–70, 219
Landon, Alfred M., 328–29
Latrobe, Osmund, 143
Lear, Ben, 544
Lee, William L. "Jerry," 352, 354, 369,
    388–89, 422, 444
Lehman, Raymond G., 543–44
Lewis, Charles W. "Jew," 421
Lim, Vicente, 359
Lincoln Highway, 22–23
Littlejohn, Robert McG., 521
Lodge, Henry Cabot, 146–47, 223
Long, Andrew Theodore, 80–82
Los Cedros, Mexico, guayule rubber
    factory, 122–23, 125
Lough, Max S., 502–3
Louisiana Maneuvers (1941), E. letters
    concerning, 530, 532, 538–46, 560–61
Luse, Arthur H., 510
Lutes, Leroy, 522–23, 560–61
Luzon, Philippine Islands, 305, 346–47,
    350, 394
Lynch, George Arthur, 398

MacArthur, Douglas: American military
  mission to the Philippines, 283–85,
  289–372; Army chief of staff, 170–72,
  198–200, 211–15, 224–47, 249–50,
  283–90; and Bonus March, 224–47;
  E. relationship with, xxvi–xxvii, 201–2,
  211–13, 230, 304, 328–29, 355–56,
  360–64, 372, 377, 383–84, 410–12,
  438–40, 453–55, 512–14, 534, 537; early
  retirement, 284, 360, 368; field marshal,
  Philippine Army, 1937–1941, 284, 304,
  306–7, 326, 534, 537; military adviser,
  Philippine Commonwealth, 283–85,
  289, 372, 379–81, 383–86, 388, 394–97,
  399–401, 406, 408, 410–13, 419, 423–24,
  429–31, 438–40, 453–55; political ambi-
  tions, 230, 363, 411; U.S. Army, Far East,
  541–42; War Policies Commission par-
  ticipation, 171–72, 198–200. *See also*
  Philippine Army; Quezon, Manuel
MacArthur, Jean Faircloth (Mrs. Douglas),
  330, 401
MacKay, Gordon W., 374–75
McAndrew, Joseph A., 434–35
McCammon, John Easton, 208–9
McCann, Kevin, ix, 114–15
McCoy, Frank Ross, 250
McFarland, Earl, 180, 188, 205
McGowan, Samuel, 168–69, 192
McIntyre, Frank, 355–56
McNair, Leslie James, 492–93, 495, 544
McNutt, Paul V., 194, 200, 330, 342, 356,
  438–39
McSwain, John J., 169, 204–6, 219, 262,
  264, 276
Magruder, Marshall, 516
Magtoto, Amado B., 344–45
Malacañan, Philippine Islands, presiden-
  tial residence. *See* Quezon, Manuel
Mangum, Hal, 536
Mangum, James E., 103, 106
Marabut, Serafin, 347, 349, 352
Marcosson, Isaac F., 266
Marks, S. J., 246
Marshall, George Catlett, 356, 386, 395,
  397, 445, 493, 505, 531, 544
Marshall, Richard J., 453, 455
Martelino, Leopoldo C., 501–2

Martelino, Pastor, 345, 502
Massachusetts legislature, gun control
  concerns, 111–12, 159–60
Mattingly, Thomas L., 390
Merillat, Louis A., 13–14
Merritt, Wesley, 400–401, 406
"Message to the Men, A" (E. speech, Camp
  Colt, Pa., 1918), 16–17
Meyer, Eugene, 196
Mexican army, E. comment on (1930), 121
Mexico, E. comment on (1930), 118,
  120–22, 124
Mickle, Gerald St. Claire, 495–96
Miles, Perry, 233, 237, 242, 246, 251
Millard School, 462–64, 491, 499
Mindanao, Philippine Islands, 296, 346
Mitchell, William DeWitt, 169–70, 219
Molex (experimental explosive), 398
Monterey, Calif., E. comment on, 116, 118
Montgomery, Robert H., 163–64, 167,
  204–6, 216–17
Moore, Mabel Frances Gill. *See* Gill
Moros, in Philippine Islands, 369–70
Moseley, George Van Horn: E. comment
  on, 100, 110–11, 144–46, 180, 183–84,
  213, 225–26, 278, 492–93; E. letters and
  memoranda to, 113–14, 160–64,
  257–58, 261–62, 264–65, 276–79,
  330–33, 541–42
Moses, Andrew, 226, 232
Murphy, Frank, 304, 350–51, 355
Mussolini, Benito, E. comment on, 446,
  494

National Defense Act (1912), 70, 72, 75–76
National Defense Act (1916), 67–68, 72,
  75–76, 156
National Defense Act (1920): E. comment
  on ramifications of, 64–65, 176–78,
  221–23; explanations of, 64–65, 99, 126,
  156
National Guard, 64, 66, 78, 243, 558
National Pistol and Rifle Matches, 1930,
  142–43
National Recovery Administration (NRA),
  143, 229, 232, 254–55
Natzel, Robert J., 466–67
Naval War College, 179

Nelson, Oliver E., 390, 407
New Deal: E. evaluations of, 249–56; effects on U.S. army, 99, 271–72
Nicholas, Richard U., 543–44
Norman, Ruby, 10–11
"Notes on Men" (E. comments on contemporaries), 224–33
Nulsen, Charles K. "Sonny," 558–59

Oboza, Federico, 398, 400
Officer Reserve Corps, 78
"On the Command and General Staff School" (E. advice to incoming students, Fort Leavenworth, Kans., 1926), 43–58
O'Neil, Ralph Thomas, 163–64, 168, 194–95
Ord, Emily (Mrs. James B.), 373–75
Ord, James Basevi: E. evaluation of, 278–79, 299, 375–76; Philippine service, 285, 293–96, 300, 305–8, 311, 327–30, 340–54, 356–60, 362, 369–71, 410, 413; USMA memorial prepared by E. (1938), 382–83
Osmeña, Sergio, 298, 337
"Our Flag" (E. speech, Camp Colt, Pa., 1918), 18
Overman Act (1918), 220

Parker, Hugh A. "Lefty," 354, 388–89, 420–22, 514–16
Parks, Floyd, 377–78
Patton, George S., Jr., E. letters to, 491–92, 497–98, 502–3
Payne, Frederick H.: addresses: —at American War College, drafted by E. (1931), 147–56; —at USMA, written by E. (1931), 172–75; assistant secretary of war, 100, 170, 553; E. view of, 146, 187–88, 226
Peabody, Hume, 351, 354
Peabody, Paul E., 351, 354
Pearson, Drew, 268–69, 412, 531
Pearson, Madison, 260–61
Peek, Ernest Dichmann, 180
Peek, George Nelson, 168–69, 188, 198, 224
Pence, Harry Langley, 185, 188

Pennsylvania State University. See Eisenhower, Milton S.
Pepke, Donn R., 466–67
Perkins, George Thompson, 398
Pershing, John J., 59–60, 80–81, 201–2, 356
Philippine Army: air corps, 312–13, 316, 320–22, 352, 354, 379; E. reports on: —to Gerow (1938), 402–6; —to Quezon (1939), 457–60, 468–89; establishment and organization of, 293–97, 302–25, 329, 361–62; fiscal problems, 332, 340–41, 344–45, 350–53, 361–63, 368, 370–72, 402–6, 413–14, 483–84; military academy, 300, 305, 473, 485–86; mobilization equipment, 335–36, 340–41, 347–48; officer corps, 298–99, 301, 306, 332, 335, 338–39, 345–47, 430, 479–81; off-shore patrols, 312–13, 316, 321–22, 353, 379, 402–3; ordnance, 302, 304–5, 307, 318–19, 322–23, 325, 327, 336, 343–45, 347–49, 397, 399–400, 402, 419; Philippine defense plan, prepared by Ord and E., 293–300; ROTC, 323, 380, 425–29, 472; War Department attitude toward, 307, 348–50, 353–54, 359, 385, 394–96. See also Boy Scouts; Philippine Constabulary; Philippine Scouts
Philippine Constabulary, 296, 299–301, 370, 380–81, 423, 484, 489
Philippine Islands: Commonwealth government, 287, 290, 293, 298; Japanese invasion of, 489; National Defense Act (1935), 284, 306; plans for independence, 286–87, 290, 330–32; U.S. high commissioner, 303–5, 330, 350–51, 356, 438–39
Philippine Scouts, 295–96, 298, 309–10, 335, 340, 345, 484–85, 489
"Plan for Industrial Mobilization, 1930" (written by E.), 145
Porter, Ray E., 550
Powers, David Lane, 260
Presidential campaign, 1936, 328–29
Presidio, Calif., 116, 460–61
Price, Xenophon H.: American Battle Monuments Commission secretary, 79–80, 102; E. letters to, 103–10

"Profits of War, The" anti–War Department article, by Forest Revere Black (*The Nation*, 1930), 144
Prosser, Harvey W., 372, 560
Public Works Administration, 211, 232, 254–55

Quartermaster general, E. report to on Army field jacket (1941), 521
Quezon, Manuel: attitude toward Moros, 369–70; E. advisory role, 299, 306, 356–59, 377, 380–81, 386, 412, 429–31, 453, 456; E. report to, 1939, 457–60, 468–89; Philippine national defense budgetary concerns, 357, 360–64; relations with MacArthur, 287–88, 298, 311, 326, 329, 355, 359, 362–63, 386, 410, 439–40, 454–55; in U.S.: —1935, 286–88; —1937, 330–31; —1942 (in exile), 489

Ramseyer, Christian William, 198, 201
Randolph, Norman, 28, 547–48
Rawls, Walter O., 522–23
Reed, David Aiken, 168–69
Replogle, Jacob L., 198, 201
Republican Party. *See* "Student in Politics, The"
Reserve Officers Training Corps (ROTC) U.S., 67, 79
Reyes, Jose de los, 296, 299, 301, 305
Ridley, Clarence S., 516
Robbins, Charles B., 194, 201
Robertson, Walter M., 548
Robinson, Joseph T., 169, 205–6, 219
Robinson, Trula, 535
Rogers, Reynolds, 554–55
Romulo, Carlos, 369–70
Roosevelt, Elliott, 553
Roosevelt, Franklin Delano, E. evaluations, xxv, 249, 251, 253–56

Sales, Oscar, 421–22
Salinas, Calif., 116–18, 125
Santos, Paulino, 296–99, 337–38, 341, 369–70, 381, 417–19
Sayre, John, 192
Schaefer, Julius Earl, 381–82, 390
Schimmelfenig, Charles A., 80

Schlesinger, W. Louis, 18–19
Scott, Frank Augustus, 165
Secretary of War. *See* War Department
Segundo, Fidel, 337–38, 501–2
Selph, Ewald E., 374–75
Sherman, John B., 251
Shinn, John B., 17, 19
Short, Walter Cowan, 119
Simonds, George Sherwin, 227, 230–31, 284, 445
Skerry, Harry Allen, 102–3
Smith, Alfred Theodore, 226, 232
Smith, Tucker, 192–93
Smith & Wesson, Inc., 111–12, 160
Sparks, Leonard Craig, 394, 396, 402
Spence, David, 116–17, 125, 132
Stanley, James G., 157, 159
Stearman Aircraft Co., 388, 390, 421–22
Stephens, Roderick, 18
Sterl, Oscar, 554–55
Sterl, William, 554–55
Stevenot, J. E., 337–38
Stevens, Luther R., 481, 489
Stone, David L., 507–8
Straight, Ronnie, 374–75
Strong, Robert William, 120, 276
"Student in Politics, The" (E. speech, Abilene, Kans., 1909), 5–7
Styer, Wilhelm Delp, 102
Sullivan, Joseph P., 549
Sutherland, Richard K., 381, 390, 534, 537
Sweeney, Walter Campbell, 409, 434, 436, 447–50, 507
Swope, Herbert Bayard, 166–67
Symonds, Charles Jacobs, 119

"Tank Discussion, A" (E. article, *Infantry Journal*, 1920), 28–34
Tanks: E. enthusiasm for, 34, 175, 244, 491, 497–98; Tank Corps, at Camp Colt, Pa., 16–17, 25–28
"Tanks with Infantry" (E. paper, Military History Institute, 1921), 35–42
Terry, Thomas A., 463–64
Thomason, Robert E., 467
"Thomason Act," 466–67, 490
Thompson, Charles Fullington, 494–95, 504–5, 507, 511
Thompson, Clark, 267–68, 270–72

Thompson, Hugh, 506
Times, Manitowoc, Wis., (anti-War Department editorial, 1930), 143–44
Torpedo boats. *See* Philippine Army, offshore patrols
"To the Graduating Class" (Payne address at USMA, written by E., 1931), 172–75
Torreón, Mexico, guayule rubber factory, 121
Trans-Continental Motor Truck Trip (1919), E. report on, 19–25
Treat 'Em Rough (Camp Colt, Pa., newsletter), 17–18
Truesdell, Karl, 164
Truscott, Lucian K., Jr., 519–20, 543
Tugwell, Rexford Guy, 256–57
Tydings-McDuffie Act (1934), 287, 290, 307, 331
Tyner, George Parker, 396–97

Ulio, James, 281, 385, 397, 406–7, 435, 437, 440–41
U.S. Army
    Army commands: Second, 531; Third, 100, 386, 529–31, 546, 560; Fourth, 400, 462, 508
    Corps: III, 100; IV, 539; VIII, 501–2; IX, 448, 461, 495, 497, 516–20, 522–23, 533, 547
    Divisions: Second Infantry, 449–50, 501, 550–51; Third Infantry, 460, 495–96, 506, 516–17, 532–33, 552; Forty-First Infantry, 494, 496, 517
    Regiments: 15th Infantry, 434, 447, 451–52, 460–64, 466, 489–90, 501–2, 509, 551–52; 19th Infantry, 111; 24th Infantry, 59; 57th Infantry, 11
U.S. Army, Philippine Department, 171, 283, 285, 292–93, 308–9, 327, 336–37, 342, 347, 349, 351, 394, 396, 412
U.S. Marine Corps, 68–69
U.S. Military Academy (USMA), West Point, N.Y., 172–75, 382–83

Valdes, Basilio, 296–97, 299, 301, 305, 417–19
Vance, John Raikes, 106–8
Vandenberg, Arthur, 169, 195, 220–21
Vanderveer, Harold C., 533

Van Duyne, Frederick William, 80
Van Fleet, James, 258–59
Van Voorhis, Daniel, 280–81
Van Zandt, James, 439, 441
Vargas, Jorge B., 337–38, 377, 410–11, 429, 431, 438, 455–58
Veterans Bureau, 103
Veterans of Foreign Wars, 164–65

Wainwright, Jonathan Mayhew, 178, 188
Walker, Fred L., 434–35, 447, 451
Wallace, Henry Agard, 256–57
Walsh, David I., 221–23
War Council, 151
War Department: budgetary concerns, 224, 249–53, 259–62, 270–72; E. special responsibilities, 111, 142, 145–46, 162, 175, 246–47; E. views on leadership of, 224–29, 231–33; industrial mobilization and procurement plans, 176–88, 211; peacetime planning responsibilities, 147–56; relations with Congress, 221–23, 247, 257–58, 260, 264–65, 267–68; relations with White House, 252–53, 268–69. *See also* Guayule rubber industry; MacArthur, Douglas; Payne, Frederick H.; Philippine Army; War Policies Commission
War Industries Board, 143, 177
"War Policies" (E. *Cavalry Journal* article, 1931), 190–201
War Policies Commission: creation and purpose of, 162, 168–69, 190–91; E. role in and comments on reports of, 111, 115, 160–72, 185–88, 200, 204–7, 215–21; public hearings, 164–69, 186, 190–200; report to White House (1932), 217–19. *See also* MacArthur, Douglas
Westover, Oscar, 398
West Point. *See* U.S. Military Academy
Wetzel, Frank J., 266–67
Whatley, Vachel Davis, Jr., 345–46, 351
Whelan, Townsend, 159–60
Whitaker, John C., 269–70
White, George A., 496, 498
Wichita, Kans., military aircraft manufacturing in, 388–89
Wile, Frederick William, 144–45
Wilkes, Gilbert Van B., 100–101, 125, 161

Willard, Daniel, 194, 197–98
Willkie, Wendell L., E. view of, 500
Winchester Repeating Arms Co., 407
Wolman, Paul, 164–65
Wood, Leonard, 250
Woodring, Harry, 231–33, 264–65
Works Progress Administration (WPA),
  211

Wyman, Willard G., 518, 520, 522–23,
  555–56
Wyoming Apartments (Washington, D.C.),
  102, 107, 556

Yeandle, William H., 117–18, 121, 126
Yellowstone Park, E. trip to (1939), 391–93

Library of Congress Cataloging-in-Publication Data

Eisenhower, Dwight D. (Dwight David), 1890–1969.
    Eisenhower : the prewar diaries and selected papers, 1905–1941 /
Daniel D. Holt, editor ; James W. Leyerzapf, associate editor ;
introduction by John S.D. Eisenhower.
        p.   cm.
    Includes bibliographical references and index.
    ISBN 0-8018-5674-4 (alk. paper)
    1. Eisenhower, Dwight D. (Dwight David), 1890–1969—Archives.
2. Generals—United States—Archives.   3. Eisenhower, Dwight D.
(Dwight David), 1890–1969—Career in the military.   4. United
States. Army—History—20th century—Sources.   5. United States—
History, Military—20th century—Sources.   I. Holt, Daniel D.,
1937–   .   II. Leyerzapf, James W.   III. Title.
E742.5.E372   1998
973.921'092—dc21
    [B]   97-16445
                                                                        CIP